HANDBOOK of
PARENTING

Theory and research for practice

HANDBOOK of
PARENTING
Theory and research for practice

Edited by
MASUD HOGHUGHI
NICHOLAS LONG

SAGE Publications
London • Thousand Oaks • New Delhi

to

*my three little princesses, two tigers
and their parents*

MH

*my parents,
John and Jean Long*

NL

First published 2004

 SAGE Publications Ltd
1 Oliver's Yard
55 City Road
London EC1Y 1SP

SAGE Publications Inc.
2455 Teller Road
Thousand Oaks, California 91320

SAGE Publications India Pvt Ltd
B-42, Panchsheel Enclave
Post Box 4109
New Delhi 100 017

British Library Cataloguing in Publication data

A catalogue record for this book is available from
the British Library

ISBN

Library of Congress Control Number 2003105476

Typeset by C&M Digitals (P) Ltd., Chennai, India
Printed in Great Britain by The Cromwell Press Ltd, Trowbridge, Wiltshire

Contents

Author Biographies

Melissa Caldwell is a doctoral student in clinical psychology at the University of Illinois, Urbana-Champaign. Her primary research interests concern the developmental antecedents and consequences of peer victimization among children and adolescents. She is also currently involved in research that examines the transactional relation between individual characteristics of children and the generation of stressful experiences.

Colleen Conley is a doctoral student in clinical psychology at the University of Illinois, Urbana-Champaign. Her research centers broadly around developmental trajectories of stress and psychopathology in children and adolescents. Most recently, she has been examining the roots of gender differences in depression that emerge in adolescence.

Shannon Dorsey, PhD is a post-doctoral fellow in the Department of Psychiatry and Behavioral Sciences at Duke University Medical Center. Her clinical training has emphasized child and family interventions, and her research has focused on parenting and its relation to child and family adjustment.

Linda Drew, PhD is a Post-Doctoral Research Fellow at the Andrus Gerontology Center, University of Southern California, USA. Her research interests are in intergenerational family relationships and the impact of society; specifically, the grandparent–parent–child relationship as affected by divorce and/or geographical separation; bereavement within the family; and the role grandparents play within society. She has co-authored with Peter Smith the chapter on 'Grandparenthood' in Marc Bornstein's *Handbook of Parenting*, 2nd edition, as well as several articles on grandparents and great-grandparents.

Thyde Dumont-Mathieu, MD, MPH is a Fellow in general academic pediatrics at the University of Connecticut School of Medicine. Her areas of research interest include parenting and child health in minority communities, cultural and social issues in child behaviour and development, child advocacy, issues in doctor–patient communication, and health promotion and education in diverse contexts.

Alison Dupre works as a Project Co-ordinator in the Family Studies Laboratory at the University of Illinois, Urbana-Champaign. She graduated in psychology from the University of Illinois. Her research interests emphasize adolescent development and stress and coping processes in peer and family relationships.

Megan Flynn is currently a Visiting Research Specialist in the Family Studies Laboratory at the University of Illinois, Urbana-Champaign. She graduated in psychology from Yale University and will soon begin her doctoral work in clinical psychology at the University of Illinois. Her research focuses on the role of stress sensitization in the onset and progression of psychopathology.

Rex Forehand, PhD is a Professor of Psychology at the University of Vermont, and a Regents Professor Emeritus of Psychology at the University of Georgia. His research has focused primarily on parenting and child psychosocial adjustment, and he is regarded as one of the field's leading experts on parenting interventions.

Stephen Frosh, PhD is Professor of Psychology and Director of the Centre for Psychosocial Studies in the School of Psychology at Birkbeck College, University of London. He was previously Consultant Clinical Psychologist and Vice Dean in the Child and Family Department at the Tavistock Clinic, London. His most recent books are *The Politics of Psychoanalysis, Young Masculinities* (with Ann Phoenix and Rob Pattman) and *After Words*.

Harriet Heath, PhD is a licensed developmental and certified school psychologist. She founded and directs the Parent Center at Bryn Mawr College in Pennsylvania. For more than 30 years she has worked with parents in public and private schools, religious settings, and mental health clinics, ranging from the Alaskan bush to Philadelphia's city center and the American School in Tel Aviv. Working with her husband her principal research has been a longitudinal study following the effects of parenting on healthy adults over a 40-year time span. She has published numerous articles for the popular press and is a columnist for parenting educator's newsletter, *Pep Talk*. She is author of the recently published award winning book, *Using Your Values to Raise Your Child to Be an Adult You Admire*, as well as a manual for parents, *Planning: A Key to the Challenge of Parenting* and a curriculum for students, *Learning How to Care: Education for Parenting*. She is past chair of the National Parenting Education Network.

Martin Herbert, PhD, FBPsS is Emeritus Professor at Exeter University. He was previously Professor of Social Work and Director of the School of Social Work, and later Professor of Psychology at the University of Leicester. He has served as a Mental Health Act Commissioner and worked as Director of Mental Health Services for children and as a consultant clinical psychologist in child and adolescent psychology. He is a Fellow of the British Psychological Society and was awarded the Monty Shapiro Prize for distinguished contribution to Clinical Psychology in 1994. He is the author of *Typical and Atypical Development: From Conception to Adolescence*.

Masud Hoghughi, PhD, FBPsS is Professor in the Department of Clinical Psychology, University of Hull and Professor of Parenting and Child Development at the University of Northumbria at Newcastle. He has spent his professional life in parallel academic and clinical settings. For years, he developed and directed Europe's largest specialized facility for the assessment and treatment of severely disordered adolescents and their families. His publications are concerned mainly with troubled and troublesome children and their families.

Judy Hutchings, PhD has worked in north Wales for the past 25 years, mainly with children who have significant behavioural problems. She currently works with a range of parents, children, specialist services and other educators concerned with children and families. Her current aim is to establish the Incredible Years programmes for parents and children across a range of settings in north Wales.

Jennifer Jenkins, PhD is Professor in the Department of Human Development and Applied Psychology at the University of Toronto. She trained as a clinical and developmental psychologist. She has carried out research in the area of developmental psychopathology, environmental risk and family interaction in clinical settings with children and families. She co-authored the book *Understanding Emotions* with Keith Oatley, and *Human Emotions* with Keith Oatley and Nancy Stein.

Carole Kaplan, FRCPsych, FRCPCH is Senior Lecturer and Consultant in Child and Adolescent Psychiatry, University of Newcastle upon Tyne and the Fleming Nuffield Unit, Newcastle. Her special interests are in the areas of child neurotic disorders, and parenting. Other appointments include member of the Advisory Board on Family Law, Children Act Sub-committee and NHS Litigation Authority.

Beth Kotchick, PhD is an Assistant Professor of Psychology at Loyola College in Maryland. She received her doctorate in clinical psychology from the University of Georgia, with a specialization in child clinical psychology. Her research has generally focused on parenting and its impact on child and adolescent psychosocial adjustment.

Nicholas Long, PhD is Professor of Pediatrics and Director of Pediatric Psychology at the University of Arkansas for Medical Sciences and Arkansas Children's Hospital. He is also Director of the Center for Effective Parenting. The primary focus of his clinical and research activities is in the area of parenting and family functioning. He is a co-author with Dr Rex Forehand of the books *Parenting the Strong-Willed Child* and *Making Divorce Easier on Your Child*.

Susan McGaw, PhD is a Chartered Clinical Psychologist, who founded the Special Parenting Service for parents with intellectual disabilities (ID) in 1988, the first of its kind in the UK. This service is well known for the development of assessment tools, theoretical models and innovative practices for use with ID parents and has published extensively in this area. She is the British Psychological Society's spokesperson on this topic.

Fiona Miller, PhD received her doctorate in School and Child Clinical Psychology from the University of Toronto in 2001. She is currently a staff psychologist in the Child Psychiatry Program at the Centre for Addiction and Mental Health – Clarke Division. Her research focuses on the role of parenting in the development and prevention of psychopathology, with a particular interest in emotion and attention regulation as factors that may mediate this connection. One current project is designed to investigate the effectiveness of community-based parent training programs for families of young children with externalizing difficulties.

Kevin Moore, PhD is Clinical Director of Community Programs and a Research Associate at the Oregon Social Learning Center (OSLC). Prior to this association, he was Director of Specialized Treatment Programs and National Director of Treatment Foster Care at Father Flanagan's Boys' Home, Boystown, Nebraska. His research interests include the use of single-subject methodologies to help guide clinical decision-making, pooled time-series, and the care and treatment of traumatized children in community-based settings.

Julie Owens MB, BS, MRCPsych is Specialist Registrar in Child and Adolescent Psychiatry, based at the Fleming Nuffield Unit, Jesmond, Newcastle.

Lee Pachter, DO is Professor of Pediatrics and Anthropology, and Head of the Division of General Pediatrics at the University of Connecticut School of Medicine. He is a pediatrician at Saint Francis Hospital and Medical Center in Hartford, Connecticut, USA. His areas of research interest include understanding the role of ethnic and cultural beliefs and practices in child health, health care, child behavior and development, minority parenting, ethnomedicine, racism and child development, and social science research methodologies.

Charlotte Patterson, PhD is a Professor of Psychology at the University of Virginia, where she teaches Developmental Psychology. Her research focuses on social and personality development among children and adolescents in the context of family, peer and school environments. She is known for her studies of children with lesbian and gay parents.

Jan Pryor, PhD is Senior Lecturer in Developmental and Family Psychology in the School of Psychology at Victoria University of Wellington, New Zealand. She is also Director of the Roy McKenzie Centre for the Study of Families. Her major research interest is in family processes and transitions and their impact on children. She is an independent consultant to the judiciary in family matters.

Christine Puckering is Consultant Clinical Psychologist, Royal Hospital for Sick Children, Glasgow. She is also Honorary Senior Research Fellow, University of Glasgow and Honorary Lecturer in Forensic Psychology, Glasgow Caledonian University. She has developed and runs the 'Mellow Parenting' programme with John Rogers. Her research and clinical interests are mainly in the areas of child and family psychology.

Gillian Pugh is Chief Executive of the London-based charity Coram Family and was previously Director of the Early Childhood Unit at the National Children's Bureau. She has published extensively, including *Contemporary Issues in the Early Years; Confident Parents, Confident Children; Preventive Work with Families*; and *Training to Work in the Early Years*. She is a visiting professorial fellow at the University of London Institute of Education, and a member of the Children's Task Force for London. She is Chair of the Parenting Education and Support Forum, a trustee of the National Family and Parenting Institute, and she works in an advisory capacity with the UK Government's Sure Start Unit and Children and Young People's Unit.

Alan Ralph, PhD is Adjunct Associate Professor of Clinical Psychology at The University of Queensland. Over the past 15 years, he has held several clinical positions, conducted research in the area of adolescent and family problems, and written numerous articles and chapters on related topics. He has developed programs to assist teenagers and their parents to manage problems commonly encountered during the transition into adolescence and adulthood and trained practitioners to implement these programs.

Karen Rudolph, PhD is an Associate Professor of Clinical and Developmental Psychology at the University of Illinois, Urbana-Champaign. Her research focuses on the development of psychopathology in childhood and adolescence. In particular, she studies how characteristics of children and their environments interact to create a risk for the emergence of depression and other disorders, with a specific focus on stress and coping processes in relationships.

Matthew Sanders, PhD is Professor of Clinical Psychology and Director of the Parenting and Family Support Centre at the University of Queensland. Over the past 25 years, he has conducted major research into the family-based treatment and prevention of behavioural and emotional problems in children. He has written extensively on parent training and evidence-based family interventions, and authored several books on the treatment of children's behaviour problems, including the popular parenting book *Every Parent: A Positive Approach to Children's Behaviour*.

Anne Shaffer is a doctoral student in clinical and developmental psychology at the University of Minnesota. Her research has focused on issues germane to child and adolescent development, with a special emphasis on child and family adjustment to stress.

Dana Smith, PhD is a research associate and clinical interventionist at the Oregon Social Learning Center. Her work focuses on prevention and intervention with adolescent female delinquent populations. Dana is also interested in the dissemination and replication of evidence-based interventions, and is involved in training and dissemination of the Multidimensional Treatment Foster Care model.

Peter Smith, PhD is Professor of Psychology and Head of the Unit for School and Family Studies at Goldsmiths College, University of London. His research interests are in social development, grandparenting, play, bullying, and evolutionary theory. He is editor of *The Psychology of Grandparenthood*, co-author of *Understanding Children's Development*, and co-editor of *Theories of Theories of Mind, The Family Systems Test* and *The Nature of School Bullying*.

Elizabeth Soliday, PhD is Associate Professor of Psychology at Washington State University at Vancouver, having gained her doctorate from the University of Kansas. Her primary research area is in child and family adjustment to chronic illness. Her projects have been funded by the National Kidney Foundation, the Carcinoid Cancer Foundation, the National Institutes of Health and the National Cancer Institute.

Peter Sprengelmeyer, PhD is the Assistant Director of OSLC Community Programs and a Research Associate at the Oregon Social Learning Center. He is also a licensed psychologist. Currently, he is working with projects within the center dealing with substance use as a co-occurring disorder and with the dissemination of empirically validated treatment approaches.

Randi Streisand, PhD is Assistant Professor of Psychiatry and Behavioral Sciences and Pediatrics at the Children's National Medical Center and the George Washington University School of Medicine and Health Sciences in Washington, DC. Her research interests are in pediatric psychology, parent–child stress and coping with chronic illness, and behavioral interventions to promote parent-child health and well-being. Dr Streisand, a pediatric psychologist, is also the author of a recently published book on child health assessment.

Erin Sutfin is a doctoral student in Developmental Psychology at the University of Virginia. Her research interests include social and emotional development during childhood and focus especially on children's gender role development. She has presented her research at the Society for Research in Child Development and at the American Psychological Association.

Kenneth P. Tercyak, PhD is a pediatric psychologist and Assistant Professor of Oncology and Pediatrics at the Lombardi Comprehensive Cancer Center and the Georgetown University School of Medicine in Washington, DC. Dr Tercyak's research addresses the interface of cancer control, behavioral science, and pediatrics, with special interests in bio-behavioral aspects of tobacco use and genetic testing for hereditary cancers among high risk children, parents, and familes.

David Utting is a writer on social policy and an Associate Director of the Joseph Rowntree Foundation. He is author of the Foundation's report on *Family and Parenthood* as well as the co-author of *Crime and the Family* and a national survey of secondary school students, *Youth at risk?* Other publications include *Reducing Criminality among Young People* and co-authorship of *What Works with Young Offenders in the Community?* He and Gillian Pugh are co-authors of *Better Results for Children and Families*, a report on involving communities in planning outcome-based services. He led the Rowntree Foundation task group that adapted the *Communities that Care* programme for use in Britain and was seconded in 1998–1999 to help establish the UK Government's *Sure Start* initiative.

Sally Wade, EdD is the Director of the Florida Partnership for Family Involvement in Education. She is also director of Family-Centered Projects at the Florida Diagnostic and Learning Resources System Center at the University of South Florida. She is a nationally recognized parent advocate who has consulted with community-based agencies regarding family-centered care and schools regarding family-friendly practices. Her professional interests include family-centered care, family support systems, family involvement policy and legislation, and training in family involvement practices.

Carolyn Webster-Stratton, PhD is a clinical psychologist and Professor of Nursing at the University of Washington, Seattle. She is a two-time recipient of the National Institute of Mental Health Research Scientist Award for her work in developing and researching violence prevention programs. She has published extensively. Her programs have been identified as a 'Blueprint Programme' for the prevention of violence and by the US Office of Juvenile Justice and Delinquency Prevention and by the American Psychological Association as one of only two effective treatments for conduct disorder. She has developed training programs for teachers, parents and children as school and community-based interventions.

Chapter Summaries

1 Parenting – An Introduction
Masud Hoghughi

This chapter introduces the concept of parenting in its widest sense. It addresses the history and evolution of parenting, its emergence into public consciousness and policy, and as a focus for research and academic interest. The author presents a comprehensive overview of parenting, encompassing its essential processes, areas of application and prerequisites.

2 The Social Context of Parenting
David Utting and Gillian Pugh

This chapter discusses the social and policy context in which a significant and growing interest in parenting has developed during the past 20 years. The authors present an overview of the public debate about families and parenting and policy initiatives. The chapter also includes a discussion of such issues as the role of research in drawing attention to parenting as a skill that can be improved and the role that voluntary/non-profit organizations have played in the spread of parenting services. The authors conclude the chapter with a discussion questioning whether sufficient public and political consensus exists to ensure the current level of services and interest in parenting are sustained.

3 Parenting in Social and Economic Adversity
Christine Puckering

This chapter has a primary focus on the link between poverty, parenting and the outcome for children. Other topics examined include teen parents and incarcerated parents. The author also discusses intervention with parents who face social and economic adversity. The chapter concludes with suggestions regarding policy and practice.

4 Parenting Across the Lifespan
Martin Herbert

This chapter focuses on the role of parents in socializing their children across the lifespan. The author discusses the various stages of development, from the prenatal period through to adulthood, and issues related to parenting at each stage. Specific areas covered include developmental tasks, attachment, and identity development. The author also briefly discusses issues pertaining to 'older' mothers. The author concludes the chapter by presenting a number of specific guidelines for use by parents through the lifespan.

5 Parental Influences on Vulnerability and Resilience
Carole A. Kaplan and Julie Owens

A major challenge for professionals working with parents and children is to help them enhance their resilience and reduce their vulnerabilities. This chapter presents a predominantly clinical perspective regarding vulnerability and resilience. The authors present a brief historical background for this topic and then go on to discuss various family factors, child factors, and environmental factors that impact vulnerability and resilience. The authors also examine the cumulative and interactional processes of such factors.

6 Parenting in Culturally Divergent Settings
Lee M. Pachter and Thyde Dumont-Mathieu

This chapter presents a view of parenting that posits that successful parenting styles and practices are relative to the specific context within which the family lives. The chapter primarily focuses on the variables that are either specific to, or have different effects on those who are parenting in culturally divergent settings, including those who have recently immigrated to another country either voluntarily or under duress, as well as ethnic minorities. Specific topics discussed include how culture affects child development, acculturation, social position factors, minority status and parenting, and challenges of the transitional process for immigrant families.

7 Religious Influences on Parenting
Stephen Frosh

This chapter examines the relationship between religion, with an emphasis on Judaism and Islam, and parenting. Although, as the author acknowledges, there is paucity of research in this area, religion has an influence on many parenting practices. The chapter discusses such influences. The author also examines the division between professional and religious views of the treatment of children and the implications of this division for practice.

8 Parenting in Reconstituted and Surrogate Families
Jan Pryor

This chapter examines issues faced by families who are not 'intact' in the biological and structural sense. The author begins with an overview of the history of families, families after divorce, stepfamilies, adoptive families, foster families, and families formed by artificial reproductive technologies. The chapter then focuses on what we know about parenting in such 'non-traditional' families and conclusions that can be drawn. In the final section of the chapter the author summarizes implications for practice and policy.

9 Sexual Orientation and Parenting
Charlotte J. Patterson and Erin L. Sutfin

This chapter begins with a review of the historical context in which lesbian and gay parenting has emerged. The authors then provide an overview of lesbian and gay parenthood today, including information about the prevalence and diversity of lesbian and gay parenting, and about the legal contexts in which these families currently live. The authors also discuss the research on lesbian and gay parents and their children as well as the implications of these research findings. The chapter concludes with a discussion of future directions for research, service, and advocacy relevant to the needs of lesbian mothers, gay fathers, and their children.

10 Grandparenting and Extended Support Networks
Peter K. Smith and Linda M. Drew

This chapter begins with a discussion of some of the major conceptual issues in studying grandparenting as well as a historical perspective on issues pertaining to the role of grandparents. The core issues examined in the chapter include the nature of contacts between grandparents and grandchildren, the issue of proximity, characteristics of grandparents and grandchildren, and direct and indirect influences of grandparents on grandchildren. The chapter also presents an overview of the various roles of grandparents and how these roles are impacted by various factors including culture and parental divorce. The chapter concludes with the authors' summarizing implications for practice related to grandparenting.

11 Parenting and Children's Physical Health
Elizabeth Soliday

This chapter synthesizes the available literature documenting the relationships between parenting factors and children's general health. The author discusses the relationship of various demographic variables and parenting process variables with children's health. The chapter also includes an overview of cognitive behavioral health interventions that involve parents. Other topics covered include family process variables, family systems interventions, and attachment. The author concludes the chapter with a discussion of implications for practice and research.

12 Parenting Chronically Ill Children – The Scope and Impact of Pediatric Parenting Stress
Randi Streisand and Kenneth P. Tercyak

This chapter examines specific issues in parenting that arise when infants, children, and adolescents experience chronic and/or life-threatening illnesses. The authors also review cross-cutting themes in parent–child stress and coping that offer multiple frameworks in which to understand such complex issues. The chapter concludes with a discussion of the practical implications of this knowledge base.

13 Parenting Influences on Intellectual Development and Educational Achievement
Sally M. Wade

This chapter provides an overview of the impact of parenting on children's intellectual developmental and academic achievement. Specific areas discussed include examples of legislation to promote parent involvement in children's education as well as a detailed discussion of the influences of parenting on early cognitive development, academic achievement, and vocational choices. The author concludes the chapter with a discussion of implications for practice, including a list of specific ways parents can promote their children's academic success.

14 Parenting Exceptional Children
Susan McGaw

This chapter describes the struggle of adults with intellectual disabilities (ID) to establish the right to become parents and to raise their children within the community. The ability and capacity of ID parents is discussed, including how their parental competency is assessed, measured and compared to that of the general parent population. The plight of their children is examined, as is the question of whether they receive 'different' or poor parenting which result in an 'exceptional' childhood. Methodological difficulties involved in conducting research on ID parents and the interpretation of findings are discussed.

15 Parenting and Antisocial Behavior
Dana K. Smith, Peter G. Sprengelmeyer and Kevin J. Moore

This chapter provides an overview of the role of parenting practices in the development, maintenance, and treatment of antisocial behavior. The role of individual child and parent factors, environmental factors, and contextual variables are discussed in the context of the impact each has, both individually and collectively, on parenting practices during early childhood, middle childhood, and adolescence. The authors conclude the chapter with a brief discussion of implications for intervention.

16 Parenting Antisocial Children and Adolescents
Beth A. Kotchick, Anne Shaffer, Shannon Dorsey and Rex Forehand

This chapter begins with a historical overview of how parents became involved in the treatment of child antisocial behaviors. The authors then discuss several core issues central to parent training, including a discussion of developmental and contextual variables. The chapter also presents an example of a well-established behavioral parent training program. The authors conclude the chapter with a discussion of challenges frequently faced by providers in accessing and implementing these parenting interventions, as well as issues related to the future direction of parent training from the clinical, research, and policy perspective.

17 Parenting and Mental Health
Colleen S. Conley, Melissa S. Caldwell, Megan Flynn, Alison J. Dupre and Karen D. Rudolph

This chapter summarizes theory and research on the impact of parental mental health, broadly construed, and associated circumstances on parenting. A brief overview of historical trends and theories in the domain of parenting research is provided, followed by a review of relevant research on personal and contextual influences on parenting. The authors conclude the chapter with a discussion on how intervention programs and social policy can be directed toward mental health promotion in the context of parenting.

18 Parenting Children with Mental Health Problems
Fiona K. Miller and Jennifer M. Jenkins

This chapter focuses on issues related to parenting children with internalizing disorders such as anxiety and depression. The authors begin with a historical overview of the perceived role of parents in children's internalizing disorders. Core issues are then discussed including a review of major internalizing disorders, child and parent effects, bi-directional influences, moderation effects, and the role of parents in the amelioration of internalizing symptoms. The authors conclude the chapter by summarizing implications for practice.

19 Assessing and Delivering Parent Support
Harriet Heath

This chapter defines support and documents the importance of having support to the well being of parents and their children. It traces the history of providing support to parents and families. It describes the functions of support and identifies potential sources of support using Bronfenbrenner's ecological framework. The chapter then turns to looking at methods for identifying and assessing parents' support systems for the purposes of developing and assessing programs and of further researching support systems and their influence.

20 Community-based Support for Parents
Judy Hutchings and Carolyn Webster-Stratton

This chapter discusses some of the challenges parents face and describes a number of interventions that have been developed to support parents and children within their own communities. The author discusses programs that support parents of young children, parents of children with behaviour problems, and parents of adolescents. A detailed overview of Carolyn Webster-Stratton's program 'The Incredible Years' is provided.

21 Towards a Multi-level Model of Parenting Intervention
Matthew R. Sanders and Alan Ralph

This chapter outlines the conceptual and empirical basis for the development of a multi-level approach to parenting education, parent training, and family intervention that focuses on the prevention and treatment of behavioral and emotional problems in children and adolescents. The authors discuss the historical context within which behaviorally oriented family interventions developed, review the evidence supporting their efficacy and effectiveness, and discuss implications for policy makers, service providers and consumers. The authors also present an overview of their Triple P – the Positive Parenting Programme.

22 e-Parenting
Nicholas Long

This chapter discusses the concept of e-parenting and the profound impact that emerging technologies will have on parents, children, and providers. The author provides a historical background of the impact of electronic technology on parenting. Core issues discussed include accessibility, potential benefits, concerns about technology dependence, concerns about privacy, the reliability and validity of information, and ethical concerns. The chapter concludes with a discussion of various issues related to implications for practice.

Epilogue: Towards a Parenting Society
Nicholas Long and Masud Hoghughi

This chapter presents a brief overview of anticipated family trends and societal issues that will impact on parenting in the 21st century. The authors then conclude the Handbook with a discussion of their thoughts on what it will take to move society towards being more supportive of parenting.

Preface

Parenting, as a process, is as old as humanity. While parenting is not rocket science, it is probably the most overwhelming and important endeavour many of us undertake in our lifetime. It would be reasonable to expect that so primordial an activity would have accumulated implicit knowledge and explicit practice as to become bullet-proof by the 21st century. It has not.

We recognize that in a rapidly changing world, there are children who are badly affected by neglectful, inappropriate and sometimes abusive parenting. We are also aware that the increasing pressures on families and the growing complexity of our social environments are creating new and additional turbulence which parents must weather. The impact of many such influences on parenting is negative, with serious long-term consequences both for the families themselves and the wider society.

Given the difficulties that parents face, it is little wonder that growing attention has been paid to parenting in recent years, including a vast number of publications for both parents and professionals. From the professional perspective, the area of parenting has traditionally been considered not a separate discipline, but rather an area of interest embedded within various disciplines such as psychology, sociology, nursing, social work, anthropology, paediatrics, child development and others. However, in recent years we have witnessed the early stages of what we believe to be the acceptance of parenting as a distinct discipline. The recognition of this newly emerging discipline was perhaps marked with the publication of the distinguished four-volume *Handbook of Parenting*, edited by Marc Bornstein in 1995 and published by Laurence Erlbaum. While acknowledging the importance of that handbook (and the five-volume second edition published in 2002), especially to academics and researchers, we have taken a different route. This *Sage Handbook of Parenting* is primarily concerned with considering theory and research evidence as a basis for practice – to be used by practitioners and students wishing to increase their understanding of parenting issues and help parenting figures who face a range of difficulties or, indeed, for those unusual parents who might wish to make use of it themselves. It is a single-volume handbook meant to provide a more general review of issues related to parenting, written primarily for the non-researcher.

This focus on practice is responsible for our decision to ask authors to include the minimum number of references in the text, so that it reads easily and coherently and can be used practically as a handbook. That the chapters are authoritative should not be in doubt; they reflect the distilled knowledge of the topic by renowned workers in the field rather than pernickety and unhelpful recourse to drowning the text in references.

Although the chapter authors were given a standardized structure for their chapters, they have each modified it to fit the content of their chapter, and we have respected their wishes in presenting the material as they saw fit. We have also kept the spelling differences between our American and other authors.

The first editor wishes to thank those parents, friends and family members who read and commented on his chapter, particularly in relation to what both it and the handbook as a whole should cover. The second editor would like to thank his colleagues and his family not only for their insights and wisdom but also for their unwavering support and encouragement.

Since the first editor has had the task of 'putting to bed' the final product, he wishes to thank his secretary and closest collaborator Doreen Kipling, to whom this public acknowledgement is, as always, but a meagre tribute.

Part I

KEY CONCEPTS

I

Parenting – An Introduction

Masud Hoghughi

SUMMARY

This chapter introduces the concept of parenting in its widest sense. It addresses briefly the emergence of parenting into public and academic awareness and gives an overview of its essential elements, areas of application and prerequisites. Certain critical areas that warrant further exploration and development are briefly outlined.

EVOLUTION

Procreation is the core, irreducible process on which the survival of the species depends. Survival is commonly accepted as the main, overarching goal of much behaviour. However, procreation is no use if offspring do not survive. To ensure survival is the chief task of parenting (Potts and Short, 1999). The human infant is a particularly vulnerable creature, unable to look after itself until well into its middle childhood. In complex modern societies, the need for parental protection and supported living is stretching beyond middle childhood, whereas searching for food and primary survival might be possible by middle childhood in simpler societies. There is, as ever, a strong case for considering both nature and nurture to be interdependently implicated in the growth of infants into effective citizens. Parenting is the critical medium for this (Collins et al., 2000).

Historically and across the globe, parents have had to cope with limited resources for sustenance; external threats to survival; poor child life expectancy; arbitrary exercise of power by rulers which threatened parents or their children; use of children as cheap labour; and wars, which reduced economic resources and frequently disrupted or permanently broke families. For many, these threats have become less intrusive, but there are still large stretches of the world where they are present. Even in developed countries, many parents still have to contend with pressures that affect and potentially undermine their effectiveness (Hoghughi, 1999). These include the following:

- relative poverty
- ill health, both physical and mental
- greater tendency to separate and re-partner
- dispersal of extended families and support networks

- conflicting demands of work and home in increasingly competitive economic environments
- greater tendency of mothers to do paid work outside the home and having to contend with the physical and emotional consequences of work
- increasing unacceptability of traditional means of corrective discipline and uncertainties about appropriate boundaries for children's behaviour
- increase in influence of peers and their culture, relative to that of parents
- greater awareness and empowerment of young people, legally and informally
- growth of urban environments and exposure of children to strong external influences, including advertising and the media
- increasing emergence of societies, particularly in the West, in which there are no longer any standard or central models of parenting

In the West, there has been a historically U-shaped relationship between wealth and number of children. The richest and the poorest always had the largest number of children and those with middle incomes the fewest. But the long-term general trend has been a gradual convergence in family sizes, not least because of the reduction in child deaths. Now, in the West, due to the changes in balance of power between men and women and economic influences on adults, fewer get married or choose to have children, with long-term economic and social consequences (Taylor and Taylor, 2001). Children have always been a significant economic drain on parents. Even in those societies where parents receive financial aid for child-rearing, this is often not regarded as adequate. Many adults who just 'managed' before, slip into poverty with the appearance of the first child and descend further with each new child (HM Treasury, 1999). Thus, at least in the material sense, having children detracts from the 'good life' to which many aspire.

The significant rise in the status of mothers as women, their increasing role as paid workers and breadwinners, and their ability to pursue careers in their own right, all press towards reduced involvement in parenting (Maitland, 2001). Nor does not having children carry any social stigma. However, despite these pressures and awareness of the costs of bringing up children in physical, economic, emotional and other terms, the biological imperative of perpetuating the species through having and raising children has largely, though variably, prevailed. It has been suggested that many men and women do not acquire their 'proper' gender role until they have a child (Arendel, 1997).

Despite significant changes, particularly in Western societies, the motivation to have children remains strong, as shown by the development and spread of fertility assistance services. This is because raising children serves many purposes – the 'goal state' to which adults aspire. These include:

- producing (hopefully) healthy and well-adapted children and thus (implicitly) perpetuating the species;
- ensuring support for parents as they grow older;
- producing and sustaining wealth through future economic activity;
- creating a citizenry for the defence and security of the homeland;
- providing a safe and protective social environment for dependent citizens;
- affirming the significance and worth of parents in contributing to continued life and progress of society;
- investing in and transferring 'social capital' to their children by transmission of values and skills; and
- providing new stimulation to and an extension of the life of parents, many of whom find 'meaning' for their own existence through having and bringing up children.

Most parents would be baffled if asked why they had or wanted children, and unlikely to give clear reasons. Having children is 'natural', a flowering of the relationship with a (loved) partner; fulfilment of a social expectation and definition of their own full male- or femalehood and the often inarticulate but telling 'just want them'. For most adults parenting serves different goals and expectations. There are also the 'accidental' parents – men and women who are sexual partners or who casually mate and produce unplanned children.

Deliberately delayed childbirth, particularly among the middle classes, suggests that children and their demands are being weighed against other personal and social goals with which they may interfere. Unless the current, almost global, push towards employment for both parents is only a passing phenomenon, it is likely that producing children will become an ever more calculated and less spontaneous act. Social evolution and psychological fulfilment may well diminish or negate the 'biological' impulse, started with separation of sex from pregnancy but propelled now by a wider array of influences. This is but one aspect of the increasing diversity of families and contexts for parenting and the often positive impact on their children (Lamb, 1999).

Parenting in Public Awareness

At one level, thinking about children must have been among the earliest cognitions of human beings regarding their own activities. Where written records are available, there are references to parenting and parental activities from the earliest times (French, 1995). As societies developed and their structures formalized, parenting became increasingly formulated in religious, economic, civic and cultural contexts. Given their vulnerability, children have probably always been regarded as special, and childhood as a distinct phase of life. Given the brutality of much life and the struggle for survival at all levels, it is likely that in the past children received the same amount of attention, relative to their 'times', as they do today (Heywood, 2001). From the 18th century onwards, they began to be seen as distinct persons rather than as mini adults or labouring hands, though industrialization extended the use of children as cheap labour.

Historically continuous male labour mobility was dramatically increased by consecutive industrial revolutions from the 18th century onwards. This factor, as well as good evolutionary reasons, always demanded that women were children's primary care-givers. From the mid-19th century onwards, public recognition grew that for some children this care was deficient and the state must intervene to protect them. Although the teachers' role as being in loco parentis had long been recognized, it was only in the 20th century that in most Western countries, the state began to adopt a parallel parenting support or substitute care role to that of biological parents. All but the least developed countries now have provisions for public care and protection of children. The death of nearly 80 children a year in the UK for example, at the hands of parents or other carers, suggests this intervention is only partially effective. For the parents, reconciling their own welfare with those of their children must have always been a complex and demanding task but its difficulties have massively increased, at least for those in the West. The economic and social context is now more complex and opaque than before, and meeting the needs of children has gained a higher legal and social priority.

Recognition of widespread child abuse and deficiencies in biological parents in the latter half of the 20th century gave particular thrust to the codification of specific child jurisprudence (Houlgate, 1980; Freeman, 1983), coinciding with the later spread of Nozick's (1977) powerful political philosophy that 'individuals own themselves'. The subtle and indirect impact of this has bred the concept that parents have their children 'in trust' (Alston et al., 1992). This means that they do not 'own' their children and cannot do with them what they want. Most national laws, certainly in the West, recognize that children should receive at least a culturally assigned minimum level of care and positive developmental opportunities and freedom from abuse. This is now enshrined in the United Nations Charter of Children's Rights. Parents are regarded as the main agents of delivery of these rights, with the state in a 'policing' and supportive back-up role. Some countries, such as New Zealand, Norway and Wales, have Children's Commissioners or Ombudsmen, to oversee the general care and protection of children and compatibility of legal and social structures with their best interests.

The relative compactness and smaller population of these countries suggests that children's issues, of which parenting and its support are major elements, are of a different order of complexity in other, equally developed countries. There is little doubt, however, that there is a gradual cultural shift in most developed countries towards recognizing qualities of parenting as the major shaper of children's state and prospects (Hoghughi and Speight, 1998).

Freud's emphasis on the central role of early specialization of children on their later adjustment was the most influential early pointer to the importance of parenting. The evidence produced was largely based on clinical cases. Quantitative research in parenting and its impact on children dates mainly from around the second quarter of the 20th century. Although childhood abnormalities and poor family histories had been considered in the context of poverty, ill health and delinquency, it was the emergence of empirical child psychiatry and psychology that gave a focus to much parenting research. These ideas and the general spirit of the times led to the work of Erikson (1950, 1964), who formulated, almost from first principles and based on acute observation of people and knowledge of cultural history, a framework for looking at lifespan development. His ideas have been profoundly influential among professionals and academics concerned with children, though less central to the understanding of influences on parenting.

The Second World War massively disrupted family life. Only by this time, there were professionals and academics who could research and report on the adverse consequences of family disruption on children. One such was Bowlby (1951), who instigated studies on the effects of removing children from their city-dwelling parents to the safety of the country in wartime Britain. Bowlby conceptualized the many disturbances of children's lives as centring on the disruption of maternal love and its consequences. His focus on the complexities of parent–child interaction and the consequent attachments opened up whole new areas of enquiry into parenting processes and outcomes. From the 1970s, research on parenting gathered pace and resulted in a series of distinguished contributions addressing some of the key issues of parenting. Bornstein's four-volume *Handbook of Parenting* (1995) demonstrated that the topic had become so fertile and complex that it could be regarded as a 'new discipline'. This has been resoundingly confirmed in the new edition of that handbook, which provides the most scholarly conspectus of the field (Bornstein, 2002).

Major Conceptual Contributions

Any list of major contributions to our view of parenting is likely to be selective and invidious, in an enterprise to which many have contributed. However, most would identify some key theoretical contributions which are now an indispensable aid to understanding parenting processes. These cannot always be neatly compartmentalized and have produced much cross-fertilization and enquiry.

Historically, pride of place must go to John Bowlby (1951, 1980) and his formulation of the concepts of maternal deprivation and *attachment*, subsequently modified and much elaborated by others. It is now evident that early maternal deprivation by itself does not have the disastrous consequences Bowlby suggested (Clarke and Clarke, 1976). Rather, damage is done by circumstances associated with maternal deprivation, such as distress, and inconsistency of care. Effects of separation from biological parents can be moderated by the child's age and the quality of substitute care, but some disruptions of attachment appear to have adverse long-term consequences. Winnicott (1958), of the same broad psychotherapeutic mould as Bowlby, introduced the humane and necessary concept of *good enough parenting* as a desirable goal of what parents do. This suggests that 'perfect' parenting, even if it could be articulated, is both improbable and unnecessary for satisfactory development of children. Realistically, the most and the best parents can do for their children is to give them a core of unconditional love and reliable care, providing a safe setting for children's own resilience and developmental potential to unfold – as demonstrated by the larger part of humanity.

Ainsworth and her colleagues, over a period of time, extended Bowlby's concept of attachment and established it in both professional and informed public consciousness, as a significant outcome of good parenting processes (Ainsworth et al., 1998). Although there are theoretical and empirical problems with the concept of attachment, there is general agreement that *secure attachment* is a crucial outcome of good parenting, creating a lifelong protective shield for the developing child against adversity (Cassidy and Shaver, 1999). Much of the material in the present book endorses this view.

Bronfenbrenner showed that parenting practices reflect and interact with the 'social and ecological context' of children and parents (Bronfenbrenner, 1979; Bronfenbrenner and Morris, 1998). The child may be the focus of parents' concerns and activities, but the effectiveness of these activities is dramatically dependent on parents' own relationships, economic circumstances, cultural context, and the wider social and political structures within which they operate. The increasing experience of parents over time, as well as their developmental perspectives also affect the way they bring up their children. The interdependent operation of a wide array of factors needs to be understood as a preliminary to making sense of parenting practices. The sophistication of many newer parenting support programmes, such as Sure Start in the UK (see chapter 2), can be traced back to Bronfenbrenner's work.

Parents' responses to the prevailing cultural climate, and their own personal styles lead to very different approaches to managing their children. As children grow older and their behaviour diversifies and becomes more complex, so they need and respond to different management approaches. Baumrind (1968, 1989) has investigated the critical issues of child management in its social and developmental context, through wide-ranging research and highly influential explorations of the topic. Most parents are seen to use a variety of styles, depending on their perception of the child's needs and age and gravity of circumstances, with few 'pure' management styles. Broadly speaking, *authoritative parenting*, which clarifies and enforces boundaries in an emotionally warm atmosphere through appropriate negotiation and reciprocity, is shown to be the most effective (Gray and Steinberg, 1999). It has the best long-term outcomes in terms of a child's self-control and parent–child harmony. It is apparent from this research and professional practice that there are wide variations, even in the West, in child management styles, dependent on social class and children's temperaments, although the wider appeal of the liberal and child-respecting views remains. However, as comments by Frosh (see chapter 7) and some glimpses of religious fundamentalist approaches to child-rearing show, child management based on religion may be narrowly culture-bound.

Children are not simply passive respondents to parenting practices. They actively shape their parents' behaviour towards themselves. Chess and Thomas (1999), through following up groups of newly born and other children, drew attention to the central importance of children's 'temperament'. Temperament is believed to be inborn, but from the first moments of life onwards, the child becomes involved in a 'biopsychosocial' complex interaction with the parents and the wider environment which influences their 'goodness of fit'. Children actively shape the quality and range of parenting practices. Thus, parent–child dealings become *transactional* (Bell and Harper, 1977; Ambert, 2001). Even in adulthood, parents' attitudes and behaviour towards their children are profoundly influenced by their perception of their children's attitude to them (Aldous et al., 1985; Samson and Rothbaart, 1994). Strong attachments are seemingly reciprocated.

Although the contributions of the foregoing principal researchers have had a profound impact on the cultural perception of parenting process, they are largely propelled by theoretical concerns. Patterson's contributions are of quite a different order. For him the practice of sorting out child and family difficulties was the starting point that led to theoretical formulations. For over three decades, he and his associates have identified parameters and processes of parent–child interactions among difficult and antisocial children (Patterson, 1975, 1982; Patterson and Forgatch, 1989). *Coercive family processes* entail inconsistent and unrewarding actions of parents in the face of children's challenges, creating a cycle of negative action and reaction. Patterson and colleagues have systematically utilized *social learning theory* to demonstrate how such processes are generated and maintained but, more importantly from a therapeutic point of view, how they can be altered by good-quality interventions. This work serves as a model of relevant, real-life, theoretically rigorous but practically useful research and accessible writing, attested by its discernible and wide-ranging impact on parenting support and education programmes. The contributions by Smith and her colleagues in chapter 15 of this volume provide an updated account of this work.

Finally, Rutter, alongside his distinguished epidemiological work and studies of much child and family psychopathology, has drawn attention to *vulnerability and resilience* as major overarching factors that are both affected by and affect the outcome of parenting practices with children (Rutter, 1985, 1999; Rutter et al., 1998). Children's susceptibility to hurt and their ability to withstand it are clearly key factors in determining the outcome of parenting under adversity which affect so many children, even in developed societies. All clinical practice with disordered children and families has to concern itself with the evaluation of these complex factors in both parents and children. In chapter 5, Kaplan and Owen set out the many facets of these concepts, where parenting practices are of central importance.

Understanding parenting practices and the outcomes drawn by the foregoing luminaries and their associates is complex enough, but the picture has been hugely enriched by many other researchers and professionals who have explored the byways of parenting practices and factors associated with them. Although it is the most natural, historically well-established and robust activity, the current view of parenting is one of almost infinite complexity. Exploration of parenting is now a veritable industry, with full-time writers for publications on parenting and regular features in professional journals. There are numerous local and national organizations concerned with research on and promotion of parenting. Depending on their level of development, many countries have, or are in the process of placing, 'parenting support' at the heart of their social policies, as shown by Utting and Pugh in chapter 2 of this volume. All this activity is not without its critics, either on empirical grounds (Harris, 1998) or from the political view that this is an aspect of state 'nannying'.

What all the research and professional activity has achieved is to support the clear message that parenting is *the* crucial process and transmission mechanism in shaping children's future. The slow recognition of this by politicians is being matched by the academics waking up to the necessity of making their work more socially relevant as a wider view of child development (Lerner et al., 2000).

THE CONCEPT OF PARENTING

'Parenting' may be defined as *purposive activities aimed at ensuring the survival and development of children*. It derives from the Latin verb *'parere'* – 'to bring forth, develop or educate'. The older function, *in loco parentis* ('in place of parents', assigned to teachers) well conveys this latter sense. The use of the verb 'parenting' is as recent as the noun 'parent' is old. As a concept, it seems largely confined to Anglophone countries, though there is evidence that its use may be spreading to other countries (Hoffmann, 2002).

The word 'parenting', from its root, is more concerned with the *activity* of developing and educating than *who* does it. In modern parlance, however, 'parent' denotes the *biological* relationship of a mother or father to a child. We qualify it by such words as 'adoptive' or 'foster' parents, 'parent surrogates' or 'carers' to keep the biological relationship distinct. On the other hand, the verb 'to parent' (or, more commonly, 'parenting') denotes a *process*, an activity and an interaction, *usually* by grown ups with children, but not necessarily or exclusively their own. 'Usually' is an important qualification because there are also 'parental children' or young carers who engage in parenting activities with their disabled or otherwise needy parents, or younger siblings (Barnett and Parker, 1998). And, of course, 'parenting' is practised by nurses, teachers and other care-givers, towards not just children but also others who might, from time to time, include friends, partners and strangers (Clarke-Stewart et al., 1995). The connotation of the word is that parenting is a positive, nurturing activity.

As parents get older, the age and power differential with the children which defined their status, becomes less stark. Care-giving roles are gradually equalized and then reversed, with most children adopting an increasingly 'parental' role, ensuring the safety and welfare of their elders. The concept has now been extended to the wide-ranging social construct of 'corporate parenting', not only concerning commercial firms looking after their employees, but also of public authorities' responsibility for children who have special needs and whom they look after (Department of Health, 1998). Given that even people who have no children of their own are somebody's child, brother or sister, aunt or uncle, almost everyone engages in 'parenting' activities. As we shall see, given the core elements of the process, the whole structure of 'social control' – formal and informal – can be construed as being an aspect of a 'parenting society'.

Thus, when we look at its reach and significance, 'parenting' emerges as probably the most fundamental and universal concern of society. It acts as the 'connective tissue' – the most prominent form of universal altruism which joins up and cuts across nations, generations, social classes, ethnic groups and religious or political creeds, where commonalities are overwhelmingly greater than the differences. Our sympathy for children in war-torn or disaster areas is an instance of this fundamental, universal parenting sentiment.

The biological connection of parents and children was fairly straightforward until the introduction of 'artificial reproductive technologies'. In this new discourse, legal definitions of who is a parent are complex and the complications arising from them far from resolved (Bainham et al., 1999). Pryor addresses some of these complexities in chapter 8 of this volume. Our concern here in this chapter and, indeed, the whole of the book is with the *activity* or *process* of parenting, neither of which presume a biological or age relationship. Thus, parenting is an activity that normally involves the children, parents and other family members in lifelong interaction. At each stage of development, participants have different conceptions of themselves as children, mothers, fathers and other care-givers. These views are affected by the context in which they operate, both within the family and outside. Issues of 'self-concept' and perceptions and presumptions of identity affect both the motivation of parents and of children's response to parenting, as brought out in many guises in the following chapters.

DIMENSIONS OF PARENTING

A notable feature of the large literature on parenting is the absence of dogmatic pronouncements and attempts at grand system-building that are evident elsewhere in the social sciences. The hallmark of this literature is recognition of the wide diversity of parenting practices, their complex and changing content, and the need to treat parents and children as particular. And yet, a coherent *discipline* can only develop if the main elements of the structure or parenting are identified and communicated.

A number of authors, such as Bronfenbrenner (1979), Belsky (1984) and Furstenberg (1985), have attempted to identify the theoretical elements of parenting. Based on these and much related work, it is possible to propose a conceptual framework of parenting (Hoghughi, 1997, 1999) that allows an evaluation of parenting practices in individual families, as well as the construction of parenting support programmes. Though clinical in origin and application, it may be useful in structuring much of the literature on parenting and considering directions for needed research.

In the present context, parenting processes are defined as *activities that are specifically aimed at promoting the child's welfare*. In turn, this can be subdivided into *parenting activities*, i.e. the core elements of necessary and sufficient parenting; *functional areas*, i.e. the main aspects of child's functioning on which they focus; and *prerequisites*, i.e. what they need in order to do their job. Between them, these provide an evaluation grid for determining parental *capacity and competence*, as a basis for supportive action and a 'conceptual map' for generating research and scientific discourse.

Parenting Activities

Parents do many things for and about their children, in a multitude of contexts, throughout their common lifespans, aimed at promoting children's welfare. Given the enormous range of what parents do, parsimony demands finding the *core* activities that are *necessary and sufficient* for 'good enough parenting'. These appear to fall into three groups: care, control and development. Each of these has two facets: (1) the *prevention* of adversity and anything that might harm the child; and (2) the *promotion* of the positive and anything that might help the child. These are usually *age and culture appropriate*, since what may be helpful with a young child may not be so with an older one, and what may be acceptable in one culture is not necessarily so in another.

CARE

'Care' comprises a cluster of activities aimed at meeting the *survival needs* of children. The work of Kellmer Pringle (1980) and others has identified a cultural consensus about what constitutes the 'needs of children'. These encompass not only the physical or 'tissue deficit' needs, such as food, warmth and shelter, but also emotional (such as love) and social needs (such as responsibility) at different developmental stages. In some countries, many of these are incorporated into laws regarding protection of children and promotion of their welfare. Thus, 'care' can best be seen as being concerned with factors that increase the child's resilience in the face of adversity and promote positive development.

Physical care includes all activities aimed at ensuring a child's survival by providing such basic necessities as food, warmth, cleanliness, sleep and satisfactory elimination of bodily wastes. It is also critically concerned with prevention of harm through accidents or preventable diseases, and if harm should occur, then providing early remedial attention.

Both systemic problems (such as poverty) and poor parenting practices result in significant proportions of children not receiving adequate physical care and protection. Even subhuman species generally provide adequate survival care. What distinguishes humans is that when we can, we go beyond this to enhance or optimize the child's state. This is evident in the diversity of food and clothing given to children, and extensive attempts to keep them in good physical shape. 'When we can' is the operative phrase, since even in advanced societies, families at the margins cannot meet some of the basic physical care needs of their children. Puckering deals focally with this and related issues in chapter 3 of this volume.

Emotional care involves ensuring that the child is not unhappy through anxiety, fear or preventable trauma. This entails giving the child respect as an individual, a sense of being unconditionally loved, and opportunities for managed risk taking and exercising choice. Its aim is to create stable and consistent positive interactions with the environment – chiefly other human beings but also the physical environment – which enable it to form secure, predictable attachments and create an optimistic orientation towards new experiences.

Social care is aimed at ensuring that the child is not isolated from peers or significant adults in the course of growth towards adolescence and beyond. Since social relationships have a profound impact on shaping children's views of themselves, and the power to affect their emotional state, they warrant close attention. Positive social care focuses on helping children to become well integrated at home and school, and accept increasing responsibility for self-management. This enables them to recognize the worth of others and seek self-development and enhancement through positive dealings with others and successful task performance.

The paramount importance of physical care as a precondition of any child's well-being is universally acknowledged and frequently written into national laws. Emotional care is more oblique and not as often the subject of focused parental activity, but it is something to which public agencies, such as social services and health clinics, are increasingly alert, as, for example, when a child is deemed not to be 'thriving'. Social care does not have a high profile and is rarely considered even by attentive parents. However, in the newer and more coherent parenting support programmes, such as Sure Start (Department of Education and Employment, 1998; see chapter 2), increasing attention is being paid to children's emotional and social care. There may be other care needs for the child, such as 'spiritual' needs, but these are neither directly related to any objective survival of the child or generally agreed upon. There is little doubt, however, that in some cultures (and fundamentalist sects) 'spiritual care' is considered to be as vital to the child's 'soul' as food is to the body (see chapter 7).

The outcome of good care is a healthy and thriving child, attachment by the child to the parenting figure(s), and the development of a firm and positive sense of self. This is the core foundation of self-esteem. A well-cared-for child will be, within genetic and constitutional limitations, healthy, emotionally resilient and socially competent, with the capacity to explore new opportunities.

CONTROL

Control comprises the range of activities concerned with *setting and enforcing boundaries* for the child, in an age- and culturally appropriate manner. As thoughts and emotions cannot be controlled, emphasis is generally on *behavioural* control and, through that, the presumed thoughts and feelings such behaviour expresses. The traditional term used in parenting literature is 'monitoring' (Stattin and Kerr, 2000), but monitoring (or 'watching over' or 'gauging impact') as an activity applies to everything that parents do with their children, from birth onwards. In relation to control, monitoring only concerns attending to and noting children's activities and making sure that they keep within reasonable boundaries. The word 'control' provokes an uneasy feeling, since it is associated with restrictive imposition of authority, but as seen in the large literature on 'social control' (e.g. Hoghughi, 1983; Cohen, 1985), the term can be both indispensable and neutral.

Control activities are guided by a complex interaction of parents' personal predisposition and cultural expectations. Such aspects as toilet training and going to school are regarded as 'unnegotiable' and almost universally applied. Others, such as table manners and spending time outside the home, on the other hand, are regulated and enforced less uniformly. A complication is that this most 'legal' of areas, often places ambiguous expectations on parents in terms of what they must/may and must not/may not do. Issues of care, being literally more vital, are more clearly defined in legal terms.

The central importance of the need for control becomes clearer as children grow older and interact with 'authority' figures, and as they become stronger, more mobile and prone to getting into trouble. Their increasing physical and social maturity, greater sense of self, and increasing autonomy renders them more problematic to control. These issues become most acute in adolescence when peer influences are at a peak (Warr, 1993). Parents' attempts at control are complicated by their own history and the type of control they experienced, their belief in the efficacy of particular methods of control, and their style of making their wishes known and gaining compliance. Parents with a harsh childhood history may just as likely reject as adopt the idea of behaving similarly towards their own children. In many countries, such as the UK, parental discipline is coming increasingly within the public purview. Parents are held publicly and legally accountable both for their children's (antisocial) behaviour, and for their own questionable attempts at control (see chapter 2).

In the West, because of the ascendancy of liberal views and respect for the individual, parents are increasingly advised to 'negotiate' boundaries and sanctions with their children, as appropriate to their ages and circumstances. There is, however, no consensus regarding the level and kind of boundaries appropriate for difficult children, how they are to be enforced, and with what consequences for breach or observance (Forehand and Long, 2002).

In the past, there were class-related standards of behaviour and sanctions, which have largely disappeared. Now, the more complex and pluralistic the society, the greater the uncertainty appears to be about what is 'appropriate behaviour'. At present, the only limited consensus seems to revolve around basic toilet habits, attending school, and prohibition of serious property offences, violence against the person and certain forms of sexual behaviour. Social and legal tolerance do not always coincide. What was previously predictable in terms of social class is no longer so, as witness the wide-ranging use of alcohol, drugs and young sex across classes. It may be unfair of wags to say that 'parents don't any longer raise their children; they simply finance them', but certainly parents are increasingly unsure of where to draw the boundaries in the face of incompatible pressures.

Setting and enforcing boundaries for children involves the whole complex psychology of shaping behaviour (Patterson and Forgatch, 1989), mixed with changing cultural and ethical considerations of what punishment or coercion is acceptable. This issue is likely to remain volatile and provocative. The already prominent (and in many Western societies largely autonomous) adolescent culture is likely to trickle down to younger ages, where children will challenge parental controls. This will demand increasing sophistication from parents in the way they set and enforce boundaries for their children. Given that most children behave in a culturally appropriate manner suggests that parents are adapting their approach to shifting social dynamics. On the other hand, the apparently greater involvement of young people in a spectrum of 'proscribed' acts, from drug-taking to serious delinquency, suggests that such adaptation is at best patchy.

DEVELOPMENT

Development activities are driven by parents' wishes for children to fulfil their potential in all areas of functioning. It is not essential to a child's survival (as in the case of care) or social functioning (as in the case of control). It is implicit in every act of encouragement or creation of new opportunities by parents. The formal social system, as funded by taxpayers, also provides a wide range of opportunities for promoting children's cultural awareness, skill development in sports, the arts and sciences, appreciation of the environment and the like.

The political thrust to this area comes from concern with social justice. Access to economic resources is a major determinant of whether and how children develop their reflective and appreciative capacities in artistic, cultural and environmental matters generally, where poorer children suffer undeserved loss. This is the core reason for the ever more explicit push towards 'social inclusivity' in access to culture, irrespective of race, gender and socio-economic level.

In addition to the 'instrumental' aspects (such as sports and education), perhaps the most important parental task in developing their children is the inculcation of values (Grusec et al., 2000). There is an understandable reluctance to prescribe values, other than in religious texts about parenting. But allowing for cultural and personal preferences, in pluralist societies such values include tolerance, wisdom, courage, fairness, inquisitiveness, temperance and respect for the equal worth of others, irrespective of their differences.

Good developmental opportunities for children result in their capacities being fully explored through experience and expression. They are 'stretched' legitimately and absorbed in socially approved and worthwhile activities, imbued with values and a sense of self that are both adaptive and rewarding.

Functional Areas

Parenting is not a single generic activity but one made up of numerous elements involving every aspect of the child's functioning. Parents themselves do not make distinctions in regard to what they do at any given time and their activities seamlessly flow from one area such as feeding, to another such as playing, and one activity almost invariably fulfils more than one purpose. However, from a professional viewpoint, particularly for purposes of parenting education and support, it may be desirable to separate out the areas of children's functioning that require parental attention. This volume focuses centrally on four major areas of children's functioning, as described below.

The classification adopted here is the simplest necessary for analytical purposes. It is not theoretical or diagnostic, but one that seems to work in research and practical settings where work with parents and children is paramount (Hoghughi, 1992). The areas of functioning cover physical health, intellectual and educational functioning, social behaviour and mental health.

Each of these areas encompasses the functioning of the child across the lifespan, from the newborn to the adult and beyond.

- *Physical health* involves all aspects of the children's physical state, survival needs and optimization of well-being; physical features (as in deformities); developmental state; physical, motor or sensory disorders and others that are physical in origin, such as Down's syndrome. The focus of parental activity is thus prevention of damage through neglect or harm, reactive care in the event of difficulty, and the provision of opportunities for positive growth. The importance of good parenting in this area is highlighted in chapters 11 and 12.
- *Intellectual and educational functioning* and problem-solving skills are essential for effective survival. Activities aim at utilizing a child's potential for acquiring intellectual and educational and work competencies. As shown in chapter 13, considerable evidence points to the incomparable power of parental support in enhancing children's educational functioning.
- *Social behaviour* covers all aspects of responsiveness to social cues and the ability to develop and respond appropriately to social relationships. In the course of growing up a child becomes aware of and learns to relate to a widening world of people and social circumstances. Parental focus on a child's social development facilitates appropriate responses to increasingly complex demands. Even more critical, however, is the recognition and internalization of cultural and legal norms of behaviour in regard to person and property. Learning to observe social distance and sanctity of persons, as well as respecting other people's property are the critical outcomes. When such learning is deficient or deviant, a child may disregard social boundaries or others' property and may be impelled to violate their persons. Unchecked non-observance or the active breach of rules leads to a pattern of antisocial or delinquent behaviour, with significant costs to the child, family and society. This is why there is so much emphasis on child management in parent training programmes, as shown particularly in chapters 15 and 16.
- *Mental health* encompasses all aspects of children's thoughts, feelings and behavioural tendencies towards themselves and others. It includes major personality variables, as well as clinical conditions (such as anxiety and

conduct disorders), and other serious mental health problems. Some children are genetically vulnerable to difficulties in this area, independent of what parents do, but there is considerable long-term research confirming the major impact of parenting practices on children's resilience, as shown in chapters 4 and 17. Yet, unlike aspects of physical care and educational support, and despite the existence of services, there is no universal 'culture' of supporting and optimizing children's mental health. There is much parents can do to increase their children's mental resilience, even when there are difficulties, as set out in chapter 18.

OPERATIONAL PREREQUISITES OF PARENTING

Depending on the quality of family relationships, parenting can be a lifelong activity. Given the preciousness of children to most parents, there is a sense of commitment and responsibility which is most demanding. What is true in all strata of society is that having children is expensive. Only the rich do not feel the economic pinch of having children (HM Treasury, 1999). Nor is parenting a purely private activity; it is a publicly recognized function, supported in developed societies by relevant fiscal and social welfare policies. Despite this, only recently have politicians recognized that financial provision is by itself not enough to ensure good-quality parenting. Economic resources are necessary for 'good enough' parenting but they are far from sufficient – as can be seen in some of the dysfunctional families of the rich.

Parents need extensive and varied resources to carry out their complex tasks, which change according to context. It is, therefore, not possible to give an exhaustive inventory. Nevertheless, in the interests of an integrated framework, an elaboration of classes of irreducible and indispensable prerequisites of parenting seems worthwhile. These include knowledge and understanding, motivation, resources and opportunity.

Knowledge and Understanding

Knowledge and understanding are concerned with parents' abilities to recognize focally their children's 'needs' through the lifespan, arising either from a deficit in the child or the urge for positive enhancement. A parent has to understand what the child's behaviour/condition signifies before responding appropriately to it.

Knowledge and understanding are the essential starting point of active parenting. They entail recognizing the child's state, interpreting it appropriately, and responding to it adequately. Parents do not come to their task totally devoid of knowledge; they bring to it a range of beliefs and competencies which are the result of their own socialization (Smetana, 1994, 2000), including any explicit learning about child development and the evolving, intimate familiarity with their own child. The knowledge element presumes the presence of acquired 'facts' about children in the functional areas previously noted and any 'needs' arising from them (e.g. 'she is crying, so must need feeding'). These 'facts' are culturally shared and validated with 'evidence', scientific and otherwise, variably percolating into the culture. This is a well-established part of most parent training and support programmes.

Apart from meeting 'ordinary' needs (such as food and warmth), parents are also often involved in 'risk assessment'. This is often done at lightning speed when the child is unwell or otherwise at risk. However, as the child grows older and matters other than pure physical health come to the fore, so the process of risk assessment becomes more complex and demanding, for example, in deciding whether a teenage child should be allowed to go to a late-night party. Risk assessment requires both child-specific and cultural knowledge. It also has to consider, critically, the costs of both a 'yes' and a 'no' decision for all concerned. This aspect of parental activity is not rigorously developed in training and support of parents, other than in the case of specific physical or mental health problems.

Understanding implies a reasonably accurate and comprehensive *interpretation* of the child's state. Although knowledge and understanding are only relevant and *useful* when allied with appropriate action, conceptually and practically they can be separated – as for example in a depressed mother who recognizes a child's distressed cry but cannot respond to it (Field, 1994). This is why immense emphasis is laid on this area in parent training, from early antenatal care onwards. Parents are also increasingly encouraged to develop some understanding of the impact of their own relationships and the quality of home atmosphere on children's behaviour (Wilson and Gottman, 1994).

Another critical element is 'assessment of impact', i.e. whether the intervention in response to a 'need' has had the desired effect. As with 'assessment of need', the complexity of this process also increases with the condition, age and maturation of the child and the wider range of 'invisible' consequences of parental intervention, for example their attempt to inculcate resistance to casual sex or drug taking. It is to this end that, increasingly, comprehensive manuals of necessary knowledge of children's age- and culture-appropriate needs are developed and disseminated (Riley et al., 1996; see chapter 21).

Motivation

Parents' own socialization gives them some knowledge of children's condition and corresponding needs. However, knowledge by itself is arid and neutral unless translated into *action*. To act on knowledge requires *motivation*. Motivation concerns parents' wishes and commitment to do whatever is necessary to maintain or improve their children's state. They acquire this motivation in the course of both their own and their children's growing up, in keeping with their personal need and social support for having children. This aspect warrants considerable elaboration, as it is often cursorily or tangentially treated in the parenting literature (Hoghughi, 1997).

Much is known technically about physiology, development, temperamental and personality correlates of motivation and how it is affected by different circumstances. Clinicians have a wide array of therapeutic measures for improving motivation at physiological, cognitive, affective and behavioural levels. And yet, it remains the most fragile aspect of human behaviour, at the mercy of sometimes minute social and personal changes of fortune. It is the 'black hole' of psychology, where much otherwise learned and high-quality clinical practice comes to grief, because we simply fail to motivate the 'patient' or the 'client' to adopt effective ways of coping with whatever is at issue, in this case 'parenting'.

Motivation for parenting entails elements of the biological urge to have children; cultural pressures; personal and social support for parenting; and constraints on it (Eggebeen and Knoester, 2001). From a historical and evolutionary perspective, most parents have looked after their children as best they could, most of the time. They have had to make considerable sacrifices in order to bring up their children. This is particularly true of women in terms of their health, mobility, wealth and opportunity to achieve personal ambitions. For some children, such as the handicapped, the sacrifice has to go on, more or less, through the common lifespan of the child and parent.

Although most parents still give their children the highest priority in principle, it is obvious that in practice significant compromises have to be made in reconciling their own personal needs with the requirements of being a good parent. For example, most women start separation and divorce proceedings in the knowledge that there will be some damage to their children (Emery, 1999). Thus, focus and priority given to children, which seem to be critical factors in high-quality parenting, are not invariable. They have to take their place in a hierarchy of needs and pressures in parents' lives.

Each parent has four roles and corresponding tasks: *self, partner, children, work.* Given the demands, conflicting burdens and complexity of each one, it is a wonder that so many families survive and do as well as they do. Currently, the most prominent problem of women's motivation in developed societies concerns their role conflict as mothers and workers (Hoffman and Youngblade, 1998). Until quite recent times, most mothers worked in the house, where children also stayed and interacted with them continuously. Now there are multiple reasons – financial, social and personal – which push or pull women to outside work. The barest minimum consequence is that they now have less time with their children. Other things being equal, inevitably they are not as physically close to their children as if they spent all their time with them. They are also frequently so fatigued or distracted that they are unable to give their children the 'quality time' they desire. The money they earn is inadequate compensation, since only some of it goes towards the child and does little to alleviate the cumulative stress, compounded when children are unwell or other family factors clash with work commitments.

Much of what men and women bring to their parenting depends on the quality of their own relationship. The impact of this on parenting is either 'additive' (when it brings additional warmth and love) or 'subtractive' (when it brings tension and distress). Further, each parent may have a 'cellular' and separate approach to parenting (e.g. harsh father, indulgent mother) or they may adopt a joint and co-operative approach to their children (Fletcher et al., 1999). Greater rates of family break up are but one indicator that parenting is subject to increasing pressure from this quarter, as it is from many others (Cummings and Davies, 1994; Wilson and Gottman, 1994; Amato and Booth, 1997). The increasing and high prevalence of single parenting presents a range of additional pressures (Fundudis, 1997).

For men, the picture has changed less, though the increasing complexity of fatherhood is now recognized in an ever-growing research and professional literature (e.g. Burghes et al., 1997;

Lipton and Barclay, 1997; Booth and Crouter, 1998). In most cultures, they have always been expected to work, spend more time away from home and less time with their children, and do more of 'their own thing' than women. The increasing employment of women has had a minor impact on the rate of employment of men, as the jobs are largely different, but in the West, it appears that more men now either choose, or are forced into, looking after their children whilst the mother is away at work. In the UK, next to the mother, they are the largest group of care-givers. In Western and developed societies, the increase in women's assertiveness regarding equality of opportunity and experience has resulted in a growing uncertainty of men regarding their own social identity. This may be one reason why many of them have difficulties and appear ready to duck out of parenting (Phares, 1996). On the other hand, in family break ups, men are increasingly contesting female custody as the 'normal' and often exclusive care-takers of their children in judicial and social contexts. Otherwise, for working men, the same issues of time, fatigue and distance in dealing with their children apply. Family break up and re-structuring is one of the most significant features of modern families, giving rise to particular tensions in parenting. This issue is covered at length by Pryor in chapter 8. Being in a minority ethnic community potentially complicates matters further (Coll et al., 1995; Sonuga-Barke and Mistry, 2000).

As is evident, therefore, the motivational element for focused, high-quality parenting is vulnerable to major social and personal pressures. And yet, in parent training and support programmes, hardly any explicit attention is paid to motivation, which so fundamentally influences what parents do (Barlow, 1997; also see chapters 3 and 20 in this volume). The available literature suggests that the main issues affecting motivation, both at the wider social level and in individual families, include the following:

- Social role and identity: how should men and women reconcile their personal aspirations with those of being a parent?
- Work and its demands: how will new and emerging labour market dynamics affect parenting tasks?
- Personal responsibility in the face of state intervention: how far can parents accept responsibility and act with corresponding authority when increasingly the state sets down the parameters of what they may and may not do, with and to their children?
- Relationship tensions and children's interests: how should parents resolve tensions in

their relationship in the knowledge of their impact on children's welfare?
- Differential income and its impact on parenting: how can parents meet their children's needs in the face of relative poverty?
- Social dislocation as a result of immigration and asylum seeking: how should societies reconcile/assimilate/integrate newly arrived families with the host culture and avoid conflict with parents' native cultural preferences?

Resources for Parenting

Academic disciplines such as social policy and sociology, national politics and clinical practice, have all dealt with the issue of resources for parenting. Indeed, the historical origins of concern with parenting can be traced back to the recognition of poverty, its impact on families and child development.

Early studies reflected the view that socio-economic adversity 'caused' inadequate and inappropriate parenting practices and poor outcomes for children. However, from the 1930s onwards, an alternative view emerged suggesting that socio-economic adversity and poor parenting practices were themselves associated with poor genetic and constitutional endowments, and that socio-economic status was only one manifestation of such differences. Although genetic differences among parents and children are recognized, claims of their paramount role in parenting are now seen as no more than deeply held prejudices. Poverty continues to be regarded as a major impediment to parenting, not least because of the personal and social factors that are associated with and result from it (Kumar, 1993).

The concept of 'resources' has not been philosophically well explored. It denotes *everything* that parents need, want or desire to deploy in raising their children. Thus, it becomes obvious that finances for obtaining goods and services are but one set of resources. Others must include psychological and social *competencies* of parents and the wider familial and cultural *environment* on which they draw. When present and of adequate standard, these are all major and invaluable aids to parenting. The core resources for parenting, apart from finance, all of which are necessary, include qualities, skills, social network and materials.

QUALITIES
Qualities are parental behaviour tendencies that arise from fundamental personality characteristics. Other things being equal, they predict the manner in which parents approach their task,

such as with warmth and intelligence. In human interactions, including parenting, the total personality is engaged. The parenting literature has tangentially identified a relatively small number of these. The 'dimensional' rather than the 'either/or' nature of personality features means that each quality ranges from 'low' through 'average' to 'high'.

Apart from the general and the common sense, little is known empirically about the interactive consequences of one or more personality characteristics for parenting. So we cannot say, for example, how parenting will unfold for an intelligent but emotionally cold mother, as opposed to a warm but not very bright mother. The main requisite qualities highlighted in parenting literature appear to include warmth, intelligence, stability and communicative ability, as well as freedom from serious physical and mental health problems.

SKILLS

The ability to parent effectively is not inborn, as is evident in much parental incompetence across the ages, cultures and psychosocial conditions. Although the motivation to have children is rooted in biology, human evolution has meant that there are no universal, inborn response patterns (apart from maternal lactation and other biological features), or competencies readily available to parents of new children. These, therefore, need to be acquired and are what, in this context, are called 'skills'. They also go from low to high, with one skill often facilitating another. They are acquired both *formally* (such as through classes in schools, maternity units and specific parenting programmes) and *informally*, through parents' own experiences, trial and error with their children, observing other parents or through the media.

Skills are required to meet the physical, emotional and social care needs of the child, to set and enforce behavioural boundaries, and to communicate with the child; persuasive ability is needed to gain resources, and management skills are required to make best use of them. The more complex the society and the more specialized the needs of children (as of the chronically ill or handicapped), the more complex and specialized the parenting skills necessary. A wide range of such skills, both general and specialized, are addressed in parenting training programmes (Smith and Pugh, 1996). They are extensively addressed in this volume, particularly from chapter 11 onwards.

SOCIAL NETWORK

The personal qualities and skills of parents are often augmented by the presence, involvement and responsiveness of other people, in the form of a network of relatives and friends, extending to other social groupings and the culture at large. Supportive people surrounding the parents are a significant source of empowerment. Parents who are visible to and integrated with benevolent social networks have, in general, much better child outcomes than those who are not, as happens in 'socially excluded' families (as shown in many of the chapters in this volume).

One of the longer term consequences of industralization, population mobility and changing family dynamics has been the gradual erosion of family ties in developed countries. Whereas at one time (as still in many developing countries) children would have had the benefit of integration into and parenting by extended families (Belle, 1989), they are now relatively isolated and face the unleavened impact of parental incapacity or incompetence. Public services provide some relief, but only *in extremis* and then often with all the limitations imposed on resources and a lack of real emotional involvement with the family.

MATERIAL RESOURCES

Material resources are generally interpreted as the money, goods and services necessary for raising children. They include food, clothing, housing, medicines, toys, educational materials and a multitude of services dictated by the prevailing standards of society. Much evidence is available showing the profound impact of inadequate material resources on parenting practices and thus child outcomes (Elder, 1985; Garmezy and Masten, 1994; Duncan and Brooks-Gunn, 1997).

The mass of evidence shows that family poverty is the single most powerful predictor of subsequent disadvantage and vulnerability in health, education, family stability, antisocial behaviour and mental health of children. However, the issue is complex, with many subtle consequences and questions about 'direction of causality'. Variations in quality and content of parenting within the same band of economic adversity have different outcomes for children (McLloyd, 1998). To this extent it is not only financial poverty itself (though that is bad enough) but also its effect in creating a 'culture of poverty' that seems to be the main source of long-term damage. The 'genteel poor' make extraordinary efforts to compensate for the effects of material poverty and work hard to manage their resources well and not appear poor. On the other hand, those who have always been poor develop a sense of hopelessness and fatalism which is even reflected in their very use of language, such as 'restricted code', passive rather than active verbs and fewer future tenses (Bernstein, 1977; Vernon-Feagaus and Farran, 1982), with which they construct social realities in which they live.

This state of poverty appears to be akin to and associated with a low-level clinical 'anxiety-depression' which saps parental energy and diffuses the effort they make on behalf of their children, as can be seen in daily clinical experience. Certainly, even in the UK, which is rich, some parents go hungry sometimes, in order to feed their children (Elder, 1985). Many cannot afford toys, 'sweet money' or other things that growing children 'need' and regard as essential (Long, 1996; Gordon et al., 2000). This is even more prominent among new economic migrants and refugees than the host population, where poverty is already significant.

Opportunity

Parents need time to do their parenting. This is so obvious as not to need belabouring and remains generally the least problematic and most readily available of all prerequisites for parenting. However, in developed societies, particularly in the rapidly evolving Western cultures, this is now an issue. Traditionally, mothers have been responsible for the care and control of their children in the early years. Fathers, when in employment, have provided the material sustenance and the funds for support of the household. With rapidly changing economic circumstances, increasing numbers of women have entered the labour market to work, full- or part-time. The time they spend at work cannot be spent with their children. Because the industrial context of women's work most often precludes taking children with them, the children have to be cared for by nurseries, child-minders, relatives, friends and others.

Research evidence on the impact of mothers' work on parenting and child outcomes is as yet ambiguous and provides support for diverse interpretations (Hoffman and Youngblade, 1998). For some families, working mothers bringing in additional money and pursuing fulfilling jobs, creates a more rewarding environment for their children and, therefore, child outcomes are better. But many mothers find the demands of work and parenting frequently incompatible; they are often tired and stressed; they are unsure of the benefits of working when so much of their income has to be spent on childcare; children get a very varied (though by no means often adverse) quality of alternative care; and outcomes for younger children, in educational

and mental health terms, may be less favourable. And, of course, there is even less contact when parents are hospitalized, incarcerated and working in distant locations.

MAJOR CONCERNS IN PARENTING

Issues of current concern in parenting range widely, both in the wider culture and within individual families. An overview of parenting literature identifies certain themes of persisting concern, though the list would no doubt vary according to author. These themes include the following:

- *Parenting and poverty* There is little doubt that good-quality parenting helps some children find a route out of poverty. Overwhelming, high-quality evidence suggests that relative and subjective poverty, particularly in many highly unequal societies in the West, is an endemic, corrosive influence. In a major and apparently growing section of society, even the best parental efforts are compromised by the undertow of failure to achieve what the rest of society regards as necessary and decent. This creates a culture of daily struggle and fatalism with low expectations and erosion of hope, which in turn leads to poor care and control of children (Department of Education and Employment, 1998). That so many children turn out reasonably is a testament to their parents' extraordinary efforts and their own resilience. No society can hope to promote better parenting without simultaneously tackling family poverty, its correlates and consequences. Awareness of this problem is not often matched by success of measures taken to combat it.

- *'Work – life' balance* This is clearly a wider concept than parenting, as it applies to all persons who work. It is now evident that in market-driven, Western societies, full employment and expected high standards of living through high output targets, pressurize parents to work ever harder. The increasing entry of women into the labour market has not taken any work pressure off men. It has placed greater demands on women themselves, who still have to do much of the parenting job, on top of the demands of their employment. Even where good childcare and other aids are available to a minority, the subjectively experienced demands on parents are increasing.

The exigencies of jobs and the consequent fatigue are not understood by the children, who continue to demand attention from parents. Parents' awareness of their own needs and the different needs of their children create a conflict of priorities which can often be only partially resolved. The resulting guilt and frustration, sometimes compounded by difficulties with the partner or lone parenthood, do not improve matters. In terms of social evolution, we do not yet appear to have adequately resolved the emerging conflict of man/woman, partner and worker roles with that of the parent.

As economic and work pressures on parents are unlikely to diminish in the foreseeable future, parents need urgent and systemic help towards better evaluation of options and practices. More focused and transparent exploration of the issues is needed, as well as greater availability of help to working parents. Highlighting what constitutes 'good enough parenting' under the prevailing social conditions, and identifying any help available, may reduce conflict between the needs of parents and their children. There is little reliable information about how best to do this, forcing parents to improvise as they go along.

- *Children in public care* All societies have children who cannot be looked after by their parents and who require substitute care. The more developed the society, the more some children appear likely to be looked after in or through public care. There are children who cannot be fostered or adopted and who present the greatest 'conglomeration of impairments' in physical and mental health terms, education and social behaviour. Their histories of disadvantage start before birth and continue through varieties of unsatisfactory care which precipitate moves from one caregiver to another. Because of this, they fail to develop adequate attachments and suffer confusion about where they belong, with attendant anger and anxiety about the shifting demands of adults. Those entrusted with looking after them, though sympathetic, often lack the skills to give them the necessary levels of care, control and opportunities for development. More importantly, they cannot give them much realistic hope for a better future.

A number of countries are attempting to legislate for and set in place high standards of public care (Department of Health, 1998). However, the reality lags significantly behind the intention, and prospects for these children, both as persons and as probable parents, are not improving. There is an urgent need to find new and better ways of parenting such children. This is not only for their sakes, as after all, they did not ask to be born, but also to mitigate their impact on society and on their own offspring.

- *Parental v peer influence* One of the possible consequences of parental preoccupation with work is that children come increasingly under peer influence from middle childhood onwards, even setting aside developmental changes. This is already a major factor in older children's behaviour. In some families and socio-economic strata, this influence is greater than that of parents, particularly where antisocial behaviour is concerned.

Little is known about how to enable parents to exert real control over their teenage children's behaviour in the face of powerful, 'pleasure-driven' peer influences, as evident in the spread of drug taking (though see chapters 15 and 16 in this book). With the continuing fragmentation and atomization of families, the need to address this issue will become ever more urgent.

- *Parenting in minority and migrant families* There is now an unprecedented movement of peoples across countries – in the form of migrant workers, refugees and others who find themselves resident in different cultures. Although there is much homogeneity of dress, behaviour and parenting practices due to globalization, nevertheless sufficient cultural specificity remains to create significant tensions in both host and minority populations. The assertion of separate identity (for example in the dress of some Moslem girls in Western schools) and exertion of parental authority and custom (such as arranged marriages with someone in the 'home' country) are all sources of possible tension between the two.

Despite uncertainties about trends, the mixing of peoples and cultures is likely to continue and even accelerate. There is a need to address this issue systematically in order to reduce tensions and enable integration without loss of cultural identity in parenting practices. To allow organic, laissez-faire evolution is an option, but not a good one if we do not learn from it and use its lessons to facilitate better parenting.

- *Parenting and mental health* What parents do with their children is fundamentally shaped by their own mental state – not just the impact of possible abnormality, but also their sense of tranquillity and self-efficacy as persons and parents. All the evidence available suggests that 'low-level' mental health problems, such as persistent stress and affective disorders are increasing, while the prevalence of more serious mental health problems remains high. Parents with such difficulties produce children who are themselves more vulnerable to mental health and other problems.

Despite considerable research, little is systematically known about how parents with mental health difficulties can be helped to mitigate the impact of their problems on their children (see chapter 17). Often work on parenting support is rendered ineffective by parents' mental condition. Any substantive work in this area is likely to produce disproportionate benefits.

- *Parental support across the social spectrum* As almost all the chapters in this book indicate, considerable effort and resources have been expended on developing parental support programmes. The emphasis on economic and other disadvantaged groups is understandable. Yet, as the following chapters also indicate, our knowledge and professional competence in providing effective parental support is patchy and, judging by its results, often unhelpful in the long run.

Maybe this is the best we can reasonably expect in complex societies. After all, parental difficulties are often hidden and parenting practices not subjected to scrutiny until something goes wrong. But society as a whole, and individual, powerless children pay a heavy price for inadequate or deviant parenting. We need much more focused, practice-orientated evidence about how best to support all parents, but particularly of the types mentioned in chapters 19, 20 and 21, in rapidly evolving social environments.

- *Research into parenting* All the above sections identify the need for more knowledge and evidence and thus research. This book presents a sample of the huge amount of information available on parenting. Much other information is not usable because it has not been produced with a view to utilization in practice.

Parenting is an applied, rapidly evolving activity. Much better practice-orientated research is needed to help support it. We have enough basic information regarding 'facts' and 'blue sky' topics in parenting to feel safe in re-orienting and promoting research into practice and its improvement. Work towards a better conceptualization of the 'dos and don'ts' of parenting in different social and family settings, in response to

particular pressures and conditions, is the prime candidate for such work.

The effort is warranted, because it would not be too extravagant to claim that there is nothing more important for society than to raise the next generation and do it better.

REFERENCES

Ainsworth, M.D.S., Blehar, M., Waters, E. and Walls, S. (1998) *Patterns of Attachment.* Hillsdale, NJ: Lawrence Erlbaum.

Aldous, J., Klaus, E. and Klein, D.M. (1985) The understanding heart: aging parents and their favourite children. *Child Development,* **56**, 303–16.

Alston, P.H., Parker, S. and Seymour, J. (1992) *Children, Rights and the Law.* Oxford: Oxford University Press.

Amato, P.R. and Booth, A. (1997) *A Generation at Risk: Growing Up in an Era of Family Upheaval.* Cambridge, MA: Harvard University Press.

Ambert, A.M. (2001) *The Effect of Children on Parents,* 2nd edn. London: The Howarth Press.

Arendel, T. (1997) *Contemporary Parenting: Challenges & Issues.* Thousand Oaks: Sage.

Bainham A., Sclater, S.D. and Richards, M. (eds) (1999) *What is a Parent: A Socio-legal Analysis.* Oxford: Hart Publishing.

Barlow, J. (1997) *Systematic Review of the Effectiveness of Parent Training Programmes in Improving Behaviour Problems in Children Aged 3–10 years.* Oxford: Health Services Research Unit.

Barnett, B. and Parker, G. (1998) The parentified child: early competence or childhood deprivation. *Child Psychology and Psychiatry Review,* **3**(4), 146–55.

Baumrind, D. (1968) Authoritarian v. authoritative parental control. *Adolescence,* **3**, 255–71.

Baumrind, D. (1989) Rearing competent children. In Damara, W. (ed.) *Child Development Today and Tomorrow.* San Francisco: Jossey Bass.

Bell, R.Q. and Harper, L.V. (1977) *Child Effect on Adults.* Hillsdale, NJ: Erlbaum.

Belle, D. (1989) *Children's Social Networks and Social Supports.* New York: John Wiley.

Belsky, J. (1984) The determinants of parenting: a process model. *Child Development,* **55**, 83–96.

Bernstein, B. (1977) Social class, language and socialization. In Karabol, J. and Halsey, S.H. (eds) *Power and Ideology in Education.* Oxford: Oxford University Press.

Booth, A. and Crouter, A. (eds) (1998) *Men in Families.* Mahwah, NJ: Lawrence Erlbaum.

Bornstein, M. (ed.) (1995) *Handbook of Parenting.* Mahwah, NJ: Lawrence Erlbaum.

Bornstein, M. (ed.) (2002) *Handbook of Parenting.* Mahwah, NJ: Lawrence Erlbaum.

Bowlby, J. (1951) *Maternal Care and Mental Health.* London: HMSO; abridged as *Child Care and the Growth of Love* (1965) Harmondsworth: Penguin.

Bowlby, J. (1980) *Attachment and Loss.* Harmondsworth: Penguin.

Bronfenbrenner, U. (1979) *The Ecology of Human Development: Experiments by Nature and Design*. Cambridge, MA: Harvard University Press.

Bronfenbrenner, U. and Morris, P.A. (1998) The ecology of developmental processes. In Lerner, R.M. (ed.) *Handbook of Child Psychology: Vol. 1 Theoretical Models of Human Development*, 5th edn. New York: John Wiley.

Burghes, L., Clarke, L. and Cronin, N. (1997) *Fathers and Fatherhood in Britain*. London: Family Policy Studies Centre.

Cassidy, J. and Shaver, R. (eds) (1999) *Handbook of Attachment: Theory, Research and Clinical Applications*. New York: Guilford Press.

Chess, E. and Thomas, A. (1999) *Goodness of Fit: Clinical Applications from Infancy through Adult Life*. London: Brunner-Routledge.

Clarke, A.M. and Clarke, A.D.D. (1976) *Early Experience: Myth and Evidence*. London: Open Books.

Clarke-Stewart, K.A., Allhusen, V.D. and Claments, D.C. (1995) Nonparental caregiving. In Bornstein, M. (ed.) *Handbook of Parenting*. Mahwah, NJ: Lawrence Erlbaum.

Cohen, S. (1985) *Visions of Social Control*. Cambridge: Polity Press.

Coll, C.T.G., Meyer, E.C. and Brillon, L. (1995) Ethnic and minority parenting. In Bornstein, M. (ed.) *Handbook of Parenting*. Mahwah, NJ: Lawrence Erlbaum.

Collins, W.A., Maccoby, E.E., Steinberg, L., Hetherington, E.M. and Bornstein, M.H. (2000) Contemporary research on parenting: the case for nature and nurture. *American Psychologist*, **55**, 218–32.

Cummings, E.M. and Davies, P. (1994) *Children and Marital Conflict*. New York: Guilford Press.

Department of Education and Employment (1998) *Sure Start: Making a Difference for Children and Families*. London: DfEE Publications.

Department of Health (1998) *Quality Protects*. London: Stationery Office.

Duncan, G.J. and Brooks-Gunn, J. (eds) (1997) *The Consequences of Growing Up Poor*. New York: Russell Sage Foundation.

Eggebeen, D.J. and Knoester, C. (2001) Does fatherhood matter for men? *Journal of Marriage and the Family*, **63**, 381–93.

Elder, G.H. (1985) Linking family hardship to children's lives. *Child Development*, **56**, 361–75.

Emery, R.E. (1999) *Marriage, Divorce and Children's Adjustment*, 2nd edn. London: Sage.

Erikson, E.H. (1950) *Childhood & Society*. New York: Norton.

Erikson, E.H. (1964) *Insight & Responsibility*. New York: Norton.

Field, T. (1994) Psychologically depressed parents. In Bornstein, M. (ed.) *Handbook of Parenting*. Mahwah, NJ: Lawrence Erlbaum.

Fletcher, A.C., Steinberg, L. and Sellers, E.B. (1999) Adolescents' wellbeing as a function of perceived interparental consistency. *Journal of Marriage and the Family*, **61**, 599–610.

Forehand, R. and Long, N. (2002) *Parenting the Strong Willed Child*, 2nd edn. Chicago: Contemporary Books.

Freeman, M.D. (1983) *The Rights and Wrongs of Children*. Dover: N.H. Pinter.

French, V. (1995) History of parenting. In Bornstein, M. (ed.) *Handbook of Parenting*. Mahwah, NJ: Lawrence Erlbaum.

Fundudis, T. (1997) Single Parents: risk and resource. *Child Psychology and Psychology Review*, **2**(1), 2–14.

Furstenberg, F.F. Jr (1985) Sociological ventures in child development. *Child Development*, **56**, 281–8.

Garmezy, N. and Masten, A. (1994) Chronic adversities. In Rutter, M., Taylor, E. and Hersov, L. (eds) *Child and Adolescent Psychiatry – Modern Approaches*. Oxford: Blackwell.

Gordon D., Middleton, S., Bradshaw, J. and Bramley, G. (principal investigators) (2000) *Poverty and Social Exclusion in Britain*. York: Joseph Rowntree Foundation.

Gray, M.R. and Steinberg, L. (1999) Unpacking authoritative parenting: reassessing a multidimensional construct. *Journal of Marriage and the Family*, **61**, 574–87.

Grusec, J.E., Goodnow, J.J. and Kuczynski, L. (2000) New directions in analyses of parenting contributions to children's acquisition of values. *Child Development*, **71**, 205–11.

Harris, J.R. (1998) *The Nature Assumption: Why Children Act the Way They Do*. Glencoe, IL: Free Press.

Heywood, C. (2001) *A History of Childhood in the West from Mediaeval to Modern Times*. Oxford: Polity Press.

HM Treasury (1999) *Tackling Poverty and Extending Opportunity*. London: HM Treasury.

Hoffman, L.W. and Youngblade, L.M. (1998) *Mothers at Work: Effects on Children's Wellbeing*. Cambridge: Cambridge University Press.

Hoffmann, E. (2002) German family structures and parenting practice. Paper presented at the 2002 German Family Organization Forum, Munich.

Hoghughi, M. (1983) *The Delinquent: Directions for Social Control*. London: Burnett Books-Hutchinson.

Hoghughi, M. (1992) *Assessing Child and Adolescent Disorders – A Practice Manual*. London: Sage.

Hoghughi, M. (1997) Parenting at the margins. In Dwivedi, K.N. (ed.) *Enhancing Parenting Skills*. Chichester: John Wiley.

Hoghughi, M. (1999) Raising the next generation and doing it better. *International Journal of Child and Family Welfare*, **4**(3), 257–72.

Hoghughi, M. and Speight, A.N. (1998) Good enough parenting for all children – a strategy for a healthier society. *Archives of Disease in Childhood*, **78**(4), 293–6.

Houlgate, L. (1980) *The Child and the State*. Baltimore: Johns Hopkins University Press.

Kellmer Pringle, M. (1980) *The Needs of Children: A Personal Perspective*, 2nd edn. London: Hutchinson.

Kumar, D. (1993) *Poverty and Inequality in the UK – The Effects on Children*. London: National Children's Bureau.

Lamb, M.E. (ed.) (1999) *Parenting & Child Development in 'Non Traditional' Families*. Mahwah, NJ: Lawrence Erlbaum.

Lerner, R., Fisher, C.B. and Weinberg, R.A. (2000) Toward a science for and of the people: promoting civil society through the application of developmental science. *Child Development*, **71**, 11–20.

Lipton, D. and Barclay, L. (eds) (1997) *Constructing Fatherhood: Discourses & Experiences*. London: Sage.

Long, N. (1996) Parenting in the USA: growing adversity. *Clinical Child Psychology and Psychiatry*, **1**(3), 469–83.

Maitland, A. (2001) The painful dilemma of kids and career. *Financial Times,* 9 April.

McLloyd, V.C. (1998) Socio-economic disadvantage and child development. *American Psychologist*, **53**(2), 185–204.

Nozick, R. (1977) *Anarchy, State and Utopia*. New York: Basic Books.

Patterson, G.R. (1975) *Families: Applications of Social Learning to Family Life*. Champaign, IL: Research Press.

Patterson, G.R. (1982) *Coercive Family Process*. Eugene, OR: Castalia Publishing.

Patterson, G.R. and Forgatch, M.S. (1989) *Parents and Adolescents Living Together*, Parts 1 and 2. Eugene, OR: Castalia Publishing.

Phares, V. (1996) *Fathers and Developmental Psychopathology*. New York: John Wiley.

Potts, M. & Short, R. (1999) *Ever Since Adam & Eve – The Evolution of Human Sexuality.* Cambridge: Cambridge University Press.

Riley, D., Salisbury, M.J., Walker, S.K. and Steinberg, J. (1996) *Parenting the First Year: Wisconsin Statewide Impact Report*. University of Wisconsin, School of Human Ecology.

Rutter, M. (1985) Resilience in time of adversity – protective factors and resistance to psychiatric disorder. *British Journal of Psychiatry*, **47**, 598.

Rutter, M. (1999) Psychosocial adversity and child psychopathology. *British Journal of Psychiatry*, **174**(6), 480–93.

Rutter, M., Culler, H. and Hagell, A. (1998) *Anti-Social Behaviour by Young People*. Cambridge: Cambridge University Press.

Samson, A. and Rothbart, M.K. (1994) Child temperament and parenting. In Bornstein, M. (ed.) *Handbook of Parenting*. Mahwah, NJ: Lawrence Erlbaum.

Smetana, J.G. (1994) *Beliefs About Parenting: Origins and Developmental Implications*. San Francisco: Jossey Bass.

Smetana, J.G. (2000) Middle-class African-American adolescents and parents' conception of parental authority and parenting practices: a longitudinal investigation. *Child Development*, **7**(6), 1672–86.

Smith, C. and Pugh, G. (1996) *Learning to be a Parent: A Survey of Group Based Parenting Programmes*. London: Family Policy Studies Centre.

Sonuga-Barke, E.J.S. and Mistry, M. (2000) The effect of extended family living on the mental health of three generations within two Asian communities. *British Journal of Clinical Psychology,* **39**, 129–41.

Stattin, H. and Kerr, M. (2000) Parental monitoring: a reinterpretation. *Child Development*, **71**(4), 1072–85.

Taylor, L. and Taylor, M. (2001) Why don't we have kids any more? *The Observer*, 3 June.

Vernon-Feagaus, L. and Farran, D.C. (1982) *The Language of Children Reared in Poverty: Implications for Evaluation and Intervention*. New York: Academic Press.

Warr, M. (1993) Parents, peers and delinquency. *Social Forces*, **72**, 247–64.

Wilson, B.J. and Gottman, J.M. (1994) Marital interaction and parenting. In Bornstein, M. (ed.) *Handbook of Parenting*. Mahwah, NJ: Lawrence Erlbaum.

Winnicott, D.W. (1958) *Through Paediatrics to Psychoanalysis*. London: Hogarth.

2

The Social Context of Parenting

David Utting and Gillian Pugh

SUMMARY

After an overview of current public debate about families and parenting and recent policy initiatives, the chapter considers some of the principal contributing influences. These include a series of rapid demographic and social changes affecting families in the final decades of the 20th century and the results from research into their underlying causes and significance. The further role of research in drawing attention to parenting as a skill that can be improved is examined. So, too, is the interest of successive political administrations in claims that a 'parenting deficit' has contributed to antisocial behaviour among children and young people. Description of the important part that voluntary (non-profit) organizations have played in the spread of parenting and family support services leads to further discussion of the recent political history of parenting. A concluding section questions whether sufficient public or political consensus yet exists to ensure that the current level of activity and interest is sustained.

This chapter considers the social and policy context in which a significant and growing interest in parenting issues has developed during the past 20 years. The use of the United Kingdom as a case history is not intended to suggest that people in Britain necessarily view or embrace parenthood in ways that are strikingly different from those living in other 'advanced' Western societies. Rather it reflects the exceptional extent to which those who make policy in Britain have, in recent years, acknowledged parenting as a political issue, and embraced the promotion of parenting services as a legitimate role for government. It is unlikely that the arguments would be dramatically different in other industrialized, Western-orientated societies.

THE CURRENT DEBATE

Parents in contemporary Britain seldom need to look far to find someone offering them advice on how best to bring up their children. The word 'parenting' can seem to be everywhere: from the magazines beside supermarket checkouts, to the posters in doctors' surgeries and church halls promising parents 'a chance to learn new skills'. The press devotes features and sections to parenting in a systematic way that would not have been conceivable 15 years ago. Their commentators have, meanwhile, joined in an argument about families and the role of parents that owes much to a widely-held dictum that readers will be more impressed by strong opinions than a strict adherence to fact. These writers set the parameters of the contemporary debate, although they cannot be said to offer a dependable guide to its detail or complexity.

On one side of the divide stand those for whom a breakdown in 'traditional family values' is to blame for a long list of social ills including incivility, crime and public disorder. This essentially conservative perspective has called for a fundamental shift in public attitudes to create a society where marriage is, again, recognized as the only acceptable basis for parenthood. Although restoration of tax breaks favouring married couples has been canvassed, informal social controls are generally favoured as agents of change over state intervention; for example, restoration of the stigma once attached to pregnancy outside marriage. Publicly funded support for families, including parenting skills programmes, are apt to be dismissed as interference by the 'nanny state'.

Ranged against them are commentators who argue that social trends such as the rise of dual-earner families and historically high levels of divorce have irrevocably altered the context of parenting and must either be accepted or positively welcomed. Decisions made by parents about personal relationships and family structure are to be treated as matters of personal freedom, privacy and choice. Yet this viewpoint is more likely to endorse the role of public policy and finances in making support available for children and families at times of stress.

A visit to the bookstore in any sizeable town offers further insight into the altered social context of parenthood and the different ways in which the term 'parenting' is applied. Publications that would once have been distributed between several different headings are now often clustered together in their own specialist 'parenting' section. Today's curious parents can choose between such enticements as *The Secret of Happy Children* (Biddulph, 1998), *Bringing Up a Boy* (Newberger, 1999), *Emotionally Intelligent Parenting* (Elias et al., 1999) and *501 Ways to be a Good Parent* (Elliott, 1996). Less enchanted mums and dads may be drawn towards *The National Childbirth Trust Book of Toddler Tantrums* (Hames, 2000) while hoping that their offspring never have recourse to *Toxic Parents: Overcoming their Hurtful Legacy and Reclaiming Your Life* (Forward, 1989).

While the sheer volume of available material is a feature of recent years, many of the available titles belong to a long tradition of guidance offered to new parents. An indispensable volume by Hardyment (1983, 1995) chronicles the erratic history of these guides, including the part played by fashion, misinformation and professional arrogance. Her exposition of changing and contradictory strands of advice stands as a caution to anyone intending to offer parents their 'expert' opinion. Her thesis that, far from undergoing steady improvement, child-raising techniques have always been tailored to the times is supported by an impressive weight of evidence.

Time will, no doubt, tell what modern-day counterparts exist for the excesses of the 1920s behaviourists Watson (1928: 'Never hug and kiss them') or Truby King (1934: 'Truby King babies are fed four-hourly from birth, with few exceptions and they do not have any night feeds'). But just as the prevailing direction of the guidance can be expected to fluctuate, so there is every reason to believe that baby-care manuals will remain as much a feature of the new century as the previous two. By contrast, public policy interest in parenting and the current debate concerning its validity is of far more recent vintage and potentially more fragile.

CURRENT POLICIES

A turning point, in terms of a political commitment to invest significant sums of public money in supporting parents as well as their children, was the election of a Labour Government under Tony Blair in 1997 and its subsequent re-election four years later. A discussion of the contributing factors to current policies follows in this chapter. From the outset, however, it is worth identifying the main components of the Blair Government's approach to family support and parenting. In England (as opposed to Scotland or Wales), these policies have included the following:

- A Sure Start programme designed to make comprehensive support services available to children under 4 years old and their families, living in disadvantaged neighbourhoods. An eventual investment of £1.4 billion was intended to result in 500 local programmes in place by 2004, reaching more than 400,000 preschool children. This was estimated to include around a third of children living in 'poor' households – defined as homes with less than half the national average income (Social Exclusion Unit, 2001; Sure Start Unit, 2001). While Sure Start is inspired by the 40-year-old Head Start preschool enrichment programme in the United States (Bronfenbrenner, 1974), it embraces a wider range of services including pre- and postnatal support, home visiting and outreach, befriending services, childcare and help for parents seeking paid work. Parenting information and support is specified as one of the core services that every local programme must provide. Sure Start also differs from its American precursor by offering universal services within targeted geographical areas, rather than access rationed through a means test on family income. Official guidance identifies the need to avoid stigmatizing families, as one of the programme's key principles (Sure Start Unit, 2001).

- A Children and Young People's Unit with a wide-ranging brief to support the Government's work in reducing poverty and social disadvantage among children aged 0 to 19. The Unit administers a Children's Fund (worth £450 million for its first three years) to pay for local services for vulnerable 5 to 13 year olds deemed 'at risk' of severe problems in adolescence and adulthood. On Track, a former Home Office initiative that includes funding for parenting programmes in the context of preventing criminality, has been placed under the aegis of the Unit. This has been recently extended to older teenagers at risk, under the Connexions (sic) programme. From December 2003, Sure Start and support for children and young people have been incorporated in a new Children, Young People and Families Directorate at the Department for Education and Skills (DfES).

- A cross-departmental Teenage Pregnancy Unit overseeing a national strategy for reducing the number of teenage pregnancies. The Unit is responsible for local teenage pregnancy co-ordinators whose preventive role is combined with a brief to develop support services for teenage parents. A Sure Start Plus programme has been introduced in areas where teenage pregnancy rates are high. As described in official guidance, it enables teenagers 'to make well informed decisions about their pregnancy and provide young parents-to-be with co-ordinated packages of support tailored to individual needs' (Sure Start Unit, 2001).

- The National Family and Parenting Institute (NFPI), a charity initiated by the Home Office, but operating independently within the voluntary (non-profit) sector. The Institute describes its role as 'working to support parents in bringing up their children, to promote the wellbeing of families and to make society more family friendly.' It has placed itself at the centre of the national debate about changing family life, defining its role as that of clarifying issues. Specific aims include providing a voice for families to

government, policy-makers and the media. Research projects have included the first attempt to map every family and parenting support service in England and Wales (Henricson et al., 2001).

No overview of the British Government's policy portfolio would be complete without mentioning the introduction of the 'Parenting Order' by which courts can compel parents of young offenders to receive counselling or guidance in controlling their children's behaviour (Crime and Disorder Act, 1998). The politics of the Parenting Order occupy the common ground between a populist view that irresponsible parenting is to blame for youth crime and measured research findings suggesting that the quality of parent–child relationships does, indeed, contribute to the risks of delinquency (Utting et al., 1993; Farrington, 1996; Rutter et al., 1998; Anderson et al., 2001). Court powers to require parents of unruly juveniles to take part in parenting skills or family support programmes have been a feature of the youth justice system in some American states for several years. In Britain they are arguably the most visible aspect of the Government's interest in parenting issues.

This might appear ironic or misleading, given the substantial public resources being invested in Sure Start and other programmes where help with parenting skills carries more positive connotations. Yet the Parenting Order is a surprisingly accurate reflection of the philosophical emphasis that the Labour Government has repeatedly placed on the responsibilities as well as rights of its citizens. Specifically, it is strongly identified with a much-quoted commitment of the Prime Minister, from his days in opposition, to be 'tough on crime and tough on the causes of crime'. In the words of a discussion paper published by the Labour spokesman and future Home Secretary, Jack Straw, shortly before taking power:

A wider acceptance is needed that having a child is not a totally private act, but one that has significance for the whole community if the child grows up into a pattern of anti-social behaviour. (Straw and Anderson, 1996)

Another driving force in the family policy agenda, coming from a different direction, has been the Government's commitment to reduce relative poverty and the wider phenomenon of 'social exclusion'. The latter term was originally coined in France to describe the way that disabled people found themselves excluded from full citizenship (Bynner, 2001). However, it is now used in Britain and other European states to describe the exclusion of individuals, families and communities from the prosperity and activity of mainstream society. At the heart of Labour's strategy lies a 20-year commitment to ending the heavy concentration of families with dependent children at the bottom of the income distribution that accumulated during the preceding 18 years of government by the Conservatives.

The evolving policy has recognized from the outset that attempts to reduce social exclusion must range across territory that includes the promotion of educational achievement and of good physical and mental health (Social Exclusion Unit, 2001). Hence the introduction of Sure Start, and other initiatives required to work across the conventional boundaries of government departments, including health and education. The primary focus is on children and young people, but this includes acceptance of the central proposition that any attempts to improve the lives and well-being of children, must also improve the lives and well-being of their parents. As expressed in *Supporting Families*, a consultation paper issued by the Home Office in 1998:

> ... the interests of children must be paramount. The Government's interest in family policy is primarily an interest in ensuring that the next generation gets the best possible start in life. (Home Office, 1998a)

CURRENT SERVICES

Although this chapter has so far emphasized the active policy role assumed by the UK Government, this does not mean that the many services now bearing the 'parenting' label in Britain necessarily owe their existence to government activity. Some parenting programmes are provided within the public sector, for example by psychiatrists and health visitors employed by the National Health Service (NHS), or by family support workers employed by local authorities. Organizations and practitioners operating within the voluntary sector are also important contributors to the range of available services. The mapping exercise carried out by the National Family and Parenting Institute (NFPI) identifies many thousands of public and voluntary sector programmes in England and Wales that fall within a broad definition of 'parenting' and family support services. From this, the NFPI deduces that an unusually well-provided locality might currently benefit from services ranging from parent–school partnerships to parenting classes facilitated by NHS health visitors, and from

family centres run by social service professionals to volunteer befriending schemes. While acknowledging the limitations of the data they had been able to collect, the authors were sufficiently enthused by the spread of activities to conclude that 'a renaissance of activity and creative thinking' has occurred among family support providers in recent years (Henricson et al., 2001).

There would certainly appear to have been an upsurge in parenting education services since the first UK studies of preparation, education and support for parents were conducted 20 years ago by Pugh and De'Ath at the National Children's Bureau (Pugh, 1979; Pugh and De'Ath, 1984). However, while funding through Sure Start and other government initiatives has enabled many parenting and family support services to expand their operations, many of these non-governmental providers pre-date the current surge of activity. They not only make a substantial contribution to the provision of services, but also play a prominent part among the forces that have propelled the Government towards its current policy position.

CONTRIBUTING INFLUENCES TO THE CURRENT SOCIAL CONTEXT

It is to these and other influences – demographic, social, organizational and political – that have contributed to the contemporary social context of parenting that we now turn in more detail. The various strands will be examined under four main headings:

- demographic and other social trends
- research and academia
- practice and practitioners
- politics and policy-makers

DEMOGRAPHIC AND OTHER SOCIAL TRENDS

As previously suggested, the level of public interest in parenting issues has risen at a time of fast-moving and well-documented changes in family life. The general direction of the relevant trends in the UK has been common to many other Western countries, but comparisons with the United States and the rest of Europe often reveal important differences of degree. Anderson (1995), a social historian, has argued that the most remarkable aspect of family life in the

20th century was the period from the end of the First World War to the mid-1960s when conformity and outward stability were more evident than in any previous century for which records exist. Yet the time between the mid-1960s and the present day has seemed to those living through it like a period of exceptional change. Some of the key trends and indicators can be summarized as follows:

- *A reduction in marriage rates* per thousand population, to their lowest levels since records began 160 years ago. The number of marriages solemnized in the UK in 1999 was about half the number 30 years earlier (Office for National Statistics, 2001a).
- *An increase in cohabitation outside marriage*: the proportion of non-married women under 50 who were cohabiting in Great Britain (excluding Northern Ireland) nearly trebled between 1976 and 1998 from 9 per cent to 29 per cent. Using a definition of 'family' that includes childless couples, it has been calculated that cohabiting couples with dependent children account for 5 per cent of families in Britain, compared with 39 per cent that are married couples with dependent children (Haskey, 2001).
- *Postponement of parenthood* has been marked by an increase in the average age for women giving birth in England and Wales from 26 in 1971 to 29 in 1999 (Office for National Statistics, 2001a). In 1979, nearly 70 per cent of births were to women in their 20s. By 1998 this had fallen to 48 per cent, while 42 per cent of births were to women in their 30s (Botting and Dunnell, 2000).
- *A greater proportion of births outside marriage*: in 1999, nearly 40 per cent of births in the UK were to unmarried mothers; five times the proportion registered in 1971. Eight out of ten births outside marriage are currently registered by both parents and six out of ten by both parents giving the same address (Office for National Statistics, 2001a).
- *The highest teenage birth rates in the European Union*: Between the 1980s and late 1990s, pregnancy and birth rates among women under 20 remained on a plateau in the UK. This contrasted with the declining levels in other parts of Europe (Office for National Statistics, 2001a).
- *Higher divorce rates*: the number of divorces in the UK doubled between 1961 and 1969 and had doubled again by 1972. Although below the peak level, divorce rates in 1999 for men and women in England and Wales

(per 1000 married population) were six times those of the early 1960s (Office for National Statistics, 2001a). It is estimated that around a quarter of children born to married couples will experience their parent's separation before their 16th birthday.

- *Growth in the proportion of children living in lone-parent families*: in Britain from 7 per cent in 1971 to 21 per cent in 2000. The rising divorce rate was the main reason in the 1970s and 1980s. Growth in the 1990s was led by an increase in the number of families headed by single mothers who had never been married (Office for National Statistics, 2001a).
- *One in seven families with dependent children are stepfamilies*: almost nine out of ten families involve at least one child from the mother's previous relationship (Office for National Statistics, 2001b).
- *More mothers in paid work*: the proportion of mothers with dependent children who were in work grew from 47 per cent in 1973 to 59 per cent in 1993. By 2000, 21 per cent of married or cohabiting mothers with children under 5 were working full-time and another 39 per cent were working part-time. Lone mothers with preschool children were only half as likely to be working. However, the equivalent proportions for mothers of children aged 11 to 15 were 39 per cent full-time and 40 per cent part-time irrespective of marital status (Office for National Statistics, 2001c).
- *Fathers in Britain working the longest hours in the European Union*: an average working week of 48 hours for fathers of children aged under 11, according to one study. More than a quarter of 33-year-old fathers in the longitudinal National Child Development Study were found to be working 50 or more hours a week in the early 1990s. Women's average time commitment to paid employment was significantly smaller (Ferri and Smith, 1996).
- *A rapid shift in the income distribution*: in the 1980s and 1990s that trebled the number of children living in families with less than half the average household income to 4.5 million (Office for National Statistics, 2002). Although a modest reduction had occurred by 2000–2001, three in ten children were in households below this relative poverty line, compared with a quarter of the population as a whole (Palmer et al., 2002).
- *A divide between 'work-rich' families where two parents are in work and 'work-poor' families where no adult in the household has*

a paid job: the number of dependent children in families without paid work in 2000 had declined by 20 per cent from a peak reached in 1994. This, however, compared with a much larger reduction in overall unemployment. An estimated 2 million children were living in 'workless' households at the turn of the 21st century (Palmer et al., 2002).

Longitudinal studies and other research (see below) have helped to cast light on the significance of these trends for parents and children. Opinion surveys, notably the annual studies of *British Social Attitudes*, also show how views of family and parenthood have gradually shifted away from a 'traditional' standpoint. For example, the proportion of British adults agreeing that 'people who want children should get married' dropped by 13 percentage points between 1988 and 1994 to 57 per cent. The proportion rejecting a statement that preschool children would suffer if their mothers had a full-time job increased. Yet the 'traditional' viewpoint still seems resilient, with dissenters remaining in a minority (Scott et al., 1998).

The sheer pace of change revealed by the trend data has stimulated extensive comment from journalists and church leaders as well as politicians and policy-makers (Utting, 1995). The focus of concern has, however, shifted in recent years. A fierce debate that raged around the issue of lone-parent families in the early to mid-1990s has abated. Other areas, where a statistical tide still seems to be flowing strongly, have moved towards the spotlight. Thus, a modest downward trend in divorce rates and a continuing rise in cohabitation and extramarital births has stimulated new interest in the stability of relationships between unmarried parents. 'Work–life balance' issues, the 'long-hours culture' and the different ways that parents manage their family and employment responsibilities have also assumed greater prominence.

RESEARCH AND ACADEMIA

Rather than attempt to review every possible research influence on current parenting policy in Britain, this section concentrates on four inter-related themes or areas where research findings appear to have made a significant impact. These concern parenting as

- a skill that can not only help or hinder children's learning and development, but is also capable of improvement or remedy;

- a factor in children and young people's antisocial behaviour, criminality and other 'problems';
- a mediator between children and stresses placed on their families, including poverty and social disadvantage, but also parental separation and family re-structuring;
- a role that may be more or less easy to fulfil in conjunction with paid work.

The title of this section reflects the fact that although empirical research findings have sometimes gained notice, even notoriety, through the interpretation placed upon them by their authors, a more common route to prominence has been through research reviews and other, more polemical, publications. The filtering role of newspapers, radio and television also needs to be recognized; not least the media's capacity for personalizing issues. This means that even studies showing modest average effects or risks have, on occasion, been presented in a sensational manner that suggests their applicability to any parent or child.

Parenting as a Skill

As suggested at the start of this chapter, the most obvious, long-term contribution from research to the social context of parenting has been through numerous books and manuals offering advice to new parents. These exemplify the ways that guidance made available to parents tends to mingle research messages with a strong dash of personal experience, theory and, sometimes, pure prejudice (Hardyment, 1995). The research sources most heavily cited are, inevitably, those concerned with children's physical and emotional growth and, in recent years, early brain development. The underlying message, in almost all cases, is that parents who understand the way that their babies develop will be better equipped to support their progress.

Some best-selling authors, notably Spock (1946, 1988, 1992), have shown willingness to modify their views with changing evidence and trends, such as the growth of maternal employment and a greater role for fathers in 'shared parenting'. The same is true of the interpretation of attachment theory, a still-developing view of parent–child relationships that has arguably influenced public policy in Britain more than any other.

Bowlby (1951, 1953) first articulated the theory in the context of bonding between mother and newborn infant and its observable role in evolutionary survival. But as subsequently modified by Bowlby (1988) and followers in the fields of psychology and psychiatry, the theory, itself, evolved. Not only did it offer recognition to the bonds between fathers and their children, but it also came to acknowledge the psychological and developmental importance to children of secure bonds of attachment within families, with friends, at school and in the wider community (Bretherton, 1991). From once seeming to insist upon the highest standards of maternal devotion in the early years of a child's life, it embraced the dictum coined from Winnicott (1958) that 'good enough' parenting is a more realistic and less guilt-inducing objective (Holmes, 1996).

No less important, it stimulated research by Rutter and others showing that insecure attachments could be remedied and that a positive bond with one parent could compensate for a poor relationship with the other. Attachments to 'significant' adults outside the family, such as teachers, were also shown to play a part in protecting children against adverse outcomes associated with persistent insecurity, including poor mental health or educational underachievement (Rutter, 1981, 1985). These findings, in turn, contributed to the case for family support services, including parenting programmes.

The 'concentric circles' of attachment theory have, in the last decade, rippled out still further to offer insights into the security, or otherwise, of the relationship between a state and its citizens. As noted in an essay by Holmes in a volume describing *The Politics of Attachment*, the heart of attachment theory remains its focus on the warmth, affection and security that one or both parents are able to provide for their children, and the potential for long-term, adverse consequences where children develop without those bonds (Holmes, 1996). Yet the fact that his fellow contributors included no less than three Labour politicians who subsequently became members of the Blair Cabinet lends credence to a view that contemporary attachment theory enjoys an influence well beyond the realms of academe (Hewitt, 1996; Jowell, 1996; Mowlam, 1996).

Prospective longitudinal research, following cohorts of children from birth or an early age, has been another important contributor to current interest in ways that parenting can influence the life chances of children. Most of the largest and most relevant studies have been conducted in Britain, Scandinavia, the United States and New Zealand (Bynner, 1999). Inevitably, it is the links established between dysfunctional parenting and children's antisocial behaviour that have received the greatest publicity and political attention (see below). But longitudinal studies also point to the positive ways in which parents, in otherwise adverse circumstances, can contribute to their children's well-being and achievements. For example, a review by Pilling of results from the National Child Development Study (NCDS) of British children born in 1958 highlighted an active interest by fathers in their children's education as a protective factor in the backgrounds of those who 'escaped' from a background of social deprivation (Pilling, 1990). Findings from the 1970 British Cohort Study (formerly the Child Health and Education Study) reported by Osborn (1990), further identified child-centred parenting, non-authoritarian parental attitudes and a strong interest in education as a distinguishing feature in the lives of high-achieving children from low-income families.

The most recent findings of the NCDS, conducted in the early 1990s when the cohort were aged 33, illuminated contemporary parenting issues, including a 'long-hours culture' in many UK workplaces that meant one in four young fathers were working more than 50 hours a week. Analysis by Ferri and Smith (1996) suggested this was a significant cut-off in terms of men's likely contribution in the home or participation in family social activities. More than half the fathers and mothers interviewed were living in dual-earner households. But while fathers were more likely to share childcare and household chores when their partners worked, it was clear that working mothers still made the main contribution. The discontent that mothers expressed with partners they thought were uninvolved in parenting increased according to the number of hours that the mothers themselves were working per week. Use of the same data set to examine the circumstances in stepfamilies produced evidence that the stepfathers in the cohort managed to be more actively involved in childcare than the biological fathers. Their lives in most other respects were shown to be remarkably similar to 'first' families, although average household incomes were lower and there were more signs of stress and conflict – especially in stepfamilies where children had been born to the 'new' relationship (Ferri and Smith, 1998).

The longitudinal studies that have influenced policy and helped to change the social context of parenting in Britain have been predominantly home-grown. By contrast, the case made for the spread of parenting education and support programmes has leaned heavily on international research. The use of American and other overseas studies has been mostly a matter of necessity. While evaluation studies of parenting education in the UK exist, few have been conducted with the methodological rigour of a randomized controlled trial, or any other design comparing the outcomes among participants with those for a control group of similar non-participants (Smith, 1996; Barlow, 1999). Hence the attention given to experiments conducted in the United States by Patterson and colleagues at the Oregon Social Learning Center (e.g. Patterson et al., 1982; Patterson, 1994) and by Webster-Stratton at the University of Washington (whose presence in the UK on sabbatical leave in 1997–1998 made her a contributor at the inception of Sure Start). The latter's Incredible Years programme using videotape 'vignettes' as discussion models for groups of parents has been researched in both clinical and community settings (see chapter 20). This has been acknowledged by UK reviewers as especially convincing evidence that parenting education can improve parent–child relationships and reduce children's conduct problems. Webster-Stratton's messages concerning the implementation methods that are most likely to engage and retain the involvement of parents in disadvantaged communities have also been influential (Webster-Stratton, 1997, 1998a, 1998b).

Scott et al. (2001a) in South London have subsequently published results from a randomized-controlled trial of a replication of Webster-Stratton's programme in the UK confirming the positive effects, in the short-term at least, on parent–child relationships and behaviour. Another study by Scott et al. (2001b) with a strong appeal to policy-makers has been an analysis of the potential cost-effectiveness of early prevention and treatment of children exhibiting antisocial behaviour. This uses longitudinal data to calculate the average cost in additional public services for young adults who have developed conduct problems (£24,324) and disorders (£70,019) during childhood, compared with those without problems (£7,423).

Prevention of Antisocial Behaviour and Crime

UK research interest in the links between parenting style and the risk that children will become involved in crime and other antisocial behaviour pre-dates the current wave of political activity by several decades. Longitudinal surveys, including data from the 1946 national cohort study analysed by Wadsworth (1979), have linked data collected on children's upbringing and family circumstances to evidence of later offending, whether self-reported or based on official records. Some of the most detailed information has come from work by Farrington, West and colleagues as part of the Cambridge Study in

Delinquent Development, following 400 South London boys from working class backgrounds, born in 1953, from their primary school years through into adulthood (West and Farrington, 1973, 1977). Family factors recorded when children were aged 8–10 years old that were found to predict later juvenile convictions and/or self-reported offending (Farrington, 2002) were as follows:

- harsh or erratic parental discipline;
- cruel, passive or neglecting attitudes by parents towards their children;
- poor parental supervision;
- conflict between parents;
- separation from parents;
- having a parent or older sibling with a criminal record;
- low family income, large family size and poor housing.

The prominence that these and other longitudinal findings have assumed in public discussion is partly attributable to a number of reviews specifically aimed at a policy-making audience (e.g. Utting et al., 1993; Farrington, 1996; Rutter et al., 1998). Although drawing attention to continuing weaknesses in the evidence, these publications have underlined the consistency with which studies in the United States and other 'Western' societies have identified major risk factors, including those of family background. UK reviewers and their counterparts in America, Australia and elsewhere (e.g. Howell et al., 1995; Developmental Crime Prevention Consortium, 1999) have contributed to a 'risk factor prevention paradigm' that offers theoretical underpinning for the possibility that parenting education and other initiatives could contribute to prevention strategies. Although there is more to be learned about the salience of particular factors and their place in causal processes, it is argued that community-wide initiatives can expect to reduce crime and antisocial behaviour by targeting a range of identified risks. This approach has been compared, by Farrington (2000) in Britain and by Hawkins and Catalano (1992) in the United States, to the public health programmes that seek to reduce the incidence of heart disease by targeting known risk factors across a broad population. From this perspective, programmes that tackle poor parental supervision and discipline will be relatively ineffective in reducing antisocial behaviour if pursued in isolation from other relevant factors, including those relating to individual children, their schools, their peers and the wider community. However, it has also been noted how the risk factors identified for young people's involvement in crime and drug misuse overlap with those for educational underachievement, teenage pregnancy and poor mental health. This means that a 'risk-focused' prevention strategy can, in theory, be used to address a range of different societal problems.

These ideas have contributed to public policy in the design of Sure Start and the work of the Children and Young People's Unit. The most sophisticated application to be found in Britain is, however, the Communities that Care (CTC) programme, using a planning and implementation process developed in the United States by Hawkins and Catalano (1992). Their 'Social Development Model' is distinctive in its insistence that the route to prevention lies in reinforcing social bonds, opportunities, cognitive skills and other protective processes capable of buffering children and young people against risk in otherwise adverse circumstances (Catalano and Hawkins, 1996). Not surprisingly, evaluated parenting programmes figure prominently in menus of 'promising approaches' that CTC communities are encouraged to replicate, depending on the results from a local audit to identify priority risk factors in their particular neighbourhood (Utting, 1999; Developmental Research and Programs, 2000).

Results from robust evaluations of parenting programmes are not only important to policymakers as indicators of 'what works', but also as evidence that the 'parenting' risk factors identified by longitudinal research are closely implicated in a causal chain linked to antisocial behaviour and other problems in childhood and adolescence (Farrington, 1996; Rutter et al., 1998). Parenting programmes available in the UK, including Webster-Stratton's Incredible Years, have tended to work with parents whose children are of primary school age or younger. So when identifying an evidence base for the introduction of the Parenting Order to be imposed by the courts on parents of juvenile offenders aged 10 to 17, the Government (Home Office, 1998b) turned directly to the United States, citing a Utah study of Functional Family Therapy (FFT) by Alexander and Parsons (1973). This showed that a time-limited programme that aimed to involve all family members in reinforcing and rewarding positive behaviour had led to significant improvements in the behaviour of adolescents referred by the juvenile court, compared with others assigned to psychodynamic family therapy, client-centred family groups, or no treatment. At least two of the local Youth Offending Teams (YOTs) charged with implementing court Parenting Orders have used Parenting Wisely, a programme based on FFT that makes use of an interactive CD-ROM (Gordon and Kacir, 1997).

Parenting as a Mediator of Family Stress

Research reviews that identify deficient parenting as a direct or proximal influence over children's conduct have gone on to suggest that other family factors, notably low income, poor housing and conflict between parents, are distal, or affect children indirectly through the stress placed on their parents. For example, a study from the Oregon Youth Study by Larzelere and Patterson (1990) found a correlation between low socio-economic status and early delinquency that was wholly mediated by parenting and observed family management practices. Likewise, studies by Conger et al. (1992, 1993, 1995) in Iowa found that links between economic pressure and antisocial behaviour among early adolescents were mediated by parental depression, conflict, hostility and poor discipline (see also Rutter et al., 1998).

The diminished quality of parenting in families under stress has also been proposed as a mediator for some of the poorer average outcomes observed among children who experience the breakdown of their parents' relationship. As one widely publicized UK review by Rodgers and Pryor (1998) puts it:

> The ability of parents to recover from the psychological distress associated with their separation is important for children's own ability to adjust. Parental distress is influenced by factors such as social and economic well-being and the presence or absence of conflict. In turn, it affects parent–child relationships and thereby influences outcomes for children.

Analysis of the major longitudinal cohort studies in Britain and elsewhere suggests that children whose parents separate, are at increased risk of behavioural problems compared with children whose birth parents remain together. They tend, on average, to perform less well in school and to achieve less in terms of jobs and earnings as adults. Work by Kiernan, among others, has also demonstrated that they are more likely to leave school and home when young and to become a parent at a young age (Kiernan, 1992, 1997). Yet, as the review by Rodgers and Pryor (1998) concludes, these different aspects of disadvantage only apply to minorities of those whose parents have separated during childhood. There is no simple or direct relationship between separation and children's adjustment, and poor outcomes are far from inevitable.

Political and media interest in these issues reached a peak in the mid-1990s when a number of Conservative Government Ministers flirted with the idea that marital breakdown and increasing lone parenthood were a cause of social dislocation – as well as increased pressure on the social security budget (see below). Support for their thinking drew on polemical analyses of research findings published by the Institute of Economic Affairs (IEA) that focused on the disruptive consequences of 'father absence' (Dennis and Erdos, 1993) and anticipated the 'replacement of the family with the mother/child unit' (Morgan, 1995). The conservative academic Charles Murray crossed the Atlantic to predict a 'neo-Victorian' revival whereby middle-class children in Britain would be raised by parents teaching 'traditional' lessons about marriage and parenthood. By contrast, a continuing expansion of single parenthood and extra-marital child-bearing in low-skill, lower class communities would create a 'new rabble' whose lives would become ever more chaotic and violent (Murray, 1994).

Murray's perceptions never gained great credence in the UK, where social attitudes researchers such as Heath (1992) found little evidence of an antisocial 'underclass' that was anti-family as well as poor. Even so, the 1990s saw the counter-arguments concerning family change and lone parenthood move away from simple assertions that the only real 'problem' created by parental separation was poverty. Emphasis was, instead, placed on the evidence collected by Kiernan that parental conflict was associated with adverse outcomes for children in two-parent settings as well as lone-parent families, and the findings by McCord in the United States that 'quality' attachments between parent and child could be protective against criminal behaviour with either one parent or two (McCord, 1982).

Although still disputed by self-styled 'family values' campaigners, the 1998 review by Rodgers and Pryor (1998) of more than 200 international research studies and meta-analyses came closer than other research to establishing a consensus. The authors distinguished between the short-term distress that most children experience when their parents separate and the long-term adverse outcomes that typically apply to minorities. While noting that a succession of changes in family structure appear to have an especially detrimental impact on children, they also found that continuing contact with the non-residential parent could benefit children's adjustment following separation. One of their chief recommendations was that separating parents should be offered better support and information with a view to minimizing the level of conflict between partners and the involvement of children in their disputes.

The Balance between Parenting and Paid Work

As previously noted, the proportion of UK mothers in paid work has grown dramatically in the past 30 years, while British fathers appear to be working the longest average hours in Europe. In the circumstances, it is not surprising that issues of parental 'work–life balance' have been widely debated. Like the findings concerning separation and divorce, results tend to be interpreted in a personal way by journalists and individual parents. Consequently, the research evidence, which is inconsistent, stands accused of oscillating between offering reassurance to working parents and fuelling their concerns. 'Parents' is, however, something of a misnomer since few studies until recent years have found much to say about the influence of working fathers – or even posed the relevant questions (Ferri and Smith, 1996; Harvey, 1999; Ermisch and Francesconi, 2001).

One example of mixed messages emerging at a time when maternal employment was growing rapidly in the UK was the 1970 British Cohort Study. Osborn and colleagues found that having a mother who worked full-time during the preschool years increased the risk of behavioural problems in 5 year olds. However, mothers who had given up their paid jobs during the preschool years were more prone to be antisocial or neurotic, while mothers from disadvantaged backgrounds were less likely to be depressed if they worked outside the home (Osborn et al., 1984). Kiernan (1996), who used the National Child Development Study of children born in 1958, showed that 16-year-old girls who had a mother in work were more likely than others to have gained qualifications, but found no equivalent effect for boys that reached statistical significance. More recently, an analysis by Joshi and Verropoulou (2000) of data on the children of the 33 year olds in the 1958 cohort suggested that mothers' employment in the first year of their children's life might lead to slightly poorer later achievement in reading, but that there was no significant effect on mathematics and behaviour. Turning to data from the 1970 cohort, they found no link between mothers' employment during the preschool years and the chances of their children becoming unemployed by age 26, or of girls becoming pregnant as teenagers. Children whose mothers had worked when the children were under 5 years old were slightly less likely to get good qualifications, but the authors concluded that family poverty and the mother's own qualifications were much stronger predictors of children's educational success.

By contrast, work by Ermisch and Francesconi (2001), using the longitudinal British Household Panel Survey, concluded that children's long-term educational attainment was adversely affected if their mothers had worked full time during their preschool years. The authors claimed particular authority for their results because their data had made it possible to compare differences between siblings. This meant they could control their results for other family variables besides parent's occupational status and parents' educational attainment. Somewhat overlooked in the media outcry that accompanied the study's publication, was the distinction made between full-time work and part-time working by mothers, where the chances of children's lower educational attainment were much reduced. Even less remarked were the findings on fathers, where sustained periods of full-time work during the preschool years had a modest negative effect on children's later attainment, very similar to that associated with part-time working by mothers.

The complex as well as contradictory results emerging from the more methodologically sophisticated studies have provided ammunition for all sides in the debate about parental employment – including those who argue strongly that paid work and the time left available for children must be an issue for fathers as well as mothers. One inherent weakness of longitudinal studies that the critics of particular findings have not hesitated to highlight is the time they take to produce results. Politicians and commentators find it all too easy to dismiss any findings they find unpalatable as 'out of date'.

A more empirical reason for treating the available research with caution has been a shortage of evidence concerning type, duration and quality of the alternative care that children receive while their parents are working (Ermisch and Francesconi, 2001). Results from America's National Institute of Child Health and Human Development (NICHD) study of early childcare are helping to fill the gap. The study, which allows data to be controlled for a battery of potential confounding factors, is the most comprehensive childcare study undertaken to date (NICHD Early Child Research Network, 2000a, 2000b). Yet its greatest claim to public attention, in Britain as in the United States, has so far been the outcry following an initial presentation of

data that linked longer periods spent in non-maternal care to higher levels of aggression and defiant behaviour in 4 year olds. The findings, at the time of writing, had yet to appear in any peer-reviewed journal article. However, the reported disagreements among investigators in this area have been memorably characterized by newspapers on both sides of the Atlantic as 'Mommy Wars'.

Practice and Practitioners

Published almost 20 years ago, the first UK-wide review of parenting education and support by Pugh and De'Ath (1984) noted that

> Structured schemes and 'schools for parents' have never really caught on in Britain to the extent that they have elsewhere. Schools for parents have been criticised for their restrictive appeal, tending to draw an 'educated and middle class elite ... and even parent–teacher associations in schools have played a minimum role in this respect in comparison to similar bodies elsewhere in Europe and in countries such as New Zealand and Japan'.

This same study quoted a government report from the, then, Department of Health and Social Security years earlier which concluded that

> ... the majority of parents would not participate in the parent education movement or attend formal further or adult education classes even if ... they were given a financial incentive to attend. Some less formal approach was needed. (Department of Health and Social Security, 1974a)

No one looking at the wide range of practice and practitioners involved in providing parenting education today could doubt that there has since been an explosion of informal support for parents. However, they might be surprised to discover that some of the more structured groups and classes that were missing 30 years ago are also very much in evidence. The UK is perhaps unique in the strength and variety of its voluntary (non-profit) sector, which some would say has grown as a direct response to relatively low levels of public funding for family support. Recent reviews of parenting education and support services illustrate the wide range of professionals from all sectors who are nowadays involved.

However, when Pugh, De'Ath and Smith updated their review in 1994, a decade after the first edition, they found that not all changes had been in the direction of expansion they had hoped to achieve. In particular, they found little evidence of a co-ordinated approach to family life education in schools and other youth settings. This suggested it had been the victim of curriculum changes in UK schools which put a much stronger emphasis on core academic subjects, leaving less time for broader topics and 'holisitic' personal and social education. The introduction of a National Curriculum continued this squeeze in the 1990s. At the time of writing, however, the Department for Education and Skills had issued new guidance on personal, health and social education, and moved towards the introduction of 'citizenship' as a new school subject.

Advancing through the 'life-cycle' to antenatal care, there are two main types of service that the state-funded National Health Service currently provides for pregnant women. Antenatal care is delivered through hospitals and general practitioners (family doctors) and is primarily concerned with the physical health of mothers and their unborn children. Antenatal classes provide information and advice to women and, to a limited extent, their partners. In addition, however, there are voluntary organizations such as the National Childbirth Trust that offer more parent-run and parent-centred groups with a stronger emphasis on peer education and mutual support that can continue after the birth. In many instances these innovative services fill gaps in statutory provision. But there is still concern that both statutory and voluntary services fail to reach some of those whose need is greatest – very young women, women from black and minority groups, those living in extreme poverty, and fathers.

The transition from pregnancy to parenthood is a challenging time for most new parents, as the heavy involvement of health professionals before and during the birth reduces, and the reality of life with a young baby become apparent along with the emotional demands of parenting. Moreover, while the National Health Service (NHS) is the main provider of care during the antenatal period, many parents look for support from informal networks and from voluntary sector organizations during the postnatal period. Prominent among these is PIPPIN, a programme developed by Parr that is based on small group sessions and which supports expectant and new parents by encouraging the development of nurturing family and parent–infant relationships (Parr, 1997).

The range of support for parents of young children – informal and more structured – is now significant. The Government's heavy investment in Sure Start programmes (see above) means that such support is likely to increase. Not unexpectedly, the review of parenting and family support services by Henricson et al. (2001) for the National Family and Parenting Institute found that a quarter of all schemes had been set up in the last five years. Just under a fifth of services were being provided on an individual basis, either through one-to-one counselling for parents, as part of a home visiting scheme, or through telephone helplines run by national voluntary organizations such as Parentline Plus. However, the main form of support was through both informal and more structured groups, and through centres providing opportunities for parents to 'drop in' and find the support they need. Some of these are provided through the statutory services. For example, many primary schools and early years centres run groups and drop-in centres for the parents of very young children, while local authority social service departments run family centres where they can refer families that are causing concern. However, the majority of support services are still located in the voluntary sector. For example, they can be found in the network of informal parent and toddler groups and playgroups affiliated to the Preschool Learning Alliance, and in the work of long-established childcare charities such as Barnardos, the NSPCC and Family Service Units. Churches and other faith groups also appear to be playing an increasing role in providing premises and actual support services.

Some of the most evident growth has occurred through the spread of parenting groups and courses. Contrary to the gloomy view of government officials 30 years ago (Department of Health and Social Security, 1974b), there has been growing recognition that bringing up children is a challenging task and that asking for help is not a sign of failure. A review of group-based parenting programmes by Smith in 1996 found 38 different programmes and approaches that had the explicit aim of helping parents improve their parenting skills and family relationships. It also identified six main theoretical approaches:

- *transactional analysis*, stressing processes important to personality development and transactions between people (Berne, 1973);
- *behavioural* (applying social learning principles as, for example, described by Patterson, 1982);
- *humanistic*, stressing the importance of parent–child empathy (for example, Parent Effectiveness Training (PET) (Rogers, 1951, 1961; Gordon, 1975);
- *psychodynamic* theories, exploring the links between inner, individual perceptions and family experiences;

- *family systems* theories stressing the importance of understanding individual children's behaviour in relation to that of other family members; and
- *Adlerian*, the ideas of Adler developed for the Systematic Training for Effective Parenting (STEP) programme (Adler, 1927, 1930; Dreikurs and Soltz, 1964; Dinkmeyer and McKay, 1976).

Smith (1996) found that the parenting programmes available in the UK divided into two broad groups: those with a behavioural focus with a main aim of changing children's behaviour; and those that mainly address interpersonal relationships within the family. Of those in the behavioural group, the most widely used model in the UK is the work of Webster-Stratton (see chapter 20), although a number of psychologists have developed their own models which are gaining popularity (see chapter 3). The 'relationships' approach also includes a number of programmes that are widely used, including courses from the Open University, the Family Caring Trust (Quinn and Quinn, 1986), a voluntary group based in Northern Ireland, and Parent Network (Davis and Hester, 1996), one of the first national parenting organizations and which is now part of Parentline Plus.

As a rough estimate, Smith, writing in the mid-1990s, thought that around 60,000 parents – about 8 per cent of UK parents – were likely to access any kind of course during their years of caring for children. In terms of users, she noted that it was mainly white, middle-class women who attended parenting groups. Since then a number of organizations, including those working in Sure Start areas, have been active in successfully broadening their appeal to low-income families and to black and minority ethnic communities. Another continuing shortcoming in UK provision, however, has been a dearth of support services for the parents of teenagers. Partly prompted by the introduction of powers for the courts to order parents of juvenile offenders to attend parenting support sessions, organizations such as the Trust for the Study of Adolescence are now working to fill the gap.

The providers of parenting courses are many and various. Smith found that, overall, the agencies providing courses included local education authorities, schools, health authorities and trusts, social service departments, voluntary organizations, churches and other faith groups, young offender institutions and prisons, and academic institutions. The two largest groups of professionals running programmes were educational psychologists and trained nurses who had qualified as health visitors, followed by social workers and teachers. Two of the most widely available programmes– Parenting Matters (formerly *Parent Link*) and the Veritas courses supported by materials from the Family Caring Trust – operate by training parents to become group leaders. The training and accreditation of more group leaders to meet demand has become an urgent priority for these and other organizations. The Parenting Education and Support Forum, established as a national 'umbrella' body for providers of parent education is currently developing a curriculum and accreditation framework.

POLITICS AND POLICY-MAKERS

While a graph depicting practitioner activity concerned with parenting through the past 30 years would show a steady, though steepening line of increase, an equivalent chart for levels of policy interest would be altogether more jagged. Analysts intent on proving that ideas become fashionable on a cyclical basis would certainly want to compare the present Labour Government's interest in parenting with the early 1970s when Sir Keith Joseph, a Conservative Cabinet Minister, launched an investigation into the transmission of social disadvantage between generations. Announcing his initiative, Sir Keith specifically contrasted the provision of medical care for mothers-to-be with the lack of effort put into preparing parents of both sexes for their role in raising children.[1] His initial ideas about families being trapped in a 'cycle of deprivation' were heavily qualified by research by Rutter and others that followed (Department of Health and Social Security, 1974a, 1974b; Rutter and Madge, 1976). But a succession of government and parliamentary reports returned to the theme of better preparation for parenthood. In the words of the 1976 Court report on the future of child health services.

'Future improvements in the health of children will depend as much on the beliefs and behaviour of parents as on the services provided.' (Committee on Child Health Services, 1976).

A 1978 policy paper on preventing child abuse from the Department of Health and Social Security, in the last days of a Labour government, called for 'education for parenthood' in schools and antenatal classes, and for a wide range of support services for parents with young children. Since the leaders of both main political parties were at this time claiming to lead 'the party of the family', it is all the more remarkable how quickly policy interest then dissipated in the 1980s. In 1983, the final report from the independent Study Commission on the Family complained that 'Political interest in the family ... seldom seems to get beyond the level of rhetoric.'

The political rediscovery of families and parenthood occurred a decade later when the divorce rate peak-level led Margaret Thatcher, the long-serving Conservative Prime Minister, to claim that children were losing their fundamental right 'to be brought up in a real family' (Utting and Laurance, 1990). As with a second wave of pronouncements under her successor, John Major, the driving force appeared to be concern over a burgeoning social security budget. The introduction of a Child Support Agency to secure child maintenance payments from non-resident fathers under Thatcher was followed by a short-lived 'back to basics' campaign under the next Cabinet. Some Cabinet Ministers took this as their cue to assert the superiority of 'traditional' two-parent families over other family structures (e.g. Peter Lilley[2] and John Redwood[3]). An immediate by-product was keener-than-usual press interest in the marital (and extra-marital) affairs of Ministers. An about-turn was signalled in 1994 when the Health Secretary, Virginia Bottomley, as the Government's official spokesman on family issues, insisted on the need for policies that 'underpin rather than undermine families'.

This was the period when the ideas of Murray in the United States concerning an antisocial 'underclass' (see above) received serious attention in some sections of the British media. An American sociologist who eventually proved more influential in the UK, however, was Amitai Etzioni whose book *The Spirit of Community* (1993) struck a chord with Tony Blair and colleagues as they started to define an ideological base for 'New Labour' after long years in opposition. Policy statements and speeches to this day insist on the need to balance rights with responsibilities in a way that echoes Etzioni's 'communitarian' thinking. Yet there has been noticeably less resonance between Labour's specific agenda on families and Etzioni's ideas, as re-packaged for the UK in a report called *The Parenting Deficit* (1995). Etzioni argued that social trends, including relationship breakdown and pressures of work, were leading parents to neglect their children's needs. But in government, Labour's perception of work as the best route out of poverty has taken precedence. The result has been policies such as the National Childcare Strategy to increase the number of affordable, alternative childcare places, and the New Deal for Lone Parents which offers advice, training and other support in moving off social security into paid work.

Even more than its Conservative predecessor, the Blair Government has been impressed by the evidence from criminological research that harsh, erratic discipline and poor parental supervision are major risk factors contributing to youth crime. The very fact that Labour, in opposition, went to the trouble of issuing a discussion paper on parenting in the name of the Shadow Home Secretary is striking (Straw and Anderson, 1996). But it was also remarkable for its repeated invocation of research evidence in support of its plans. Calls for policy to be 'evidence-based' have remained a feature of Labour in government, with a specialist unit attached to the Prime Minister's office for that purpose. Initiatives such as Sure Start and the Children and Young People's Unit not only justify their existence on the basis of existing research, but also include a strong commitment to evaluation. Even so, there are a host of practical reasons why the conflicting priorities and timescales of politicians and researchers are unlikely to produce a match made in heaven. This may especially be the case where community-based services for children and families are concerned (Glass, 2001).

Another noteworthy feature of Labour's subsequent government consultation paper, *Supporting Families,* was the way it defined the extent and limits of government involvement. Carefully placing itself between 'back to basics' fundamentalism and 'anything goes' liberalism, the Government defined its role as that of offering support to parents, but not trying to substitute for them. In other words,

> There needs to be a clear understanding of the rights and responsibilities which fall to families and to government. Parents raise children, and that is how things should remain. More direct intervention should only occur in extreme circumstances, for example in cases of domestic violence or where the welfare of children is at stake. (Home Office, 1998a)

While stating that 'marriage is still the surest foundation for raising children', the Government remained careful to assert that many lone parents raise their children 'every bit as successfully'. The consultation paper also suggested that lessons had been learned from the previous administration's unhappy experience in relation to well-publicized pronouncements on families: 'We must not preach and we must not give the impression that members of the Government are any better than the rest of the population. They are not.'

CONCLUSIONS

This chapter has identified some unusually rapid changes in the social and political context of parenting that have taken place in Britain on the cusp of the 20th and 21st centuries. It has highlighted demographic, social and economic trends, by no means unique to the UK, which mean that the circumstances in which parents raise children can be very different from those of 30 years ago. The increasing number of families where both parents are in work and the contrast in living standards with those where no adult has a paid job is one example. Another is the diversification of family structures: although most children still grow up with their two birth parents, a large and growing minority of parents are unmarried – at least to begin with. Moreover, a substantial minority of children are, at any one time, being raised by a lone parent, either because their parents have not lived together since they were born or because their parents' relationship has come to an end through bereavement or separation. The number of stepfamilies has also increased. These are real changes that, one way or another, have touched the lives of every family.

Given the evidence of ways in which the quality of parenting can make it easier or harder for children to 'escape' from poverty and adjust to family change, it is not altogether surprising that politicians and other policy-makers have become interested in the scope for parenting and family support services. The remarkable feature of the Sure Start programme and other policy initiatives taken by the current Labour Government is, perhaps, that it has taken so long to happen. It is, after all, 40 years since the Democrat's 'War on Poverty' led to the creation of Head Start in the United States.

Factors that have previously inhibited UK policy development in this area have included a banal, though realistic, fear among politicians that pronouncements on family and parenthood issues will expose their own lives to unwanted scrutiny by the media. At a more cerebral level, there has been a genuine debate concerning the appropriate positioning of a line between the state's legitimate interest in the welfare of children and unwarranted intrusion into the private lives of individuals and families. The British Government has worked out a formula designed to justify its stance while holding its opponents in check. The nub of this has been to define its role in terms of making publicly funded support available for parents, rather than explicit intervention in their lives.

Those parts of the formula that are most obviously a 'political fix' have led to accusations of inconsistency. Critics from both a liberal and a conservative perspective have wondered whether declarations of respect for family diversity really square with an avowed determination to strengthen the institution of marriage (Home Office, 1998a). A more substantive concern is whether tensions can be resolved between pushing parents of young children towards paid work as part of an anti-poverty agenda, and the promotion of better parent–child relationships. Research, as seen, has only limited guidance to offer policy-makers on the apparent trade-offs, where children's long-term prospects are concerned, between improving family income and reduced time spent interacting with children at home. Crucial questions about the quality and quantity of alternative childcare also remain unanswered (Ermisch and Francesconi, 2001).

Other steps taken to increase support for children, young people and families, including an increase in funding for parenting education, have attracted less controversy. Even the power for criminal courts to make Parenting Orders has gained wider acceptance than once seemed probable; not least because implementation has depended heavily on practitioners who are well aware of the pitfalls of reinforcing parents' feelings of impotence and stigma. Sure Start, still the flagship family support initiative, appears to inspire genuine affection, not least among parents who use its services. The fact that an elaborate programme of longitudinal evaluation is under way contributes to confidence that the model of making comprehensive, multi-agency support services available in disadvantaged communities will endure. The American experience with Head Start also suggests that preschool enrichment programmes can attract bipartisan support, making them resilient to changes of administration and altered spending priorities.

There is, as yet, no equivalent political consensus in the UK. The current policy interest in parenting and family support in the UK must, therefore, still be deemed vulnerable to shifts in political priorities. An instructive analysis of the debate about family support services by Hardiker and colleagues (Hardiker et al., 1991; Hardiker, 1995) attempted a match between ideology and different levels of prevention. This equated a commitment to invest public money in primary prevention through universal services, with the most liberal (or even socialist) agendas. Secondary prevention, targeting help on a smaller population of children and parents experiencing stress, was associated with a more philanthropic and paternalist strand of liberalism. By contrast, a belief that publicly funded support was only warranted at times of suspected child abuse, offending and other crises – tertiary prevention – was identified with a conservative outlook of keeping state intervention to a minimum. Thus, while the Blair Government's programme might fairly be said to reflect the second tier, with even some elements of the first, it is entirely conceivable that a change of administration would send the pendulum swinging back towards the third. This will be even more so if the switch in ideology were to coincide with a squeeze on public spending.

Accusations by political opponents that Labour is running an interfering 'nanny' state have, at the time of writing, been muted. The loudest criticism has come from those in journalism and the outside world who portray the Government's initiatives as part and parcel of a wider agenda to establish a 'parenting industry' in the UK. According to Furedi, a prominent academic objector, we are witnessing a 'professionalization' of parenting where all parents are treated as potential failures, instead of the small minority who genuinely need help:

> Unable to work out effective social policies that can tackle the real problems facing British society, some politicians have been persuaded that if they can re-educate parents everything would turn out fine. Politicians, who have failed to provide Britain with a decent system of education, somehow assume that nevertheless they are fit to educate parents. (Furedi, 2001)

If the rhetoric seems overblown, one reason might be because the impact of policies promoting parenting education and family support services is, in reality, still far from universal, as seen above. Government funding may have brought about a significant increase in those numbers, but it should be noted that even Sure Start at its peak in 2004 will only reach about 400,000 preschool children in England. While parenting and family support services have expanded rapidly in recent years, there is an open question over their capacity to reach the two-thirds of low-income families who live outside Sure Start areas, never mind more advantaged households. How the experience of Sure Start, the Children and Young People's Unit and other special programmes might be used to reorganize 'mainstream' children's services delivered by local authorities is a critical issue that is only beginning to be addressed (Chief Secretary to the Treasury, 2003). Indeed, leaders of the statutory public services that are required by law to provide for all children 'in need' have begun to protest that their funding is being unfairly squeezed, while talented staff are being lured away from them.

The special initiatives may have increased the thickness of icing, but local social services directors are now voicing alarm that the actual cake beneath is growing smaller.

Notwithstanding the proliferation of relevant material in newspapers and magazines, the current judgement must be that the impact of formal parenting and family support services in the UK is still limited. The political context is, likewise, one where the Government has engaged in some innovative and thoughtful policy-making, but has yet to secure an enduring consensus for the changes it has made.

NOTES

1   Joseph, Sir K. Speech to the annual meeting of the Pre-School Playgroup Association, 1972.
2   Lilley, P. Speech to the Conservative Way Forward Group, 7 October 1993.
3   Redwood, J. Speech to the Conservative Political Centre Summer School, Cardiff, 2 July 1993.

REFERENCES

Adler, D. (1927) *Understanding Human Nature.* New York: Greenberg.
Adler, D. (1930) *The Education of Children.* New York: Greenberg.
Alexander, J.F. and Parsons, B.V. (1973) Short-term behavioral intervention with delinquent families: impact on family process and recidivism. *Journal of Abnormal Psychology,* **18**, 219–25.
Anderson, B., Beinart, S., Farrington, D.P., Langman, J., Sturgis, P. and Utting, D. (2001) *The Risk and Protective Factors for Youth Crime: Prevalence, Salience & Reduction.* London: Youth Justice Board for England and Wales.
Anderson, M. (1995) *Today's Families in Historical Context.* Paper for a joint seminar organized by the Church of England Board for Social Responsibility and the Joseph Rowntree Foundation. Cited in Utting, D. (1995).
Barlow, J. (1999) What works in parent education programmes? In Lloyd, E. (ed.) *Parenting Matters: What Works in Parenting Education?* Barkingside, Essex: Barnardo's.
Berne, E. (1973) *What Do You Say After You say Hello?* New York: Bantam.
Biddulph, S. (1998) *The Secret of Happy Children.* London: Thorsons.
Botting, B. and Dunnell, K. (2000) Trends in fertility and contraception in the last quarter of the 20th century. *Population Trends,* **100**, 20–31.
Bowlby, J. (1951) *Maternal Care and Mental Health.* Geneva: World Health Organisation.
Bowlby, J. (1953) *Childcare and the Growth of Maternal Love.* London: Penguin.

Bowlby, J. (1988) *A Secure Base: Clinical Applications of Attachment Theory.* London: Routledge.

Bretherton, I. (1991) Roots and growing points of attachment theory. In Parkes, C.M., Stevenson-Hyde, J. and Marris, P. (eds) *Attachment Across the Life Cycle.* London: Routledge.

Bronfenbrenner, U. (1974) *Is Early Intervention Effective? A Report on Longitudinal Evaluations of Pre-school Programs,* Vol. 2. Washington, DC: DHEW Office of Child Development.

Bynner, J. (1999) *Risks and Outcomes of Social Exclusion. Insights from Longitudinal Data. Report for the Organization for Economic Cooperation and Development (OECD).* London: Institute of Education.

Bynner, J. (2001) Childhood risks and protective factors in social exclusion. *Children and Society,* **15**(5), 285–301.

Catalano, R.F. and Hawkins, J.D. (1996) The social development model: a theory of antisocial behavior. In Hawkins, J.D. (ed.) *Delinquency and Crime. Current Theories.* Cambridge: Cambridge University Press.

Chief Secretary to the Treasury (2003) *Every Child Matters,* Cm 5860. London: Her Majesty's Stationery Office.

Committee on Child Health Services (1976) *Fit for the Future* (court report). London: Her Majesty's Stationery Office.

Conger, R.D., Conger, K.J., Elder, G.H. Jr, Lorenz, F.O., Simons, R.L. and Whitbeck, L.B. (1992) A family process model of economic hardship and adjustment of early adolescent boys. *Child Development,* **63**, 526–41.

Conger, R.D., Conger, K.J., Elder, G.H. Jr, Lorenz, F.O., Simons, R.L. and Whitbeck, L.B. (1993) Family economic stress and adjustment of early adolescent girls. *Developmental Psychology,* **29**, 206–19.

Conger, R.D., Patterson, G.R. and Ge, X. (1995) It takes two to replicate: a mediational model for the impact of parents' stress on adolescent adjustment. *Child Development,* **66**, 80–97.

Davis, H. and Hester, P. (1996) *An Independent Evaluation of Parent-Link: A Parenting Education Programme.* London: Parent Network.

Dennis, N. and Erdos, G. (1993) *Families Without Fatherhood.* London: Institute of Economic Affairs (IEA) Health and Welfare Unit.

Department of Health and Social Security (1974a) *The Family in Society: Preparation for Parenthood.* London: Her Majesty's Stationery Office.

Department of Health and Social Security (1974b) *The Family in Society: Dimensions of Parenthood.* London: Her Majesty's Stationery Office.

Department of Health and Social Security (1978) *Violence to Children: A Response to the First Report from the Select Committee on Violence in the Family (1976–77).* London: Her Majesty's Stationery Office.

Developmental Crime Prevention Consortium (1999) *Pathways to Prevention: Developmental and Early Intervention Approaches to Crime in Australia.* Canberra: National Crime Prevention.

Developmental Research and Programs (2000) *Communities That Care: Prevention Strategies: A Research Guide to What Works.* Seattle: Developmental Research and Programs Inc.

Dinkmeyer, D. and McKay, G. (1976) *Systematic Training for Effective Parenting.* Circle Pines, MN: American Guidance Service.

Dreikurs, R. and Soltz, V. (1964) *Happy Children: A Challenge to Parents.* New York: Hawthorn.

Elias, M., Tobias, S. and Friedlander, B. (1999) *Emotionally Intelligent Parenting. How to Raise a Self-disciplined, Responsible, Socially-skilled Child.* London: Hodder & Stoughton.

Elliott, M. (1996) *501 Ways to Be a Good Parent. From the Frantic Fours to the Terrible Twelves.* London: Hodder & Stoughton.

Ermisch, J. and Francesconi, M. (2001) *The Effects of Parent's Employment on Children's Lives.* London and York: Family Policy Studies Centre and Joseph Rowntree Foundation.

Etzioni, A. (1993) *The Spirit of Community. Rights, Responsibilities and the Communitarian Agenda.* London: Fontana Press.

Etzioni, A. (1995) *The Parenting Deficit.* London: DEMOS.

Farrington, D.P. (1996) *Understanding and Preventing Youth Crime.* York: Joseph Rowntree Foundation and York Publishing Services.

Farrington, D.P. (2000) Explaining and Preventing Crime: The Globalization of Knowledge. *Criminology,* **38**(1), 1–24.

Farrington, D.P. (2002) Key results from the first forty years of the Cambridge Study in Delinquent Development. In Thornberry, T.P. and Krohn, M.D. (eds) *Longitudinal Research in the Social and Behavioral Sciences.* New York: Kluwer and Plenum, pp. 137–83.

Ferri, E. and Smith, K. (1996) *Parenting in the 1990s.* London: Family Policy Studies Centre and Joseph Rowntree Foundation.

Ferri, E. and Smith, K. (1998) *Step-parenting in the 1990s.* London: Family Policy Studies Centre and Joseph Rowntree Foundation.

Forward, S. (1989) *Toxic Parents: Overcoming Their Hurtful Legacy and Reclaiming Your Life.* New York: Bantam.

Furedi, F. (2001) *Paranoid Parenting. Abandon Your Anxieties and be a Good Parent.* Harmondsworth, Middlesex: Penguin.

Glass, N. (2001) What works for children: the political issues. In Utting, D. (ed.) *Made to Measure? Evaluating Community Initiatives for Children.* Special issue of *Children & Society,* **15**(1), 14–20.

Gordon, T. (1975) *Parent Effectiveness Training.* New York: Peter Wyden.

Gordon, D.A. and Kacir, C. (1997) Effectiveness of an interactive parent training program for changing behavior for court-referred parents. Website abstract.www.familyworksinc.com/research_articles/index.html

Hames, P. (2000) *The National Childbirth Trust Book of Toddler Tantrums. How to Tame your Child's Temper.* London: Thorsons.

Hardiker, P. (1995) The social policy contexts of services to prevent unstable family life. Unpublished paper for a Joseph Rowntree Foundation seminar series on family and parenthood.

Hardiker, P., Exton, K. and Barker, M. (1991) *Policies and Practices in Preventive Child Care*. Aldershot: Avebury/Gower.

Hardyment, C. (1983) *Dream Babies*. London: Jonathan Cape.

Hardyment, C. (1995) *Perfect Parents. Baby-care Advice Past and Present*. Oxford: Oxford University Press.

Harvey, E. (1999) Short-term and long-term effects of early parental employment on children of the National Longitudinal Survey of Youth. *Developmental Psychology*, **35**, 445–59.

Haskey, J. (2001) Cohabitation in Great Britain: past, present and future trends – and attitudes. *Population Trends*, **103**, 4–25.

Hawkins, J.D. and Catalano, R.F. (1992) *Communities That Care. Action for Drug Abuse Prevention*. San Francisco: Jossey Bass.

Heath, A. (1992) The attitudes of the underclass. In Smith, D.J. (ed.) *Understanding the Underclass*. London: Policy Studies Institute.

Henricson, C., Katz, I., Mesie, J., Sandison, M. and Tunstill, J. (2001) *National Mapping of Family Services in England and Wales*. London: National Family and Parenting Institute.

Hewitt, P. (1996) Preface. In Kraemer, S. and Roberts, J. (eds) *The Politics of Attachment*. London: Free Association Books.

Holmes, J. (1996) Attachment theory: a secure base for policy? In Kraemer, S. and Roberts, J. (eds) (1995) *The Politics of Attachment*. London: Free Association Books.

Home Office (1998a) *Supporting Families. A Consultation Document*. London: The Stationery Office.

Home Office (1998b) *The Parenting Order*. Guidance Document. London: Home Office.

Howell, J.C., Krisberg, B., Hawkins, J.D. and Wilson, J.J. (eds) (1995) *A Sourcebook. Serious, Violent and Chronic Juvenile Offenders*. London: Sage.

Joshi, H. and Verropoulou, G. (2000) *Maternal Employment and Child Outcomes*. London: The Smith Institute.

Jowell, T. (1996) The Life of a Legislator. Can Politicians be Normal people? In Kraemer, S. and Roberts, J. (eds) *The Politics of Attachment*. London: Free Association Books.

Kiernan, K.E. (1992) The impact of family disruption in childhood on transitions made in young adult life. *Population Studies*, **46**, 213–34.

Kiernan, K.E. (1996) Lone motherhood, employment and outcomes for children. *International Journal of Law, Policy and the Family*, **10**, 233–49.

Kiernan, K.E. (1997) *The Legacy of Parental Divorce: Social, Economic and Demographic Experiences in Adulthood*. Centre for Analysis of Social Exclusion Case Paper 1. London: London School of Economics.

Larzelere, R.E. and Patterson, G.R. (1990) Parental management: mediator of the effect of socioeconomic status on early delinquency. *Criminology*, **28**(2), 301–24.

McCord, J. (1982) A longitudinal view of the relationship between paternal absence and crime. In Gunn, J. and Farrington, D.P. (eds) *Abnormal Offenders, Delinquency and the Criminal Justice System*. Chichester: John Wiley, pp. 113–28.

Morgan, P. (1995) *Farewell to the Family? Public Policy and Family Breakdown in Britain and the USA*. London: Institute of Economic Affairs (IEA) Health and Welfare Unit.

Mowlam, M. (1996) The political context. In Kraemer, S. and Roberts, J. (eds) *The Politics of Attachment. Towards a Secure Society*. London: Free Association Books.

Murray, C. (1994) *Underclass: The Crisis Deepens*. Choice in Welfare Series 20. London: Institute of Economic Affairs (IEA) Health and Welfare Unit.

Newberger, E.H. (1999) *Bringing up a Boy. The Nature and Nurture of Male Character*. London: Bloomsbury.

NICHD Early Child Care Research Network (2000a) Characteristics and quality of child care for toddlers and preschoolers. *Applied Developmental Science*, **4**, 116–35.

NICHD Early Child Care Research Network (2000b) The relation of child care to cognitive and language development. *Child Development*, **71**, 958–78.

Office for National Statistics (2001a) *Social Trends No. 31*. London: The Stationery Office.

Office for National Statistics (2001b) Demographic indicators. England and Wales. *Population Trends*, **104**, 5.

Office for National Statistics (2001c) *General Household Survey*. London: The Stationery Office.

Office for National Statistics (2002) *Households Below Average Income – 1994/5 to 2000/01*. London: Department for Work and Pensions.

Osborn, A.F. (1990) Resilient children: a longitudinal study of high achieving socially disadvantaged children. *Early Child Development and Care*, **62**, 23–47.

Osborn, A.F., Butler, N.R. and Morris, A.C. (1984) *The Social Life of Britain's Five-Year Olds: A Report of the Child Health and Education Study*. London: Routledge & Kegan Paul.

Palmer, G., Rahman, M. and Kenway, P. (2002) *Monitoring Poverty and Social Exclusion, 2002*. York: Joseph Rowntree Foundation.

Parr, M. (1997) *Description of a Study Evaluating a New Approach to Preparation for Parenting for Women and Men in the Transition to Parenthood (Hertfordshire Longitudinal Study 1989–1993)*. Stevenage, Hertfordshire: PIPPIN.

Patterson, G.R. (1982) *A Social Learning Approach Vol. 3: Coercive Family Process*. Eugene, OR: Castalia Publishing.

Patterson, G.R. (1994) Some alternatives to seven myths about treating families of antisocial children. In Henricson, C. (ed.) *Crime and the Family Conference Report. Proceedings of an International Conference, held in London, 3 February 1994*. London: Family Policy Studies Centre.

Patterson, G., Chamberlain, P. and Reid, J.B. (1982) A comparative evaluation of a parent-training program. *Behavior Therapy*, **13**, 638–50.

Pilling, D. (1990) *Escape from Disadvantage*. London: Falmer Press.

Pugh, G. (ed.) (1979) *Preparation for Parenthood*. London: National Children's Bureau.

Pugh, G. and De'Ath, E. (1984) *The Needs of Parents. Practice and Policy in Parent Education*. London: National Children's Bureau.

Pugh, G., De'Ath, E. and Smith, C. (1994) *Confident Parents, Confident Children*. London: National Children's Bureau.

Quinn, M. and Quinn, T. (1986) *What Can a Parent Do? Handbook for the Veritas Basic Parenting Programme*. Newry, Co. Down: Family Caring Trust.

Rodgers, B. and Pryor, J. (1998) *Divorce and Separation. The Outcomes for Children*. York: Joseph Rowntree Foundation.

Rogers, C. (1951) *Client Centred Therapy*. Boston: Houghton Mifflin.

Rogers, C. (1961) *On Becoming a Person: A Therapist's View of Psychotherapy*. Boston: Houghton-Mifflin.

Rutter, M. (1981) *Maternal Deprivation Re-Assessed*. London: Penguin.

Rutter, M. (1985) Resilience in the face of adversity: protective factors and resistance to psychiatric disorder. *British Journal of Psychiatry*, **147**, 598–611.

Rutter, M. and Madge, N. (1976) *Cycles of Disadvantage: A Review of Research*. Studies in Deprivation and Disadvantage No 1. London: Heinemann.

Rutter, M., Giller, H. and Hagell, A. (1998) *Antisocial Behavior by Young People*. Cambridge: Cambridge University Press.

Scott, J., Braun, M. and Ahrin, D. (1998) Partner, parent, worker: family and gender roles. In Jowell, R., Curtice, J., Park, A., Brook, L., Thomson, K. and Bryson, C. (eds) *British Social Attitudes and European Social Attitudes: The 15th Report. How Britain Differs*. Aldershot: Ashgate.

Scott, S., Spender, Q., Doolan, M., Aspland, H., Spender, Q. and Jacobs, B. (2001a) Multicentre controlled trial of parenting groups for childhood antisocial behaviour in clinical practice. *British Medical Journal*, **323**(7306), 194–6.

Scott, S., Knapp, M., Henderson, J. and Maughan, B. (2001b) Financial costs of social exclusion: follow up study of children into adulthood. *British Medical Journal*, **323**(7306), 191–3.

Smith, C. (1996) *Developing Parenting Programmes*. London: National Children's Bureau.

Social Exclusion Unit (2001) *Preventing Social Exclusion. Report by the Social Exclusion Unit*. London: Social Exclusion Unit (Cabinet Office).

Spock, B. (1946) *Common Sense Book of Baby and Child Care*. New York: Duell Sloan (revised editions in 1957, 1968 and 1979).

Spock, B. (1988) *Parenting*. New York: Simon & Schuster.

Spock, B. with Rosenberg, M.B. (1992) *Dr. Spock's Baby and Child Care for the Nineties*. New York: Simon and Schuster.

Straw, J. and Anderson, J. (1996) *Parenting. A Discussion Paper*. London: The Labour Party.

Study Commission on the Family (1983) *Families in the Future. A Policy Agenda for the '80s*. London: Study Commission on the Family.

Sure Start Unit (2001) *Sure Start. Making a Difference for Children and Families*. Annesley, Nottingham: Department for Education and Skills (DfES) Publications.

Truby King, M. (1934) *Mothercraft*. Melbourne, Australia: Whitcomb & Tombs.

Utting, D. (1995) *Family and Parenthood. Supporting Families, Preventing Breakdown*. York: Joseph Rowntree Foundation.

Utting, D. (ed.) (1999) *A Guide to Promising Approaches in the UK*. London: Communities that Care.

Utting, D. and Laurance, J. (1990) Family fallout. *Sunday Correspondent*, 15 July 1990.

Utting, D., Bright, J. and Henricson, C. (1993) *Crime and the Family. Improving Child-rearing and Preventing Delinquency*. London: Family Policy Studies Centre.

Wadsworth, M. (1979) *The Roots of Delinquency*. London: Martin Robertson.

Watson, J.B. (1928) *Psychological Care of the Infant and Children*. New York and London: Allen & Unwin.

Webster-Stratton, C. (1997) From parent training to community building. *Families in Society: The Journal of Contemporary Human Services*, March/April, 156–70.

Webster-Stratton, C. (1998a) Preventing conduct problems in Head Start children: strengthening parenting competencies. *Journal of Consulting and Clinical Psychology*, **66**, 715–30.

Webster-Stratton, C. (1998b) Parent training with low-income families: promoting parental engagement through a collaborative approach. In Lutzker, J.R. (ed.) *Handbook of Child Abuse Research and Treatment*. New York and London: Plenum Press.

West, D.J. and Farrington, D.P. (1973) *Who Becomes Delinquent?* London: Heinemann.

West, D.J. and Farrington, D.P. (1977) *The Delinquent Way of Life*. London: Heinemann.

Winnicott, D.W. (1958) *Through Paediatrics to Psychoanalysis*. London: Hogarth.

3

Parenting in Social and Economic Adversity

Christine Puckering

SUMMARY

Most parents rear their children in what are, for their societies, 'normal' or 'average' circumstances. Some are better off and presumably give an advantage to their children. At the opposite end there are those who, for a variety of social, economic and personal reasons, suffer from disadvantages and adversities. We should expect that these adversities will be communicated by parents and reflected in what they do with their children.

This chapter briefly examines poverty in parents, and historical and current attempts to alleviate its effects on children. Adolescent parents, parents in prison and those with learning difficulties are then discussed as clear examples of 'socially excluded parents'. The choice is not random, and studying specific groups discloses a more pervasive underlying pattern. Finally, one programme specifically addressing the personal and parenting needs of very disadvantaged groups is described.

The most important and universal adversity is poverty. This is not only because it affects parents' access to goods and services which they might utilize for rearing their children, but also by virtue of the impact of poverty on the parents themselves – the way it affects their thoughts and feelings about themselves and their children. The major emphasis of this chapter will, therefore, be on poverty. Furthermore, there will be an inevitable UK bias in the exposition of this chapter because the author's work is grounded in the UK with seriously disadvantaged parents, particularly mothers. However, the issues that the chapter raises can, with minor variations, be applied to other countries and cultures where social and economic adversity, whether absolute or relative, also reign.

The link between poverty, parenting and the outcome for children is both obvious and complex. The connection between poverty and inequalities in health and development is clear, but the mechanisms may involve a range of factors, with parenting as a strong candidate. Like age, poverty is also accompanied by other features. Asking who is poor at parenting would identify parents with mental and physical illness, poor education, low literacy and many for whom the 'cycles of disadvantage' have gone through several generations.

Common patterns may be seen in women who, having experienced harsh or neglectful parenting, fail in school, truant and may become depressed and get into petty crime, early drinking and drugs. Seeking better relationships, they move early into sexual relationships, and early child-bearing, often with partners as deprived and unskilled in relationships as themselves.

Lacking a secure attachment base and skills in empathy, they visit their misfortunes on their children. Even where they try to avoid the harsh upbringing they experienced, it is hard for them to find another model. Lacking material and educational resources, they are ill-equipped to access help, feeling judged and marginalized. It is difficult, and may be fruitless, to try to disentangle whether poverty and poor parenting are causes or effects, but the results for the children are dire.

PARENTING AND POVERTY

Poverty can be described in terms of whether it is 'absolute', 'relative' or 'subjective' (Hagenaars and de Vos, 1988). Absolute poverty is distinguished by a deficit in the minimum of basic requirements of food, clothing and shelter. Relative poverty is the lack of access to commodities that are common in the society, and is defined by a proportion of the average expectations for that society. Subjective poverty is a personal feeling of disadvantage, of not having enough to get along. Poverty and deprivation can thus be interchangeably used.

While in the UK there is no formally defined poverty line, proxies can be used. In schools, for example, the number of children eligible for free school meals is taken as an index of deprivation. Poverty is not the same as low socio-economic status (SES). Low SES is usually defined by some composite of family income with parental education, parental occupation, and lifestyle. Poverty is more volatile than SES, as a family's income may fall or rise year by year, while education and occupation are relatively stable.

In the UK, 50 per cent of *average national income* after housing costs is widely used as an index of poverty. This is a relative poverty measure, and is not an indication of the ability of a family to meet basic needs based on other, absolute indices, such as food. Using this index, the national charity, Child Poverty Action Group (CPAG) estimates that more than 1 in 3 children in the UK were living in poverty in 1998/9, an *increase* since 1979 when the figure was 1 in 10. Children are more likely than any other group to be living in poverty. Over half of lone parents live in poverty and couples with children are the largest number of people in poverty. A similar threefold rise in poverty among children has been identified between 1979 and the mid-1990s, with an estimated 4.4 million children living in poverty in 1997–8 (Gordon et al., 2000). Thus the UK has one of the highest rates of poverty among developed societies (Bradshaw and Sainsbury, 2000).

The term 'social exclusion' has been coined to describe the lack of voice and participation in community life that comes with poverty. Spending on children in families from a range of incomes varies less than might be expected. Spending on children in poor families remains relatively high, while spending on the women in the family contracts. A child-centred index of poverty has been developed, based on the availability to the child not only of necessities of food, clothing and developmental opportunities, but also participation in sport and community activities (Gordon et al., 2000). The most deprived children are more likely to be

- in households where no-one is in paid employment,
- in single-parent families,
- aged between 2 and 4 years old,
- in families with three or more children,
- to have a parent with a chronic illness, and
- of a non-white ethnic group.

Health and Development

Poverty is a marker for many hazards in childhood. There are significant differences in stillbirths, perinatal and infant mortality according to income levels. Children of unskilled and poor-earning fathers have double the risk of death due to accidents, injury and poisoning (BMA, 1999). Manual workers produce more children with low birth-weight and chronic illness. From the start, children of poorer parents are less likely to be breast fed, more likely to move onto an unsuitable weaning diet of crisps, sweets and soft drinks, and less likely to have fresh fruit and vegetables in their diet (Acheson, 1998; Law, 1999). Such a start in life immediately sets in train a course of events that have long-term repercussions for health and energy. As well as physical health, the Mental Health Foundation reports socio-economic disadvantage as a significant risk factor for a variety of mental health and development factors, including anxiety disorders, disruptive behaviour disorders and attention deficit problems (Mental Health Foundation, 1999).

Poverty and low socio-economic status act as good predictors for this wide variety of health and development problems. Some of these may be under the control of parents in relatively clear ways, for example the early feeding of the infant, while others (such as accidents) may be indirectly attributable, for example, to poorer housing or parental supervision. Views of the origin and cures for these ills have alternated through the generations, with the moral turpitude of the individual parent or social inequalities being the extreme positions. The solutions generated by these views are represented by the two main strands of social welfare interventions, that is the 'rescue' of the individual, via compensatory education or psychotherapy, or community building and community action to support families. Rescue is seen in contrast to prevention. The current legislative framework of the Children Act 1989 and the Children (Scotland) Act 1995 have moved attention significantly towards a prevention model of improving family support. In the same domain, Sure Start programmes have also chosen children under three years old as a group with the most capacity for growth and so the greatest potential for help towards an enduring preventive impact (see chapter 2).

Historical Perspective

The link between poverty, parenting and child welfare has been long known. It was not lost on the Pilgrim Fathers, who in Boston mandated parents to rear their children with 'basic education and marketable employment skills' in order to ensure their economic and physical welfare (Ross, 1979).

Victorian concern for the welfare of the poor led to the construction of Booth's maps of London, which carefully delineated the social geography of poverty (Booth, 1889). This was taken up by Joseph Rowntree who mapped poverty in York, and began a philanthropic study of both the causes and effects of poverty. He concluded that poverty impinged most on the very young and the very old. The causes of poverty included unemployment, low wages, illness of the chief wage earner and large family size. These views influenced family welfare policies, with a direct bearing on children (Ward, 2000).

Studies of the early records of the Children's Society, originally known as the 'Waifs and Strays Society', showed the major role of poverty in the separation of children from their parents. While the public view was that the children in care were there because they were orphans or the victims of abuse, in reality many were there because their parents could not afford to support them, or were commonly imprisoned for theft. Allowance was made for an illegitimate child whose mother was 'striving to retrieve her character' and who was expected to contribute to the upkeep of the child. The voluntary societies saw themselves as catering for the 'deserving poor', considering these a cut above the presumably undeserving poor for whom the only alternative was the workhouse. Children of widows were admitted to care homes, as the only employment open to women was as charwomen or seamstresses or live-in jobs in service which, although better paid, excluded their living with their children. Widowers were assumed to be able to care for their children, because men's employment opportunities and pay were better.

An employed man seeking support for his family could only do so under the Poor Law. This Act was specifically intended to discourage 'mendacity' or dependence on charity by stigmatization and making the granting of support a harsh choice of the workhouse or no support. It was politically unacceptable to allow that an independent labourer might be unable to support a family because employment was irregular and wages too low. The fault must then lie in the individual rather than in the system. Handing out money, the system of 'out-relief' that allowed pauper families to stay together in their own homes, was seen as an encouragement to laziness. In the workhouse, the conditions were made deliberately harsh. The Poor Law was designed to both deter and punish those seeking support. Husbands and wives were separated, and their children over the age of 7 years housed separately. Children's active parenting was an accidental and marginal activity.

The voluntary societies, in theory, catered for a more respectable stratum of society, although in practice there was considerable overlap. The cost of this advantage was that families had to sign over the future of the child to the Society, including the possibility of the child being fostered, which sometimes meant barely more than being put to service or sent to the colonies. The Society would pay foster carers an allowance to help support the child, but did not on the whole consider making such an allowance to the parents to help them keep the family together, which was seen as fostering dependency. Returning to their family was considered a waste of the careful training in skills and religious ethics that had been instilled in the children by the agency. The role of the agency was to 'rescue' the children from bad environments and bad influences. Removing children from the malign influence of feckless parents was seen as a positive step, and no notion of supporting parents to care for their children was even considered.

Interventions

A dawning recognition of the relationship between poverty, health and child development was the mainspring for the founders of the Peckham Experiment in South London. The

McMillans opened the first school clinic in Bow in London, and subsequently the Open Air Nursery School in Peckham and the Deptford Clinic, in 1910. Promotion of healthy and well-educated families was seen as a means of bettering their lot, and improving society. The philosophical and political foundations of these movements were often in puritan and later in socialist Christianity. Many of them wilted (though some continue to thrive) after the development of the National Health Service in the UK. Equivalent services continue in other countries, both as substitutes for and as complements to statutory services.

Despite high principles and humanitarian ideals, projects based on social reform failed to move families out of poverty, and the growing emphasis on the significance of the first five years of a child's life shifted the focus of attempts to improve the welfare of children in poverty from family health and health promotion, to accelerated or enhanced stimulation of high-risk infants. This was in essence a swing from prevention to rescue. In the 1960s the concept of 'compensatory education' was developed (Fein, 1980). From these the Head Start movement in America was developed, and later Sure Start initiatives in the UK. These combined, to varying degrees, community or political measures to address poverty, parenting interventions to address the effects of parents as conduits of disadvantage, and individual child interventions at what might seem to be the most malleable point of the cycle of disadvantage.

Major cross-sectional and longitudinal studies suggested that there was a 'critical period' in early development, with the children achieving half their adult intelligence between conception and four years of age (Bloom and Steinhart, 1993). Accelerating and ensuring healthy development in the first four years was intended to ameliorate the adverse effects of environmental deprivation. The model was focused on individual enhancement for the child, while some programmes emphasized a more holistic intervention including attention to extra-familial obstacles to good parent–child interaction, such as public services and community attitudes (Halpern, 1988).

Effects of Poverty on Parenting

The effects of poverty on parenting are largely indirect. This is because children are not independent economically and, therefore, any restrictions on their income and its consequences come via parents. Like other parents, poor ones vary in age, marital status, mental health and support networks. Poverty, however, increases the likelihood that the total burden on parents will exceed their coping resources. Poverty may magnify vulnerabilities in the parents as well as exposing the child to adverse effects of neighbourhoods and poor housing (Solnit, 1983; Halpern, 1988). Further, the children themselves are likely to be more vulnerable, by dint of low birth-weight, prematurity and poor antenatal care, including maternal drug use in pregnancy. The risk of intellectual and psychological disorders in young children appears to double with each additional environmental risk factor, with maternal mental illness, lack of positive child-centredness, family size, lack of support, minority ethnic status and socio-economic factors particularly prominent (Sameroff et al., 1987). While not all these factors have a direct connection with poverty, they act as markers of the families who appear in major studies as experiencing economic deprivation and social exclusion.

A degree of casualness or lack of child-centredness is described by several authors observing patterns of parenting in chronic poverty. Children receive abundant love both from parents and other family members, but it is provided idiosyncratically and when the parent is available rather than in sensitive response to the infant's need (Escalona, 1987). Patterns of parenting observed in such settings over a prolonged period are characterized as 'inconsistent' (Jeffers, 1967). The same behaviour in the child might provoke anger one day, pleasure the next and be ignored on the third. Mother's mood is affected by 'crisis events', and these mood changes are reflected in her interaction with the child. In a similar vein, children are alternately ignored and enjoyed, depending on the other preoccupations of the mother (Rainwater, 1970). Mothers (who may be predominantly black, from other poor minority ethnic groups or the endemically poor) appear to treat childcare as a routine activity, and rarely manifest a deep psychological investment in the child. In a study of families with premature infants, for example, problems and crises of the parents interfered with their ability to respond sensitively to the child, despite best intentions (Bromwich, 1978).

A lack of enjoyment of the child and an over-investment in material and physical well-being has been repeatedly described (Jeffers, 1967; Crittenden and Bonvillian, 1984). This may be an attempt to compensate for the deprivations the mother may have experienced in her own childhood, and also an attempt to make up with material goods the deficits the mother is aware of in her emotional relationship with the child (Halpern, 1993). Not infrequently, families living in poverty will put themselves into debt to give their children the most lavish Christmas and birthday gifts, but are unable or unwilling to play with their children, or to take pleasure in their company.

Conditions for the infant born in poverty often involve a negative triad of a constitutionally vulnerable infant, and a vulnerable and overwhelmed parent, in an unsupportive social and community context (Halpern, 1993). As a result of the unpredictability of care and crises in the child's life, the child may fail to develop a secure sense of a base and fail to be socialized into an understanding of time, cause and effect, a sense of self-efficacy and identity that provide a foundation for later adjustment to school. The probable mechanisms for the translation of poverty into poor parenting are set out elsewhere in this book (see chapter 1).

Conclusions

Poverty exists within the most affluent of societies. Inequalities in material resources are reflected in inequalities in health and opportunities for development for children. The 'cycle of disadvantage' identified in the 1980s continues to trap some families. Neither socio-political reform nor individual therapeutic input alone will solve all the problems. Increasing the income of parents who have themselves experienced poor parenting is unlikely to improve the outcome for children automatically, without specific change in parental attitudes and behaviour. However, the demoralization of families who live in overcrowded housing, on minimal incomes with no hope of improvement, will always vitiate attempts to 'rescue' individual children.

To a large extent, the issue of family and child poverty is a political one, and the influence of scientific evidence and good childcare practice may be only marginal in a larger political agenda. Childcare and mental health professionals will have their own positions on their individual and professional role in influencing politics. However, they can contribute their understanding to the debate and to designing and running services that reach out actively and effectively to families who are disenfranchised and socially excluded. In a study in South London of the effects of a volunteer befriending programme for depressed and isolated families (Newpin), it was the social and cultural impoverishment that was most striking. Although the local council and library might offer children's resources and activities that were free, these families did not know about them and would not use them, without some prompting and support.

The role of health and social work practitioners as social activist has a long tradition, often with a religious, humanitarian or political motive. Latterly, these motives may have been eroded, but the evidence base should empower those concerned with the welfare of children to continue acting in their interest.

ADOLESCENT PARENTING

The rate of births to teenage mothers is higher in the UK than anywhere else in Europe, and has been on a rising curve. The reasons for this are many, and include the following:

- the diminishing stigma attached to unmarried parenthood,
- the widening gap between rich and poor,
- lower age of sexual maturation,
- a greater sense of hopelessness and helplessness in seriously disadvantaged young people, leading to
- a restriction of life opportunities and early sexual activity (Ladner and Gourdine, 1985).

This carries hazards both for child and parent, whose own options for education and employment are seriously curtailed, perpetuating and exacerbating the circumstances that may have led to the birth of the child. Comprehensive reviews have detailed the short- and long-term effects of teenage pregnancy on both the mother and the child and show it to be both a manifestation and origin of adverse parenting (Brooks-Gunn and Furstenberg, 1986).

Factors that have been shown to be associated with teenage pregnancy and parenting include parents' lack of future plans and career aspirations. Adolescents who have a clear future orientation are less likely to become pregnant, though some young women see motherhood as a complete future (Jessor, 1992). This is congruent with the evidence that the majority of pregnant teenagers do not plan their pregnancy (Kaufman, 1996). Girls at highest risk are those who

- reach puberty before they have the maturity or cognitive ability to take control of situations,
- live in high-risk, poor socio-economic environments,
- themselves grow up in a single-parent household,
- have been sexually abused,
- have five or more siblings,
- have a sister or friend who became a teenage mother,

- drop out of school, and
- experience low parental supervision (Jessor, 1992).

The risk increases with the number and severity of risk factors. Parents who are moderately strict are less likely to have daughters who become pregnant early, less than either those who are extremely lax or overly strict (Whitehead, 1994).

From a psychological viewpoint, poor experiences in childhood, including lack of nurturance and secure attachment, and early sexual abuse produce a complex picture. Becoming pregnant may bring the girl closer to her own mother, produce at least a fleeting closeness to a sexual partner, and a feeling of being special, however temporary. However, the feelings of being needed and loved may not survive the demands of raising a baby, particularly as the child becomes less passive and more challenging (Musick, 1993).

Less is known about teenage fathers, some of whom may not be aware or not choose to acknowledge that they are fathers (Kaufman, 1996). The limited data that do exist suggest that these young men may have suffered similar life events with resulting low self-esteem to the girls, as well as family violence, dropping out of school and being involved in substance misuse and delinquency (Kaufman, 1996). Clearly their own life opportunities are low, as is their ability to offer a secure and supportive relationship to a child.

Many pregnant teenagers have a long history of disinterest in school, truancy and low educational achievement. This can be compounded by early child-bearing (Osofsky and Osofsky, 1970). The birth of a child to an adolescent mother brings in its wake further social disadvantage, with more pregnant girls living in poverty, being unemployed or holding lower paid jobs than their peers (Furstenberg et al., 1987). The best predictor of positive parenting behaviour appears to be the age of the child and the satisfaction of the mother with her social support network, mainly her own mother (Nitz et al., 1995). Relationships of conflict, usually with her own mother or the baby's father, unsurprisingly, seem to relate to negative maternal behaviour. The strongest predictor of positive parenting behaviours in a number of studies (holding a number of factors constant) appears to be the mother's IQ. In those with lower IQs, it was the birth of additional children that spelled trouble (Whiteside-Mansell et al., 1996).

Biological Risks

There have been a number of studies suggesting that there is an elevated physical risk to teenage mothers, including toxaemia, anaemia and hypertension. Their children are at higher risk from prenatal complications, low birth-weight, prematurity and infant mortality (Klein, 1974; Fielding, 1978; Dwyer, 1984). Some of these risks can be reduced by good antenatal care (Robins et al., 1975; McCarthy et al., 1997) and may be attributable less to teenage pregnancy than to its associated constellation of social adversity, including poverty and inadequate nutrition (Hollingsworth et al., 1983). Very young mothers (under 15) appear to remain at longer term risk and, clearly, their own developmental immaturity may significantly impede adequate parenting (McCormack, 1985).

Developmental and Mental Health Risks

There is a significant link between child behaviour problems and being born to a teenage mother. In a study examining the effects of community violence on 9–12 year olds, being born to an adolescent mother significantly increased a child's exposure to those environmental and family factors that are damaging to mental health (Osofsky et al., 1993). A constellation of disadvantage in health, emotional and educational outcomes seem destined for the majority of children of adolescent parents.

Adolescent mothers may be at an increased risk of depression, especially when the reasons why young women may become pregnant at an early age are taken into account (Osofsky and Eberhard-Wright, 1988; Garrison et al., 1989). Strong evidence exists that maternal depression has an adverse effect on cognitive, social and behavioural development of their infants. There is also some evidence for sensitive periods in the early months of a child's life when a mother's postnatal depression may particularly impact on the fundamental learning experiences for the child (Hay and Kumar, 1995; Sharp et al., 1995; Murray et al., 1996).

UK studies of postnatal depression attribute the poor cognitive development of the children to the quality of mother–child interaction. They differ slightly in the details of the patterns of adverse consequences they detect and particularly whether boys are more vulnerable and whether language development is most at risk. However, the consistent message is that postnatal depression is a powerful negative factor in cognitive progress as well as emotional development of children. There are variations in rates of postnatal depression, some of those in continental Europe being lower than in the UK.

A number of researchers attribute most of the apparent cognitive disadvantage suffered by the children of depressed mothers to the adverse social and marital factors associated with depression rather than depression *per se* (Kurstjens and Wolke, 2001). At this point, the arguments start to become circular, and indeed the same unfavourable social and family influences that provided the platform for teenage pregnancy may predispose the young woman to depression and also leave her ill-equipped to make a sound relationship with her child. The best we can do is to keep an open mind about 'causes' but recognize that teenage parenting in developed societies is fraught with problems.

Within an adolescent sample, higher self-esteem in the mother appears related to a more realistic understanding of child development, better empathy, less expectation that the child will act as a support to the parent, and less reliance on physical methods of discipline (Hurlbut et al., 1997).

Given that the mothers in some studies were followed from pregnancy only until the child was six months old, evidence of physical discipline is particularly worrying. Indeed, some evidence exists that the children of teenage mothers are at more risk of physical abuse at the hands of their mothers, which is frequently a reason why the children are removed into foster care (Miller, 1998). This does not mean, of course, that some teenage mothers do not actively protect and nurture their children. There are, indeed, some studies that suggest they are no different from other mothers in this respect. The balanced view must be, however, that teenage parenting is not the best medium for a child's development.

The children of adolescent mothers do not seem to fare well academically. A 17-year follow up found major discrepancies between the achievements of the children of adolescent mothers and a matched group whose mothers were older (Furstenberg et al., 1987). The reasons may include poorer genetic endowment, more constitutional difficulties, poorer schooling and similar factors. However, undoubtedly, one major factor is inadequate and inappropriate parenting.

Parenting Activities

Several descriptive and observational studies have shown a poorer quality of interaction between adolescent mothers and their children, affecting both maternal sensitivity and stimulation offered to the child by her. Teenage mothers seem to be more unrealistic in their expectations of the child's development, frequently demanding more and better than the child can developmentally manage (Osofsky and Osofsky, 1970;

Field, 1980; Roosa et al., 1982). Perhaps partly as a result of this they tend to be more negative in their assessment of the child and punitive in their management strategies (Field, 1980; Frodi and Lamb, 1980; Frodi, 1981).

The interaction of adolescent mothers and their infants at four and twelve months of age appears to be less rich and less stimulating than adult single mothers (Barratt and Roach, 1995). Teenage mothers appear less vocal to their infants, smile less and offer them interactions using toys less frequently at four months. At twelve months the pattern of stimulation is similarly impoverished. The infants in return smile and vocalize less. This is the case even when other possible confounding facts such as class, education and ethnicity have been controlled, leaving the age of the mother as the best explanation of the difference found. This has been confirmed in other studies. Lower frequencies of vocalization by teenage mothers have been identified (Field, 1980; Sandler et al., 1981; Roosa et al., 1982; Landy et al., 1983; Garcia-Coll et al., 1987; Culp et al., 1998), as have low rates of smiling at various ages (Levine et al., 1985; Lamb and Ketterlinus, 1990; Stern, 1995). Adolescent mothers appear also less likely to demonstrate toys or tasks for their infants with direct consequences for their intellectual and emotional development (Levine et al., 1985; Stern, 1995). What, of course, this shows fundamentally, is that teenage mothers are generally more preoccupied and unhappy and have less to smile about.

Parenting is itself a developmental process, hence the need to look at patterns over time. Dividing young mothers into five parenting patterns dependent on their initial scores and at 12 and 28 and 36 months, on average the scores of young mothers appear below those of older mothers, implying a lower level of sensitive responsiveness (Caldwell and Bradley, 1979; Whiteside-Mansell et al., 1996). However, the largest group of the young mothers eventually gain average and stable scores, with only a minority falling into the more worrying categories. Children's birth-weight, and cognitive and social development is positively associated with parenting patterns. The higher the level of intellectual functioning within the mother, the fewer the number of subsequent children, and the better their material circumstances, the better off the children will be.

Intervention

In view of the considerable body of evidence that teenage mothers and their children are at risk of long-term ill effects on their health, well-being and development, interventions have been designed for both mothers and children, keeping in mind that the mothers in this situation have not completed what might be seen as their own development to adulthood. Data from the Hull House programme (an integrated service beginning in pregnancy for teenagers in Chicago) describes three aims for the young women:

- to delay subsequent pregnancies
- to improve education and job opportunities
- for the infants increase birth-weight, reduce perinatal complications, and promote knowledge of child development and parenting.

A cohort design was used, comparing each year's intake with young women's own experiences in the year preceding the programme.

Despite the availability of a wide range of services within the programme, the rate of subsequent pregnancies was high and entry into jobs low. Contraceptive knowledge increased significantly, as did their knowledge of childcare. Of course, knowledge may be a necessary but not sufficient basis for action. The analysis does not deal effectively with the issue of those young women who did not choose to join the programme or who dropped out prematurely. Few social indices predicted non-attendance, except the number of children the mother already had (McCarthy et al., 1997). The provision of these programmes requires substantial funding. Given the promise of only modest improvements for a minority of participants, on the basis of these and similar findings from replications, they are unlikely to become public policy (Weatherley, 1991).

A wide range of ploys have been used to reach vulnerable teen parents. For example, in an attempt to reach non-participants, an interactive programme was developed to teach teenage parents effective non-coercive parenting skills, utilizing laser-disc technology (Lagges and Gordon, 1999). The target group did show an improvement in knowledge, but without a measure of behaviour change the real world impact of the programme remained speculative. Similar improvements in knowledge have been achieved by sending monthly parenting booklets, based on exploration of good parenting models (Dickenson and Cudabek, 1992). Knowing that the highest risks to infants have been identified in those mothers with IQs below 70, whose literacy skills may be limited, the effectiveness of this approach may be confined to a less severely affected group. However, demands on literacy and comprehension can be controlled in the design of the booklet.

Adolescent mothers have a poorer knowledge of infant development and understanding of child and parent roles. It has been shown that after a six-month course of weekly home visits, by a trained 'paraprofessional', their knowledge had improved to the level of more mature mothers. Safety had improved in their homes and they also had increased involvement with community agencies that might help them to sustain and develop the pattern of changes they had begun (Culp et al., 1998).

Recognizing the need for something more than a brief intervention for pregnant teenagers, the efficacy of offering a mentor to pregnant teenagers who screened positive for risk factors for child maltreatment has been assessed. The young women involved in the programme had intensive home visiting for two years. The study group had about one-third of the expected rate of low birth-weight, no infant mortality and a reduced rate of neglect. The provision of the long-term support of a 'mother figure' or role model helped the young women (many of whom had had poor experiences of being parented) to use health, education and support services effectively. This pattern of service may help to provide the positive experience that more fortunate mothers-to-be get from their own mothers. The importance of both the instrumental and specific psychological support that a good mother figure may offer to facilitate the role change from daughter to mother is replicated by the mentoring process (Stern, 1995)

A different model has been aimed at promoting education for the mother, with the hope that this might break the cycle of disempowerment and disadvantage. Even for teenagers who had been poor students before the programme, a two-year school-based intervention made good academic progress, and longer participation in the programme was predictive of wider spacing of subsequent children (Seitz et al., 1991). Given the significance of teenage pregnancy as a precursor of poor parenting, it seems that a range of attempts at improving the mother's own state and her parenting practices will repay rich dividends.

Conclusions

The evidence of the adverse effects of early child-bearing is clear. There are health risks to the baby, negative parenting patterns, and a poor outcome for the mothers in terms of education, employment and social integration. Even the most intensive intervention programmes have had only minimal success.

If the fundamental difficulty lies in the powerlessness, low expectations and low self-esteem of the parent-to-be, then prevention may rely on taking better care of the adolescent. For girls who do become mothers at an early age, programmes that work are those that mentor and support them over a prolonged period. To some extent, this is a parental role, and replicates what a good parent might have done, both before the pregnancy and in supporting the young adult and new mother. Access to good childcare, continuing education for the mother and, perhaps most importantly, a long-term and consistent relationship with a good role model and mentor are all essential. Education and childcare alone are unlikely to have sufficient impact if deficits in self-esteem underlie early child-bearing. While psychotherapy might address the relationship issues, there is more chance of engaging the young mother in a supportive network when this is based around her immediate agenda of progress for herself and care for her child. Combining practical and therapeutic work offers the best chance to make a change in the trajectory of the mother and child. Befriending may be more potent than high-tech solutions.

If learning to be a parent is seen as a developmental process, then it becomes clear that a brief training is not going to equip a child to face a major challenge, if they begin from a standing start. Learning to make a relationship begins at birth, and if the mother has not had the benefit of good relationships in the past she may lack the capacity to respond empathetically to her child. Parenting is firstly about a relationship, and only secondarily about skills.

INCARCERATED PARENTS

Prevalence

An estimated 250,000 children in America have a parent in prison, and conversely half of all prison inmates have children (Courtier, 1995; Harris, 1996). The rate rises to nearer 75 per cent when female prisoners only are examined (Bloom, 1964). The impact of this on their children is partly mediated by who is then available to look after the children. Some 90 per cent of male prisoners report that their children remain in the care of their mother, but 50 per cent of the children of incarcerated mothers are cared for by grandparents, about a quarter are with their fathers, and other relatives care for about one-fifth. Official figures estimate that the remaining children are in foster care, with research quoting over 10 per cent in public care (Beckerman, 1998). While women are still by far the minority in prison, the rate for women is rising at a higher rate than for men.

In the UK, there has been a fivefold increase in the number of women in prison over a ten-year period. The majority of the women are imprisoned for non-violent crime, often property crime related to supporting their own or a partner's drug habit. The pattern appears to be similar in most Western countries and is probably even worse in developing countries.

Consequences for Children

The relationship between parents in prison and their children is obviously particularly difficult. As well as the problems of good childcare and maintaining the continuity of the relationship, the factors that lead to offending behaviour are likely to be the same as those that undermine good parenting. Drug and alcohol misuse is common in men, and is now rapidly spreading to women, with deleterious effects on the mental health of the parents and the welfare of the children (Harm et al., 1998). These patterns usually (but not invariably) obtain in families that are also disadvantaged in other ways, such as knowledge of children's needs, and ability to meet them, both in terms of personal competence and external resources.

The children therefore suffer a double jeopardy in terms of poor parenting history and the added separation and disruption of care due to incarceration. Studies tend to be descriptive, or to suffer methodological limitations, but they show that the experience of separation is likely to be traumatic, and also to have negative reverberations for the child's carers. Having to decide whether or not to sustain a marriage or relationship with a partner in prison may increase the preoccupation of the remaining parent. Children of incarcerated fathers tend to remain in the care of their mothers. Loss of a mother into the prison system more often implies a complete change of care-takers. However, behavioural problems in the children are more closely related to previous marital turmoil, instability and psychopathology of the remaining care-taker than to separation alone (Gabel, 1992). Financial disadvantage can also be assumed, on top of the emotional hazards. The loss of one income often tips families from borderline coping to poverty, thus triggering many other stresses on and distortions of parenting practice.

A degree of sentimentality towards children has been described in imprisoned parents. But this overt expression of love for the child is often unmatched by any real empathy, so that the children feel at best unattached and, at worst, rejected and stigmatized by peers and adults alike (Yochelson and Samenow, 1997). Studies of views of mothers in prison suggest that they rate the same sorts of issues and values as being of importance as other mothers (Leflore and Holston, 1990). However, the majority of inmate mothers, who, in the study, were serving terms of an average of six years and, therefore, were not available to care for their children, still felt they were 'successful' or 'very successful' as parents. This suggests a lack of insight into the impact of their imprisonment on their children and a poor and unrealistic understanding of what parenting entails. It is not unreasonable to infer that people who are not deterred by their status as parents of dependent children from high-risk offending are unlikely to be generally and realistically concerned parents.

Arguments about the effects of parental incarceration on children can be made only through extension from related literature, as actual studies of the imprisoned population are relatively scanty. Intergenerational transmission of criminal attitudes is strong. Juvenile crime is significantly more common in children with a parent in prison, even when other socio-economic risks are taken into account (Robins et al., 1975). Children also experience poorer school progress than their peers and are more likely to repeat patterns of adult offending and the poor parenting that is associated with it (Lanier, 1991).

Family Factors and Intergenerational Continuity

Imprisoned parents themselves usually come from troubled backgrounds. Mothers of incarcerated 16-year-old girls, for example, have been found to have had an average of four marriages, and a large number of children, often by different fathers. Many of the girls' parents also have criminal records. It is clear that such parents cannot give the quality and continuity of parenting the girls would have needed (Rosenbaum, 1989).

The links are also evident in the reverse directions. It is clear that abused children often progress to later behavioural deviance and criminal activities (Bolton et al., 1977; Alfaro, 1981; Gray, 1986). Of families reported for child abuse or neglect in the 1950s, 50 per cent had at least one child who was subsequently identified as delinquent by court records (Alfaro, 1981). Children whose parents experienced a period of imprisonment are themselves six times more likely to be imprisoned at a later date (Beckerman, 1998).

Mothers in prison have reported behaviour problems in their children during the sentence and an even higher rate of behaviour difficulties after release, making them a high-risk group for coercive patterns of parenting (Fritsch and Burkhead, 1981). In a population study, more than half the mothers and fathers in a community sample described at least one episode of violence towards their children in the year preceding the study, in the context of discipline (Gelles, 1978). This sort of difficulty in managing child behaviour is a clear trigger for frustration and abuse, and the raised frequency of behaviour problems in the children during and after imprisonment may create a vicious circle with parents who have pre-existing anger-management difficulties.

Child's Understanding of Absence

From the child's point of view, the imprisonment of a parent may follow periods of less than optimal parenting. This is then compounded by forcible separation and the unwillingness of family and friends to discuss their parents' situation. Children are drawn into and bound by a 'conspiracy of silence'. Thus they are unable to discuss their own fears or feelings, but are discouraged from mentioning their parent's imprisonment at all for real or imagined fear of stigma or discrimination (Johnston and Gabel, 1995; Kampfner, 1995). The behavioural and emotional problems in the children of incarcerated parents may relate more to the children's confused and negative understanding of the separation and the levels of actual care they receive than separation alone (Gabel, 1992). A clear pattern of temporary behavioural symptoms in children immediately following the incarceration of a parent, and more serious antisocial behaviour among a few older children, has also been identified (Sack et al., 1976). The clear implication is the need to focus and alleviate the child's troubled state when such trauma occurs, as with parents' hospitalization, but with the added weight of stigma and all other disadvantages.

Substitute Care and Contact

As well as the difficulty of establishing suitable childcare, the style of the substitute carer can be inconsistent with the parent's methods, and practical problems of transport and timing may make prison visiting difficult. One-third of imprisoned women have no visits from their children during their prison sentence (Koban, 1983). The child's carer, whether that be the mother's family, father's family or foster parents, may be reluctant to bring children to prison. Facilities in the prison are usually poor, in terms of space and recreational materials for children and parents. Prison staff can regard family visits as burdens, or risks from a security point of view (Lange, 2000). Over and above any possible benefit to the child, the evidence is that ex-inmates who live with their families after parole have lower rates of re-offending (Holt and Miller, 1972; Boudouris, 1996). Some studies suggest that most imprisoned fathers appear to be willing to involve themselves in active parenting programmes, even though only a third of them were visited in prison by their children (Hairston, 1990).

The UN Convention on the Rights of the Child and various laws concerning child welfare endorse the right of children to have contact with both parents, and the responsibility of the parent to foster that right. However, where sentences are very long or where parents are so damaged that contact is detrimental to the children, then difficult decisions may need to be made about permanent alternative care for them. The majority of women in jail have long histories of family and personal problems. The feasibility of good long-term plans for family reunification and rehabilitation may be limited by the availability of effective counselling, substance abuse treatment, vocational training, work or activity opportunities, and meaningful support to face the challenge of developing a safe and supportive family for the child outside the damaging confines of the jail (Beckerman, 1998).

Intervention

The theoretical parenting knowledge of women in prison does not appear to be grossly impaired, though programmes of parenting education significantly increase their knowledge (Dinkmeyer and McKay, 1989). The relationship of knowledge to practice in the groups remains less clear. More compelling is the evidence of the impact of such programmes on long-term recidivism. They seem to be significantly better for women who have completed such programmes (Showers, 1993). A similar drop in recidivism has been found after programmes to support family relationships (Bayse et al., 1991). Attempts at educating fathers show that it is possible to improve attitudes to parenting.

There is often little impact on the fathers' self-esteem or the children's self-perceptions, which is unsurprising since the fathers and children often have little opportunity to consolidate and put into practice the gains in attitude with actual

contact (Harrison, 1997). An optimistic picture of the ability of mothers with substance-abuse problems to respond to a parent education programme has been painted. However, it is essential to emphasize the importance of opportunities to consolidate new skills either in face to face, written or telephone contact with their children (Harm et al., 1998). It remains unknown whether the increase in knowledge and more appropriate parenting attitudes would translate into changed behaviour after release.

Overall, there is recognition that children with parents in prison are a particularly vulnerable group, subject to multiple disadvantage both from the effects of separation and the adverse factors associated with their parents' criminal behaviour. The parents will often have experienced disadvantaged childhoods, and have poor models of parenting, if not outright abuse and damage. The child's current carer may also be struggling with economic and emotional adversities, and may feel unable or unwilling to support the child's emotional development or continuing contact with the incarcerated parent. There is a growing body of evidence to suggest that parents in prison have the will to engage in parenting programmes and are able to gain in knowledge of child development and parenting skills. How effectively these gains can be translated into practice after release depends on the level of support that can be offered to the parents to allow them to escape the cycle of difficulties, including substance misuse, that may have led to imprisonment. Indications of the lowering of recidivism rates for inmates who return to a family setting and for those who participate in parenting education programmes suggest that this is a worthwhile avenue to pursue, both for the child and the parent.

Conclusions

There are two strands of evidence that shape thinking about how to reduce the adverse impact of imprisonment on parenting. The first is the increased risk that children whose parents have been imprisoned will themselves end up in prison. It is not possible to tease out to what extent it is the imprisonment or the attitudes and behaviour of the parent that is communicated to the children, that influences the outcome. The second is that separation from parents is likely to bring with it both direct effects on the behaviour and educational progress of the child and a cascade of other difficulties with substitute carers and maintaining a relationship across time and space.

There is good evidence that being able to maintain strong links with and return post-sentence to a family environment may be one of the strongest factors in reducing recidivism in the parent. There may be very strong reasons then to examine the advantages and disadvantages of custodial sentences for parents, and particularly for women who are increasingly being incarcerated, largely for non-violent crimes, and often to support their own or another's drug habit. Apart from strict retribution, there may be much more value to children, families and society in keeping parents out of prison than in locking them up.

Parenting programmes in prison are of some value in increasing prisoners' understanding of the importance of good parenting and in changing knowledge of child development and attitudes to discipline for children. Although there remains a query as to how effectively changes in knowledge translate into changed behaviour, parenting programmes in prison settings should have a high priority, in view of their opportunities to access a marginalized group. The input of health visitors and other health care and child development workers in prison is welcomed by the inmates, and may offer a significant benefit in systems that too often increase the brutalization of prisoners rather than improve their coping skills and capacity to relate.

'MELLOW PARENTING'

Behavioural parent training programmes are effective in changing children's behaviour and promoting school readiness but there is good evidence that not all families are able to use these programmes (Webster-Stratton, 1991). Low socio-economic status, lack of social support, poor marriages and parental mental ill health are all factors that reduce the likelihood of engaging in such programmes. Conversely, however, it seems that offering parents support to improve their social integration, self-esteem and depression, fails to make a direct impact on parenting (Cox et al., 1990; Oakley et al., 1997).

A practical model of intervention with severely disadvantaged parents, combining the best available practice to support parents and very structured work on parenting has been developed by the present author, called 'Mellow Parenting'. The term has been deliberately adopted as a reminder to parents and others of the overall emotional focus and tone of all interactions in what are often dramatically 'unmellow' circumstances. Evaluation of the programme shows that it is possible to engage severely disadvantaged, socially excluded families in intensive work, involving one day a week over 14 weeks (Puckering et al., 1994, 1996).

The daily programme involves psychotherapeutic support for the parents and direct work on parenting, using video and 'hands-on' practice. About one-quarter of the parents have been physically or sexually abused in childhood, three-quarters report the experience of a harsh or indifferent parent, and a third have spent some of their childhood in foster care or children's homes. Almost none have any educational qualifications. Two-thirds of the mothers entering the programme are suffering from a diagnosable psychological disorder, and two-thirds report having no partner, friend or family member in whom they feel able to confide.

Despite these burdens, the vast majority attend almost all of the 14 weekly sessions, with hardly any dropouts. The engagement of the family is seen as a substantial endeavour in its own right by most such projects, notably Newpin in the UK. It is evident that many of these families have suffered long histories of coercion, in their own experience of parenting, school non-attendance and failure, and fraught current relationships both with partners and professionals. To begin the therapeutic relationship, it is, therefore, helpful to approach them with an 'offer' of a contact, with no agenda that they 'should' join because it would be good for them or their children. Not being told what to do immediately marks this as something different from the previous experience.

Negotiation with statutory bodies such as social services and child protection agencies has been necessary at times to deflect their wish to 'do the best' for the family by engaging them in a programme the agency thought might help. Once a family decided to join the Mellow Parenting Programme, however, strenuous efforts were made to facilitate their attendance, including transport, availability of childcare and a pleasant and welcoming environment. Three weeks into a group, one mother whose children were on the child protection register said, 'I started coming to the group to learn how to manage my children better, but now I am coming because I enjoy it.'

The provision of lunch, eaten with staff, parents and children together, opportunities to have fun with the children, and a respect for the wishes and views of the parents is an enjoyable and empowering experience for downtrodden families. With care given to avoid being intrusive or demanding, families who missed a session are contacted and offered any necessary support in attending the next session. The motivation to attend is high. One mother stood in tears at the door of the family room explaining that she could not come that morning as her son had been refused a place in the crèche that day as he had diarrhoea, which might affect the other children. One of the staff offered to push him in his buggy round the park for two hours so she could at least attend the personal group.

Marked positive effects of the group, compared with many other parenting programmes in neighbouring family centres (in central Scotland), are seen across a range of parental, child and interaction measures. Increased positive interaction between the mothers and their children has been shown to be maintained over a 12-month follow-up period. The average verbal IQ of the children involved has been increased by nine points, about two-thirds of a standard deviation. Mothers attribute positive changes in their lives, including increased confidence, and getting on better with their children, to the effects of the group.

Realistically, given the lifelong disadvantage of the families, it is unlikely that a 14-week intervention would put everything right. But by the middle of the sessions, women appear better able to take a future perspective and plan the steps they need to take to achieve their aims. Asked whether the group had helped with her key problems, one mother reported, 'Yes, in a way, but I still have some things to sort out in myself.' Another mother reported that she wanted to 'get some exams behind me and work with the homeless'.

Mothers appreciate being able to discuss personal things without fear of being judged, and trusting, being heard, and learning from each other: 'It helped you to discuss things I've never been able to discuss before' and 'Everyone thinks they are the only ones with problems with their children. Going to the group helps realize you are not alone.'

Themes that emerge from the groups and the feedback from the parents reinforce the conception that the origins of parenting lie in the competence of the parent in making and maintaining relationships. Those who for various reasons are not good at relationships, are less good at relating to their children. Women entering the group, in an atmosphere where they can trust that they will not be judged, reveal that having experienced poor parenting they want to avoid inflicting the same punitive patterns on their children. One commonly seen pattern is of excessive indulgence, until the importunate demands of the children become intolerable and the parent explodes. This is characteristically followed by

further indulgence to make reparation for the parent's guilt. One parent who had experienced harsh and punitive treatment said, 'I don't like the way my parents treated me, and I don't want to do that to my children, but I don't know what else to do.' In the group, parents can discover that it is possible to be 'firm and fair', and that setting limits does not provoke loss of the child's love.

Insecurity in relationships is also seen in the repeated failure of the women to make good sexual relationships. Often the pattern is of intense and rapid attachment to men who seem initially to be perfect, but rapidly turn out to be as needy, deprived and lacking in security in making relationships as the women themselves. The pattern is then for the relationship simply to break down, or become violent as the man attempts to assert his 'right' to the woman's devotion. Patterns of attachment between group members can also demonstrate the same over-intense, over-involvement which forms rapidly but soon becomes intolerable in intensity or demands on one or both of the parties. The opportunities to experience this in a controlled and contained environment, to learn to regulate intimacy, and to make a 'good' ending to the group, are all delicate but powerful learning experiences.

Parents begin to make the links between their own previous experience and their parenting. Mothers described their understanding of their problems before the group in anonymous feedback. One mother reported, 'I was all mixed up with my own childhood. I was letting it run over into my children.' One mother, whose stern demeanour began to relax in play sessions with her child, said, 'I am enjoying the childhood I never had.'

A deliberate approach of 'parenting the parent' is not made explicit in the group, although elements of this are probably present. What has become clear is that the whole group process is 'reflexive', with the relationship of the group leaders to the parents and the parents to the children being analogous.

CONCLUSIONS

Parents on the whole want to do the job well, but feel desperately uncertain as to whether they are doing the job well enough. Where they themselves have experienced unhappy childhoods and poor parenting, they are doubly anxious but also defensive. The first requirement for engaging a parent in change is to allow them to feel heard and not judged. Parents are hypervigilant to criticism and even the most valuable advice can be taken to imply that they were 'doing it wrong before'. The more vulnerable the parents, the more fragile their self-esteem and the more likely they are to read criticism into advice. For this reason, good behavioural programmes can fail to reach those parents who need it most.

The messages of children's legislation are sound. The job of the helping agencies is to empower and support parents in doing their job, not to supplant them. The most significant mechanism may be through the development of better self-esteem in young people and young parents. More recognition of the importance of parenting and the difficulties of the tasks it entails is helpful, and also the message that no-one gets it right all the time and that it is possible to ask for help without it being a sign of failure. Respect for the parent as an individual is paramount. One parent in a recent five-year follow-up of a parenting project said, 'You believed in me, and so I believed in myself. When I go down I just think that I can get up one step of the ladder, and then I know I can climb up again.' She was clear that the maintenance of the positive effects of the group depended not on being free of subsequent personal and family problems, but her belief that she could weather the downs and climb back up the ladder. Fostering such a belief does not guarantee that parents will be perfect, only that they will continue to strive for themselves and their children.

IMPLICATIONS FOR PRACTICE

It is easy to assume that poverty means feckless-ness and poor parenting, as has been done historically. The majority of professionals in health, education and social welfare are from middle classes and relatively affluent backgrounds. Almost by definition, these professionals have survived or even thrived in the education system, and have little conception of how intimidating and alienating contact with services can be. Add to this, poverty and lack of educational success, linked to lack of self-confidence and self-esteem, and a gulf of mutual misunderstanding and mistrust grows.

However, poverty, and the reasons for it, are strongly associated with poor health and educational failure for children. As a single crude indicator of children's development and well-being, poverty works quite efficiently.

The introduction of childcare and protection legislation in developed countries has marked a major change in thinking in child welfare, but the ghosts of the Poor Law, and the stigmatization it involved, have not yet entirely vanished. There are still 'Children's Centres' and nurseries that offer good quality care to children, but regard the parents of the children as part of the children's problems, rather than partners in promoting good experiences for the children. The wish to 'rescue' the children is taken to imply freeing them from the adverse effects visited on them by their parents' failings. Rescue and prevention are seen as inimical and mutually exclusive.

The thinking behind the legal and political movements underlying the Children Act and Sure Start has been a positive force in children's welfare. However, the realities of the situation in practice do not always achieve the laudable aims of the policy. Parent help programmes must be multi-disciplinary to meet the overall objectives, but agencies are loath to give up their domains, and health, social work and education do not easily rescind line management of key staff. Also, justice services are to a large extent separate from everybody else, even though the major costs of failure of good parenting falls to them eventually.

Reasonable claims can be made that professionals need to keep strong links with their own discipline to maintain continuing professional development and absorption of relevant material. In health, except in universal services such as health visiting, most professional activity is measured by referrals, a method that unfairly disadvantages proactive, preventive work. In social work, the pressure on services and widespread understaffing means that many services are only able to offer a 'fire-fighting' service responding to child protection emergencies. Even children on the 'child protection register' may not have an allocated case-worker. In that environment the aims of prevention, the Children Act or Sure Start, cannot begin to be implemented, and parental adversity will continue to haunt some children and reduce their opportunities to thrive for the rest of their lives.

REFERENCES

Acheson, D. (1998) *Independent Enquiry into Inequalities in Health*. London: HMSO.

Alfaro, J.D. (1981) Report on the relationship between child abuse and neglect and later social deviant behaviour. In Hunter, R.J. and Walker, Y.E. (eds) *Exploring the Relationship between Child Abuse and Delinquency*. Montclair, NJ: Allanheld, Osmun, and Co., pp. 175–219.

Barratt, M.S. and Roach, M.A. (1995) Early interactive processes: parenting by adolescent and adult single mothers. *Infant Behaviour and Development*, **18**, 97–109.

Bayse, D.J., Algid, S.A. and Van Wyk, P.H. (1991) Family life education: an effective tool for prisoner rehabilitation. *Family Relations*, **40**, 254–7.

Beckerman, A. (1998) Charting a course: meeting the challenge of permanency planning for children with incarcerated mothers. *Child Welfare*, **77**, 513–29.

Bloom, B.S. (1964) *Stability and Change in Human Characteristics*. New York: Wiley.

Bloom, B. and Steinhart, D. (1993) Incarcerated mothers and their children: maintaining family ties. In *Female Offenders: Meeting the Needs of a Neglected Population*. Laurel, MD: American Correctional Association.

Bolton, F.G., Reich, J.W. and Gutierres, S.E. (1977) Delinquency patterns in maltreated children and siblings. *Victimology*, **2**, 349–57.

Booth, C. (1889) *Life and Labour of the People in London*. London: Macmillan.

Boudouris, J. (1996) *Parents in Prison: Addressing the Needs of Families*. Lanham, MD: American Correctional Association.

BMA (1999) *Growing up in Britain*. London: BMA.

Bradshaw, J. and Sainsbury, R. (2000) *Getting the Measure of Poverty: The Early Legacy of Seebohm Rowntree*. Aldershot: Ashgate.

Bromwich, R. (1978) *Working with Parents and Families*. Austin, TX: Pro-Ed.

Brooks-Gunn, J. and Furstenberg, F.F. (1986) The children of adolescent mothers: physical, academic and psychological outcomes. *Developmental Review*, **6**, 224–51.

Caldwell, B. and Bradley, R.H. (1979) *The Home Observation for the Measurement of the Environment*. Little Rock, AK: University of Arkansas at Little Rock.

Courtier, L. (1995) Inmates benefit from family services programs. *Corrections Today*, **57**, 100–7.

Cox, A.D., Puckering, C., Pound, A., Mills, M. and Owen, A. (1990) The evaluation of a home visiting and befriending scheme. London: Newpin. Final report to the Department of Health.

Crittenden, P. and Bonvillian, J. (1984) The relationship between maternal risk status and maternal sensitivity. *American Journal of Orthopsychiatry*, **54**, 250–62.

Culp, A.D., Culp, R.E., Blankemeyer, M. and Passmark, L. (1998) Parent Education Home Visitation Program: Adolescent and non-adolescent mother comparison after six months of intervention. *Infant Mental Health Journal*, **19**, 111–23.

Dickenson, N.S. and Cudabek, D.L. (1992) Parent education for adolescent mothers. *The Journal of Primary Prevention*, **13**, 23–35.

Dinkmeyer, D.S. and McKay, G.A.D. (1989) *STEP: Systematic Training Effective Parenting*. Circle Pines, MN: American Guidance Service.

Dwyer, J. (1984) Teenage pregnancy. *American Journal of Obstetrics and Gynecology*, **118**, 393–405.

Escalona, S. (1987) *Critical Issues in the Early Development of Premature Infants*. New Haven, CT: Yale University Press.

Fein, G. (1980) The informed parent. In Kilmer, S. (ed.) *Advances in Early Education and Day Care*, Vol. 1. Greenwich, CT: JAI Press, pp. 155–85.

Field, T.M. (1980) Interaction patterns of pre-term and term infants with their lower and middle class teenage mothers. In Field, T.M. Goldberg, S. Stern, D. and Sostek A.M. (eds) *High Risk Infants and Children: Adult and Peer Interactions*. New York: Academic.

Fielding, J. (1978) Adolescent pregnancy revisited. *New England Journal of Medicine*, **299**, 893–6.

Fritsch, T.A. and Burkhead, J.D. (1981) Behavioural reactions of children to parental absence due to imprisonment. *Family Relations*, **30**, 83–8.

Frodi, A.M. (1981) Contribution of infant characteristics to child abuse. *American Journal of Mental Deficiency*, **85**, 341–9.

Frodi, A and Lamb, M. (1980) Infants at risk for child abuse. *Infant Mental Health Journal*, **1**, 240–7.

Furtsenberg, F.F., Brooks-Gunn, J. and Morgan, S.P. (1987) Adolescent mothers and their children in later life. *Family Planning Perspectives*, **19**(4), 142–51.

Gabel, S. (1992) Behavioural problems in the sons of incarcerated or otherwise absent fathers: the issue of separation. *Family Process*, **31**, 303–14.

Garcia-Coll, C.T., Hoffman, J. and Oh, W. (1987) The social ecology and early parenting of Caucasian adolescent mothers. *Child Development*, **58**, 955–63.

Garrison, C.Z., Scluchter, M.D., Schoenbach, V.J. and Kaplan, B.K. (1989) Epidemiology of depressive symptoms in young adolescents. *Journal of the American Academy of Child and Adolescent Psychiatry*, **28**, 343–51.

Gelles, R.J. (1978) Violence towards children in the United States. *American Journal of Orthopsychiatry*, **48**, 580–92.

Gordon, D., Adelman, L., Ashworth, K., Bradshaw, J., Levitas, R., Middleton, S., Pantazis, C., Patsios, D., Payne, S., Townsend, P. and Williams, J. (2000) *Poverty and Social Exclusion in Britain*. York: Joseph Rowntree Foundation.

Gray, E. (1986) *Child Abuse: Prelude to Delinquency?* Chicago: National Committee for Prevention of Child Abuse, Sept 1986.

Hagenaars, A. and de Vos, K. (1988) The definition and measurement of poverty. *Journal of Human Resources*, **23**, 211–21.

Hairston, C.F. (1990) Men in prison: family characteristics and parenting views. *Journal of Offender Counseling, Services and Rehabilitation*, **14**, 23–30.

Halpern, R. (1988) Parent support and education for low income families: historical and current perspectives. *Children and Youth Services Review*, **10**, 283–303.

Halpern, R. (1993) Poverty and infant development. In Zeanah, C.H. (ed.) *Handbook of Infant Mental Health*. New York: Guilford Press.

Harm, N.J., Thompson, P.J. and Chambers, H. (1998) The effectiveness of parent education for substance abusing women offenders. *Alcoholism Treatment Quarterly*, **16**, 63–77.

Harris, Z. (1996) How to help children when mothers go to jail. *American Jails*, **9**, 31–6.

Harrison, K. (1997) Parental training for incarcerated fathers: effects on attitudes, self esteem and children's self perceptions. *Journal of Social Psychology*, **137**, 588–93.

Hay, D. and Kumar, R. (1995) Interpreting the effects of mother's postnatal depression on children's intelligence:

a critique and reanalysis. *Child Psychiatry and Human Development*, **25**, 165–81.

Hollingsworth, D.R., Kotchen, J.M. and Felice, M.E. (1983) Impact of gynaecological age on outcome of adolescent pregnancy. In McAnarney E.R. (ed.) *Premature Adolescent Pregnancy and Parenthood*. New York: Grune and Stratton, pp. 169–94.

Holt, N. and Miller, D. (1972) *Explorations in Inmate–Family Relationships*. Sacramento, CA: California Department of Corrections.

Hurlbut, N.I., Culp, A.M., Jambunathan, S. and Butler, P. (1997) Adolescent mother's self esteem and role identity and their role in parenting skills knowledge. *Adolescence*, **32**, 639–54.

Jeffers, C. (1967) *Living Poor*. Ann Arbor, MI: Ann Arbor Press.

Jessor, R. (1992) Successful adolescent development among youth in high-risk settings. *American Psychologist*, **48**, 117–26.

Johnston, D. and Gabel, K. (1995) Incarcerated parents. In Gabel, K. and Johnston, D. (eds) *Children of Incarcerated Parents*. New York: Lexington Books.

Kampfner, C.J. (1995) Post traumatic stress reactions. In Gabel, K. and Johnston, D. (eds) *Children of Incarcerated Parents*. New York: Lexington Books.

Kaufman, J. (1996) Teenage parents and their offspring. In Sechzer, J. and Pfafflin, S. (eds), *Women and Mental Health. Annals of the New York Academy of Sciences*, **789**, 17–30.

Klein, L. (1974) Early teenage pregnancy, contraception and repeat pregnancy. *American Journal of Obstetrics and Gynecology*, **120**, 249–56.

Koban, L.A. (1983) Parents in prison: a comparative analysis of the effects of incarceration on the families of men and women. *Research in Law, Deviance and Social Control*, **5**, 171–83.

Kurstjens, S. and Wolke, D. (2001) Effects of maternal depression on cognitive development of children over the first 7 years of life. *Journal of Child Psychology and Psychiatry*, **42**, 623–36.

Ladner, J. and Gourdine, R.M. (1985) Black mothers and their daughters: some preliminary findings. In Benson, V.L. and Robertson, J.F. (eds) *Grandparenthood: Research and Policy Perspectives*. Beverly Hills, CA: Sage.

Lagges, A.M. and Gordon, O.A. (1999) Use of an interactive laserdisc parent training program with teenage parents. *Child and Family Behaviour Therapy*, **21**, 19–37.

Lamb, M.E. and Ketterlinus, R.D. (1990) *Parental Behavior: Adolescent*. New York: Garland.

Lange, S.M. (2000) The challenges confronting children of incarcerated parents. *Journal of Family Psychotherapy*, **11**, 61–8.

Lanier, C.S. (1991) Dimensions of father–child interaction in a New York State prison population. *Journal of Offender Rehabilitation*, **16**, 27–42.

Landy, S., Montgomery, J.S., Schubert, J., Cleland, J.F. and Clark, C. (1983) Mother–infant interaction of teenage mothers and the effect of experience in observation sessions on the development of their infants. *Early Child Development and Care*, **10**, 165–86.

Law, C. (1999) *Inequalities in Health: The Evidence*. Bristol: Policy Press.

LeFlore, L. and Holston, M. (1990) Perceived importance of parenting behaviours as reported by inmate mothers: an exploratory study. *Journal of Offender Counselling and Rehabilitation*, **14**, 5–21.

Levine, L., Garcia Coll, C.T. and Oh, W. (1985) Determinants of mother–infant interaction in adolescent mothers. *Pediatrics*, **75**, 23–9.

McCarthy, P., Sundby, M., Merland, J. and Luxemberg, M. (1997) Identifying attendance correlates or a teen and young adult parenting program. *Family Relations*, **46**, 107–12.

McCormack, M.C. (1985) The contribution of low birth weight to infant mortality and child morbidity. *New England Journal of Medicine*, **312**, 82–90.

Mental Health Foundation (1999) *The Fundamental Facts*. London: Mental Health Foundation.

Miller, S. (1998) *Crime, Control and Women: Feminist Implication of Criminal Justice Policy*. Thousand Oaks, CA: Sage.

Murray, L., Hipwell, A., Hooper, R., Stein, A. and Cooper, P.J. (1996) The cognitive development of 5-year-old children of postnatally depressed mothers. *Journal of Child Psychology and Psychiatry*, **37**, 927–35.

Musick, J. (1993) *Young, Poor and Pregnant*. New Haven: Yale University Press.

Nitz, K., Ketterlinus, R.D. and Brandt, L.J. (1995) The role of social support, and family environment in adolescent mother's parenting. *Journal of Adolescent Research*, **10**, 358–82.

Oakley, A., Rajan, L. and Turner, B.A. (1997) Evaluating parent support initiatives: lessons from two case studies. *Health and Social Care in the Community*, **6**, 1–13.

Osofsky, J.D. and Eberhart-Wright, A. (1988) Affective exchanges between high risk mothers and their infants. *International Journal of Psychoanalysis*, **69**, 221–31.

Osofsky, J.D. and Osofsky, H.D. (1970) Adolescents as mothers: results of a program for low-income pregnant teenagers with some emphasis upon infant's development. *American Journal of Orthopsychiatry*, **40**, 825–34.

Osofsky, J.D., Wewers, S., Fick, A., Hann D.M. and Richters, J. (1993) Children's exposure to chronic community violence: what are we doing to our children? *Psychiatry*, **56**, 36–45.

Puckering, C., Rogers, J., Mills, M., Cox, A.D. and Mattsson-Graff, M. (1994) Process and evaluation of a group for mothers with parenting difficulties. *Child Abuse Review*, **3**, 299–310.

Puckering, C., Evans, J., Maddox, H., Mills, M. and Cox, A.D. (1996) Taking control: a single case study of Mellow Parenting. *Clinical Child Psychology and Psychiatry*, **1**, 539–50.

Rainwater, L. (1970) *Behind Ghetto Walls: BlackLife in a Federal Slum*. Chicago: Aldine.

Robins, L.N., West, P.A. and Herjanic, B.L. (1975) Arrests and delinquency in two generations. *Journal of Child Psychology and Psychiatry*, **16**, 125–40.

Roosa, M.W., Fitzgerald, H.E. and Carlson, N.A. (1982) Teenage and older mothers and their infants: a descriptive comparison, *Adolescence*, **17**, 1–17.

Rosenbaum, J.L. (1989) Family dysfunction and female delinquency. *Crime and Delinquency*, **35**, 31–44.

Ross, C.J. (1979) Early skirmishes with poverty: the historical roots of Head Start. In Zigler, E. and Valentine, J. (eds) *Project Head Start: A Legacy of the War on Poverty*. New York: Free Press, pp. 21–42.

Sack, W., Seidler, J. and Thomas, S. (1976) The children of imprisoned parents. *American Journal of Orthopsychiatry*, **46**, 618–28.

Sameroff, A., Seifer, R., Barocas, R., Zak, M. and Greenspan, S. (1987) Intelligence quotients of four year old children: social and environmental risk factors. *Pediatrics*, **79**, 343–50.

Sandler, H.M., Vietze, P.M. and O'Connor, S. (1981) Obstetric and neonatal outcomes following intervention with pregnant teenagers. In Scott, K.G., Field, T. and Robinson, E.G. (eds) *Teenage Parents and Their Offspring*. New York: Grune and Stratton.

Seitz, V., Apfel, N.H. and Rosenbaum, L.K. (1991) Effects of an intervention program for pregnant adolescents: educational outcomes at two years post partum. *American Journal of Community Psychology*, **19**, 911–30.

Sharp, D., Hay, D., Pawlby, S., Schmucker, G., Allen, H. and Kumar, R. (1995) The impact of postnatal depression on boy's intellectual development. *Journal of Child Psychology and Psychiatry*, **36**, 1315–37.

Showers, J. (1993) Assessing and remedying parenting knowledge among woman inmates. *Journal of Offender Rehabilitation*, **20**, 35–46.

Solnit, A. (1983) Foreword. In Provence, S. and Naylor, A. (eds) *Working with Disadvantaged Parents and Their Children*. New Haven, CT: Yale University Press.

Stern, D. (1995) *The Motherhood Constellation*. New York: Basic Books.

Ward, H. (2000) Poverty and Family Cohesion. In Bradshaw, J. and Sainsbury, R. (eds) *Getting the Measure of Poverty: The Early Legacy of Seebohm Rowntree*. Aldershot: Ashgate.

Weatherley, R. (1991) Comprehensive services for pregnant and parenting adolescents: historical and political considerations. *Evaluation and Program Planning*, **14**, 17–25.

Webster-Stratton, C. (1991) Coping with conduct-problem children: parents gaining knowledge and control. *Journal of Clinical Child Psychology*, **20**, 413–27.

Whitehead, B.D. (1994). The failure of sex education. *American Educator*, **19**, 22–9.

Whiteside-Mansell, L., Pope, S.K. and Bradley, R. (1996). Patterns of parenting behavior in young mothers. *Family Relations*, **45**, 273–81.

Yochelson, S. and Samenow, S.E. (1997) *The Criminal Personality*. Northvale, NJ: Jason Aronson.

4

Parenting Across the Lifespan

Martin Herbert

SUMMARY

The influence of parenting and family life as major sources of environmental change is the main focus of this chapter. Individuals experience their life-cycle and cope with various life tasks in the context of the life-cycle of their families. An important area is generational and intrafamilial relationships in family life, parental roles and associated parenting practices, their contribution to good citizenship and, conversely, the rising tide of antisocial behaviour manifested by children and adolescents. The socialization of children and its successes and failures is a particular theme.

The chapter examines the developmental tasks that face children and adolescents as they grow up; and later, the shifts in their personal development as they move from youthful maturity as parents, to middle age. What is personally learned has its roots in individual experiences of being parented and grandparented, observations of other parents 'on task', plus contributions from the media. Fine-tuning and more radical modifications of one's child-rearing 'theories' are likely to emerge in the daily trial and error of actually raising a child.

BACKGROUND

The role of parents in socializing their children across the lifespan is the focus of this chapter. The term 'lifespan' refers not only to parents' concerns for their children's developmental needs as they grow up, but also their own parenting tasks at different stages of the family cycle. The remit of the chapter is already wide. Thus, the emphasis is mainly on family life in industrialized societies. An important area of interest is the generational and intrafamilial changes in family life, parental roles and associated parenting practices, and their contribution to good citizenship.

THE VARIETY OF PARENTAL ROLES AND FAMILY PATTERNS

The impressive longevity and universality of the family (family groupings go back some half a million years to the Pleistocene period) suggest that it is an institution of inestimable value to the survival of the individual and the human species. This durability does not mean that the family as such, or the parents who bring each new family unit into existence, are unchanging entities. They have always been, and continue to be, susceptible to the impact of social, economic and historical forces (Mount, 1983). Unlike many of their predecessors, contemporary families in industrial societies tend to be relatively small units of parent(s) and offspring, in response to changing economic and social circumstances.

Increasingly long lives and decreasing fertility have modified the structure and life-cycle of the family (Berryman, 2000). One indication of the latter is the increased independence and autonomy of young people. Other changes are evident in the decreasing insistence on marriage as a context for child-bearing, and an increasing dissociation of couplehood from parenting (Birth Statistics, 1998). There is an increase in the number of single-parent families. In 1994, 26 per cent of families with children were headed by a single parent, on their own because of death, divorce or separation – unmarried/unpartnered through circumstances or choice. About four out of ten first marriages ended in divorce and more in separations. All these changes have had their impact on the traditional roles of parents, their style of child-rearing and their offspring's reactions to those who care for them (see Herbert and Harper-Dorton, 2002; also chapter 2).

There may have been radical changes in the inner and outer shape of the family, but not its popularity or significance in the lives of its members. It is clear that despite ups and downs of fortunes of families and quite diverse experiences of their members, they continue to be hugely popular. Men and women continue to mate, produce and look after children, and show greater allegiance to their families than to any other social obligation (Mount, 1983). Reconstituted families are a common phenomenon. Re-marriages are popular. In about one out of every three marriages, one or both partners have been married before. For the offspring, becoming someone's stepchild – a likely consequence – is not always a welcome life event or an easy adaptation. The difficulties are legendary, as are the dilemmas facing even the most well-intentioned step-parent in a reconstituted family.

THE BEGINNING OF PARENTHOOD

The Prenatal Period

Pregnancy has been described as a unique and critical transition in the life of a woman; in the words of Pines (1972), 'a point of no return [which] implies the end of the woman as an independent single unit and the beginning of the unalterable and irrevocable mother–child relationship'. The father's attachment to his child should not be left out, although it differs in some respects from the maternal bond, as we shall see.

The child's first 'home' within the mother's womb, is an environment that is generally hospitable, as shown by the majority of babies who are born healthy. Good environmental conditions and support during the mother's confinement makes possible a good outcome for their infant. At the other extreme, results of inhospitable prenatal environments caused by the parents are to be seen in infants born with a drug addiction, with acute foetal alcohol syndrome, syphilis or with infections such as the HIV/AIDS virus (Herbert, 2003).

Bonding to the Unborn Baby

It is debatable whether the positive feelings for the unborn child that many mothers-to-be experience during pregnancy represent an 'attachment' or can legitimately be called 'love'. Nevertheless, surveys indicate that this is what many feel toward the foetus inside them (Herbert and Sluckin, 1985). Can parental viewing of the early foetus (before 'quickening') by means of ultrasound imagery accelerate bonding with the baby-to-be? Should we, however, try to extend bonding back in time to the mere existence of the foetus, as some physicians have suggested? Would it not make sense in adaptational terms if there were no such attachment to an unborn child or a neonate? After all, stillbirth after 24 weeks' gestation accounts for 0.5 per cent of births in England and Wales (Birth Statistics, 1998). Parents do tend to suffer traumatic grief for many months after such losses. There is some evidence that siblings of stillborn infants (perceived as the 'vulnerable', 'replacement' child, engendering over-protective parenting) are more vulnerable to psychological problems in later life, notably distortions of their attachment to their mothers (Hughes et al., 2001).

Birth

With the birth of the first child the tasks of the parents, the roles they occupy and their orientation toward the future, all change radically (Macfarlane, 1977; Etchegoyan, 2000). The changes in responsibilities and routines for the partners will alter their relationship, placing a strain on it until a new equilibrium is established in their lives. Any stress, if extreme in sound and fury, is likely to have adverse effects on the baby's well-being. Like her infant, the mother is not a blank page on which the experience of mothering will be etched. In general, whether she has had previous children is a potent influence on her actions with a new baby. Women with many children, as one might expect, appear more efficient than first-time mothers in managing their child, and are less likely to be influenced by outside disturbances. They respond more quickly to their babies' crying and are more likely to feed them subsequently (for a review, see Herbert, 2003). They are less likely than first-time mothers to feel an initial indifference to the newborn baby – a not uncommon, but disconcerting experience, for many women (Robson and Kumar, 1980). 'Initial' is the crucial word here as most mothers, in time, fall in love with their infants.

Doubtless the dawning realization of the unconditional responsibility for a totally dependent child has its impact on women, particularly (but not exclusively) first-time mothers and, notably, exhausted ones. It is quite normal for what are called the 'baby blues' to distress a mother about three to five days after she has given birth. They last between a week and ten days and affect some 80 per cent of mothers. The sudden change in hormone levels, such as the dramatic reduction in progesterone and oestrogen following childbirth, is thought to be a principal cause of this malaise and of more serious postnatal depression (Herbert, 2003). Infants are very susceptible to 'unnatural disruptions' in the interactional sequences (for example, a depressed mother's blank face or mistiming of her reactions) between them and their mothers.

Babies are usually a great joy to their parents. The reciprocal interactions of parent and child are in a state of constant adjustment as each reinforces the other positively or, sometimes, negatively. Any mother who has had several children and can thus compare her babies, knows that they differ markedly in temperament from the very beginning. Thomas et al. (1968) carried out influential research with New York families which demonstrated just how important these constitutional aspects of personality – the temperamental qualities of the child – are in the unfolding of normal and dysfunctional behaviour. Though clearly parents vary, it seems 'rewardingness' or 'punitiveness' are not apparently qualities inherent in the parent, but are elicited by a particular child and its activities. Children's temperamental attributes interact with parental characteristics – a phenomenon referred to as 'goodness of fit'. A matching temperament makes for happy and relaxed relationships. Some 40 per cent of the New York experimental sample fell into the so-called 'easy' category, a group of children who were highly rewarding to rear. A mismatch of temperament tended to result in an extended series of mutually unrewarding interactions. Thomas et al. (1968) found that 10 per cent of their sample of infants were 'difficult'. Parents had to cope with children whose disorganized condition made their management exhausting and distressing.

Parents (especially those who have enjoyed an 'easy' child) are sometimes disconcerted by the fractious temperament of their next baby, by his or her resistance to changes of routine and even the simplest training requirements. This is what one mother said to the author about her infant:

> From the first day that I saw my son I realized that he was more lively than his sister and wouldn't be content to be in a room by himself. He would scream; and I went through endless months wondering if I was feeding him correctly, whether he had a pain or was unhappy. He would not sleep during the day like other babies, and eventually not at night either. When I went to cuddle him he would scream, bite or kick and this showed itself particularly at bath time and changing time.

This extreme example is fortunately relatively uncommon, but one well known to child psychologists and psychiatrists to whom such infants are frequently referred later in their young lives (Herbert, 1998). There is evidence that even as early as the second year of life, and before the manifestation of symptoms, children who were later to develop behaviour problems requiring clinical attention showed particularly difficult temperamental attributes.

In the New York research, 15 per cent of the babies were 'slow to warm up'. These infants combined negative responses of mild intensity to new stimuli with slow adaptability after repeated contact. Infants with such characteristics differed from the difficult children in that they withdrew from new situations quietly rather than loudly. They did not usually exhibit the intense reactions, predominantly negative mood and behavioural irregularity, as did the difficult children.

Temperament should not be regarded as a fixed, unmodifiable 'entity'. Environmental factors shape the manner in which temperament is displayed as the child gets older and, indeed, changes in temperament over time have been shown to be correlated with parental characteristics. Although difficult children adjusted slowly, many did so to a reasonable degree, especially those with resourceful, robust parents. Conversely and probably due to parenting practices, 18 per cent of the easy children also developed behavioural problems.

LIFESPAN NEEDS AND TASKS

Among the basic needs of children as they grow up, are the following:

- physical care and protection,
- affection and approval,
- stimulation and teaching,
- discipline and controls that are consistent and appropriate to the child's age and development,
- opportunity and encouragement to acquire gradual autonomy, so the child takes gradual control of his or her own life.

Research evidence suggests that what is important in child-rearing is the general emotional and social climate in the home, for example the attitudes and feelings of the parents, which form a background to the application of specific methods for raising their children and meeting their needs. It is *how* the young child is looked after that is crucial and it is the social and psychological context of care that matters, rather than its timing and mechanics (Herbert and Harper-Dorton, 2002). For example, feeding, potty training and the like, are important elements of the child's daily activities; but it is the social interactions they generate and the manner in which parents undertake these tasks that give them significance. The mother who is most effective is one who does, with a sense of confidence, what she and the community to which she belongs, believe is right for the child (Becker, 1964; Baumrind, 1971).

Reference has been made to the dynamic interactions of parents and their offspring. It is useful to consider children and adolescents and their dilemmas in the context of how they interact with parents who are not without their own preoccupations and difficulties. The family-life map is a useful visual device for bringing together the life-events, transitions, interactions, and developmental (life) tasks of different members of a family living together (Figure 4.1).

Developmental Tasks

By the child's first birthday the most dramatic development and growth have already taken place. In just 12 months they have been faced with several challenging developmental tasks. The early tasks include beginnings of talking and controlling elimination. Later they involve the development of self-control over aggressive and sexual inclinations, acquiring a moral sense and social skills, adjusting to school life and mastering academic competencies, and becoming self-directed and self-confident. Some are vital psychological tasks. They arise in sequence at recognized periods of a child's life, although on variable timescales. Successful accomplishment of developmental tasks leads to a sense of

satisfaction and achievement both in child and parent and makes success with later tasks more likely. Failure hinders the individual's subsequent psychosocial endeavours which, in turn, lead to personal distress and disapproval by society. Engaged parents become worried when their child struggles with any of these challenges, and some seek professional advice.

The Eriksonian Model of Development

There are many developmental theories and perspectives (e.g. Crain, 1985; Goodnow and Collins, 1990; Garbarino and Binn, 1992) but, over the past 40 years or so, one has come to dominate thinking about lifespan development. This is the view developed by Erikson (1985), which combines a range of perspectives.

The developmental tasks postulated by Erikson centre on attitudes and behaviour that enter into the child's evolving personality, and more particularly, his or her sense of identity. Erikson regards early personality development as a series of stages in the development of *patterns of reciprocity* between the 'ego' and 'alter', i.e. self and others. The stages are 'psychosocial' events, in the sense that they represent biological developmental processes interacting with facilitative or hindering influences in the environment, notably the family. He provides intuitively meaningful terms to describe the child threading his or her way between opposing forces of 'altruism and self-centredness', while trying to find a mature balance between selfish individualism and a need to conform, with a degree of self-denial, to the rules and mores of family and community. An extreme lack of balance in reciprocity between self and others (in either direction) gives rise to unsatisfactory social relationships. There are potential 'identity crises' between trust and mistrust, confidence and doubt and other crucial stage-related attitudes that children internalize as they grow up.

Although these stages are described as if the alternatives are complete opposites, Erikson sees children as occupying positions between the extremes. Where they are depends on the persons with whom, and situations in which, they are interacting. They tend to show a predominance of one or other attitude if they have been exposed to certain kinds of experience.

Psychosocial stages of development

- From birth to about four years of age the child needs to develop a sense of trust (in

TIM Age 22 months	ANNE Age 10 years	PETER: Age 14 years	MOTHER Age 38 years	FATHER Age 45 years	GRANNY Age 69 years
LIFE TASKS • Develop motor skills • Develop self-control • Elaborate vocabulary • Explore his world – make 'discoveries'	LIFE TASKS • Cope with academic demands at school (under-achieving) • Developing her sense of self • Learn to be part of a team	LIFE TASKS • Adjust to physical changes of puberty • Adjust to sexual awareness • Cope with the opposite sex (shyness) • Deepen friendships (intimacy)	LIFE TASKS • Review her life and commitments • Adjust to loss of youth and (in her perception) 'looks' • Cope with an adolescent	LIFE TASKS • Review commitments in mid-life • Develop new phase in relationship with wife • Face physical changes – some limitations on athletic/sexual activity	LIFE TASKS • Deal with increasing dependence on others • Come to terms with old age/death • Cope with loss of peers
LIFE EVENTS • Parents insist on obedience now • Adjust to temporary separations when mother works • Not the centre of attention and 'uncritical' deference	LIFE EVENTS • Afraid to go to school (cannot manage maths) • Bullied by a girl in her class • Jealous of attention Tim gets (calls him a spoiled brat) • Worried about father's health	LIFE EVENTS • Worried about his skin (acne) and size of his penis • Has a girlfriend – his first • Upset by his parents' quarrels • Complains that his mother is always watching him	LIFE EVENTS • Coping with late child – an active toddler • Has taken part-time job to relieve feeling trapped • Feels guilty • Bouts of depression • No longer enjoys sex	LIFE EVENTS • Threat of redundancy • High blood pressure • Worried about drifting apart from his wife • Had a brief affair • Feels unattractive	LIFE EVENTS • Poor health • Gave up home when bereaved (may have made a mistake!) • Enjoys the little one, but • Feels 'claustrophobic' with all the activity/squabbles
TODDLERHOOD	PREPUBESCENCE	ADOLESCENCE	MID-LIFE		RETIREMENT

Figure 4.1 *A family-life map: transitional stages of life*

parents and others) and, later, a growing autonomy. The major hazards to the development of a perception of a trustworthy and predictable world, in which children initiate their independence-seeking, are social and physical conditions that interfere with their sense of personal adequacy and/or which hinder their acquisition of skills (e.g. Seligman, 1975; Amato and Keith, 1991).

- During the next stage, from approximately 4 to 5 years, there is a sense of initiative, a period of vigorous reality testing, imitation of adult patterns of behaviour and imaginative play. Overly strict discipline, interference and over-protection can disrupt the successful achievement of these attributes, making for poor spontaneity and uncertain testing and appreciation of realities (Browne and Herbert, 1997).

- A sense of duty and accomplishments is the next developmental task – from 6 to 11 years – when the child puts aside much of the fantasy and play-life and undertakes real tasks at school and develops academic and social skills. Excessive demands or competition and personal limitations which lead to persistent failure can create a crisis in this important stage and result in feelings of inferiority and poor work habits (Lewis, 2001).

- From 12 to 15 years, children consolidate their sense of identity, clarifying who they are and, broadly, what their role in life is to be. Society may create difficulties for the early adolescent by failing to provide clearly defined or valued roles and standards for the young person (Erikson, 1968).

- In later adolescence, from 15 to adulthood, normally an increasing search for intimacy develops – a wish to establish close personal relationships with members of both sexes outside the family (see Coleman and Hendry, 1999).

PARENTING INFANTS

Early Attachments

An *initial two-way attachment* of mother and her infant is essential for the parents' successful meeting of children's needs and tasks. Parental bonds and relationships have their own complex, many-sided developmental histories, stretching over many years. All relationships have to have a beginning. Close mother–infant contact is regarded as desirable, whenever possible. Where better to begin than with the newborn child placed in its mother's arms? Mothers tend to welcome it, and lactation is facilitated. Mutual awareness and familiarity have an opportunity to develop (Herbert et al., 1982; Sluckin et al., 1983). What then follows is foundational learning – learning (for mother and infant) how to relate to a stranger. Among the factors that influence the way a mother behaves and relates to her offspring are her age, her cultural and social background, her own experience of being parented, her personality, her previous experience with babies, and her experiences during pregnancy and birth.

'Maternal Bonding' Theory

Maternal bonding theory enjoyed (or suffered) from the 1980s onwards, the usually uncritical discussion afforded to new fads and fashions in childcare. Although past its heyday, it is worth commenting on a theory that proved so controversial. Put briefly, it was proposed that in some mammalian species including our own, mothers become 'bonded' to their infants (imprinted) through close contact very soon after birth, with the implication that the 'bond' or tie was so strong as to be biological. During the hours following birth, tactile, visual and olfactory stimulation of the mother by her baby was thought to be the critical period for her becoming attached to it (Klaus and Kennell, 1982).

Where the mother's initial responsiveness was disrupted by separation from the baby (for example, the infant having to go into intensive care) there was a risk, it was feared, of long-term adverse consequences for the mother–child relationship. There would be enormous difficulties in establishing contact between mother and child, with the result that she might feel unattached and alienated towards it, and normal bonding would not develop. Therefore, immediately after the birth of her baby, the mother was made to hold and fondle the baby, in order to become emotionally tied to it. It was even postulated that if the attachment to the child proved to be inadequate, the longer term harmful consequences could lead to child abuse.

At the theoretical level, the premise of a *critical period* for mothers was awesome, considering that concepts such as imprinting could not explain the origins of fatherly love or the committed attachments of adoptive and long-term foster parents to their children. At the applied level these ideas influenced day-to-day practice in maternity hospitals, homes and nurseries.

These ideas also influenced decisions made in courts of law; for example, whether a child was to be taken away from its parents, or which of the contesting parents was to be given custody. Clearly, empirical evidence was needed. The most rigorously controlled studies indicated that close contact soon after birth makes no difference to mothering effectiveness or to mother-love, either as reported by mothers or as inferred from their behaviour. With regard to the risk of child abuse, the results of various studies indicated that the hypothesized relationship between mother–newborn bonding and maltreatment did not exist (see the review by Herbert and Sluckin, 1985).

It is reassuring to observe the various ways in which maternal feelings arise and grow. When reports of the development of mother-love are scrutinized, it becomes apparent that the growth of maternal attachment is usually a gradual process. Mothers generally expect to have positive feelings toward their infants at the time of birth. Indeed, some mothers do report an instant love toward their newborn babies. Others report that they feel nothing initially. Specific love, the bond to the child, tends to develop slowly but surely, gradually growing stronger (Harlow, 1971). Very much later it may weaken, but it probably never vanishes. The course of the growth of paternal love appears to be essentially similar.

Representational Models of Mothers

There are other influences on care-giving relationships that are cognitive rather than emotional in origin – perceptions of the infant that Bowlby (1981) referred to as mothers' 'representational models'. He suggested that these internal working models are stable within individuals, and that they guide behaviour in care-giving relationships. What, perhaps, is surprising is that they influence parental interpretations of the infant's characteristics and behaviour not only after birth, but also prenatally. There is evidence that feelings of expectant mothers can predict their security of attachment over a year later (Herbert, 2003).

Paternal Bonding

It is not always the female who cares for the baby. This is so even in some animal species: male marmosets, for example, carry the infant at all times except when it is feeding. Most fathers develop a strong love for their offspring, even if they were nowhere near the delivery room when their children were born. A study of first-time fathers suggests that they began developing a

bond with their infant during the first three days after the birth and often earlier. They tended to develop a feeling of preoccupation, absorption and interest (see Lewis, 1986). There are no clear indications that early contact by the father with the newborn facilitates this paternal bonding. Nevertheless, the opportunity for father and infant to get to know one another early is important, especially as contemporary Western society is witnessing a more participative role in childcare by the father. Additionally, there is a massive increase in the number of single-parent families, and in not a few, the father is the caregiver. They are also the main carers, numerically, after mothers.

Child-to-Mother Attachment

Ethologists discovered that during a restricted period just after hatching, goslings instinctively follow the first large moving thing they see. Many of us remember pictures of Konrad Lorenz being followed by his animal 'offspring'. These young creatures not only tend to follow this moving object but they come to prefer it to all others, and after a time will follow no others. The fascinating question that arises from this type of early learning (referred to as imprinting) is whether the human child's attachments, preferences or other behaviours are also acquired during restricted periods of development on an imprinting-like basis. The most influential writings have been those of Bowlby (1981) who argued initially that the period in the infant's life when a major new relationship to the mother was being formed, was a 'critical' one for determining the nature of that relationship and, in turn, the child's normal development. He concluded, while studying infants in institutions and orphanages that were set up as a result of the Second World War, that early separation of mother and child resulted in serious physical, mental and emotional damage to children – an outcome that he termed 'maternal deprivation'.

In the wake of these important findings for interpretations, there have been debates about whether the young child's mother is the person who should devote herself (without separation required by a regular job outside the home) to this task (Belsky, 2001). Are fathers and surrogate care-givers 'good enough' for a responsibility that has such massive implications for the child's well-being? Bowlby modified his views over time as new research evidence emerged. Studies indicated that children were more likely to suffer emotional and/or developmental problems through remaining in very disturbed, though intact homes rather than through losing relationships when parents separate. Bowlby remained firm in the belief (shared by Belsky) in the importance of intimate and consistent relationships in the early nurturing of a child, despite evidence suggesting that substitute care, when good, can mitigate or eliminate the adverse effects of periods of separation of children from parents. The work of Mary Ainsworth et al. (1978) showed that a mother may be physically present but 'emotionally remote'. A child of such a mother, often insecure in his or her attachment, can also be said to be 'maternally deprived'.

The Development of Sociability

Social life for the newborn baby means a gradually widening circle of significant people, most crucially a mother or mother-substitute. It is highly advantageous if infants show signs of being sociable – seeking attention and smiling, for example – at a very early age. Particularly important are their attraction to the kind of auditory and visual stimuli provided by care-givers to babies. They lock onto face-like patterns, but not onto other complex and symmetrical arrangements, when they are only 30 minutes old. They turn their heads to patterned sounds, particularly those sounds within the frequency range of human speech. For the all-important human need to communicate, the very young infant's signalling repertoire – crying, cooing, smiling and arm movements – are effective in eliciting nurturing behaviour from the mother or care-giver (see review by Herbert, 2003).

Martin Seligman (1975) conveys the importance of this phase so elegantly that it would be a pity not to quote him in full:

The infant begins a dance with his environment that will last throughout childhood. I believe it is the outcome of this dance that determines his helplessness or mastery. When he makes some response, it can either produce a change in the environment or be independent of what changes occur. At some primitive level, the infant calculates the correlation between response and outcome. If the correlation is zero, helplessness develops. If the correlation is highly positive or highly negative, this means the response is working; and the infant learns either to perform that response more frequently or to refrain from performing it, depending on whether the correlated outcome is good or bad. But over and above this, he learns that responding works, that in general there is synchrony between responses and outcomes. When there is asynchrony and he is helpless, he stops performing the response and further, he learns that in general responding doesn't matter. Such learning has the same consequences that helplessness has in adults:

lack of response initiation, negative cognitive set, and anxiety and depression. But this may be more disastrous for the infant since it is foundational.

Even very young babies exhibit a need to be competent, to master or deal effectively with their own environment. Psychologists consider this tendency to be related to such motives as mastery, curiosity and achievement.

Parenting Preschool Children

By about four months old, infants generally behave in much the same friendly way towards people as they did earlier, but will react much more markedly to their mother or whoever else has been the constant care-giver. They will smile and coo and follow her with their eyes more than they will other people. Attachment behaviour is best demonstrated when the mother leaves the room and the baby cries or tries to follow her. It is also evident when not just anyone can placate the infant. At six months, about two-thirds of babies appear to have a close attachment to their mothers, indicated by separation protests of a fairly consistent sort. Three-quarters of babies are attached by nine months. This first attachment is usually directed at the mother, and only very occasionally towards some other familiar figures. During the months after, children first show evidence of emotional bonds to others; one-quarter of them will show attachment to other members of the family. By the time they are 1½ years old, all but a few children will be attached to at least one other person (usually the father) and often to several others (usually older children).

For Bowlby and Ainsworth, the ability to use an attachment figure as a secure base affords a haven of safety, and also provides the confidence necessary to explore and master the environment. Ainsworth and her colleagues developed a test of infants' responses to a 'strange situation'. In this experimental method, a mother enters a room with her infant. Some minutes later a stranger enters too. After a few minutes the mother departs unobtrusively, leaving her baby alone with the stranger. The mother then returns and the stranger leaves the room. Ainsworth and her colleagues, by using this method, were able to identify four distinct styles of attachment:

- The 'securely attached' infant reacted positively to the stranger when the mother was present, but was visibly fearful and cried when she left. When she returned, the upset infant went to her and was quickly comforted.

- The 'insecure/avoidant' infants were somewhat indifferent to their mother when she was in the room, and they may or may not have expressed distress when she left. When she returned, they made no move to interact with her, and stiffened or looked away.
- The 'insecure/ambivalent' infants were distressed on entering the room and showed little exploration. They were very upset when the mother left. When she returned they wished to be near her, but resisted all her efforts to comfort them. They struggled if picked up, and showed a great deal of angry behaviour.
- The 'disorganized' infant showed incomplete, interrupted movements, and freezing. There was fear of the parent. The main feature was the lack of a coherent attachment strategy.

Ainsworth's findings suggest that *maternal sensitivity* is influential in determining the child's reactions. Sensitive mothering in response to the infant's behaviour was exhibited in the homes of the securely attached infants. Insecurely attached, anxious and avoidant infants were found to have their interactive behaviour rejected by the mothers. In the case of the insecurely attached, anxious and resistant infants, a disharmonious and often ambivalent mother–infant relationship was evident. The resistant and ambivalent behaviours shown were seen as a result of inconsistent parenting. Although these findings are not rigorously repeated and the details are debatable, there is currently a general consensus among child psychologists regarding their pertinence and importance (see Browne and Herbert, 1997).

PARENTING OLDER SCHOOL-AGE CHILDREN

In order to achieve trust, autonomy and initiative it is necessary for the child to interact with an increasing number of people. By attending school, his or her social universe is significantly extended. There is a marked contrast between the playful existence of the preschool child with a nurturant mother near at hand, and the life of the school-going youngster. Even in today's more informal play and nursery schools, children are faced with exacting disciplines and intellectual demands that can constitute quite an ordeal.

In Erikson's framework of psychosocial development, the theme of this period of life involves the gradual laying aside of fantasy and play and undertaking real tasks, developing academic and social competencies, and in essence developing a sense of duty and accomplishment. The pragmatic–optimistic nature of school-aged children shows itself in their concern with how things work, and how to produce things of meaning and value that will receive others' approval. Success in small endeavours feeds a sense of optimism about mastering new skills and acquiring new abilities. 'Achievement motivation' is one of the earliest and most stable attributes displayed by children, especially if fuelled by parental encouragement and/or pressure.

At this stage of development, children are likely to be mildly but firmly pressed into the adventures of discovering that they can learn to accomplish what they would never have thought of themselves. The attractiveness of such activities lies in the very fact that they are not the products of fantasy but reality, practicability and logic. They provide a sense of participation in the real world of adults. Children are, therefore, probably as amenable as they are ever likely to be to learning, and open to the direction and inspiration of others. Emotional problems, excessive competition, personal limitations or other conditions that lead to experiences of failure, hinder childhood pragmatism and optimism and retard acquisition of social competencies. They may result in crises that create a sense of inadequacy and incompetence.

Perhaps one of the most serious consequences of emotional and behavioural problems is their deleterious effect on children's learning in the classroom and hence their scholastic and social achievement. Even when highly intelligent, those pupils with psychological difficulties tend to have real difficulties in school performance (Goldstein, 1995). The greater the number of problems manifested by the child, the poorer, on the whole, is school performance and the longer term outlook.

Social and Moral Development

One of the child's major acquisitions on the road to becoming a social being is the development of 'internal controls' over behaviour, the internalization of standards of conduct and morality implied by the term. The work of Baumrind (1971) and others shows that 'authoritative' parents raise children who have high self-esteem and who cope confidently with life. These parents tend to direct their children's activities in a rational manner determined by the issues involved in particular disciplinary situations. They encourage verbal give-and-take and share with the child the reasoning behind their policy. They value the child's self-expression but encourage respect for authority and social requirements.

The mother, for example, appreciates *both* independent self-will and disciplined conformity. Therefore, she exerts firm control at those points where she and her child diverge in viewpoint, but she does not hem in the child with restrictions. She recognizes her own special rights as an adult, but also the child's individual interests and special ways. She affirms the child's present qualities, but also sets standards for future conduct. She uses reason as well as personal power to achieve her objectives. Her decisions are not based solely on the consensus of the group or the individual child's desires, but she also does not regard herself as infallible or divinely inspired. This approach to parenting has been categorized as 'democratic'.

PARENTING TEENAGERS

The event that makes adolescence stand out from the rest of childhood is the radical nature of the growth that takes place around age 12 years in girls and 14 years in boys. The changes due to the action of hormones are quite dramatic and transform children into young adults. There are theorists who reject the notion of adolescence as a distinct stage of development, repudiating the idea that at puberty children take on a qualitatively different *persona*, more or less overnight. The alternative view is that the child grows by imperceptible degrees into a teenager, and the adolescent turns by degrees into an adult. Some cultures, notably preliterate ones, have 'rites of passage' that move children on directly from their childhood status to an adult one. In reality, the different theories make little difference to parenting practice, since they both urge alertness to the change.

Many parents now anticipate their child's adolescence with apprehension, so ingrained are the stereotypes in the media of alienated 'changelings' or horror stories about the approaching rebellious stage of development. They may construe the teenage years as something to be confronted rather than shared, endured rather than enjoyed – a recipe for a self-fulfilling prophesy (Herbert, 1987). Their anxieties may be about the possible loss of the closeness, affection and parental authority they see as important in their relationship with their children. Although in Western societies it may be a common parental attribution that adolescence

is marked by challenges to adult authority, conflict between parents and offspring is not so generally anticipated in societies where filial piety and respect are encouraged, indeed insisted on (see chapter 7).

Undoubtedly, adolescence can be traumatic for some individuals, but it is by no means necessarily or even largely so. The popular and professional notion that adolescence *is* different from the whole of development that precedes it, and the whole of development that follows it, is of relatively recent origin and not well supported by evidence. Certainly psychiatrists, with their biased sample of clinic-attending youngsters, have tended to take a jaundiced view of adolescence. Clinicians tend to see disturbed or deviant young people. It is clear from evidence based on unbiased community samples rather than impressionistic data, that adolescence, despite its difficulties, is negotiated successfully by most children who have authoritative, as opposed to authoritarian or permissive, parents. There is essentially a continuity of the central aspects of personality (the 'propriate functions') from childhood, through adolescence and on to adulthood.

Nevertheless, many of the physical and psychological changes that are features of adolescence, notably as young people establish their sense of identity, are dramatic enough. An understanding of these processes can be of benefit to young people in transition from childhood to adulthood, and to their parents (Herbert, 1997).

Stages of Identity Formation

Among the stage-appropriate tasks of adolescence is the formation of an identity – one that includes self-awareness and social sensitivity. If youngsters are undermined by criticism or rejection, they are likely to feel unworthy and inferior and display aggressive or attention-getting behaviour. These betray defensiveness and anxiety. Many of the difficulties are social ones – the problems of getting along with peers, with teachers, with their own parents and also with themselves. Aristotle suggested that friendly relationships require a liking for oneself. Young people need to like themselves, to rely on themselves, and to know themselves. As we see below, this is not always the case when teenagers are developing their self-image.

Erikson (1968) proposes several ways in which children and adolescents cope with the formation of their sense of who and what they are, and how they feel about themselves and others (see Figure 4.2). Although there is no

Approximate age periods	Characteristics to be achieved	Major hazards to achievement	Facilitative factors
Birth to 18 months or so	Sense of trust or security	Neglect, abuse or deprivation of consistent and appropriate love in infancy, harsh or early weaning	If parents meet the preponderance of the infant's needs, the child develops a strong sense of trust
Around 18 months to 3 years	Sense of autonomy – child viewing self as an individual in his/her own right, apart from parents although dependent on them	Conditions that interfere with the child's achieving a feeling of adequacy or the learning of skills such as talking	If parents reward the child's successful actions and do not shame his or her failures (e.g. in bowel or bladder control) the child's sense of autonomy will out-weigh self-doubt/shame/guilt
3 to 5 years	Sense of initiative – period of vigorous reality testing, imagination and imitation of adult behaviour	Overly strict discipline, internalization of rigid ethical attitudes which interfere with the child's spontaneity and reality testing	If parents accept the child's curiosity and do not put down the need to know and to question, the child's sense of initiative will be enhanced
5/6 to 11 years	Sense of duty and accomplishment – laying aside of fantasy and play, undertaking real tasks, developing academic and social competencies	Excessive competition, personal limitations, or other conditions which lead to experience of failure, resulting in feeling of inferiority and poor work	If the child encounters more success than failure at home and at school he or she will have a greater sense of industry than of inferiority
12 to 15 years	Sense of identity – clarification in adolescence of who one is, and what one's role is	Failure of society to provide clearly defined roles and standards; formation of cliques which provide clear but not always desirable roles and standards	If the young person can reconcile diverse roles, abilities and values and see their continuity with past and future, a sense of personal identity will be developed and consolidated

Figure 4.2 *Developmental tasks: facilitative and adverse influences on sense of self (based on Erik Erikson's theorizing)*

universal endorsement of the following stages of identity formation in adolescence, they are helpful in elucidating the issues in this difficult area.

- *Foreclosure*: vocational, political or religious decisions (for example, strict adherence to a clearly defined religious or ethnic lifestyle) are made for the adolescents by parents, and the adolescents accept these decisions without entering into a prolonged decision-making process about their own identity. Young people of this type tend to endorse authoritarian values.
- *Identity diffusion*: this occurs if the young person makes no firm commitment to personal, social, political or vocational beliefs or plans. Teenagers devote themselves to excitement and fun, drifting from situation to situation without establishing any long-term plans or a coherent view of their identity.
- *Moratorium*: the adolescent experiments with a number of roles before settling on a clear identity. Some of these roles may be negative (delinquent) or non-conventional (drop-out). They may be staging posts on the way to forming a stable identity. The balance of power and influence between parents and 'outsiders' is significant. In many ways, young people of this age turn their backs on adults and become immersed in the community of peers. If the balance is tilted too much in favour of peer group or too much parental influence, the effects distort development.
- *Achieving a clear identity*: Here the adolescent achieves a well-defined identity following a successful moratorium. She or he develops a strong commitment to social and moral values (for example, vocational, social, political and religious) and usually enjoys a good psychosocial adjustment in adulthood.

Teenage Pregnancy

Very early parenthood is likely to disrupt the development of a mature sense of identity. In Britain, about 8000 of the 90,000 adolescents who become pregnant every year are under 16 years old; many are 14 years old or younger (see Gerard, 2000). In the US, it has been estimated recently that over 50 per cent of teenage mothers not enrolled in educational or vocational programmes will become pregnant again within a very short period of time (US Bureau of the Census, 1993). The empirical evidence drawn from a vast literature on adolescent parents (mainly mothers) presents an almost wholly negative picture of the unpreparedness of teenagers for the burdens of parenthood.

The following are among the correlates of early pregnancy:

- tendency to drop out of school
- conduct problems
- disciplinary difficulties
- deficits in social skills and problem-solving
- poor resources in the home backgrounds
- disturbed childhood experiences
- diminished social and psychological coping skills
- vulnerability to physical and emotional abuse
- a raised risk of birth complications
- an adverse influence on siblings
- dependency on drugs

In relation to their care of infants, teenage parents tend to

- show less responsive and sensitive interactions than adult mothers
- display poor play skills with their children
- express less satisfaction with parenting than older mothers
- appear less sensitive to their children's needs
- be at greater risk of abusing their children
- have poor outcomes (e.g. learning difficulties) with their children

Teenage fathers appear to be no more ready to assume the responsibilities of parenthood than are adolescent mothers.

This litany of risks is related to the social, emotional, educational and physical disadvantages frequently found in the girls' backgrounds (Herbert and Harper-Dorton, 2002). Teenage parenthood is thought to be a central link in this 'cycle of disadvantage'. Their children are thus of particular interest in the study of intergenerational transmission of poverty, mental disorders and other social problems. Children born of teenage parents are likely to be reared, at least in their early years, by parents who struggle in many ways – finding and keeping jobs, paying bills and enrolling in vocational and training programmes, with frequent unemployment and poverty.

Grandparents play an important role (often an intensive, ongoing and 'hands on' role) in supporting and mentoring teenage mothers, notably by encouraging and helping them to stay on at school. This is one of the major influences mitigating the adverse effects of the young mothers' future opportunities for living a reasonable life (see chapter 10).

PARENTING YOUNG ADULTS

Among middle-aged parents whose younger child, now a young adult, is about to leave high school, women tend to mention the approaching departure of the youngest child as a forthcoming change but do not generally believe that it will be a difficult time for them. Parents do sometimes create problems for themselves by trying to live through their children, drawing vicarious satisfaction from their activities. In this context, it is commonly asserted that middle age is a more difficult phase of life for the woman than for the man. The changes in her life are in many ways more obvious. The children are becoming less dependent, if not totally independent of her, when until this period her maternal interests may have been uppermost in her life. Although her concern continues, her direct role as a mother is coming to an end. But we must not exaggerate the 'empty nest' phenomenon. Most men ignore the imminent event in their conversations with researchers, their attention being already directed to their own retirement and future.

Marriages/partnerships may be undergoing greater strain at this juncture than at any time since the initial impact of the intimacy of living together, when the couple first set up home. This is not to say the relationship is necessarily poor or terminal; but coping with self-willed older teenagers is difficult, especially if a person is not getting full support from his or her partner. Difficulties in marriage may become more exposed and more abrasive, if offspring are rebelling, getting into serious trouble, or playing one parent off against the other. This age group has been referred to as the 'middle generation'. Some parents feel trapped by the competing needs of ageing parents and demanding offspring. The dilemma is most severely felt by parents (mainly women) who look forward to resuming a career they gave up, now that their children are self-sufficient, but are prevented from taking up this (or other) 'liberating' opportunities by needing to care for elderly, infirm parents. Others find the advice, support and caring of their parents (especially in their role as grandparents) a 'blessing' (see reviews by Nortman, 1974; East, 1992; Blake and Lile, 1995; Zippay, 1995).

Parenting in Older Mothers

At one time gynaecologists considered a woman of 30 or more an 'elderly first-time mother'. In recent decades there has been a marked rise in the number of women commencing motherhood while at the two extremes of the fertility continuum – adolescence and middle age. For couples who delay having children into their thirties, the children will reach their 'teens' when they are in their forties or fifties – the 'prime of life' as many see it. But what do the teenagers

make of them? Adolescent offspring may well think of this time of life as 'old age', a time of life when a whole generation seems to have forgotten its youth and has often lost its zest for living.

The percentage of women aged 35 and over giving birth for the first time has continued to rise, now reaching 15 per cent. Thus, a small but increasing proportion of 21st century adults (around 10 per cent of those born in 1992, for instance) will be the children of mothers who are 35 or more years older than themselves and who, in many instances, are also grandmothers. Berryman and Windridge of the Leicester Motherhood Project address some of the issues generated by the trend to later child-bearing being recorded in the UK, USA, Australia and much of the developed world. They have posed, *inter alia*, the following questions in their longitudinal project:

- Are older women more or less at risk in terms of their own physical and psychological well-being and that of their baby either during pregnancy, at birth, or in the long term?
- Do older women, possibly with many years of life experience, find it more or less difficult to adjust to the physical and emotional changes of pregnancy, birth and motherhood than do 'average age-range' women?
- Do maturity and increased experience (potential correlates of increased age) have positive benefits for those having babies later in life?
- Do the marital/partner relationships of older women differ from those of 'average age-range' women, and if so, does this have implications for their adjustment to pregnancy and motherhood?

The answers to these questions, according to the evidence, are generally in the positive direction (Berryman, 2000). Attitudes to the over-thirties have changed in recent times, partly because of the generally reassuring research findings, and also as a result of the trend in the Western world to delay childbirth. Delayed child-bearing provides young adults an extended time for their careers and for establishing their lives as a couple before including a child in their family. Overall, women of higher socio-economic status and with more education tend to be of later age at childbirth and of lower fertility than is the typical pattern. However, there are wide variations from country to country in the reasons for postponing motherhood. Feminist ideology is an evident factor in the timing of first births in American women but it is, for example, less evident in a sample of Swedish women (op. cit.).

Scrutiny of the available evidence shows that the physical risks of pregnancy in older women have been exaggerated. Most older first-time mothers, for example, breastfed their babies. Some young mothers do not breastfeed. Older mothers more often than younger mothers take their baby into bed with them. In general issues of childcare, the similarities between younger and older parents significantly outweigh the differences (see reviews by Nortman, 1974; Welles-Nystrom, 1997; Berryman, 2000).

IMPLICATIONS FOR PRACTICE

Notwithstanding variations in family pattern and style of parenting, all societies seem to be broadly successful in the task of transforming helpless, self-centred infants into more or less self-supporting, responsible members of their communities. Indeed, there is a basic 'preparedness' on the part of most infants to be trained to behave appropriately. This involves teaching them to conduct themselves in a socially 'normal' manner. Two persons are involved: a learner and a teacher. The lessons in social behaviour are not always effective or appropriate. Despite extensive research, there is much doubt as to how different qualitative methods of child-rearing (for example, breast feeding versus bottle feeding, or fixed-interval feeding versus on-demand feeding, or early or late weaning) influence the development of the child's personality. The available evidence suggests negligible long-term effects for these very early events (Becker, 1964; Herbert, 1974).

What is more certain is that environmental influences are mediated by learning processes. The vast majority of childhood behaviours are learned, including the problematic ones that adults find so disturbing. Much unusual and dysfunctional behaviour and cognition in children is on a continuum with normal (functional, non-problematic) activity and thought. These phenomena do not differ in general (although there are important exceptions) from their normal counterparts in the development, persistence and the way in which they can be modified. Unfortunately (and it is the case with all forms of learning) the very processes that help the child adapt to life can, under certain circumstances, contribute to maladaptation. An immature child who learns by imitating an adult does not understand when a parent may unwittingly reinforce antisocial, coercive behaviour by attending or giving in to it. The youngster who learns adaptively on the basis of normal conditioning

processes to avoid or escape from dangerous situations, can also learn in the same way (maladaptively) to avoid school or social gatherings (Herbert, 2002).

Many persons other than parents have an influence on children's personality and behaviour. But parents can encourage a strong 'immune system' in their offspring – protection against some of the stresses and snares of growing up. The developmental literature (Herbert, 1974, 1998) provides clear guidelines to supplement social learning theory in such cases:

- strong ties of affection and respect between themselves and their children
- firm social and moral demands being made on their offspring
- the consistent use of sanctions
- techniques of punishment that are psychological rather than physical, such as threats to withdraw approval
- an intensive use of reasoning and explanations
- responsibility given to children and adolescents

These generalizations can be put more specifically as guidelines for use by parents through the lifespan, as below:

- *Guideline 1: Foster bonds of respect and affection.* Such bonds tend to facilitate teaching endeavours. The more affection there is as a foundation for disciplinary tactics, the more attention will be given as the child is 'on the same side' as the care-giver). He or she will identify with what is being said.
- *Guideline 2: Make firm social and moral demands (set limits).* This means establishing and conveying a reasonably coherent idea of the aims and objectives that lie behind the training and supervision of young people. Children whose parents set firm limits for them grow up with more self-esteem and confidence than those who are allowed to behave in any way they like. It is important to give children a reasonable amount of freedom of choice within those limits (Baumrind, 1971).
- *Guideline 3: Prepare children for life by developing family routines.* Most routines are useful shortcuts to living. For example, routines help a child master and carry out on 'auto-pilot' such daily tasks as feeding, washing, dressing, going to bed, and helping him or her to achieve more with less effort.
- *Guideline 4: Teach children the family rules.* Everyone needs some self-discipline or rules of conduct in order to adjust his or her needs and desires to those of others. Children

need the affection and approval of people around; being self-centred and egotistical will alienate others and lose this approval.

- *Guideline 5: Choose rules carefully.* It is crucial to ensure that children know precisely what the rules and constraints are, and what is expected of them. Rules and limits are most effective when they are relatively uncomplicated, fair, understandable and applied justly and consistently so that they can anticipate what will happen if they transgress them.
- *Guideline 6: Be consistent.* When teaching a child to distinguish between right and wrong, or between appropriate and inappropriate social actions, it is important to be consistent. It is confusing if he or she is punished for a behaviour one day and gets away with it on another.
- *Guideline 7: Be persistent.* Parents often stand out against rebellious, non-compliant behaviour for some time, only to give in eventually. The child soon learns that the meaning of parents' word is ambiguous and that if he or she uses 'coercive' strategies (e.g. temper tantrums or aggression), the parent will give way. The intermittent reinforcement of defiant behaviour will entrench it very strongly.
- *Guideline 8: Give explanations/reasons.* Children are more likely to internalize standards if those standards are justified in terms of their intrinsic value and when given reasons that indicate their meaning, rather than in terms of the punishment that follows from their violation. The former encourages children to 'tell themselves' what they can or should not do, while the latter simply teaches them what they must not do when observed. When young, they cannot comprehend unaided the reasons for training. Later on, when in a position to understand explanations, they may be side-tracked. Worse still, there maybe no sense in the demands made upon them, because what is being asked is unreasonable and/or inappropriate.
- *Guideline 9: Tell children what they should do, not only what they should not do.* Explain clearly to children what is required of them. Emphasize the positive, not only the negative. By attending to positive actions, parents make them more likely to occur.
- *Guideline 10: Give responsibility.* Giving young people responsibility provides them with the opportunity to practise and to be responsible. It is an essential element of healthy psychological growth.

- *Guideline 11: Listen carefully to what the child says.* Children's communications are often in code. Parents need to be empathetic, hearing, not just listening, to what their children are saying, using what has been called 'the third ear' – an ear tuned to the subtext, the hidden messages.

Evidence (e.g. Lidz, 1968; Herbert, 1974; Bandura, 1977, 1981; Patterson, 1982; Newman and Newman, 1991; Dadds, 1995; Mason et al., 1998) suggests that in parenting across the lifespan, the following attributes are associated with the well-being of family group members:

1. time spent in shared activity
2. minimal social withdrawal, avoidance and segregated activity
3. a high rate of warm interactions, and a low rate of critical or hostile interactions amongst members
4. full and accurate communication between members
5. favourable evaluations of other members; low levels of criticism of other members
6. favourable meta-perceptions, that is, members likely to assume that other members have a favourable view of them
7. high levels of perceived affection between members
8. high levels of satisfaction and morale, and much optimism about the future stability of the family group
9. Frequent mutual enhancement of self-confidence (perceived self-efficacy)
10. minimal coercive interactions

Families that lack the characteristics listed above make their members vulnerable to psychological distress. Particularly at risk are those family members who are already vulnerable for other reasons – the young, the elderly, those suffering from other types of stress such as hospitalization, alcohol dependence, or coping with a large number of children.

A coalition between the parents (in a two-parent home) is advantageous not only to give unity of direction to their children, but also to provide each of them with the emotional support essential for carrying out his or her cardinal functions. This is not to suggest that children from one-parent families will necessarily have more problems than children from two-parent families. There is little hard evidence to confirm this fear. Children from one-parent homes are no more likely to become delinquents, dropouts, vandals or drug addicts than those with two parents. The worst fears of commentators that single parenting is fraught with dangers for the offspring would seem to be misplaced. This is especially the case if the lone parent has reasonable financial resources, a decent home in which to rear the children, and high-quality child-minding and/or nursery/preschooling if the single parent (and it is increasingly a father) goes out to work.

Young children often exhibit regressive or 'going backwards' reactions that reflect feelings of loss and abandonment, following the separation of their parents. Preschool children usually appear to be very sad and frightened, and they become clinging and demanding. Children attending school or nursery may become very anxious about attending and may protest strongly when left. Vivid fantasies about abandonment, death of parents, and harm, are encountered. Some children, following the break-up of their families, express aggression toward other children. With older children, although grief and sadness remain a prominent feature, anger becomes more marked. This is usually directed at the parents, especially the one with whom the child is living. A marital separation may result in children re-appraising their own relationships with their parents, while questioning the nature of other social relationships. Children of divorced parents tend to enter into sexual relations early, make poorer occupational choices, and develop less-stable long-term relationships. Research also indicates that more children of divorced parents are in danger of developing long-term problem behaviours, depression and anxieties (see Amato and Keith, 1991; Herbert and Harper-Dorton, 2002; see chapter 8).

This depressing litany of prognoses involves far too many global and unqualified generalizations. It is potentially misleading as there are many moderating and protective factors to produce less unhappy outcomes for some individuals. As with single parenting, the social and economic consequences of the break-up can play a subversive role. There is also evidence that adverse outcomes for the children are more likely to arise from unbroken but disharmonious homes that are immersed in frequent hostile confrontation, than from homes that split up. If parents and children, post-divorce, can retain intact emotional relationships, and parents strive to be united in supporting their children, their offspring's grief and resentment may be made more tolerable.

CONCLUSIONS

One of the main objectives of training and education is the preparation of children for their future. Some of the influences on pro-social behaviour, and causes of childhood and adolescent antisocial or dysfunctional behaviour have been described. A significant number of the latter can be prevented or mitigated by sensitive and sensible parenting. It is doubtful whether any child has all of his or her individual needs satisfied by parents. Parents are not infallible, as they are only human. This, in part, is why the term 'good enough parenting' has entered the professional vocabulary. To quote Bruno Bettelheim (1987):

> In order to raise a child well one ought not try to be a perfect parent, as much as one should not expect one's child to be, or become, a perfect individual. Perfection is not within the grasp of ordinary human beings ... But it is quite possible to be a good enough parent.

REFERENCES

Ainsworth, M.D.S., Behar, M., Waters, E. and Wall, S. (1978) *Patterns of Attachment: A Psychological Study of the Strange Situation*. Hillsdale, NJ: Lawrence Erlbaum.

Amato, P.R. and Keith, B. (1991) Parental divorce and the well-being of children: a meta-analysis. *Psychological Bulletin*, **110**, 26–46.

Bandura, A. (1977) *Social Learning Theory*. Englewood Cliffs, NJ: Prentice-Hall.

Bandura, A. (1981) Self-efficacy mechanisms in human agency. *American Psychologist*, **37**, 122–47.

Baumrind, D. (1971) Current patterns of adult authority. *Developmental Psychology Monographs*, **1**, 1–102.

Becker, W.C. (1964) Consequences of different kinds of parental discipline. In Hoffman, M.L. and Hoffman, L.H. (eds) *Review of Child Development Research*. New York: Russell Sage Foundation.

Belsky (2001) Developmental risks (still) associated with child care. *Journal of Child Psychology and Psychiatry*. **42**, 845–59.

Berryman, J.C. (2000) Older mothers and later motherhood. In Sherr, L. and St Lawrence, J.S. (eds) *Women, Health and the Mind*. Chichester: John Wiley.

Berryman, J.C. and Windridge, K. (1998) *Motherhood after 35: Mothers and Four-year-olds. A Report on the Leicester Mother and Child Project*. Leicester: Leicester University and Néstle.

Bettelheim, B. (1987) *A Good Enough Parent*. New York: Knopf Publications Random House.

Birth Statistics (1998) *Birth Statistics: Review of the Registrar General on Births and Patterns of Family Building in England and Wales, 1996*. Series FMI no. 25. London: HMSO.

Blake, H. and Lile, B. (1995) The impact of type of school-based programs on self-efficacy development of teen-aged parents. *Dissertation Abstracts International Section A: Humanities and Social Sciences*, **55**, 3078.

Bowlby, J. (1981) *Attachment and Loss: Attachment*. New York: Basic Books.

Browne, K. and Herbert, M. (1997) *Preventing Family Violence*, Chichester: John Wiley.

Carter, E.A. and McGoldrick, M. (1989) *The Family Life Cycle*, 2nd edn. Boston, MA: Allyn and Bacon.

Coleman, J. and Hendry, I. (1999) *The Nature of Adolescence*, 3rd edn. London: Routledge.

Crain, W.C. (1985) *Theories of Development: Concepts and Applications*. Englewood Cliffs, NJ: Prentice-Hall.

Dadds, M.R. (1995) *Families, Children and the Development of Dysfunction*. Thousand Oaks, CA: Sage.

East, P.L. (1992) Pregnancy risk among the younger sisters of pregnant and child-bearing adolescents. *Journal of Developmental and Behavioral Pediatrics*, 13, 128–36.

Erikson, E.H. (1968) *Youth, Identity and Crisis*. New York: Norton.

Erikson, E.H. (1985) *Childhood and Society*, 35th anniversary edn. New York: Norton.

Etchegoyan, A. (2000) Perinatal mental health: psychodynamic and psychiatric perspectives. In Reder, P., McClure, M. and Jolley, A. (eds) *Family Matters: Interfaces between Child and Adult Mental Health*. London: Routledge.

Garbarino, J. and Binn, J.L. (1992) The ecology of childbearing and child-rearing. In Garbarino, J. (ed.) *Children and Families in the Social Environment*, 2nd edn. New York: Aldine de Gruyter.

Gerard, N. (2000) Feature article on adolescent sexuality. *Observer Review*, 15 October 2000.

Goldstein, S. (1995) (ed.) *Understanding and Managing Children's Classroom Behavior*. New York: John Wiley.

Goodnow, J.J. and Collins, A.W. (1990) *Development According to Parents: The Nature, Sources and Consequences of Parents' Ideas*. Hillsdale, NJ: Erlbaum.

Harlow, H.F. (1971) *Learning to Love*. San Francisco: Albion.

Herbert, M. (1974) *Emotional Problems of Development*. London: Academic Press.

Herbert, M. (1987) *Living with Teenagers*. Oxford: Basil Blackwell.

Herbert, M. (1997) *Conduct Disorders of Childhood and Adolescence*, 2nd edn. Chichester: John Wiley.

Herbert, M. (1998) *Clinical Child Psychology: Social Learning, Development and Behaviour*, 2nd edn. Chichester: John Wiley.

Herbert, M. (2002) Behavioural therapies. In Rutter, M. and Taylor, E. (eds) *Childhood and Adolescent Psychiatry*. Oxford: Blackwell.

Herbert, M. (2003) *Typical and Atypical Development: From Conception to Adolescence*. Oxford: Blackwell.

Herbert, M. and Harper-Dorton, C. (2002) *Working with Children and Adolescents and Their Families*. Leicester: BPS Books / New York: Lyceum.

Herbert, M. and Sluckin, A. (1985) A realistic look at mother–infant bonding. In Chiswick, M.L. (ed.) *Recent Advances in Perinatal Medicine*. Oxford: Churchill Livingstone.

Herbert, M., Sluckin, W. and Sluckin, A. (1982) Mother-to-infant bonding. *Journal of Child Psychology and Psychiatry*, 23, 205–21.

Hughes, P., Turton, P., Hopper, E., McGauley, G.A. and Fonagy, P. (2001) Disorganized attachment behaviour among infants born subsequent to stillbirth. *Journal of Child Psychology and Psychiatry*, 42, 795–801.

Klaus, M.H. and Kennell, J.H. (1982) *Parent–Infant Bonding*. St Louis, MO: Mosby.

Lewis, C. (1986) The role of the father in the human family. In Sluckin, W. and Herbert, M. (eds) *Parental Behaviour*. Oxford: Basil Blackwell.

Lewis, V. (2001) *Development and Handicap*. Oxford: Basil Blackwell.

Lidz, T. (1968) *The Person: His Development throughout the Life-cycle*. London: Basic Books.

Macfarlane, J.W. (1977) *Psychology of Childbirth*. Cambridge, MA: Fontana.

Mason, M.A., Skolnick, A. and Sugarman, S.D. (1998) *All our Families*. New York: Oxford University Press.

Mount, F. (1983) *The Subversive Family: An Alternative History of Love and Marriage*. London: Unwin.

Newman, B. and Newman, P. (1991) *Development through Life*, 5th edn. Pacific Grove, CA: Brooks/Cole.

Nortman, D. (1974) *Parental Age as a Factor in Pregnancy Outcome and Child Development*. Reports of Population/Family Planning. No. 16. New York: Population Council.

Patterson, C. (1982) *Coercive Family Process*. Eugene, OR: Castalia.

Pines, D. (1972) Pregnancy and motherhood: interaction between fantasy and reality. *British Journal of Medical Psychology*, 45, 333–43.

Robson, K.S. and Kumar, H.A. (1980) Delayed onset of maternal affection after childbirth. *British Journal of Psychiatry*, 136, 347–53.

Seligman, M.E.P. (1975) *Helplessness*. San Francisco: Freeman.

Sluckin, W., Herbert, M. and Sluckin, A. (1983) *Maternal Bonding*. Oxford: Basil Blackwell.

Thomas, A., Chess, S. and Birch, H.G. (1968) *Temperament and Behaviour Disorders in Children*. Hillsdale, NJ: Lawrence Erlbaum.

US Bureau of the Census (1993) *Current Population Reports. Population profile of the United States*. Washington, DC.

Welles-Nystrom, B.L. (1997) The meaning of postponing motherhood for women in the United States and Sweden aspects of feminism and radical timing strategies. *Health Care for Women International*, 18, 279–99.

Zippay, A. (1995) Expanding employment skills and social networks among teen mothers: case study of a mentor program. *Child and Adolescent Social Work Journal*, 12, 51–69.

5

Parental Influences on Vulnerability and Resilience

Carole A. Kaplan and Julie Owens

SUMMARY

There is now a significant and high-quality literature on vulnerability and resilience, as the list of references at the end of this chapter indicates. The purpose of this chapter is to present a predominantly clinical perspective on this issue, to highlight those points which workers with parents, in and out of clinics, need to bear in mind from this body of evidence. This chapter addresses the historical background, family factors, individual child factors, environmental factors, cumulative and interactional processes and social policy.

INTRODUCTION

All parents wish to do the best for their children. Often, their greatest fear is that they themselves may in some way damage their children, or perhaps exacerbate, rather than ameliorate, their difficulties. Influences that parents have on their children are many and various. Some will be positive, others less so. However, any study of human life shows that there is never only one single, direct cause of a child's woes. There is always some interaction, often complex, between the parent, the child, the family and their environments.

The major challenge for professionals working with parents and children is to help them enhance their resilience and reduce their vulnerabilities. This requires great skill, often working in the absence of much hard evidence,

and using as much a creative as a scientific resource.

For most of us, life includes adversity as well as opportunity. Many parents and professionals would wish to shield children from the more negative of these. The additive and interactional effects of different negative factors may be overwhelming at times. However, a life free from adversity may also not be ideal, and cushioning children from stress and challenge may not be the best of childhood experiences or the best preparation for adulthood. Parental influence thus has to encompass a 'filter' to shield children from too much adversity as well as helping them to face the difficulties that they will necessarily confront, as they develop towards independence. To understand vulnerability and resilience requires consideration of all the attributes of individuals within the context that they function, in the broadest possible terms.

HISTORICAL BACKGROUND

Since their advent, care professions have tried to ameliorate the effects of adversity, to treat disease, help the impoverished and educate the illiterate. Over time, the focus of concern has changed. Initially concern was with discovering the relationship with infection and other forms of ill health. Consideration then shifted to the effects of early employment on children still immature and at early stages of development. By the mid-20th century, the more basic issues having been addressed, attention shifted to those matters which impeded children's psychological growth, such as maternal and other deprivations (Bowlby, 1951). Professional research has become ever more elaborate, with the elucidation of complex models, mediating factors and sophisticated research designs attempting to disentangle complex sets of cause, process and effect variables. There are multiple interactions between individuals and the environmental and ecological organizational systems within which they operate. Our understanding of these has become gradually more extensive, if not always more secure.

The essential human skills of parenting are becoming less a matter of private family life and more a matter of public concern. School children, those about to marry, and parents of unborn or newly arrived children, are all targets of public programmes to teach them parenting skills. This may be a reflection of the historical changes to family life. Children learn to take care of others by not only being cared for themselves, but also by watching and taking part in the care of their siblings and other family members. Families today seldom include grandparents in the immediate home environment, and children experience a more distant relationship with members of the extended family when compared to the past. In addition, in affluent societies and families, leisure is often an organized affair and time for families to spend together is sometimes severely limited.

The concerns of research over the past half century have shifted: the 1940s started studies of patterns of family relationships and child-rearing; the effects of attachment and peer relationships became the focus in the 1950s; and studies of temperament and environmental factors dominated in the 1960s and 1970s (Thomas et al., 1968). Studies of individual capacity to perform functions such as planning became prevalent in the 1980s and 1990s (Quinton, 1994). In relation to childhood experiences relating to mental health outcomes, the 1940s saw descriptions of the 'schizophrenogenic' mother (Reichard and Tillman, 1950) and 'refrigerator' parenting (Kanner, 1949). Over the decades, there was a shift in emphasis to studies of interactions between parents and children to which both parties made a contribution, and then in the 1970s (Rutter, 1971; Brown and Harris, 1978) and 1980s, studies of life events that may adversely mark the children. The research became far more sophisticated, evaluating the different contributions of risk and resilience factors in terms of parental influences and childhood attributes.

Thus over time there has been a great shift in emphasis in the expert advice given to parents. It is just as well to consider that some advice did a lot of damage, particularly in a situation where parents were made to feel guilty about the way they cared for their children. The earlier simplistic explanations that something about parents, or what they did, resulted in damage to a child are now largely discredited. The obvious exception to this is, of course, in cases of child abuse.

Some of the most useful work is helping parents to see that their influence on their children is mediated and balanced by many factors. As an example, a depressed mother who has difficulty empathizing with her child while ill, does not lose a previously good relationship with the child. This is particularly so if there are other members of the family who can support the child and mother, and where the child can be helped to understand that his or her mother is ill.

Vulnerability and Resilience

'Vulnerability' refers to the susceptibility to be hurt or damaged by adversity. A child may be 'vulnerable' physically (such as brittle bones), intellectually (such as having learning difficulties), in terms of family (depressed parent), socially (belonging to an ethnic minority), or in terms of mental health (having a tendency to anxiety). Much is known about vulnerability and a large number of 'risk factors' (such as those cited) have been identified that increase the chances of negative outcomes for children.

Vulnerability may be regarded as the result of 'multi-factorial' risk factors that may exist within the child (genetic, physical), the family (break-up, violence) and the wider community (poor housing, social stigma). These factors combine in a 'synergistic' or multiplying manner to affect the individual. However, the development of maladaptive behaviour or even psychopathology is dependent on the interplay with the child's resilience.

'Resilience', at the other end of the spectrum from vulnerability, refers to the ability to withstand

and emerge without serious harm from the experience of adversity. It is a matter of degree – the higher the presumed resilience, the lower the impact of the adversity. It is a judgement that can only be made retrospectively, though evidence has pointed to a number of 'protective factors' that shield the child from the full face of negative experiences. Vulnerability and resilience have been conceptualized by some writers as being the opposite ends of a 'dimension', capable of being broken down into the sources of impact on the child, as the above factors indicate.

The concept of 'resilience' is relatively new and as a result there is little 'hard' scientific evidence to support the ways in which factors may operate to provide resilience. However, there are a number of likely ways in which these protective processes may work:

- Reducing the risk by affecting the nature of the risk factor itself or altering the exposure to or involvement in the risk; for example, a child who is sociable may be able to spend more time with friends and playing sport, thus keeping out of the way of domestic violence.
- Reduce the likelihood of negative chain reactions arising from the risk; for example a child who is helped by a homework club to succeed at school while the mother recovers from a depressive disorder.
- Promote self-esteem and self-efficacy through the availability of secure and supportive personal relationships, or success in achieving tasks; for example, a child who is included in a football team when his parents are separating.
- Open up new and positive opportunities and offer turning points, where a risk path may be re-routed; for example, movement to a new neighbourhood after the separation of parents may allow for the opportunity to go to youth clubs and take up new activities, where previously unknown skills are revealed.

There is often a delicate balance between risk and resilience. In child clinics, it is common to find that some children in a family cope with serious adversity, whilst others seem floored with minor difficulties. Equally, there are children who cope in some settings, but not others.

The interplay between vulnerability and resilience is complex and not yet adequately understood. However, what is apparent is that factors affecting vulnerability and resilience act as 'mediators' or 'moderators'. Mediating factors include events, circumstances and personal characteristics that form a link between underlying 'causal' influences and eventual outcomes. Moderators change the relationship between two factors; for example, grandparents' support may moderate the relationship between parental conflict and children's psychological distress.

Current thinking suggests that multiple factors operate in combination to produce vulnerability and resilience. It is also apparent that resilience is not necessarily conferred by the absence of risk. The absence of many or serious risk factors does not automatically ensure that an individual will adapt successfully, although it may reduce the level of dysfunction in such a protected group.

A great deal of research is still required to investigate the constructs of vulnerability and resilience, as there is still much to be learned. Of particular interest when considering parental influence is whether risk factors do harm through undermining the development of protective factors, such as support systems, self-esteem, or academic competence, as this may affect the 'critical development' tasks of a child. In turn, this may lead to an inability to develop adequate protective resources early in life that not only cause problems then, but also lead to later increased exposure to stress and vulnerability to dysfunction.

Another key question is to what extent adverse effects persist, even after good-quality care is re-established. Studies of institutional deprivation (Rutter, 2002) show a combination of restoration to normal functioning in the majority, with a minority showing clinically important difficulties for up to two years after restoration of normality. To what extent this is true of children exposed to other forms of risk remains to be elucidated.

Problems, risks and resilience require a consideration of the people and context within which they develop. Changes in one individual are both the cause and consequence of changes in others and over time. Small changes can have a large impact. It is tempting to think that the interactions and interdependency of so many risk and resilience factors are so complex that they are impenetrable. However, it may be that their very complexity makes them more amenable to change. A belief that people are capable of change throughout their lifespan, and that the degree of 'plasticity' in children is great, can drive important initiatives on individual, family and national bases.

FAMILY FACTORS

It seems to be generally accepted in most societies that the most beneficial experience of family life for a child is to grow up in a family where there are two harmonious parents of different gender. However, many children have the experience of living in single-parent families and large numbers of others experience many different family configurations during their early years. Others have the experience of the care and influence of two parents of the same gender, and less often, there are children who experience parenting from a parent with a re-assigned gender (see chapter 8).

In most Western countries, there is a desire, in the community as well as in law, to enable children to experience the care of two parents. Parents carry responsibility (not always legal) for their children's care for life. The exception is where adoption is the course that must be followed, as influence from the biological parent(s) is judged too adverse an experience for the child.

Factors Associated with Resilience

It is a complex and difficult task to provide parental care for one or more children. When this is shared by two adults in a mutually supportive and caring relationship, the difficulties are diffused by sharing and diversifying core advantages. Other things being equal (such as when a parent is not mentally ill and in need of special care), there is greater capacity to absorb the physical demands of caring, and the opportunity to provide differing relationships for the children. However, there is also the potential for conflict between parents and this must be dealt with in a way that is not damaging. Parents need to adopt a consistent approach to discipline, moral attitudes, standards of behaviour, support for education, love, positive regard and respect for members of the family. This early formative experience sets a template for future positive experiences in the child's life.

However, many parents do not live in such a positive relationship, and regard their difficulties as a personal failure. This is particularly the case when their own families of origin are recalled as being characterized by affection, involvement and a capacity to disagree without catastrophic consequences. Other parents, by contrast, recall little affection, harsh discipline, marked discord and other adversities. This may lead to a rejection of much of their own early life experiences and a desire to provide a different kind of parental influence for their children. Whatever individuals' experience may be, their own childhood experiences have a critical impact on the relationships they, in turn, form with their children. It is interesting to note that the formal assessment of parental bonding has increasingly

become part of routine clinical assessment. For example, someone who has had a childhood filled with rejection and insecurity in terms of their relationship with a parent, may find that their attachment to their own child is influenced by this experience. Factors such as these can be assessed using questionnaires such as the Parenting Bonding Instrument or the Adult Attachment interviews, which can be used to look at an individual's relationship with their parents and their children.

Whatever the configuration of the family, at least one good relationship with a close adult (such as grandparent) seems essential for the healthy development of a child. This should encompass warm acceptance, empathy and respect. It may be hard to achieve in a family where there are multiple stresses, but it is striking how even limited pleasant interactions can provide a basis for the development of positive self-regard. All families have disagreements and periods of disharmony, and a cognitive challenge to the emotional reactions engendered can be helpful. Difficulties are not necessarily disasters, and if the strengths of the relationships are great enough, these stresses may serve to strengthen the relationships and enrich family life. Positive reframing of serious family disharmony in this way can be helpful, as will be the creation of family and individual histories of coping with problems.

It is also worth considering the attributes that each individual brings to these interactions, and the capacity to learn from them. These are clearly diverse and complex. The preponderance of one attribute (such as a child's anxiety-proneness) or the sum of the total interaction (such as an insecure child) will clearly colour the impact of family events.

The 'style' of parents' interactions with their children is most important in the development of vulnerability or resilience. Of central importance is the parent–child relationship and the resulting 'attachment' (Ainsworth et al., 1978).

Whilst most children form an attachment with their care-givers, the quality of this relationship varies greatly. Research has led to a classification into secure and insecure attachments. 'Secure attachments' are characterized by meeting the child's emotional and other needs as well as providing consistent control, discipline and structure. 'Insecure attachments' are divided into the following:

- *avoidant* – characterized by reflecting or insensitive behaviour which lacks tenderness on the part of the parent,
- *resistant/ambivalent* – characterized by minimal or inconsistent parental responsiveness, and

- *disorganized/disorientated* – the parents'
  behaviour is unpredictable, overrides the
  infant's cues and gives double messages.

Children brought up by nurturing, responsive and
yet behaviourally demanding parents are less
likely to show disturbance than those brought up
by parents who are emotionally cold and yet
rigid in enforcing rules and harsh in their discipline. Parents' own experiences of childhood
care have been linked to the kind of attachment
they develop with their children. Evidence suggests that over half of children have secure
attachments but a large minority do not. Of these,
children who have a 'chaotic' attachment to
parents may have the poorest outcome in terms
of social and behavioural adaptations.

Thus cycles of disadvantage can be established where poor parental experiences lead them
to behave damagingly towards their children
through lack of capacity or competence for warm
emotional expressions. It is often difficult to
know how best to break them. However, an amelioration of early negative experiences can be
achieved for many, often by the process of
parents' understanding their own life histories,
and actively working towards not repeating them
with their children.

An affectionate and confident approach to
parenting may promote resilience through strong
attachment. When this is accompanied by the
parents' constant awareness of where their
children are, and what (in general terms) they are
doing and (possibly) feeling, then, in psychoanalytical terms, the children have the sense of
being 'held' in the parents' minds. This kind of
'containment' is significant for children's mental
health. Where it is inadequate, this can be a
central aim of the therapeutic work with the
child. If a child knows that a parent is always
available and involved in his or her life, this provides a sense of being important and valued. This
affects the way children feel about themselves
and affects their interactions with others. The
way this is done must, of course, be tailored to
the child's developmental stage. The need for
constant supervision of a toddler is very different
from knowledge of the whereabouts of a
teenager, but the principle of holding them is the
same, and the link between parent and child
retains its essence.

The other major domain of functioning for a
child is school. Thus, the quality of interaction
between parents and school is of great importance in promoting children's resilience. In the
UK, the state takes the view that ensuring that a
child receives education is the responsibility of
the parent, and action may be taken against

parents who do not enforce this. Good parental
influence goes far beyond getting the child
through the school gates and includes a close
involvement with education from the earliest age
(Utting, 1996).

Playing in a manner that promotes learning (as
well as the other positive effects of such a plea-
surable experience) is important for the
preschool child. Once the child is in formal education, an active interest and involvement in
school and home-based activity provides many
opportunities for wide-ranging development of
positive experiences. The child receives a clear
message that education is valued and important.
Educational activity is also a source of stimulation and pleasure, and an opportunity for praise
and approval from parents as well as teachers and
peers. The involvement of parents themselves in
reading (the presence of books in the home is a
major factor associated with good educational
achievement) and other homework reinforces
this. Even when parents may regard themselves
as incompetent educationally (for example, if
they struggle to read or calculate) this can be
turned to both the child's and the parent's advantage, by the parent learning to read with their
child. This emphasizes and confirms a close
bond between them, a sense of partnership and
sharing in a goal, whilst retaining appropriate
boundaries between parent and child. Both individuals acquire new skills that they share and
value, the acquisition of which is initiated
and maintained by the parent, at least initially,
and valuable one-to-one time is established.

The extended family can provide considerable
support for children. Caring grandparents who
become involved in the care of their grandchildren can form a very special relationship with
them, and this is to their mutual benefit. Many
grandparents comment on the advantages of the
slight distance conferred by not providing all the
daily care of the child, and children, of course,
regularly talk about how lovely it is to have
grandparents who 'spoil' them. Support for
parents is thus provided by grandparents and
other members of the extended family and can be
highly valued. Sometimes this allows mothers to
seek employment, which can promote aspirations in daughters particularly, but must be
balanced against those studies that report negative effects on children of full-time maternal
employment (see chapter 10).

Factors Associated with Vulnerability

Overt conflict in the family is hard for children to
deal with, particularly if it is violent, sustained

and frequent. Some children become directly involved in the conflict and are harmed both physically and psychologically. The child's reaction to the conflict is often complex, ill-absorbed and distressing even if not always expressed. Some children will try to distract their parents from the arguments by whatever means, often with the result that they themselves are blamed for the conflict. A child's method of distracting may be to display disruptive or aggressive behaviour or self-harm, with the result that the parents sometimes unite to chastize him. If the parents continue, the child is blamed for the conflict on the grounds that if the child were not difficult, they would not disagree on how to handle him, thus damaging their own relationship. Other children may become ill, engage in self-harm, suffer from eating or sleeping disorders, run away or other maladaptive acts, demanding parental unity in caring for them. These reactions may have a temporary effect of reducing conflict, but often they are short-lived, as the underlying family tensions burst forth and create a spiral of worsening reactions which warrant serious attention by clinicians.

A child who feels responsible for parental conflict, particularly if this ultimately leads to breakdown or parental separation, will feel deeply guilty. This sense of guilt is exacerbated by difficulties over contact, particularly where the parent who does not live with the child does not maintain contact. Such children may then feel that the parent never loved or cared for them and never wanted them and that this led to the parent's departure. Alternatively, they may blame the parent with whom they live for driving the other parent away. Highly charged disputes over contact serve to emphasize the complex and often damaging dynamics in these families. Given children's often 'secret' preoccupation with these dynamics, it is hardly surprising that children from separated families tend to achieve less academically, and later, as adults, are at increased risk of behavioural, physical and mental health problems, substance misuse problems and, for the girls, to become sexually active and leave home at an earlier age.

It is most important not to attribute these differences (when compared to children from intact families) to the separation alone. There is a process of conflict and unravelling that begins well before the final event, and it is this, as much as the final outcome, that can be difficult for children, and its impact and concurrent consequences are a source of vulnerability (see chapter 8).

Thus, there is work to be done with children and families, to help them realize that there are times when relationships do not last, and that,

although breakdown is not desirable, it is also not uncommon. There is now increasing awareness of the need to help children when families fall apart, though there are few readily accessible services. Evidence shows clearly that information for parents who are considering separation is valued. This acquaints them with the mechanisms of divorce, but also, more importantly, the likely impact on children, and provides advice on how to tell the children about what is happening in the family. Similarly children also benefit from knowing the 'truth', rather than letting them brood on their unspoken fears. It is better to talk frankly to them about difficulties and plans to separate. Children worry about where they will live, with whom, where the departing parent will go, when and how often they will meet, where will they go to school, what their grandparents and peers will think, whether there will be enough money, and countless other anxieties. It is as obvious as it is necessary to emphasize that these issues are best dealt with in a calm manner by the parents. The issue of contact can be very troublesome and sometimes a structured approach worked out by both parents, for example by using a 'Parenting Plan', can be helpful. This is a structured document that identifies the boundaries of the above issues and facilitates negotiation between parents regarding the most important aspects of separation as they relate to the children.

Separation and divorce are hard for children to deal with. There is a considerable sense of loss and a demand for readjustment. This has to be done whilst in the care of parents who are themselves stressed and who cannot continue parental care in the same way as before. The familiar features of life are disrupted and significant uncertainties and threats must be dealt with. Yet the vast majority of children survive parental separation without too much harm. It is likely that this is as a result of their own resilience and sense of self-esteem, combined with good relationships (which may go through a difficult period, but recover) and successful experiences with parents in their own lives. Parents can help this by keeping children informed of what is going on, considering their feelings and wishes in the actions they take, and trying to keep their lives as stable as possible. A positive attitude to challenges in life is helpful and parents who are able to abandon conflict and a sense of victimization, and who can embrace the present and future positively, make an enormous contribution to their children's welfare.

Affecting all child–parent relationships is the children's capacity to identify and adjust to change. Changes in childhood are noted by the expansion of life and social skills, and marked by physical maturation and ceremonies such as changing schools. Parents need to be sensitive to these changes in their children and recognize their pattern of changing needs. The very close supervision of a young child must evolve into the increasing freedom of the young teenager and the ultimate assistance to leave home. Many parents find this hard, and benefit from discussions with other parents in the same position. Sometimes, when there is significant difficulty with this stage of transition, the roots lie in the parent's own fears of ageing, concerns about the new shape of family life and their own experiences of separation.

Sometimes parents try to delay their children's growth into adulthood, with often serious consequences for the child. Apart from the obvious retardation and distortion of development, the children express considerable resentment at their parents' behaviour, which becomes evident when they compare themselves with peers. Depending on the child's temperament and the strength of peer influences, they may resort to asserting independence, which may place them at risk, deeply distress the parent and lead to a further cycle of unhappiness and rejection.

It is understandably hard for some parents to accept that their children are turning from totally dependent infants to fully autonomous adults. There is for some sadness and a sense of loss about times past. However, helping a young person achieve independence successfully is the ultimate goal of parenting, even though achieving this can be hard, and requires a considerable adjustment from parents. Helping parents reflect on their own life and childhood experiences in a clinical or counselling context can help them recognize what they need to do to help their own offspring towards maturation and independence.

Children also need help to realize that their parents are changing and have to cope with themselves. Children who understand this can smooth their own path to both independence and their parents' to greater freedom. Children and parents need to realize that they need 'space' to grow and change.

PARENTAL ABUSE

Among the worst negative experiences a child can have is to be abused by a parent. This may be physical, sexual or emotional abuse. In clinical experience, usually one type of abuse is accompanied by others, though there are significant individual and social class variations. The kind of emotional, physical and behavioural disturbance that children may reveal varies across the full spectrum of psychiatric and psychological disorders and the severity varies markedly. The appropriately horrified social and legal response to abuse fails to recognize that children do survive such significant adversity and become 'victim survivors' who do not perpetuate the cycle of abuse but instead become good parents. It is hard to predict which children will overcome this kind of negative life event. However, evidence suggests that those who have had some positive experiences, particularly with non-abusing adults and peers prior to, or even during chronic abuse, preserve a sense of self which promotes resilience.

Those children who have areas where they are accepted and can succeed, such as at school or in sport, seem to have an advantage. Most important of all appears to be the relationship the child has with the non-abusing parent. Such parents, even if unaware of the abuse, rapidly respond to the allegations, act protectively and will start an active reparative process with their child. Building a sense of mutual trust and respect, nurturing children's positive attributes, understanding their difficulties and shaping behaviour and attitudes, are all part of this long process of acceptance. The actual experience of abuse and its associations, as well as the continuing relationship with the perpetrator, must all be unravelled so that the child can be helped to understand his or her experience and move forward positively. Arrangements for contact, as well as for care of the child, must be considered very carefully. The best help a child can get following abuse is in the form of confirmation of her or his value as a person, freedom from blame, and conveying support and the view that the impact of and coping with the abuse will change with time. Many forms of therapy have been offered to victims of abuse, which have included de-briefing, group therapy, individual therapy and medication. No one form of therapy has emerged as the panacea, and multimodal therapy may be needed over a long period of time. Of course, the work is not with the child alone; the parent with whom the child lives, siblings and the perpetrator all need help and support if the family as a whole is to provide a safe and nurturing environment in which growth can occur.

Parental Illness

Parental illness appears to be a risk factor that makes the child more vulnerable to developing emotional and behavioural and perhaps mental health problems (Rutter and Quinton, 1984). The way that this risk operates may be direct (for example, a genetic predisposition to developing a mental illness) or indirect, through the effects of parents' illness on their behaviour towards their children or the complications that can arise as a result of parents' hospitalization. Many parents with a mental illness do an excellent job of caring for their children and, given the incidence of mental illness in the community, this is of great importance. Clearly, if a parent's behaviour is bizarre and poses a danger to the child (for example, if the child is the subject of the delusional ideas in the parent) then this may pose a significant risk to the child whilst the parent is unwell. However, once parents have recovered from the acute episode, they are often in the best position to explain to the child how the illness affected them and to demonstrate their response to treatment as a significant contribution to the child's ability to cope. It may be true that the child is at risk of developing the same illness as the parent. Thus, to witness resilience in the parent contributes significantly to the child's coping abilities. This appears to be particularly relevant where there is an acute episode of illness that is relatively short-lived. However, if the parent experiences ongoing difficulties, for example with a depression that may be resistant to treatment, or where there are many negative features of a schizophrenic illness, the risk to the child may be more insidious. Where there has been a good relationship between parent and child this may become eroded, the child mourns the good parent that was, and resents this very different parent, a situation that is compounded by fear, incomprehension, a sense of responsibility and exposure to pressures that have to be faced alone.

A similar situation is also found where there is serious chronic physical ill health in a parent and the child becomes a carer. As a result, the child takes on age-inappropriate responsibility, and the boundaries of who manages whom may be broken down. There is often role reversal to a major degree in the burden of care and the child has very few opportunities to enjoy the normal activities of childhood and to receive the kind of care a comparable child receives. This burden appears to increase children's vulnerability to further stresses that for others may not pose an adaptive threat. Where possible, the best way forward is not to remove the child from the care of the parent, where there is often deep attachment, but rather to give assistance in their tasks. This provides relief without casting doubts on the child's ability and willingness to play an important role in the care of the parent. This is a difficult task, to be undertaken with sensitivity, and the best results are often found where the parent has been supportive to help the child accept assistance and have the capacity to enjoy age-appropriate activities.

Criminality

The origins and development of criminality are complex, but there is a strong association between parental criminality and juvenile delinquency. Twin and adoption studies of adult recidivist criminals suggest that there is probably a small genetic influence. However, it seems that familial and socio-economic difficulties contribute the greatest risk to children. The Newcastle Longitudinal Study (Kolvin et al., 1988) have convincingly demonstrated the cumulative nature of risk factors in the development of criminality. This study showed that when deprivation increased over time, the subsequent rate of offending increased, and when deprivation decreased, the rate of criminality decreased. This is encouraging as it raises the possibility that if deprivation can be reduced, so can the risk. The effects of offending often entail considerable hardship for the family of the criminal who is imprisoned. There is financial hardship, the loss of a significant member of the family, and sometimes significant social stigma (see chapter 3).

Where there is a pattern of recidivism in the parent, many families adapt quite well. However, this is heavily dependent on the strength and resilience of the remaining parent, most often the mother. Where there is interpersonal violence in the family, there may be considerable relief when the offending parent is incarcerated, and fear when the release date approaches. This creates serious difficulties for children who live in a tense atmosphere and who may experience frequent changes of address, coupled with frequently expressed fear and hostility. This is confusing, and children often react in ways that vary from the aggressive to the withdrawn, imposing further stress on a family already in difficulty.

The best guiding principle is to encourage parents to maintain consistency, familiarity and stable relationships, for example, in relation to housing, schooling, friends and extended family members. Wherever possible, contact should be maintained with the absent parent in order to dissipate fears and anxieties. It may be necessary to supervise contact visits, and watch over the balance of negative effects for the children as against any advantages. Whatever is decided, children need and are helped by support if they are to make sense of what is happening around them.

Loss and Bereavement

Loss and bereavement are significant events for children as well as adults. The loss of a parent or sibling can be devastating to a young child, dramatically increasing their vulnerability to other future 'life events' or adversities. Of great importance is the quality of the attachment between parent and child, or child and sibling, before the death. Risk is reduced if it is possible to prepare for the death, for example, when the illness is serious and carries a risk of death. Children often inhabit worlds in which they believe themselves to be both powerful and responsible. Time to explore feelings and fantasies, such as worries that something they did led to the illness or death, can be very helpful. Enabling children to anticipate and cope with impending bereavement by giving them information about what is likely to happen, exploring beliefs about death, and helping them accept the permanent separation, are all strategies that reduce vulnerability. Loss is a major risk factor for children, but helping them understand and accept death and loss before the event, has a significant positive effect. Previous experience of death can be 'helpful' too, for example, the death of an elderly grandparent or a pet, as the child's knowledge of death is greatly expanded, and there is experience of life after bereavement. Each of these can, of course, increase vulnerability, depending on the child's temperament and the impact of the loss event.

For many professionals, the experience of dealing with a bereaved child can be painful, particularly if they are unprepared. Children who are bereaved may present difficulties in many ways. These include having unusual and frightening experiences, such as 'seeing' or 'hearing' the dead person. This can unsettle both the child and the adults involved. Often it seems necessary to 'breathe deeply' and adopt a calm approach. If there are any severe or persistent symptoms in the child, these should be assessed. By and large, reassurance and acknowledgement of the pain and grief, exploration of feelings of anger and guilt, helping to mark memories of the departed so that they are not lost, and primary focus on the child are helpful. It can be useful too to ask whether the child ever feared the person when alive, as there would be no reason to fear them when dead. A positive 're-framing' of these experiences can help the child and reduce distress. A process of 'guided mourning' which includes more than one member of the family can also be considered. This sharing of grief in a structured way can reduce the stress and vulnerability for everyone around the child. Adults should be encouraged to talk about the dead person, and the child helped to see that the subject does not have to be avoided, even if it upsets people.

Generally, children are remarkably resilient in the face of adversity. The challenge for parents and professionals is how to identify and promote this. The individual and temperamental features may be a 'mixed bag', each having two aspects, one that promotes resilience, the other vulnerability.

Gender

In adults, women have a greater vulnerability to psychiatric disorders (particularly if they have experienced early adversity), but in childhood it seems that girls cope better. Thus the female gender is a resilience factor in childhood. The usual explanation is that girls have greater socialization skills and this enables them to cope better. The different expectation of the genders in terms of their behaviour and roles in society doubtless also plays a part.

Intelligence

Intelligence is a major resilience factor. The more able children have greater experience of success, encounter less stress and have greater capacity to make sense of their life experiences. Associated individual characteristics may also promote resilience. Attributes such as the capacity to reflect on difficulties and take a problem-solving (as opposed to an emotional or denial) approach, help children to cope better with adversity.

The ability to plan action and a belief that the child can exercise some control are also very positive. These are all interesting features of resilience, and whilst many may be regarded as innate, many can be modelled and taught by parents. Clearly, intelligence cannot be sensibly separated from the rest of the child's personality. It can, therefore, only be regarded as a protective factor, 'other things being equal'. High intelligence can inhabit an otherwise highly vulnerable personality, as in the case of some schizophrenics.

Communication Skills

Communication skills can be enhanced by parental demonstration and encouragement. Children and adults who communicate well, find that other people react positively. If positive regard and respect for others is also conveyed in the process of learning good communication, it will be a major benefit. Positive attitudes and problem-solving approaches to difficulties are attractive and bring not only the rewards of a greater chance of success but also the benefit of other people's approval. This approach can be identified and encouraged by parents, through 'operationalizing' and demonstrating and encouraging the child to copy.

The competence to reflect on a problem, consider its implications and then to plan an approach to dealing with it, can be taught. Parents often have this skill but use it automatically without making it explicit. It can be helpful to children to have this articulated by their parents, and then helped to do the same in relation to their own problems. The more often this skill is practised, the better and more 'automatic' it becomes, thus conferring resilience.

Sense of Homour

Sense of humour has also been identified as contributing to resilience. A sense of humour is a great asset in anyone, particularly a parent, as the capacity to defuse difficult situations makes life easier. Humorous people often find the funny or absurd aspects of an otherwise grave situation, thus reducing its impact. The more fun a parent and child can have together the better, and often advice to 'go and enjoy something together' can mobilize resources to help cope with adversity.

Religious Belief

Religious belief is often associated with strong community networks and this itself is a major source of support at times of adversity. Religion also confers 'cause and effect' explanations as well as a means of explaining and coping with adversity (see chapter 7). Clearly this is a complex matter, raising issues about the kind, intensity and consequences of particular belief systems, which can only be sensibly evaluated as part of the total 'life space' of parents and children.

Temperament

Temperament can be defined as the 'how' of behaviour. For example, if two children ride a bike, one may do so carefully and slowly, and the other do so fast and rather recklessly. Both are doing the same thing, but the way that they do it is very different, and could be considered a reflection of their temperament. Temperament has

been extensively studied because an individual's characteristics influence their vulnerability or resilience in everyday life as well as in special adversity. There are a number of important studies of temperamental attributes in children and the way in which they may have contributed to an individual's long-term development.

The individual attributes of a person are easily conceived of as making an important difference to the way in which he or she copes with, is perceived by, and interacts with their environment. In an adult, the term 'personality' is usually used to describe these characteristics, but in children the term 'temperament' is used more often.

Children who have an easy temperament often seem to have an unfair advantage in life. They are easy, placid babies who smile a lot, fit into a routine and adapt to change without problems. These happy, rewarding children are a joy for parents to care for, and forming strong, positive relationships with them is easy. At the other end of the spectrum is the child with the 'difficult temperament', who never seems to be at ease, cries easily, complains a lot, is unpredictable and difficult to care for. They do not like their routines upset and react intensely when the unexpected happens. These children can make the most competent and caring parent feel inadequate, as what is done for them does not often seem to be good enough (Robbins, 1966). The combination of a child with a difficult temperament and a parent under stress can be seriously distressing, with two angry and unhappy people locked in a cycle of negative interactions. Parents can be helped during these difficult years by recognizing that their child has a particular kind of temperament (sometimes similar to another member of the family), that others would also find it difficult, and that the children are not finding life very easy either. The 'goodness of fit' between parent and child is worth exploring, particularly where one parent is finding it easier to cope than the other. Parents may love their children but have to learn to like them. In some cases this does not happen.

It has been suggested that some children have the ability to select what is best in their environment from many different sources, in part because they possess a quality that was valued by parents and others, thus building up their self-esteem. The importance of a 'good fit' between child and parent or older siblings is very important as the child is valued and rewarded by the parent who in turn is rewarded by the child's reaction, thus continuing the cycle of positive and possibly protective interactions. The 'goodness of fit' is equally applicable in relation to community resources for a child who derives some degree of resilience from these positive interactions.

However, a difficult temperament is not all negative. It is true that in a stable community at peace, the association between a difficult temperament and antisocial behaviour and possible criminality in later life have been described in research. However, this is based on retrospective studies and the majority of children who have a 'difficult' temperament do eventually settle into well-adjusted lives. Often, it is the 'easy' child who is at a disadvantage in times of deprivation, severe adversity and war. The 'difficult' child demands and gets attention (and food), whereas the easy, compliant child may be neglected (Werner and Smith, 1982). This can be observed in families under stress where the 'noisy' child is cared for 'to keep them quiet', whereas the quiet one is ignored. Parents need to tune into both the assessment and response to their children's temperaments.

When a family is caring for a child with a difficult temperament, clear behaviour strategies can be helpful. At times parents may feel almost persecuted by their unsettled, difficult children and become angry, depressed or both. It is usually one parent who bears the brunt of this difficulty and the support of the other parent becomes indispensable. Ways of handling the child should be worked out between the parents and caring shared in an explicit way. Discussions of what the nature of temperament is can be helpful, for some parents, reference to the relevant research.

RISK FACTORS

Genetics

The study of genetics has grown exponentially in recent years, and yet, despite the claims of some zealots, it remains difficult to tease out the relative contribution of genetic endowment to human behaviour. Genetic influences range from looks and diseases where there is a clear pattern of inheritance, to the more vague ideas of children being temperamentally similar to their relatives in various ways. Interactions between genetic and environmental factors are complex. Traditionally, medical genetics has concentrated on single-gene ('Mendelian') disorders where genetic conditions associated with human disease can easily be mapped and are seen not to be affected by environmental conditions (such as Down's syndrome). More recently, as studies have become more sophisticated, techniques have been developed that make it possible to

consider the significance of the effect of the environment on the activity of genes.

In recent years, interest has also focused on 'behavioural genetics' which explores the significance of inheritance on variations in human behaviour. These developments have major implications for the study of psychological disorders or behavioural traits that run in families. As a great simplification, it seems that most psychological traits have a 'heritability' of 50 per cent (that is, genetic differences between individuals) and account for about half of the variation observed in the population (Goodman and Scott, 1998). There are exceptions to this generalization, such as in autism which *may* have a heritability of over 90 per cent, and anger-proneness problems which are probably only affected to a small extent by genetic influences.

Genetics are often blamed for the difficulties a child may have. It is not uncommon to try to explain severe behavioural difficulties in a child on the basis that this has been inherited from an antisocial parent. The research is helpful here, as there is little evidence that genes have more than a potentially small effect in relation to conduct disorders. It is also useful to remember that each parent contributes half the child's genetic endowment. Thus, any vulnerability and resilience features emerge in the children as a complex of features. A common difficulty arises when one parent sees a problematic child as being 'just like' the other parent. If the relationship between the parents is poor, the result of such comparison can be unfortunate for the child who, almost inevitably, seems to live out the negative prophecies made by the complaining parent. Parents should be helped to see the complexity of their product and avoid devaluing comparisons. This advice applies equally to the positive talents that a parent may hope the child will inherit.

Learning Disability

In the same way that good intellectual ability and often associated academic success are seen as resilience factors, learning disability and developmental delays are factors that confer vulnerability. One of the most important things that parents can give children is a sense that they are valued in and for themselves, rather than for any particular characteristics. Emphasis on what children are able to do, and their strengths, rather than their weaknesses, is critical. The first step is for parents to realize what difficulties and challenges the children have to face, but separate these from the intrinsic worth of the child. Some parents believe that their child is 'lazy' and 'could try harder', when in fact she or he has a learning disability. Learning disabled people have no less need for positive self-esteem and such an approach is inimical to its development. Parents become increasingly frustrated and annoyed with the apparent failure of the child to try harder and a cycle of anger and sadness is created that is hard to break. Relevant factual information available through or from the school can help. Parents sometimes do not have confidence in teachers and do not believe their assessments of their child. It is helpful to have this identified and dealt with directly. The opposite can also happen, where parents receive continuing complaints from teachers about their child, when parents believe the child to have learning difficulties or some other difficulty, and the school attributes disruptive behaviour or poor learning to wilfulness. Psychological assessment and intervention can be crucial in all of these situations (see chapter 14).

Physical Illness

Physical illness, particularly chronic illness, is also a risk factor for children. Long periods away from school, particularly if intermittent, disrupt educational progress, peer relations and a sense of belonging as well as an ability to have some control over plans for the future. Illness itself may cause a loss of confidence in self and future, and living in an environment of anxiety and sometimes fear adds to the problem. The sense of being different and less able than one's peers is often underlined by the need to take medication and frequent inability to take part in physical and other activities. Children do not often understand their illness and react with anxiety and frustration. Additionally, they pick up their parents' worries about themselves. In the case of older children, there is also often a high level of worry about the prognosis, the treatment and the implications for the future, such as fertility, the heritability of the disorder and other issues (see chapter 12).

Teenage Pregnancy

This issue causes widespread concern on an individual, professional and political level. The reasons for young girls becoming pregnant are many. Becoming pregnant in the early teenage years is a significant risk to young people on physical, social, educational and emotional levels (Fundudis, 1997). These young girls are often not capable of caring for themselves, without having to cope with the needs of a dependent infant. The disapproval of family and friends can be very harsh, and rejection by family, school and community can lead to serious emotional and social dislocation. It is usually the girl who bears the brunt of this, in some cases suffering 'post-traumatic stress disorder' and depression, particularly where such pregnancies are not an accepted part of the local community. Obstetric services appear to recognize that support and acceptance of the teenager's decision to proceed or terminate the pregnancy is needed. Information about the physical change processes is important as a means of optimizing the mother and baby's state. The majority of such pregnancies occur among the poorer and less well-endowed girls (and fathers are often transitory). The unborn children are at risk of malnourishment, effects of substance use or transmitted diseases. Most developed countries have services for such girls, encompassing working with parents towards acceptance and care of their daughter, and with schools regarding continuation or reinsertion into education. Despite these, the future social and emotional well-being of both very young mother and her child are at high-level risk.

THE ENVIRONMENT

Resilience

SOCIAL NETWORK

A supportive network in the community can be a significant source of resilience for children. Children receive care from a meaningful group of adults who know them and who have an interest in the good functioning of the community. A community that has such an identity works well to support the individuals that compose it, nurtures the children within it, and promotes a positive identity both for individuals and itself. A wider range of caring and positive experience is made available to the children, from which both young and old benefit. Children are made aware of different role models and ways of assuming responsibility as well as developing a sense of belonging to a group wider than their immediate family. Cohesive communities with common values and standards of behaviour are beneficial and where there is high rate of engagement of members of the neighbourhood in community activities and initiatives friendships are forged and new skills learned which all promote resilience. With appropriate models, tolerance and respect for others can also be fostered. In Western urban societies, where most parenting takes place, such communities are disappearing fast. The relative exceptions are religious communities and those formed by minority ethnic groups and these have their own problems.

GOOD HOUSING

Good housing and a standard of living reasonably above poverty levels are major resilience factors in children's lives. Families who do not have to struggle with the basics of daily living are in better health and have more resources of all kinds (particularly their own positive attention) to give their children. The children are not marked out from their peers by virtue of poverty. Parents who are poor often find the normal demands that children make, for example to own the same clothes and toys as their peers, hard to bear. Promoting a shared sense of what a family can and cannot manage is thus worthwhile. Straitened circumstances demand rigorous planning for the expenditure of meagre resources and can promote pride in achievement of a desired goal. These are opportunities that children in more affluent families are likely to miss. However, the poverty and poor housing that often goes with it are unmitigated sources of disadvantage and vulnerability for parents and thence their children.

Research has not yet settled the question of whether, in Western societies, maternal work outside the home is a risk factor for children or not. Clinical experience, focused as it always is on alleviating difficulties, is also an inadequate guide. Studies so far have produced mixed results. Some studies (notably a recent one for the Rowntree Foundation; see Bachett-Milburn et al., 2001) show that full-time maternal work outside the home when children are very young is associated with poor academic achievement, early adult unemployment and psychological distress.

On the other hand, other studies have shown that where there is good nursery or childcare provision, maternal work outside the home is associated with positive outcomes for children. The greater financial resources, maternal fulfilment and time out from the stresses of rearing children, all contribute to this. In advising parents, where necessity does not dictate matters and children have no special needs, maternal working would seem worthwhile if parents can spend good quality time with their children and provide a strong emotional base for the growing child (see chapter 1).

In the UK, changes in employment over the last decade have led to a widening gap between 'work-rich' and 'work-poor' families. This has led to an increasing disparity in the income available to families, and currently one in three children live in poverty (Smith, 1999). Paternal unemployment or low earnings are the main cause of child poverty. As well as providing an income, employment also provides other opportunities for parents such as status, increased social contacts, information and wider access to other resources shown to impact positively on parental mental health and, therefore, child-rearing.

The adverse impact on children of inequality and poverty includes worse health and educational outcomes and, therefore, reduced capacity for positive adaptation in adulthood. Although this may be the general effect, there are also children who 'escape' their adverse backgrounds and achieve significant success. Factors such as stable families, an interest in education and intrinsic features all play a role for these resilient children.

SCHOOL ATTENDANCE

Attendance at a school that takes positive measures for suffering behaviour and attitudes of its pupils and has a strong anti-bullying policy is another strong resilience factor for a child. School is such an important part of a child's life, not only in the amount of time spent there, but also in terms of the enormous amount to be learned in all domains of functioning academically, emotionally and socially. The role models that are available, the focal attention on the child's performance, both academic and non-academic, have a lifelong influence on the child. There is considerable evidence showing that where parents take a positive interest and are actively involved in the child's school life, there are significant benefits in both academic and social terms. Furthermore, from a clinical viewpoint, positive collaboration between parents and teachers provides both parties with greater knowledge about the child and allows a more consistent application of behavioural boundaries. This issue becomes both more important and more difficult as the child grows older and comes increasingly under peer pressure.

Risk Factors

Social housing policy has an important role to play in the establishment of well-balanced communities that allow the maintenance of connections with extended families. Unfortunately, often poor and already stressed families are accommodated in temporary, low-standard housing. As a result, children are subject to overcrowded conditions, discontinuous and poor schooling, poor social and health care from over-stretched and poor services, and exposure to greater physical injury and malign social influences, which are more frequent in deprived communities. Such children, with fewer competencies and developed capacities, have a lesser potential for independent and effective social functioning.

Any factor that leads to families being isolated from their communities leads to increased vulnerability and risk. This may arise from prejudice about ethnic and religious affiliations, often resulting in hostile acts towards minorities, which have an adverse impact on children. Children of parents who are 'different' in some way, perhaps because of illness, appearance, or life-style, are often victimized, not always in obvious ways. Apart from prejudiced targeting by racist members of the community and its impact, there are also forms of discipline and sheer ignorance of the needs and difficulties of children in some minority ethnic families (like those in the majority) which are likely to add to children's vulnerability. This is exacerbated when children are moved frequently and their homes, schools and wider environments change, as is often the case. Parents normally make (or are forced to make) such changes for the better welfare of the family. It is important to advise them to maintain as much consistency as possible, in terms of familiarity of objects (even if only a few), food and particularly routines such as bedtime rituals. This would go some way to countering the anxiety and dislocation so often associated with change.

DISASTERS

Great adversity is usually associated with disasters, natural or human-made, and children feel vulnerable at these times. The level of shock and bereavement is often unimaginable – children lose parents, siblings, friends, homes, possessions, schools, and sometimes whole neighbourhoods. Life before the disaster does not resemble that which follows it. In addition, there is a constant fear that another catastrophe may befall them. As a variety of events have shown, developed societies are no more immune to such disasters than are others, although shootings in an American school are somewhat different from a civil war in Africa. By the same token, evidence suggests that, at least in the short term, the Western child who has grown up in a relatively more stable environment is likely to feel more vulnerable and be more marked by traumatic events than his counterparts elsewhere.

There do not appear to be any particular ways of safeguarding children against such experiences. Not many parents, family members or teachers attempt to inure children by familiarizing them with serious (accounts of) adversity. When such events occur, reassurance, good physical care and the opportunity for safe expression of distress are necessary. Evidence suggests, however, that attempts to 'counsel' traumatized children may in fact heighten and prolong their distressed reactions. Overall, the principles of psychological support such as preserving a sense of worth, capacity for caring, and a sense of efficacy, provide appropriate pointers for parents in these extreme conditions.

Some of the factors that conferred resilience while life was predictable, may now confer vulnerability. Positive temperament may be severely strained and undermined. Problem-solving skills that were effective in normal times may not appear to work in extreme conditions, and the skills of social communication and reflection many not be as effective as impulsive and aggressive actions in the face of disaster.

Cumulative Processes

There are a number of important questions to ask in relation to the way in which different factors in a child's life interact. A large body of research evidence supports the idea that rearing experiences in the course of growing up have a substantial effect on an individual's development. Risks arise when there is a lack of dependable, harmonious, focused and committed relationships, or when the relationships are negative ... and engender uncertainty (Rae-Grant et al., 1989). The effects of adversity are diverse, and there is little evidence for age-sensitive periods, although at least psychodynamically, there is an argument for early life experiences being more significant. Very little is known about the mechanisms that mediate this.

Over recent years, much of the research has pointed to the importance of chronic, rather than acute adversity, as being significant in the development of vulnerability. This has particular importance in childhood as any chronic adversity has the potential to affect the long-term development of an individual child. Rutter, considering the indirect long-term effects of risk factors on young children, states:

> the ways in which early experiences exerted long term effects, stemmed from their influences in both making negative experiences more likely to occur later and through rendering individuals more vulnerable to such experiences (Rutter and Smith, 1995).

It is apparent that risk factors frequently co-occur. For example, the death of a parent is often associated with loss of income and thus the possibility of having to move house and school, with the potential for subsequent loss of contact with family and friends. Thus one adversity may lead to other negative experiences. Parental divorce or separation, or repeated parental absence due to, for example, imprisonment, have similar and emerging effects and strain children's adaptive ability.

Many studies have demonstrated the serious effects of cumulative disadvantage and adversity on children. Rutter (1985, 1987) demonstrated the synergistic effects of a number of risk factors associated with familial adversities and the subsequent development of psychiatric disorders in the offspring. The studies showed that a child with only one risk factor had only a slightly raised (1–2 per cent) probability of developing a mental health problem. However, with three risk factors the rate increases to about 8 per cent, and with four or more risk factors the rate increases to 20 per cent. The kinds of risk factors described included severe marital discord, low social status, overcrowding, large family size, parental criminality and maternal psychiatric disorder.

SOCIAL POLICY

The social policy of governments in most developed countries has tried to utilize this knowledge about vulnerability and resilience, as well as making assumptions about remedies, by legislating as well as using other forms of government influence to try and change social traditions and responses.

Strategies to give parents information about the skills of parenting, and to help them to increase awareness of what children need, has been incorporated in parenting classes and information meetings associated with divorce, and may also be considered at the times of other important life events. The effectiveness of these initiatives has yet to be demonstrated. Indeed, the level of penetration of these ideas into the thinking of the general population is far from clear and it is by no means certain that directive approaches are accepted by the general public. We are a long way from knowing whether strategies such as these make any difference to children individually or collectively, or to the contexts within which they grow and develop.

CONCLUSION

It is apparent that the factors associated with vulnerability and resilience are continually interacting and this can result in many different outcomes. Parents' hopes and fears for their children usually centre on the desire that they should reach an independent adult life complete with the capacity to achieve their full potential.

Children have individual characteristics of genetic endowment, temperament, health attributes, and family environment, which influence the extent to which they may be vulnerable or resilient in different life circumstances. The interactional and cumulative effects may be mediated or moderated, but however this operates, the role of parents in their child's development is critical and of central importance.

As professionals, citizens and parents, we would all wish to reduce the risks that our children face, manage their vulnerabilities and promote their resilience. To do this, we must take account of individual differences, variations in relationships and great unevenness in the quality of the social environment.

REFERENCES

Ainsworth, M.D., Blehar, M.C., Waters, E. et al. (1978) *Patterns of Attachment*. Hillsdale, NJ: Erlbaum.

Bachett-Milburn, K., Cunningham-Burley, S. and Kemmer, D. (2001) *Experiences of Lone and Partnered Working Mothers in Scotland*. York: Joseph Rowntree Foundation.

Bowlby, J. (1951) *Maternal Care and Maternal Health*. Geneva: World Health Organization.

Brown, G.W. and Harris, T.O. (1978) *Social Origins of Depression: A Study of Psychiatric Disorder in Women*. London: Tavistock.

Fundudis, T. (1997). Single parents: risk or resource? *Child Psychology and Psychiatry Review*, **2**, 2–13.

Goodman, R. and Scott, S. (1998) Nature, nurture and family adversities. In *Child Psychiatry*. Oxford: Blackwell Science, pp. 208–17.

Kanner, L. (1949) Problems of nosology and psychodynamics in early infantile autism. *American Journal of Orthopsychiatry*, **19**, 416–26.

Kolvin, I., Miller, F.J.W., Fleeting, M. and Kolvin, P.A. (1988) Social and parenting factors affecting criminal offence rates. *British Journal of Psychiatry*, **152**, 80–90.

Quinton, D. (1994). Cultural and community influences. In Rutter, M. and Hay, D. (eds) *Development through Life: A Handbook for Clinicians*. Oxford: Blackwell Scientific, pp. 159–84.

Rae-Grant, N., Thomas, B.H., Offord, D.R. and Boyle, M.H. (1989). Risk, protective factors and the prevalence of behavioural and emotional disorders in children and adolescents. *Journal of the American Academy of Child and Adolescent Psychiatry*, **28**(2), 262–8.

Reichard, S. and Tillman, C. (1950). Patterns of parent–child relationships in schizophrenia. *Psychiatry*, **13**, 247–57.

Robbins, L. (1966). *Deviant Children Grown Up.* Baltimore: Williams & Wilkins.

Rutter, M. and Quinton, D. (1984) Parental psychiatric disorder: effects on children. *Psychological Medicine*, **14**(4), 853–80.

Rutter, M. and Smith, D.J. (1995) *Psychosocial Disorders in Young People: Time Trends and their Causes.* Chichester: John Wiley.

Rutter, M. (1985) Resilience in the face of adversity – protective factors and resistance to psychiatric disorder. *British Journal of Psychiatry*, **47**, 598.

Rutter, M. (1987). Continuities and discontinuities from infancy. In Osofsky, J. (ed.) *Handbook of Infant Development.* New York: John Wiley.

Rutter, M. (1971) Parent–child separation: psychological effects on the children. *Journal of Child Psychology and Psychiatry*, **12**, 233–60.

Rutter, M. (2002) Maternal deprivation. In Bornstein, M. (ed.) *Handbook of Parenting*, 2nd edition. Mahwah, NJ: Lawrence Erlbaum.

Smith R. (1999) Eradicating child poverty. *British Medical Journal*, **319**, 203–04.

Thomas, A., Chess, S. and Birch, H.G. (1968) *Temperament and Behaviour Disorders in Childhood.* New York: New York University Press.

Utting, D. (1996) Reducing criminality among young people: a sample of relevant programmes in the United Kingdom. London: Home Office.

Werner, E.E. and Smith, R.S. (1982) *Vulnerable but Invincible: A Study of Resilient Children.* New York: McGraw-Hill.

6

Parenting in Culturally Divergent Settings

Lee M. Pachter and Thyde Dumont-Mathieu

SUMMARY

As the world becomes more of a global village, interlinked through multinational media, the Internet, and global markets, we are provided with increasing opportunities to learn about other cultures, and gain a truer world view. Diversity within countries is increasing as well, and most are likely to have very mixed populations.

It is the goal of this chapter to present a view of parenting that posits that successful parenting styles and practices are relative to the specific context within which the family lives. This *adaptive contextual* approach will provide a framework for evaluating parenting practices in different cultures, settings, and environments in a relativistic manner. We will primarily focus on the variables that are either specific to, or have differential effects on those who are parenting in culturally divergent settings. These include parents who have recently immigrated to another country either voluntarily or under duress, as well as ethnic minorities.

This growing diversity, and the increase in opportunities afforded by newer technologies, results in more and more parents rearing their children in environments that offer heterogeneity of experiences and interaction with different cultures. As we become more aware of the diversity of beliefs, values, and experiences regarding parenting and child-rearing in different cultures, it becomes more obvious that the universal goals of parenting can be accomplished in many different ways, and that the mainstream approach commonly seen in the majority cultural group is no more or less 'valid' than other approaches.

THEORETICAL CONSIDERATIONS

The concept of a 'mainstream' implies a particular accepted and expected way of doing things. This way is presumably derived through a process accounting for the 'majority' viewpoint, as well as the identification of a 'right' way of doing things. In the case of parenting that would mean there is a given way that most parents rear their children, and as such there is one accepted way of parenting. Hidden within this concept of a 'mainstream' is the idea that all parents are undertaking the task of parenting within the same context. Thus, not only do they have the same goals, they also face the same challenges. This assumption is only partially correct.

LeVine (1977) has proposed three universal goals relating to parenting: (i) ensuring the physical survival and health of the child; (ii) providing an environment for successful progression through the developmental stages into adulthood to assure self-maintenance in maturity; and (iii) teaching/modeling normative cultural and societal values. Although many would agree that these goals are indeed 'universal,' the specifics of what it takes to successfully accomplish these goals are not necessarily universal. In this sense, LeVine saw parenting as an adaptive process. What is being adapted to are the specific contexts that the family is situated in. For example, in contexts where child survival is threatened (e.g. areas with endemic infectious diseases, or in high violence areas such as where there is war or neighborhood violence) parenting practices will emphasize the goal of 'physical survival and health of the child' aspects to a greater degree than the goals of developing behavioral capacities for self-maintenance in maturity or attaining normative cultural or societal values. In contexts where child survival is less of an issue, behavioral attainment of self-sufficiency and cultural values and norms will take on a greater priority.

In order to understand the specifics of parenting in ethnic minority families, it is important to appreciate that although minority and majority families may share a common geographical, political and temporal environment, significant differences in context exist, and need to be taken into account when evaluating parenting strategies. Such contexts may include cultural differences from the majority mainstream culture, economic conditions, social class distinctions, temporal and spatial disruptions due to migration, and the effects of minority status in and of themselves (i.e. separate from cultural and socio-economic issues).

Historically, the study of ethnic and minority parenting and child development has been dominated by a perspective which emphasized that variations seen among ethnic and racial groups are due to deficiencies; that is, certain groups are culturally deprived vis-à-vis middle-class mainstream culture (Sears, 1975). More recent approaches assume a 'culturally different' perspective; that is, variations seen among individuals and groups that diverge from the white middle-class mainstream are not deficient but instead are legitimate adaptations of parenting and child development to differing contexts (Garcia Coll et al., 1996; Garcia Coll and Pachter, 2002). As discussed above, some of these contextual differences include ethnicity and culture, socio-economic position, and

minority status. Each of these factors will be discussed separately.

CULTURE AND PARENTING

A cultural group can be defined as a collective of individuals who share common beliefs, practices, ideals, values, traditions, and behaviors. Harkness, Keefer and Super define it as 'the way of life of a people, including both the external, socially constructed environments for living … and the internalized rules, expectations, and values that guide communication, thinking, and behavior' (Harkness et al., 1999). An ethnic group is a group that – in addition to sharing common beliefs, values, and practices – traces its origins to a particular area, region, or country.

Ogbu (1999) defines culture as 'a people's adaptive way of life' and speaks of six components: (1) the customary ways of behaving; (2) the assumptions, expectations, and emotions underlying those customary behaviors; (3) the artifacts, or things that have meanings to the people; (4) economic, political, religious, and social institutions; (5) patterns of social relations; and (6) cultural frame of reference – how people talk, feel, think, relate to others, and strive to achieve.

Super and Harkness developed a model that explains how culture influences child development. According to this model (known as the 'cultural niche'), culture affects child development through its influence on (1) the physical and social environment in which child-rearing occurs; (2) customs of child-rearing and child-care; and (3) the parent's (care-taker's) psychology (Super and Harkness, 1986). All of these factors are mediated through parents. For example, the culturally influenced physical environment that parents provide for the growing child may contribute to differences in child development seen in different cultures (Pachter and Harwood, 1996). Sleep behavior in infancy provides one example. In the United States, infant sleep patterns suggest that a maximum sleep-episode time increases during the first few months of life, with an average of two to four hours per sleep episode at one month of age, to an average of up to eight hours by age four to five months. This pattern has been interpreted to suggest that an increase in maximum sleep time over the first year of life is a good indication of physiological and neurological maturation. In East Africa, however, an infant's sleep pattern is much different. At one month of age, the average maximal sleep time is about three hours, and this remains constant for most of the first year of life. When compared to US norms (and the developmental implications that are based on it, i.e. longer sleep intervals indicating developmental maturation), East African infants would appear to be delayed. In fact, the differences in sleep patterns are a result of different cultural norms relating to the physical home environment. In the US, parents prepare the home for a new child by creating a separate space for the infant to sleep in (usually in a separate room). In this environment, frequent awakenings are inconvenient for the parent, who must leave the bed and the room to attend to the child. Thus, longer sleeping episodes are reinforced. In East Africa, infants co-sleep in bed with the parents, and awakening does not trigger the need for the structured parental behavior that occurs in US families; in East Africa, the infant can feed off the mother's breast at will. In this context there is less parental need to reinforce longer sleeping cycles (Harkness, 1980). Therefore a pattern that might be considered pathological in one cultural context is in fact normal within another cultural context. This is an example of viewing heterogeneity of parenting patterns from a 'culturally different' as opposed to a 'culturally deficient' perspective.

The second component of the model – customs of child-rearing – includes the common (and often unconscious) practices that are usually taken for granted within a culture. For example, modes of ambulating with an infant may include carrying the infant on the mother's back, holding the infant in front with the baby's head facing back over the shoulder, carrying in a perambulator or baby carriage, etc. Some cultures have the infant carried during regular activities of the mother; other cultures have the infant carried only during times of transportation. These customary methods create different developmental environments for the infant, including visual experiences, spatial orientation, physical activity, and social interaction (Super and Harkness, 1986). These different environments will affect what are considered child developmental norms; for example, the age of attainment of milestones such as crawling and walking.

The third component of the developmental niche – care-taker psychology – includes the beliefs and values that are culturally constructed and that pertain to parenting, childhood, child-rearing, and child behavior/development. Super and Harkness call these 'parental ethnotheories.' For example, results of a study of mothers' perceptions of normal infant and child development showed differences among African-American, Puerto Rican, West Indian/Caribbean, and Anglo-American mothers as to when children should attain common developmental milestones (Pachter and Dworkin, 1997). These differences persisted after controlling for maternal age, socio-economic status, number of children, and educational level. In another study, Harwood and colleagues studied mothers' beliefs regarding socialization goals for their children and found that middle-class Puerto Rican and US 'Anglo' (i.e. of northern European background) mothers had different goals. Puerto Rican mothers emphasized qualities including 'proper demeanor' (being respectful, obedient, and accepted by the community) whereas Anglo mothers emphasized qualities related to 'self-maximalization' (being self-confident, independent, and exhibiting individuality) (Harwood, 1996). This pattern conforms to normative cultural values that have been often identified in the Puerto Rican culture (*respeto, simpatía*). This study illustrates that parental beliefs about child behavior are in part culturally constructed.

Another cross-cultural study of Swedish, Italian, and American mothers demonstrated different interpretations of the maternal role, as well as goals expressed for their children (Welles-Nystrom and Richman, 1994). As in the prior study, US mothers expressed a desire for a higher degree of autonomous behavior for themselves and their children. Swedish mothers indicated that being a good mother meant integrating the role of mother with other aspects of life; the Italian mothers expressed the view that motherhood was a central part of being a woman, and therefore were not able to identify specific criteria for being a 'good' mother. This study shows that even among industrialized Western societies, differences in care-taker beliefs, attitudes, and practices are culturally constructed. It also reminds one that although culture is often related to ethnicity and race, they are different constructs.

There is usually as much variation in beliefs and behaviors *within* a cultural group as between groups. This point is important to recognize if one is to steer free of stereotyping. Culture is a dynamic concept, and what is the 'cultural norm' may likely change over time. The sources of intracultural variation are many and include personal and family beliefs (which are independent of cultural input), past experiences, as well as acculturation, which is the process through which cultural adaptation and change occurs. During the process of acculturation, families combine ethnic/minority and majority cultural parenting values. Typically, families who live in an ethnic enclave, who have older, more traditional family members living in the household or close by, or who speak their original language, may have more traditional, less acculturated beliefs and practices (Harwood, 1981). These factors can guide clinicians as they familiarize themselves with their patients' cultural viewpoints. This type of assessment is at best a rough estimate though; the best way to assess a family's approach to parenting issues is to ask directly.

Traditionally, acculturation has been conceptualized as a unidimensional process of learning about a new culture, progressively adapting beliefs and practices of the new culture, and deciding what aspects are to be retained or sacrificed from the culture of origin. More recent views of acculturation emphasize the multidirectional and multidimensional nature of the process, acknowledging that cultural contact affects, modifies, and changes the host group as well as the minority group (Berry, 1997). Also, the process of change occurs along multiple dimensions (e.g. ethnic pride, loyalty, language, retention of traditions, and so forth). Degree of cultural retention or change differs among these dimensions; it is not an 'all or nothing' phenomenon. Individuals and families who have the ability to retain aspects of their original culture while being able to live with a sense of ease and competency in the host culture (i.e. are 'bi-cultural') may be seen as having the best adjustment to the multicultural context of modern life (Szapocznik et al., 1980).

The concept of acculturation is particularly salient for parenting and child development. One can conceptualize childhood and adolescence as stages of cultural change in which the individual slowly acculturates into the 'culture' of adulthood in their society. Change always incurs conflict, and some of the intergenerational conflicts that occur in families can be seen as consequences of the different points of view of parents and children during this process of acculturation to adulthood. For the minority parent and child, an additional acculturative stress may occur; that is, intergenerational differences in the balance between tradition and adaptation to the majority cultural style. The rate and degree of acculturation will often vary by age and generation. Younger family members may be able to incorporate host culture values, attitudes, and behaviors to a greater degree and at a faster pace than their parents and other older relatives. Likewise, different generations may place greater or lesser value on the traditions and lifestyles of one's original culture. These issues may serve as an additional flashpoint for intergenerational conflict in the ethnic minority family.

Culture and cultural change have a major impact on all families. For families from the majority culture, these issues relate mostly to a *diachronous* orientation (i.e. a change of culture over time). For the minority family, culture and cultural change have the potential to be much larger issues, because in addition to the temporal aspects of cultural change, the minority parent and child must deal with possible discordance between the cultural values of the majority group and the traditional and ethnic cultural values and lifestyles of the family. It becomes a *synchronous* (present-time, cross-sectional) as well as a diachronous issue for the minority family.

SOCIAL POSITION FACTORS

In most societies, individuals are situated in a hierarchy of positions that are unequal with regard to power, property, status, and psychic gratification (Tumin, 1967). These factors relate to the properties of social stratification. In many Western industrial and post-industrial societies, social stratification occurs primarily along lines of race, ethnicity, and class, although other factors such as gender, age, and religion are also important.

One of the outcomes of the process of social stratification is the creation of unequal distribution of resources, including those that promote optimal environments for parenting, such as housing stock, disposable income, quality daycare, preschools and schools, commerce, quality health care, and jobs. Those families who do not have access to the physical and economic capital that promote parenting and child development are at a disadvantage (Lamberty et al., 2000). Some of this disadvantage may be offset by strong social links and community cohesion. Community strengths are essential to acknowledge if one is to steer clear of the 'deficit' model of minority parenting, and allow for the acknowledgment of positive or promoting influences that act to counteract some of the negative aspects of living on the underside of social stratification. Belonging to an ethnic community may help neutralize some effects of living in a racist society by helping to reject negative messages, or transforming them so that they have a less negative impact (Barnes, 1991). Conversely, minority families living in an affluent neighborhood consisting primarily of majority group members, but without much of a social network (e.g. a black family living in a white suburb) may not have the same burden of low economic and material capital, but may suffer the consequences of discrimination without the buffer of social support that may be available in an ethnic community

(Tatum, 1992). The importance of social capital (Coleman, 1990; Putnam, 1995) independent of economic or physical capital is becoming more and more recognized as a potent influence on the lives of children, families, and communities (Pachter, 2000).

MINORITY STATUS AND PARENTING

Being a minority has effects on parenting and child development which are separate from those that can be attributed to culture and social class. Teaching children about prejudice, discrimination, and racism is a parenting task that all parents should prioritize. However, teaching children how to deal with racism, prejudice, and discrimination is a difficult task *required* of ethnic and minority parents. Since parents are the prime socializing agents for young children, their attitudes and responses to prejudice and discrimination will have great effects on their children's behavior, self-esteem, response to stress, academic performance, and social attitudes. On one hand, minority parents need to impart to their children the philosophy that hard work will result in rewards (i.e. meritocracy); on the other hand, they need to prepare their children for the fact that discrimination and prejudice may likely influence outcomes as well.

Teaching children how to deal with discrimination is part of the process of racial socialization, which is part of learning how to live in a society where race status has salience, particularly for minority individuals. Racial socialization includes learning about group identity and cultural socialization (teaching about heritage, history, customs, and traditions), preparation for bias (promotion of an awareness of prejudice and discrimination), socialization of mistrust (warning children to be wary of interacting with individuals from outside their racial/ethnic group; relaying a sense of distrust), and egalitarian socialization (promoting an appreciation of all peoples and groups) (Hughes and Chen, 1999). Messages regarding racial socialization that parents give to children can be deliberate and/or unintended, verbal and non-verbal, and proactive or reactive.

There is much variation in beliefs among minority parents regarding how important it is to teach about race (Spencer, 1985). In one study, two out of three African-American parents said that they discuss issues regarding racial socialization with their children – such as emphasizing racial pride, cultural heritage and tradition,

positive self-image, and understanding of racial restrictions and blocked opportunities, and the fundamental equality of all people (Thorton et al., 1990).

What parents teach their children about race and society changes depending on the child's developmental and chronological age. In a study of African-American parent–child communication, Hughes and Chen found that African-American parents discussed mistrust and preparation for bias more commonly with children 9 to 14 years old than with 4- to 8-year-olds, whereas the frequency of parents' cultural socialization messages did not vary with the age of the child (Hughes and Chen, 1997). Perhaps parents feel the need to protect their children from learning of the bias and mistrust that they will likely face, or parents may feel that their younger children are not ready to learn about this negative aspect of life. It may also be that parents wait for their children to cue in to the bias before discussing it with them, and older children are more likely to encounter racial and ethnic bias.

Racial socialization is an important component of minority parenting across socio-economic strata, although the specific content and approach may differ depending on variables such as socio-economic status, household composition, and parenting style. Differences among parental style and content of racial socialization – like other parenting processes – have profound influences on critical aspects of child development. For example, Bowman and Howard (1985) found that emphasis on cultural socialization, preparation for bias/discrimination, and egalitarian socialization was associated with children's motivation, achievement, and prospects for upward mobility.

Sometimes racial socialization messages may be a source of cognitive dissonance for the child. For example, teaching children the importance of working hard to achieve one's goals (i.e. the basis of meritocracy) – an important societal value – may be at odds with racial socialization messages that prepare minority children for bias (i.e. promotion of an awareness of prejudice and discrimination). Likewise, Ogbu (1991) finds the potential for similar contradictory messages with regard to school and education. On the one hand, parents stress the importance of getting a good education in order to secure good employment; on the other hand, as part of racial and ethnic socialization they also teach their children that US society does not reward African-Americans and whites equally for similar school credentials or educational accomplishments. In Ogbu's opinion, these conflicting messages may contribute to the disengagement found among some minority youths toward school. Marshall (1995) found that among middle-income African-American children, those who received more ethnic socialization from parents had poorer school performance. The fact that this study was conducted with middle-class African-American families whose children attended predominantly white schools speaks to the importance of context.

In addition to the intracultural variations in ethnic socialization discussed above, there are also different general approaches seen among different ethnic groups. For example, one study of ethnic and racial socialization in Japanese-American, African-American, and Mexican-American teen–parent dyads found that African-American and Japanese-American parents discussed issues concerning adaptation to the overall society more than Mexican-American parents did, and compared to the other groups African-American parents more frequently discussed prejudice as a problem (Phinney and Chavira, 1995). Again, these intercultural differences can be explained through appreciating differences in context among the groups (e.g. cultural values and attitudes, circumstances surrounding migration/immigration, social position, and extent and form of prejudice).

SPECIAL CONSIDERATIONS FOR IMMIGRANT FAMILIES

Parents who have recently immigrated to their current country of residence often face issues specific to the immigration experience, regardless of class, race, or ethnicity. Recent immigration represents an additional contextual variable that may have an effect on parenting and child-rearing. Rumbaut (1997) and Waters (1997) draw three conclusions based on the research available on immigrant families. First, they remind us that there is no singular immigrant family experience. Secondly, they suggest that the strong family ties and educational aspirations/ achievements (the so-called 'immigrant ethos') seem to erode with time in the adopted country. Lastly, they state that ethnicity has a strong effect on the immigrant family's outcomes and experiences.

The presumption that there is a singular immigrant experience is particularly ironic in countries with a long tradition of immigration from all over the world. Perhaps the myth of the general immigrant experience facilitates an expectation that the playing field is a level one for each individual entering the new homeland, and that the varying levels of success are solely dependent on the effort (or lack thereof) of the individual. Although it is true that all immigrant families

undergo a process of transitioning into the new environment, this process differs for each family due to the varying contexts from which and to which each family immigrate. Each family brings with them various amounts of capital (social, economic, political, psychological) depending on the circumstances of their immigration and the social position that they occupy in their new environment. Factors such as inability to speak the language, racial discrimination, and ethnicity may all influence the transition process. For example, an immigrant family who immigrates to a country where their particular ethnic group is discriminated against may face a different transition process than an immigrant family who is of the ethnic majority in their new homeland. The minority family may have held a higher social position in their native land, but in their new homeland find themselves in a lower position. Their prior educational, economic, and social achievements in their native land may now be of little value. They may not be able to find comparable employment and no longer hold the leadership positions they held in their prior community. In addition to ethnicity, other factors may create unequal experiences. For example, two immigrant families from the same place of origin but who have different skin color (e.g. a dark-skinned Puerto Rican family and a lighter-skinned Puerto Rican family) may have differing opportunities in the host environment despite coming from the same country and culture.

The Transition Process: Challenges

Immigration is a displacement process. The family members who immigrate leave behind familiar places, routines, friends, and lifestyles. An additional challenge faced by many recent immigrant families is the disruption of the family unit. Most families do not immigrate as one unit, but by 'serial migration' (Waters, 1997). One parent may be granted entry with some or all of the children. This results in a family separation period that incurs loss and grieving in both parent and child. Furthermore, when family members are eventually reunited there occurs an adjustment period of varying length, depending on factors such as length of absence, age of children, etc. During certain critical periods such as adolescence, this adjustment process may provide an additional stress on the parent–child relationship.

Such disruptions in family structure and function may place the child at risk for mental health problems. The occurrence of such problems depends on the balance of risk and protective factors. These factors include the age at which the child migrated, time of separation, level of family economic resources, trauma/loss, self-esteem, language proficiency, level of encountered racism/discrimination, family supports, coping mechanisms, and level of acculturation/biculturalism (de Leon Siantz, 1999). Rumbaut (1994) found that the factors affecting the psychological well-being in immigrant children include gender (girls reported lower self-esteem and higher depression) and parent–child conflict (which best predicted self-esteem and depression). These findings provide clinicians working with immigrant families specific areas to assess. In addition to inquiring about physical and economic well-being, assessing social well-being by inquiring about social networks, parental acceptance at work and in the community, social support systems, and connectedness to formal and informal community resources will help the clinician gain an understanding of how the family is adapting to their new environment.

Arredondo-Dowd (1981) has proposed a theoretical model for understanding the transitional process that occurs as the immigrant family works through their feelings of loss and grief. The first phase is characterized by feelings of shock and disbelief which accompany the adaptation to a new environment. This environment may not only be physically different, but may operate under different rules and norms. The immigrant must re-learn all the 'givens' under which he or she is used to functioning. For example, a mother and her school-aged children emigrating from a warm climate to a colder one will need to learn how to dress differently. They will find that the community is constructed differently than the one back home – outdoor markets, for example, may be replaced by more formal indoor supermarkets. The way that neighbors interact with each other are probably much different. Interpersonal codes – smiles, touch, space, tone of voice – may be different. The school-aged child who has been taught to show respect for the teacher by maintaining a certain distance and only speaking when called upon may be reported as being aloof or an under-achiever at a parent–teacher conference. All of these experiences may lead to a sense of being overwhelmed.

The second phase consists of feelings of despair and pain, as attempts to fit in continue without the benefits of the familiar social networks and supports. This phase may be especially difficult for parents who struggle with the balance, wanting their families to succeed in the new context while maintaining a cultural and behavioral link with their native culture. The third

phase culminates in the acceptance of life in a new environment and context through a successful balance of continuity and change. These phases very likely will occur at different rates and at different levels for all individuals, and often occur over generations. For example, older adults who immigrate to a new homeland may never get over the homesickness associated with the second phase. Those family members who immigrate first may have a more difficult time getting through these phases than family members who come over later, since they may have the benefit of moving to an environment with social support systems and structures in place.

Language Barriers

Language issues are perhaps one of the more formidable challenges faced by many immigrant families. Language discordance may create problems for parents who seek employment, advocate for their children in school, and navigate the daily experience of shopping and obtaining services. The rate of language acquisition is variable, and often children seem to be able to acquire the new language faster than their parents. This may set up a type of role reversal in which the parent is dependent on the child to translate for them. This is potentially damaging to the parent–child relationship for several reasons. It upsets the traditional role of the parent as provider for the child, as well as potentially putting the child in the position of having to broker information to his or her parent that may be inappropriate for the child (e.g. bad news, health-related matters, developmentally advanced concepts and terms). For these reasons, a young child should never be put in the position of interpreting for his or her parents.

Another issue that arises relating to language is the real concern that the child may lose their native language. Many children of immigrants learn a new language at the expense of their original language (Garcia Coll and Magnuson, 1997). The loss of the native language may potentially add to the distance between parent and child over time as their ability to communicate effectively may diminish. Ironically, parents are often the ones insisting that the child learn the new language quickly, often at the expense of the language of origin, in order to help the child to 'fit in' to the new system. The significance of the loss of the native language may not be recognized immediately. It may only become apparent when, for example, the grandmother comes to live with the family, and the child is unable to have a meaningful conversation with her. This language loss may affect the ability of the child to maintain his or her cultural heritage and identity. It may bring into question – in their own minds or in others – whether they are a true member of the cultural group.

Immigration to a new homeland under the best of circumstances requires courage. It involves being willing to leave behind all that is familiar – including loved ones, friends, family members, and social networks – to forge new relationships in a new environment in the hope of a better life. Each family member will face a transition process as they adapt to the new setting and attempt to 'fit in' – into the neighborhood, the community, at work, school, daycare, and society at large. One often finds that the realities of their new life are vastly different than they had imagined. The family unit may encounter new challenges as the goals and styles of parenting may be different than 'at home.' Parent and child may undergo periods of grief and loss as they transition into their new lives in their new homeland. The child health-care practitioner may be of assistance to the child and family at each step of this journey by first recognizing that such a process is occurring, undertaking a comprehensive needs assessment, and becoming a resource for the family.

CONCLUSIONS AND IMPLICATIONS FOR PRACTICE

As LeVine pointed out almost 25 years ago, the goals of parenting are universal, but the methods, orientations, and approaches to achieving those goals are specific to the context in which the family exists (LeVine, 1977). Parents of ethnocultural minority status want the same things for their children that parents from the majority culture want – health, happiness, success, and security. What those 'things' mean, and how they are obtained, vary by context. By context we mean the specific circumstances that the family lives in and needs to react to. Contextual factors include the physical environment, family structure and function, cultural beliefs and practices, social position (poverty, wealth, etc.), social environment (living in a homogeneous or diverse setting), and social stratification mechanisms such as bias, racism, and discrimination. Some of these issues are salient for all families, minority and majority; others are specific to minority families. We have attempted to demonstrate how a knowledge of the family's context will help those interested in child health and development better understand the rationale for diverse parenting styles and practices.

Clinicians who work with children, parents and families from diverse ethnocultural backgrounds need to be aware of the role of cultural beliefs, socio-economic factors, and social position on a parent's approach to parenting, as well as the resources made available to the parent and family. First and foremost the clinician should not assume that the definition of what makes a 'good parent,' or what is 'normal child' behavior and development is the same between and among members of different ethnocultural groups.

In this age of patient/client-centered care, the most important questions a clinician asks of a parent is 'How is your child doing?' and 'Do you have any concerns about your child's health, behavior, or development?' The answers to such questions are strongly influenced by the respondent's personal, familial, social, and cultural background. Do not assume that the response 'She's doing fine' has the same meaning to the parent as to you the clinician. Ask open-ended questions about behavioral and developmental perceptions and expectations. Also, ask questions about family background, parent's fears and concerns for their children, and expectations for their and their children's future, as answers will provide valuable information which may help put child-rearing practices into perspective.

When differences in parenting style or practices are encountered, the clinician should determine whether the practices are detrimental or just different. We have been surprised at the number of times when parenting practices at first seemed inappropriate, but after obtaining information about the circumstance of the family's life found that the style was in fact a successful adaptation to a context very different from that of the typical majority 'mainstream' family. Any judgment regarding the appropriateness of a parenting practice or style needs to be analyzed from a 'goodness of fit' perspective – can the practice be seen as an adaptive response to specific circumstances, and in that light will it contribute to a potentially successful outcome for the child and the family? When dealing with different beliefs and practices, it is always helpful to remember that many different roads can lead to the same destination.

REFERENCES

Arredondo-Dowd, P.M. (1981) Personal loss and grief as a result of immigration. *The Personnel and Guidance Journal*, **59**, 376–8.

Barnes, E.J. (1991) The black community as the source of positive self concept for black children: a theoretical perspective. In Jones, R.L. (ed.) *Black Psychology*, 3rd edition. Berkeley, CA: Cobb and Henry, pp. 667–92.

Berry, J.W. (1997) Immigration, acculturation, and adaptation. *Applied Psychology: An International Review*, **46**, 5–68.

Bowman, P.J. and Howard, C. (1985) Race related socialization, motivation, and academic achievement: a study of Black youth in three generation families. *Journal of the American Academy of Child and Adolescent Psychiatry*, **24**, 1134–41.

Coleman, J.S. (1990) *The Foundations of Social Theory.* Cambridge, MA: Harvard University Press.

Council of Economic Advisors (1998) *Changing America: Indicators of Social and Economic Well-Being by Race and Hispanic Origin* (http://www.whitehouse.gov/WH/EOP/CEA/html/publications.html).

De Leon Siantz, M.L. (1999) Children in crisis: the mental health status of immigrants and migrant Hispanic children. In Fitzgerald, H.E., Lester, B.M. and Zuckerman, B.S. (eds) *Children of Color: Research, Health and Policy Issues.* New York: Garland Press.

Garcia Coll, C. and Magnuson, K. (1997) The psychological experience of immigration: a developmental perspective. In Booth, A., Crouter, A.C. and Landale, N. (eds) *Immigration and the Family: Research and Policy on U.S. Immigrants.* Mahwah, NJ: Lawrence Erlbaum.

Garcia Coll, C. and Pachter, L.M. (2002) Ethnic and minority parenting. In Bornstein, M.H. (ed.) *Handbook of Parenting*, 2nd edition, Vol. 4. Mahwah, NJ: Lawrence Erlbaum.

Garcia Coll, C., Lamberty, G., Jenkins, R., McAdoo, H.P., Crnic, K., Wasik, B.H. and Vasquez Garcia, H. (1996). An integrative model for the study of developmental competencies in minority children. *Child Development*, **67**, 1891–914.

Harkness, S. (1980) The cultural context of child development. *New Directions for Child Development*, **8**, 7–13.

Harkness, S., Keefer, C.H. and Super, C.M. (1999) Culture and ethnicity. In Levine, M.D., Carey, W.B. and Crocker, A.C. (eds) *Developmental-Behavioral Pediatrics*, 3rd edn. Philadelphia, PA: W.B. Saunders.

Harwood, A. (1981) Guidelines for culturally appropriate health care. In Harwood, A. (ed.) *Ethnicity and Medical Care.* Cambridge, MA: Harvard University Press, pp. 482–508.

Harwood, R.L., Schoelmerich, A., Ventura-Cook, E., Schulze, P.A. and Wilson, S.P. (1996) Culture and class influence on Anglo and Puerto Rican mothers' beliefs regarding long-term socialization goals and child behavior. *Child Development*, **67**, 2446–61.

Hughes, D. and Chen, L. (1997) When and what parents tell children about race: an examination of race-related socialization among African-American families. *Applied Developmental Science*, **1**, 200–14.

Hughes, D. and Chen, L. (1999) The nature of parents' race-related communications to children: a developmental perspective. In Balter, L. and Tamis-Lemonada, C.S. (eds) *Child Psychology: A Handbook of Contemporary Issues.* Philadelphia, PA: Psychology Press, pp. 467–90.

Lamberty, G., Pachter, L. and Crnic, K. (2000) Social stratification: implications for understanding racial, ethnic, and class disparities in child health and development.

Session presented at the Second Annual Meeting of Child Health Services Researchers, Los Angeles (http://www.ahrq.gov/research/chsr2soc.htm).

LeVine, R.A. (1977) Childrearing as cultural adaptation. In Leiderman, P.H., Tulkin, S.R. and Rosenfeld, A.H. (eds) *Culture and Infancy.* London: Academic Press, pp. 15–27.

Marshall, S. (1995) Ethnic socialization of African American children: implications for parenting, identity development, and academic achievement. *Journal of Youth and Adolescence*, **24**, 377–96.

Ogbu, J.U. (1991) Minority coping responses and school experience. *Journal of Psychohistory*, **18**(4), 433–57.

Ogbu, J. (1999) Cultural context of children's development. In Fitzgerald, H.E., Lester, B.M. and Zuckerman, B.S. (eds) *Children of Color: Research, Health and Policy Issues.* New York: Garland Press.

Pachter, L. (2000). Social stratification and child health status. Paper presented at the Second Annual Meeting of Child Health Services Researchers, Los Angeles.

Pachter, L.M. and Dworkin, P.H. (1997) Maternal expectations about normal child development in 4 cultural groups. *Archives of Pediatrics & Adolescent Medicine* **151**, 1144–50.

Pachter, L.M. and Harwood, R.L. (1996) Culture and child behavior and psychosocial development. *Journal of Developmental and Behavioral Pediatrics*, **17**(3), 191–8.

Phinney, J.S. and Chavira, V. (1995) Parental ethnic socialization and adolescent coping with problems related to ethnicity. *Journal of Research on Adolescence*, **5**, 31–53.

Putnam, R.D. (1995) Bowling alone: America's declining social capital. *Journal of Democracy*, **6**(1), 65–78.

Rumbaut, R.G. (1994) The crucible within. *International Migration Review*, **28**(4), 748–94.

Rumbaut, R.G. (1997) Ties that bind: immigration and immigrant families in the United States. In Booth, A., Crouter, A.C. and Landale, N. (eds) *Immigration and the Family: Research and Policy on U.S. Immigrants.* Mahwah, NJ: Lawrence Erlbaum.

Sears, R.R. (1975) Ancients revisited: a history of child development. In Hetherington, E.M. (ed.) *Review of Child Development Research*, Vol. 5. Chicago: University of Chicago Press, pp. 1–73.

Spencer, M.B. (1985) Cultural cognition and social cognition as identity correlates of black children's personal-social development. In Spencer, M.B., Brookins, G.K. and Allen, W.R. (eds) *Beginnings: The Social and Affective Development of Black Children.* Hillsdale, NJ: Lawrence Erlbaum.

Super, C.M. and Harkness, S. (1986) The developmental niche: a conceptualization at the interface of child and culture. *International Journal of Behavioral Development*, **9**, 545–69.

Szapocznik, J., Kurtines, W.M. and Fernandez, T. (1980) Bicultural involvement and adjustment in Hispanic-American youths. *International Journal of Intercultural Relations*, **4**, 353–65.

Tatum, B. (1992) *Assimilation Blues: Black Families in a White Community.* Northampton, MA: Hazel-Maxwell.

Thorton, M.C., Chatters, L.M., Taylor, R.J. and Allen, W.R. (1990) Sociodemographic and environmental correlates of racial socialization by Black parents. *Child Development*, **61**, 401–09.

Tumin, M.M. (1967) *Social Stratification*. Englewood Cliffs, NJ: Prentice Hall.

Waters, M.C. (1997) Immigrant families at risk: factors that undermine chances for success. In Booth, A., Crouter, A.C. and Landale, N. (eds) *Immigration and the Family: Research and Policy on U.S. Immigrants.* Mahwah, NJ: Lawrence Erlbaum.

Welles-Nystrom, B., New, R. and Richman, A. (1994) The 'good mother': a comparative study of Swedish, Italian, and American maternal behavior and goals. *Scandanavian Journal of Caring Science*, **8**, 81–6.

7

Religious Influences on Parenting

Stephen Frosh

SUMMARY

This chapter sets out to examine the relationship between religion and parenting practices. Such an examination is complicated by the diversity of religious beliefs and practices and the paucity of research material on the topic. The emphasis in this chapter is on two of the three great deistic religions – Judaism and Islam. 'Christianity' is now part of the mainstream of Western societies, imbuing their value and legal systems. Judging by the available material, it seems to exert no *particular* influence.

It is clear from the material available that there is a great division and perhaps even opposition between professional and religious views in the treatment of children. The former emphasizes the primacy of the welfare of the child, and the latter the primacy of religion and parental authority. These issues have practical implications for practice of parenting support and research with religious groups.

INTRODUCTION

In recent years, it has become commonplace to acknowledge the importance of religion as a force in people's lives. In the context of the Iranian revolution, the fatwa against Salman Rushdie, the various 'Jihads', and most recently the 'September 11th' events, this acknowledgement has also taken on the panicky aura of a potential 'clash of civilizations' between the liberal, mainly secular West and the (Islamic) fundamentalist East. It is a mostly unvoiced irony that ranged on the 'secular' side in one of the most religious countries in the world, the United States of America, in which (Christian) religious fundamentalism is a major reactionary force.

This is an irony which also reveals how easily appeals to religious values can be used in the service of racism and xenophobia. More generally, however, despite postmodernism, global capitalism and the rhetoric of multiculturalism, religion retains a powerful hold in most cultures, including those of the West. The effects of this can be seen in many areas, but most significantly in the discussions on moral and ethical issues which erupt periodically, and which centre particularly on family life.

These issues include the regulation of sexuality and the transmission of moral values, but they also permeate a range of questions around parenting, for example the inculcation of beliefs, modes of discipline, educational priorities and citizenship. Religion, of various kinds and to varying degrees, is consequently a major influence on the lives of many parents, possibly increasingly so in the light of migration and the effect this has on polarizing, or at least highlighting, the alternative lifestyles available in contemporary society. The rise of fundamentalism fuels this, but it is not only at the fundamentalist end of the spectrum that real questions arise about the place of religion in parenting. The major concerns include whether religious influences on parenting are harmful or beneficial, for example, in the spheres of education and mental health. More broadly, the issue of what difference it makes to be a 'religious' parent is one of social and psychological significance.

Although the importance of religion might seem obvious, one of the most striking aspects of this topic from an academic point of view is the paucity of literature on the subject, particularly from a psychological perspective. This is despite a plethora of materials from religious organizations giving parenting advice (running to hundreds of publications); increasing concern over the wilder shores of religious indoctrination (including post-September 11th questions about the socialization of 'terrorists' or 'martyrs'); and, most academically, a long history of anthropological interest in the religious activities and symbolism of non-Western cultures, including initiation rites.

Clearly, coming to grips with the issues around religion and parenting is important for a number of reasons. Socially, the context is one in which, despite the secularization of Western society, religion continues to have a significant influence on major sectors of the population and, in some respects, is even growing in importance. For example, fundamentalist renderings of religion, notably within Christianity (especially in the USA) and Islam, have received major boosts from events in the Middle East, patterns of migration and the activities of the political Right. It is perhaps these versions of religious orthodoxy which pose the most radical problems for conventional Western secular understandings of normative or standard parenting. In addition, the advocacy and support of multiculturalism in professional and political circles makes the understanding of differences in religious values and their roots urgently pressing.

Conceptually, the relationship between communal beliefs and values and child-rearing poses many questions. Little is known about how these intersect with the prevalent 'liberal consensus' among mental health and childcare professionals, which holds the welfare of the individual child as paramount. Practically, too, there are implications in terms of understanding and learning from the impact of religious belief on what parents do, the effects on child development and mental health, and the appropriateness of different forms of intervention in parenting among religious families. Finally, there would seem to be potentially rich pickings for researchers here

in areas similar to those outlined above, most especially perhaps in tracking the developmental trajectories for children in religious families.

Why, then, is there such a paucity of academic literature on the subject? As this chapter shows, this situation is not an accident, but is rather symptomatic of a deep divide between some core values of religious parenting and Western psychological assumptions. The challenge posed by religious world views to the liberal position of most childcare professionals and academics is at times so unexpectedly and embarrassingly profound, that many of them do not know what to do with it. Instead, they have tended to treat religion as a kind of voluntary or neutral 'add on' to the important issues determining quality of parenting; for example, marital harmony or attachment relationships.

This view of religion might be true for many Westerners who have only mild religious affiliations. However, what the new strands of religious fundamentalism appearing in the West have revealed is that for those parents for whom religion is central to their lives, its effect is not neutral at all; it is the bedrock on which the basic values and assumptions of the parenting process are built. In order to explore this argument, it is helpful to focus on some of the issues surfacing in Western constructions of religious orthodoxy using, as illustration, the community with which the present author is most familiar – an orthodox Jewish community. The aim is to lay some groundwork for a consideration of the assumptions about what parenting is for and how these assumptions might impact on religious parents. One objective is to convey the importance of recognizing the way religious values operate in Western contexts, both for clinical and research purposes.

CORE ISSUES

Perhaps two brief clinical examples will be a useful way in here. The first arose after allegations of sexual abuse surfaced in an ultra-orthodox Jewish boys' school. The author and a colleague were asked to see several of the boys involved to assess their therapeutic needs. Although we had long been inured to the ambiguities of sexual abuse work, it still came as a surprise and a disappointment to encounter strong hostility in a situation in which we had been asked to help. The hostility was politely and respectfully expressed: the fathers brought their sons to see us because their Rabbi, with whom we had done substantial amounts of previous work, had told them they had to do so. Each father told us that he had come with his son because the Rabbi had ruled that he should, but there was really no problem and we need not waste our time with them. In this way, they both obeyed their Rabbi's injunction and sabotaged it.

The parents seemed to believe that we were not just mistaken in raising the issue of possible sexual abuse with the children, but that we were actively doing damage. Talking about 'these things' would stir up trouble, in terms of the emotional consequences for the boys. Also, our investigations would reveal something distasteful going on in the community, thus bringing it into disrepute and damaging the advance of religion. Because of this, it was clear to some fathers that we had acted improperly in such circumstances: they believed that the Jewish way 'is to sweep it under the carpet'. It seemed clear at the time that while some of the fathers were unusual in the openness of their hostility, their attitude was very much in line with the general view of the parents involved: that however good our credentials might be, even with their Rabbi's blessing, our attempt to talk about sexual abuse openly was mistaken and possibly religiously wrong.

The second example was from an earlier piece of work with a sophisticated ultra-orthodox family, where both parents were professionals. Faced with a highly resistant and at times delinquent adolescent daughter, they had sought help on their own initiative, albeit after seeking the approval of their Rabbi in America. Family work with them went reasonably well and quite a lot of tension was eased, but what was most remarkable was one small interchange that could be interpreted as a signal not to cross a significant boundary. In one session, having listened to a catalogue of criticisms of the daughter's behaviour (she wanted a radio so that she could listen to pop music, she wanted her ears pierced, and she was saying that she might want to go to college), the author suggested this was a common adolescent stage in which a child starts to make bids for independence whilst remaining attached. The parents exchanged glances and then the mother said, 'Independence is not a term we use, it's not something we look for in our children'.

There are a number of features of these examples that point to some of the core issues in religion and parenting. Both cases reveal the clinician being tripped up by the sudden exposure of a set of assumptions about child-rearing, community life and religious values, which seem to come from somewhere else, despite the apparent cultural similarity between him and the families concerned. The assumptions suggest that helping

a child overcome a possible trauma is *not* more important than preserving the good name of the community, and that achieving autonomy and independence is not an appropriate developmental aim. Two world views are in conflict here: one derived from a Western focus on the needs and well-being of the child, which at its most benevolent might be called a 'humanistic' view; the other relating to the priority given to the collective, the community, and through that to a very specific view of 'the proper path of life'. In this view, a child who is deviant or who disobeys his father is a cancer in the body politic, to use the conventional image, and it is a religious duty to 'wipe him out'. The quotations are from the commentary to Denteronomy 21, 18–21 by the most important Jewish commentator on the Bible, the eleventh century French rabbi, Rashi.

While this position is not actually held to in contemporary religions, it does symbolize a real clash of sympathies in relation to parenting priorities. Religion often aims to *enforce* the 'proper path' (witness, for example, the violence of the so-called 'right to life' movement) and if this means brushing aside individual sensitivity, then so be it. Given a secular social context for parenting in which the happiness and, specifically, the 'welfare of the child' is of paramount legal and pedagogic concern, this makes for interesting and often uncomfortable dilemmas.

The paucity of research in this area might also be due to unvoiced Western assumptions that the value systems of all cultures should be similar when it comes to child-rearing. But these assumptions are spurious and actively misleading, and themselves represent a mode of 'imperialism' that is being challenged by religious communities throughout the West. Liberal academics espouse critical, rational modes of thought based on evidence and argument; orthodox religious groups replace these with 'revelation' and authority-based directives. Liberal humanism is based on a democratic urge, however well or badly that might have been achieved. Religious orthodoxy is not democratic. One cannot vote on religious practices. Obedience to the teachings is demanded as these have been passed down through religious authorities who sometimes lay claim to their own authority on the basis of charisma and learning, but mostly on the basis of *who* (what previous authority) has conferred it upon them. This is particularly the case with fundamentalist versions of religion, where the task is the maintenance of traditional authority structures and beliefs, which are seen as more important than the welfare of individuals. In this view, religion is not about anyone's 'best interests' but is about following certain 'laws' which are immutable, because they are believed to be literally 'God-given'. Faced with the choice between authority and humane insight, the fundamentalist chooses authority every time.

This should not be taken to mean that all religious affiliations are the same, or that only fundamentalist influences demand attention. Indeed, the common failure to imagine the huge range of religious positions may be one of the factors contributing to support for fundamentalist authoritarianism in religion. Outsiders (e.g. the state through its funding agencies, the media, and professionals in health and social services) relate to minority communities through representatives of religious orthodoxy rather than, for example, dissenting groups (Sahgal and Yuval-Davis, 1992). What actually exists in many religious communities, what differentiates them from homogeneously fundamentalist, authoritarian structures, is a healthy *uncertainty* about truth, whereby many community members are connected through primarily cultural and ethnic affinities rather than firmly held religious beliefs. Thus, the degree to which even orthodox religions pursue uniform child-rearing is enormously varied, from a rigid authoritarian, father-dominant style at one extreme to laissez-faire and liberal parents at the other. A common professional problem is the tendency to lump together all modes of religion, often seeing them as the same (mainly exotic) 'cultures' without recognizing real divergences and conflicts.

In this context, it is difficult to hold on to a coherent notion of what might be meant by 'religious' influences on parenting. Nevertheless, it is important to recognize the degree to which religion manifests itself not just as the espousal of certain values, but as the regulation of action – a position shared by orthodox Judaism through the detailed legal code of Halachah (rabbinic law) and Islam through the Shar'ia (law made by Mullahs), both of which are complex sets of rules for conduct with little parallel in Western secular law.

Much of this regulatory and prescriptive legislation relates to parenting: indeed, about a third of the legal injunctions in the Quran are concerned with the family and appropriate relations within it (Ahsan, 1995). Muslim parents traditionally have had enormous moral and quasi-legal authority over their children, effectively including the right to manage their affairs and direct the course of their lives in all its moral, social and religious detail (Akhtar, 1995). The guidance parents offer must, however, conflict neither with the explicit dictates of the Quran nor with the prophetic exemplar (the normative conduct of Mohammed). There are also some specific circumstances in which children may legitimately rebel against a misuse of parental powers. Importantly, these are religious circumstances – in

particular, if parents try to bring up their children to be idolaters (Akhtar, 1995).

This is relevant where a child adopts fundamentalist practices against the wishes of a more liberal parent, something which often happens in the Jewish community and, as is already evident, will become more common amongst Western Muslims. Under these circumstances, finding 'the proper path of life' involves going against the authority of parents, who, at the extreme, may even be rejected or denounced.

On a more familiar level, there has been a pained debate in religious communities about the extent to which the religious injunction to 'honour your father and mother' holds when, for example, parents encourage children to engage in illegal activities or make them the victim of (particularly sexual) abuse. While to outsiders it might be assumed that by such behaviour a parent relinquishes the claim to moral authority, not all religious leaders have seen things that way. In some religions, children are not even supposed to speak of their parents to outsiders, whether for good or ill. Several family therapists trying to work with orthodox Jewish families, for example, have come up against interpretations of 'speaking evil' rules which mean that nothing can be said about parents without their explicit permission and their presence. Although religious authorities (e.g. the main London orthodox rabbinical court) have tended to rule that children whose parents abuse them should be exempt from the requirement to show them honour, there are very strong prohibitions against revolt, and some of the court's own practices (e.g. their refusal to give evidential weight to the testimony of children and women) militate against a more liberal dissent from parents' views.

Thus, as we have seen, despite the significance of religion in some minorities, there is a strikingly weak literature on the topic of religious influences on parenting. This is partly because of a failure amongst secular Western professionals and researchers to appreciate the diversity of religious life. At its extremes, there is a radical discontinuity between Western humanist perceptions of the role of parenting and those held by religious believers. Specifically, the Western tradition places the welfare of the individual child at the centre of its concerns and assumes that this will be true in all contexts, despite variations in cultural practices. For religious parents, however, it may be that promoting the continuity of the community and upholding the 'truth of the religious path' is more important than maximizing the freedom, autonomy and independence of the individual child. Thus, their approach to parenting is likely to be religion-centred rather than child-centred.

This does not mean that they have a free hand, for example, to discipline children as harshly as they like, or to abuse them. On the contrary, often there is a very strong commitment to the idea of the well-being of children in religious communities, although abuse and harshness are not absent. Kate Loewenthal, writing about the pressures of bringing up a large family, comments, 'The believing Jew (and believers of other religious traditions) feels that each soul that is brought into a human body is precious; each has spiritually significant tasks to accomplish; the parents are privileged to be the means of enabling this … Each child is precious, a spiritual gem' (Loewenthal and Brooke-Rogers, 2001, p. 9). Nevertheless, the idea that each child has 'spiritually significant tasks to accomplish' and that parents are 'the means of enabling this' is not a common notion directing the work of Western psychologists and childcare professionals. Despite some similarities of outlook, child-rearing practices in religious communities are organized and priorities established by religious rules of conduct rather than by those apparently shared in secular cultures.

The more strongly held the religious position, the more complex all this becomes. The various tensions here involve the active wish of parents to transmit something of their own allegiances – their identities – to their children, measured against a set of liberal values that emphasize individual freedom to make some kind of choice. This choice is always constrained, at least by the forces in its social context. There is also the additional and specific problem that fundamentalist cultures do not recognize the legitimacy of 'choice', let alone of liberal values. Indeed, each framework is in part built around the repudiation of the other, through a process of scrutiny, judgement and ostracism. Liberals refute the authoritarianism of fundamentalists either as something 'primitive' or as an understandable but pernicious defensiveness; fundamentalists reject the secular, pluralistic, fragile morality of the West which, they argue, so often fails to provide any sense of 'roots'.

In this debate, there is no evidence to suggest that the rigid morality of fundamentalist religion produces children with less robust mental health outcomes than the liberal framework characteristic of pluralist Western society. However, absence of evidence one way or another does not support either case. Even in areas where the oppressive nature of the religious outlook seems obvious, for example, in sexual repressiveness and the subjugation of women, there are many speaking from within fundamentalist communities who claim otherwise. Most people in the West would agree that a fundamentalist community's failure to educate a child so that she or he has the best capacity to make informed choices between different careers and lifestyles is a constraint on freedom. However, there are many religionists who argue that there can be a similar loss of freedom when religious and communal values, which are part of a child's family tradition, are not inculcated in the child. For example, it has often been pointed out that male circumcision carried out for religious reasons contravenes the rights of children to physical integrity. Similarly, many practices appear to negate the right of women to equality. Importantly, these values are accepted as universal and not culture-bound, and are enshrined in UN resolutions and charters (Katz, 1999). From the child protection perspective, therefore, male circumcision should provoke prevention and intervention. However, from a religious perspective, circumcision itself may be seen as a fundamental injunction; *not* to circumcise a male child will therefore be wrong on religious grounds, as it contravenes the explicit 'command of God'. It also carries a variety of perceived risks and consequences, both for the individual child and his family, who might find themselves excluded from the community, and for the community itself, which might experience the repudiation of a defining feature of its way of life. Rational arguments about 'right' or 'wrong' are deemed irrelevant where religious authority is concerned.

Continued negation of the right of women to equality with their menfolk in Islam and Judaism (and some fundamentalist Christian sects) is similarly justified by the (male) religionists as deriving from authoritative religious 'commandments'. Despite some dissent by women and attempts at their 'liberation' by some men, the practices continue, since they are critical to maintaining the very fabric of those religions as they stand.

These examples suggest that there is a fundamental incommensurability between the professional discourse of child protection and the humane discourse of equality of men and women on the one hand and the religious view on the other. Thus, the argument between them can only be resolved on grounds of value rather than fact, that is, by asserting the superiority of one set of values over the other, even if this assertion may be based on fundamental notions of justice and human worth. Appealing, for example, to mental health outcomes (even if they could be shown to be different in the two systems) is not the point: secularists will not adopt religious beliefs because this might make their children less likely to go off the rails; and religious believers will not give up their ideologies in order to make someone else happy, whether that someone else be the representatives of the state or their own child.

On the whole, in the West, it is Western liberal perspectives that have absorbed much of the Christian belief systems that dominate the area of parenting and normative child development, especially in terms of interventions. In this sense, expectations of cultural 'sensitivity' derived from 'multiculturalism' are largely one-way: from the point of view of the state, it is always the other who has to change because the state represents the majority. Even when multiculturalism leads to the relaxing of Western values in order to make room for the co-existence of ethnically and religiously diverse citizens, Western values are not themselves usually pressured to change by other cultural positions. They continue to retain the assumption of superiority, even if unvoiced. Ilan Katz (1999), contributing to the debate on child protection, gives the example of how in many Muslim communities in the UK, it is viewed as abusive not to send children to a religious school. Further, the same Muslims do not regard it as abusive physically to chastise a child who refuses to go to school. He notes: 'It is quite likely that physical chastisement will result in the intervention of child protection agencies, but very unlikely that a parent not sending a child to a religious school would be deemed to be an appropriate trigger for a child protection enquiry'.

Again we need to remember that the assumption that all enlightened cultures have the same developmental aims, for instance to promote autonomy, independence and individual happiness, is simply unfounded. Western professionals and academics are caught up in a long history of imperialist reasoning when they take their own culture as the measure by which all others are to be judged. The purpose of a religious upbringing is 'to serve God', usually by ensuring that children carry on the religious tradition, even if this means severely restricting their lifestyles and developmental, not to say career, possibilities. The idea, for example, that a Muslim girl might be sent away to be married to a Muslim boy she has never met before seems anathema to Western consciousness, organized as it is around notions of individual choice and romantic love. However, if it preserves the girl's religious (and sexual) integrity, then it might well be seen from within the community as justifiable.

Children's individual rights to self-determination may be respected at the extreme, in the sense that they can usually choose to cut themselves off from their community. However, they are not accepted as a principle because, unlike liberal humanistic views, the individual human subject is not the basic unit of the moral order. The community and, behind it, the religious 'truth' inscribed in its texts and supported by its authorities, is more primary, more 'fundamental'. Most religious cultures allow some specific laws to be transgressed in order to save life, as they place strong value on the preciousness and even 'holiness' of the individual souls with which they have been entrusted. However, they do not organize themselves to promote individual development or happiness, but to maintain order and tradition, without which religious culture and its integrity will be lost.

The idea that the community's 'entitlements' might be more important than those of the individual child is a considerable challenge to the liberal view that places the rights of the individual at the centre of moral systems, and makes the optimal development of the child's individuality the goal of parenting. Indeed, in the classic 'rights versus duties' tension of citizenship, fundamentalists quite straightforwardly emphasize the primacy of duties. The 'best interests of the child' are less significant than the best interests of the community as judged by those vested with religious authority, such as the Mullah or the Rabbi. It can often be argued that these two poles are not apart but go together – it is in the 'best interests of the child' to be acceptable to the community – though not always. When in conflict, preservation of the community and its traditional religious values is of paramount concern – passing down the truth to the next generation. It is important to note here that while this primacy of the community's interests occurs particularly strongly in totalitarian and authoritarian systems (of which religious fundamentalism is the most vibrant contemporary example) it cannot be dismissed *a priori* as an irrational or pernicious occurrence. All religious and most other communities have this concern; the differences lie in the degree to and methods by which they are willing to subjugate the interests of individuals. Fundamentalist leaders might not step back from the demand that children are sacrificed in the interests of the social–religious order, as many recent examples show, and in so doing they reveal their extremism. But it is not only fundamentalist cultures that demand such steps, as we see from time to time, in wars and other events.

PRACTICE OF PARENTING

An important qualification needs to be made here, in order to ameliorate any sense that religious parents can and will do *anything* to preserve the integrity of 'the proper path'. Not only do all the major religions lay down stringent rules about decent behaviour towards others, including children, but there is also a good deal of dissent and divergence within communities from which the outside might look quite homogeneous. These can be made more acute in Western settings in which religious cultures come into close contact with an increasingly secular wider society, especially through children. For example, as Akhtar (1995) has indicated, Muslim parents commonly experience the following anxieties about bringing up children in non-Muslim societies, anxieties undoubtedly shared by other religious groups, including religious Christians:

- monitoring and 'control' of juvenile sexuality in a permissive culture where sexual experimentation from adolescence onwards is the norm;
- ambiguous moral attitudes to boy–girl relationships, including self-determination of sexual acts;
- ready access to information about the technology of contraception – themes that are part of the biology syllabus of British schools and must therefore be taught by law – and also a whole sex education curriculum, using models and aids such as condoms;
- widespread drug use and abuse by teenagers to which their children may be exposed;
- some kinds of contemporary music which might encourage dissenting beliefs and attitudes such as, for example, the acceptability of sexual experimentation and defiance of parental authority;
- lapses in strict religious observance, especially for those who leave home to go to university and live independently in a secular environment for a prolonged period.

These anxieties may indicate a genuine 'generation gap' between elders who place most emphasis on the preservation of a religious culture, believe themselves to be in the right, and who seek to 'protect' young people from the 'corrupting influence' of the wider society. The fact that these anxieties are grounded in the wish to perpetuate and defend male supremacy and restrict sex to a male-dominated marriage, do not alter their power over religionists.

Young people, on the other hand, themselves might see their religious heritage as one amongst many possible paths which they could take, or as something to be held on to only to the degree that it does not constrain their other choices

adversely. Given their immersion in a modern society, to which they are exposed whatever the constraints of home and community environments, young people in religiously orthodox cultures have to grapple with choices that simply might not have been available to their elders. Evidence suggests that, particularly amongst Muslim children, the impact of religious values is to strengthen notions of 'proper conduct' and family and community ties. This does not usually mean that children adopt all religious injunctions, but their religious beliefs place limits on their behaviour and give greater cohesion to their lives, to the extent that they observe religious injunctions. So, for example, some Muslim boys will go out with non-Muslim girls but would not consider marrying them (Frosh et al., 2002).

Alternatively, the entwining of religion and notions of correct conduct may provoke more conflict, as in the many examples of difficulties surrounding arranged marriages. A common response of religious parents under such circumstances is to become coercive in ways that are clearly counter-productive, not just from the point of view of a Western child-centred discourse, but in its own terms. For example, it is claimed (Akhtar, 1995) that Muslim adolescents in Britain are often coerced into marriage or engagement in order to legalize and control their sexuality, before the freedom of the surrounding culture gets to work. However, this can result in the disintegration of the extended family, with children who refuse to accept parental choices and increasingly make their own decisions about marriage partner, place of residence and lifestyle. There may even be a 'disintegration of faith-based identity', particularly amongst girls, under the impulse of parental pressure towards academic achievement and acceptance of unfairly arranged marriages.

The word 'unfairly' is important here from a religious perspective, suggesting not only that coercive arranged marriages can lead to disintegration of family and faith, but also that they are religiously *wrong*. In the case of arranged marriages, the Quran makes it clear that they must be fair and appropriate, which means that parents do not have complete control over their children's destinies. An important point here, from a professional point of view, is that only a religious authority would be able to rule on whether a parent was behaving unfairly, an issue that often arises in clinical work when trying to establish the boundaries of appropriate parenting.

The factors described above have considerable practical importance in areas central to parental activities and boundaries of decision-making, for instance in education, child protection and psychological intervention. In psychological therapies, there is the obvious problem of working within strict authority structures, understanding the complexity of the culture and community pressures, being curious about yet not subverting deeply held religious beliefs, and working with family conflicts that are related to belief (Loewenthal, 1999). In particular, strictly religious communities turn to their religious leaders on matters relating to religious law, including its impact on many features of daily life. In any intervention, whether therapeutic or research based, participants are likely to ask whether the religious authority has given approval, and most would refuse to co-operate if approval had been withheld. This is one reason why anyone who works with religious communities (or some individuals) needs to form working alliances with the religious authorities who govern and are respected within these communities. Clearly, sometimes it is necessary to act irrespective of religious authority; more frequently, guidance on what is reasonable, from a religious point of view, would be readily given. This is sometimes regarded as an imposition by secular authorities, but it is important to remember that there are many different sources of legitimation.

There is some evidence that religious parents are more likely to have harmonious family relationships rather than the converse, and less likely to use physical punishment against their children. This is contrary to what might have been predicted from some of the earlier comments and from suggestions that religious parents are likely to be more punitive and engage in harsher discipline than do secular parents (Loewenthal, 2001). For example, in a study of African-American families in the rural south of the USA, Brody et al. (1998) found higher religious activity among the parents to be associated with lower levels of conflict between them, more cohesive family relationships and fewer problems among their adolescent children.

Reviewing the literature on the relationship of fathering and religious belief, Dollahite (1998) argues that religion generally has a positive influence on men and supports 'responsible' fathering, specifically through moral persuasion, personal example, community support and explicit teaching of marriage and family life. The research he quotes suggests that American men know that a sense of 'meaning', direction, solace, and involvement with a caring community and religious practices in which these are embedded are important in raising children. For these parents, 'religion, consisting of a covenant faith community with teachings and narratives that enhance spirituality and encourage morality, is the most powerful, meaningful, and sustained influence for encouraging men to be fully involved in children's lives' (Dollahite, 1998, p. 3).

There is also research evidence suggesting that religious attitudes, and perhaps the structures of communal support that often accompany them, are helpful in the parenting of children with specific difficulties and disabilities. For example, some evidence comes from interviews with Church of Jesus Christ of Latter-Day Saints ('Mormon') fathers of children with special needs (Marks and Dollahite, 2001). The focus of enquiry was the meaning of religion in relation to responsible, involved parenting for these fathers and their families. Interviews showed that although the fathers' experiences with religion were sometimes challenging, religion was meaningful and influential in supporting them in their efforts to be responsible and focused on relations. Religion was an important resource for these fathers, affecting how they coped, the perspective they took, the way they experienced their parenting, and how they created their life stories (Dollahite et al., 1998). Research has also been done with parents of Mexican and Puerto Rican origin living in the USA who had young children with developmental delays, to determine the role of religion in their lives. These results indicated that parents largely viewed themselves as religious, were affiliated with a formal religion and participated in religious activities. Most parents viewed both church and faith as supportive, but faith was shown to provide more support, suggesting that the important factor for them was not simply connection with a community (Skinner et al., 2001).

Enquiries into the culture of American 'conservative Protestantism' show that religious values are an important predictor of child-rearing attitudes and practices in a number of ways (Wilcox, 1997). Specifically, while conservative Protestant parents maintain strict discipline, they also show an unusually warm and expressive style of parent–child interaction. This is further supported by the parenting advice given to them by religious leaders. In addition, data from the 1987–1988 US National Survey of Families and Households shows that parents with conservative theological beliefs are more likely to praise and hug their children than are parents with less conservative views (ibid.). Effect of parental religiosity and racial identity on their reports of child behaviour problems in a sample of low-income African-American children has also been studied (Christian and Barbarin, 2001). Results from interviews and questionnaires administered in the early 1990s showed that children of parents attending church at least weekly had fewer problems compared to those whose parents attended less frequently. These data seem to confirm the importance of religion as a socio-cultural resource in African-American families, one that is associated with the resilience of children at risk of behavioural or emotional maladjustment.

A further study of young people from a very religious and homogeneous community, members of the Church of Jesus Christ of Latter-Day Saints attending Brigham Young University, also shows a protective effect of parental religiosity on mental health, this time in regard to drug use, which had a very low (self-reported) incidence (Merrill et al., 2001). The most commonly reported reasons for abstention from drugs were that drug use would violate the young person's religious beliefs and personal moral code. Protective factors against drug use included parental positions of responsibility in the church and frequent family discussions involving religion and Christian conduct. Mothers' views of religion were a stronger inhibitor of previous drug use than fathers' views, positions of church responsibility held by the parents, or arguments about religious teachings with parents. Discussion on topics of Christian conduct was more strongly associated with no previous drug use than were either church attendance or discussions on topics of religious doctrine. Taken together, these findings suggest that cohesive family life combined with religious belief, and a context in which religiously informed behaviour could be discussed, are of preventive value in the high-risk area of drug taking and probably associated behaviours. Interestingly, despite overt paternal dominance, it is the maternal communication and presumably relationship that is the more powerful buffer against adverse influences.

These are all admittedly limited data, but they suggest that the structure of religion, both in terms of its inculcation of beliefs and ethics and its community, can have a beneficial effect on practice of parenting. However, there are drawbacks too. For instance, one significant factor is the large size of many religious families which results from the prohibition of contraception (except for strict medical reasons) and the advocacy of (often youthful) marriage towards a state of 'spiritual completion'. In some of these communities, there is an average of five children per family, with families of ten or more children being commonplace (Holman and Holman, 2002). In these circumstances, with the added problem of the economic privation produced by large families, maternal depression is quite common. This may be offset to some extent by community organizations and by the benefits of

living in an environment of close relatives and contacts. The mental health effects of these difficulties on children in religious communities have not been researched. However, given the strength of the link between maternal depression and children's problems, difficulties are likely to be substantial (Loewenthal and Goldblatt, 1993).

In child protection, issues of punishment, neglect of children's wishes over arranged marriages and circumcision have already been mentioned, as has the intractable problem of the 'closed' nature of many religious communities to outside scrutiny. There have been suggestions in the literature that religion promotes child abuse, at least to the extent that it endorses physical means of punishment. There are widely varying Christian sources advocating the use of corporal punishment 'for the good of the child' which can easily drift into child abuse (Capps, 1992). There is also evidence in contemporary Christian writings that physical and psychological abuse, shaming and humiliating children is rationalized in the name of principled child-rearing (De Jonge, 1995). That these may form the basis for creating a cycle of violence within families and subcultures seems to be ignored.

Studies of undergraduates and their parents show a relationship between fundamentalism and support for corporal punishment, although associated right-wing authoritarian attitudes appear to be at least as important as religious beliefs (Danso et al., 1997). Conservative Protestants (and to a lesser extent Catholics) seem to endorse authoritarian parenting disproportionately (that is, to value obedience at the expense of autonomy), linked to three core religious beliefs: biblical literalism, the belief that human nature is sinful, and punitive attitudes toward sinners (Ellison and Sherkat, 1993). However, although such studies demonstrate that conservative Protestant parents support corporal punishment more strongly and use it more frequently than other parents (Ellison, 1996), it remains unclear whether this form of religious conservatism is linked with actual child abuse, unless the term is extended to imply all physical forms of discipline.

On the other side, a study of British adults suggests that there was no relationship between recalled parental religiosity and the use of physical punishment with children under 13 years of age. The more religious parents were less likely to use physical punishment on adolescents over 13 years. When parents did use physical punishment, the more religious were less likely to accompany it with shouting and saying damaging things, and more likely to be recalled as having a child-oriented motive. The more religiously active parents were also recalled as having a better and more positive relationship with their children (Steley, 1996; Loewenthal, 2001). Other studies also support the general claim that 'religiosity' amongst parents is positively related to harmonious relationships with children, irrespective of particular religious denomination, and this is probably due primarily to the way most religions promote strong family ties (Pearce and Axin, 1998).

Thus, it appears that there is evidence both 'for' and 'against' religiosity in relation to parenting practices and their consequences. So religiosity itself does not appear a significant factor. As elsewhere, parental personalities and family histories and cultures seem to be the more influential factors in determining parental behaviour towards the child.

When child abuse and protection becomes an issue in religious communities, there can be substantial difficulties for secular state agencies in trying to gain access (Shor, 1998). Given that the good standing and reputation of the community is linked to promoting religious belief, then anything that brings shame on the community can be seen as an anti-religious act. When problems occur, this can mean that the community turns silent in order to prevent outsiders knowing of its troubles. As several high-profile instances in the Catholic and Jewish communities have shown, this can act solidly against child protection work, even when these nominally have the support of religious authorities.

In the clinical vignette given earlier, the community can be seen virtually to shut down in the face of child protection investigations from outside; in extreme cases, forms of excommunication have been exerted on those who use the secular, state system as a port of call for protective activity. Very commonly, particularly in the case of sexual abuse where an abuser is known within the community, religious authorities will take responsibility for intervening. The consequence is often that the suspected abuser moves out of the community, with the risk exported elsewhere. All this can be extremely frustrating for child protection authorities, who may find themselves unable to establish the standing of accusations or meet the protective and therapeutic needs of children involved.

In the area of education, there is a substantial and visible impact of religion on what parents will tolerate. As noted above, the biology and sex education of state schools is often problematic for religious parents. That is why, in the USA, the largest group of 'home educators' are Christians wishing to ensure that their children are not exposed to education on sexuality – as well as wishing to inculcate in them minority attitudes such as 'creationism'. Research on fundamentalist Christian parents in the USA suggests that such parents significantly boost the educational attainment of male children who follow their beliefs, but also that they are deleterious to the educational attainments of girls, particularly those who eventually move away from fundamentalist attitudes themselves (Sherkat and Darnell, 1999). More generally, most religious parents wish to have single-sex schooling for their children, at least once they get to adolescence, which can mean that they have great trouble finding anything suitable within the state sector (Ahsan, 1995).

There is also the broader question of what is taught, how much of the curriculum can be devoted to religious instruction, and how to ensure that this is of the 'right kind'. For all these reasons, schooling in religious communities is usually private: children go to single-sex schools where the curriculum is heavily loaded towards religious instruction and sometimes (though by no means universally) where secular studies are relegated to secondary importance. Nevertheless, religious schools in Britain feature well in 'league tables' for secular outcomes.

There are several further consequences of this situation, varying somewhat across different religious groups. For example, in the strictly orthodox Jewish community, schooling follows a distinctive pattern: parents wish to give their children a 'Torah education', demanding single-sex schooling and a very high proportion of time spent in studying religious texts. Few of the schools meeting the requirements of strictly orthodox parents receive state or local authority funding, meaning that parents have to use private funds, thus adding to the economic pressure of having to provide for large families. This in turn may be an important risk factor for psychiatric morbidity among adults in this community (Loewenthal and Goldblatt, 1993). It is also probably linked to child mental health difficulties, although very little is known about psychiatric morbidity among children in the strictly orthodox Jewish or Muslim communities since there is reluctance to admit to problems and to seek help, especially outside the community. Fear of stigmatization is a powerful factor driving the widespread view that she or he 'will grow out of it'.

IMPLICATIONS FOR PRACTICE

Religious values and beliefs have implications for design of schools and curricula and in methods of psychological work with parents who are affiliated to religious communities. In particular, issues such as authority and independence, beliefs about gender roles and 'correct behaviour', and questions of transmission of religious values need to be understood and worked with, rather than against.

It is important for professionals to support community-based initiatives, despite difficulties of confidentiality, because without this there is likely to be a substantial gap between the needs of the community and their take-up of provision. There are many ways in which parents in religious communities might feel misunderstood by secular professionals. Whilst 'cultural awareness' educational programmes are of value here, they cannot always address the gulf between the ideological standpoints of religious and secular cultures. Moreover, simply feeling comfortable enough to accept help is a major issue when it comes to parenting and mental health provision, something which is more likely to occur when services are provided from within communities rather than from outside (Loewenthal, 1999). The most significant move forward, however, will perhaps be achieved when parenting and child mental health professionals recognize that religious beliefs and practices are not best understood as an optional 'add-on' to the mores of Western secular culture – something exotic to be learnt about and acknowledged but not taken seriously. Rather, they represent, at least at their extremes, an ideology that in important and relevant respects is opposed to the one almost universally adopted by those who operate health and education services.

In research terms, it will also be apparent from the paucity of empirical data in this chapter that very little is known about the extent of actual variations in parenting behaviour between members of different religious and secular groups. In addition, the degree of heterogeneity that exists amongst parents who are members of religious communities is worthy of research, as it will allow some calibration of 'normality' in those communities as well as increased understanding of the degree to which variations from apparently accepted or prescribed practices are themselves normative. The degree of conflict represented by this heterogeneity, whether it varies across cultures, and how much it is changing over time, are all relevant concerns.

There is also a real opportunity to examine the relative mental health outcomes of radically different sets of parenting values, particularly in relation to fundamentalism. So little is known about the frequencies of parenting difficulties and mental health problems in children in religious communities, that it is not even possible at this stage to say with confidence whether current services are meeting the needs of such communities appropriately. Some basic research is required, but in order to do it researchers will have to work industriously to cultivate good relationships with community organizations and religious authorities – and this takes imagination, diplomacy and commitment.

REFERENCES

Ahsan, M. (1995) The Muslim family in Britain. In King, M. (ed.) *God's Law versus State Law*. London: Grey Seal, pp. 21–30.

Akhtar, S. (1995) Relationships between Muslim parents and children in a non-Muslim country. In King, M. (ed.) *God's Law versus State Law*. London: Grey Seal, pp. 31–43.

Brody, G., Stoneman, Z. and Flor, D. (1998) Parental religiosity and youth competence. *Developmental Psychology*, **32**, 696–707.

Capps (1992) Religion and child abuse: Perfect together. *Journal for the Scientific Study of Religion*, **31**, 1–14.

Christian, M. and Barbarin, O. (2001) Cultural resources and psychological adjustment of African American children: effects of spirituality and racial attribution. *Journal of Black Psychology*, **1**, 43–63.

Danso, H., Hunsberger, B. and Pratt, M. (1997) The role of parental religious fundamentalism and right-wing authoritarianism in child-rearing goals and practices. *Journal for the Scientific Study of Religion*, **35**, 496–511.

De Jonge, J. (1995) On breaking wills: the theological roots of violence in families. *Journal of Psychology and Christianity*, **14**, 26–37.

Dollahite, D. (1998) Fathering, faith and spirituality. *Journal of Men's Studies*, **7**, 3–15.

Dollahite, D., Marks, L. and Olson, M. (1998) Faithful fathering in trying times: religious beliefs and practices of Latter-day Saint fathers of children with special needs. *Journal of Men's Studies*, **7**, 71–93.

Ellison, C. (1996) Conservative Protestantism and the corporal punishment of children: clarifying the issues. *Journal for the Scientific Study of Religion*, **35**, 1–16.

Ellison, C. and Sherkat, D. (1993) Obedience and autonomy: religion and parental values reconsidered. *Journal for the Scientific Study of Religion*, **32**, 313–29.

Frosh, S., Phoenix, A. and Pattman, R. (2002) *Young Masculinities: Understanding Boys in Contemporary Society*. London: Palgrave.

Holman, C. and Holman, N. (2002) *Torah, Worship and Acts of Loving Kindness: Baseline Indicators for the Charedi Community in Stamford Hill*. Leicester: De Montfort University.

Katz, I. (1999) Is male circumcision morally defensible? In King, M. (ed.) *Moral Agendas for Children's Welfare*. London: Routledge.

Loewenthal, K.M. (1999) Religious issues and their psychological aspects. In Bhui, K. and Olajide, D. (eds)

Cross Cultural Mental Health Services: Contemporary Issues in Service Provision. London: W.B. Saunders, pp. 54–65.

Loewenthal, K.M. (2001) *The Psychology of Religion.* Oxford: Oneworld.

Loewenthal, K.M. and Brooke-Rogers, M. (2001) Culturally and religiously sensitive psychological help – from a Jewish perspective. In King-Spooner, S. and Newnes, C. (eds) *Spirituality and Psychotherapy.* Ross-on-Wye: PCCS Books.

Loewenthal, K.M. and Goldblatt, V. (1993) Family size and depressive symptoms in orthodox Jewish women. *Journal of Psychiatric Research,* **27**, 3–10.

Marks, L. and Dollahite, D. (2001) Religion, relationships, and responsible fathering in Latter-day Saint families of children with special needs. *Journal of Social and Personal Relationships,* **18**, 625–50.

Merrill, R., Salazar, R. and Gardner, N. (2001) Relationship between family religiosity and drug use behavior among youth. *Social Behavior and Personality,* **29**, 347–58.

Pearce, L. and Axin, W. (1998) The impact of family religious life on the quality of mother–child relations. *American Sociological Review,* **63**, 810–28.

Sahgal, G. and Yuval-Davis, N. (eds) (1992) *Refusing Holy Orders.* London: Virago.

Sherkat, D. and Darnell, A. (1999) The effects of parents' fundamentalism in children's educational attainment: examining differences by gender and children's fundamentalism. *Journal for the Scientific Study of Religion,* **38**, 23–35.

Shor, R. (1998) The significance of religion in advancing a culturally sensitive approach towards child maltreatment. *Families in Society,* **79**, 400–9.

Skinner, D., Correa, V., Skinner, M. and Bailey, D. (2001) Role of religion in the lives of Latino families of young children with developmental delays. *American Journal on Mental Retardation,* **106**, 297–313.

Steley, J. (1996) Parental Discipline and Religious Commitment as Recalled by Adult Children. Unpublished MPhil thesis, University of London.

Wilcox, W. (1997) Conservative Protestant child-rearing: authoritarian or authoritative? *American Sociological Review,* **63**, 796–809.

8

Parenting in Reconstituted and Surrogate Families

Jan Pryor

SUMMARY

Parenting issues in families that are not 'intact' in the biological and structural sense are reviewed and discussed. These include one-parent families, stepfamilies, adoptive and foster families, and families formed by artificial reproduction techniques. Family structure in itself does not account for differences in parenting quality. Rather, adults' and children's histories of relationships are important in determining the nature of parent–child relationships. The main implication of these conclusions is that the fostering of stability in children's lives is pivotal to their well-being, regardless of family structure.

INTRODUCTION

Parenting is a challenge in all families, even those who have the obvious advantages of two competent and harmonious parents with children who are wanted and loved. However, when there are variations in family structure and relationships, such as reconstituted households or those where children are not the biological offspring of the parents, then there are extra challenges to be faced. In stepfamilies, for instance, one parent is not biologically related to the children of the other, and is usually fulfilling a parenting role whilst the other biological parent may still be involved in the children's lives. In families where children are adopted, neither parent is usually related to the children, and there may, if the adoption is open, be the added complication of ongoing relationships between children and at least one of their biological parents. Families created by new technologies present perhaps the most interesting situations, since the complications of parent–child relationships are even more impressive. A child in such a family may, for example, have two social parents, two genetic parents, and one surrogate mother.

In this chapter, parenting issues faced by families who are not 'intact' in the biological and structural sense will be considered. Intact families are often referred to as 'nuclear', and for the purposes of comparison this term will be interpreted to mean families in which two married heterosexual parents live with their biological children conceived and born by natural means. Where there is evidence available that assesses parenting and parent–child relationships in non-nuclear families, the findings will be discussed. The implications arising from these for families themselves, for practice and for policy will also be considered.

HISTORICAL BACKGROUND

The history of families tells us that children have not always been brought up by their biological parents. Prior to the 18th century, it was the norm in Europe for children to be sent to live in other households as apprentices or servants, and indeed a family was defined as those living in a household, including servants and others. There were, too, many orphans as a result of high levels of maternal mortality, so that many children did not grow up in two-parent families with their biological parents. Though children and looking after them has always been important, the reality of frequent child mortality is likely to have mitigated parental preoccupation with their children. Surrogate parenting was, then, commonplace and it was not until what we know as the nuclear family emerged, and mortality and fertility declined, that what we now refer to as intact families became the norm. Throughout most of the 19th and the first half of the 20th centuries, nuclear families prevailed in Western countries. Increasingly, children became the foci of their parents' lives as their survival became more likely and families restricted the numbers of children they bore. Families became truly nuclear in the sense that they relied on a small and isolated group of biologically related people within the household unit for emotional, psychological and physical support. This trend endured into much of the next century.

FAMILIES AFTER DIVORCE

Stable and relatively inflexible gender roles meant that parenting in this nuclear group was predominantly the domain of mothers. None the less, it was not until the beginning of the 20th century that it was considered appropriate for mothers to have custody of children after divorce. Until then they were the property of their fathers and, in the comparatively rare cases that divorces occurred, children remained in their fathers' households. Early in the 20th century, the 'doctrine of tender years' emerged, which held that children were properly to be raised by their mothers even in the event of divorce. This view was buttressed by the writings of John Bowlby who asserted that mothers were of primary importance to children, with fathers best seen in the role of supporters of the mothers' parenting. Freud saw the mother–child relationship as 'unique, without parallel, established unalterably for a whole lifetime as the first and strongest love-object and as the prototype of all later love relations – for both sexes' (Freud, 1940). The 'mother mystique' emerging from all this meant that children usually lived with their mothers after divorce. This has gathered pace so that mothers are usually the primary parents after separation, though the pattern may be changing, particularly for teenage children.

This means that women most often head lone-parent households. In the UK, over 18 per cent of children lived in lone-parent households in the 1990s (Haskey, 1994); of these, less than 10 per cent lived with fathers. In the US, 27 per cent of children lived with a lone parent (Saluter, 1996) and 14 per cent of these lived with their fathers (Rawlings and Saluter, 1996). In practice, therefore, large numbers of children are being parented primarily by mothers. There has been a particular focus on the economic stresses faced particularly by lone mothers, and on the more general stress of parenting alone. Women who may not have been in the workforce before divorce are often forced to get a job, either part- or full-time, in order to support themselves and their children. Lone parents, then, find themselves single-handedly balancing work and parenting with varying degrees of support from ex-partners and extended family members.

Parenting by fathers after divorce has been a comparatively neglected topic. Many men lose contact with their children (Seltzer, 1991) and for some others, parenting is at best a part-time endeavour confined, by and large, to the entertainment of their children. Increasingly, however, men are becoming more involved with children after separation (Gibson, 1992; Simpson et al., 1995; Maclean and Eekelaar, 1997). This has led to the recent examination of parenting by fathers after divorce. Other influences have also encouraged an examination of fathering, including the understanding from developmental psychology research about the importance of men in their children's lives (Lamb, 1995); the impact of the men's movement; and the voices of children themselves that articulate their desire to have their fathers involved in their lives.

STEPFAMILIES

Stepfamilies have always existed, although in the past they were most likely to be formed as the result of the death of a parent. Today they are, in the main, a result of divorce. The majority of adults re-partner after separation, with two-thirds of women and three-quarters of men in the US marrying after divorce (Bumpass et al., 1990).

Put another way, in the US, one in two marriages involve a person who has been previously married (Hetherington and Henderson, 1997). In the UK, Australia and New Zealand, one-third of marriages include one divorced partner (Haskey, 1994; Funder, 1996; Statistics New Zealand, 1996). Not all re-partnerships are marriages, however. Over half of adults in stepfamilies in the US cohabit for a time before marrying (Thompson, 1994).

Another way in which stepfamilies are formed is through the partnership of women who have conceived a child while un-partnered. In Europe, 70 per cent of women in this situation go into partnerships (Kiernan, 1999). In the US, too, children born to lone mothers are very likely to enter a stepfamily before the age of 16 (Aquilino, 1996). In these families, children have not usually experienced parental separation and may not have known their biological fathers before entering a stepfamily.

The majority of stepfamilies are those in which children are living with their biological mothers, who continue their parenting roles through the transitions of divorce and re-partnering. In stepmother families, where children are the biological offspring of their fathers, stepmothers usually take on primary parenting roles with children who are not theirs, especially if children are young (Ferri and Smith, 1998). In stepfamilies, then, we need to consider the parenting of both the biological parent and of the step-parent, and to distinguish the situations in stepfather and stepmother households.

In stepfather families, children continue in the main to be parented by biological parents, that is, their mothers. In stepmother families where their resident biological parent is their father, they are more likely to be parented primarily by a non-biological parent, that is, their stepmother. So children in stepmother families have to adapt to being parented by someone who is not related to them and who may be a comparative stranger. For children in stepfather families, this adaptation does not have to be made although they and their mothers have to get used to a relationship that is no longer the exclusive one they may have had when they lived as a one-parent family.

Biological parents may have to contend with tensions between the demands of their new partners and those of their own children. For children, there is the adjustment to be made to having another adult in the house who not only absorbs their parents' attention but may also adopt and exercise a parenting role toward them. In turn, step-parents face the challenges of integrating themselves into family groups that have existed without them and of both establishing and maintaining partner relationships, and forging relationships with sometimes recalcitrant and resentful stepchildren.

Therapists who work with stepfamilies have suggested that the adults sometimes attempt to model themselves on intact families, and to adopt parenting roles that worked in their original households (Visher and Visher, 1990). This may be a result of the desire to seem 'normal' and to establish relationships as close and loving as those assumed to exist in biologically related families. Sadly this approach does not work smoothly, since older children do not adapt easily to a strange adult moving into a disciplinary role with them, especially if their own father or mother is still involved in their lives. Children may resist step-parents' approaches to parenting and discipline; they may also move regularly between houses so that daily routines are impossible to put in place. In some ways, then, step-parents find themselves without 'scripts' about how to parent since the original family model does not work. Much as they may want to, instantly loving relationships are not possible to create, and perhaps the best they can do is to develop workable relationships at least in the first instance.

Unfortunately, the difficulties faced by stepfamily living mean that they falter and dissolve more often than first-marriage families. In the US, 54 per cent of remarried women, and 64 per cent of remarried men, divorce a second time (Martin and Bumpass, 1989). In a New Zealand cohort of families with children, 53 per cent of stepfamily households dissolved within five years of formation (Fergusson et al., 1984). In turn, parents, displaying what might be described as the triumph of hope over experience, often enter further partnerships so that children experience multiple family transitions. In the same New Zealand cohort, for example, nearly one in five children had lived in three family situations by the age of nine.

ADOPTIVE FAMILIES

The history of parenting in adoptive families is not well known. In the past, adoptions tended to be secret and children were not told that they were not their parents' biological offspring. This situation may have arisen from a general ambivalence about non-biological parent–child relationships, and the persistent negative association for men and women between infertility and self-esteem. Birth mothers, too, were not likely to reveal the existence of illegitimate children in a climate of social opprobrium. Despite more recent trends toward open adoption, there still exists a 'DNA mystique' in which biological connectedness is seen as the 'gold standard' for parent–child relationships, and that sustains the continuing feeling of subtle difference in regard to adoptive families.

Because of this, there is a widely held assumption that children in adoptive families are at risk, although the few studies that have systematically compared their outcomes present a mixed picture. In some ways adopted children do better, and in other ways worse, than their non-adopted siblings (Sharma et al., 1998), age at adoption being a crucial factor in this regard. The younger the age at adoption, the better the outcome will be in general. Overall, there are few differences in outcomes and it is probable that any disadvantages they may face arise as much from the climate of ambivalence they face from peers and others who know about their status, as from internal family dynamics (Ambert, 2001). Another source of possible disadvantage for adopted children lies in the conditions of their antenatal life and birth; mothers who relinquish their children may not take care of themselves during pregnancy to the same extent as those who keep their children. They may smoke and drink more, and be more likely to have birth complications (Golombok et al., 1990).

Unlike parents who have conceived and borne their children, adoptive parents do not have the antenatal period in which to develop a relationship with the unborn child. Neither, in the normal course of events, do they have contact with their child in the perinatal and neonatal period. The transition to parenthood is, then, different for parents who adopt if they have been unable to have their own biological children. They face challenges beyond those for biological parents since, in common with others who have experienced infertility such as those who conceive with the help of reproductive technology, they have sometimes endured intrusive medical procedures in their bid to overcome infertility. They have had to come to terms with the failure of these efforts, in the context of their own and others' views about the desirability of biological parent–child relationships.

It is estimated that one million children in the US live in adoptive families. These households are heterogeneous, because they vary widely in their formation and composition. For example, adoptions may be transracial or international; they may be by gay or lesbian couples, or single adults, or step-parents. There are also variations in children who are adopted in terms of age, disability, and previous histories of fostering. It is likely, therefore, that family relationships and parenting will vary considerably across adoptive households.

FOSTER FAMILIES

Fostering of children who cannot, for various reasons, be parented by their biological parents, has been a part of human society throughout history and across cultures. It has both similarities and differences compared with adoption. As in adoptive families, the parent–child relationship is not a biological one although an extended family member may foster children. Both fostering and adoption can happen at various stages in a child's life, and the earlier they occur, the less likely that a child will have had adverse parenting experiences. Because both fostered and adopted children are relinquished by their often disadvantaged parents, they may also share the risk of a less than optimal prenatal environment. The consequences of inadequate antenatal care, smoking, and substance abuse include, for example, pre-term birth and growth retardation.

Major differences lie in the different perceptions and contexts inherent in fostering and adoption. Regardless of the age of children, adoptive parents intend from the start to include them as permanent members of their families. Their intention is to form a family, or to add a child to their existing family. Their commitment to their children will, then, be greater than that of foster parents. Foster parents, in contrast, may be less likely to make a total emotional investment in children whom they anticipate losing, although many foster relationships become permanent arrangements. So although the majority are loving and adequate parents, their temporary status as 'professional care-givers' means that they are much less likely to be totally and unconditionally accepting of their foster child. Added to this, foster parents are paid for their parenting, so that at least a part of their motivation for caring for children may be economic.

Another difference lies in the fact that foster parents often care for more than one non-related child. Their household typically encompasses their own biological children, and one or more foster children who may or may not themselves be siblings. Children who are fostered, then, have to adjust not just to new parents but also to a variety of siblings.

Finally, foster children who are not placed at or near birth are likely to have been relinquished by parents who have not parented them satisfactorily. They may have been exposed to insensitive parenting, neglect, or even rejection and maltreatment. They may also have experienced more than one foster placement, so that several attachments have been made and broken. This is also the case for many children who are adopted, especially in the UK and the US. In practice, most fostering also takes place beyond infancy.

Impermanence, professional status of parents, and children's previous histories are, therefore, important factors that may impinge on parenting in foster families.

FAMILIES FORMED BY ARTIFICIAL REPRODUCTIVE TECHNOLOGIES (ART)

Families produced as a result of new reproductive technologies are comparatively recent, and present particularly complex relationship constellations for their members. Beside the relatively simple scenario where sperm is supplied by a donor because a husband is infertile, many more complicated arrangements arise that raise questions about parenting and about children's understanding of family relationships. A particularly challenging situation, for example, is posed for the French child whose mother bore him at the age of 62 and who is his biological (because she bore him) and social (because she is raising him) mother. His genetic (and possibly social father) is his uncle, and his genetic mother is a woman who donated an ovum. Other complicated relationships include the situation where a mother may carry a child by surrogacy for her infertile daughter, thus being her granddaughter's 'carrying mother'.

By definition, families formed through the use of artificial reproductive technologies are formed through processes that arise as a result of infertility in one or both parents. There are several consequences of this. Parents will have experienced interventions, both medical and social, that do not conform to the usually straightforward process of sexual intercourse leading to pregnancy and childbirth. They are likely to have had long periods of uncertainty about whether or not they will have children, and of waiting. There are also varying degrees of genetic relatedness between them and their children, ranging from none to one or the other parent contributing genetic material to their offspring.

ART parents are also likely to be older than those with naturally conceived children by the time they take on parenthood, and may be materially better off, especially in countries where the cost of fertility treatment is high. These parents, then, come to parenting with a constellation of factors some of which they share with adoptive parents, and others that are unique to them. Van Balen (1998) has described four commonly held assumptions about families formed in this way. One is that the child is seen as a precious gift to be protected, leading to over-protective behaviours by parents. Another is that children are so wanted that they are 'over desired', leading to high and unrealistic expectations of and about them. A third is that because ART parents have had years of living without children, they will find it more difficult than most to adapt to the demands of parenting, since they have become used to a lifestyle without responsibilities. And finally, because of the nature of their conception and birth, their children may be perceived as different, and parental attitudes and behaviour toward their children will be affected by these perceptions.

It is not surprising, then, that parenting and outcomes for in vitro fertilisation (IVF) children have confidently been predicted to be problematic. In regard to scientific developments in human reproductive technology, Snowden (1998) has suggested that 'it is difficult not to exaggerate their potential effect on the biological, personal, and social experience of human life as we know it today.'

Overall, the experiences of separation, divorce, stepfamily formation, and adoptive, fostering and IVF family living bring with them several crucial factors that may have an impact on parenting, and that are not characteristic of nuclear families. Table 8.1 shows the presence or absence of these factors in the families discussed here.

Transitions made by parents are almost always accompanied by distress and stress, which has an impact on their ability to parent effectively. The emotional energy required to cope with the loss of a partnership and the structural changes such as moving houses and neighbourhoods mean that they often have depleted resources for looking after their children. Similarly, family transitions for children are well documented as being stressful and likely to affect their behaviour in the short term, as well as their well-being in the medium and long term (Pryor and Rodgers, 2001).

The question of biological relationship is addressed as potentially a major factor in relation to parenting in stepfamilies (e.g. Hetherington et al., 1999). It is assumed that any deficiencies in step-parent–stepchild relationships are a product of a lack of 'ownness' or genetic relationship between adult and child. Thus it is also a potential issue for ART and adoptive parents.

The experience of infertility, too, is one that brings its own stresses and disappointments that

Table 8.1 *Factors present in reconstituted and non-nuclear families that may have an impact on parenting*

Factor	Lone-parent families	Stepfamilies	Adoptive families	Foster families	ART families
Parents have experienced transitions	Yes	Yes	No	No	No
Child has experienced transitions	Yes	Yes	Maybe	Yes	
No or partial genetic relationship between parents and child			Yes	Yes	Yes
Experience of infertility			Yes	Maybe	Yes
Potential or real social stigma	Yes	Yes	Yes	Yes	Yes
Possibly more than two parenting figures		Yes	Yes	Yes	Yes
Possible ethnic or cultural differences between child and parents		Yes	Yes	Yes	Yes

may be linked with future parenting behaviour for reasons described above. Parents may, for example, be over-anxious about children whom they have obtained after taking sometimes extreme measures.

Social stigma is apparent in the accounts of individuals in families who are not nuclear, and has led, for example, to the former National Stepfamily Association in the UK being re-named. It is also apparent in the accounts of some children whose parents have divorced, when they say they do not want their friends or teachers to know (Douglas and Murch, 2002). In practice it is almost impossible to measure the impact of stigma on parent–child relationships since they are so dependent on the psychological state and well-being of those involved in them.

Sustaining relationships with multiple parenting figures is not an uncommon experience for large numbers of children. This is especially the case in those stepfamilies who have relationships with non-resident parents and often two step-parents. In situations of open adoption, and possibly even in ART families where donor parents are known to children, children are also likely to sustain relationships with several parents, and to make their own sense of those relationships. Again, the implications of this factor for parenting are complex and not well examined. Children are remarkably pragmatic about families, and accept a wide range of structures as 'family' (Pryor and Rodgers, 2001; Anyan and Pryor, 2002). Their ability to accept and benefit from a variety of parenting figures is, therefore, likely to depend primarily on how the complex of relationships is handled by adults in their lives.

Finally, ethnic and cultural differences may have an impact on adoptive and foster families in particular, but also potentially in stepfamilies and ART families. Physical differences between parents and children are an obvious potential source of unfamiliarity. So too are attitudes to and expectations of families, especially those held by children who are beyond infancy when adopted or fostered. And, when children reach adolescence, issues of cultural and ethnic identity come to the fore and require addressing by young people and their parents.

The conduit through which these factors have their impact on children is primarily in their effect on parenting and parent–child relationships. Parenting, then, is central to our concern for children in these families, since it orchestrates and funnels these and other diverse factors.

PARENTING IN NON-TRADITIONAL FAMILIES: WHAT DO WE KNOW?

In examinations of parenting in non-nuclear or non-traditional families, comparisons are most frequently made with intact families, that is, households with two heterosexual married parents and their biological children. In some cases these may not be the most appropriate comparisons to be made. For example, in considering parent–child relationships in stepfamilies, a more appropriate comparison might be with lone-parent families where children have also experienced parental separation. Similarly, in families formed as a result of artificial reproductive technologies the common experience of infertility in most adoptive families might serve as a more salient comparison (and in fact these comparisons are made by some researchers).

Parenting in Lone-Parent Households

Numerous studies in the US and the UK have documented that as a group lone parents are more likely to show poor parenting techniques than those in intact families (Hetherington and Clingempeel, 1992; Emery, 1994; McLanahan and Sandfur, 1994; Simons, 1996; Dunn et al., 1998; Hetherington, 1999). They are, for example, more likely than mothers in intact families inappropriately to leave their children alone at times, and less likely to provide supervision, help with school work, and set rules for TV watching (McLanahan and Sandfur, 1994). Separated mothers are more likely to display negative attitudes to their children, and less likely to behave positively toward them, than mothers in intact and stepfamilies (Deater-Deckard and Dunn, 1999). In general, authoritative parenting, encompassing high levels of support and appropriate monitoring, is less often seen in lone-parent than other households (Avenevoli et al., 1999).

Most of the studies that report these findings are based on cross-sectional comparisons of intact and lone-parent families. However, it is not clear from cross-sectional comparisons whether inadequate parenting arises as a result of the stresses of separation and parenting alone, or whether separated mothers still displayed poor parenting when they were in partnerships. Some longitudinal studies have found that women who subsequently separated showed high levels of negative behaviour and low levels of control of their children *before* the separation (Hetherington et al., 1999). This may reflect the fact that partnerships deteriorate some time before parents part and conflict is often present as a lead-up to separation, so that reduced parenting skills may reflect the stress of parents in the lead-up to the separation. Family transitions are, though, usually accompanied by a deterioration in parenting quality (DeGarmo and Forgatch, 1999), whether they be from intact to lone-parent households, or from lone-parent to stepfamily formation. This suggests the significant impact of stresses associated specifically with the transitions from one family form to another, such as moving house and neighbourhoods, and economic change. Some time after a transition, the quality of parenting usually returns to levels similar to those before separation, although conflict between mothers and children in lone-parent

households may persist (Hetherington and Clingempeel, 1992).

Parenting by Non-residential Parents

In the majority of situations, non-residential parents are fathers. For many children, fathers are completely absent from their lives after divorce, so they do not experience parenting of any kind from them (Seltzer, 1991). Increasingly, however, fathers are remaining in contact with their children and there are two main factors that are likely to influence this increase in contact. One is the payment of child support, which has become institutionalized in most countries. There is a positive association between payment of child support and contact with children (Seltzer, 1991; Arditti, 1992) although the direction of this relationship is not clear. For some men, the fact that they contribute economically to their children's upbringing may lead them to demand more contact. On the other hand, fathers who want to be involved with their children may be more likely to pay child support. The second factor is the increasing incidence of joint custody for children. By definition, this means that fathers with shared custody are more likely than those without legal or residential custody to have regular contact with their children.

Contact does not automatically mean that fathers are involved in parenting their children. For many, contact means entertainment in the form of movies, playgrounds, and take-away food. In practice it is difficult for non-residential parents to be heavily involved unless their children stay with them regularly so that active parenting skills are called upon and developed in a manner appropriate to children's age and gender. To the extent that parents *are* involved with their children's lives and can provide both support and monitoring, their children benefit (Amato and Gilbreth, 1999). Non-residential mothers are more likely than non-residential fathers to be involved in the lives of their children (Gunnoe, 1993), something that can be an important challenge for stepmothers, as discussed below.

Men as Lone Parents

Boys, and older children are most likely to live with their fathers (Australian Bureau of Statistics, 1991; Maccoby and Mnookin, 1992; Cancian and Meyer, 1998). Perhaps because fathers are a minority of lone residential parents, there is little research that examines their parenting. Fathers themselves report good relations with their children and fewer problems than lone mothers after separation (Furstenberg, 1988). None the less, one in four lone fathers say they feel uncomfortable in that role (DeMaris and Greif, 1997). This may be because men often gain custody as a result of problematic mother–child relationships, maternal mental health, or problems with a mother's new partner. The circumstances under which men come to be lone parents, therefore, are often associated with difficult events that may add stress to their parenting efforts. In general, lone fathers have better economic resources but fewer social supports than lone mothers (Downey, 1994), reflecting more general gender differences. The stresses on their ability to parent will be more likely to be personal and social, than economic.

Parenting in Stepfamilies

When a stepfamily is formed, several changes in family dynamics occur that call for considerable adaptation by adults and children. From one perspective, it might be anticipated that in re-partnering, a lone mother is improving the situation for her children. Household income rises (McLanahan and Sandfur, 1994), alleviating economic stress that is often associated with poor parenting (Simons, 1996). Re-partnering also means that a second adult who is another potential parenting figure is present, or at least provides a source of support for the first parent. However, there are also some challenges to be faced that might mitigate these advantages, principally the adaptation of existing relationships to the changed situations, and the establishment of new ones.

Parenting by Mothers in Stepfather Families

Parenting and parent–child relationships are often poor in the period after a stepfamily household is formed, probably because of the adaptations required. In the early stages of stepfamily formation, mothers in stepfamilies report being more negative and less positive in interactions with their children (Bray and Berger, 1993; Dunn et al., 1998). They are more likely to show disengaged parenting, typified by low levels of support and control, than those in first-marriage families (Hetherington and Clingempeel, 1992).

Interactions, of course, are two-way, and children have been found to display negative behaviour toward their mothers soon after stepfamily formation (Vuchinich et al., 1991; Hetherington and Clingempeel, 1992; Bray and Berger, 1993). The quality of parent–child

relationships is determined, therefore, not just by the behaviour and attitudes of mothers, but also by the behaviour of their children who, in the case of stepfamilies in the early stages, may be negative and difficult.

Several factors are important here, however. One is the time since the stepfamily formed. In families that have been established for several years, parenting is of much the same quality as that shown in first-marriage families (Hetherington et al., 1999). The changes and disruptions associated with early life in a stepfamily appear to contribute to a lowering of parenting standards because of the changes called for from all family members and the depletion of energy for parenting in adults, as they establish their own new relationship. The quality of parenting tends to return in time either to levels shown before re-partnering or to those in first-marriage families.

A second factor is the age of children at the time of re-partnering. Relationships between mothers and young children appear to be comparatively resilient, settling down to function well over time. This may be because of the relative dependence of younger children in comparison with adolescents, and their readiness to accept the presence of another adult in the family. However, those families in which children are older, and particularly if they are early adolescents, are more fraught. For these young people, issues of developing autonomy from parental authority, peer relationships, and burgeoning sexuality make it more difficult to adjust to the changes in their family structure and dynamics. Parent–child relationships and parenting may never be restored to the same levels of good functioning as those of adolescents and parents in first-marriage families, and in one study, by the age of 15 years, one-third of boys and one-quarter of girls had disengaged from their stepfamily households (Hetherington, 1993).

A third factor is the gender of the child. Girls whose mothers re-partner have more fraught relationships with their mothers than do boys. It has been suggested that this is because a girl and her lone mother form a particularly close relationship, which is disrupted by the intrusion into their lives of another person who absorbs much of the mother's attention and detracts from the mother–daughter relationship. Boys, on the other hand, may benefit from the presence of a male adult in the household and there is some inferential support for this view, as they are likely to have experienced difficult relationships with their mothers in lone-parent households (Hetherington, 1993). It may be that the new family constellation eases the mother–son relationship.

A fourth factor relates to the particular aspect of parenting being considered. A recent study using panel data from the National Survey of Families and Households in the US found that when lone mothers re-partnered they showed less harsh discipline techniques, and their children reported closer mother–child relationships than when their mother had been single (Thomson et al., 2001). Supervision of the child, however, did not improve with re-partnering or remarriage, perhaps because the associated residential changes disrupts or reduces monitoring by parents.

Parenting by Stepfathers

Men who move into parenting roles in relation to their partners' children face the task of building relationships with young people to whom they are not biologically related. The children usually have a non-resident father who is more or less involved in their lives, but the day-to-day parenting falls to their mother and their stepfather. There are several potential disadvantages. First, stepfather and stepchildren have not shared the infancy and early childhood of the children, the time when shared histories are established and children and adults adapt to each other. Second, children may resent the intrusion of another adult into their lives in a parenting role. Third, they may see their stepfather as competition for their mother's attentions. And fourth, children often have a biological father whom they regard as their 'proper' father. How, then, do stepfathers parent their stepchildren?

Like mothers in stepfamilies, they are less likely than fathers in intact families to monitor children's behaviour (Hetherington and Clingempeel, 1992; Voydanoff et al., 1994; Hetherington et al., 1999). Some studies suggest that, compared with fathers in intact families, stepfathers show high levels of warmth (Vuchinich et al., 1991). Stepfathers, therefore, are likely to engage in 'permissive' parenting, that is, high levels of warmth and low levels of control. Although it is generally accepted that authoritative (high warmth, high control) parenting is optimal for children in all family structures, those studies that have examined parenting in stepfamilies have usually not included permissive parenting, as a typology. In one that did, family happiness and the quality of the stepchild–step-parent relationships were highest in families where stepfathers were high in warmth and low in control or monitoring (Crosbie-Burnett and Giles-Sims, 1994). This finding makes sense in light of the fact that the majority of children, especially adolescents, in stepfamilies regard their stepfather as a friend rather than as a parent (Buchanan et al., 1996; Gorrell Barnes et al., 1998). Permissive parenting, then, may be optimal for stepfathers, although it is likely that it will be most successful where mothers are authoritative parents so that monitoring is available for children from at least one parent.

Parenting in Stepmother Families

Remarkably little research has taken place that examines the parenting by fathers in stepmother families, probably because as a group they are a small minority of stepfamilies, and because fathers' new partners usually assume primary parenting. We can assume, though, that men who have been lone parents before re-partnering will remain in active parenting roles vis-à-vis their children, particularly in comparison with stepfathers.

It was noted earlier that non-residential mothers often remain involved in their children's lives. They stay in telephone and written contact, and take a direct monitoring role more than non-residential fathers do (Thompson, 1994; Hetherington and Henderson, 1997; Stewart, 1999). This makes the task of being a stepmother somewhat difficult if she takes a major parenting role in the family (Ferri and Smith, 1998). There is little doubt, too, that the continuing spectre of the wicked stepmother exacerbates the challenges faced by women put into this difficult position. Furthermore, stepmothers are often childless when they come into the family so that they take on the parenting of someone else's children with little or no experience.

It is not surprising, then, that the little we know about stepmother families suggests that parenting by stepmothers is difficult. They have reported being less involved with stepchildren both positively and negatively (Thompson et al., 1992) and children in stepmother families do not ease their task. They are less likely to be satisfied with the degree of closeness with stepmothers than with stepfathers (Funder, 1996) and more likely to dislike their stepmother than children are to dislike their stepfather (Gorell Barnes et al., 1998). So stepmothers are often in difficult situations where they are expected to be a primary parent yet face resistance from stepchildren. Stepfathers, in contrast, can be more peripheral in the lives of stepchildren since their partner is usually in the primary parenting role. It is perhaps not surprising, then, that Coleman and Ganong (1997) reported that 'many stepmothers were dissatisfied enough with their role as residential or non-residential stepmother that they would advise women against marrying men who have children from previous relationships.'

Parenting after Multiple Transitions

As we have seen, parenting is usually compromised as parents traverse transitions across several family structures (DeGarmo and Forgatch, 1999), since the distress and disruption accompanying a separation and re-formation of a household detracts from parents' abilities to maintain optimal standards of support and monitoring (Capaldi and Patterson, 1991). Adolescents whose parents have had several partnership transitions report that their parents provide less supervision, show lower levels of acceptance, and engage in more conflict than those whose parents who had few or no separations (Kurdek et al., 1995). In families where there have been few transitions, positive relationships between parents and children are more likely and negative relationships less likely (Dunn et al., 2000). Not surprisingly, multiple transitions raise the risks for children of adverse outcomes in the medium and long term, including high levels of offending (Fergusson et al., 1992), poorer educational outcomes (Kurdek et al., 1995) and producing a child during adolescence (Wu and Martinson, 1993).

Parenting in Adoptive Families

The process of securing a child for adoption can be a frustrating experience that puts stresses on relationships. However, in some ways adoptive parents may have an advantage in that they are likely to be of comparatively higher socio-economic status, and to have had considerable time to prepare for being parents since their decision to do so is, by definition, a deliberate one. Furthermore the shared tribulations of facing infertility and remaining a couple (because some do not), and preparing for adoption may strengthen, rather than weaken, their relationship. Indeed, in an Israeli study of the transition to parenthood by adoptive couples, it was found that in comparison with parents of naturally conceived babies, adoptive parents adapted and coped better a few months into parenthood (Levy-Schiff et al., 1991).

There is a remarkably persistent mythology about 'bonding' that suggests not having contact with their children antenatally and perinatally confers a disadvantage on adoptive parents. However, the notion of bonding derives from animal models and is not supported by research with human parent–infant pairs. Far more crucial is the establishment of secure attachment relationships, and these do not start to develop until the infant is several months old. For infant adoptions, then, the lack of opportunity to 'bond' in the antenatal and neonatal period should not in itself be a disadvantage for subsequent parent–child relationships and parenting in general. In a study that compared attachment classifications at 11–18 months of age, no differences were found in groups of non-adopted and adopted infants of the same race (Singer et al., 1985).

A potentially significant aspect of adoptive families is that parents and children are not genetically related, and parents in particular know from the start that their children are not biological products of themselves. One predictor of parent–child relationships in adoptive families is the degree to which parents feel compatible with their children (Grotevant and Kohler, 1999). Compatibility involves feeling harmony with each other, and this implies communication at a variety of levels. As children get older, the perspectives on compatibility of both parents and children may become more important. Adolescents become more aware of themselves in relation to others and understand more fully the potential significance for their sense of themselves of the lack of biological relationship with their parents. So the importance of feeling compatible will increase as issues of personal identity become more salient in adolescence.

Another aspect of parenting particularly, but not exclusively, in adoptive families is the extent to which parents feel a sense of entitlement to parent their children (Cohen et al., 1996). Although they have legal rights as parents, this does not mean that they will necessarily feel psychologically or emotionally entitled, and this may affect their ability to monitor and discipline their children. Cohen et al. (1996, p. 442) suggest that entitlement 'refers to the parents' presumption that they are indeed the child's parents with attendant rights to command authority and set expectations' and they have operationalized the concept into four factors: parenting doubts, distance, discipline success, and discipline comfort.

The most notable findings of Cohen and colleagues were the few differences that existed between adoptive and non-adoptive families on these factors. They found that distance was the factor most likely to predict difficulties and subsequent referral of their children for clinical help. Distance encompassed feelings in parents of rejection by the child, and feelings that the child did not feel, or may not in the future feel, like part of the family. It resembles, then, the notion of compatibility or similarity in that it involves mutual ease and good communication.

Although there has been no empirical investigation of the links amongst feelings of entitlement, parenting styles, and outcomes for children, parenting that involves high levels of emotional support but low levels of monitoring ('permissive' parenting) is linked with poor impulse control in children, low levels of persistence and, in adolescence, excessive reliance on peers and less involvement in academic pursuits (Baumrind, 1991; Lamborn et al., 1991; Kurdek and Fine, 1994). Not feeling entitled to monitor and discipline children at the same time as loving them suggests a form of permissive parenting. We might thus expect that if adopted children are more likely to be parented this way, then they will show higher levels of problem behaviour both concurrently and later. But overall this is not the case, reflecting the finding that 'lack of entitlement' is not confined to adoptive parents.

It is widely accepted now that secrecy about the fact that a child is adopted is ill-advised, and parents must face and handle sensitively the task of telling their children that they are adopted. Most do this around the age of three or four years, and often use stories as vehicles for explaining the concepts. Children are usually pragmatic and accept their adopted status; however, when they reach adolescence issues of identity arise that lead them to ponder their biological origins. Parents of adopted adolescents often find themselves dealing with issues and potential conflicts beyond those that normally accompany adolescence.

It is at this age that children may seek specific knowledge of their biological parents in order to determine their contribution to their identity in both biological and psychological domains. For some, curiosity about physical and personality resemblance leads them to want to find and meet their birth parents as a way of giving better definition to their burgeoning self-concept. For some adoptive parents, their children's mission is seen as a threat to the rapidly changing relationship that they have with their young people; they fear that their children may want to abandon them in favour of biological parents. Most parents realize, however, that the likelihood of adolescent children changing loyalties is low and that finding out about their genetic origins is an important process of self-discovery and self-understanding.

Age at Adoption

Unlike former times, children who are beyond infancy are being increasingly adopted as neonates become less available to adoptive parents. They include those who have special needs, and those whose biological parents have become or been deemed unable to care for them. For these children, there has been a life before adoption in another family or institution, so that the transition to being adopted is qualitatively different from those adopted in infancy before the child's memory and early learning patterns and relationships are established. Issues of attachment and sometimes abuse or neglect become salient for older children. Although there is evidence that, at least for those who were 11 years old or younger at the time of adoption, successful adaptation is possible (Hodges and Tizard, 1989), parenting of children adopted beyond infancy entails extra challenges for parents. Their earlier experiences of forming relationships are likely to be mixed and by definition unsatisfactory, leading to probable social and behavioural difficulties throughout childhood and in adolescence (Howe, 1996). The older they are at the time of first living with their adoptive parents, the greater the difficulties are likely to be.

Open Adoption

In the last three to four decades, adoptions have become increasingly open, that is, information about and contact between adopted children and their birth parents have been allowed and encouraged. This trend has been viewed with alarm by some adoptive parents who have been concerned that such knowledge and communication might lead to compromised relationships between themselves and their adopted children. However, pressure for more open adoptions has come from the experiences of adopted children who, in adolescence, seek knowledge of their genetic as well as their social heritage in constructing a life story and full identity for themselves.

What is the impact of such openness on adoption? In one study that addressed this, Grotevant et al. (1994) compared adoptive families with four levels of openness on measures reflecting the concerns of advocates for and against open adoption. They included aspects of adoptive parents' feelings about the adoption and their child, and their attitudes to the birth parents. The results are strikingly supportive of openness. Parents in fully disclosed adoptive groups were significantly more likely to communicate fully with their child about the adoption; to show empathy for the concerns of their adopted child; to be more empathetic toward birth parents; and to acknowledge the child's interest in his or her background. They were also less likely to fear the reclaiming of the child by the birthmother, and (for fathers) to feel a greater sense of permanence about their child.

Finally, their narratives about adoption were judged to be more coherent if the adoption was fully disclosed than if it was confidential.

Grotevant et al. point out that there are two main domains that are important in these findings. The first is the notion of 'shared fates' between the adoptive family and the birth family, linked by the child. Not only birth parents, but also grandparents and siblings, are likely to make up the constellation of the birth family contacts, especially as the adopted child reaches adolescence and seeks out the less immediate family members. Second, the concepts of entitlement, permanence and coherence about their roles suggest that adoptive parents can and do take on that identity, rather than pretending to be biological parents. A caution about the optimistic findings in this study, however, is that the children were between the ages of 4 and 12 years at the time it was carried out. A crucial question lies in the possible differences in the children's well-being and family dynamics as they move into adolescence, when more challenging issues of identity become paramount. On the basis of these findings the open and supportive parenting style practised by the adopting parents is likely to have more positive outcomes than the alternative, although it is still not known whether or not it is beneficial for adolescents.

Transracial Adoption

For children adopted from one culture into another, there are additional issues of cultural difference between them and their parents, especially if they are beyond infancy at the time of adoption and have significant experiences of their birth culture. Physical differences may well be apparent between parents and children. Singer et al. (1985) noted that infants adopted transracially were more likely than those adopted intraracially to be insecurely attached at 18 months old; however, this did not appear to be because of lack of social support or problematic pre-placement history. They noted that most studies of inter-racially adopted children indicate good adjustment. Rather, they believed that the higher rates of insecure attachment in transracially adopted children occurred because it took more time for parents to adapt to infants of a different race, but that these initial differences became less serious.

There is remarkably little research that compares parenting by adoptive parents directly with that of biological parents. This is perhaps because it is only relatively recently that adoptive families have become more visible with the reduction in confidentiality and closed adoption. Some studies of children born by artificial reproductive technologies have included groups of adoptive families (e.g. Golombok et al., 1999, 2001). These find few or no differences in parenting practices between adoptive parents and biological parents on a range of measures that include emotional involvement, parental warmth and dependability, and affection.

Parenting in Foster Families

For reasons discussed earlier, several factors suggest that parenting in foster families will be more difficult than in intact families. A significant factor is the past history of the child. If she or he is beyond the neonatal period then issues of attachment arise, since attachments are typically formed with care-givers from about six months of age onward. Foster parents of children who are beyond infancy, then, forge relationships with children who have experienced the loss of at least one important person in their lives with whom they have had a primary relationship, even if that relationship was insecure or unsatisfactory. Furthermore, insecure relationships may have been accompanied by inadequate care and neglect. However, at least one study has found that infants placed in foster care between birth and 20 months of age form secure attachments with foster parents at the same rate as biological parent–infant pairs (Dozier et al., 2001). In these early months, the role of age in determining attachment formation is not clear. Younger infants (6 to 12 months) seem to stabilize their attachment behaviour relatively quickly in comparison with older (12 to 20 months) infants (Stovall and Dozier, 2000), but three months after fostering, these age differences are not apparent in the security of attachments formed.

Although there is little evidence available about attachment formation in children fostered beyond two years of age, we might expect that as memory processes become more sophisticated and experience of poor parenting is longer, so too will difficulties increase. Indeed, rejection by birth parents (which presumably reflects a poor relationship) has been found to be a major predictor of the breakdown of permanent placement in unrelated families of children in middle childhood (Rushton et al., 2000).

The second major factor in parenting in foster families is the constellation of attitudes and expectations held by the parents themselves, including impermanence and the consequent possible lack of emotional investment. In the studies of early-fostered children mentioned above, parents' 'state of mind' about their own attachment experiences proved to be salient for the kind of attachments formed between fostered infants and themselves. Those who were autonomous, or secure in their accounts of themselves in regard to attachments, were more likely than those who were non-autonomous to form secure attachments with their infants. Significantly, foster parents are less likely to provide nurturance to babies who do not elicit it (unlike most biological mothers), and fostered infants themselves appear to have low expectations of nurturance. Hence the relationship is likely to be comparatively low-key in terms of its emotional involvement. In his study of late-placed children, Rushton found that half of the parents reported difficulties with being emotionally responsive to their children, although only one in five had problems with monitoring and discipline. It appears, then, that warmth and emotional support may be comparatively lacking between foster parents and children, probably because of difficult parent–child relationships rather than particular characteristics of foster parents.

Overall, parenting in foster families presents potent difficulties for parents and children. Even toddlers show subtle differences in their behaviour and expectations of nurturing, and older children, especially if they have experienced adversity, come to the parent–child relationship with anxieties about relating and often have behaviour problems as a result of their experiences. Foster parents too have low expectations of permanence and of the possibilities of establishing close and enduring relationships with their children. The presence in foster families of unrelated siblings also contributes to the challenges faced in parenting in foster families.

Parenting in Families Formed by Artificial Reproductive Technologies (ART)

Perhaps because of the complexities anticipated by the formation of families by ART, there is a small but impressive body of recent and current research from several countries that is addressing the experience and well-being of these families as they increase in number. In Australia, a prospective study of women pregnant through IVF treatment found high levels of anxiety during pregnancy, and anticipation of infant difficulty, in comparison with a control group of naturally conceived infants (McMahon et al., 1997). IVF infants were perceived as comparatively difficult by their mothers when their infants were 4 and 12 months of age (Gibson

et al., 1998). However, the authors note that these anxieties were not unrealistic given the high risks of failure inherent in such pregnancies and, significantly, they did not lead to compromised mother–infant interaction at 12 months of age (McMahon et al., 1995). Attachments between mothers and infants at one year were as likely to be secure in the IVF group as in the naturally conceived group (Gibson et al., 2000).

Parent–child relationships in families with preschool children born by IVF in Belgium (Colpin et al., 1995) and Holland (van Balen, 1996) have been compared with those of naturally conceived parent–child pairs. No differences were found in the Belgian group on measures of parent–child relationship or parental psychosocial functioning. Dutch IVF mothers reported comparatively *higher* levels of emotional involvement and parenting pleasure, and saw their children as less obstinate and more sociable than did the mothers of naturally conceived children. They also reported low levels of parenting stress. Taiwanese mothers and their three- to seven-year-old children have also been examined on measures of parenting and family functioning (Hahn and DiPietro, 2001). Teacher ratings of these families indicated that IVF mothers showed greater warmth, but not over-protectiveness or intrusiveness toward their children. Teachers also reported fewer behaviour problems in IVF than in naturally conceived children. Mothers themselves reported high feelings of protectiveness toward their children, but apparently these feelings did not translate into over-protective behaviour.

These findings clearly contradict the pessimistic predictions that parenting in ART families will be compromised by experiences of infertility treatment, complicated genetic relationships, and distorted parental perceptions of their much-wanted children. Their enjoyment of parenting and their positive perceptions of their children indicate that their parenting practices are likely to be optimal.

These cross-sectional studies are supported by the findings of a longitudinal study of children born by IVF, adopted children, and naturally conceived children that has been carried out by Golombok and her colleagues. The first assessment when the children were between four and eight years old (Golombok et al., 1995) found that mothers of IVF children were warmer, more emotionally involved, and experienced less parenting stress than mothers of naturally conceived children. Adoptive parents were similar to IVF parents, leading the authors to conclude that a strong desire for children is more important in relation to good parenting than a genetic relationship.

When the children were 12 years old, these families were examined again and perceptions of children, parents and teachers obtained (Golombok et al., 2001). Comparisons were made between groups who had experienced infertility (IVF and adopted versus naturally conceived) and between IVF and adopted groups. At this stage, parental behaviour was somewhat different. Mothers in the infertility groups were found to be less sensitively responding to their adolescents than mothers in the natural conception group, and fathers and mothers in the adoptive families showed less warmth toward their teenagers than those in the IVF families. On the other hand, mothers who had experienced infertility were seen by their children as more dependable than those in the natural conception group. In comparisons of control and discipline, however, adolescents in families who had experienced infertility saw their parents as less likely to discuss issues with them than those who were naturally conceived. On measures of child and parent affection and emotional involvement, no differences amongst groups were found. Measures of disputes, discipline and aggression showed no differences.

The few differences that were found, overall, were both positive and negative but suggest that as adolescence approaches, parental behaviour may change in subtle ways. It is impossible to determine from these studies whether these arise from changes in adolescent behaviour and perceptions or from changes in parental attitudes. The children were in very early adolescence, and we do not know whether differences in parenting might escalate or diminish as they become older. As with adopted children (and young people in general), issues of identity become increasingly salient. For ART teenagers, their biological identity is particularly complicated.

The findings suggest, overall, that method of conception is not a strong factor in determining parenting practices and children's responses. Support for this conclusion comes from comparisons that have been made amongst three- to eight-year-old children born by donor insemination and egg donation in order to examine degrees of genetic relatedness (Golombok et al., 1999). Again, few differences were found, and those that were found favoured families in which there was no genetic link between mothers and children.

To date, then, studies in a variety of countries using a range of measures and informants indicate that there are few systematic differences in family functioning amongst families formed by ART and those either adopted or naturally conceived. This in turn indicates the probable

insignificance of this variable for parenting practices. Predictions of over-protection and unreasonable expectations of children are not borne out by the evidence and, indeed, ART parents appear to be less stressed by parenting and warmer and happier as parents than those with naturally conceived children. Van Balen suggests that 'a coherent picture arises: there are many similarities between IVF families and normally fertile families, but when differences are found, the situation appears to be better in IVF families' (van Balen, 1998).

However, caution is necessary since we have no studies that follow children into middle and late adolescence, a period when questions of identity become paramount and when family cohesion usually decreases. In stepfamilies, parent–adolescent relationships often become more vexed than in intact families (Hetherington, 1993) and, for possibly different reasons, this may happen also in ART families. We have yet to learn whether openness about young people's genetic origins will affect their acceptance and adjustment toward their varied inheritance as they come to terms with the existence of a variety of parents including genetic, carrying and nurturing fathers and mothers. In the meantime, research is encouraging in providing evidence for the capacities of ART parents to provide supportive family environments for their children.

WHAT CAN WE CONCLUDE?

It is important to remember that even within the same grouping, such as stepfamilies or adoptive families, there are likely to be variations that are disguised by the overall findings. Nevertheless, the overall findings are the best bases we have for making evidence-based comments about reconstituted and surrogate families.

It is apparent that parenting in lone-parent and stepfamilies compares adversely with that in intact families. However, these differences are notable mainly in the early phases after the transition from the previous family structure, and even out as family situations become more stable – usually about two years later.

Families that have experienced multiple transitions are particularly at risk in this regard. The little evidence we have regarding foster families suggests that parent–child relationships may be somewhat fraught, because of parental expectations and the child's past history.

There is substantial support, though, for concluding that at least in childhood the quality of parenting in adoptive and especially in ART families compares favourably with that seen in naturally conceived children and their parents. This is despite their common experiences of infertility, and the partial or absent biological relationships between parents and children. These findings lead to some perhaps surprising conclusions.

First, family structure *in itself* is not predictive of parenting quality. The differences where they do exist between lone-parent, step-parent and intact family households largely disappear over time, and are accounted for by other factors such as the disruption associated with transitions and the formation of new household structures, conflict, a reduction in household income, but not with the presence or absence of two biological parents of both sexes. The evidence from open adoption, too, suggests that the traditional structure of nuclear families is in itself unimportant for parenting. Children are able to encompass several parenting figures into their lives successfully, as they do in stepfamilies and in open adoption. The key to their success, however, seems to lie in the ability of adults to manage their own relationships well. An important caveat here is that these findings apply predominantly to the childhood years. The situation may be different for adolescents, as has been indicated throughout this chapter.

Children's perspectives on families are informative in this regard. When asked whether particular groupings of individuals constitute families, they are remarkably accepting and pragmatic, with a considerable majority seeing lone-parent (whether mother or father), stepfamily groupings, families with gay and lesbian parents, and cohabiting parents and children as legitimate families (Gilby and Pederson, 1982; O'Brien et al., 1996; Anyan and Pryor, 2002). Table 8.2 shows the levels of endorsement of family types by 232 adolescents in a recent New Zealand study. So it is adults and communities that are likely to have problems with non-traditional family households and to be the sources of stigma that might have an impact on the well-being of children in these families.

Second, biology and genetic relationships do not appear to be important predictors of parenting. Adoptive parents, especially those who adopted their children in infancy, and ART parents are quite as competent, involved and committed to their children as are biological parents. Where differences exist, they are usually in favour of ART parents. Although this should come as no surprise when we consider the long historical view of families and parenthood and the variation in religious and social structures, it does not support a view of parenting that is often applied to troubled step-parent–stepchild relationships, that biological

Table 8.2 *Percentage of adolescents endorsing groupings as a family (from Anyan and Pryor, 2002)*

	Per cent
Married parents and children	99.6
Lone mother with children	92.6
Cohabiting parents and children	88.4
Lone father with children	86.6
Grandparents	86.0
Aunt, uncle and cousin	86.0
Two women and a child	80.0
Family without love	64.3
Non-resident father and children	62.8
Married couple, no children	62.1
Non-resident mother and children	56.3
Lone mother's partner and children	54.3
Residential family friend	49.3

relationships are of paramount importance (see e.g. Daly and Wilson, 1998). The belief that a genetic relationship is important for good parenting clearly does not apply.

What, then, *does* matter? The evidence points to family members' histories of relationships and change as being central to the quality of parent–child relationships. For parents, transitions present stresses and challenges that sap their emotional and other resources, and jeopardize their ability to parent consistently, and the evidence is clear that parenting deteriorates during and after structural change in a household. Moreover, the number of relationship changes parents themselves have experienced before their current partnership is linked with the quality of their parent–child relationships, and with the relationships their partners have with their children (Dunn et al., 2000). The findings discussed here of reduced quality of parenting in the initial phases for lone-parent and step-parent families, and the significant problems faced by children whose parents have had several transitions, support the conclusion that adult transitions are a significant risk factor for their children, presumably through their impact on parents' own state and parenting practices.

For children, transitions often mean changes in relationships, with the loss of some relationships, and the sometimes-unwanted acquisition of others. For children in foster families and those who are adopted after infancy, their history of previous relationships and adverse parenting are significant in shaping their relationships with their new parents. A central mechanism is likely to be the loss of significant attachment figures, especially fathers, mothers or both. When these losses are multiple then children's abilities to form secure relationships with parenting figures are undermined.

The major corollary of this is that stability of relationships is a crucial aspect of parenting and well-being for children. From the children's perspective, the *quality* of the relationships they have with parents and others is of course important, and there are instances where a relationship is best severed. However, the avoidance of loss or diminution, where possible and appropriate, is clearly in children's best interests. For parents, stability of supportive relationships and the absence of change and loss buttress their ability to parent effectively. The fact that parenting practices settle down in lone-parent and stepfamilies over time indicates that stability increases the ability of both adults and children to sustain reasonable parent–child relationships.

Developmental Considerations

It is apparent that the age of children is a major factor in considering parenting practices in the diverse families considered in this chapter. The capacities, cognitions and needs of children at different ages and stages call for developmentally sensitive approaches to parenting. There is also the cumulative impact of earlier experiences as children grow up that needs to be considered. In particular, unsatisfactory or abusive early relationships can affect the ways in which children form subsequent relationships in their lives.

Young children are especially vulnerable to the making and breaking of significant relationships. Their ability to trust themselves and others in relational matters is substantially established in the early years. Sensitive, responsive parenting is essential to the establishment of trust and security, and although insecure relationships are not necessarily predictive of later difficulties, repeated experiences of insecure and disrupted attachments can put them at risk for later difficulties with relationships and self-concept. In the early years, children are typically egocentric in their dealings with the world. This confers the risk of self-blame when things go wrong, a phenomenon often noted when parents separate.

In middle childhood the establishment of friendships with peers becomes paramount. Poor peer relations are associated with both difficulties at home, including those associated with poor parenting, and with unsatisfactory functioning, such as low self-esteem. Hence children in this age group thrive in peer-related and school-related activities when their parents are able to provide effective parenting at home.

Adolescence, as we have seen repeatedly in this chapter, is an especially vulnerable time for identity and self-concept. Cognitive changes mean that teenagers are able to imagine alternatives to the ways they and the world might be, and to think in abstract ways. There is typically an intense focus on questions of who they are as physical and psychological changes occur. For these reasons, it is perhaps not surprising that there is some evidence that adopted adolescents and their families face challenges in their relationships (Howe, 1996), although as yet the experiences of adolescents in ART families have not been examined. For those adopted and ART children who are aware of their different origins, questions of genetic identity will become important, as they enter adolescence, in regard to their physical changes, their personalities and other characteristics.

A second characteristic of adolescence is the emergence of the need for autonomy from parents. In stepfamilies, parent–adolescent relationships deteriorate to a greater extent than they do in intact families (Hetherington and Jodl, 1994) and this is especially the case if children are going through adolescence when their stepfamily is formed. Many of them never establish a satisfactory relationship with a step-parent. For these young people, the pressure to accept the parenting of an adult who has not been a part of their earlier lives comes up against their developing autonomy, creating disruption in family relationships. It is no coincidence that adolescents in stepfamilies are more likely to leave home, and to leave home because of conflict, than those in lone-parent or intact families (Kiernan, 1992).

Implications for Parenting Practice

In several ways these findings are cause for optimism. If structural conformity and biological relationships were necessary aspects of good parenting, then the rapidly increasing diversity of family forms would be alarming. However, families formed by ART, stepfamilies, and adoptive families are becoming increasingly numerous and the findings reported here suggest that such families have the potential to be, and in many cases are, robust and healthy environments for children. The major challenges for society are to reduce suspicion and stigmatization of 'different' families, and to find effective ways to promote stability in relationships for children.

This last point does not imply that dysfunctional or unhappy families should be discouraged from dissolving. It does mean, however, that although parents divorce each other, they do not or should not divorce their children. It also suggests that support for parents and parenting at the time of transitions such as separation and stepfamily formation is important. Help with relationships for families before they reach the stage of becoming irredeemable are also to be encouraged.

The task for parents in all families is to maintain practices that include love and support, monitoring and boundary setting, and promotion of healthy development. In families that are the result of structural transitions, such as lone-parent and stepfamilies, there are the added challenges of maintaining parenting throughout stressful events, and of minimizing instability. In lone-parent families, continuing contact, where appropriate (that is, when issues of abuse, for example, do not exist), with non-resident parents contributes to the stability of relationships for children and the sharing of the parenting load for parents. It is also important for both parents to maintain consistent monitoring and to co-operate as far as possible in order to avoid children 'playing parents off' against each other in areas of discipline. It is sometimes tempting to be lenient or inconsistent with children through feelings of guilt, or lack of energy, or fear of alienating them. Children also need reassurance that their parents have not and will not stop loving them even though they may have stopped loving each other.

The formation of a stepfamily is usually a second transition for children and their biological parents, and introduces a third parenting adult into the children's lives, at least potentially. The research evidence and clinical writing suggest that stepfathers parent best by being friendly, supportive, but relatively uninvolved in monitoring and discipline. Stepchildren prefer to view step-parents as friends rather than parents (Buchanan et al., 1996; Funder, 1996), especially if they are teenagers, and tend to resent attempts at control by stepfathers.

Although still sparse, the evidence suggests that in adoptive, foster and ART families openness about biological origins is helpful for parent–child relationships. Adolescents are less likely to face crises of identity if they have good social and biological information about all their parents. This suggests the importance of telling children early about their origins, and providing as much information as possible for them as they need it for developing full and satisfying self-concepts.

These considerations lead to the following conclusions for practice and policy:

- Families need support for parenting, especially in the early phases of transitions, such as separation and stepfamily formation.
- Foster families will benefit from advice and help in parenting children with histories of difficult relationships.

- Adoptive families need support and therapeutic help up to and beyond legal adoption, especially in situations of late adoption.
- It should not be assumed that families produced by artificial reproductive technologies will have difficulties in parenting or parent–child relationships.
- Openness with children about their biological origins appears to be advantageous, although there is no evidence yet either way for adolescents.
- Stability of relationships for children is of paramount importance. Where possible and appropriate, relationships with parents and extended kin should be maintained through separation, divorce and beyond.
- Families of adolescents may need help in accepting that adolescents may not be open to parenting from step-parents in their lives and may not form a close relationship with them at all.

AUTHOR'S VIEW

As family structures become more diverse, so too do parenting arrangements and practices. Children are parented by a wide variety of people, including same-sex couples, unrelated but committed adults, extended family members, older siblings, teachers and mentors. Attempts to curtail diversity are at best misguided and may lead at worst to the imposition of continuing misery on unhappy families, as in attempts to stop divorce or return to fault-based divorce. Social stigmatization of same-sex, adopting and step-families is similarly misguided and undermines families' efforts to find their own best ways of supporting their members. History tells us that nothing much has changed. We have merely found more ingenious ways to form families in order to adapt to the changes and demands we face. As secrecy becomes both less possible and less desirable, children and families deserve information, respect, and full support as they adapt and thrive.

Parenting, in its broadest sense, remains pivotal to the well-being of children and is the conduit through which most other factors impinge upon them. The major elements of unconditional love and respect, monitoring and boundary setting, and fostering good development, apply across all settings. Recognition and respect for the diversity of settings in which they are applied is essential if we are to socialize our children as well-functioning adults in a rapidly changing world. This means moving beyond limiting notions of family structure, biological imperatives and heterosexual presumptions, and facing the challenge of fostering the stability of individual families so that children and their parents can thrive.

REFERENCES

Amato, P. and Gilbreth, J.G. (1999) Nonresident fathers and children's well-being: A meta-analysis. *Journal of Marriage and the Family*, **61**(August), 557–73.

Ambert, A.-M. (2001) *The Effect of Children on Parents*, 2nd edition. Binghamton, NY: Haworth Press.

Anyan, S. and Pryor, J. (2002) What is in a family? Adolescent perceptions. *Children & Society*, **16**, 1–12.

Aquilino, W. (1996) The life course of children born to unmarried mothers: childhood living arrangements and young adult outcomes. *Journal of Marriage and the Family*, **58**, 293–310.

Arditti, J.A. (1992) Factors related to custody, visitation, and child support for divorced fathers: an exploratory analysis. *Journal of Divorce & Remarriage*, **17**, 23–41.

Australian Bureau of Statistics (1991) Australia's one parent families. Canberra: Australian Bureau of Statistics.

Avenevoli, S., Sessa, F.M. and Steinberg, L. (1999) Family structure, parenting practices, and adolescent adjustment: an ecological examination. In Hetherington, E.M. (ed.) *Coping with Divorce, Single Parenting, and Remarriage. A Risk and Resiliency Perspective*. Mahwah, NJ: Lawrence Erlbaum, pp. 65–90.

Baumrind, D. (1991) Effective parenting during the early adolescent transition. In Cowan, P.A. and Hetherington, E.M. (eds) *Family Transitions*. Hillsdale, NJ: Lawrence Erlbaum, pp. 111–63.

Bowlby, J. (1969) *Attachment and Loss, Vol. 1. Attachment*. London: Hogarth.

Bowlby, J. (1977) The making and breaking of affectional bonds. *British Journal of Psychiatry*, **130**, 201–10.

Bray, J.H. and Berger, S.H. (1993) Nonresidential parent–child relationships following divorce and remarriage. In Depner, C.E. and Bray, J. (eds) *Nonresidential Parenting. New Vistas in Family Living*. Newbury Park: Sage, pp. 156–81.

Buchanan, C.M., Maccoby, E.E. and Dornbusch, S.M. (1996) *Adolescents after Divorce*. Cambridge, MA: Harvard University Press.

Bumpass, L.L., Sweet, J.A. and Castro-Martin, T.C. (1990) Changing pattern of remarriage. *Journal of Marriage and the Family*, **52**, 747–56.

Cancian, M. and Meyer, D. (1998) Who gets custody? *Demography*, **35**(2), 147–57.

Capaldi, D.M. and Patterson, G.R. (1991) Relation of parental transitions to boys' adjustment problems: I. A linear hypothesis. II. Mothers at risk for transitions and unskilled parenting. *Developmental Psychology*, **27**, 489–504.

Cohen, N.J., Coyne, J.C. and Duvall, J.C. (1996) Parents' sense of 'entitlement' in adoptive and nonadoptive families. *Family Process*, **35**, 441–56.

Coleman, M. and Ganong, L.H. (1997) Stepfamilies from the stepfamily's perspective. *Marriage & Family Review*, **26**(1/2), 107–21.

Colpin, H., Demyttenaere, K. and Vandemeulebroecke, L. (1995) New reproductive technology and the family: the parent–child relationship following *in vitro* fertilisation. *Journal of Child Psychology and Psychiatry*, **36**(8), 1429–41.

Crosbie-Burnett, M. and Giles-Sims, J. (1994) Adolescent adjustment and stepparenting styles. *Family Relations*, **43**, 394–9.

Daly, M. and Wilson, M. (1998) *The Truth about Cinderella: A Darwinian View of Parental Love*. London: Weidenfeld & Nicolson.

Deater-Deckard, K. and Dunn, J. (1999) Multiple risks and adjustment in young children growing up in different family settings. In Hetherington, E.M. (ed.) *Coping with Divorce, Single Parenting, and Re-marriage*. Mahwah, NJ: Lawrence Erlbaum.

DeGarmo, D.S. and Forgatch, M.S. (1999) Contexts as predictors of changing maternal parenting practices in diverse family structures. In Hetherington, E.M. (ed.) *Coping with Divorce, Single Parenting, and Re-marriage. A Risk and Resiliency Perspective*. Mahwah, NJ: Lawrence Erlbaum.

DeMaris, A. and Greif, G.L. (1997) Single custodial fathers and their children. In Hawkins, A.J. and Dollahite, D.C. (eds) *Generative Fathering. Beyond Deficit Perspectives*. Thousand Oaks, CA: Sage, pp. 134–46.

Douglas, G. and Murch, M. (2002) *The Role of Grandparents in Divorced Families*. Family Studies Research Centre, University of Wales.

Downey, D. (1994) The school performance of children from single-mother and single-father families: economic or interpersonal deprivation? *Journal of Family Issues*, **15**(1), 129–47.

Dozier, M., Chase Stovall, K., Albus, K.E. and Bates, B. (2001) Attachment for infants in foster care: the role of caregiver state of mind. *Child Development*, **72**(5), 1467–77.

Dunn, J., Deater-Deckard, K., Pickering, K. and O'Connor, T.G. (1998) Children's adjustment and prosocial behaviour in step-, single- and nonstep-family settings: findings from a community study. *Journal of Child Psychology and Psychiatry*, **39**(8), 1083–95.

Dunn, J., Davies, L.C., O'Connor, T.G. and Sturgess, W. (2000) Parents' and partners' life course and family experiences: links with parent–child relationships in different family settings. *Journal of Child Psychology and Psychiatry*, **41**(8), 955–68.

Emery, R.E. (1994) *Renegotiating Family Relationships. Divorce, Child Custody and Mediation*. New York: The Guilford Press.

Fergusson, D., Horwood, J. and Shannon, F. (1984) A proportional hazards model of family breakdown. *Journal of Marriage and the Family*, **46**, 539–49.

Fergusson, D., Horwood, L.J. and Lynskey, M.T. (1992) Family change, parental discord and early offending. *Journal of Child Psychology and Psychiatry*, **33**(6), 1059–75.

Ferri, E. and Smith, K. (1998) *Step-parenting in the 1990s*. London: Family Policy Studies Centre.

Freud, S. (1940) An outline of psychoanalysis. In Strachey, J. (ed.) *The Standard Edition of the Complete Psychological Works of Sigmund Freud*. London: Hogarth, pp. 137–207.

Funder, K. (1996) *Remaking Families*. Melbourne: Australian Institute of Family Studies.

Furstenberg, F.F. (1988) Child care after divorce and remarriage. In Hetherington, E.M. and Arasteh, J.D. (eds) *Impact of Divorce, Single Parenting, and Stepparenting on Children* Hillsdale, NJ: Lawrence Erlbaum, pp. 245–61.

Gibson, F.L., Ungerer, J.A., Leslie, G.I., Saunders, D.M. and Tennant, C. (1998) Development, behavior and temperament: a prospective study of infants conceived through in vitro fertilization. *Human Reproduction*, **13**, 1727–32.

Gibson, F.L., Ungerer, J.A., McMahon, C.A., Leslie, G.I. and Saunders, D.M. (2000) The mother–child relationship following in vitro fertilisation (IVF): infant attachment, responsivity, and maternal sensitivity. *Journal of Child Psychology and Psychiatry*, **41**(8), 1015–23.

Gibson, J. (1992) Non-custodial fathers and access patterns. Canberra: Family Court of Australia.

Gilby, R.L. and Pederson, D.R. (1982) The development of the child's concept of family. *Canadian Journal of Behavioral Sciences*, **14**, 111–21.

Golombok, S., Bhanji, F., Rutherford, T. and Winston, R. (1990) Psychological development of children of the new reproductive technologies: issues and a pilot study of children conceived by IVF. *Journal of Reproductive and Infant Psychology*, **8**, 37–43.

Golombok, S., Cook, R., Bish, A. and Murray, C. (1995) Families created by the new reproductive technologies: quality of parenting and social and emotional development of the children. *Child Development*, **66**, 285–98.

Golombok, S., Murray, C., Brinsden, P. and Abdalla, H. (1999) Social versus biological parenting: family functioning and the socioemotional development of children conceived by egg or sperm donation. *Journal of Child Psychology and Psychiatry*, **40**(4), 519–27.

Golombok, S., MacCallum, F. and Goodman, E. (2001) The 'test tube' generation: parent–child relationships and the psychological well-being of in vitro fertilization children at adolescence. *Child Development*, **72**(2), 599–608.

Gorrell Barnes, G., Thompson, P., Daniel, G. and Burchardt, N. (1998) *Growing Up in Stepfamilies*. Oxford: Clarendon Press.

Grotevant, H.D. and Kohler, J.K. (1999) Adoptive families. In Lamb, M. (ed.) *Parenting and Child Development in 'Nontraditional' Families*. Mahwah, NJ: Lawrence Erlbaum, pp. 161–90.

Grotevant, H.D., McRoy, R.G., Elde, C.L. and Fravel, D.L. (1994) Adoptive family system dynamics: variations by level of openness in the adoption. *Family Process*, **33**(June), 125–46.

Gunnoe, M.L. (1993) Noncustodial mothers' and fathers' contribution to the adjustment of adolescent stepchildren. Unpublished doctoral dissertation, University of Virginia, Charlottesville.

Hahn, C.-S. and DiPietro, J.A. (2001) In vitro fertilization and the family: quality of parenting, family functioning, and child psychosocial adjustment. *Developmental Psychology*, **37**(1), 37–48.

Haskey, J. (1994) Stepfamilies and stepchildren in Great Britain. *Population Trends*, **76**, 17–28.

Hetherington, E.M. (1993) An overview of the Virginia Longitudinal Study of Divorce and Remarriage with a focus on early adolescence. *Journal of Family Psychology*, **7**(1), 39–56.

Hetherington, E.M. (ed.) (1999) *Coping with Divorce, Single Parenting, and Remarriage*. Mahwah, NJ: Lawrence Erlbaum.

Hetherington, E.M. and Clingempeel, W.G. (1992) *Coping with Marital Transitions*. Chicago: Society for Research in Child Development.

Hetherington, E.M. and Henderson, S.H. (1997) Fathers in stepfamilies. In Lamb, M.E. (ed.) *The Role of the Father in Child Development*. Chichester, John Wiley, pp. 212–26.

Hetherington, E.M. and Jodl, K.M. (1994) Stepfamilies as settings for child development. In Booth, A. and Dunn, J. (eds) *Stepfamilies. Who Benefits? Who Does Not?* Hillsdale, NJ: Lawrence Erlbaum, p. 233.

Hetherington, E.M., Henderson, S.H. and Reiss, D. (1999) *Adolescent Siblings in Stepfamilies: Family Functioning and Adolescent Adjustment*. Ann Arbor, MI: Society for Research in Child Development.

Hodges, J. and Tizard, B. (1989) Social and family relationships of ex-institutional adolescents. *Journal of Child Psychology and Psychiatry*, **30**(1), 77–97.

Howe, D. (1996) Adopters' relationships with their adopted children from adolescence to early adulthood. *Adoption and Fostering*, **20**(3), 35–43.

Kiernan, K. (1999) European perspectives on non-marital childbearing. *Population Trends*, **98** (Winter 1999), 11–20.

Kiernan, K.E. (1992) The impact of family disruption in childhood and transitions made in young adult life. *Population Studies*, **46**, 213–34.

Kurdek, L.A. and Fine, M.A. (1994) Family acceptance and family control as predictors of adjustment in young adolescents: linear, curvilinear, or interactive effects? *Child Development*, **65**, 1137–46.

Kurdek, L.A., Fine, M.A. and Sinclair, R.J. (1995) School adjustment in sixth graders: Parenting transitions, family climate, and peer norm effects. *Child Development*, **66**, 430–45.

Lamb, M. (1995) Paternal influences on child development. In van Dongen, M.C.P., Frinking, G.A.B. and Jacobs, M.J.G. (eds) *Changing Fatherhood an Interdisciplinary Perspective*. Amsterdam: Thesis Publishers.

Lamborn, S.D., Mounts, N.S., Steinberg, L. and Dornbusch, S.M. (1991) Patterns of competence and adjustment among adolescents from authoritative, authoritarian, indulgent, and neglectful families. *Child Development*, **62**, 1049–65.

Levy-Schiff, R., Goldshmidt, I. and Har-Even, D. (1991) Transition to parenthood in adoptive families. *Developmental Psychology*, **27**(1), 131–40.

Maccoby, E.E. and Mnookin, R.H. (1992) *Dividing the Child: Social and Legal Dilemmas of Custody.* Cambridge, MA: Harvard University Press.

Maclean, M. and Eekelaar, J. (1997) *The Parental Obligation. A Study of Parenthood Across Households.* Oxford: Hart Publishing.

Martin, T.C. and Bumpass, L.L. (1989) Recent trends in marital disruption. *Demography*, **26**, 37–51.

McLanahan, S. and Sandfur, S. (1994) *Growing Up with a Single Parent: What Hurts, What Helps.* Cambridge, MA: Harvard University Press.

McMahon, C.A., Ungerer, J.A., Beaurepaire, J., Tennant, C. and Saunders, D.M. (1995) Psychosocial outcomes for parents and children after *in vitro* fertilization: a review. *Journal of Reproductive and Infant Psychology*, **13**, 1–16.

McMahon, C.A., Ungerer, J.A., Beaurepaire, J., Tennant, C. and Saunders, D.M. (1997) Anxiety during pregnancy and fetal attachment after in vitro fertilization conception. *Human Reproduction*, **12**, 101–7.

O'Brien, M., Alldred, P. and Jones, P. (1996) Children's constructions of family and kinship. In Brannen, J. and O'Brien, M. (eds) *Children in Families: Research and Policy*. London: Falmer Press, pp. 84–100.

Pryor, J. and Rodgers, B. (2001) *Children in Changing Families. Life after Parents Separate.* Oxford: Blackwell Publishers.

Rawlings, S. and Saluter, A. (1996) *Household and family characteristics: March 1994*. Washington, DC: US Department of Commerce.

Rushton, A., Dance, C. and Quinton, D. (2000) Findings from a UK based study of late permanent placements. *Adoption Quarterly*, **3**(3), 51–71.

Saluter, A. (1996) *Marital status and living arrangements: March 1994. Current population reports, population characteristics P20–484.* Washington, DC: US Department of Commerce.

Seltzer, J.A. (1991) Relationships between fathers and children who live apart: the father's role after separation. *Journal of Marriage and the Family*, **53**, 79–101.

Sharma, A.R., McGue, M.K. and Benson, P.L. (1998) The psychological adjustment of United States adopted adolescents and their nonadopted siblings. *Child Development*, **69** (June), 791–802.

Simons, R.L. (1996) *Understanding the Differences between Divorced and Intact Families. Stress, Interaction, and Child Outcome.* Thousand Oaks, CA: Sage.

Simpson, B., McCarthy, P. and Walker, J. (1995) Being there: fathers after divorce. Newcastle upon Tyne: Relate Centre for Family Studies.

Singer, L.M., Brodzinsky, D.M., Ramsay, D., Steir, M. and Waters, E. (1985) Mother–infant attachment in adoptive families. *Child Development*, **56**, 1543–51.

Snowden, R. (1998) Psychosocial discontinuities introduced by the new reproductive technologies. *Journal of Community and Applied Psychology*, **8**, 249–59.

Statistics New Zealand (1996) Marriage and divorce. In *Demographic Trends*. Wellington: Statistics New Zealand.

Stewart, S.D. (1999) Nonresident mothers' and fathers' social contact with children. *Journal of Marriage and the Family*, **61**, 894–907.

Stovall, K.C. and Dozier, M. (2000) The evolution of attachment in new relationships: single subject analyses for ten foster infants. *Development and Psychopathology*, **12**, 133–56.

Thompson, R.A. (1994) The role of the father after divorce. *The Future of Children. Children and Divorce*, **4**(1), 210–35.

Thomson, E., McLanahan, S.S. and Curtin, R.B. (1992) Family structure, gender, and parental socialization. *Journal of Marriage and the Family*, **54**, 368–78.

Thomson, E., Mosley, J., Hanson, T.L. and McLanahan, S.S. (2001) Remarriage, cohabitation, and changes in mothering behavior. *Journal of Marriage and the Family*, **63** (May), 370–80.

Van Balen, F. (1996) Child-rearing following in vitro fertilization. *Journal of Child Psychology and Psychiatry*, **37**(6), 687–93.

Van Balen, F. (1998) Development of IVF children. *Developmental Review*, **18**, 30–46.

Visher, E.B. and Visher, J.S. (1990) Dynamics of successful stepfamilies. *Journal of Divorce & Remarriage*, **14**, 3–12.

Voydanoff, P., Fine, M. and Donnelly, B.W. (1994) Family structure, family organisation, and quality of family life. *Journal of Family and Economic Issues*, **15**(3), 175–200.

Vuchinich, S., Hetherington, E.M., Vuchinich, R.A. and Clingempeel, W.G. (1991) Parent–child interaction and gender differences in early adolescents' adaptation to stepfamilies. *Developmental Psychology*, **27**(4), 618–26.

Wu, L. and Martinson, B. (1993) Family structure and the risk of a premarital birth. *American Sociological Review*, **58**, 210–32.

9

Sexual Orientation and Parenting

Charlotte J. Patterson and Erin L. Sutfin

SUMMARY

In this chapter, we first review the historical context in which lesbian and gay parenting has emerged. We then provide an overview of lesbian and gay parenthood today, including information about the prevalence and diversity of lesbian and gay parenting, and about the legal contexts in which lesbian and gay families currently live. We then describe the results of research on lesbian and gay parents and their children, and discuss some implications of the research findings for theories of psychological development and for the politics of family life. The chapter concludes with a discussion of future directions for research, service and advocacy relevant to the needs of lesbian mothers, gay fathers, and their children.

It is generally expected that both parents and their children are heterosexual. Not only are they expected to be heterosexual in their orientation, but they are also generally expected to exemplify heterosexuality in their attitudes, values, and behavior. From such a perspective, children with lesbian and gay parents seem not to exist, and the idea of lesbian or gay parenthood may be difficult to imagine. In contrast to such expectations, however, many lesbian women and gay men are parents.

HISTORICAL BACKGROUND

The emergence of large numbers of openly self-identified lesbian women and gay men is a relatively recent historical phenomenon (Boswell, 1980; Faderman, 1981, 1991; D'Emilio, 1983). Although the origins of homophile organizations date to the 1950s and even earlier (D'Emilio, 1983, Faderman, 1991), the origins of contemporary gay liberation movements in the US are generally traced to police raids on the Stonewall bar in the Greenwich Village neighborhood of New York City in 1969, and to resistance shown by gay men and lesbian women to these attacks (D'Emilio, 1983; Adam, 1987). In the years since

that time, more and more gay men and lesbian women have abandoned secrecy, declared their identities, and begun to work actively for gay and lesbian rights (Blumenfeld and Raymond, 1988).

With greater openness among lesbian and gay adults, the number of families in which one or more of a child's parents identify as lesbian or gay is increasing, and the diversity of family forms is becoming more apparent. Many such families involve children from a previous marriage. Others involve children born or adopted after the parents have identified themselves as gay or lesbian. In the last 15 to 25 years, such families have been the subject of increasing attention in the media and in the popular press (Schulenberg, 1985; Rafkin, 1990; Gross, 1991; Goleman, 1992; Martin, 1993).

Although it is widely believed that family environments exert important influences on children who grow up in them, authoritative scholarly reviews of such matters are only now beginning to consider children growing up in families with gay and/or lesbian parents (Lamb, 1999). Given the multiplicity of new gay and lesbian families, and in view of their apparent vitality, scientists today are faced with remarkable opportunities to study the formation, growth, and impact of new family forms.

To the extent that parental influences are seen as critical in psychosocial development, and to the extent that lesbians and/or gay men may provide different kinds of influences than heterosexual parents, then the children of gay men and lesbians can been expected to develop in ways that are different from children of heterosexual parents. Whether any such differences are expected to be beneficial, detrimental, or non-existent depends, of course, upon the viewpoint from which the phenomena are observed. Lesbian and gay families with children thus present an unusual opportunity to test basic assumptions that many scientists have long taken for granted (Patterson, 2000; Stacey and Biblarz, 2001).

ISSUES AT THE CORE
OF THE CHAPTER

How many lesbian and gay families with children are there in the world today? What are the important sources of diversity among them? And what is the nature of the legal contexts within which lesbian and gay families are living? In this section, we discuss each of these questions in turn.

Prevalence of Gay and Lesbian Parenthood

For many reasons, no accurate count of the numbers of lesbian and gay families with children is available. First, the numbers of lesbian and gay adults in the world today cannot be estimated with confidence. Because of fear of discrimination, many take pains to conceal their sexual orientation (Blumenfeld and Raymond, 1988; Herek, 1995). It is especially difficult to locate gay and lesbian parents. Concerned that they might lose child custody and/or visiting rights if their sexual orientation were to be known, many lesbian and gay parents attempt to conceal their gay or lesbian identities (Pagelow, 1980), sometimes even from their own children (Dunne, 1987).

Despite acknowledged difficulties, estimates of the numbers of gay and lesbian families with children in the United States have been offered (see Patterson and Friel, 2000, for a review and critique). One approach to making estimates of this kind is to extrapolate from what is known or believed about base rates in the population. For example, there are about 106 million women and about 98 million men over 18 years of age in the United States today (U.S. Bureau of the Census, 2000). If one assumes that about 4 per cent of the population is gay or lesbian, that would place the numbers of lesbian and gay adults in the United States today at about 4.2 million and 3.9 million, respectively. According to some large-scale survey studies (e.g., Bell and Weinberg, 1978; Blumstein and Schwartz, 1983), about 10 per cent of gay men and about 20 per cent of lesbians are parents, most of whom have children from a heterosexual marriage that ended in divorce. Calculations using these figures suggest that there may be well over a million gay or lesbian parents in the United States today. If, on average, each parent has two children, that would mean that there may be more than two million children with lesbian and gay parents in the United States today.

The accuracy of such estimates is, of course, no better than that of the figures on which they are based (Michaels, 1996). The data upon which the above estimates were based (Bell and Weinberg, 1978) were drawn from a large and diverse sample of lesbian and gay adults, but the sample was not intended to be representative of the population of the United States; indeed, all the respondents lived in a single geographical area. Moreover, the average age of the respondents was 35 years of age, so ultimate levels of fertility could not be assessed. For these and related reasons (Patterson and Friel, 2000), the Bell and Weinberg (1978) data, though valuable, cannot be seen as definitive.

Recently, efforts have been made by Badgett (1998) and by Patterson and Friel (2000) to estimate the numbers of lesbian and gay parents in the United States by drawing on data from nationally representative (or near-representative) samples of American adults of child-bearing age. Badgett (1998) used data from voter exit polls, and Patterson and Friel (2000) used data from the National Health and Social Life Survey (NHSLS, Laumann et al., 1994). The researchers estimate that there are between one and five million lesbian and gay parents in the United States today, with the lower numbers taken from the very most conservative assessments on the NHSLS (Patterson and Friel, 2000), and the higher numbers drawn from the more liberal assessments employed in the NHSLS and in the voter exit polls (Badgett, 1998; Patterson and Friel, 2000). Projecting from these estimates of the numbers of parents, and assuming that each parent has on average only one child, then there would be between one and five million children with lesbian and gay parents in the United States today. If one makes estimates assuming that each parent has more than one child, then estimated numbers of children with lesbian and gay parents would of course be larger.

Although the exact numbers will probably never be known with certainty, either in the United States or abroad, it does seem clear that substantial numbers of people are involved. In addition to those who had children in the context of a heterosexual marriage, many lesbian and gay adults are also having children after assuming non-heterosexual identities, so the characteristics of the population may also be changing (Ricketts, 1991; Martin, 1993; Patterson, 1994b; Gartrell et al., 1996; Stacey and Biblarz, 2001). Whatever estimates one adopts, it seems clear that many children are growing up with lesbian or gay parents.

Diversity among Lesbian Mothers, Gay Fathers, and Their Children

The numbers of lesbian and gay families with children would thus appear to be sizeable. In considering the numbers, however, it is important not to overlook the many sources of diversity among these families. In an effort to begin to describe the diversity that characterizes gay and lesbian families with children, some of the differences among such families are examined next.

As suggested above, one important distinction among lesbian and gay families with children involves the sexual identity of parents at the time of a child's birth or adoption. Probably the largest group of children with lesbian and gay parents are those who were born in the context of heterosexual relationships between the biological parents, and whose parent or parents subsequently identified as gay or lesbian. These include families in which the parents divorced when the husband came out as gay, families in which the parents divorced when the wife came out as lesbian, families in which the parents divorced when both parents came out, and families in which one or both of the parents came out and the parents decided not to divorce. Gay or lesbian parents may be single, or they may have same-sex partners. A gay or lesbian parent's same-sex partner may or may not assume step-parenting relationships with the children. If the partner has also had children, the youngsters may or may not also assume step-sibling relationships with one another. In other words, gay and lesbian families with children born in the context of heterosexual relationships are themselves a relatively diverse group.

In addition to children born in the context of heterosexual relationships between parents, lesbians and gay men are believed increasingly to be choosing parenthood (Pies, 1985, 1990; Patterson, 1994a, 1994b). Many such children are conceived by means of donor insemination (DI). Lesbians who wish to bear children may choose a friend, relative, or acquaintance to be the sperm donor, or may choose instead to use sperm from an unknown donor. When sperm donors are known, they may take parental or avuncular roles relative to children conceived via DI, or they may not (Pies, 1985, 1990; Patterson, 1994a, 1994b). Gay men may also become biological parents of children whom they intend to parent, whether with a single woman (who may be lesbian or heterosexual), with a lesbian couple, or with a gay male partner. Many adoption agencies are open to working with lesbian and gay prospective adoptive parents (Brodzinsky et al., 2003), and options pursued by gay men and lesbians include both adoption and foster care (Ricketts, 1991). Thus, many children are today being brought up in a diverse array of lesbian and gay families.

In addition to differences in parents' sexual identities at the time of a child's birth, another set of distinctions concerns the extent to which family members are related biologically to one another (Pollack and Vaughn, 1987; Riley, 1988; Weston, 1991; Patterson, 1998). Although biological relatedness of family members to one another is taken for granted less and less as heterosexual stepfamilies proliferate, it is often even more prominent as an issue in lesbian and gay than in heterosexual families (Wright, 1998). When children are born via DI into lesbian families, they are generally related biologically only to the birthmother, not to her partner. Similarly, when children are born via surrogacy to a gay couple, only the father who served as a sperm donor is likely to be biologically related to the child. In adoption and foster care, of course, the child will probably have no biological relation to any adoptive or foster parent.

Another issue of particular importance for lesbian and gay families concerns custodial arrangements for minor children. As in heterosexual families, children may live with one or both biological parents, or they may spend part of their time in one parent's household, and part of their time in another's. Many lesbian mothers and gay fathers have, however, lost custody of their children to heterosexual spouses following divorce, and the threat of custody litigation probably looms larger in the lives of many divorced lesbian mothers than it does in the lives of divorced heterosexual ones (Pagelow, 1980; Lyons, 1983). Although no authoritative figures are available, it seems likely that a greater proportion of gay and lesbian than of heterosexual parents have lost custody of children against their will. Probably for this reason, more lesbians and gay men may be noncustodial parents (do not have legal custody of their children) and nonresidential parents (do not live in the same household with their children) than might otherwise be expected.

Beyond these basic distinctions, many others can also be considered. Other important ways in which lesbian and gay families with children may differ from one another include income, education, race/ethnicity, gender, and culture. Difficulties and ambiguities in the definition of sexual orientation should also be acknowledged (Brown, 1995; Fox, 1995). Although such variability undoubtedly contributes to differences in the qualities of life, little research has yet been directed to understanding such differences among lesbian and gay families.

Legal and Public Policy Issues

When considering the environment within which lesbian and gay parenting takes place, it must be acknowledged that the legal system in the United States and in many other countries has long been hostile to lesbians and to gay men who are or who wish to become parents (Falk, 1989; Editors of the Harvard Law Review, 1990; Polikoff, 1990; Rivera, 1991; Patterson and Redding, 1996). Lesbian mothers and gay fathers have often been denied custody and/or visiting of their children following divorce (Falk, 1989). Although some jurisdictions now have laws stipulating that parental sexual orientation as such cannot be a factor in determining child custody following divorce, in other areas, gay or lesbian parents are regarded as unfit parents (Patterson and Redding, 1996). Regulations governing foster care and adoption in many areas have also made it difficult for lesbians and gay men to adopt or to serve as foster parents (Ricketts and Achtenberg, 1990). It is clear from recent research (King and Black, 1999) that college students in the United States expect children of lesbian mothers to have more behavior problems than other children, and this bias may be shared by at least some judges and policy-makers around the world.

One of the central issues underlying judicial decision-making in custody litigation and in public policies governing foster care and adoption has been questions about the fitness of lesbians and gay men to be parents. Specifically, policies have sometimes been constructed and judicial decisions have often been made on the assumptions that gay men and lesbians are mentally ill and hence not fit to be parents, that lesbians are less maternal than heterosexual women and hence do not make good mothers, and that lesbians' and gay men's relationships with sexual partners leave little time for ongoing parent–child interactions (Falk, 1989; Editors of the Harvard Law Review, 1990). Because these assumptions have been important in denying or limiting gay and lesbian parental rights, and because they are open to empirical evaluation, they have guided much of the research on lesbian and gay parents that will be discussed below.

In addition to judicial concerns about parents themselves, three principal kinds of fears about effects of gay and lesbian parents on children have also been reflected in judicial decision-making about child custody and in public policies, such as regulations governing foster care and adoption (Patterson and Redding, 1996; Patterson, 1997). One of these concerns is that development of sexual identity among children of lesbian and gay parents will be impaired. For instance, it may be feared that children will themselves grow up to be gay or lesbian, an outcome which is often viewed as negative. Another concern is that gay and lesbian parents will have adverse effects on other aspects of their children's personality development. For example, it may be feared that children in the custody of gay or lesbian parents will be more vulnerable to behavior problems or to mental breakdown. A third general concern is that these children will have difficulties in social relationships. For instance, it may be believed that children will be teased or stigmatized by peers because of their parent's sexual orientation. Because such concerns have often been explicit in judicial determinations when lesbian or gay parents' custody or visitation rights have been denied or curtailed (Falk, 1989; Editors of the Harvard Law Review, 1990; Patterson and Redding, 1996), and because these assumptions are open to empirical test, they have provided an important impetus to research.

PRACTICE OF PARENTING

Case reports about lesbian mothers, gay fathers, and their children began to appear in the psychiatric literature in the early and mid-1970s (e.g., Osman, 1972; Weeks et al., 1975), but systematic research on these families is a more recent phenomenon. Despite the diversity of lesbian and gay parenting communities, research to date has with few exceptions been conducted with relatively homogeneous groups of participants. Samples of parents have been mainly Caucasian, well-educated, affluent, and living in major urban centers. Any studies that provide exceptions to this rule are specifically noted as such. In this section, research on those who became parents in the context of heterosexual relationships, before coming out as lesbian or gay, is presented first. Studies of lesbians who became parents after coming out are described next. Other recent reviews of research on lesbian and gay parents have been provided by Brewaeys and Van Hall (1997), Kirkpatrick (1996), Patterson (1997, 2000), Perrin (1998) and by Tasker and Golombok (1997).

Lesbians and Gay Men Who Became Parents in the Context of Heterosexual Relationships

One important impetus for research in this area has come from extrinsic sources, such as judicial concerns about the psychological health and well-being of lesbian mothers as compared with heterosexual mothers. Other work has arisen from concerns that are more intrinsic to the families themselves, such as what and when children should be told about their parents' sexual orientation. Because studies tend to focus either on mothers or on fathers, we present first the research on mothers, then that on fathers. Although some of these parents may not have been married to the heterosexual partner with whom they had children, it is likely that most of the research participants were married. To avoid the use of more cumbersome labels, then, we refer to divorced lesbian mothers and to divorced gay fathers.

DIVORCED LESBIAN MOTHERS

Because the overall mental health of lesbian mothers as compared to heterosexual mothers has often been raised as an issue by judges presiding over custody disputes (Falk, 1989), a number of studies have focused on this issue. Consistent with data on the mental health of lesbian women in general (Gonsiorek, 1991), research in this area has revealed that divorced lesbian mothers score at least as high as divorced heterosexual mothers on assessments of psychological health. For instance, studies have found no differences between lesbian and heterosexual mothers on self-concept, happiness, overall adjustment, or psychiatric status (Falk, 1989; Patterson, 1995b, 1997, 2001).

Another area of concern has focused on maternal sex-role behavior, and its potential impact on children (Falk, 1989). Stereotypes suggest that lesbians might be overly masculine and/or that they might interact inappropriately with their children. In contrast to expectations based on the stereotypes, however, neither lesbian mothers' reports about their own sex-role behavior nor their self-described interest in child-rearing have been found to differ from those of heterosexual mothers. Reports about responses to child behavior and ratings of warmth toward children have been found not to differ significantly between lesbian and heterosexual mothers (Thompson et al., 1971; Mucklow and Phelan, 1979; Kweskin and Cook, 1982).

Some differences between lesbian and heterosexual mothers have also been found. Lyons (1983) and Pagelow (1980) reported that divorced lesbian mothers had more fears about loss of child custody than did divorced heterosexual mothers. Similarly, Green et al. (1986) found that lesbian mothers were more likely than heterosexual mothers to be active in feminist organizations. Given the environments in which these lesbian mothers were living, findings like these are not surprising. How such differences may affect parenting behavior, if at all, is at present unknown.

A few other scattered differences seem more difficult to interpret. For instance, Miller et al. (1981) reported that lesbian mothers in the sample were more child-centered than heterosexual mothers in their discipline techniques. In a sample of African-American lesbian mothers and African-American heterosexual mothers, Hill (1987) found that lesbian mothers reported being more flexible about rules, more relaxed about sex play and modesty, and more likely to have non-traditional expectations for their daughters.

Several studies have also examined the social circumstances and relationships of lesbian mothers. Divorced lesbian mothers have consistently been reported to be more likely than divorced heterosexual mothers to be living with a romantic partner (Pagelow, 1980; Kirkpatrick et al., 1981; Harris and Turner, 1985/1986). Whether this represents a difference between lesbian and heterosexual mother-headed families, on the one hand, or reflects sampling biases of the research, on the other, cannot be determined on the basis of information in the published reports. Information is sparse about the impact of such relationships in lesbian mother families, but what has been published suggests that, like heterosexual step-parents, co-resident lesbian partners of divorced lesbian mothers can be important sources of conflict as well as support in the family (Kirkpatrick, 1987).

Relationships with the fathers of children in lesbian mother homes have also been a topic of study. Few differences in the likelihood of paternal financial support have been found for lesbian and heterosexual families with children. Kirkpatrick and her colleagues (1981) reported, for example, that only about half of heterosexual mothers and about half of lesbian mothers in the sample received any financial support from the fathers of their children.

Findings about frequency of contact with fathers are mixed, with some (e.g., Kirkpatrick et al., 1981) reporting no differences in frequency of contact as a function of maternal sexual orientation and others (e.g., Golombok et al., 1983) reporting more contact with fathers among lesbian mothers than among heterosexual mothers.

Although most research has involved assessment of possible differences in personality and social behavior between lesbian and heterosexual mothers, a few studies have reported other types of comparisons. For instance, in a study of divorced lesbian mothers and divorced gay fathers, Harris and Turner (1985/1986) found that gay fathers were likely to report greater financial resources and to say that they encouraged more sex-typed toy play among their children, whereas lesbian mothers were more likely to describe benefits such as increased empathy and tolerance for differences among their children as a result of having lesbian or gay parents. In comparisons of relationship satisfaction among lesbian couples who did or did not have children, Koepke et al. (1992) reported that couples with children scored higher on overall measures of relationship satisfaction and of the quality of their sexual relationship. These findings are intriguing, but much more research will be needed before their implications are clear.

Another important set of questions, as yet little studied, concerns the conditions under which lesbian mothers experience enhanced feelings of well-being and support. Rand and her colleagues (1982) reported that the psychological health of lesbian mothers is associated with mothers' openness about their sexual orientation with employers, ex-husbands, children, and friends, and with their degree of feminist activism. Kirkpatrick (1987) reported that lesbian mothers living with partners and children had greater economic and emotional resources than those living alone with their children. Much is still to be learned about determinants of individual differences in psychological well-being among lesbian mothers.

Many other issues that have arisen in the context of divorced lesbian mother families are also in need of study. For instance, when a mother is in the process of coming out as a lesbian to herself and others, at what point in that process should she address the topic with her child, and in what ways should she do so, if at all? And what influence ought the child's age and circumstances to have in such a decision? Reports from research and clinical practice suggest that early adolescence may be a particularly difficult time for parents to initiate such conversations, and that disclosure may be less stressful at earlier points in a child's development (Patterson, 1992, 1997), but systematic research on these issues is just beginning. Similarly, many issues remain to be addressed regarding stepfamily and blended family relationships that may emerge

as a lesbian mother's household seeks new equilibrium following her separation or divorce from the child's father (Wright, 1998).

DIVORCED GAY FATHERS

Although considerable research has focused on the overall psychological adjustment of lesbian mothers as compared with that of heterosexual mothers, no published studies of gay fathers make such comparisons with heterosexual fathers. This fact may be attributable to the greater role of judicial decision-making as an impetus for research on lesbian mothers. In jurisdictions where the law provides for biases in custody proceedings, these are likely to favor female and heterosexual parents. Perhaps because, other things being equal, gay fathers are extremely unlikely to win custody battles over their children after divorce, fewer such cases seem to have reached the courts. Consistent with expectations based on this view, only a small minority of divorced gay fathers have been reported to live in the same households as their children (Bozett, 1980, 1989; Bigner and Bozett, 1990).

Research on the parenting attitudes of gay versus heterosexual divorced fathers has, however, been reported (Barret and Robinson, 1990). For example, Bigner and Jacobsen (1989a, 1989b) compared gay and heterosexual fathers, each of whom had at least two children. Results showed that, with one exception, there were no significant differences between gay and heterosexual fathers in their motives for parenthood. The single exception concerned the greater likelihood of gay than heterosexual fathers to cite the higher status accorded to parents as compared with non-parents in the dominant culture as motivation for parenthood (Bigner and Jacobsen, 1989a).

Bigner and Jacobsen (1989b) also asked gay and heterosexual fathers in their sample to report on their own behavior with their children. Although no differences emerged in the fathers' reports of involvement or intimacy, gay fathers reported that their behavior was characterized by greater responsiveness, more reasoning, and more limit-setting than did heterosexual fathers. These reports by gay fathers of greater warmth and responsiveness, on the one hand, and greater control and limit-setting, on the other, are strongly reminiscent of findings from research with heterosexual families, and would seem to raise the possibility that gay fathers are more likely than their heterosexual counterparts to exhibit authoritative patterns of parenting behavior such as those described by Baumrind (Baumrind, 1967; Baumrind and Black, 1967). Caution must be exercised, however, in the interpretation of results such as these, which stem entirely from paternal reports about their own behavior.

In addition to research comparing gay and heterosexual fathers, a few studies have made other comparisons. For instance, Robinson and Skeen (1982) compared sex-role orientations of gay fathers with those of gay men who were not fathers, and found no differences. Similarly, Skeen and Robinson (1985) found no evidence to suggest that gay men's retrospective reports about relationships with their own parents varied as a function of whether or not they were parents themselves. As noted above, gay fathers and lesbian mothers have been compared showing that, although gay fathers had higher incomes and were more likely to report encouraging their children to play with sex-typed toys, lesbian mothers were more likely to believe that their children received positive benefits such as increased tolerance for diversity from growing up with lesbian or gay parents (Harris and Turner, 1985/1986). Studies like these begin to suggest a number of issues for research on gender, sexual orientation, and parenting behavior, and it is clear that there are many valuable directions that future work in this area could take.

A great deal of research in this area has arisen from concerns about the gay father identity and its transformations over time. Thus, Miller (1978, 1979) and Bozett (1980, 1981a, 1981b, 1987) sought to provide a conceptualization of the processes through which a man who considers himself to be a heterosexual father may come to identify himself, both in public and in private, as a gay father. Based on extensive interviews with gay fathers both in the United States and in Canada, authors have emphasized the centrality of identity disclosure and of the reactions to disclosure by significant people in a man's life. Miller (1978) suggests that, although a number of factors such as extent of occupational autonomy and amount of access to gay communities may affect how rapidly a gay man discloses his identity to others, the most important of these is likely to be the experience of falling in love with another man. It is this experience, more than any other, it appears, that leads a man to integrate the otherwise compartmentalized parts of his identity as a gay father. This hypothesis is very much open to empirical evaluation, but such research has not yet been reported.

Lesbians and Gay Men Choosing to Become Parents

Although for many years lesbian mothers and gay fathers were generally assumed to have become parents in the context of previous heterosexual relationships, both men and women are believed increasingly to be undertaking parenthood in the context of pre-existing lesbian and gay identities (Crawford, 1987; Patterson, 1994a, 1994b; Beers, 1996; Gartrell et al., 1996, 1999). A substantial body of research addresses the transition to parenthood among heterosexuals (Cowan and Cowan, 1992), but very little research has explored the transition to parenthood for gay men or lesbian women. Many issues that arise for heterosexual parents-to-be also face lesbian women and gay men (such as concerns about how children will affect couple relationships, and economic concerns about supporting children), but gay men and lesbian women must also cope with many additional issues because of their situation as members of stigmatized minorities. These issues are best understood when viewed against the backdrop of heterosexism and anti-gay prejudice.

Anti-gay prejudice is evident in institutions involved with health care, education, and employment that often fail to support, and in some cases, are openly hostile to lesbian and gay families (Casper et al., 1992; Martin, 1993; Perrin, 1998; Casper and Schultz, 1999). Lesbian and gay parents may encounter anti-gay prejudice and bigotry even from members of their families of origin (Pollack and Vaughn, 1987). Many if not most of the special concerns of lesbian and gay parents and prospective parents stem from problems created by such hostility.

A number of interrelated issues are often faced in particular by lesbians and gay men who wish to become parents (Crawford, 1987; Martin, 1989, 1993; Patterson, 1994b; Beers, 1996). One of the first needs among prospective gay and lesbian parents is for accurate, up-to-date information on how lesbians and gay men can become parents, how their children are likely to develop, and what supports are available to assist them. In addition to such educational needs, lesbians and gay men who are seeking biological parenthood are also likely to encounter various health concerns, ranging from medical screening of prospective birthparents to assistance with DI techniques, prenatal care, and preparation for birth. As matters progress, a number of legal concerns about the rights and responsibilities of all parties are likely to emerge. Associated with all of these will generally be financial issues; in addition to the support of a child, auxiliary costs of medical and legal assistance may be considerable. Finally, social and emotional concerns of many different kinds are also likely to emerge (Pies, 1985; Pollack and Vaughn, 1987; Rohrbaugh, 1988; Patterson, 1994b).

As this brief outline of issues suggests, numerous questions are posed by the emergence of prospective lesbian and gay parents. What are the factors that influence lesbians' and gay men's inclinations to make parenthood a part of their lives? What effects does parenting have on lesbians or gay men who undertake it, and how do these effects compare with those experienced by heterosexuals? How effectively do special services such as support groups serve the needs of lesbian and gay parents and prospective parents for whom they were designed? What are the elements of a social climate that is supportive for gay and lesbian parents and their children? As yet, little research has addressed such questions.

In one study of gay men who were not parents, Beers (1996) found that about half of the participants reported that they would like to become parents. Interestingly, those who expressed a desire to become parents were also described as being at higher levels of psychosocial development (assessed within an Eriksonian framework) and at higher levels of identity formation with regard to their gay identities. There were no differences, however, in retrospective reports of experiences with their own parents (Beers, 1996). These results suggest the possibility that internalized negative attitudes about homosexuality may be associated with reluctance on the part of gay men to become parents, but further evidence on this point is lacking.

The earliest studies of child-bearing among lesbian couples were reported by McCandlish (1987) and by Steckel (1985, 1987). Both investigators reported research based on small samples of lesbian couples who had given birth to children by means of DI. Their focus was primarily on the children in such families, and neither investigator conducted systematic assessments of mothers. McCandlish (1987) did, however, highlight some events and issues that were significant among families in her sample. For instance, she noted that, regardless of their interest in parenting prior to the birth of the first child, the non-biological mothers in each couple unanimously reported an 'unexpected and immediate attachment' to the child (McCandlish, 1987, p. 28). Although both mothers took part in parenting, they reported shifting patterns of caregiving responsibilities over time, with the biological mother taking primary responsibility during the earliest months, and the non-biological mother's role increasing in importance after the child was 12 or more months of age. Couples also reported changes in their own relationships following the birth of the child, notably a reduction or cessation in sexual intimacy. That lesbian couples reported less sexual activity after the birth of a child in the McCandlish (1987) study would seem to be at odds with the finding reported by Koepke and her colleagues (1992) that lesbian couples with children were more satisfied with their sexual relationship than were

those without children. Further research will be needed to provide a definitive interpretation of these apparently contradictory results, and to clarify the associations of such variables with the qualities of actual behavior in parenting roles.

A study by Hand (1991) examined in detail the ways in which a small group of lesbian and heterosexual couples with children under 2 years of age shared childcare, household duties, and occupational roles. The principal finding was that lesbian couples reported sharing parental duties more equally than did heterosexual couples. Lesbian non-biological mothers were significantly more involved in childcare than were heterosexual fathers. The lesbian non-biological mothers also regarded their parental role as significantly more salient than did heterosexual fathers. Lesbian biological mothers viewed their maternal role as more salient than did any of the other mothers, whether lesbian or heterosexual. Fathers viewed their occupational roles as more salient than did any of the mothers, whether lesbian or heterosexual.

Another study conducted at about the same time (Osterweil, 1991) involved a larger group of lesbian couples with at least one child between 18 and 36 months of age. Consistent with Hand's results for parents of younger children, Osterweil reported that biological mothers viewed their maternal role as more salient than did non-biological mothers. In addition, although household maintenance activities were shared about equally, biological mothers reported having more influence in family decisions and more involvement in childcare. Osterweil (1991) also reported that the couples in her study scored at about the mean for normative samples of heterosexual couples in overall relationship satisfaction. Taken together, results of the Hand and Osterweil studies thus suggest that lesbian couples who have chosen to bear children are likely to share household and childcare duties more equally than do heterosexual couples, and that lesbians are relatively satisfied with their couple relationships.

In the context of the Bay Area Families Study, Patterson (1995b) studied 26 families headed by lesbian couples who had children aged between 4 and 9 years. Consistent with results of other investigators (Osterweil, 1991; Koepke et al., 1992), Patterson (1995b, 2001) found that lesbian parents' mental health and their relationship satisfaction were generally high, relative to norms for heterosexual couples. Although they reported sharing household tasks and decision-making equally, couples in this study reported that biological mothers were more involved in childcare and that non-biological mothers spent longer hours in paid employment. The differences reported by Patterson (1995b) between lesbian parents' involvement in childcare were smaller by far, however, than those reported by Hand (1991) between heterosexual parents. Within this context, Patterson (1995b) also found that children were better adjusted and parents were more satisfied in lesbian mother families when childcare was shared more equally between parents.

Chan, Brooks, Raboy and Patterson (1998) studied 80 families formed by lesbian and by heterosexual parents via DI, and reported similar findings, as did Tasker and Golombok (1998) with a group of 99 lesbian and heterosexual in British families. In this latter study, lesbian couples with children who had been conceived via DI were more likely to share childcare duties evenly than were heterosexual couples who had conceived children via DI or than heterosexual couples who had conceived children in the conventional way.

A study of gay couples choosing parenthood was conducted by McPherson (1993) who assessed division of labor, satisfaction with division of labor, and satisfaction with couple relationships among 28 gay and 27 heterosexual parenting couples was assessed. Consistent with evidence from lesbian parenting couples (Hand, 1991; Osterweil, 1991; Patterson, 1995b; Chan et al., 1998; Tasker and Golombok, 1998), McPherson (1993) found that gay couples reported a more even division of responsibilities for household maintenance and childcare than did heterosexual couples. Gay parenting couples also reported greater satisfaction with their division of childcare tasks than did heterosexual couples. Finally, gay couples also reported greater satisfaction with their couple relationships, especially in the areas of cohesion and expression of affection.

Sbordone (1993) studied 78 gay men who had become parents through adoption or through surrogacy arrangements and compared them with gay men who were not fathers. Consistent with Skeen and Robinson's (1985) findings with divorced gay fathers, there were no differences between fathers and non-fathers on reports about relationships with the men's own parents. Gay fathers did, however, report higher self-esteem and fewer negative attitudes about homosexuality than did gay men who were not fathers.

An interesting result of Sbordone's (1993) study was that more than half of the gay men who were not fathers indicated that they would like to rear a child. Those who said they wanted children were younger than those who said they did not, but the two groups did not otherwise differ (for example, on income, education, race, self-esteem, or attitudes about homosexuality). Given that fathers had higher self-esteem and fewer negative attitudes about homosexuality than either group of non-fathers, it appeared that gay fathers' higher self-esteem might be a result rather than a cause of parenthood.

As this brief discussion has revealed, research on lesbians and gay men who have chosen to become parents is as yet quite sparse. Most research has been conducted on a relatively small scale, and many important issues have yet to be addressed. Existing research suggests, however, that lesbian and gay parenting couples are more likely than heterosexual couples to share tasks involved in childcare relatively evenly, and perhaps also to be more satisfied than heterosexual couples with their arrangements. Much remains to be learned about the determinants of lesbian and gay parenting, about its impact on lesbian and gay parents themselves, and about its place in contemporary communities.

Research on Children of Lesbian and Gay Parents

As with research on parents, an important impetus for studies of children with lesbian and gay parents has been the issues raised by the courts in the context of child custody hearings. Reflecting concerns that have been seen as relevant in the largest number of custody disputes, most of the research on children of gay and lesbian parents compares the development of children with custodial lesbian mothers to that of children with custodial heterosexual mothers. Because many children living in lesbian mother-headed families have undergone the experience of parental separation and divorce, it has been widely believed that children of divorced but heterosexual mothers provide the best comparison group. Research has also focused mainly on age groups and topics relevant to the largest numbers of custody disputes. Thus, most research compares children of divorced custodial lesbian mothers with children of divorced custodial heterosexual mothers, and most studies focus on school-aged children. Other recent reviews of this literature have been offered by Tasker and Golombok (1991, 1997), Patterson (1995b, 1997, 2000), Victor and Fish (1995), Brewaeys and Van Hall (1997), Parks (1998), and Perrin (1998).

One main area of concern discussed by judges in custody proceedings involves the development of sexual identity among children of lesbian and gay parents (Patterson, 1992, 1997). Studies of gender identity and of gender role behavior have, however, revealed few if any significant differences between children of lesbian or gay parents, on the one hand, and those of heterosexual parents, on the other. For instance, in one study (Gottman, 1990), adult daughters of divorced lesbian mothers did not differ on indices of gender role preferences either from adult daughters of divorced heterosexual mothers who had remarried or from adult daughters of divorced heterosexual mothers who had not remarried. Results of other studies have been similar (Green, 1978; Hoeffer, 1981).

An area of perennial interest in the area of sexual identity is that of the development of sexual orientation. Are the offspring of lesbian and gay parents themselves more likely to become lesbian or gay? Research to date gives precious little evidence to support the view that having homosexual parents predisposes a child to become gay or lesbian (Patterson, 1992; Tasker and Golombok, 1997). In Gottman's (1990) study, for example, the percentage of adult daughters who self-identified as lesbian did not differ as a function of mothers' sexual orientations. Similar results have been reported by other investigators (Golombok and Tasker, 1996; Bailey and Dawood, 1998).

Other concerns voiced by judges about lesbian mother homes include worries about other aspects of personal development, and about social relationships among the children (Patterson, 1992). Research relevant to these issues has, however, found no evidence to sustain any of these concerns. Children of lesbian mothers have proven to have no particular behavioral or emotional problems, no special difficulties with self-concept (Huggins, 1989), and no evidence of disruption in their social relationships with children or adults. For example, Golombok, Spencer and Rutter (1983) compared school-aged children of divorced lesbian mothers to same-aged children of divorced heterosexual mothers on a wide array of assessments of behavioral problems, issues in peer relations, and relationships with adults. They found no differences, except that lesbian mothers reported that their children had more contact with their fathers than did heterosexual mothers. Children's contacts with fathers were also studied by Kirkpatrick and her colleagues (1981), who reported no differences between children of divorced lesbian and divorced heterosexual mothers. Overall, then, the picture drawn by the existing research is one of great similarity between children of lesbian and heterosexual divorced mothers.

Some research has also been conducted to describe development among children born to or adopted by lesbian parents. The earliest studies in this area reported similarities in overall patterns of development among young children born to lesbian couples and children born to heterosexual couples (Steckel, 1985, 1987; McCandlish, 1987). This general pattern of findings has also been reported in studies by Patterson and her colleagues (1994a, 2001), by Flaks and his colleagues (1995), by Gartrell and her colleagues (1996, 1999), and by Golombok and her colleagues (Golombok et al., 1995,1997). Results of research on lesbian child-rearing converge on the conclusion that children of lesbian mothers are developing in a normal fashion.

Despite the diversity evident within gay and lesbian communities, research on variations among lesbian and gay families with children is as yet quite sparse. Existing data suggest that children may fare better when mothers are in good psychological health (e.g., Patterson, 2001). Children have also been described as more well-adjusted when their lesbian mothers reported sharing childcare duties more evenly (Chan et al., 1998). Existing data also suggest the value of a supportive milieu, in which parental sexual orientation is accepted by other significant adults, and in which children have contact with peers in similar circumstances. Research findings are still few in number, however, and much remains to be learned in this area.

AUTHORS' OVERVIEW

Research on lesbian mothers, gay fathers, and their children, though relatively new, has already made a number of contributions. Systematic study of lesbian and gay families with children began in the 1970s, in the context of judicial challenges to the fitness of lesbian and gay parents. For this reason, much research has been designed to evaluate negative judicial presumptions about the psychological health and well-being of parents and children in lesbian and gay families. Although much remains to be done to understand the conditions that foster positive mental health among lesbian mothers, gay fathers, and their children, the results of the early research were exceptionally clear. Findings of studies to date provide no reason under the prevailing 'best interests of the child' standard to deny or curtail parental rights of lesbian or gay parents on the basis of their sexual orientation, nor do they provide any support for the belief that lesbians or gay men are less suitable than heterosexuals to serve as adoptive or foster parents.

With these conclusions in mind, researchers are now beginning also to turn their attention to issues of diversity among gay and lesbian families, and are starting to explore conditions that help gay and lesbian families to flourish. This transition, now well under way, appears to be gathering momentum, and it suggests that research on lesbian and gay families has reached a significant turning point (Patterson, 1992, 1997; Stacey and Biblarz, 2001). Having addressed negative assumptions represented in psychological theory, judicial opinion, and popular prejudice, researchers are now in poised to explore a broader range of issues.

From a methodological viewpoint, a number of directions seem especially promising. Longitudinal research is needed to follow families over time and illuminate how changing life circumstances affect both parents and children. There is also a clear need for observational studies, and for work conducted with large samples. A greater focus on family interactions and processes as well as on structural variables is also likely to be valuable (Patterson, 1992, 1997, 2000).

From a substantive point of view, many issues relevant to lesbian and gay families are in need of study. First and most obvious is that studies representing the demographic diversity of lesbian and gay families are needed. With few exceptions (most notably, the work of Golombok and her colleagues in the UK), existing research has involved mainly Caucasian, well-educated, middle-class families who live in urban or suburban areas of the US. More work is needed to understand differences that are based on race and ethnicity, family economic circumstances, and cultural environments. Research of this kind should elucidate differences as well as commonalities among lesbian and gay families with children.

Future research should also, insofar as possible, encompass a larger number of levels of analysis. Existing research has most often focused on children or on their parents, considered as individuals. Valuable as this emphasis has been, it will also be important to consider couples and families as such. Assessments of dyadic adjustment or family climate could enhance our understanding of individual-level variables such as self-esteem. When families are considered at different levels of analysis, nested within the neighborhood, regional, and cultural contexts in which they live, a more comprehensive understanding of lesbian and gay families is likely to emerge.

In this effort, it will be valuable to devote attention to family process as well as to family structure. How do lesbian and gay families negotiate their interactions with institutional settings such as the school and the workplace (e.g., Casper and Schultz, 1999)? How are family processes and interactions affected by economic, cultural, religious, and legal aspects of the contexts in which families live (e.g., Badgett, 1998)? How do climates of opinion that prevail in their communities affect lesbian and gay families, and how do families cope with prejudice and discrimination when these are encountered?

Gender is a matter deserving of special attention in this regard. Inasmuch as lesbian and gay relationships encourage the uncoupling of gender and behavioral roles, one might expect to find considerable variability among families in the ways in which they carry out essential family, household, and childcare tasks (Hand, 1991; Osterweil, 1991;

McPherson, 1993; Patterson, 1995b; Chan et al., 1998; Tasker and Golombok, 1998). In what ways do non-traditional divisions of labor affect children who grow up in lesbian and gay homes? And in what ways does the performance of non-traditional tasks affect parents themselves? In general terms, it will be valuable to learn more about the relative importance of gender and behavioral roles in lesbian and gay families with children.

One additional issue that should be given special emphasis involves the conceptualization of parents' sexual identities. So far, scant attention has been devoted to the fluidity of sexual identities over time, or to the implications of any such fluidity for parents and children (Brown, 1995). For instance, many parents are probably bisexual to some degree, rather than exclusively heterosexual, gay, or lesbian, yet this has rarely been noted or studied directly in the existing research literature. Substantial numbers of adults (who may also be parents) identify themselves as bisexual (Fox, 1995). Future research might benefit from closer attention to issues in assessment of parental sexual orientation.

Although research to date on lesbian mothers, gay fathers, and their children has been fruitful, there is yet much important work to be done. Having addressed some of the heterosexist concerns of jurists, theorists, and others, researchers can now examine a broader range of issues raised by the emergence of different kinds of lesbian and gay families with children. Results of future work in this area have the potential to increase our knowledge about gay and lesbian parenthood, stimulate innovations in our theoretical understanding of human development, and inform legal rulings and public policies relevant to lesbian mothers, gay fathers, and their children.

IMPLICATIONS FOR PRACTICE

Directions for Research

One of the important directions for research is assessment of the climate for lesbian and gay parenting in various areas. What are the important criteria that should be used in such an assessment, and how do different locales measure up against them? One approach might be to use local indicators as rough indices. For example, a local gay/lesbian rights law would be a positive indicator with regard to the climate for lesbian and gay parenting, as would the accomplishment of second-parent adoptions. On the other side, negative indicators would include the existence of sodomy laws and/or other adverse legal precedents. One might also review regulations pertaining to adoption and foster-care placements. Ratings of this sort could be useful for couples and individuals seeking parenthood, parents considering relocation, and for activists and advocacy groups deciding how best to direct their activities.

The climates of local communities might also be assessed with the needs of lesbian and gay parents and their children in mind. For instance, one might ask whether or not there are gay and lesbian parent groups already in existence, whether or not any second-parent adoptions have been completed within this community, and whether or not relevant health care and medical resources are available to lesbian and gay families. Such assessments should be geared to specific locales, because communities that are located in geographical proximity to one another may vary tremendously in the climates they provide for gay and lesbian families with children.

Such efforts to examine and to describe the atmosphere for lesbian and gay family life also raise questions about what aspects of a community make it an attractive place for gay and lesbian parents and their children to live. Such characteristics might in some cases be similar to those for heterosexual families (such as safe streets, good schools) whereas in other cases, they might vary even among lesbian and gay families as a function of the family's other identities, interests, or needs. For instance, multiracial families might value especially the opportunity to live in multiracial neighborhoods.

It would also be valuable to learn more about the effectiveness of existing services for lesbian and gay families. Although many new services and programs have emerged for prospective parents as well as for parents and their children, there have been few attempts to evaluate their effectiveness. How effectively do available services fill the needs that they are intended to address? What populations are targeted by existing programs, and with what success do programs and services reach the communities for which they are intended? What are the essential elements of effective programs? And how can existing programs be improved? All of these are critical questions for community-oriented research on lesbian and gay parenting services (see D'Augelli and Garnets, 1995).

Finally, the knowledge base relevant to gay and lesbian parenting is still somewhat limited. Courts need accurate information about the impact, if any, of parental sexual orientation upon the development of children. Lesbians and gay men interested in parenting often want descriptive information about child and adolescent development among the offspring of lesbian and gay parents. Many lesbians and gay men considering parenthood also have questions about the ways in which parenthood can be expected to affect existing couple relationships in lesbian and gay families. Others are concerned about relationships with members of their families of origin as well as with friends, neighbors, and colleagues. Still others focus on family members' interactions with institutional contexts such as educational, legal, and medical settings. Scientists want to develop a better understanding of the important variables in parenting, and this requires greater knowledge about parenting and about child development in gay and lesbian families. Such topics are open to empirical study, and the work has begun, but much remains to be accomplished.

Directions for Service

There are a number of ways in which efforts to provide improved services for lesbian and gay parents might be directed. In part because services for lesbian and gay parents are so new, and in part because of widespread discrimination, expanded services are needed at all levels. At the US national level, an organization such as the Family Pride Coalition has the potential to develop lists of health care, legal, and other resources on a local basis, as well as to provide technical assistance to local groups. At regional and local levels, individual parent groups are mounting educational events and other programs in support of lesbian and gay parenting in local communities. Even in major urban areas, however, most such programs are in a nascent state, depend heavily on the efforts of volunteers, and reach mainly affluent, well-educated segments of lesbian and gay communities. In many smaller towns and rural areas, there are as yet no services at all.

One of the major needs, then, is for expansion of services. Programs and services should be developed by and for low-income and ethnic minority lesbian and gay individuals and couples who are parents or who wish to become parents. Of necessity, such work would involve identification of medical, legal, and other resources that are open to members of sexual minorities as well as to ethnic minorities and low-income communities. Services could also be developed for the children of lesbian and gay parents.

In seeking to expand services for sexual minority parenting communities, it will be important not to overlook important resources outside lesbian and gay communities themselves. For instance, building public library collections in areas relevant to lesbian and gay parenting can provide an important resource that is available to large numbers of people, regardless of sexual orientation. Educational institutions such as high schools, colleges, and universities can also provide important resources for prospective lesbian and gay parents by including accurate information in the curriculum, by providing speakers and other relevant programing, and by making available to students articles, books, and video materials that relate to parenting by individuals with sexual minority identities (Casper and Schultz, 1999). Similarly, religious groups can offer meaningful support by providing special activities for lesbian and gay families with children, and by educating all members of congregations about lesbian and gay parenting (Kahn, 1991).

Another major aim of service to prospective lesbian and gay parents is to eliminate discrimination against lesbian and gay parents and their children. To the degree that this effort meets with success, many of the special needs of gay or lesbian parents and their children will decrease in significance. Although it is unlikely that anti-gay prejudice will be eliminated in the foreseeable future, work in this direction is nevertheless of great importance. Prevention efforts relevant to lesbian and gay parenting should be designed to counter unfavorable stereotypes of lesbians and gay men with accurate information about the realities of life in lesbian and gay families, and to provide an understanding of psychosocial processes underlying prejudice and discrimination.

Directions for Advocacy

Among the greatest current needs of lesbian and gay families with children is for activism to promote social and political change. Gay and lesbian parents and their children have issues in common with those of many other families, but they also have unique concerns that arise from prejudice against lesbian and gay parents and their children.

The basic issues of children and families are, in many cases, also the issues of lesbian and gay families with children. For instance, many families with children would benefit from enhanced safety in their homes and neighborhoods, higher quality schools, flexible working hours for parents, and better access to health care. A more equal distribution of economic resources would benefit children in economically stressed lesbian and gay families, just as they would benefit children in other economically disadvantaged homes. In other words, a common stake is held by gay, lesbian, and heterosexual parented families in many issues of public policy relevant to families with children.

Even allowing for overlap with the needs of other families, though, lesbian and gay parents and their children also have a unique agenda. These families are less likely than heterosexual families to enjoy legal recognition for their family relationships, equal access to medical care, or freedom from harassment, bigotry, and hate crimes. The quality of life for lesbian and gay parents would be greatly enhanced if they could be confident that their sexual orientation would not be held against them as they pursue parenthood, bring up their children, or seek custody of their children after a partner's death or the break-up of parents. Like the offspring of heterosexual parents, children of lesbian and gay parents would feel more secure if their relationships with parents were protected by law. Accomplishment of such aims is an important goal for advocacy efforts on behalf of lesbian and gay families with children (Polikoff, 1990; Rubinstein, 1991; Patterson and Redding, 1996).

It is clear that there is much work to be done to improve the lives of lesbian and gay parents and their children. Although research to date has been productive, although many advances in services have been made and important advocacy campaigns have been mounted, there is still much to do. As stated above, research can be helpful in identifying issues that need to be addressed through service and advocacy efforts. However, it is through the intertwining of research, service, and advocacy that the lives of lesbian and gay parents and their children can most likely be improved.

REFERENCES

Adam, B.D. (1987) *The Rise of a Gay and Lesbian Movement*. Boston: Twayne Publishers.

Badgett, M.V.L. (1998) The economic well-being of lesbian, gay and bisexual adults' families. In Patterson, C.J. and D'Augelli, A.R. (eds) *Lesbian, Gay and Bisexual Identities in Families: Psychological Perspectives*. New York: Oxford University Press, pp. 231–48.

Bailey, J.M. and Dawood, K. (1998) Behavior genetics, sexual orientation, and the family. In Patterson, C.J. and D'Augelli, A.R. (eds) *Lesbian, Gay and Bisexual Identities in Families: Psychological Perspectives*. New York: Oxford University Press, pp. 3–39.

Barret, R.L. and Robinson, B.E. (1990) *Gay Fathers*. Lexington, MA: Lexington Books.

Baumrind, D. (1967) Childcare practices anteceding three patterns of preschool behavior. *Genetic Psychology Monographs*, **75**, 43–88.

Baumrind, D. and Black, A.E. (1967) Socialization practices associated with dimensions of competence in preschool boys and girls. *Child Development*, **38**, 291–327.

Beers, J.R. (1996) The desire to parent in gay men. Unpublished doctoral dissertation, Columbia University, New York.

Bell, A.P. and Weinberg, M.S. (1978) *Homosexualities: A Study of Diversity among Men and Women*. New York: Simon and Schuster.

Bigner, J.J. and Bozett, F.W. (1990) Parenting by gay fathers. In Bozett, F.W. and Sussman, M.B. (eds)

Homosexuality and Family Relations. New York: Harrington Park Press, pp. 155–75.

Bigner, J.J. and Jacobsen, R.B. (1989a) The value of children to gay and heterosexual fathers. In Bozett, F.W. (ed.) *Homosexuality and the Family.* New York: Harrington Park Press, pp. 137–62.

Bigner, J.J. and Jacobsen, R.B. (1989b) Parenting behaviors of homosexual and heterosexual fathers. In Bozett, F.W. (ed.) *Homosexuality and the Family.* New York: Harrington Park Press, pp. 163–72.

Blumenfeld, W.J. and Raymond, D. (1988) *Looking at Gay and Lesbian Life.* Boston: Beacon.

Blumstein, P. and Schwartz, P. (1983) *American Couples.* New York: Morrow.

Boswell, J. (1980) *Christianity, Social Tolerance, and Homosexuality: Gay People in Western Europe from the Beginning of the Christian Era to the Fourteenth Century.* Chicago: University of Chicago Press.

Bozett, F.W. (1980) Gay fathers: how and why they disclose their homosexuality to their children. *Family Relations,* **29,** 173–9.

Bozett, F.W. (1981a) Gay fathers: evolution of the gay-father identity. *American Journal of Orthopsychiatry,* **51,** 552–9.

Bozett, F.W. (1981b) Gay fathers: identity conflict resolution through integrative sanctioning. *Alternative Lifestyles,* **4,** 90–107.

Bozett, F.W. (1987) Children of gay fathers. In Bozett, F.W. (ed.) *Gay and Lesbian Parents.* New York: Praeger, pp. 39–57.

Bozett, F.W. (1989) Gay fathers: a review of the literature. In Bozett, F.W. (ed.) *Homosexuality and the Family.* New York: Harrington Park Press, pp. 137–62.

Brewaeys, A. and Van Hall, E.V. (1997) Lesbian motherhood: the impact on child development and family functioning. *Journal of Psychosomatic Obstetrics and Gynecology,* **18,** 1–16.

Brodzinsky, D.M., Patterson, C.J. and Vaziri, M. (2003) Adoption agency perspectives on lesbian and gay adoptive parents: a national study. Unpublished manuscript, Rutgers University, Piscataway, NJ.

Brown, L. (1995) Lesbian identities: conceptual issues. In D'Augelli, A.R. and Patterson, C. (eds) *Lesbian, Gay and Bisexual Identities Across the Lifespan.* New York: Oxford University Press, pp. 3–23.

Casper, V. and Schultz, S. (1999) *Gay Parents, Straight Schools: Building Communication and Trust.* New York: Teachers College Press.

Casper, V., Schultz, S. and Wickens, E. (1992) Breaking the silences: lesbian and gay parents and the schools. *Teachers College Record,* **94,** 109–37.

Chan, R.W., Brooks, R.C., Raboy, B. and Patterson, C.J. (1998a) Division of labor among lesbian and heterosexual parents: associations with children's adjustment. *Journal of Family Psychology,* **12,** 402–19.

Chan, R.W., Raboy, B. and Patterson, C.J. (1998b) Psychosocial adjustment among children conceived via donor insemination by lesbian and heterosexual mothers. *Child Development,* **69,** 443–57.

Cowan, C.P. and Cowan, P.A. (1992) *When Partners Become Parents: The Big Life Change for Couples.* New York: Basic Books.

Crawford, S. (1987) Lesbian families: psychosocial stress and the family-building process. In Boston Lesbian Psychologies Collective (ed.) *Lesbian Psychologies: Explorations and Challenges.* Urbana: University of Illinois Press, pp. 195–214.

D'Augelli, A.R. and Garnets, L. (1995) Lesbian, gay and bisexual communities. In D'Augelli, A.R. and Patterson, C.J. (eds) *Lesbian, Gay and Bisexual Identities Across the Lifespan.* New York: Oxford University Press, pp. 293–320.

D'Emilio, J. (1983) *Sexual Politics, Sexual Communities: The Makings of a Homosexual Minority in the United States, 1940–1970.* Chicago: University of Chicago Press.

Dunne, E.J. (1987) Helping gay fathers come out to their children. *Journal of Homosexuality,* **13,** 213–22.

Editors of the Harvard Law Review (1990) *Sexual Orientation and the Law.* Cambridge, MA: Harvard University Press.

Faderman, L. (1981) *Surpassing the Love of Men.* New York: William Morrow.

Faderman, l. (1991) *Odd Girls and Twilight Lovers: A History of Lesbian Life in Twentieth Century America.* New York: Columbia University Press.

Falk, P.J. (1989) Lesbian mothers: psychosocial assumptions in family law. *American Psychologist,* **44,** 941–7.

Flaks, D.K., Ficher, I., Masterpasqua, F. and Joseph, G. (1995) Lesbians choosing motherhood: a comparative study of lesbian and heterosexual parents and their children. *Developmental Psychology,* **31,** 105–14.

Fox, R.C. (1995) Bisexual identities. In D'Augelli, A.R. and Patterson, C.J. (eds) *Lesbian, Gay and Bisexual Identities Across the Lifespan.* New York: Oxford University Press, pp. 48–86.

Gartrell, N., Hamilton, J., Banks, A., Mosbacher, D., Reed, N., Sparks, C.H. and Bishop, H. (1996) The national lesbian family study: I. Interviews with prospective mothers. *American Journal of Orthopsychiatry,* **66,** 272–81.

Gartrell, N., Banks, A., Hamilton, J., Reed, N., Bishop, H. and Rodas, C. (1999) The national lesbian family study: II. Interviews with mothers of toddlers. *American Journal of Orthopsychiatry,* **69,** 362–9.

Goleman, D. (1992) Studies find no disadvantage to growing up in a gay home. *New York Times,* 2 December 1992, C-14.

Golombok, S. and Tasker, F. (1996) Do parents influence the sexual orientation of their children? Findings from a longitudinal study of lesbian families. *Developmental Psychology,* **32,** 3–11.

Golombok, S., Spencer, A. and Rutter, M. (1983) Children in lesbian and single-parent households: psychosexual and psychiatric appraisal. *Journal of Child Psychology and Psychiatry,* **24,** 551–72.

Golombok, S., Cook, R., Bish, A. and Murray, C. (1995) Families created by the new reproductive technologies: quality of parenting and social and emotional development of the children. *Child Development,* **66,** 285–98.

Golombok, S., Tasker, F.L. and Murray, C. (1997) Children raised in fatherless families from infancy: family relationships and the socioemotional development of children of lesbian and single heterosexual mothers. *Journal of Child Psychology and Psychiatry*. **38**, 783–91.

Gonsiorek, J.C. (1991) The empirical basis for the demise of the illness model of homosexuality. In Gonsiorek, J.C. and Weinrich, J.D. (eds) *Homosexuality: Research Implications for Public Policy*. Beverly Hills, CA: Sage Publications.

Gottman, J.S. (1990) Children of gay and lesbian parents. In Bozett, F.W. and Sussman, M.B. (eds) *Homosexuality and Family Relations*. New York: Harrington Park Press.

Green, R. (1978) Sexual identity of 37 children raised by homosexual or transsexual parents. *American Journal of Psychiatry*, **135**, 692–7.

Green, R., Mandel, J.B., Hotvedt, M.E., Gray, J. and Smith, L. (1986) Lesbian mothers and their children: a comparison with solo parent heterosexual mothers and their children. *Archives of Sexual Behavior*, **7**, 175–81.

Gross, J. (1991) New challenge of youth: growing up in a gay home. *New York Times*, 11 February 1991, A-1, B-7.

Hand, S.I. (1991) *The Lesbian Parenting Couple*. Unpublished doctoral dissertation, The Professional School of Psychology, San Francisco.

Harris, M.B. and Turner, P.H. (1985/1986) Gay and lesbian parents. *Journal of Homosexuality*, **12**, 101–13.

Herek, G. (1995) Psychological heterosexism in the United States. In D'Augelli, A.R. and Patterson, C.J. (eds) *Lesbian, Gay and Bisexual Identities over the Lifespan: Psychological Perspectives*. New York: Oxford University Press, pp. 321–46.

Hill, M. (1987) Child-rearing attitudes of black lesbian mothers. In the Boston Lesbian Psychologies Collective (ed.) *Lesbian Psychologies: Explorations and Challenges*. Urbana: University of Illinois Press, pp. 215–26.

Hoeffer, B. (1981) Children's acquisition of sex-role behavior in lesbian-mother families, *American Journal of Orthopsychiatry*, **5**, 536–44.

Huggins, S.L. (1989) A comparative study of self-esteem of adolescent children of divorced lesbian mothers and divorced heterosexual mothers. In Bozett, F.W. (ed.) *Homosexuality and the Family*. New York: Harrington Park Press, pp. 123–35.

Kahn, Y.H. (1991) Hannah, must you have a child? *Out/Look*, Spring 1991 (Issue 12), 39–43.

King, B.R. and Black, K.N. (1999) College students' perceptual stigmatization of the children of lesbian mothers. *American Journal of Orthopsychiatry*, **69**, 220–7.

Kirkpatrick, M. (1987) Clinical implications of lesbian mother studies. *Journal of Homosexuality*, **13**, 201–11.

Kirkpatrick, M. (1996) Lesbians as parents. In Cabaj, R.P. and Stein, T.S. (eds) *Textbook of Homosexuality and Mental Health*. Washington, DC: American Psychiatric Press, pp. 353–70.

Kirkpatrick, M., Smith, C. and Roy, R. (1981) Lesbian mothers and their children: a comparative survey. *American Journal of Orthopsychiatry*, **51**, 545–51.

Koepke, L., Hare, J. and Moran, P.B. (1992) Relation- ship quality in a sample of lesbian couples with children and child-free lesbian couples. *Family Relations*, **41**, 224–9.

Kweskin, S.L. and Cook, A.S. (1982) Heterosexual and homosexual mothers' self-described sex-role behavior and ideal sex-role behavior in children. *Sex Roles*, **8**, 967–75.

Lamb, M.E. (ed.) (1999) *Parenting and Child Development in Nontraditional Families*. Hillsdale, NJ: Erlbaum.

Laumann, E.O., Gagnon, J.H., Michael, R.T. and Michaels, S. (1994) *The Social Organization of Sexuality: Sexual Practices in the United States*. Chicago: University of Chicago Press.

Lyons, T.A. (1983) Lesbian mothers' custody fears. *Women and Therapy*, **2**, 231–40.

Martin, A. (1989) The planned lesbian and gay family: parenthood and children. *Newsletter of the Society for the Psychological Study of Lesbian and Gay Issues*, **5**, 6 and 16–17.

Martin, A. (1993) *The Lesbian and Gay Parenting Handbook: Creating and Raising Our Families*. New York: HarperCollins.

McCandlish, B. (1987) Against all odds: lesbian mother family dynamics. In Bozett, F. (ed.) *Gay and Lesbian Parents*. New York: Praeger, pp. 23–36.

McPherson, D. (1993) Gay parenting couples: parenting arrangements, arrangement satisfaction, and relationship satisfaction. Unpublished doctoral dissertation, Pacific Graduate School of Psychology.

Michaels, S. (1996) The prevalence of homosexuality in the United States. In Cabaj, R.P. and Stein, T.S. (eds) *Textbook of Homosexuality and Mental Health*. Washington, DC: American Psychiatric Press, pp. 43–63.

Miller, B. (1978) Adult sexual resocialization: adjustments toward a stigmatized identity. *Alternative Lifestyles*, **1**, 207–34.

Miller, B. (1979) Gay fathers and their children. *Family Coordinator*, **28**, 544–52.

Miller, J.A., Jacobsen, R.B. and Bigner, J.J. (1981) The child's home environment for lesbian versus heterosexual mothers: a neglected area of research. *Journal of Homosexuality*, **7**, 49–56.

Mucklow, B.M. and Phelan, G.K. (1979) Lesbian and traditional mothers' responses to adult responses to child behavior and self concept. *Psychological Reports*, **44**, 880–2.

Osman, S. (1972) My stepfather is a she. *Family Process*, **11**, 209–18.

Osterweil, D.A. (1991) Correlates of relationship satisfaction in lesbian couples who are parenting their first child together. Unpublished doctoral dissertation, California School of Professional Psychology, Berkeley/Alameda.

Pagelow, M.D. (1980) Heterosexual and lesbian single mothers: a comparison of problems, coping and solutions. *Journal of Homosexuality*, **5**, 198–204.

Parks, C.A. (1998) Lesbian parenthood: a review of the literature. *American Journal of Orthopsychiatry*, **68**, 376–89.

Patterson, C.J. (1992) Children of lesbian and gay parents. *Child Development*, **63**, 1025–42.

Patterson, C.J. (1994a) Children of the lesbian baby boom: behavioral adjustment, self-concepts, and sex-role identity. In Greene, B. and Herek, G. (eds) *Contemporary Perspectives on Lesbian and Gay Psychology: Theory, Research, and Applications*. Beverly Hills: Sage Publications, pp. 156–75.

Patterson, C.J. (1994b) Lesbian and gay couples considering parenthood: an agenda for research, service, and advocacy. *Journal of Gay and Lesbian Social Services*, **1**, 33–55.

Patterson, C.J. (1995a) Lesbian mothers, gay fathers, and their children. In D'Augelli, A.R. and Patterson, C.J. (eds) *Lesbian, Gay and Bisexual Identities Across the Lifespan*. New York: Oxford University Press, pp. 262–90.

Patterson, C.J. (1995b) Families of the lesbian baby boom: parents' division of labor and children's adjustment. *Developmental Psychology*, **31**, 115–23.

Patterson, C.J. (1997) Children of lesbian and gay parents. In Ollendick, T. and Prinz, R. (eds) *Advances in Clinical Child Psychology*, Vol. 19. New York: Plenum Press, pp. 235–82.

Patterson, C.J. (1998) Family lives of children with lesbian mothers. In Patterson, C.J. and D'Augelli, A.R. (eds) *Lesbian, Gay and Bisexual Identities in Families: Psychological. Perspectives*. New York: Oxford University Press, pp. 154–76.

Patterson, C.J. (2000) Family relationships of lesbians and gay men. *Journal of Marriage and the Family*, **62**, 1052–69.

Patterson, C.J. (2001) Families of the lesbian baby boom: maternal mental health and child adjustment. *Journal of Gay and Lesbian Psychotherapy*, **4**, 91–107.

Patterson, C.J. and Friel, L.V. (2000) Sexual orientation and fertility. In Bentley, G.R. and Mascie-Taylor, N. (eds) *Infertility in the Modern World: Biosocial Perspectives*. Cambridge: Cambridge University Press, pp. 238–60.

Patterson, C.J. and Redding, R. (1996) Lesbian and gay families with children: public policy implications of social science research. *Journal of Social Issues*, **52**, 29–50.

Perrin, E.C. (1998) Children whose parents are lesbian or gay. *Contemporary Pediatrics*, **15**, 113–30.

Pies, C. (1985) *Considering Parenthood*. San Francisco: Spinsters/Aunt Lute.

Pies, C. (1990) Lesbians and the choice to parent. In Bozett, F.W. and Sussman, M.B. (eds) *Homosexuality and Family Relations*. New York: Harrington Park Press, pp. 137–54.

Polikoff, N. (1990) This child does have two mothers: redefining parenthood to meet the needs of children in lesbian mother and other nontraditional families. *The Georgetown Law Review*, **78**, 459–575.

Pollack, S. and Vaughn, J. (eds) (1987) *Politics of the Heart: A Lesbian Parenting Anthology*. Ithaca, NY: Firebrand Books.

Rafkin, L. (ed.) (1990) *Different Mothers: Sons and Daughters of Lesbians Talk about Their Lives*. Pittsburgh: Cleis Press.

Rand, C., Graham, D.L.R. and Rawlings, E.I. (1982) Psychological health and factors the court seeks to control in lesbian mother custody trials. *Journal of Homosexuality*, **8**, 27–39.

Ricketts, W. (1991) *Lesbians and Gay Men as Foster Parents*. Portland, ME: National Child Welfare Resource Center for Management and Administration.

Ricketts, W. and Achtenberg, R. (1990) Adoption and foster parenting for lesbians and gay men: creating new traditions in family. In Bozett, F.W. and Sussman, M.B.

(eds) *Homosexuality and Family Relations*. New York: Harrington Park Press, pp. 83–118.

Riley, C. (1988) American kinship: a lesbian account. *Feminist Issues*, **8**, 75–94.

Rivera, R. (1991) Sexual orientation and the law. In Gonsiorek, J.C. and Weinrich, J.D. (eds) *Homosexuality: Research Implications for Public Policy*. Newbury Park, CA: Sage, pp. 81–100.

Robinson, B.E. and Skeen, P. (1982) Sex-role orientation of gay fathers versus gay nonfathers. *Perceptual and Motor Skills*, **55**, 1055–9.

Rohrbaugh, J.B. (1988) Choosing children: psychological issues in lesbian parenting. *Women and Therapy*, **8**, 51–63.

Rubenstein, W.B. (1991) We are family: a reflection on the search for legal recognition of lesbian and gay relationships. *The Journal of Law and Politics*, **8**, 89–105.

Sbordone, A.J. (1993) Gay men choosing fatherhood. Unpublished doctoral dissertation, Department of Psychology, City University of New York.

Schulenberg, J. (1985) *Gay Parenting: A Complete Guide for Gay Men and Lesbians with Children*. New York: Anchor.

Skeen, P. and Robinson, B. (1985) Gay fathers' and gay nonfathers' relationships with their parents. *Journal of Sex Research*, **21**, 86–91.

Stacey, J. and Biblarz, T.J. (2001) (How) Does the sexual orientation of parents matter? *American Sociological Review*, **65**, 159–83.

Steckel, A. (1985) Separation-individuation in children of lesbian and heterosexual couples. Unpublished doctoral dissertation, The Wright Institute Graduate School, Berkeley, CA.

Steckel, A. (1987) Psychosocial development of children of lesbian mothers. In Bozett, F.W. (ed.) *Gay and Lesbian Parents*. New York: Praeger.

Tasker, F.L. and Golombok, S. (1991) Children raised by lesbian mothers: the empirical evidence. *Family Law*, **21**, 184–7.

Tasker, F.L. and Golombok, S. (1997) *Growing Up in a Lesbian Family: Effects on Child Development*. New York: Guilford.

Tasker, F.L. and Golombok, S. (1998) The role of co-mothers in planned lesbian-led families. In Dunne, G.A. (ed.) *Living Difference: Lesbian Perspectives on Work and Family Life*. New York: Harrington Park Press, pp. 49–68.

Thompson, N., McCandless, B. and Strickland, B. (1971) Personal adjustment of male and female homosexuals and heterosexuals. *Journal of Abnormal Psychology*, **78**, 237–40.

Victor, S.B. and Fish, M.C. (1995) Lesbian mothers and their children: a review for school psychologists. *School Psychology Review*, **24**, 456–79.

United States Bureau of the Census (2000) http://www.census.gov/population/estimates/nation2/html

Weeks, R.B., Derdeyn, A.P. and Langman, M. (1975) Two cases of children of homosexuals. *Child Psychiatry and Human Development*, **6**, 26–32.

Weston, K. (1991) *Families We Choose: Lesbians, Gays, Kinship*. New York: Columbia University Press.

Wright, J.M. (1998) *Lesbian Stepfamilies: An Ethnography of Love*. New York: Harrington Park Press.

10

Grandparenting and Extended Support Networks

Peter K. Smith and Linda M. Drew

SUMMARY

Grandparenting is an important part of the life-cycle. Grandparent–grandchild contacts are often quite frequent and usually satisfying. Proximity is an important variable, although becoming less so now, with technological advances such as email. This contact allows grandparents to influence their grandchildren in many ways, directly and indirectly. There are distinctive roles in grandparenting, which vary between individuals, historical periods, and cultures. An important element of this is often acting as surrogate parents. Parental separation or divorce can greatly affect grandparents and their relations with grandchildren. This chapter sets out the major issues in this area.

INTRODUCTION

Grandparents and grandchildren have been described as being a 'vital connection' (Kornhaber and Woodward, 1981). Grandparenting is certainly an important part of the life-cycle; about three-quarters of adults will become grandparents. In the developed countries, the average age of becoming a grandparent is around 50 years for women and 52 years for men. With high death rates not coming in until the late 70s (mostly men) and 80s (especially women), this means that many will remain grandparents for some 25 years or about a third of their lifespan, and children will often grow up with both sets of grandparents. The three-generation family is now the most common modal. It can be considered normative today for children up to early adulthood to have grandparents, and for people in their late 50s onwards to have grandchildren (Rossi and Rossi, 1990).

This is a dramatic change from a century ago. It has been shown in the US context that of those born at the beginning of the 20th century, only about one-fifth had *any* grandparent still living by

age 30. For those born now, almost four-fifths will still have at least one grandparent alive by the same age. This change is part of a larger demographic shift from a 'pyramidal' age structure of the population, to a 'beanpole' structure. The pyramidal structure, typical through human history, has a predominantly young society and large families with limited intergenerational presence. The beanpole structure is the opposite, with smaller families and extended kin groups but greater intergenerational length, including grandparents, and extending to great-grandparents (Bengtson, 2001).

MAJOR CONCEPTUAL ISSUES

Development takes place in an historical context. Bengtson's approach illustrates this. He distinguishes *period* effects (historical period), *cohort* effects (when you were born while living in an historical period), and *lineage* effects (different generations within a family structure). Historical and cohort effects are important in studying grandparenting. The present cohort of grandparents in their 70s, for example, as well as being older than parents and grandchildren, will also have experienced less formal schooling.

An emphasis on *lineage* rather than *age* is appropriate for this topic, where we are primarily looking at the generational relationship of grandparenthood. Terms such as 'grandparent', 'parent', 'child', and 'grandchild' are relative; someone may be both a parent and a child, for example. Many researchers use generational labels such as G1, G2, G3 to avoid this ambiguity. However, this device has its own difficulties, as if G1 refers to a grandparental generation, then there is no appropriate label for any great-grandparents. In this chapter, we take grandchildren as the reference point, and refer to their parents, grandparents, and great-grandparents.

Grandparents can of course vary in age a great deal, whereas lineage remains constant. Age of grandparent can be considered as one factor (among many others) affecting grandparental relations. Another factor to be considered is culture. Most of our evidence on grandparenthood comes from modern urban, industrial societies, particularly the USA and to a lesser extent Western Europe. Generational relations would have been (and still are) very different in agrarian societies, being embedded in a system with strong kinship ties and strong expectations of reciprocity; parents tended to have many children, mortality was relatively high, and parents expected children to support them in old age. The urban-industrial revolution reduced the importance of kinship and parentage; and the concept of child-rearing changed from one of lifelong reciprocity to one of launching children into an autonomous maturity in which their future relationship with parents was optional (Caspi and Elder, 1988).

IMPORTANCE IN RESEARCH, COMMENTARY, POLICY AND PRACTICE

Falling fertility and increasing longevity have led to the demographic ageing of Western industrialized societies. Population ageing is shared by all these nations, but they differ in degree and speed of the process. In the last few decades, there has been an increase in divorce rates and in numbers of reconstituted families and step-kin; greater health and financial security in older generations; and with this some greater ambiguity in the role of grandparental lineage.

These demographic changes may even have influenced the extent to which grandparenting has been an object of social scientific and psychological research in the last 20–30 years, in addition to demographic changes. Three other reasons for the greater focus on grandparenting research have been suggested (Tinsley and Parke, 1984):

- the broader perspective of developmental and family psychologists beyond the parental dyad and 'nuclear family' to wider social networks:
- greater consideration of a lifespan framework and processes of intergenerational influence; and
- overcoming some methodological difficulties associated with working with grandparents.

Theoretical and statistical models need to be complex to cope with the three-way or multiple relations and patterns of direct and indirect influence entailed in analysing grandparent–grandchild influence and interaction.

Besides an increase in research on grandparenting, there are now a number of websites for grandparents (such as http://www.grandparenting.org/kornhaber.htm), and popular books on the topic. There are important policy issues regarding grandparents helping parents of young children getting into the workforce (by providing surrogate care for young children); and for rights of access to grandchildren when parents divorce. Courses in grandparenting may also be important in helping maximize the potential of this role in society (Werner, 1991).

HISTORICAL BACKGROUND

Some early articles about grandparents appeared in the 1930s and 1940s, influenced by the psychoanalytical perspective that was powerful at the time. These articles were usually written by psychiatrists or other clinicians, and gave a rather negative view of grandparental influence. For example, an early article by a medical practitioner criticized the 'malignant influence of grandmothers' who interfered with the mother's child-rearing in old-fashioned and didactic ways (Vollmer, 1937). The conclusion was that grandparents were not suitable as 'custodians' of the care and rearing of their grandchildren. They were seen as disturbing factors against which parents should protect the child to the best of their ability.

A more balanced view started to emerge in the 1950s. It was acknowledged that there were potential problems in grandparents living with their children and grandchildren. On the other hand, if they managed to establish positive relationships, they could make the transition from a position of responsibility in the family to one of being interested and helpful. The difficulty was seen as lying in the diffusion of boundaries for both parents and children through interference in such issues as discipline (Staples, 1952).

From the 1960s, grandparents started to be presented much more favourably in publications on the topic. This may reflect some actual changes in grandparental attitudes and behaviours. Although the early studies are probably unrepresentative in terms of sampling, it does seem that earlier in the century more grandparents were co-resident, and had a more authoritative attitude to their families. By the 1960s, however, many grandparents accepted a 'formal' or 'fun-seeking' role, clearly demarcating grandparental and parental roles. In an early study, only a very small proportion of grandparents saw themselves as 'reservoirs of family wisdom'. This decrease in formality and authority probably allowed more indulgent and warm relationships between grandparents and other family members (Neugarten and Weinstein, 1964).

From the 1970s, writings on grandparenthood continued this more positive picture. Grandparenthood was investigated (primarily in North America) for the importance of grandparents as support and socialization agents and as valued intergenerational family members (Tinsley and Parke, 1984). In the early 1990s, Smith edited a selection of studies of grandparenthood from different industrialized countries, helping to balance the great bulk of research from the USA (Smith, 1991). Over the last two decades, there has been a considerable increase in research on grandparenting. These generally have a more positive view of the role than was given in the earlier studies, while recognizing that difficulties can occur, as in any relationships.

CORE ISSUES

The Nature of Contacts between Grandparents and Grandchildren

Grandparents play an important and supportive role in the lives of grandchildren, and grandparent–grandchild contacts can be mutually rewarding. The consensus of a considerable number of studies on contemporary grandparents and grandchildren is that they see each other moderately frequently, and the relationship is usually (though not invariably) quite close and satisfying, rather than involving conflict.

How close grandparents and grandchildren live – their physical proximity – has been found to be the most important factor in frequency of contact and level of emotional closeness between grandparents and grandchildren. In many countries (such as the US, UK and Poland), the majority of grandparents have been found to live fairly close to their grandchildren (an average distance of 30 miles/50 km is typical) and they see their grandchildren weekly or at least monthly. In Finland, the vast majority of grandparents, even when quite elderly, see their grandchildren at least once a week; and most see the relationship in positive terms (Hurme, 1988). In Germany, grandparents typically see grandchildren weekly, or more often for preschool grandchildren (Sticker, 1991).

Generally, grandchildren ranging in age from young children to adulthood feel a strong emotional bond with their grandparents, and this is reciprocated. Over four-fifths of US grandfathers said they felt very close to the grandchild with whom they had most contact, and ranked grandfatherhood as the third most important role in their life, after being a spouse or parent (Kivett, 1985). Similarly in the UK, most grandparents state that their relationship with their grandchild was closer than any or most relationships they have had (Drew, 2000). The predominant tendency is for grandparents to see grandchildren often enough to share a quite close and satisfying relationship. However, there is variation in contact and satisfaction in grandparent–grandchild relationships: as in any other forms of human relationship. Some grandchildren may not like their grandparents; one Polish student reported, 'I don't like my grandmother; she's sloppy and disagreeable ... I don't like visiting her'; and another, 'she's always running about, grumbling, nagging and shouting' (Tyszkowa, 1991). The relationship of the grandparent has usually been generalized to all of their grandchildren; but different grandchildren will have different needs and personalities. Grandparents, not surprisingly, spend more time with those grandchildren they regard as 'special' than those they describe as 'irritating'.

Grandparents engage in a wide range of activities with grandchildren, such as giving treats, providing a 'sense of family', imparting family history, taking part in family events, playing games, going on trips, baby-sitting, 'making you feel good', giving emergency help, giving personal advice, being 'someone to talk to', joining in religious activity, and giving advice on school. Intimate conversations have been reported in a number of studies: 'with Grandma I can talk about my problems'; '... we talk about everything, also about confidences which concern our family as a whole'. The majority of grandparents in the US have been shown to talk to their grandchildren about personal concerns. Sometimes, being close but not an authority figure, grandparents can act as confidants in situations where an older child might not wish to confide in a parent (Hodgson, 1992).

In summary, most grandparents see many grandchildren at least once a month, sometimes much more often, and generally the relationship is seen as positive, emotionally rewarding, and important, by both generations.

Is Proximity Important?

An important factor in the frequency of contact and level of emotional closeness between grandparents and grandchildren is their proximity. At least, this was found to be the case in research through the 1980s and early 1990s. While many grandparents and grandchildren live within 30 miles (50 km) of each other, in the US a quarter live more than 500 miles (800 km) away, and this greater distance is the strongest factor in predicting (lower) frequency of contact. In almost all cases, the grandchild with whom a grandfather had the most contact with was also the closest geographically (Kivett, 1985; Hodgson, 1992). In Finland, a sharp decline in frequency of contact with 12-year-old grandchildren was found when grandparents lived more than 20 km away, although there was little change in the perceived importance of the relationship, up to 60 km (Hurme, 1988).

Changes in transportation and communication provide other avenues to maintain contact, so these patterns may be changing in contemporary times. For decades, the telephone has been available, although expensive for frequent long-distance use. Telephone contact plays an important role in sustaining the relationship between adolescent grandchildren and paternal grandparents, and the frequency of telephone calls is a more effective predictor of grandparent–grandchild closeness than letters. In a US national study, about two-thirds of grandparents communicated with their grandchildren weekly or more via the telephone. However, contact was more likely to be initiated by grandmothers, younger grandparents, and those with younger grandchildren (Silverstein and Marenco, 2001).

Although little research evidence is available, it is clear that many grandparents now use email and text messages to maintain contact with grandchildren. In a UK study, it has been found that grandparents who lived a long way away from their school-age grandchildren, and saw them yearly, felt as emotionally close to them as to their grandchildren who lived closer and whom they saw weekly. All the grandparents who were separated geographically (ranging from 70 to 450 miles or 110–725 km) from their grandchildren had some form of indirect contact with their grandchildren: about half spoke on the phone weekly, almost as many spoke on the phone twice weekly or wrote letters once a month, and about one in ten emailed twice weekly (Drew, 2000). In the UK, recent data show that the vast majority of grandparents and grandchildren kept in regular telephone contact and some via email. It is a common experience that distances seem to shrink when daily email contact across countries and continents can be maintained (Age Concern, 1998).

Characteristics of Grandparents and Grandchildren

Factors specific to the grandparent and grandchild that might impact the grandparent–grandchild relationship are gender, lineage (paternal or maternal), age and health of the grandparents, and age and gender of the grandchildren.

Age of grandparent can be an important consideration, just as age of the grandchild can. In a US national study, younger grandparents tended to live closer and have greater contact, while older grandparents provided more financial assistance (Silverstein and Marenco, 2001). College-aged grandchildren identified reasons for closeness with younger and older grandparents: for younger grandparents (aged 50–60), reasons were more to do with love and appreciation, intimacy, and shared activities, while older grandparents, especially those over 75, received more reasons to do with affection and other positive sentiments for the grandparent.

No special connection between age of grandparent and satisfaction with the role of grandparent or in the amount of help given to grandchildren has been found. However, younger grandparents (ranging in age from 45 to 69) express greater responsibility for grandchildren's discipline and for giving child-rearing advice than older grandparents. This may be due to the age of the grandchild. In an Italian study, grandchildren aged 8–9, 12–13 and 16–17 years were questioned. The youngest group more often described playing with grandparents, especially maternal grandparents, while older grandchildren saw their grandparents as somewhat less important, but also as more patient and understanding than parents (Battestelli and Farneti, 1991). As children develop rapidly, it is more likely that changes in the age of the grandchild are responsible for this trend rather than historical period, or age of grandparent.

Effects of age of grandparent are often confounded with grandparent health. Older grandparents are less likely to be in good health, and this can affect the relationship. Mild health problems may not decrease the satisfaction with a relationship, but more serious illnesses such as Alzheimer's disease, not surprisingly, may decrease levels of intimacy and affection, although not nurturance for the grandparent (Creasey et al., 1989).

Just as mothers are more often the closer parent to children, many studies find that grandmothers are more involved with grandchildren than grandfathers, and grandchildren feel closer to grandmothers at all ages. Similarly, the usual finding is that maternal grandparents are more involved than paternal grandparents. 'Sex role' beliefs may influence grandchildren in identifying the grandmother as having a greater influence on their values, and feeling closer to them. However, traditionally closer mother–daughter relationships may be influential in grandchildren of all ages having closer relationships with maternal than paternal grandparents (Smith and Drew, 2002).

Compared to grandfathers, grandmothers tend to anticipate and become involved in the nurturing role sooner and have greater satisfaction with their current and expected grandparenting role. Gender roles place importance on emotional interactions for grandmothers and granddaughters, while grandfathers and grandsons focus on doing things together, and instrumental and practical support, such as financial or career advice. However, when involved, the evidence is that grandfathers are able to nurture and respond to children's needs as effectively as grandmothers. Some grandfathers are more nurturing than they were as fathers. The differences may lie in personal perception of the role and variations of human interactions, or in the diverse cultural norms of relations between genders in different societies (Rossi and Rossi, 1990; Kornhaber, 1996).

Direct and Indirect Influences of Grandparents on Grandchildren

What influence do grandparents have on the development of grandchildren? These are generally distinguished as *direct influences*, resulting from contact and face-to-face interaction, and *indirect influences*, mediated by other means such as parental behaviour (Tinsley and Parke, 1984).

INDIRECT INFLUENCES

One source of indirect influence of grandparents is via financial support. Grandparents can often help grandchildren by assisting the middle generation (parents) financially, for example, in buying a home, or a better home than could otherwise be afforded. In a US national sample, about one-third of grandparents gave gifts or money to their grandchildren (Silverstein and Marenco, 2001). These grandparents were more likely to be older. Grandparents may also give emotional support, for example when parents experience family stress, separation or divorce, as seen later. This can help the grandchildren, quite aside from any direct contact that may take place.

More subtly but just as powerfully, grandparents, by acting as parents themselves, will have influenced the way in which their children act as parents to the children. To some extent, parents take their own parents as models of the parenting process. Some studies have looked at transmission of general parenting qualities such as warmth, autonomy, depression and aggression. In a Finnish sample there were significant correlations between grandparental and parental child-rearing attitudes and practices (Ruoppila, 1991). In the US, the quality of the grandparents' marriage was found to be repeated in the marital happiness of their adult children and the transfer of skills through the generations, from grandparent to parent to grandchild (Rossi and Rossi, 1990). A modest relationship through the generations (grandmother to adult daughter to granddaughter) has been found for 'autonomy' and 'warmth'. In a sample of Dutch grandmother–mother pairs, there were strong grandmother–mother links for educational level, affection and conformity; and also from grandmother affection to mother's psychological well-being (Vermulst et al., 1991).

Intergenerational influences have also been found for antisocial behaviour, drug abuse and psychopathology. The use of physically aggressive and punitive techniques in the grandparent–parent generation predicts similar behaviour in the parent–grandchild generation and antisocial behaviour in the grandchildren. In the Berkeley Guidance Study in the US, links were found between problem behaviour and unstable ties in the family across four generations of women (Caspi and Elder, 1988). Relations between grandparent and maternal drug abuse and behavioural/developmental problems in grandchildren aged 2 to 8 years have been found, especially for boys. When both the parent and grandparent are depressed, the grandchild is at a high risk for anxiety, and about half of these grandchildren had some form of psychopathology (Warner et al., 1999).

Some generational transmission may be through modelling of 'parenting behaviours', while some of it may be genetic. Another sort of explanation has been put forward by attachment theory. In infancy, attachment type is assessed by the 'Strange Situation' (SS), yielding classifications of *'secure'*, *'avoidant'*, *'ambivalent'* and *'disorganized'* attachment with the mother or care-giver. Attachment theory argues that these behavioural patterns acquired in infancy and childhood become internalized representations, reflecting trust or ambivalence learnt in primary relationships. They become 'internal working models of relationships'. In adult life these are assessed by the 'Adult Attachment Interview' (AAI), which yields four categories (Van Ijzendoorn, 1995):

- 'autonomous' – recalling earlier attachment-related experiences objectively and openly, even if these were not favourable;
- 'dismissive' – earlier attachment-related experiences seen as of little concern, value or influence;
- 'preoccupied' – still dependent on parents and actively struggling to please them; and
- 'unresolved' – a trauma involving, or early death of, an attachment figure, which has not been worked through.

There is a moderate predictive link between the child's SS category with (usually) its mother and the mother's AAI classification reflecting her model of the relationship with her own parents (her child's grandparents). Studies in this area are fraught with methodological and other complications, which make interpretation difficult. From the small number of studies available, however, it appears that there is a strong carry-over of attachment style from childhood to adulthood.

Part of this intergenerational transmission appears to be due to maternal sensitivity to infant signals. Available evidence shows these links across three generations – grandmother–mother–infant triads – show similar attachment styles (Benoit and Parker, 1994).

Attachment theory emphasizes consistency over generations, but it also predicts that adults can work through or resolve unsatisfactory relations with their parents and modify their 'internal working models' or the way they perceive and respond to key relationships through self-reflection, with the aid of therapy or counselling. A current and continuing study of survivors of the Holocaust in World War II finds that, although many survivors (now grandparents) score 'unresolved' on the AAI, due to the traumatic way in which they lost their parents at an early age, few of their children score unresolved. Their grandchildren appear to be indistinguishable from the remaining population in terms of attachment characteristics (Bar-On et al., 1998).

DIRECT INFLUENCES

Examples of the direct influence of grandparents on grandchildren are giving gifts, being a companion and confidant, acting as an emotional support or 'buffer' at times of family stress, passing on family history or national traditions, and acting as a role model for ageing. The most direct form of grandparent–grandchild influence is through acting as a surrogate parent. There are three levels at which this can happen:

- temporary childcare or daycare when the grandchild goes to the grandparent's house;
- co-resident grandparenting, where grandparents live in a three-generation household with the grandchild; and
- the grandparent-maintained household or 'skipped generation' family, in which the grandchild is cared for directly by the grandparent(s).

We review these three areas below.

PRACTICE OF GRANDPARENTING

Childcare

Grandparents are often relied on to provide baby-sitting or regular childcare to help parents, who may be working full-time, while the children are young. The majority of grandparents in the US seem to provide childcare or baby-sitting for their younger grandchildren. Those grandparents who live either with or near their grandchildren and those with a college education appear more likely to offer this service to parents. The decision to care may be initiated by the grandparent. Many grandparents are not paid for the childcare provided, and the most frequent pattern is maternal grandparents who care for their daughter's children.

There are advantages for all three generations when the grandparent provides childcare. Parents are confident that their children are in a loving safe environment, they have reduced expenses, and are able to be better employees, through timekeeping and reduced preoccupation with their child's welfare. Grandchildren are in a stable environment and develop an emotionally close relationship with their grandparent. For grandparents, the rewards are in helping their adult child, in being a part of the emotional development of their grandchildren, and increasing their own sense of emotional well-being. However, not all grandparents are happy to provide this service, especially those who do not want to be tied down every day looking after grandchildren as they feel they are done with parenting (Silverstein and Marenco, 2001).

Grandparents who Parent Their Grandchildren

The most intensive form of childcare occurs in grandparent-maintained households – grandparents who parent their grandchildren. The 1997 US Census Bureau indicated that 1.3 million grandparents were rearing grandchildren between 1980 and 1992, an increase on previous figures. The reasons for the adoption of this role change range from parental incapacity due to drug use, teenage pregnancy (of their daughter), divorce, mental and physical illness AIDS, and child abuse to parental incarceration and no doubt others. Grandparent-headed households appear to be more common in African-American and then Latino or Hispanic than European-American families. No similar information is available for other multi-ethnic countries.

Grandchildren reared in grandparent-headed households are reported to have poorer academic performance than similar children in parent-headed households. This may be because these families are often poor, with less adequate health care. Many grandparents who are raising their grandchildren are in good health and work outside the home. African-American grandparents appeared more satisfied with this role, while more European-American grandmothers report feeling trapped in their role – not having enough time for themselves, lacking privacy, and having to tolerate unwanted change in their home environment. However, both African-American and European-American grandmothers have high levels of satisfaction with themselves as a function of their grandparent role. African-American grandmothers are more likely to have friends or other family members rearing grandchildren and feel less tired or isolated. But for some, there is a price to pay. Some grandparents who look after their grandchildren have a higher incidence of depression, anxiety and risk for physical and emotional health problems (Kennedy and Keeney, 1988).

Grandparenting Role and Psychological Well-being

The grandparenting role is largely a matter of individual adaptation and may not be equally significant to all grandparents. Nevertheless, a substantial majority of grandparents in a US national study reported that the grandparent role was extremely important to their sense of self (Silverstein and Marenco, 2001). Although the grandparental role is developed through the process of interaction with grandchildren, the 'meaning' of grandparenthood also emerges in part from past relationships with one's own grandparents and observations of one's own parents as grandparents. The individual meaning of the grandparent role is certainly a major factor in the importance placed on the grandchild relationship and how it is enacted. There is no way of predicting it until it happens.

Researchers have identified typologies or different styles of grandparenting. In brief, grandparenthood holds significant positive meaning for most grandparents in multiple and often overlapping ways. These include fulfilling an emotional need; a sense of biological renewal in the continuation of family characteristics; being a teacher or resource person; and seeing the grandchild as an extension of themselves. A few grandparents, however, feel remote from the relationship. The meaning of the grandparenting role is very specific to the individual and has been found to vary between gender and lineage (Neugarten and Weinstein, 1964).

Changes in Roles with Time and Culture

In the Pacific Rim countries of China, Japan and Korea, family ties including grandparental bonds tend to be especially close, and many grandparents still live in three-generation households. In a study of elderly people in the Philippines, Taiwan and Thailand, almost half lived with young grandchildren (Hermalin et al., 1998). The majority of older parents in Beijing, China, live with an adult child, usually with a grandchild present. Preschool care by grandparents in China has been associated with rather better school performance than parental care (Falbo, 1991). There are possible complications in this finding (such as socio-economic status), but frequency of grandparental contact, plus grandparents' educational attainment, predict better language and mathematics scores in first- and fifth-grade children. Korean grandmothers have been credited with increasing their grandchildren's resiliency by providing sources of attachment, affection and knowledge, as well as having indirect positive effects through their support of parents (Hwang and St James-Roberts, 1998).

In the USA, several studies have documented the particular importance of grandparents, especially the maternal grandmother, in African-American households. Currently about half of African-American children live in single-parent female-headed households, about three times the figure for European-American families. Also, the generation gap tends to be shorter. There is thus more opportunity in African-American families for younger grandparents to be involved with and support their grandchildren (Burton and Dilworth-Anderson, 1991).

Expectations and practice of grandparental roles and behaviour, in Western societies, changed over the 20th century. Western grandparents have, by and large, settled into a 'supportive' role in which they are available to help parents, but do not interfere with parental decisions. A US study found that grandmothers could give a list of rules that they used to regulate their behaviour with their grandchildren (Johnson, 1983). These rules suggested they should be an advocate, mediator, support, and source of enjoyment; they should not be too intrusive, overprotective, parental or too old-fashioned. Most contemporary UK grandparents seem able to find a balance in their role of supporting the family through emotional and practical help, but of non-interference in the parenting style of their adult child and son/daughter-in-law.

Changes in grandparental role can lead to intergenerational difficulties and disagreements. This can happen through historical time, but also through processes of 'acculturation', changes in the cultural behaviour and thinking of an individual or group through contact with another culture. Children of immigrant parents and grandparents more rapidly adopt the language, styles and customs of a new, larger culture they are in, than the older generations, leading to changes in perceptions of the parent or grandparent role. In a study of Muslim mothers who lived in extended families in Britain, acculturation was found to contribute to disagreements in child-rearing practices with grandmothers, often resulting in the mothers having unusually high levels of depression and anxiety (Sonuga-Barke et al., 1998). The more closely adapted the intergenerational family, the greater amount of discrepancy found in child-rearing practices, with grandmothers being more 'authority orientated' and mothers more child-centred.

In the USA, the extent of absorption in the new culture of adult Mexican-American grandchildren has been found to affect the amount of contact they reported with their grandparents. However, grandparents did not feel a sense of loss of closeness. In a comparison of Mexican-American and Euro-American adult grandchild and grandparents, similar high scores of affection were found for both ethnic groups (Giarrusso et al., 2001). However, the new culture did not appear to have affected Mexican-American grandsons' family orientation since they indicated greater affection for their grandfathers than grandfathers reported for grandsons, in keeping with Mexican cultural values. Indo-American grandparents appear more accepting of their grandchildren moving away from the culture, than they are of their adult children (Pettys and Balgopal, 1998). They believed it was necessary for their grandchildren to change in order to get ahead in the American culture that they perceived as positive, whereas they expected their adult children to stay close to their ethnic origins. In Greece, a study of families with a Greek father and a British mother identified differing views of grandparents and parents from two distinct cultural backgrounds (Anderson, 1999). These differences made the grandparents difficult for grandchildren to accommodate when they were developing their own cultural identity.

Grandparents, Grandchildren and Parental Divorce

Separation and divorce have become more common events over the last few decades in many countries, including the US and the UK (Rodgers and Pryor, 1998). When parents separate and divorce, this can have a tremendous impact on grandparent–parent–grandchild relationships. The relationship of grandparents to parents, particularly to a custodial parent (or one who has care and control of the grandchildren), becomes a crucial factor in their relationships with the grandchildren. If the grandparent–parent relationships are harmonious, this opens opportunities for a supportive role: grandparents can provide stability, support and nurturance to the grandchild(ren) and family, often also providing financial assistance or childcare. Grandparents can negotiate relationship difficulties between the parent and grandchild and be a 'stress buffer' and source of emotional stability during times of family distress, which can benefit grandchildren even when their relationship with the grandparent is not intense (Smith and Drew, 2002).

After parental divorce a significant increase in contact occurs for some grandparent–grandchild pairs, notably for those maternal grandparents who can respond flexibly to their daughter and live close to their grandchildren. However, other grandparents can experience significantly reduced contact, especially when the grandparent–parent relationship has been difficult. If, as is usually the case, the children reside with their mother after divorce, then paternal grandparents may have to 'tread carefully' in obtaining access to their grandchildren. With about half of non-custodial fathers in the UK, USA and Canada gradually losing all contact with their children, paternal grandparents are at a higher risk of losing contact with their grandchildren than are maternal grandparents (Kruk, 1994).

The consequences of unwanted loss of contact with grandchildren can be devastating for grandparents. Researchers have studied reactions of grandparents to the family rupture. They find that after loss of contact with their grandchildren due to parental divorce, grandparents report symptoms of bereavement and damage to their physical and emotional health. Some join support groups, where these are accessible. Following loss of contact with a grandchild due to divorce and also to family feud, there are for many a range of negative consequences, including intense chronic grief, symptoms of post-traumatic stress, both preoccupation with and tendency to avoid thinking about their grandchildren, mental health problems, and lowered life satisfaction, with some being clinically depressed (Drew and Smith, 2002). One grandparent stated, five years after loss of contact with their granddaughters, 'My life ended when I lost my granddaughters … I hurt the same depth of hurt day after day. I still see my psychologist every week'. Another grandparent reported 'a feeling of sadness that my son is being deprived of his daughter's "baby years" and that my granddaughter is being deprived of her Daddy's company and influence' (Drew, 2000).

Many grandparents continued to 'hope' for a reunion with their grandchildren. While this may not be totally unrealistic, it may make it difficult to work through the grief process. As one grandparent stated, 'I miss her [granddaughter] so much, my family will never be complete until she returns to us. I know she is out there somewhere and I shall see her again one day. I'll never give up hope till my dying days. I have eight grandchildren and one lost, but one day there will be nine.'

Grandparents can sometimes negotiate a better relationship with the custodial parent, in order to have contact with their grandchild. The personality, resources and coping strategies of grandparents can be important in this. Grandparents who have a greater sense of positiveness and competence in the grandparenting role find ways to be involved in their grandchild's life, even when obstacles stand in the way. As another option, grandparents may consider mediation or gaining legal support for contact with their grandchildren, as discussed below. With time, also, grandchildren become more independent. Young adult granddaughters who had a close intimate relationship with their grandmother have been shown to bypass the parent generation and maintain contact after parental divorce.

Step-grandparenthood

After divorce, remarriage can produce complicated three-generation family relationships. A grandchild could have three types of step-grandparent, resulting from a *parent* remarrying (the most usual), a *grandparent* remarrying, or from the *parent of a step-parent* remarrying. One study obtained the views of mothers on grandparent relations with grandchildren and step-grandchildren (Henry et al., 1992). The relationships were perceived as 'different', with more step-relationships described as 'remote'. A comparison of US grandchildren's perceptions of grandparents and step-grandparents by their college-aged grandchildren found that grandparent–grandchild relationships were closer, with more frequent contact, greater emotional involvement, and role expectations, than step-grandparent–grandchild relationships (Sanders and Trygstad, 1989). All the same, about half their grandchild sample saw the step-grandparent relationship as important. The differences appeared to be partly, but not completely, a product of the length of time for which they had known the (step-)grandparent.

Death of a Grandchild

The probability of a child under the age of 15 dying has decreased from 62 per cent in 1900 to 4 per cent in 1976 (Uhlenberg, 1980). This probably explains why only seven studies to date have investigated how the death of a grandchild affects grandparents, and on their role within the family following bereavement. In all these studies, despite the varying ages of the grandchildren, family characteristics, or causes of the death (such as accident, or sudden infant death syndrome), grandparents reported great anguish, grief, sadness, and emotional and physical pain as they suffered a threefold grief – for their grandchild, their adult child, and themselves (White, 1999). Grandparents can provide a great source of emotional and practical support to the parents and siblings (of the child who has died) after bereavement, which is special and unique to the grandparent role.

Grandparents and Lesbian Mothers

Little is known about the grandparent role in lesbian families. One study looked at lesbian-mother families with children aged 4–9 years, who lived with either their biological or adopted lesbian mother (Patterson et al., 1998). The majority of grandchildren were in monthly contact with their grandparents. They had more frequent contact with biological grandparents and had fewer behaviour problems than those with less frequent contact. Another study of lesbian mothers with children aged 5 years who had been conceived through donor insemination found that the arrival of children led to improved relationships with (grand)parents in most of the cases and increased contact for over half (Gartrell et al., 1999). There do not appear to be any grandparenting studies of the apparently rare cases where the child stays with a gay father and his partner. Because of the rarity of the cases, no generalizations can be made. The welfare of the child, which includes contact with grandparents, has to be individually evaluated. On the face of it, there are no reasons why considerations regarding lesbian mothers should not equally apply to gay fathers, in relation to their children and contact with grandparents.

Grandparents of Grandchildren with Disabilities

Grandparents can be vital sources of emotional and practical support when a grandchild has a disability. None the less, sometimes the grandparent's immediate inability to accept a grandchild's disability can be a source of added stress to the family system. The birth of a grandchild with a disability evokes emotions that are different from those experienced when the grandchild is healthy. The grandparents often experience anxieties for their newborn grandchild's health, their adult child's ability to cope, and their role as a grandparent (Myer and Vadasy, 1986).

In these circumstances, grandparents may frequently be trapped in disappointment and grieve for their grandchild as well as their adult child. Grandparents who attend support or educational groups related to their grandchild's disability may have more positive feelings. Grandparent education about their grandchild's disability is associated with greater acceptance and more

involvement with their grandchild. Educational workshops for grandparents about their grandchild's deafness, for example, have been shown to be helpful not only in educating the grandparent but in assisting them to let go of their denial about their grandchild's disability (Schilmoeller and Baranowski, 1999).

As with grandchildren generally, it is maternal grandparents who typically provide most emotional support to families with disabled grandchildren. One study found maternal grandparents to be more likely to learn sign language to communicate with their deaf grandchild than paternal grandparents (Nybo et al., 1998). Maternal grandmothers are apparently also able more accurately to assess the development of their grandchild with autism than the paternal grandmother (Glasberg and Harris, 1997).

Great-grandparents

The parental role is well established with rules, rewards and sanctions; the grandparent role is more variable. The more extended intergenerational roles, such as great-grandparenthood, are still more ambiguously defined. 'Role salience' or relevance has been found to decrease consistently with each generation, from parent to grandparent to great-grandparent. Three particular roles have been identified for the great-grandparent:

- personal and family renewal,
- 'diversion' in their lives, and
- a mark of their longevity.

Psychological well-being has been found to be associated with investment in the great-grandparenting role through the parent and grandparent role.

One study of great-grandmothers aged 75 to 89 years showed, for example, that they saw their role as intrinsic to the family system – they initiated family gatherings or were the cause of them. Great-grandparents took gift-sending to their great-grandchildren seriously, and this allowed them to stay visible in their great-grandchild's lives. Many provided childcare. There was sometimes competition with grandparents for the (great-)grandchild's attention. One great-grandmother interviewed, referred to her great-grandchildren as 'my daughter's grandchildren'. However, from the perspective of adult great-grandchildren, the role of the great-grandparent is not always so clear. Although about one-third of great-grandchildren reported having respect for their great-grandparents and about a quarter seeing them as a teacher, over half report having little to no contact with their great-grandparent while growing up or currently (Wentowski, 1985).

So far as contact is concerned, in Finland for example, elderly people see great-grandchildren much less frequently than grandchildren – monthly compared to weekly (Ruoppila, 1991). In the USA, a study found that one 92-year-old great-grandmother saw some local great-grandchildren weekly, but had never seen some non-local great-grandchildren at all (Wentowski, 1985). In this study, even the youngest and healthiest great-grandmothers (aged 66 and 71) were not so involved with great-grandchildren as with grandchildren. Health may be a factor in the amount of contact between great-grandparents and grandchildren, as are also proximity and the quality of the relationship of and with the two middle generations of parent and grandparent.

AUTHORS' OVERVIEW

Future Directions for Theory and Research in Grandparenting

Despite much productive work and many interesting findings, there are limitations to research on grandparenting to date. In particular, a wider range of methodologies might be usefully employed. Most studies have employed interviews or else structured or semi-structured questionnaires. These may not always be reliable indices of behaviour. A few studies of grandparental relationships have used direct observation of behaviour in standard situations. More naturalistic home observations of grandparent–grandchild interaction would be useful. So too would be more projective or open-ended methods, for example, analysis of essays children have written about their grandparents or drawings done by grandchildren of grandfathers and grandmothers. Case studies and more qualitative approaches can add important insights and complement more quantitative results.

Wider Cultural Comparisons

With some exceptions, most research on grandparenthood has been carried out in the USA. This has included description of subcultural variations, not only African-American families but other ethnic groups. A greater number of comparable studies of grandparenthood in different cultures, including Eastern as well as Western, non-industrial as well as urban, will give a more generalizable and representative picture of the variety of grandparenting.

The Need for Theory

Research in grandparenthood would benefit from greater theoretical underpinning. Many articles simply describe the amounts and kind of contact between grandparents and grandchildren, the influence of such factors as type of grandparent, age of grandchild, proximity, and so forth. It is important to get this descriptive information, but also to look for a wider theoretical framework in which to interpret the information. The use of family systems theory (which has been used in studies of grandchildren with disabilities) provides one promising approach. Other possibilities are attachment theory (in understanding intergenerational transmission and conflict), intergenerational solidarity (in understanding the strength of the relationship between parents, grandparents and grandchildren), and evolutionary theory (in understanding kinship asymmetries). Rather than seeing these perspectives as opposed, it would be helpful to work towards some expansion and integration (Smith and Drew, 2002).

IMPLICATIONS FOR PRACTICE

Grandparents in Society

In the USA, there are now courses for grandparents. These are aimed at educating grandparents to help strengthen families. The components include:

- sharing feelings and ideas with others,
- listening to the views of younger people,
- learning about lifespan development,
- improving family communication skills, and
- focusing self-evaluation.

Education programmes have been used to evaluate the needs of Mexican-American, Japanese and Taiwanese grandparents. Interventions following these programmes have been self-evaluated and reported to be effective (Strom and Strom, 1989).

Grandparents who look after or 'parent' their grandchildren are providing a service to their communities as well as their families and need support at a national and community level to continue effectively. The American Association of Retired Persons provides support, advice and education to grandparent care-givers. The

Brookdale Grandparent Caregiver Information Project, again in the USA, has been tracking some of the smaller community organizations that provide support to custodial grandparents. These services help grandparents to feel less isolated and better able to cope with the demands and challenges of their new role, but they suffer from lack of financial support and proper evaluation.

There have also been attempts to enlist the help of grandparents who were the primary caregivers for children receiving mental health treatment. There are intergenerational programmes such as the Three Generation Project which aim to help both new parents and grandparents cope with shifts in family relationships that the transition to (grand)parenthood brings. One study described an evaluation of bringing grandparents into family therapy sessions (Ingersoll-Dayton and Neal, 1991).

There are also 'foster grandparent' programmes. These attempt to enlist the help of the elderly towards caring and companionship for a 'variety of high-risk children and youths'. In some schemes, they receive a small, tax-free payment. These take place in hospitals, residential institutions, daycare programmes, and family shelters. The evaluation of these programmes appears to be positive (Werner, 1991). Clearly, there is a burgeoning recognition of the importance of grandparents as a community resource. Thus, such initiatives are likely to spread.

Obtaining Contact after Parental Divorce: The Courts or Mediation?

An important issue for grandparents is their access and 'visitation rights' to grandchildren of a non-custodial parent. A review in 1989 of the then legal situation in the USA found that statutes granting grandparents legal standing to petition for legally enforceable visits to their grandchildren, even over parental objections, had been passed in all 50 states. However, in many states these laws have since been rescinded due to parents challenging the laws on the basis that the statute is an infringement of their fundamental constitutional right to raise their children as they see fit. Contact orders are transferable from state to state as of December 1998, when the Visitation Rights Enforcement Act became law. In a recent landmark decision, the US Supreme Court struck down the law in Washington State that gave grandparents rights to contact with their grandchildren. This decision leans towards the rights of parents against the rights of children and welfare of children, who, as shown, benefit from grandparent contact (Kornhaber, 1996).

In the UK, the 1989 Children Act highlights the interests of children, and also allows any person (not just grandparents or relatives) to request a leave to seek an order for contact with a child. When deciding whether to grant a leave, the court will consider the applicant's connection with the child. But even if the grandparent has obtained a contact order, there is little that holds the parent to abide by the court ruling. Parents who defy the court can be held in contempt and serve 28 days in prison. However, few grandparents would wish to take such action and risk their grandchildren being placed in care for the duration of parents' imprisonment. Additionally, this sort of action by the grandparent would only increase the anger of the parents, leaving the grandparent with less long-term opportunity of seeing their grandchildren. All these court proceedings are very expensive, and often beyond the means of grandparents who have retired and are on fixed incomes (Douglas and Lowe, 1990).

There are considerable problems in using legal measures, which are probably best seen as a last-resort option, which even when granted may not always be properly enforceable. Grandparents often stress the importance of attempting non-legal forms of resolution first, such as mediation, while opting for legal action as a final resort. Mediation has been found to be effective in some cases; however, sometimes legal contact orders are the only way of preserving the child's continued contact with their grandparent.

Dos and Don'ts

- DO develop a strong and long-lasting relationship with your grandchild by *listening* and *talking* to your grandchild.
- DO talk to your grandchild about family history or 'When I was your age ...'
- DO promote the 'total family', to which all three [or more] generations belong.
- DO use the telephone, letters and email to maintain emotional closeness with grandchildren.
- DO seek support from peers, support groups or professionals if you find yourself raising your grandchild in your home.
- DO keep the child's parents 'on board' and informed of what you are doing.
- DON'T give up if your grandchild is not talkative. Find a way to involve their parent to stimulate conversation.
- DON'T let any negative characteristics of the parent or your grandchild prevent the development of a loving relationship.

- DON'T feel you *must* provide financial support to your grandchild(ren); *only* do this if you are in the financial position to do so and have the desire.
- DON'T miss out on the experience of being a grandparent; most grandparents find it a very rewarding experience which increases emotional well-being.
- DON'T disrespect or disregard parents' wishes while *listening* and *talking* to your grandchildren.
- DON'T miss out on one-to-one interactions directly to influence your grandchild through childcare opportunities that meet you and your adult child's needs.
- DON'T assume you have no rights to see your grandchildren when there is a breakdown in the parents' relationship. Get information from law centres, Citizens Advice Bureaux, other information sources or the internet regarding your rights.
- DON'T allow cultural differences between you and your grandchildren to distort or damage the relationship.
- DON'T treat your gay grandchild or the child of your gay son or lesbian daughter differently from your other grandchildren, just because their sexual preferences are different.
- DON'T expect the parents to help you accept your grandchild's disability – it is your task, if you want all the positive aspects of what can still be a rewarding relationship
- DON'T feel you are taking over your children's role by wanting to know your grandchild or great-grandchild.

REFERENCES

Age Concern (1998) *Across the Generations.* London: Age Concern.

Anderson, M. (1999) Children in-between: constructing identities in the bicultural family. *Royal Anthropological Institute*, **5**, 13–26.

Bar-On, D., Eland, J., Kleber, R.J., Krell, R., Moore, Y., Sagi, A., Soriano, E., Suedfeld, P., van der Velden, P.G. and van Ijzendoorn, M.H. (1998) Multigenerational perspectives on coping with the holocaust experience: an attachment perspective for understanding the developmental sequelae of trauma across generations. *International Journal of Behavioural Development*, **22**, 315–38.

Battestelli, P. and Farneti, A. (1991) Grandchildren's images of their grandparents: a psychodynamic perspective. In Smith, P.K. (ed.) *The Psychology of Grandparenthood: An International Perspective.* London: Routledge, pp. 143–56.

Bengtson, V.L. (2001) Beyond the nuclear family: the increasing importance of multigenerational bonds. *Journal of Marriage and the Family*, **63**, 1–16.

Benoit, D. and Parker, K. (1994) Stability and transmission of attachment across three generations. *Child Development*, **65**, 1444–56.

Burton, L.M. and Dilworth-Anderson, P. (1991) The intergenerational family roles of aged Black Americans. In Pfelfer, S.K. and Sussman, M.B. (eds) *Families: Intergenerational and Generational Connections.* Binghampton, NY: Haworth Press, pp. 311–30.

Caspi, A. and Elder, G.H. (1988) Emergent family patterns: the intergenerational construction of problem behaviour and relationships. In Hinde, R.A. and Stevenson-Hinde, J. (eds) *Relationships within Families: Mutual Influences.* Oxford: Oxford University Press, pp. 218–40.

Creasey, G.L., Myers, B.J., Epperson, M.J. and Taylor, J. (1989) Grandchildren of grandparents with Alzheimer's disease: perceptions of grandparent, family environment, and the elderly. *Merrill-Palmer Quarterly*, **35**, 227–37.

Douglas, G. and Lowe, N. (1990) Grandparents and the legal process. *Journal of Social Welfare Law*, **2**, 89–106.

Drew, L.M. (2000) What are the implications for grandparents when they lose contact with their grandchildren? Unpublished PhD thesis, University of London, England.

Drew, L. and Smith, P.K. (2002) Implications for grandparents when they lose contact with their grandchildren: divorce, family feud and geographical separation. *Journal of Mental Health and Aging*, **8**, 95–119.

Falbo, T. (1991) The impact of grandparents on children's outcomes in China. *Marriage and Family Review*, **16**, 369–76.

Gartrell, N., Hamilton, J., Banks, A., Mosbacher, D., Reed, N., Sparks, C.H., Bishop, H. and Rodas, C. (1999) The National Lesbian Family study: 2. Interviews with mothers of toddlers. *American Journal of Orthopsychiatry*, **69**, 362–9.

Giarrusso, R., Feng, D., Silverstein, M. and Bengtson, V. (2001) Grandparent–adult grandchildren affection and consensus: cross-generational and cross-ethnic comparisons. *Journal of Family Issues*, **22**, 427–55.

Glasberg, B.A. and Harris, S.L. (1997) Grandparents and parents assess the development of their child with autism. *Child and Family Behavior Therapy*, **19**, 17–27.

Henry, C.S., Ceglian, C.P. and Matthews, D.W. (1992) The role behaviors, role meanings, and grandmothering styles of grandmothers and stepgrandmothers: perceptions of the middle generation. *Journal of Divorce and Remarriage*, **17**, 1–22.

Hermalin, A.I., Roan, C. and Perez, A. (1998) Challenges to comparative research in intergenerational transfers. Paper presented at the World Congress of Gerontology, Adelaide, Australia.

Hodgson, L.G. (1992) Adult grandchildren and their grandparents: the enduring bond. *International Journal of Aging and Human Development*, **34**, 209–25.

Hurme, H. (1988) *Child, Mother and Grandmother: Intergenerational Interaction in Finnish Families.* Jyvaskyla: University of Jyvaskyla Press.

Hwang, H.J. and St James-Roberts, I. (1998) Emotional and behavioural problems in primary school children from nuclear and extended families in Korea. *Journal of Child Psychology and Psychiatry*, **39**, 973–9.

Ingersoll-Dayton, B. and Neal, M.B. (1991) Grandparents in family therapy: a clinical research study. *Family Relations*, **40**, 264–71.

Johnson, C.L. (1983) A cultural analysis of the grandmother. *Research on Aging*, **5**, 547–67.

Kennedy, G.E. and Keeney, V.T. (1988) The extended family revisited: grandparents rearing grandchildren. *Child Psychiatry and Human Development*, **19**, 26–35.

Kivett, V.R. (1985) Grandfathers and grandchildren: patterns of association, helping, and psychological closeness. *Family Relations*, **34**, 565–71.

Kornhaber, A. (1996) *Contemporary Grandparenting*. Newbury Park, CA: Sage.

Kornhaber, A. and Woodward, K. (1981) *Grandparents/ grandchildren: The Vital Connection*. Garden City, NY: Doubleday.

Kruk, E. (1994) Grandparent visitation disputes: multigenerational approaches to family mediation. *Mediation Quarterly*, **12**, 37–53.

Myer, D.J. and Vadasy, P.F. (1986) *Grandparent Workshops: How to Organize Workshops for Grandparents of Children with Handicaps*. Seattle, WA: University of Washington Press.

Neugarten, B.L. and Weinstein, K.K. (1964) The changing American grandparent. *Journal of Marriage and the Family*, **26**, 199–204.

Nybo, W.L., Scherman, A. and Freeman, P.L. (1998) Grandparents' role in family systems with a deaf child: an exploratory study. *American Annals of the Deaf*, **143**, 260–7.

Patterson, C.J., Hurt, S. and Mason, C.D. (1998) Families of the lesbian baby boom: children's contact with grandparents and other adults. *American Journal of Orthopsychiatry*, **68**, 390–9.

Pettys, G.L. and Balgopal, P.R. (1998) Multigenerational conflicts and new immigrants: an Indo-American experience. *Families in Society: The Journal of Contemporary Human Services*, **74**, 410–23.

Rodgers, B. and Pryor, J. (1998) *Divorce and Separation: The Outcomes for Children*. England: Joseph Rowntree Foundation.

Rossi, A.S. and Rossi, P.H. (1990) *Of Human Bonding: Parent–Child Relations Across the Life Course*. New York: Aldine de Gruyter.

Ruoppila, I. (1991) The significance of grandparents for the formation of family relations. In Smith, P.K. (ed.) *The Psychology of Grandparenthood: An International Perspective*. London: Routledge, pp. 123–39.

Sanders, G.F. and Trygstad, D.W. (1989) Stepgrandparents and grandparents: the view from young adults. *Family Relations*, **38**, 71–5.

Schilmoeller, G.L. and Baranowski, M.D. (1999) Intergenerational support in families with disabilities: grandparents' perspectives. *Families in Society: The Journal of Contemporary Human Services*, **79**, 465–76.

Silverstein, M. and Marenco, A. (2001) How Americans enact the grandparent role across the family life course. *Journal of Family Issues*, **22**, 493–522.

Smith, P.K. (1991) Introduction: the study of grandparenthood. In Smith, P.K. (ed.) *The Psychology of Grandparenthood: An International Perspective*. London: Routledge, pp. 1–16.

Smith, P.K. and Drew, L. (2002) Grandparenthood. In Bornstein, M. (ed.) *Handbook of Parenting, Volume 3: Being and Becoming a Parent*, 2nd edition. Mahwah, NJ and London: Lawrence Erlbaum, pp. 141–72.

Sonuga-Barke, E.J.S., Mistry, M. and Qureshi, S. (1998) The mental health of Muslim mothers in extended families living in Britain: the impact of intergenerational disagreement on anxiety and depression. *British Journal of Clinical Psychology*, **37**, 399–408.

Staples, R. (1952) Appreciations and dislikes regarding grandmothers as expressed by granddaughters. *Journal of Home Economics*, **44**, 340–3.

Sticker, E.J. (1991) The importance of grandparenthood during the life-cycle in Germany. In Smith, P.K. (ed.) *The Psychology of Grandparenthood: An International Perspective*. London: Routledge, pp. 32–49.

Strom, R. and Strom, S. (1989) Grandparents and learning. *International Journal of Aging and Human Development*, **29**, 163–9.

Tinsley, B.J. and Parke, R.D. (1984) Grandparents as support and socialization agents. In Lewis, M. (ed.) *Beyond the Dyad*. New York: Plenum.

Tyszkowa, M. (1991) The role of grandparents in the development of grandchildren as perceived by adolescents and young adults in Poland. In Smith, P.K. (ed.) *The Psychology of Grandparenthood: An International Perspective*. London: Routledge, pp. 50–67.

Uhlenberg, P. (1980) Death and the family. *Journal of Family History*, **5**, 313–20.

Van Ijzendoorn, M.H. (1995) Adult attachment representations. *Psychological Bulletin*, **117**, 387–403.

Vermulst, A.A., de Brock, A.J.L.L. and van Zutphen, R.A.H. (1991) Transmission of parenting across generations. In Smith, P.K. (ed.) *The Psychology of Grandparenthood: An International Perspective*. London: Routledge, pp. 100–22.

Vollmer, H. (1937) The grandmother: a problem in child rearing. *American Journal of Orthopsychiatry*, **7**, 378–82.

Warner, V., Weissman, M., Mufson, L. and Wickramaratne, P.J. (1999) Grandparents, parents, and grandchildren at high risk for depression: a three-generation study. *Journal of American Academy of Child Adolescent Psychiatry*, **38**, 289–96.

Wentowski, G.J. (1985) Older women's perceptions of great-grandmotherhood: a research note. *Gerontologist*, **25**, 593–6.

Werner, E.E. (1991) Grandparent–grandchild relationships amongst US ethnic groups. In Smith, P.K. (ed.) *The Psychology of Grandparenthood: An International Perspective*. London: Routledge, pp. 68–82.

White, D.L. (1999) Grandparent participation in times of family bereavement. In de Vries, B. (ed.) *End of Life Issues*. New York: Springer Publishing, pp. 145–66.

Part II

FUNCTIONAL AREAS

11

Parenting and Children's Physical Health

Elizabeth Soliday

SUMMARY

The purpose of this chapter is to synthesize available literature documenting relationships between dimensions of parenting, which include contextual factors, cognitive behavioral factors, parenting process and relational variables, and children's health variables. The chapter also includes an overview of cognitive behavioral health interventions that involve parents. Implications for practice and research are also addressed.

PARENTING AND CHILDREN'S HEALTH

In the past three decades, a substantial body of research exploring psychosocial factors and physical health has been published, partly because medical and mental health professionals have increasingly recognized that most aspects of physical health can be influenced by both physiological and psychosocial processes. This trend reflects the shift away from the mind–body dualism that characterized Western cultural perspectives on physical health during the early part of the 20th century. In the new millennium, researchers and clinicians can no longer ignore the critical role of psychological factors in health, in the onset and course of acute illness, and in chronic illness management.

Researchers and clinicians acknowledge that parents are one of the primary psychosocial agents in the physical health of children. At early ages in particular, children rely almost wholly on their parents to ensure their physical health and well-being. Parents are responsible for reading their children's physical distress cues, for responding to their health care needs, for adhering to necessary treatments, and for implementing healthy practices and preventive health measures such as immunizations. In short, parents are responsible for ensuring that their children are healthy and that they survive.

Although other forces, such as school, community, peers, and television become more important in the health socialization process as children grow older (Tinsley, 1992; Lau et al., 1990), documented relationships between parents' and children's health behaviors such as eating habits, exercise, smoking behavior, body weight, and health care utilization continue throughout childhood into adulthood (Lau et al., 1990; Kedler et al., 1994; Rosso and Rise, 1994).

DEFINING CHILDREN'S HEALTH

Defining 'children's health' presents special challenges. In general, the concept of children's health differs from adult health. As children grow and develop, different health concerns will predominate. For example, in infancy and early childhood, the prevailing health-related concerns may be the absence of identifiable pathology and achieving developmental milestones in feeding and walking. At these ages, failure to achieve developmental milestones would factor differently into perceptions of the child's health than the presence or absence of such skills in older child or adult populations.

In addition to developmental concerns, children's health must be defined as a multidimensional construct encompassing a wide range of potential outcome variables. The multidimensional nature of children's health is best understood as the child's ability to participate fully in developmentally appropriate physical, psychological, and social tasks (Lewis et al., 1989). This definition is reflected in the World Health Organization's 1978 definition of children's health as, 'a state of complete physical, mental, and social well-being, and not merely the absence of disease or infirmity'. Additional factors to be included in defining children's health are 'health behavior', which includes healthy practices and disease-prevention behaviors, and can occur on behalf of or on the part of the child. Identifiable disease pathogens and health care utilization patterns are also components of children's health (Starfield, 1992).

Following from the above concerns related to developmental issues and multidimensional definitions of children's health is measurement. Although extensive discussion of pediatric health measurement is beyond the scope of this chapter, it is important to note the primary factors that complicate synthesis of research. Psychosocial studies conducted on pediatric health traditionally include health behavior variables, most often health care utilization such as clinic services and hospitalizations, as the focal outcome (Lewis et al., 1989). Professionals believe that health care utilization is an important variable, as it is considered a primary health behavior and as such should be included in any discussion of physical health (Bonner and Finney, 1996). In addition, use of services is important to measure because of its economic and social implications. However, it should be noted that utilization correlates only moderately with measures of functional status, and it is an indirect rather than a direct measure of health (Lewis et al., 1989). Other variables, for example exposure to environmental toxins (such as lead), vaccination rates, adequate nutritional intake, subjective (somatic) complaints, perceptions of well-being, and achievement of normal development, would also provide valuable information on children's health. These variables are less frequently the focal outcomes in studies of parenting influences and children's health.

Measurement strategies may also complicate synthesis of available research. Regardless of the focal outcome variable, the most frequently used, efficient, and cost-effective measurement strategy is self-report. Self-report can be obtained using symptom checklists, illness histories, and standardized questionnaires, as well as population-based strategies such as epidemiological surveys. Unfortunately, the validity of self-report may be limited by a variety of factors including social desirability, the informant's psychological status, and the quality of the assessment device (Rand and Weeks, 1998).

Furthermore, very young children's state of health is almost completely subject to parental interpretation. As children develop, parents continue to rely on children's behavior and verbal reports of how they are feeling, and these two sources do not always agree, especially for vague somatic complaints. For example, markedly different correlations have been reported between parents and school-age children across three health variables (symptom report, physician visits, school days missed). Correlations within each group were much higher across the three measures (Meade et al., 2001). Consistency across parents and older adolescent pairs is even weaker (Baker et al., 2000). Although objective measures such as laboratory findings and vital statistics may appear to be more appealing alternatives, these procedures can be expensive, time-consuming, difficult to obtain, and their validity may also be limited. In sum, the potential effects of subjective versus objective measurement strategies, the child's developmental status, and the informant should all be considered when synthesizing research on parenting and children's health.

DEMOGRAPHIC VARIABLES AND CHILDREN'S HEALTH

In examining studies of psychosocial influences on children's health, most researchers would agree that demographic variables provide descriptive information and are presumably difficult or impossible to modify. None the less, demographic variables have a role in theoretical models of parenting and children's health outcomes. Addressing demographic variables in models of children's health acknowledges the fact that neither the parent–child relationship nor children's health occur in isolation. Instead, parenting issues in general should be considered within a broader cultural context that includes family's social status, their work, neighborhood, health care institutions, and the interrelationships among those entities (Bronfenbrenner, 1977). Related to this, demographic variables have been found to play a mediating role in the major models of children's health and behavior to be reviewed later in this chapter. Demographics also play a role in individuals' responses to psychosocial intervention (Nader et al., 1996), which is necessary to consider when developing health interventions. Given the importance of contextual variables as factors and/or mediators in children's health, the major demographic variables related to parenting and children's health will be reviewed briefly.

Family (Parent) Income

Numerous research studies have documented that, in general, children in low-income families have higher rates of acute illnesses, lower rates of immunization, and are at higher risk for many negative health outcomes (Starfield, 1992; Halfon and Newachek, 1993). Health service utilization patterns in low-income families differ from higher income groups. Research indicates that lower income children receive fewer regular outpatient clinic services, but have higher rates of emergency hospital visits (Lombrail et al., 1997). The specific role of income in children's health is not well understood. It could simply be that lower income individuals are exposed to more health risks and have more difficulty accessing adequate clinic-based health services for preventive and acute care concerns. Access to adequate treatment may be the inhibited by the absence of or inadequate medical insurance, a lack of transportation, the need for childcare for well children, and inaccessibility of health care during off-work hours.

Maternal Education

Income-related differences in children's health are greatly reduced or disappear altogether after accounting for the effect of maternal education, and this finding has emerged across a number of studies (Molina and Aguirre-Molina, 1994). Higher levels of maternal education have been associated with higher levels of pediatric outpatient clinic use and higher rates of preventive health measures, such as immunizations (Mechanic, 1964; Newachek and Halfon, 1986; Taylor and Cufley, 1996). In studies assessing beliefs related to the importance of preventive health care, maternal education has been associated with stronger beliefs in preventive health care (Cheng et al., 1996). However, research findings related to more positive health outcomes as a function of higher maternal education have not been consistently reported (Wolfe, 1980; Horowitz et al., 1985).

Family Structure

Family structure refers to the composition of family members in a household, and ranges from traditional, two-parent nuclear families, to nontraditional families formed by single parenthood, divorce, or death of a spouse. One-parent families may also contain unrelated partners or may become remarried families. Findings on associations between family structure and children's health are mixed. Negative effects of nontraditional family structure on children's health have been reported (Soliday et al., 2001; Soliday and Lande, 2002), though other researchers have indicated no differences in children's health by family type (Manne et al., 1995). Yet others have reported significant effects, mediated by family process variables such as cohesion and adaptability (Silver et al., 1996). Interpretation of findings related to family structure can be complicated by the presence of pre-existing or ongoing marital/partner conflict, family income, sample size, and definition of family status (Dunn et al., 1998; Cherlin, 1999; Hetherington and Stanley-Hagan, 1999).

Ethnicity

Because parenting practices and child socialization are embedded in an ethnic/cultural context, a child's cultural milieu should be more frequently addressed in studies of parenting influences on children's health. Studies on the general topic of children's health status indicate that ethnic minority children are at higher risk for a number of negative health outcomes, including findings of higher rates of infectious disease, higher rates of obesity, and lower rates of physical activity and higher body fat (Heckler, 1986; Alexander et al., 1991; Anderson et al., 1998). Determining the effects of ethnic status is complicated by family income and social class factors. Ethnic differences may be reduced or disappear altogether after controlling for family income (Arcia, 1998; Lindquist et al., 1999), and not all studies find health differences as a function of ethnicity (Cullen et al., 2000). Although many studies of parenting and children's health include ethnic minority samples, fewer studies examine ethnicity as a variable in children's health outcomes. Further study of whether or how ethnicity relates to parenting and children's health may help clarify the process by which ethnic minority children come to suffer poorer health outcomes, which would be useful for designing interventions.

Summary of Research on Demographic Factors

Family demographics play a role in children's health, with a higher risk of negative health outcomes at least partly a function of low family income, low maternal education, and ethnic minority status. These findings are not consistent across studies, and demographic variables explain only part of the variance in children's health outcomes. Importantly, demographic variables such as maternal education and income are frequently confounded with each other. The more current and widely accepted psychosocial models of children's health are multivariate. They address demographic factors as contextual and/or mediating variables rather than direct influences on health outcomes, and their primary focus is on psychological characteristics that are presumably modifiable.

PARENTING PROCESS VARIABLES AND CHILDREN'S HEALTH

In contemporary multivariate models of parenting and children's health, parenting dimensions are best viewed as process variables. The *Oxford English Dictionary* defines 'process' as an action or series of actions or events – a definition that describes the manner by which parents nurture

and facilitate their children's development, including their physical health. Parenting is generally viewed as dynamic, and as involving a series of actions and interactions on the part of parents that include emotions, cognitions, and behaviors in fostering children's growth and development (Belsky, 1984; Dix, 1991). Conceptualizing parenting as a dynamic rather than a static process allows researchers to identify areas for potential improvement/ intervention. A selection of the parenting process variables that have received the greatest amount of research support as they relate to children's health will be presented to provide an overview. These process variables include cognitive behavioral factors such as attitudinal variables and modeling; family process variables, specifically family environment quality; and relational processes, or attachment.

COGNITIVE BEHAVIORAL VARIABLES

At the center of current views of parenting are cognitions and emotions, with parents' own cognitive-affective processes viewed as driving their parenting behavior. These processes are also viewed as potentially modifiable over the course of the developing parent–child relationship (Teti et al., 1996). Additionally, cognitive factors are widely presumed to play an important role in health behavior and health behavior change, and as a result, a number of cognitive and attitudinal variables have been researched as they relate to health behavior. Understanding parents' health-related beliefs and attitudes is especially important to optimize children's well-being because children depend on parents to ensure their health. Cognitive behavioral variables with the widest research support include health knowledge, health beliefs, health locus of control, self-efficacy, and modeling.

Health Knowledge

Studies indicate that parents' health knowledge plays a role in their health behavior, and that their knowledge is influenced by demographic characteristics. For example, a group of researchers examined how demographic factors, knowledge, and perception of immunizations influenced parents' decisions to immunize their children (Impicciatore et al., 2000). Mothers of children younger than six years were interviewed on their vaccine-related knowledge and the immunization status of their children. Mothers' knowledge of vaccine schedules increased with education and maternal age. In a multivariate model, the most significant predictors of optional immunizations were satisfactory information on immunization and positive attitudes toward immunization; these findings emerged after controlling for maternal education.

In older children, the degree to which parental health knowledge influences children's knowledge may be mediated by parent–child communication. For example, researchers have examined parents' knowledge of AIDS, communication frequency, and accuracy of information imparted to their elementary-age children (Sigelman et al., 1995). Children whose families spent more time communicating about AIDS had greater knowledge of HIV transmission myths. However, this relationship only held when children's reports of the amount of communication were used rather than parents' reports, which correlated 0.37. This study exemplifies the differential impact that informant (parent versus child) may have on findings, which is especially critical when addressing serious health issues such as AIDS.

Health Beliefs

One of the most extensively studied social cognition models in health psychology is the Health Belief Model (HBM), devised by Rosenstock (1974). The HBM has provided a useful framework in predicting variability in health-related behaviors. Within this model, it is presumed that cognitive/self-regulation processes (i.e. goal-setting, cognitive preparation, monitoring, and evaluating) relate to behavior. Research on health beliefs provides a basis for understanding the cognitive determinants of behavior and behavior change.

Within the HBM, cues to take action (physical symptoms) stimulate attitudes reflecting readiness to act. In pediatric health, parents may rely on behavioral cues such as crying or disturbed sleep patterns, or specific physical cues such as elevated temperature, coughing, or a rash (Polic, 1998). Based on the specific cues they receive, parents then choose their course of action, such as taking their children to a health care provider due to concern over the child's symptoms. 'Readiness' variables are cognitive appraisals of the disease or situation, and are subdivided into the HBM's multiple dimensions, which include 'susceptibility,' or the perceived probability of experiencing a potentially harmful condition, and 'severity,' or the condition's degree of perceived threat. 'Benefit' focuses on the perceived effectiveness of specific behaviors in reducing the condition's threat. 'Barriers' relate to negative aspects of specific health behaviors. 'Motives' refers to the internal cues (such as physical symptoms) or external cues (for example advice from a friend) that stimulate health behavior (Janz and Becker, 1984).

Related to children's health, a number of parental actions on behalf of their children's health have been consistently predicted using HBM constructs (Norman, 1995; Sheeran and Abraham, 1995). For example, parents' health beliefs as they related to parents' reports of teaching their children injury risk prevention behavior, such as burn prevention, bicycle safety, and safe food preparation, have been assessed (Peterson et al., 1990). Parents' reported attitudes and health beliefs predicted ten safety teaching behaviors, explaining from 3 to 22 per cent variance.

Many health belief studies have focused on health care utilization (e.g. use of preventive and acute care clinic services) as the primary health status/outcome variable. Interestingly, child health service utilization is only modestly related to children's actual physical condition (Janicke and Finney, 2000). Because of this modest relationship, focus on factors related to use of health services has increased to keep pace with the growing reliance on evidence-based medicine and managed health care.

Although HBM constructs have consistently predicted pediatric health service utilization, researchers agree that the explanatory power of HBM constructs in health-related behavior is at best moderate. Furthermore, the most consistent and strongest health belief predictor across studies is 'barriers'. To increase the model's explanatory power, contemporary views have grown to address more complex, multivariate relationships between beliefs and behavior. Researchers have proposed a set of interrelated factors, including economic/environmental variables such as parental educational level, social class, family structure, and the child's symptoms. These are thought to directly affect 'readiness' variables, which in turn predict parents' decisions to seek pediatric services (Zambrana et al., 1994; Sheeran and Abraham, 1995).

Researchers have studied the relative importance of maternal health beliefs and demographic variables in a complex model predicting emergency department (ED) utilization (Wasilewski et al., 1996). For 0- to 1-year-old infants, a health belief variable (i.e. mother's worry about the child's illnesses) was the strongest predictor of utilization. The second most important predictor was a demographic variable, single-parent status. In a sample of children with asthma, studies have reported that parents receiving Medicaid (free medical help), who perceived their children's condition as severe, and who held inaccurate beliefs about asthma, made higher use of ED services (Jones et al., 1988). Demographic variables predicting high utilization included younger age of child and lower income.

Studies testing multivariate models of ED behavior indicated predictive effects of demographic and health belief variables. In one study, adherence to pediatric ED after-care instruction was assessed in parents of children with minor conditions (Soliday and Hoeksel, 2000). The health beliefs 'barriers' and 'susceptibility' and child age significantly predicted parents' adherence to instructions given to them for home care procedures, medication purchase, and dosage. However, parents' level of education, ethnic or marital status were not significant factors in this study. In another study, public insurance status, a proximal indicator of low family income, predicted higher pediatric ED utilization together with higher perceived barriers and benefits of care. (Soliday and Hoeksel, 2001).

Health Locus of Control

The Health Locus of Control (HLOC) theoretical framework is based on Rotter's early work indicating individual differences in the degree to which individuals perceive reinforcement to be dependent on their own actions (Rotter, 1966). Individuals with internal 'locus of control' perceive reinforcement or events as largely a consequence of their own actions. External 'locus of control' refers to reinforcement as contingent not on one's own behavior, but on fate, luck, or powerful others. In a series of studies, a Health Locus of Control model and scale have been developed to assess situation-specific application of HLOC constructs to predicting health behavior (Wallston et al., 1976, 1978; Wallston, 1991). In the HLOC model, health is viewed as a general construct, predicted by three subdimensions: internal control, control by powerful others (such as physicians), and 'chance' locus.

In one study, low- and middle-income African-American and Caucasian mothers reported on their degree of perceived control, powerful others' control, and chance control over their children's health (Tinsley and Holtgrave, 1989). Utilization information (including immunizations and well-baby checkups) was obtained through medical records. Analyses indicated that mothers' higher perceived control over their children's health predicted appropriate and timely utilization of services. Results were maintained after controlling for family income.

In another other study of parents' health beliefs and health behavior on behalf of their children, health beliefs of parents who decided to follow up on school nurse referrals for identified pediatric health problems to those who did not follow up were compared (Bush, 1997). No differences on health locus of control or any other health belief variable (barriers, beliefs, severity, susceptibility, motivation) were found between families who reported following up versus those who did not follow up with nurse referrals. The primary limitation of this study was that health beliefs were assessed after parents should theoretically have followed up; in other words, a retrospective rather than prospective approach was used. Therefore, health beliefs could have changed as a result of the follow-up experience.

Self-efficacy

Self-efficacy is defined as individuals' judgments about their competency at a particular task or in a particular setting (Bandura, 1982, 1986; Bandura and Wood, 1989). Bandura's social-cognitive theory proposes that individuals high in self-efficacy judge themselves as competent and effective in a given task, and they persist in their efforts to achieve success even in the face of obstacles, whereas those low in self-efficacy give up prematurely even though success may be achievable (Bandura, 1986). The relationship between self-efficacy beliefs and actual success is believed to be bi-directional, with one's history of successes and failures feeding into perceived self-efficacy. Self-efficacy will also depend on emotional state and modeling of effective behavior.

Several studies have found positive relationships between self-efficacy and pediatric health variables. One, for example, focused on efficacy and health beliefs (barriers, benefits, susceptibility, severity) in a study predicting parental attempts to prevent injuries to their children (Russell and Champion, 1996). In a sample of mothers of 1- to 3-year-old children, higher self-efficacy was the only health belief variable that significantly predicted either lower observed hazard accessibility or lower observed hazard frequency. A higher sense of self-efficacy accounted for a large portion of each respective outcome. Higher maternal age, education, and income also significantly predicted more positive outcomes in injury prevention. In other words, mothers' perceived personal ability to execute actions may be more useful in predicting behavior and planning for behavioral change than their perceived susceptibility to injury. Similar findings emerged in a study of parents' readiness to immunize their children (Taylor and Cufley, 1996). The results showed that mothers' reporting self-efficacy in a group of fully immunized children was significantly higher than self-efficacy reported by mothers of children who were not fully immunized, but there were no differences between groups on other health beliefs, including barriers, benefits, and susceptibility.

A study of children's self-reported efficacy and disease management behaviors found that children with the greatest self-management skills were those who had the highest scores on perceived self-efficacy, those who had participated in asthma education, and those who had experienced previous hospitalization (Clark et al., 1988). Self-efficacy appears to be a useful predictor of subsequent disease management in children, particularly for those who have experienced serious illness. Examining the parents' role in the development of high self-efficacy is likely to prove useful in efforts designed to improve children's self-management when they are ill.

Multiple Cognitive-Behavioral Constructs

In an effort to increase the explanatory power of cognitive behavioral variables in predicting health outcomes, several pediatric studies include multiple cognitive behavioral constructs. For example, in mothers in single- and two-parent households with children aged 10–14 years, health beliefs correlated with parents' reports of engaging in health promotion activities (Ford-Gilboe, 1997). Higher maternal education was the only demographic predictor of higher health promotion behavior. After controlling for maternal education, mothers' self-efficacy and family cohesion remained strong predictors of health promotion behavior. Although not significant predictors by themselves, locus of control and family income seem to increase the predictive ability of other factors.

In a chronically ill population, researchers examined three cognitive behavioral factors believed to affect mothers' management of asthma: illness knowledge, practical problem-solving skills, and maternal expectations regarding asthma management (Wade et al., 2000). After establishing the baseline asthma morbidity, ineffective problem-solving strategies were most consistently associated with objective measures of how bad the asthma morbidity became. More positive care-taker expectations were related to better child functioning status. Care-giver knowledge of asthma was not related to the morbidity measures.

Another study linked cognitive, affective, and behavioral factors to children's health, thus providing insight into the process by which parents may shape specific child health-related behaviors (Lees and Tinsley, 2000). In a sample of kindergartners and first graders, mothers were randomly assigned to engage in teaching their children about either health prevention or making friends. Higher maternal control, maternal positive affect, and mother's maternal direct teaching during the health prevention task was related to healthier behavior (such as selecting healthy foods and avoiding risky behaviors) in their children. Mothers' belief that children learn through processes of social learning and exploration led to higher use of direct teaching tactics. Mothers who believed that their children's healthy behavior was due to children's and adults' efforts rather than maturational/biological factors tended to take a positive, active teaching role in health socialization. More direct maternal control and teaching related to healthier child behavior.

Social Learning/Modeling

Researchers have long assumed that children's eating habits, activity levels, stress management, and substance use are directly associated with having those specific behaviors modeled for them by their parents (Mullen, 1983; Kedler et al., 1994; Kannel et al., 1995). In a conceptual model specifying the role of both cognitive and behavioral processes in the acquisition of behavior from models, Bandura (1977, 1982) argued that while imitating others is central in the process of learning behavior, cognitive processes play a role as well. Children choose whether to imitate others based on several factors; among those most central are the relevance of the model and the perceived consequences of the act. Because parents are among the most important models in a child's environment, particularly in early childhood, it follows that children would be likely to imitate parents' health-related behaviors. Furthermore, children are more likely to imitate and subsequently repeat a behavior if the behavior is reinforced. Parental social learning influences – imitation and reinforcement – have been examined as they relate to pediatric health variables which include illness orientation, illness behavior, utilization, unexplained pain, and the development of specific health practices.

A number of studies examine the impact of behavioral factors on children's health related attitudes and behavior. In an early study, Mechanic (1964) examined relationships between maternal variables and children's illness orientation, that is, symptom-reporting when ill, risk-taking behavior, and knowing when a doctor is necessary. Among the many self-reported parenting variables examined, mothers' attentiveness to illness-related symptoms was only modestly related to children's illness orientation. Retrospective reports of parenting experiences from adult patients have also been collected. For example, diabetics whose parents stopped working when ill were themselves more likely to be 'avoidant' compared with diabetics whose parents were 'non-avoidant' (Turkat, 1982). Although patient groups were highly similar on physician-rated illness parameters, those patients with a family history of avoidance had significantly more clinic visits, hospital admissions, more illness days, and lower self-reported quality of life than patients without a family history of avoidance. Illness reinforcement did not differentiate between avoidant and non-avoidant groups.

In another noteworthy study of illness behavior attributable to parental modeling, researchers tested whether the ways mothers taught their daughters to respond to menstrual symptoms contributed to the development of somatic complaints and illness behavior (Whitehead et al., 1986). Adult nursing students completed questionnaires on maternal encouragement of the sick role for menstrual and cold symptoms (for example, being excused from chores during illness or menstruation) and maternal modeling of menstrual distress. Their mothers completed parallel forms. Significant, positive correlations resulted between maternal encouragement of the sick role for menstrual symptoms, modeling of sick role behavior for menstrual symptoms, and dependent variables including number and frequency of menstrual symptoms, visits to health care services, and number of absences from work or school. The pattern of relationships between subjects' and their mothers' reports was highly consistent, excluding the number of clinic visits.

Although the above studies provide important insight into relationships between social learning influences in childhood and later health experiences, they employ a retrospective methodology. Retrospective reports of parental socialization are subject to selective memory effects and the influence of current stressors (Hyman and Loftus, 1998; Ornstein et al., 1998). Therefore, studies on concurrent relationships between children's health variables and their modeling experiences would expand the validity of conclusions based solely on retrospective reports. Studies of concurrent relationships between social learning influences and health experiences have results similar to those using retrospective reports.

For example, in a study of two groups of children, one with explained pain (due to sickle cell disease) and one group with unexplained pain (abdominal or chest), four-fifths of those with unexplained pain (UP) identified a salient model for their pain (Osborne et al., 1989). Of the UP children who identified a pain site, two-thirds shared at least one pain site with the model. Pain intensity and frequency were highly correlated with that identified in the model. In the UP group, 25 per cent of the models children identified for their pain were parents. Children did not necessarily perceive consequences of their own pain behavior as similar to consequences for the model; UP children were more likely to report positive or neutral consequences of their pain. In another study with similar outcomes, researchers assessed a variety of maternal and family factors as they related to adolescents' reports of recurrent abdominal pain (Kaufman et al., 1997). Half of these adolescents' mothers reported a personal history of abdominal pain, compared to much smaller proportions of the control group.

Other studies examine parental influence in the use of health services. Findings indicate that maternal clinic utilization was the strongest predictor of child utilization, although maternal education, health status, family income, structure, and size were also significant predictors (Newachek and Halfon, 1986). There is a similar pattern of health service utilization by adolescents across three types of symptoms, including influenza, fatigue, and serious symptoms (blood in urine, lump in abdomen). The relationship between parental and child utilization increased in strength with increasing chronological age of the adolescent (Quadrel and Lau, 1990).

It has been proposed that parents' behaviors, for example, buying and preparing food, engaging in health-related activities, seeking health care, and engaging in health-related risk behavior such as substance use, are the primary forces in shaping children's health behavior (Lau et al., 1990). Parents may hold beliefs that directly impact their own health behavior, which are then transferred to their children via the parenting role. Evidence suggests that the most enduring influences on the college students' health beliefs and behaviors were the beliefs and behaviors of their parents in areas such as alcohol consumption, eating habits, exercise, smoking, and wearing seat belts.

Parental Supervision

Another specific parenting behavior that has been examined as it relates to children's subsequent health behavior is the amount of direct supervision parents provide during children's chronic illness management. A study hypothesized that adolescents more closely supervised by their parents during hypoglycemic (extremely low blood sugar) and hyperglycemic (extremely high blood sugar) episodes would be likely to respond appropriately to these potentially dangerous events (Johnson et al., 2000). Counterintuitively, inappropriate responses to hyperglycemia occurred more frequently when supervised as opposed to unsupervised by a parent. Because adolescents were the subject of the study, it is possible that they had higher levels of diabetes self-care knowledge than their parents; diabetes education efforts may have focused on the adolescents themselves rather than parents. In addition, adolescents showed excellent knowledge about hypo- and hyperglycemic events, but apparently did not translate their knowledge into high rates of appropriate behavioral response to different conditions.

HEALTH INTERVENTIONS BASED ON COGNITIVE BEHAVIORAL MODELS

The integration of mental health professionals into primary health care facilities and treatment teams has led to numerous psychologically based interventions targeted toward improving children's health. Methodologically sound interventions in which researchers and clinicians identify specific psychosocial variables considered important in physical functioning, and in which the mechanism of action is defined, are emerging. A sample of interventions focusing on cognitive behavioral constructs is presented below to provide a general sense of available interventions, their strengths, and areas for further learning (see chapter 12; also see Lemanek and Koontz, 1999; Hughes et al., 2001; Walker and Roberts, 2001).

Interventions targeted at improving health knowledge have proven to be successful. In a general pediatric outpatient population, an intervention to improve parental knowledge of febrile convulsions, which are frequently seen in pediatric practice, has been shown to be effective (Wassmer and Hanlon, 1999). Parents who received structured information on this condition

from a health care provider showed significantly higher knowledge than those who had not received the information, and the information was retained at a 9-month follow-up. In another study, the goal was to reduce unnecessary emergency demand (Shields et al., 1990). These researchers provided a four-session educational intervention to parents and children with asthma, focusing on prevention and intervention of asthma attacks, medication management, and appropriate health care utilization. Post-intervention, families in the intervention group showed significantly higher knowledge than those in a control group. However, no differences on health care utilization resulted.

Another intervention targeting asthma patients focused on improving parental self-efficacy. It was hypothesized that increasing parental self-efficacy in a large sample of mothers of pediatric asthma patients with moderate to severe asthma would in turn lead to improved asthma self-management skills (Hanson, 1998). Over 24 months, self-efficacy increased in both the intervention and usual care group to a significant degree. A similar improvement in self-management skills also resulted; however, a change in self-efficacy scores was not associated with a change in parents' asthma self-management skills.

In the studies above, the cognitive variables that were the focus of the intervention – knowledge and self-efficacy – improved as a result of intervention. However, behavior change was either nonspecific to the intervention or did not result at all. In chronic illness populations in particular, most individuals have a certain level of factual knowledge, and above that threshold, knowledge may be less important than practical problem-solving skills. Some interventions conducted with healthy and chronic illness populations integrate components targeted toward behavior change, such as daily illness or health management and skills for coping with the consequences of behavior change, leading to more positive outcomes in terms of actual behavior change.

In a study of cardiovascular risk reduction involving families at high risk for cardiovascular disease, parents and elementary-age children attended classes focusing on nutrition and physical activity. Skills-based training in coping, maintenance of new health behavior, and stress management were emphasized (Bindler et al., 2000). Significant improvements for both intervention and control groups were found on a variety of cardiovascular health measures, which were maintained at one-year follow-up. Improvement in the control group was attributed to recent cardiovascular events in those families, which may have motivated program participants to improve their health. This anecdotal finding provides evidence for Bandura's proposal that behavior change is more likely to occur with increased salience of a model and perceived consequences of the act (Bandura, 1982), although the duration and nature of such effects remains to be determined in further research.

Another study examined implementation of an educational program for families with a child who had cystic fibrosis (CF) (Bartholomew et al., 1997). The program focused on improving parents' and children's knowledge of CF, their self-efficacy in treating the disorder, and their self-management. Behavioral components of the program included goal setting, reinforcement, modeling, skill training, and self-monitoring delivered in written patient education materials. At a 24-month post-test, care-givers (mostly mothers) and children reported significant improvements in CF knowledge, self-efficacy, self management, and three aspects of problem solving, compared to controls who received usual care. In adolescents, no differences were found on problem solving, self-efficacy or pulmonary function tests. Across ages, other measures of health status showed improvement resulting from program participation. In addition to providing support for the notion that effective programs provide education and focus on altering behaviors, these results also highlight the importance of tailoring programs to children's changing developmental needs.

SUMMARY AND COMMENT ON COGNITIVE BEHAVIORAL STUDIES

Studies examining parents' cognitive behavioral variables such as health knowledge, health beliefs, self-efficacy, and modeling have explained children's health outcomes including health care utilization, preventive health, injury prevention practices, health teaching behaviors, illness-related avoidance, and pain behavior. Among the most consistent predictors of children's health variables are health beliefs and self-efficacy. Comprehensive models that integrate demographic/contextual factors and include a wider range of cognitive constructs explain a greater amount of variance in health outcomes. Interventions targeting cognitive constructs have resulted in increased knowledge. Programs directly addressing behavioral aspects of health such as illness management are more likely to promote behavior change effectively.

Although cognitive behavioral models consistently explain about half of the variance in children's health variables, their limitations should be noted. First, both basic research and intervention studies are cross-sectional rather than developmental. This methodological approach reflects the reality of conducting research with clinical populations. However, the question of how parents' cognitive behavioral influences change over the course of children's development is important not only for further specifying the nature of psychosocial influences on children's physiological functioning, but on designing appropriately timed interventions. Second, most available cognitive behavioral research is correlational: whether parental cognitive behavioral variables influence children's health or vice versa remains an open question. Bandura (1986) proposed that behavior, the environment, and personal factors operate in a continuously reciprocal fashion, which suggests that the direction of influence may be especially challenging to determine. Prospective, longitudinal designs and contemporary data analytic strategies such as structural equations and growth curve modeling may provide more insight into this issue.

FAMILY PROCESS VARIABLES

The research discussed thus far has focused on parents' cognitions and behaviors that relate to children's health variables. According to family systems theorists, influences on children's physical and psychological well-being involve multiple family members and family process variables, which have bi-directional effects (Minuchin, 1974; Moos and Moos, 1994). It has been suggested that, for example, in diabetic children, poor outcomes were not solely a function of poor disease management, but family process variables as well (Minuchin et al., 1975). Dysfunctional family processes such as overprotection, rigidity, and poor conflict resolution have been proposed as the family process variables which in turn trigger physiological processes that exacerbate the disease process. Central to this model is a focus on family pathology and dysfunction. Subsequent studies have widened the scope to include both functional and dysfunctional processes (Moos and Moos, 1994). Thus a positive family environment can buffer the effects of ongoing stressors. Positive family environments have been characterized by high cohesion, where family members support one another. In addition, a high degree of encouragement to express needs and desires directly, called 'expressiveness', and low levels of conflict among family members, also characterize a positive family environment.

In one study, adolescents who reported the healthiest behavior also reported highest family cohesion and most positive scores on adaptability; those reporting poorest health behavior had lowest family cohesion (Bourdeaudhuij and Van Oost, 1998). Similar findings emerged when using parent rather than adolescent reports of family process variables. However, results from parent reports did not replicate. In another study of family process, mothers in families with low adaptability scores had the lowest leadership (family member most often responsible for making family health decisions) scores (Phipps, 1991). Balanced fathers (neither extremely rigid nor extremely chaotic) participated in health decisions more frequently than extreme fathers. The most chaotic families endorsed the highest levels of sick role behavior, defined as being recognized by the family as ill.

In chronic illness populations, studies linking family process variables with children's health variables have yielded equivocal results. In children with diabetes, for example, both family structure and family environment significantly predict children's behavior problems, with those from nontraditional families low in expressiveness at highest risk (Silver et al., 1996). Another study focused on the effects of family environment medical indicators in children with kidney disease (Soliday et al., 2001). A multivariate model including child age, diagnosis, and family environment variables successfully predicted medical service utilization and number of medications. Higher family conflict and nontraditional family structure predicted a higher number of prescribed medications; higher family cohesion predicted fewer hospitalizations. By contrast, others have found that high inflexibility, considered a less positive family attribute, is associated with better medical outcomes in children with diabetes (Klemp and LaGreca, 1987). Other diabetes researchers have found no significant relationships between family system variables and adjustment outcomes (Kovacs et al., 1989).

All the above family system studies are cross-sectional, leaving open the question of whether family processes are negatively influenced by parenting a chronically ill child or whether less positive family processes place an ill child at risk for poorer health. Although family systems theorists would propose that multiple, bi-directional parent–child transactions occur throughout development, one longitudinal study provides insight into the direction of influence. Researchers applied a 'homeostatic' model to children with cystic fibrosis, proposing that existing family processes shift to adapt to children's physical decline as a compensatory mechanism to maintain balance (Wilson et al., 1996). In a sample of CF children followed for two years, family functioning improved following a clinically significant decline in children's health. Physical deterioration led to improved family environment, which in turn related to improvement in the children's objectively measured health status, less rapid physical decline, and improvement in the children's depression. This cycle was not observed in a comparison sample of children with CF whose health did not decline significantly. Although this study had a small sample, it provides compelling preliminary insight into the association between parenting process variables and pediatric health, illustrating the complex transactions between psychosocial and physiological variables as well as developmental change.

In addition to specifying the complex transactions that occur between family process variables and physiological functioning, researchers have begun to expand family process theories to explain the specific physiological mechanisms by which family process variables influence children's physical functioning. It has been proposed that family process variables influence one another and interact with individuals' bio-behavioral reactivity (Wood, 1993). 'Reactivity' is defined by two mechanisms: (1) bio-behavioral reactivity, or the degree or intensity to which a person responds physiologically to emotional stimuli; and (2) interpersonal responsivity, which is the degree or intensity to which individuals respond to one another. Bio-behavioral reactivity can either buffer or exacerbate physiological processes related to disease activity. For example, a child with an immune system disease in an indulgent family where parents are in conflict showed serious relapses when family difficulties intensified and when the child had to transition to regular school (Wood, 1993).

FAMILY SYSTEM INTERVENTIONS

The majority of family system interventions focus on treating chronically ill pediatric patients due to the tremendous impact that childhood illness can have on the entire family. Family system interventions vary in terms of the intensity of the intervention and the level of expertise necessary for implementing the intervention, both of which may have some bearing on outcomes (Campbell and Patterson, 1995).

A study was concerned with a multifamily group intervention for adolescents with diabetes and their parents (Satin et al., 1989). Over six sessions, both control and experimental group families received education on diabetes management; support was also provided. The experimental group also received a 'parent simulation' intervention in which parents simulated diabetes care on themselves for one week. Adolescents in both groups improved on objective indicators of diabetes management, observed self-care behaviors, and attitudes toward their illness.

In another study addressing pediatric chronic illness patients' needs, clinicians worked with asthmatic children and parents (Tal et al., 1990). Six sessions of asthma education and coping skills training were provided. In comparison to a no-treatment control group, children in the education group showed improvement in asthma self-management. Higher independence scores were obtained on a measure of family environment. Another study concerned a cognitive behavioral family intervention for children with recurrent abdominal pain and their mothers (Sanders et al., 1994). In the cognitive behavioral group, patients received six sessions of treatment emphasizing parent management of child's pain, and direct instruction in self-management was provided. Reduction of pain was found for both the treatment group and the standard care group, although the cognitive behavioral intervention group had lower relapse rates, less activity limitation due to pain, and more satisfied parents.

The efficacy of a family psychoeducational intervention for parents or primary care-givers of children with sickle cell disease, a hematological disorder resulting in frequent severe pain episodes, has been evaluated (Kaslow et al., 2000). The intervention focused on improving disease knowledge, psychological adjustment, family and social functioning, and social support. Family intervention yielded more improvements in child and primary care-giver disease knowledge than did standard treatment and the children in the experimental group maintained their disease knowledge at follow-up.

SUMMARY AND COMMENT ON FAMILY PROCESS RESEARCH

Research focusing on family processes has provided a fair amount of evidence on associations between family functioning and children's health. Family variables, including family conflict, family cohesion, adaptability, and expression of needs and desires, have been found to predict objective measures of children's health. Similar to studies on parents' cognitive behavioral factors in children's health, most family process studies rely on cross-sectional data. Direction of effect is implied by the selection of particular models and hypotheses, but causality cannot be determined by actual study data. Although one recent study helps delineate the nature of transactions between parenting process and pediatric physiological functioning, further longitudinal studies are needed to better understand transactions between family variables and the developmental course of positive health as well as chronic illness. Family interventions generally involve parents (most often mothers), children, and other family members in treatment. Effective interventions tend to be eclectic, focusing on improving cognitive elements such as knowledge and illness self-management. The eclectic nature of family system intervention may be due to previously demonstrated effectiveness of cognitive behavioral approach in mental health as well as a general shift toward symptom-focused psychosocial interventions. It remains to be determined whether systematic treatment of family variables such as cohesion, which has been found in basic research studies to influence disease course, would lead to improved outcomes.

ATTACHMENT

In addition to cognitive behavioral and family process variables, researchers have focused on interpersonal relationships as they relate to child health. This work has been inspired by early findings linking other dimensions of social relationships such as social support to health outcomes including immune system functioning and the course of chronic illness (Cohen and Wills, 1985; Gardner et al., 2000; Stoney and Lentino, 2000). Based on those findings, researchers have begun examining the link between the early attachment relationship and later physical health outcomes.

According to Bowlby (1982), human infants form relationships, or attachments, with their care-givers as a means of ensuring their safety and survival. Both care-giver and infant are involved in forming the attachment relationship: to ensure safety, infants are equipped with specific behaviors that predispose care-givers to remain within close proximity, and infants seek the proximity of care-givers in times of distress or in unfamiliar situations. Based on care-givers' responses to infants' proximity-seeking during times of need and distress, infants develop what Bowlby termed the 'internal working model', which is a mental representation of interpersonal relationships.

Ainsworth (1978) theorized that attachment relationships vary in quality. Infants whose care-givers accurately read their cues (sensitivity) in a timely fashion (contingency) are likely to develop secure attachment relationships. Because their care-givers have adequately met their needs, securely attached infants will develop internal working models of relationships leading them to view others as helpful and responsive. Infants with less consistent and sensitive care-giving experiences are likely to develop insecure attachments. Those whose care-givers respond negatively to their distress cues may avoid contact with others (avoidant); those whose care-givers respond inconsistently or unpredictably may develop ambivalent (resistant) relationships. Attachment theory has spawned decades of research linking attachment relationship quality to children's later adjustment in areas such as academic functioning, social competence and adjustment including peer relations, and general psychological adjustment (Pianta et al., 1997; Bohlin et al., 1998; Booth et al., 1998; Lewis et al., 2000).

Relating attachment theory to physical health, it has been proposed that two mechanisms are involved in connecting attachment and children's health (Feeny and Ryan, 1994). First is the influence of care-givers' own health on parenting behavior. Parental illness and sick role behavior may influence parents' contingency and sensitivity, or responding to infant needs in a timely and appropriate manner, which in turn influence the child's attachment style. The second mechanism by which the attachment relationship may affect physical health is the child's help-seeking behavior. Conditions such as fatigue, pain, and sickness activate the attachment system. How the child and care-giver respond to negative physical symptoms and/or states would vary by the quality of attachment. Children with secure attachments would be likely to express distress and seek help because they have historically experienced sensitive and responsive care-giving. Children with avoidant attachments would suppress their distress due to a history characterized by lack of responsiveness and discouragement of help-seeking behavior. Children with ambivalent attachments may exaggerate their symptoms to arouse responses from inconsistent care-givers (Mikail et al., 1994; Feeny, 2000).

Feeny and Ryan (1994) tested the hypothesis that parental health is related to parental physical illness, which in turn relates to subsequent attachment style and symptom reporting. College-age subjects reported on early family experiences of illness, attachment style, emotionality, and subjective measures of health, including self-reported symptoms and health service utilization. Results generally supported the hypotheses: a path model indicated that parental overindulgence (e.g. overprotection, bringing special treats when ill) related to anxious/ambivalent attachment, which related to the students' negative emotionality, which in turn related to symptom reports. Further analyses of attachment groups indicated that secure attachment was associated with reports of less parental illness and lower rejecting parental responses to ill health. An anxious/ambivalent attachment style related to higher negative emotionality and higher self-reported symptoms. Avoidant attachment style related to lower parental overindulgence and fewer self-reported health care visits.

The non-organic failure to thrive (NOFT) population lends itself well to studying associations between attachment and health because it has been suggested that insecure attachments are over-represented in NOFT samples (Chatoor et al., 1998), and the health outcomes within clinical samples vary greatly (Boddy et al., 2000). In a prospective study examining the association between attachment and children's health, Brinich et al. (1989) examined direct relationships between attachment quality and physical growth outcomes of children with an early history of NOFT. In a follow up conducted at age 42 months, no differences in nutritional status (weight for height) resulted as a function of attachment classification at age 12 months. However, children classified as insecure had twice the number of hospitalizations as children classified as secure, the majority of which were related to the NOFT diagnosis.

It has been hypothesized that attachment may affect children's health through parents' health-related behavior and children's help-seeking (Feeny and Ryan, 1994; Feeny, 2000). A potential physiological mechanism by which attachment relationship quality may affect children's health is bio-behavioral. From this perspective, the quality of the relationship with parents may indirectly affect physical health via effects on stress hormones and other physiological responses.

Within the bio-behavioral model, family processes influence and interact with emotional processes in ways that either buffer or exacerbate biological processes of the disease. In other words, the pathway from family variables to physical outcomes is *emotional regulation* (Wood et al., 2000). Emotional regulation is reflected in the degree to which a child responds physiologically, emotionally, and behaviorally to emotional stimuli, including stress. Reactivity is presumably influenced by temperament and parenting patterns. Because reactivity is mediated by the autonomic nervous system, psychological and physical health are influenced by it to a greater or lesser degree depending on

- the degree and intensity of reactivity, and
- the degree to which a specific physical condition is influenced by psychological and behavioral factors.

The autonomic nervous system regulates the activity of cardiac muscle, smooth muscle, and glands, and it consists of sympathetic and parasympathetic branches (Stoney and Lentino, 2000). The sympathetic nervous system prepares an individual for action, resulting in increased heart rate and respiration. The parasympathetic system counterbalances the arousal of the sympathetic system. In certain chronic conditions such as cardiovascular disease, extreme emotional responses such as prolonged anxiety, anger, fear, and interpersonal relationship stress may negatively impact the disease process (Barefoot et al., 2000; Rutledge et al., 2001; Searle and Bennett, 2001).

The bio-behavioral family model has been tested in a study of children with asthma (Wood et al., 2000). The authors proposed that witnessing a high degree of family conflict and marital distress would result in increased rates of children's stress hormones, but that the time required to recover from this arousal would depend on family process variables, including attachment. Because asthma is a disorder involving inflammation of the airways, elevated and/or sustained arousal may result in airway constriction. Children with asthma were exposed to an emotionally challenging film, and family discussion tasks followed to elicit family patterns of attachment, conflict, and triangulation (placing the child in a loyalty conflict between parents). Higher triangulation was associated with vagal activation during baseline, the movie, and family tasks. The results are complex and not easy to generalize, but they indicate a probable pathway by which family

variables, including the attachment relationship, may operate as a risk factor for physical morbidity. Supportive evidence is also found from a case study on an intervention to improve parent–child attachment (Minde, 1999). In children with serious illnesses, increasing parent consistency and sensitivity led to improved children's health.

Results from attachment studies are compelling in several ways. Studies focusing on the attachment process as it relates to children's health provide preliminary evidence suggesting physiological pathways by which psychosocial variables may influence child health. Efforts to establish the link between psychological and physiological variables warrant high regard due to the expense and intensive involvement of study participants and researchers. Further research on attachment could employ additional objective measures of physiological functioning to expand the current understanding of how relationship processes influence physical health.

IMPLICATIONS FOR CONTINUED RESEARCH

As the work presented in this chapter demonstrates, research has established connections between parenting dimensions and children's health that had received scant attention in the past. However, information on the physiological mechanisms by which parenting may influence children's health is only beginning to emerge. Continued inquiry into how dimensions of parenting affect physiological processes such as vagal activation, hormonal activity, and immunological functioning will provide scientific evidence for the process by which seemingly unrelated variables such as parents' views and their children's physical health are, indeed, related. Advanced physiological measurement strategies and greater accessibility to those strategies will help open the doors to more researchers interested in pursuing these questions.

Greater focus on paternal as well as maternal influences is warranted. Fathers have been grossly under-represented in the parenting literature, yet it has been established that fathers significantly influence children's development and the family system (Phares, 1992; Phares and Compas, 1992; Lamb, 1995).

Consistent with the general under-representation of fathers in the parenting literature, the overwhelming majority of studies mentioned in this chapter use the term 'parent' when referring to samples consisting completely or almost completely of mothers only. Fathers participated in several of the studies, but in proportions too small to consider separately. When the proportion of fathers is large enough to analyze as a factor, differential effects on children's health variables have resulted (Phipps, 1991; Wood et al., 2000), indicating the need for additional research including both parents. A similar need to explore effects of ethnicity and nontraditional family structure becomes evident upon reviewing available literature. To maximize relevance, study samples should reflect the changing demographics of families, who are becoming increasingly diverse in both structure and ethnicity.

A further area for study is the influence of parenting practices on children's health in a life-span developmental perspective. Current knowledge on how parents' attitudes, beliefs, and behavior in family relationships influence children's health comes primarily from assessments conducted at single points in time, with few studies conducted over developmental sequences. The challenges inherent in conducting longitudinal research – or any research involving clinical samples, for that matter – can be addressed through multi-site collaboration and increased research support for such endeavors.

IMPLICATIONS FOR PRACTICE

Child and family practitioners have much to gain from available research on parenting and children's health. Although individual studies may not directly address practice concerns, applications related to assessment and intervention can be drawn from the cumulative body of research.

Related to assessment, multimodal assessment from multiple informants will lend more accurate information on the health variable of interest than, for example, parental self-report alone. Research has shown that parent and child reports of child's health correlate weakly. As practitioners are well aware, self-report data carry limitations, but they are frequently used because of their time and cost efficiency. However, the measurement validity gained from direct observations of behavior and/or objective reports should be considered in an overall cost–benefit analysis. For example, objective methods may be especially valuable when a distressed parent is the only informant

for an infant or young child because the parent's report is likely to be biased by her/his own distress.

A second implication for practice relates to intervention. Interventions targeted toward altering parents' views appear to improve knowledge of specific child health issues, but programs that are primarily educational have little effect on parents' behavior. Intervention programs that integrate behavioral components – for example, specific skills training – do appear to have a greater effect on direct indicators of children's health. But, the specific components that make these programs effective remain to be specified. It also remains to be determined whether altering family processes such as cohesion and conflict leads to improved health outcomes in children. Case studies attempting to improve attachment suggest that children's health may improve following an improvement in the parent–child relationship, but this early indication remains to be systematically established with larger samples.

Determining the efficacy of a given intervention requires repeated assessment. Case studies and several studies with small samples mentioned in this chapter indicate improvements on subjective and objective measures of children's health. In addition to helping to establish the efficacy of a given intervention, repeated assessment may shed greater light on the direction of influence between parenting and children's health. No study has firmly established that specific parental beliefs or behaviors directly cause specific child health outcomes. Until such a study is published, practitioners should continue treating parents and children as a reciprocally influencing, transactional system rather than one in which there is a unidirectional influence from parent to child.

One critical practice-related conclusion is that many interventions – particularly those focusing on preventive health care – meet with only limited success. The majority of child health interventions are currently targeted toward the family only. Major developmental transitions, the influence of other socializing influences such as peers, community, and media, and the interaction between parenting and other external influences are other variables that influence children's health. Similar to demographic variables, external influences are factors over which the practitioner (or the parent) may have little control. However, improving intervention effectiveness may ultimately rely on greater collaboration among larger socializing agents such as communities and those serving individual families and children.

Research has established that parents influence their children's health in a variety of ways, ranging from their cognitions, to the behavior they model for their children, to the quality of parent–child relationships and the family environment. Researchers and clinicians should bear in mind that studying psychosocial aspects of parenting, whether cognitions, behavior, or relationship quality, will only account for those aspects of physical health outcomes that can be explained by psychological variables. Like all aspects of clinical health psychology, other forces within and external to the individual influence health and health behavior. However, because children must depend directly on parents to ensure their health and well-being, continued attention to the critical role that parents play in children's physical health early and later in life remains essential.

REFERENCES

Ainsworth, M.D., Blehar, M.C., Waters, E. and Wall, S. (1978) *Patterns of Attachment*. Hillsdale, NJ: Erlbaum.

Alexander, M.A., Blank, J.S. and Clark, L. (1991) Obesity in Mexican-American school children: a population group at risk. *Public Health Nursing*, **8**, 53–8.

Anderson, R.E., Crespo, C.J., Bartlett, S.J., Lawrence, J.C. and Pratt, M. (1998) Relationship of physical activity and television watching with body weight and level of fatness among children. *Journal of the American Medical Association*, **179**, 938–42.

Arcia, E. (1998) Latino parents' perception of their children's health status. *Social Science & Medicine*, **46**, 1271–4.

Baker, C.W., Whisman, M.A. and Brownell, K.D. (2000) Studying intergenerational transmission of eating attitudes and behaviors: methodological and conceptual questions. *Health Psychology*, **19**, 376–81.

Bandura, A. (1977) Self-efficacy: toward a unifying theory of behavioral change. *Psychological Review*, **84**, 191–215.

Bandura, A. (1982) Self-efficacy mechanisms in human agency. *American Psychologist*, **37**, 122–47.

Bandura, A. (1986) *Social Foundations of Thought and Action: A Social-Cognitive Theory*. Englewood Cliffs, NJ: Prentice-Hall.

Bandura, A. and Wood, R. (1989) Effect of perceived controllability and performance standards on self-regulation of complex decision making. *Journal of Personality and Social Psychology*, **56**, 805–14.

Barefoot, J.C., Brummett, B.H., Helms, M.J., Mark, D.B., Siegler, I.C. and Williams, R.B. (2000) Depressive symptoms and survival of patients with coronary artery disease. *Psychosomatic Medicine*, **62**, 790–5.

Bartholomew, L.K., Czyzewski, D.I., Parcel, G.S., Swank, P.R., Sockrider, M.M., Mariotto, M.J., Schidlow, D.V.,

Fink, R.J. and Seilheimer, D.K. (1997) Self-management of cystic fibrosis: short-term outcomes of the Cystic Fibrosis Family Education Program. *Health Education & Behavior*, **24**(5), 652–66.

Belsky, J. (1984) The determinants of parenting: a process model. *Child Development*, **55**, 83–96.

Bindler, R.M., Short, R.A., Cooney, S.K., Domitor, P., Garabedian, H., Hain, R., Johnson, C., Lammers, G., Provo, M., Repovich, W., Schwartz, A. and Van Cott, N.M. (2000) Interventions to decrease cardiovascular risk factors in children: the northwest pediatric heart project. *National Academics of Practice Forum*, **2**, 43–8.

Boddy, J., Skuse, D. and Andrews, B. (2000) The development sequelae of non-organic failure to thrive. *Journal of Child Psychology and Psychiatry and Allied Disciplines*, **41**, 1003–14.

Bohlin, G., Hagekull, B. and Rydell, A. (1998) Attachment and social functioning: a longitudinal study from infancy to middle childhood. *Social Development*, **9**(1), 24–39.

Bonner, M.J. and Finney, J.W. (1996) A psychosocial model of children's health status. In Ollendick, T.H. and Prinz, R.J. (eds) *Advances in Clinical Child Psychology*, vol. 18. New York: Plenum Press, pp. 231–82.

Booth, C.L., Rubin, K.H. and Rose-Krasnor, L. (1998) Perceptions of emotional support from mother and friend in middle childhood: links with social-emotional adaptation and preschool attachment security. *Child Development*, **69**, 427–42.

Bourdeaudhuij, I.D. and Van Oost, P. (1998) Family characteristics and health behaviors of adolescents and families. *Psychology and Health*, **13**, 785–803.

Bowlby, J. (1982) *Attachment and Loss, Vol. 1: Attachment*, 2nd edition. New York: Basic Books.

Brinich, E., Drotar, D. and Brinich, P. (1989) Security of attachment and outcome of preschoolers with histories of nonorganic failure to thrive. *Journal of Clinical Child Psychology*, **18**, 142–52.

Bronfenbrenner, U. (1977) Toward an experimental ecology of human development. *American Psychologist*, **32**, 513–31.

Bush, M.R. (1997) Influence of health locus of control and parental health perceptions on follow-through with school nurse referral. *Issues in Comprehensive Pediatric Nursing*, **20**, 174–82.

Campbell, T.L. and Patterson, J.M. (1995) The effectiveness of family interventions in the treatment of physical illness. *Journal of Marital and Family Therapy*, **21**, 545–83.

Chatoor, I., Ganiban, J., Colin, V., Plummer, N. and Harmon, R.J. (1998) Attachment and feeding problems: a reexamination of nonorganic failure to thrive and attachment insecurity. *Journal of the American Academy of Child and Adolescent Psychiatry*, **37**, 1217–24.

Cheng, T.L., Savageau, J.A., DeWitt, T.G., Bigelow, C. and Charney, E. (1996) Expectations, goals, and perceived effectiveness of child health supervision: a study of mothers in a pediatric practice. *Clinical Pediatrics*, **35**, 129–37.

Cherlin, A.J. (1999) Going to extremes: family structure, children's well being, and social science. *Demography*, **36**, 421–8.

Clark, N.M., Rosenstock, I.M., Hassan, H. and Evans, D. (1988) The effect of health beliefs and feelings of self efficacy on self management behavior of children with a chronic disease. *Patient Education and Counseling*, **11**(2), 131–9.

Cohen, S. and Wills, T.A. (1985) Stress, social support, and the buffering hypothesis. *Psychological Bulletin*, **98**, 310–57.

Cullen, K.W., Baranowski, T., Rittenberry, L. and Olvera, N. (2000) Social-environmental influences on children's diets: results from focus groups with African-, Euro-, and Mexican-American children and their parents. *Health Education Research*, **15**, 581–90.

Dix, T. (1991) The affective organization of parenting: adaptive and maladaptive processes. *Psychological Bulletin*, **110**, 3–25.

Dunn, J., Deater-Decherd, K., Pickering, K., O'Connor, T.G., Golding, J. and the ALSPAC Study Team (1998) Children's adjustment and prosocial behavior in step-, single-parent, and non-step family settings: findings from a community study. *Journal of Child Psychology, Psychiatry and Allied Disciplines*, **39**, 1083–95.

Feeney, J.A. (2000) Implications of attachment style for patterns of health and illness. *Child: Care, Health, and Development*, **26**, 277–88.

Feeney, J.A. and Ryan, S.M. (1994) Behavior and family experiences of illness in a student sample. *Health Psychology*, **13**, 334–45.

Ford-Gilboe, M. (1997) Family strengths, motivation, and resources as predictors of health promotion behavior in single-parent and two-parent families. *Research in Nursing & Health*, **20**, 205–17.

Gardner, W.L., Gabriel, S. and Diekman, A.B. (2000) Interpersonal processes. In Cacioppo, J.T., Tassinary, L.G. and Bernston, G.G. (eds) *Handbook of Psychophysiology*, 2nd edition. New York: Cambridge University Press, pp. 643–64.

Halfon, N. and Newachek, P.W. (1993) Childhood asthma and poverty: differential impacts and utilization of health services. *Pediatrics*, **91**, 56–61.

Hanson, J. (1998) Parental self-efficacy and asthma self-management skills. *Journal of the Society of Pediatric Nurses*, **3**(4), 146–54.

Heckler, M.M. (1986) Report of the secretary's task force on Black and minority health. *Hispanic Health Issues*. Washington, DC: Department of Health and Human Services.

Hetherington, E.M. and Stanley-Hagan, J. (1999) The adjustment of children with divorced parents: a risk and resiliency perspective. *Journal of Child Psychology, Psychiatry, and Allied Disciplines*, **40**, 129–40.

Horowitz, S.M., Morgenstern, H. and Berkman, L.F. (1985) The impact of social stressors and social network on pediatric medical care use. *Medical Care*, **23**, 946–59.

Hughes, J.N., La Greca, A.M. and Conoley, J.C. (eds) (2001) *Handbook of Psychological Services for Children and Adolescents*. New York: Oxford University Press.

Hyman, I.E. and Loftus, E.F. (1998) Errors in autobiographical memory. *Clinical Psychology Review*, **18**, 933–47.

Impicciatore, P., Bosetti, C., Schiavio, S., Pandolfini, C. and Bonati, M. (2000) Mothers as active partners in the prevention of childhood diseases: maternal factors related to immunization status of preschool children in Italy. *Preventive Medicine: An International Journal Devoted to Practice and Theory*, **31**(1), 49–55.

Janicke, D. and Finney, J.W. (2000) Determinants of children's primary health care. *Journal of Clinical Psychology in Medical Settings*, **7**, 29–39.

Janz, N.K. and Becker, M.H. (1984) The health belief model: a decade later. *Health Education Quarterly*, **11**, 1–47.

Johnson, S.B., Perwien, A.R. and Silverstein, J.H. (2000) Response to hypo- and hyperglycemia in adolescents with Type 1 Diabetes. *Journal of Pediatric Psychology*, **25**, 171–8.

Jones, S.L., Jones, P.K. and Katz, J. (1988) Health belief model intervention to increase compliance with emergency department patients. *Medical Care*, **26**, 1172–84.

Kannel, W.B., D'Agostino, R.B. and Belanger, A.J. (1995) Concept of bridging the gap from youth to adulthood. *The American Journal of the Medical Sciences*, **310**, 15–21.

Kaslow, N.J., Collins, M.H., Rashid, F.L., Baskin, M.L., Griffith, J.R., Hollins, L. and Eckman, J.E. (2000) The efficacy of a pilot family psychoeducational intervention for pediatric sickle cell disease (SCD). *Families, Systems & Health*, **18**, 381–404.

Kaufman, K.L., Cromer, C., Daleiden, E.L., Zaron-Aqua, A., Aqua, K., Greeley, T. and Li, B.U. (1997) Recurrent abdominal pain in adolescents: Psychosocial correlates of organic and nonorganic pain. *Children's Health Care*, **26**, 15–30.

Kedler, S.D., Perry, C.L., Klepp, K.I. and Lytle, L.L. (1994) Longitudinal tracking of adolescent smoking, physical activity, and food choice behaviors. *American Journal of Public Health*, **84**, 1121–6.

Klemp, S.B. and LaGreca, A.M. (1987) Adolescents with IDDM: the role of family cohesion and conflict. *Diabetes*, **36**, 18A.

Kovacs, M., Kass, R.E., Schnell, T.M., Goldston, D. and Marsh, J. (1989) Family functioning and metabolic control of school-aged children with IDDM. *Diabetes Care*, **12**, 409–14.

Lamb, M.E. (1995) *The Changing Role of Fathers. Becoming a Father: Contemporary, Social, Developmental, and Clinical Perspectives*. New York: Springer.

Lau, R.R., Quadrel, M.J. and Hartman, K.A. (1990) Development and change of young adults' preventive health beliefs and behavior: influence from parents and peers. *Journal of Health and Social Behavior*, **31**, 240–59.

Lees, N.B. and Tinsley, B.J. (2000) Maternal socialization of children's preventive health behavior: the role of maternal affect and teaching strategies. *Merrill-Palmer Quarterly*, **46**, 632–52.

Lemanek, K.L. and Koontz, A.D. (1999) Integrated approaches to acute illness. In Russ, S.W. and Ollendick, T.H. (eds) *Handbook of Psychotherapies with Children and Families*. New York: Kluwer Academic/Plenum Publishers.

Lewis, C.C., Pantell, R.H. and Kieckhefer, G.M. (1989) Assessment of children's health status: field test of new approaches. *Medical Care*, **27**, 54–65.

Lewis, M., Feiring, C. and Rosenthal, S. (2000) Attachment over time. *Child Development*, **71**(3), 707–20.

Lindquist, C.H., Reynolds, L.D. and Goran, M.I. (1999) Sociocultural determinants of physical activity among children. *Preventive Medicine*, **29**, 305–12.

Lombrail, P., Vitoux-Brot, C., Bourrillon, A., Brodin, M. and Depouvourville, G. (1997) Another look at emergency overcrowding: accessibility of the health services and quality of care. *International Journal of Quality in Health Care*, **9**, 225–35.

Manne, S.L., Lesanics, D., Meyers, P., Wollner, N., Steinherz, P. and Redd, W. (1995) Predictors of depressive symptomatology among parents of newly diagnosed children with cancer. *Journal of Pediatric Psychology*, **20**, 491–510.

Meade, J.A., Lumley, M.A. and Casey, R.J. (2001) Stress, emotional skill, and illness in children: the importance of distinguishing between children's and parent's reports of illness. *Journal of Child Psychology and Psychiatry and Allied Disciplines*, **42**, 405–12.

Mechanic, D. (1964) The influence of mothers on their children's health attitudes and behavior. *Pediatrics*, **33**, 444–53.

Mikail, S.F., Henderson, P.R. and Tasca, G.A. (1994) An interpersonally based model of chronic pain: an application of attachment theory. *Clinical Psychology Review*, **14**(1), 1–16.

Minde, K. (1999) Mediating attachment patterns during a serious medical illness. *Infant Mental Health Journal*, **20**, 105–22.

Minuchin, S. (1974) *Families and Family Therapy*. Cambridge, MA: Harvard University Press.

Minuchin, S., Baker, L., Rosman, B.L., Liebman, R., Milman, L. and Todd, T.C. (1975) A conceptual model of psychosomatic illness in children. *Archives of General Psychiatry*, **32**, 1031–8.

Molina, C.W. and Aguirre-Molina, M. (1994) *Latino Health in the U.S.: A Growing Challenge*. Washington, DC: APHA.

Moos, R.H. and Moos, B.S. (1994) *Family Environment Scale Manual*, 3rd edition. Palo Alto: Consulting Psychologists Press.

Mullen, P.D. (1983) Promoting child health: channels of socialization. *Family and Community Health*, **5**, 52–68.

Nader, P.R., Sellers, D.E., Johnson, C.C. and Perry, C.L. (1996) The effect of adult participation in a school-based family intervention to improve children's diet and physical activity: the child and adolescent trial for cardiovascular disease. *Preventive Medicine*, **25**, 455–64.

Newachek, P.W. and Halfon, N. (1986) The association between mother's and children's use of physician services. *Medical Care*, **24**, 30–8.

Norman, P. (1995) Applying the health belief model to the prediction of attendance at health checks in general practice. *British Journal of Clinical Psychology*, **34**, 461–70.

Ornstein, P.A., Ceci, S.J. and Loftus, E.F. (1998) Adult recollections of childhood abuse: cognitive and developmental perspectives. *Psychology, Public Policy, and Law*, **4**, 1025–51.

Osborne, R.B., Hatcher, J.W. and Richsmeier, A.J. (1989) The role of social modeling in unexplained pediatric pain. *Journal of Pediatric Psychology*, **14**, 43–61.

Peterson, L., Farmer, J. and Kashani, J.H. (1990) Parental injury prevention endeavors: a function of health beliefs? *Health Psychology*, **9**, 177–91.

Phares, V. (1992) Where's Poppa? *American Psychologist*, **47**, 656–64.

Phares, V. and Compas, B.E. (1992) The role of fathers in child and adolescent psychopathology: make room for daddy. *Psychological Bulletin*, **111**, 387–412.

Phipps, S.A. (1991) Family systems functioning, family health roles, and utilization of physical health services. *Lifestyles: Family and Economic Issues*, **12**, 23–41.

Pianta, R.C., Nimetz, S.L. and Bennett, E. (1997) Mother–child relationships, teacher–child relationships, and school outcomes in preschool and kindergarten. *Early Childhood Research Quarterly*, **12**, 263–80.

Polic, M. (1998) Parents' perception of children's health and illness. *Studia Psychologica*, **40**, 79–93.

Quadrel, M.J. and Lau, R.R. (1990) A multivariate analysis of adolescents' orientations toward physician use. *Health Psychology*, **9**, 750–73.

Rand C.S. and Weeks, K. (1998) Measuring adherence with medication regimens in clinical care and research. In Shumaker, S.A. (ed.) *The Handbook of Health Behavior Change*. New York: Springer.

Rosenstock, I.M. (1974) The health belief model and personal health behavior. *Health Education Monographs*, **2**, 324–508.

Rosso, I. and Rise, J. (1994) Concordance of parental and adolescent health behaviors. *Social Science & Medicine*, **38**, 1299–305.

Rotter, J.B. (1966) Generalized expectancies for internal U.S. external control of reinforcement. *Psychological Monographs: General and Applied*, **80**(1), 1–28.

Russell, K.M. and Champion, U.L. (1996) Health beliefs and social influence in home safety practices of mothers with preschool children. *Image: Journal of Nursing Scholarship*, **28**(1), 59–64.

Rutledge, T., Reis, S.E., Olson, M., Owens, J., Kelsey, S.F., Pepine, C.J., Reichek, N., Rogers, W.J., Merz, C. N., Sopko, G., Cornell, C.E. and Matthews, K.A. (2001) Psychosocial variables are associated with atherosclerosis risk factors among women with chest pain: the WISE study. *Psychosomatic Medicine*, **63**, 282–8.

Sanders, M.R., Shepherd, R.W., Cleghorn, G. and Woolford, H. (1994) The treatment of recurrent abdoinal pain in children: a controlled comparison of cognitive behavioral family intervention and standard pedatric care. *Journal of Consulting and Clinical Psychology*, **62**, 306–14.

Satin, W., LaGreca, A.M., Zigo, M.A. and Skyler, J.S. (1989) Diabetes in adolescence: effects of multifamily group intervention and parent simulation of diabetes. *Journal of Pediatric Psychology*, **14**, 259–75.

Searle, A. and Bennett, P. (2001) Psychological factors and inflammatory bowel disease: a review of a decade of literature. *Psychology, Health & Medicine*, **6**(2), 121–35.

Sheeran, P. and Abraham, C. (1995) The health belief model. In Conner, M. and Norman, P. (eds) *Predicting Health Behaviour*. Buckingham, UK: Open University Press.

Shields, M.C., Griffin, K.W. and McNabb, W.L. (1990) The effect of a patient education program on emergency room use for inner-city children with asthma. *American Journal of Public Health*, **80**, 36–8.

Sigelman, C.K., Mukai, T., Woods, T. and Alfeld, C. (1995) Parents' contributions to children's knowledge and attitudes regarding AIDS: another look. *Journal of Pediatric Psychology*, **20**, 61–77.

Silver, E.J., Stein, R.E. and Dadds, M.R. (1996) Moderating effects of family structure on the relationship between physical and mental health in urban children with chronic illness. *Journal of Pediatric Psychology*, **21**, 43–56.

Soliday, E. and Hoeksel, R. (2001) Psychosocial predictors of pediatric patients' emergency room and hospital service utilization. *Psychology, Health, and Medicine*, **6**, 5–12.

Soliday, E. and Hoeksel, R. (2000) Health beliefs and pediatric emergency department after-care adherence. *Annals of Behavioral Medicine*, **22**(4), 1–9.

Soliday, E. and Lande, M.B. (2002) Family structure and the course of steroid-sensitive nephrotic syndrome. *Pediatric Nephrology*, **17**, 41–4.

Soliday, E., Kool, E. and Lande, M.B. (2001) Family environment, child behavior, and medical indicators in children with kidney disease. *Child Psychiatry and Human Development*, **31**, 279–95.

Starfield, B. (1992) Child and adolescent health status measures. *Future of Children*, **2**, 25–39.

Stoney, C.M. and Lentino, L.M. (2000) Psychophysiological applications in clinical health psychology. In Cacioppo, J.T., Tassinary, L.G. and Bernston, G.G. (eds) *Handbook of Psychophysiology*, 2nd edition. New York: Cambridge University Press.

Tal, D., Gil-Spielberg, R., Antonovsky, H., Tal., A. and Moaz, B. (1990) Teaching families to cope with childhood asthma. *Family Systems Medicine*, **8**, 135–44.

Taylor, J.A. and Cufley, D. (1996) The association between parental health beliefs and immunization status

among children followed by private pediatricians. *Clinical Pediatrics*, **35**, 18–22.

Teti, D.M., O'Connell, M.A. and Reiner, C.D. (1996) Parenting sensitivity, parental depression and child health: the mediational role of parental self-efficacy. *Early Development and Parenting*, **5**, 237–50.

Tinsley, B.J. (1992) Multiple influences on the acquisition and socialization of children's health attitudes and behavior: an integrative review. *Child Development*, **63**, 1043–69.

Tinsley, B.J. and Holtgrave, D.R. (1989) Maternal health locus of control beliefs, utilization of childhood preventive health services, and infant health. *Developmental and Behavioral Pediatrics*, **10**, 236–41.

Turkat, I.D. (1982) An investigation of parental modeling in the etiology of diabetic illness behavior. *Behavior Research Therapy*, **20**, 547–52.

Wade, S.L., Holden, G., Lynn, H., Mitchell, H. and Ewart, C. (2000) Cognitive-behavioral predictors of asthma morbidity in inner-city children. *Journal of Developmental and Behavioral Pediatrics*, **21**, 340–6.

Walker, E. and Roberts, M.C. (eds) (2001) *Handbook of Clinical Child Psychology*, 3rd edition. New York: John Wiley.

Wallston, K.A. (1991) The importance of placing measures of health locus of control beliefs in a theoretical context. *Health Education Research*, **2**, 251–2.

Wallston, K.A., Wallston, B.S., Kaplan, G.D. and Maides, S.A. (1976) Development and validation of the health locus of control (HCL) scale. *Journal of Consulting and Clinical Psychology*, **44**, 580–5.

Wallston, K.A., Wallston, B.S. and De Vellis, R. (1978) Development of the multidimensional health locus of control (MHLOC) scales. *Health Education Monographs*, **6**, 160–70.

Wasilewski, Y., Clark, N.M., Evans, D., Levison, M.J., Levin, B. and Mellins, R.B. (1996) Factors associated with emergency department visits by children with asthma: implications for health education. *American Journal of Public Health*, **86**, 1410–15.

Wassmer, E. and Hanlon, M. (1999) Effects of information on parental knowledge of febrile convulsions. *Seizure*, **8**, 421–3.

Whitehead, W.E., Busch, C.M., Heller, B.R. and Costa, P.T. (1986) Social learning influences on menstrual symptoms and illness behavior. *Health Psychology*, **5**, 13–23.

Wilson, J., Fosson, A., Kanga, J. and D'Angelo, S.L. (1996) Homeostatic interactions: a longitudinal study of biological, psychosocial and family variables in children with cystic fibrosis. *Journal of Family Therapy*, **18**(2), 123–9.

Wolfe, B.L. (1980) Children's utilization of medical care. *Medical Care*, **23**, 1196–207.

Wood, B.L. (1993) Beyond the 'psychosomatic family:' a biobehavioral family model of pediatric illness. *Family Process*, **32**, 261–78.

Wood, B.L., Klebba, K.B. and Miller, B.D. (2000) Evolving the biobehavioral family model: the fit of attachment. *Family Process*, **39**, 319–44.

World Health Organization (WHO) (1978) *Primary Health Care. Report of the International Conference on Primary Health Care*, Alma Ata, USSR. Geneva: World Health Organization.

Zambrana, R.E., Ell, K., Dorrigton, C., Wachsman, L. and Hodge, D. (1994) The relationship between psychosocial status of immigrant latino mothers and use of emergency pediatric services. *Health and Social Work*, **19**(2), 93–102.

12

Parenting Chronically Ill Children – The Scope and Impact of Pediatric Parenting Stress

Randi Streisand and Kenneth P. Tercyak

SUMMARY

Parenting children with a chronic illness represents an important area of interest for practitioners and researchers alike. This is because children with long-term medical problems constitute a significant portion of health care patients, and the stresses faced by parents raising such children are formidable.

The goal of this chapter is to explore particular issues in parenting that arise when infants, children, and adolescents experience chronic and/or life-threatening illness. In addition to describing the emergence of this special area of parenting research, we review cross-cutting themes in parent–child stress and coping that offer multiple frameworks in which to understand these complex psychological processes. Along with a detailed exploration of prior work conducted with parents of children with illnesses such as diabetes, cancer, and other serious health threats, we discuss the practice implications of this knowledge.

INTRODUCTION

All parents are challenged with the task of promoting normal, healthy development in their children. This includes promoting not only physical growth and maturation, but also social, emotional, and intellectual development as well. For parents of children with a chronic illness, these challenges are intensified, because helping children to achieve their developmental milestones must occur within the parameters of the child's medical adversity. At times, childhood illness interrupts or delays normal development. This can result in a widening gap between the resources, skills, and achievements of ill children relative to their healthy peers, thereby further increasing the worries, stresses, and burdens faced by their parents.

Decades of explanatory behavioral research on children with chronic illness has brought to light the unique circumstances that they and their parents must confront on an everyday basis. As a result of this body of research, it is widely understood that pediatric illness and in-patient medical care are acutely stressful events, and that the stress associated with these events can profoundly impact upon long-term outcomes. On a more positive note, findings from these studies can also be used to guide clinical practice to promote enhanced quality of life among children, parents, and their family members.

The impact that the illness has on the parent is thought to play a role in how the child adapts to the medical adversity (Melamed and Ridley-Johnson, 1988). For example, negative behavioral and emotional responses (such as anxiety) on the part of the parent can affect the child's recovery process (such as observed distress during medical procedures). Positive associations between parent and child distress highlight that family impact is an important consideration for health care providers and practitioners who work with children and their family members in these circumstances. That is, health professionals must be keenly aware of the behavioral impact of the illness on the child and on his or her parents (Chan and Leff, 1982).

HISTORICAL BACKGROUND

There is a longstanding tradition of health professionals working closely with parents of chronically ill children to assist in the management of disease burden, as well as developmental and behavioral side-effects. On both sides of the Atlantic, and in other areas of the world, consultation–liaison models in child psychiatry and pediatrics, behavioral pediatrics, and pediatric psychology have been established and evaluated (Rothenberg, 1968; Graham, 1994; Roberts and McNeal, 1995; Rodrigue et al., 1995). Clinical implementation of these models in hospitals and out-patient settings helps ensure that the medical care children receive includes a strong focus on family life. These approaches also recognize the importance of the parenting role in promoting child development under adverse medical conditions, and minimizing negative child outcomes. Below, we detail some of the professional achievements and milestones that led to psychosocially enhanced children's medical services, and highlight the richness and diversity of approaches that have led to the current focus on the impact of children's illness on parents.

Early Pioneers

In the early 20th century, Arnold Gesell, who was both a psychologist and physician, wrote and lectured about psychological principles in pediatric medicine, and the relationship between child behavior and development (Gesell, 1940). It was Gesell who intensively studied infant

mental abilities and later amassed a film library of observational data on the development of children from birth through adolescence. As a result of this work, he identified behavioral norms occurring within each developmental phase. This achievement played an important role in parenting during the 1940s and 1950s, as many practitioners used this knowledge to identify children in need of special services.

By the middle of the 20th century, pediatrician Benjamin Spock's book *Common Sense Book of Baby and Child Care* (1946) was published for the first time. This book would later go on to sell more than 50 million copies worldwide, and was translated into more than 30 languages. Spock's message of patience, tolerance, and love for children influenced the attitudes and practices of generations of parents throughout the US, UK, and other parts of the world.

However, these and other popular resources primarily concentrated on physically healthy children; far less was known about parenting in the face of medical adversity, such as physical handicaps or chronic illness. Like Gesell, many believed that the study of normal development would ultimately lead to a more complete understanding of deviant processes. Subsequent advances in medical diagnosis and treatment would make it possible to explore similar issues among the chronically ill.

Emerging Focus on Physical Illness

In the early 1960s, Green and Solnit wrote about 'vulnerable child syndrome'. At its core, this syndrome described the altered relationship between parent and child when the child experienced an acute illness, and was not expected to, yet ultimately did survive. Green and Solnit (1964) recognized that children with significant illness histories would often be viewed by their parents in a new light as being almost fragile. They hypothesized that this skewed parental view would lead to child maladjustment over time. At the time, this and other early parent–child frameworks were particularly important because they helped to set the stage for closer examination of long-term relationships between parents and children in the context of medical crisis.

In the latter part of the 20th century, theoretical models began to emerge that specifically focused on factors affecting psychosocial adjustment among children with chronic conditions. These include a disability–stress–coping model, and a transactional stress and coping model. They both emphasized the importance of parental adjustment and other familial/social factors in promoting child behavioral functioning under adverse medical circumstances (Thompson, 1985; Wallander et al., 1989). These models, and others discussed later in this chapter, have been instrumental in promoting theory-based research on parent–child behavioral interactions occurring within medical contexts.

THEMES IN CHILD HEALTH, PARENTING, STRESS AND COPING

Across all serious pediatric illnesses, there are five main points to consider when assessing the social, behavioral, and psychological sequelae of the illness. The first of these areas, stress faced by parents, is at the core of this chapter. The second area, prevalence, tells us how widely parent–child stress exists within medical settings. Third are the conceptual models that offer a framework for understanding complex interactions. Fourth, natural illness and developmental processes are important because they underlie key outcomes of interest. And finally, we consider the application of our understanding in each of these areas to determine individual needs and resources, including the potential for interventions.

Pediatric Parenting Stress

'Pediatric parenting stress' is the term we use to refer to the stress faced by parents of children with chronic illness (Streisand et al., 2001). We favor this term over others (for example, 'parenting stress', 'care-giver burden') because we feel it more firmly establishes interrelationships among three central features: (1) child health; (2) parental roles, responsibility, and burden; and (3) psychological and behavioral response and adaptation to illness.

First and foremost, the term 'pediatric' (though meaning 'related to children' in general) specifically applies to the development and care of infants, children, and adolescents with some type of illness. Second, the term 'parenting' in this context makes explicit reference to interactions between parents and their children, and not just children and a wider range of care-givers, because of the intensity of the parent–child relationship. Finally, a substantial body of research supports the notion that 'stress' – a transactional process between an individual and his or her environment – could arise from multiple sources, including parents' concern related to their children's health status.

Sources of stress among parents of children with chronic illnesses include the following:

- negotiating complex health care systems;
- learning to communicate with providers around the jargon of the child's disease;
- parents' emotional reactions to the child's diagnosis, illness trajectory, and treatment; and
- limitations the child's illness may place on parent role functioning (for example, in their professional lives and in caring for the ill child's healthy siblings).

While areas other than the four mentioned above certainly contribute to the experience of stress among parents of children with illness, these are among the most salient, relevant, and important to parents' daily lives in this context. To the extent that stress in these domains can be better understood, professionals involved in the care of ill children and their families will be better able to offer assistance to aid their coping and adaptation. This goal would include ways to strengthen the parenting role and general psychological functioning of parents (Johnston and Marder, 1994).

In the absence of professional guidance, some parents may become so preoccupied with their child's health risks, as to engage in over-protective behavior and thus provoke a range of negative clinical outcomes (Thomasgard and Metz, 1997). Though some parents internalize their distress in an attempt to conceal it from the family, others externalize their feelings in equally unhealthy ways. Why is it that some parents are more resilient and ready to take charge when faced with hospitalization or illness in their child compared to other parents? Investigations into the coping mechanisms that underlie such processes have shed light on this issue, and generate important ideas for assisting those in greatest need (Burke et al., 1991).

EPIDEMIOLOGY OF BEHAVIOR PROBLEMS AMONG CHRONICALLY ILL CHILDREN

It has been estimated that up to 50 per cent of all general pediatric clinic visits reflect behavioral, psychological, and educational concerns (Costello, 1986). A range of other studies estimate that overall prevalence rates of behavioral disturbance among children seen in primary care are over 10 per cent (Jellinek et al., 1999). These findings contribute to growing concerns about psychosocial morbidity among pediatric patients, and the need to promote effective behavioral screening and treatment. As children with a chronic illness are seen by medical professionals more often than healthy children, pediatric specialists working with such families may be even more likely to learn about behavioral, psychological, or educational concerns than general practitioners.

As mentioned previously, parents are children's most important health resource, helping them to manage the illness, while continuously bringing the child's medical needs to the attention of health care providers. Parents are an integral component of the identification and management of behavioral concerns, and the nature and quality of their communications with professionals about such problems often determine if and when intervention services are offered (Garrison et al., 1992; Horwitz et al., 1998). A study by Sharp et al. (1992) of child health visits concerned with reviewing children's conditions found that physicians very often created opportunities for parents and children to express psychosocial concerns. As professionals, one of our most important goals should be to help parents seize upon these opportunities so that they and their children receive the care and support they deserve. This may include offering anticipatory guidance about what behaviors to expect from a child as he or she matures with the illness, teaching parenting strategies to manage negative behavior, or to provide a referral to a behavior specialist who can help the parent learn to cope more effectively.

Prevalence

Prevalence rates of childhood chronic illness and disability illustrate the significant proportion of children affected by these conditions worldwide (see Table 12.1). While families of children with an illness contend with a host of physical and medical demands (for example, invasive procedures, complex medication regimens, in-patient hospitalization), many families also face a concomitant set of child behavioral and psychosocial complications. Research has consistently demonstrated that across illness types, parents of children with an illness experience significant levels of stress (Goldberg et al., 1990; Eiser et al., 1991; Quittner et al., 1998; Streisand et al., 2001). Other sequelae may include conflict with partners, increased behavioral problems in the child, uncertainty about the future, and poorer family functioning.

Theoretical Models of Parent, Child, and Family Adaptation

While few families remain unchanged after experiencing a child's illness, many factors affect the severity of the impact that the illness will bring to the child and his or her family. These models overlap, as they must, since they describe the same phenomena. Their differences lie primarily in emphasizing elements, process, and outcome in these families. Some highlight the bi-directional influences on the child and family (Fiese and Sameroff, 1989). Others take into account how parent-related variables influence family adaptation (Wallander et al., 1989) or how influences from other areas, such as the child's school and community, impact upon parent or family adjustment (Kazak, 1989).

Parent and family adjustment may also be related to family characteristics (for example, adaptability and cohesion; Chaney and Peterson, 1989), parents' perception of the child's health risk (Youngblut and Shiao, 1993), or other family demographic characteristics, such as employment and socio-economic status (Walker et al., 1989). For example, studies suggest that children in families with lower levels of cohesion and adaptability have poorer overall functioning, that mothers who perceive their children to be at greater risk experience more distress themselves, and that working mothers and mothers with higher household incomes may experience less distress.

Illness Trajectory

For those who take a predominantly social-ecological perspective (Kazak, 1989), the illness itself plays a large role in determining how some families manage with a child's illness. For example, an illness associated with a significantly shortened life expectancy, such as cystic fibrosis, might engender more significant long-term worries in parents than an illness that requires ongoing treatment, yet has a more positive prognosis, such as asthma.

The stage of the illness, or where children are in the illness trajectory, also affects how families respond (Gravelle, 1997). For example, a study of Chinese parents of children being treated for cancer found that the diagnosis and terminal phases of the child's illness were seen as the most difficult or most stressful time by the families (Martinson et al., 1997). Even the time period just prior to the actual diagnosis can be extremely difficult for families, with parents wondering why their child's health is failing.

Table 12.1   *Worldwide prevalence of common pediatric illnesses by age and gender*

Condition	Gender	Age group (years)	Prevalence rate (per 100,000)
Asthma	Males	0–4	1,669
		5–14	2,885
	Females	0–4	1,168
		5–14	2,053
Diabetes mellitus	Males	0–4	6.2
		5–14	15.7
	Females	0–4	6
		5–14	16.7
Epilepsy	Males	0–4	389
		5–14	571
	Females	0–4	395
		5–14	573
Leukemia	Males	0–4	4.4
		5–14	10.6
	Females	0–4	4.4
		5–14	9.5
Lymphomas and multiple myeloma	Males	0-4	3.8
		5–14	15.5
	Females	0–4	1.9
		5–14	9.2
Spina bifida	Males	0–4	46
		5–14	35
	Females	0–4	96
		5–14	87

Adapted from Murray and Lopez (1996).

During the period of time prior to diagnosis, stress may come as children and parents endure countless medical tests to determine the etiology of the child's symptoms (Horner, 1997).

Stress and Coping

Similar to the social-ecological model, the disability–stress–coping model (Wallander et al., 1989) views family members as an integrated whole, where a medical stressor or illness influencing the behavior of one individual has implications for all family members. In this model, the developmental phase of the child (infancy, school-age, adolescence), as well as that of the family (recent marriage or divorce, new family), affects the impact of the illness. It is therefore critical for practitioners to consider both the age and developmental level of the child, and to be aware of the risks to normal development faced by children with an illness. Figure 12.1 outlines the major tasks for children at different phases of development and the challenges of the illness at each developmental

phase. These issues are discussed later in the chapter.

In terms of the implications of stress related to the illness, it is important to recognize several lines of evidence which suggest that even subtle, illness-related variations in parents' stress symptoms impact upon both the parent and child. For example, it has been shown that parents caring for children with physical limitations are at risk of experiencing poor mental health states (Wallander et al., 1989). Further, such stress has been shown to play a role in information learning, processing, and recall (Gillis, 1993), which could compromise parental comprehension of, and adherence to, the child's prescribed treatment. Stress on the part of parents may also be directly related to stress subsequently experienced by children facing health threats (Melamed and Ridley-Johnson, 1988; Johnson and Tercyak, 1995), possibly suggesting systemic family modeling of anxiety and worry. Finally, elevated stress levels among parenting figures could negatively impact upon children's own ability to adhere to their medical regimen by creating maladaptive preoccupations and

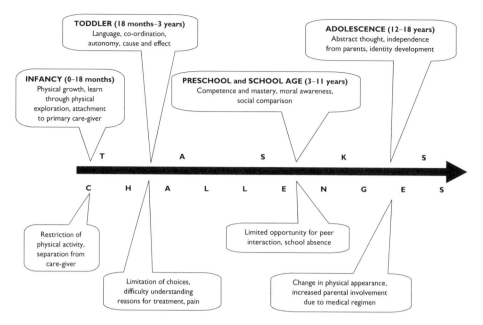

Figure 12.1 *Major developmental tasks, and corresponding challenges posed by illness, from birth to 18 years old*

behavior (Hanson et al., 1995; Auslander et al., 1997).

How parents cope with these issues, and the social support available to them, are two of the most important determinants of outcomes. Parents who effectively utilize family support, those who maintain a positive outlook, and those who manage to integrate the child's medical care/daily regimen into their normal routines perceive less burden (Ray and Ritchie, 1993).

In a Finnish study of parents of children with a chronic illness (diabetes, rheumatoid arthritis, asthma), several forms of social support, including emotional support, instrumental support, and support from health care staff were identified (Hentinen and Kyngas, 1998). Higher levels of emotional and instrumental support were closely associated with more positive adaptation.

Researchers have also sought to determine if there are basic differences in the coping styles of mothers and fathers. It has been found, for example, that mothers and fathers rely on different strategies to support themselves when their children are affected by chronic illness (Copeland and Clements, 1993). Fathers may be more likely than mothers to use 'reasoning' strategies, whereas mothers may be more likely than fathers to use 'releasing' and 'relating' strategies. Reasoning strategies include seeking information about the illness and teaching the

child about his or her disease. Releasing strategies include physical and emotional activities that expend energy (for example, exercising, crying), and relating strategies include communicating with others and involvement in support and religious groups.

Patterns in Children's Illness and Development

Of course, the degree of impact further depends on several other factors, and may be moderated by both stage of illness and phase of child development. In terms of the stage of illness, psychological sequelae usually begin to emerge in parents at the time of the child's diagnosis, and may ultimately alter family life for years to come. In terms of the child's development, hospitalization during infancy is consistently noted as being one of the most highly stressful events for parents (Goldberg et al., 1990; Coffman et al., 1993). Regardless of age at diagnosis or treatment, health care providers must work towards helping families maintain a sense of normalcy. Further, they must strive to keep the child on the same developmental trajectory as if the illness was not present. As such, we now turn our attention to the topic of development, and the potential issues faced by parents of ill children at the various phases.

INFANCY

From birth to 18 months, infants develop through two primary avenues: (1) exploration of their environment, and (2) attachment to their care-giver(s). Physical illness during this period may impede either or both of these avenues of exploration, significantly impacting both the infant and the parent.

In terms of exploration, being in a hospital room or connected to medical equipment for extended periods of time is confining and restricting. While a short period of restricted movement is unlikely to be detrimental to the infant's long-term development, prolonged restriction can slow the rate at which the infant progresses to the next developmental phase and a referral to a physical therapist may be necessary.

Physical confinement due to illness may also impact the infant's ability to form an attachment to care-givers, and an insecure attachment may result from parents' lack of resolution about the diagnosis (Marvin and Pianta, 1996). This phenomenon is similar to that of infants who are physically deformed or delayed in their social responsiveness, who, by the nature of their disability (for example, craniofacial anomaly), may provide less feedback or positive reinforcement to parents in their care-giver role (Perrin and Gerrity, 1984).

While parents of children of all ages have an innate desire to protect their children, parents of infants may also feel at fault for 'causing' the infant's difficulties (perhaps through passing on inherited diseases), or feel incapable of managing their child's care (Stevens, 1994). Some may even come to question their competency in general parenting. For example, many illnesses preclude parents from continuing a typical feeding routine – a task that helps most parents develop confidence in their parent role. It is not surprising, then, to find that across illness groups much research has demonstrated greater stress in parents of infants who are ill as compared to parents of healthy infants (Goldberg et al., 1990; Stephenson, 1999).

PRESCHOOL

Similar to infants, toddlers and preschoolers, or children aged 18 months through 5 years, are largely dependent on their parents or care-givers. By 18 months, most children are comfortably mobile, and movement restrictions due to illness are, therefore, less likely to cause significant delays in motor development or disruptions in attachment at this phase.

Instead, challenges to parenting are more related to helping children understand their illness, and helping them to co-operate with treatment. Because of their use of 'magical thinking', children may come to believe they are to blame for the illness or painful medical regimens, and parents may feel at a loss over how to explain the need for various procedures to them.

Development of self-control is also important for toddlers and preschoolers. Yet this can also be affected by illness when children are precluded from making choices, or parents are reluctant to set appropriate limits on behavior. For example, when children are in hospital, medical staff frequently enter the child's room to perform various procedures, often with little warning or advance notice given. They typically do not offer any choice over the timing of procedures, or even preference for physical placement or location of venipuncture lines (left or right arm) or devices to monitor vital signs. Similarly, when preschoolers start feeling better and regain their strength and activity levels, parents may allow these children to act out in ways that would not have been tolerated prior to the child's illness. No matter what the medical circumstance, self-control cannot be learned unless children's negative behaviors are limited and corrected.

SCHOOL AGE

For school-aged children (6–11 years), accomplishing developmental tasks is largely affected by interactions with peers, with children at this age using social comparison to help them judge their competencies in various domains of life. Disruption in normal routines due to illness can limit children's opportunities for social interactions, or even cause them to look and/or feel different from peers. This may hamper the personal growth typically gained from peer interaction. Irregular school attendance due to illness also limits children's opportunities to succeed, and may reduce their likelihood of future achievement unless corrective steps are taken.

ADOLESCENCE

Perhaps the largest body of literature related to children's health and their development focuses on the transition to adolescence (ages 12–18 years). Many challenges occur at this phase, including identity formation, struggling with body image issues, and the move towards independence. These tasks may be particularly challenging for the adolescent with an illness. For example, the treatment of various illnesses (such as cancer) can significantly alter their appearance. To the teenager, adverse changes in physical appearance, such as hair loss, can be devastating. It is not surprising, then, that adolescents with chronic illnesses are at greater risk for developing behavioral or emotional problems than are their healthy peers (Wallander and Varni, 1995).

For all adolescents, regardless of health status, formation of an individual identity is a major task of this developmental phase. It is normal for adolescents to report a decline in closeness to their families during this transition, and many note spending significantly less time with parents than at previous ages (Larson and Richards, 1991). This path towards independence can lead many parents to struggle with their new role in their teenager's lives, and may even adversely affect parents' own mental health (Silverberg and Steinberg, 1990).

The task of independence poses particular challenges for parents of children who are ill. Just when parents are beginning to relinquish some responsibilities for the adolescent, an illness can easily overwhelm and alter this situation, necessitating parents once again to become intimately involved in every aspect of the teenager's life. This causes difficulties for the adolescent, the parent, and also the parent–adolescent relationship.

APPLICATION OF THEORY TO ASSESSMENT

The need to consider the impact of the child's illness on not only the child, but also on his or her parents or family members has been a consistent theme in this chapter. Now we will turn to putting our knowledge into practice by highlighting the ways in which practitioners can assess the need for intervention among these individuals. Through careful assessment, practitioners can determine which parents are at risk, and who might benefit from behavioral counseling.

As noted earlier, impact or stress is multidimensional. Assessing how families appraise the specific stressor, or child's illness, is the cornerstone to understanding the stress faced by these parents. Two parents faced by the same adversity, or with children diagnosed with the same illness at the same developmental period, are likely to respond in different ways. One parent, for example, may not consider himself or herself to be experiencing excessive stress, while the other may appraise the situation as stressful, or feel that the demands of the illness outweigh his or her available resources. The stress may impact on their physical or psychological state, intimate relationships, work, and response to the rest of the family.

Once the degree and point of impact or stress has been determined, practitioners may focus on how parents cope with the child's illness. They, as well as parents, learn that coping is a highly individual response to a stressor, there being no 'right' or 'wrong' way of coping, though clearly some ways are more disruptive than others. Such value-laden judgments as 'right' and 'wrong' have no place when working with families, and are counterproductive to the goal of assisting them.

Similarly, practitioners should not expect how a parent copes at one point in time during the child's illness to be the same as how he or she copes with future difficulties. Coping patterns most certainly change over time. All too often, hospital staff form an impression of parents based upon their initial distress when the child is diagnosed. However, after the initial shock and grief over the diagnosis dissipate, many parents return their energies to the problem-focused approaches often demanded by the condition of the child and the imperative of managing it as well as possible.

The assessment of parental stress may demand a referral for psychological intervention. The assessment of coping can be particularly helpful to health care professionals in such ways as understanding how much information parents like to be given, what resources they use to manage upsetting thoughts, and how bad news should be given to them. Developing a greater appreciation and awareness of individual differences in response to stressful situations associated with children's illness is important because practitioners will find it facilitates their communication with the parent.

Formal clinical assessment of stress and coping resources in parents is often not appropriate, unless the condition causes serious concern. In such cases, choice of measurement would be based on the particular stressor, for example, parental anxiety, depression, daily hassles, parent–child communication or family functioning. Where possible, we also believe that measures specifically designed for parents of children with an illness are particularly useful. By using pediatric-specific assessment tools, practitioners may be better able to identify the specific origin of stress and how individuals cope with particular medically related difficulties (Rodrigue et al., 2000; Streisand et al., 2001, in press).

IMPACT ON PARENTAL FUNCTIONING AND PARENTING PRACTICES

Earlier in this chapter we reviewed some of the ways in which illness, development, and parenting characteristics can play a role in parent's adjustment to a child's chronic illness. We now turn to the literature to describe specific ways in which parents are impacted, as well as how bringing up a child with an illness may alter parenting practices. Below, we highlight five distinct medical challenges to illustrate the varied difficulties inherent in parenting a child with an illness: physical limitations, diabetes, asthma, cystic fibrosis, and cancer.

Physical Limitations

Given the limitations in exploring their environment, children with limited physical motility, including those in wheelchairs, and those with hearing and visual impairments, are prone to many and diverse frustrations and psychosocial challenges. Parents of these children face difficult tasks, such as getting their children enrolled in suitable schools, and helping them adjust to having a limited number of opportunities for social interaction. Though the range and availability of such schools vary across countries and localities, compared with schooling and social development of normal children, there are always difficulties.

Children with visual impairments have an increased number of behavioral and social skills problems (Teare, 1984; Ammerman et al., 1989, 1991; Tirosh et al., 1998). Parents of these children have been found to

- have a range of difficulties starting from the birth of the visually impaired child,
- hold unrealistic expectations for the child's abilities, and
- have a tendency toward over-protection.

Other work suggests that similar issues are faced by parents of children with hearing impairments. Such parents report greater life stress and, in particular, stress related to conflict in their many parental and personal roles, or concerning finances and occupation (Meadow-Orlans, 1995).

Investigations with hearing-impaired children have been conducted in several different countries, all yielding a consistent finding: increased stress in parents of these children (Horsch et al., 1997; Lampropoulou and Konstantareas, 1998). Parent factors have been shown to play a role in parental adjustment to a child's hearing impairment. Within a sample of Greek parents of hearing-impaired children, for example, it was found that parents who reported lower self-esteem endorsed higher levels of stress (Konstantareas and Lampropoulou, 1995).

Parents of children with physical limitations, such as those with spina bifida or cerebral palsy, have similarly been found to have a difficult adjustment period characterized by shock and disbelief, which often occurs around the time of the child's birth and subsequent diagnosis. Compared to parents of healthy children, research has shown that parents of these children express elevated symptoms of depression (Miller et al., 1992), reduced parental satisfaction and competence, and a greater sense of social isolation (Holmbeck et al., 1997).

Both illness severity (Havermans and Eiser, 1991) and parental coping characteristics (Miller et al., 1992) have been associated with parental stress outcomes. Parents of children with more severe limitations, and those utilizing more emotional coping strategies, generally report greater levels of parenting stress. The impact of the child's physical disability on the marital relationship is less clear, with some studies citing increased marital discord, or citing the child's disability as the main cause for rupture (Tew et al., 1974; Havermans and Eiser, 1991). However, other studies have found no decrease in marital satisfaction as compared to parents of healthy children (Holmbeck et al., 1997).

Diabetes

Parents of children with diabetes must assist their children in adhering to a complex daily medical regimen that consists of multiple insulin injections and blood glucose tests, careful nutrition planning, and participating in regular physical exercise. The goal of properly adhering to the regimen is for children to attain prolonged periods of near-normal blood glucose levels. However, given the complexity of the different aspects of the regimen, non-adherence often occurs (Johnson, 1994). It has been suggested that parents must remain active in their children's diabetes management from the time of diagnosis through to adolescence (Anderson et al., 1997).

Research studies have examined several family and parenting variables related to outcome in children with diabetes, as well as the impact of the illness on parents' own functioning. In regard to children's metabolic control, it has been shown that parental warmth is associated with better adherence, and parental restrictions associated with poorer metabolic control (Davis et al., 2001). In terms of other child-rearing practices, parents of children with diabetes generally use less limit-setting of their children's behavior than parents of healthy children (Ievers et al., 1994). This finding may stem from the fact that parents are reluctant to stipulate any more rules governing the child's behavior when so many already exist that are related to the medical regimen. Similarly, parents may feel guilty that children need daily injections or continuous restrictions on food intake and therefore may not enforce traditional family rules such as the child making his or her bed, or helping with normal household chores.

Family structure and disease impact have also been explored, with parents of children with diabetes from single or reconstituted families reporting poorer family organization and greater childhood behavior problems than parents of children from intact two-parent families (Overstreet et al., 1995). Similarly, children from single-parent families have been found to have poorer metabolic control than children from two-parent families (Thompson et al., 2001), suggesting that the family structure may directly impact parents' ability to help children adhere to the daily regimen.

In terms of impact on the parents themselves, a number of studies suggest that parenting a child with diabetes is associated with less parenting satisfaction and lower efficacy related to parenting (Rodrigue et al., 1994), as well as elevated risk for poor mental health outcomes. Specifically, parents of children with diabetes experience significant stress, which places them at risk for anxiety and depression (Johnson, 1994).

Longitudinal investigations are currently examining how mental health outcomes in parents change over the course of the child's illness. Findings so far indicate that parents have an easier time coping with their child's diabetes management over time (Kovacs et al., 1990). Overall, diabetes management clearly impacts the entire family, and may affect not only parenting practices, but parent mental health outcomes. Health care professionals must consider the role of the family when examining children's adherence or metabolic control, as the effects on family or parenting stress and metabolic control are likely to be bi-directional, with each impacting upon the other, and both therefore playing an important role in adjustment (Viner et al., 1996).

Asthma

Asthma is the most common chronic illness in childhood. While most affected children are able to lead a normal life with the use of daily medication, illness severity varies, and some children experience repeated hospitalization and/or extended school absences. The role of parents in asthma management is focused on assisting the youngsters with adherence to medication, which typically involves daily use of inhalers. The chronic and often unpredictable nature of the illness is one of the reasons that parenting a child with asthma can be particularly challenging. While earlier research focused on identifying family or parenting practices that may have contributed to the onset of asthma, contemporary thinking is that children's asthma attacks may be triggered by family stress, but family or parenting difficulties *per se* do not cause a child to have asthma (Carson and Schauer, 1992).

Similar to research within the area of childhood diabetes, family characteristics and parenting practices, as well as parent mental health outcomes, have been explored in childhood asthma. While some researchers suggest that parents of children with asthma are more critical and negative than parents of healthy children (Schobinger et al., 1993), others have found no difference between the parenting practices of healthy children and children with asthma (Eiser et al., 1991). Parents of these children have been found to experience significantly greater stress (Eiser et al., 1991), be at risk for depression (Hookham, 1985), and have increased rates of marital discord and divorce (Faleide et al., 1988) as compared to parents of healthy children.

Cystic Fibrosis

Similar to asthma, cystic fibrosis also affects the lungs, with respiratory difficulties posing the most significant problem for these children. Cystic fibrosis is a chronic, terminal illness, and is the most common terminal genetic disorder among Caucasian children. Like the previously mentioned illnesses, cystic fibrosis requires significant effort on the part of parents and children to manage the illness. Parents must assist children in adhering to a daily regimen involving inhalants, physical therapy on the chest, following a prescribed nutrition plan, and taking enzyme medication. Coupled with the everyday demands of the regimen, parents of children with cystic fibrosis live with the knowledge that their child's illness is terminal, and the uncertainty of knowing when the child will become seriously ill and threatened.

While parents of children with cystic fibrosis have been found to use parenting practices rather similar to those used by parents of healthy children (involvement, responsiveness, guidance), studies have found these parents to be less likely to set limits on their children's behavior

(Ievers et al., 1994). Perhaps the most common finding in parents of children with cystic fibrosis is increased levels of general and parenting stress (Quittner et al., 1992, 1998; Thompson et al., 1994). These parents have also been found to exhibit increased symptoms of depression (Quittner et al., 1992). In terms of the impact of illness on the parents' relationship, earlier investigations found increased levels of marital discord (Quittner et al., 1992). However, a more recent study shows greater 'role strain' yet no differences in marital satisfaction (Quittner et al., 1998).

Perhaps more so than in the previously mentioned illnesses (physical disability, diabetes, asthma), the stage of the illness in cystic fibrosis plays a significant role in parental impact. For example, Quittner et al. (1998) highlighted the importance of understanding the context of the parental stress, rather than conducting global assessments of parental functioning. Given the terminal nature of the disease, with most children leading relatively normal lives for years until becoming increasingly ill, it is understandable that parents' stress and adjustment vary as a function of the child's health. This may account for the equivocal findings noted above, and underscores the importance of considering the illness itself as one part of the larger system affecting the child and family.

Cancer

Within childhood cancer, issues of prognosis, illness severity, and duration of illness and treatment vary greatly, with some children remaining on treatment for over two years at a time. Parents of children with cancer encounter stressors similar to parents of children with other illnesses, such as assisting children with medical procedures, hospitalizations, and adjusting to school absences. In addition, given the physical side-effects of many types of cancer treatment (for example, chemotherapy and resulting hair loss), parents usually must help their children adapt to a changing physical appearance. Unfortunately, while increasing numbers of children with cancer are being successfully treated, some parents of children with cancer will also experience the terminal phase of their child's illness.

The idea that parenting practices in parents of children with cancer differ from practices in parents of healthy children has been widely explored. For example, Hillman (1997) compared the practices of parents of children with cancer to those of parents of healthy children. On dimensions measured, the groups differed significantly on discipline and over-protectiveness issues. Specifically, parents of children with cancer were, not surprisingly, more likely to endorse 'I tend to spoil my child' and 'I worry about the health of my child.' While other studies have also demonstrated increased over-protectiveness in these parents (Wasserman et al., 1987), others have found no differences in such parenting practices. It has been suggested that a lack of healthy comparison samples or use of non-standardized assessment measures may be possible reasons why previous studies have found differences in parenting practices (Davies et al., 1991).

Regardless of whether changes in parenting practices occur or not, it is clear that parenting a child with cancer has a profound impact on the parents' own functioning. Mothers and fathers may experience the impact differently (Brown and Barbarin, 1996; Martinson et al., 1997), and may parent the child differently – a not unusual issue, exaggerated by the child's condition. In terms of the emotional impact on parents, parents of children with cancer have been found to display a wide range of symptoms including significant levels of stress, anxiety, depression, and even symptoms of post-traumatic stress disorder (Kazak and Meadows, 1989; Speechley and Noh, 1992; Streisand et al., 2001). These symptoms can affect parents both while their children are being treated for cancer, and when their children are considered to be cured or off treatment.

Some investigations suggest that the level of emotional support that parents have during their child's illness plays a role in the parents' experience of anxiety and depression (Speechley and Noh, 1992). In addition to the emotional impact, it has been suggested that parents of children with cancer may also experience significant physical symptoms, particularly in cultures that are more accepting of physical rather than psychological difficulties (Martinson et al., 1997).

IMPLICATIONS FOR PRACTICE

As a child's illness can affect both child and parents in myriad ways, health care teams should strive towards promoting greater awareness of these issues among parents, alerting them to the potential difficulties in terms of the child's developmental phase, as well as stage of the illness. In addition to working towards preventing such problems from occurring, health care workers should also assist in the early identification of those families in greatest need. The fact that our knowledge is far from complete and has to take account of parents' ways of coping simply makes the task more difficult.

By addressing children's and parents' difficulties early, later phases of child and family development are less likely to be adversely affected, with an increased likelihood of achieving positive outcomes. This investment in early intervention has led to major initiatives in promoting development among ill children, including home visiting, in hospital behavioral intervention, and out-patient management.

Home Visits

Home visiting programs for families caring for medically ill children are an important way of assisting parents to develop their child-rearing skills. These programs often target high-risk parents, including those with chronically ill children. Though programs vary substantially in their scope, most provide parent education, training, social support, and co-ordination with other social service agencies.

The effectiveness of home visiting programs has been demonstrated in a small number of studies conducted by the American Academy of Pediatrics (1998) with expectant couples, families of newborns, and during early childhood. An Australian randomized controlled study of nurse home visits with families of at-risk infants has demonstrated beneficial effects on mothers' psychological functioning and parent–infant bonding (Armstrong et al., 1999). In one of the earliest studies to include parents in preparing for their child's medical procedures, researchers provided home preparation for the child's tonsillectomy (Wolfer and Visintainer, 1979). Parents who were provided a preparation book reported better adjustment than those without such preparation.

Intervention for In-Hospital Procedures

Interventions conducted within the hospital setting focusing on parents also show encouraging results. In a randomized controlled trial conducted with parents of children undergoing bone marrow transplantation, Streisand et al. (2000) administered a multi-part in-hospital training program that included the following:

- education about children's behavioral responses to illness, medication, and medical procedures;
- strategies for relaxation and positive coping; and

- strategies for communicating with the child, other family members, and members of the health care team.

While there were no statistically significant differences between the intervention and control groups, trends in the data suggest that parents often used the strategies they learned to help manage their stress levels.

Other studies have focused on interventions with both hospitalized children and their parents. For example, in an attempt to prepare children with congenital heart disease for cardiac surgery, Campbell et al. (1995) randomized child–caregiver pairs to a treatment or standard care group. Parents in the treatment group reported greater confidence in their ability to care for their child both in the hospital and following discharge.

Out-patient Management

Many childhood illnesses do not require frequent hospitalization and are managed at home. In a stress management program for parents of children with severe handicaps, researchers designed a training program for parents consisting of self-monitoring of stressful events, progressive muscle relaxation, and modification of cognitions associated with distress (Singer et al., 1998). After eight group sessions, parents in the intervention condition reported significantly lower levels of anxiety as compared to those in the no-treatment control group.

Similarly, in an intervention designed to reduce distress in children undergoing endoscopy, parents were included in a behavioral intervention program for children (Young and Schnee, 1997). Parents and their children were divided into one of three conditions: (1) standard medical treatment, (2) hypnotherapeutic intervention, or (3) counseling. While no differences in child or parent distress were noted between groups, the authors believed that in order for parents to serve as role models for their children, they may have needed more intensive training than was offered by the intervention.

While the available data on interventions are somewhat limited, initial findings from studies of parenting and chronic illness suggest the potential for improving parent well-being and child health outcomes. Although there are no specific interventions for parents in such circumstances that have been empirically validated, we offer some general guidelines for practitioners working with these families. Table 12.2 includes a number of examples of ways in which practitioners can support parents in their efforts to parent

Table 12.2 *Suggestions for practitioners on parenting a child with a chronic illness*

Do	Don't
• Help parents become educated about the child's illness, treatment, and potential impact on the child's behavior	• Assume that parents fully understand how the child and family will be affected
• Assist parents in communicating about the illness to the child in honest, simple, and developmentally appropriate terms	• Expect parents to know how best to communicate with their child about the illness
• Encourage parents to help their child lead as normal a life as possible	• Recommend that parents restrict children from social, educational or occupational activities as a result of the illness
• Suggest that parents maintain a family routine, including the use of consistent discipline	• Encourage parents to bend the rules for their child if they feel guilty about the illness
• Promote parents' expression of fears and concerns, while at the same time helping them to remain calm and realistic	• Tell parents to imagine or prepare for the worst
• Recognize when parents are overwhelmed and may be in need of intervention	• Assume that parents' stress, anxiety, or depressive symptoms will decrease on their own

children with a chronic illness, and it also suggests areas for practitioners to avoid.

Throughout this chapter we have attempted to emphasize the importance of parents' keeping children on the same developmental track despite living with a chronic illness. We believe that in doing so, parents themselves are more likely to stay on their own track of parenting, and ultimately preserve their emotional well-being.

AUTHORS' OVERVIEW

This chapter began with an introduction to the diverse history of research focused on parents of children with chronic illness. The roots of this work can be traced to early pioneers in the fields of pediatrics, child psychiatry, and child psychology, and the coming together of these specialties to focus on common issues pertaining to growth and development among ill children. Further, in the light of an emerging focus on comprehensive child health care, psychological and behavioral adjustment and the well-being of parents fall within this purview.

Several cross-cutting themes in child health, parenting, and stress and coping have been identified. These include the concept of 'pediatric parenting stress' (or the stresses faced by parents of children with chronic illness), the prevalence of behavior problems among ill youngsters, theoretical models of parent, child, and family adaptation to illness (family systems theory, illness trajectory and social-ecological model, disability–stress–coping model), the convergence of children's illness (diagnosis, acute in-hospital treatment, out-patient management, follow-up care) with developmental phases (infancy, toddler, preschool and school age, adolescence), and how this can result in children 'getting off track.'

Recognizing the importance of maintaining children's developmental progression during illness periods, it is critical that professionals work closely with parents of children with physical limitations and conditions such as diabetes, asthma, cystic fibrosis, and cancer to assess their strengths and resources, as well as intervene when necessary and appropriate. We offer below, the major implications of the relevant research in terms of do's and don'ts for those who wish to help parents of ill children.

Do

• help parents learn about the child's illness, treatment, and potential impact of it on the child's behavior;
• assist parents in communicating about the illness to the child in honest, simple, and developmentally appropriate terms;
• encourage parents to help their child lead as normal a life as possible, particularly in social and activity terms;
• suggest that parents maintain a family routine, including the use of consistent discipline;
• promote parents' expression of fears and concerns, while at the same time helping them to remain calm and realistic;

- recognize when parents are overwhelmed and may be in need of help.

Don't

- assume that parents fully understand how the child and family will be affected;
- expect parents to know how best to communicate with their child about the illness;
- recommend that parents restrict children from social, educational, or occupational activities as a result of the illness;
- encourage parents to bend the rules for their child if they feel guilty about the illness;
- tell parents to imagine or prepare for the worst;
- assume that parents' stress, anxiety, or depressive symptoms will decrease on their own.

REFERENCES

American Academy of Pediatrics, Council on Child and Adolescent Health (1998) The role of home-visitation programs in improving health outcomes for children and families. *Pediatrics*, **101**(3), 486–9.

Ammerman, R.T., Van Hasselt, V.B., Hersen, M. and Moore, L.E. (1989) Assessment of social skills in visually impaired adolescents and their parents. *Behavioral Assessment*, **11**(3), 327–51.

Ammerman, R.T., Van Hasselt, V.B. and Hersen, M. (1991) Parent–child problem-solving interactions in families of visually impaired youth. *Journal of Pediatric Psychology*, **16**(1), 87–101.

Anderson, B., Ho, J., Brackett, J., Finkelstein, D. and Laffel, L. (1997) Parental involvement in diabetes management tasks: relationships to blood glucose monitoring adherence and metabolic control in young adolescents with insulin-dependent diabetes mellitus. *Journal of Pediatrics*, **130**(2), 257–65.

Armstrong, K.L., Fraser, J.A., Dadds, M.R. and Morris, J. (1999) A randomized, controlled trial of nurse home visiting to vulnerable families with newborns. *Journal of Paediatrics and Child Health*, **35**(3), 237–44.

Auslander, W.F., Thompson, S.J., Dreitzer, D. and Santiago, J.V. (1997) 'Mothers' satisfaction with medical care: perceptions of racism, family stress, and medical outcomes in children with diabetes. *Health and Social Work*, **22**(3), 190–9.

Brown, K.A.E. and Barbarin, O.A. (1996) Gender differences in parenting a child with cancer. *Social Work in Health Care*, **22**(4), 53–71.

Burke, S.O., Kauffmann, E., Costello, E.A. and Dillon, M.C. (1991) Hazardous secrets and reluctantly taking charge: parenting a child with repeated hospitalizations. *Image – The Journal of Nursing Scholarship*, **23**(1), 39–45.

Campbell, L.A., Kirkpatrick, S.E., Berry, C.C. and Lamberti, J.J. (1995) Preparing children with congenital heart disease for cardiac surgery. *Journal of Pediatric Psychology*, **20**(3), 313–28.

Carson, D.K. and Schauer, R.W. (1992) Mothers of children with asthma: perceptions of parenting stress and the mother–child relationship. *Psychological Reports*, **71**(3, part 2), 1139–48.

Chan, J.M. and Leff, P.T. (1982) Parenting the chronically ill child in the hospital: issues and concerns. *Children's Health Care*, **11**(1), 9–16.

Chaney, J.M. and Peterson, L. (1989) Family variables and disease management in juvenile rheumatoid arthritis. *Journal of Pediatric Psychology*, **14**(3), 389–403.

Coffman, S., Levitt, M.J. and Guacci-Franco, N. (1993) Mothers' stress and close relationships: correlates with infant health status. *Pediatric Nursing*, **19**(2), 135–40.

Copeland, L.G. and Clements, D.B. (1993) Parental perceptions and support strategies in caring for a child with a chronic condition. *Issues in Comprehensive Pediatric Nursing*, **16**(2), 109–21.

Costello, E.J. (1986) Primary care pediatrics and child psychopathology: a review of diagnostic, treatment, and referral practices. *Pediatrics*, **78**(6), 1044–51.

Davies, W.H., Noll, R.B., DeStefano, L., Bukowski, W.M. and Kulkarni, R. (1991) Differences in the child-rearing practices of parents of children with cancer and controls: the perspectives of parents and professionals. *Journal of Pediatric Psychology*, **16**(3), 295–306.

Davis, C.L., Delamater, A.M., Shaw, K.H., La Greca, A.M., Eidson, M.S., Perez-Rodriguez, J.E. and Nemery, R. (2001) Brief report: parenting styles, regimen adherence, and glycemic control in 4- to 10-year-old children with diabetes. *Journal of Pediatric Psychology*, **26**(2), 123–9.

Eiser, C., Eiser, R.J., Town, C. and Tripp, J.H. (1991) Discipline strategies and parental perceptions of preschool children with asthma. *British Journal of Medical Psychology*, **64**(1), 45–53.

Faleide, A.O., Galtung, V.K., Unger, S. and Watten, R.G. (1988) Children at risk of allergic development: the parents' dyadic relationship. *Psychotherapy and Psychosomatics*, **49**(3–4), 223–9.

Fiese, B.H. and Sameroff, A.J. (1989) Family context in pediatric psychology: a transactional perspective. *Journal of Pediatric Psychology*, **14**(2), 293–314.

Garrison, W.T., Bailey, E.N., Garb, J., Ecker, B., Spencer, P. and Sigelman, D. (1992) Interactions between parents and pediatric primary care physicians about children's mental health. *Hospital and Community Psychiatry*, **43**(5), 489–93.

Gesell, A. (1940) *The First Five Years of Life: A Guide to the Study of the Preschool Child, From the Yale Clinic of Child Development*. New York: Harper and Brothers.

Gillis, J.S. (1993) Effects of life stress and dysphoria on complex judgments. *Psychological Reports*, **72**(3), 1355–63.

Goldberg, S., Morris, P., Simmons, R.J., Fowler, R.S. and Levison, H. (1990) Chronic illness in infancy and parenting stress: a comparison of three groups of parents. *Journal of Pediatric Psychology*, **15**(3), 347–58.

Graham, P.J. (1994) Paediatrics and child psychiatry: past, present and future. *Acta Paediatrica*, **83**(8), 880–3.

Gravelle, A.M. (1997) Caring for a child with a progressive illness during the complex chronic phase: parents' experience of facing adversity. *Journal of Advanced Nursing*, **25**(4), 738–45.

Green, M. and Solnit, A.J. (1964) Reactions to the threatened loss of a child: a vulnerable child syndrome. *Pediatrics*, **34**(1), 58–66.

Hanson, C.L., DeGuire M.J., Schinkel, A.M. and Kolterman, O.G. (1995) Empirical validation for a family-centered model of care. *Diabetes Care*, **18**(10), 1347–56.

Havermans, T. and Eiser, C. (1991) Mothers' perceptions of parenting a child with spina bifida. *Child: Care, Health and Development*, **17**(4), 259–73.

Hentinen, M. and Kyngas, H. (1998) Factors associated with the adaptation of parents with a chronically ill child. *Journal of Clinical Nursing*, **7**(4), 316–24.

Hillman, K.A. (1997) Comparing child-rearing practices in parents of children with cancer and parents of healthy children. *Journal of Pediatric Oncology Nursing*, **14**(2), 53–67.

Holmbeck, G.N., Gorey-Ferguson, L., Hudson, T., Seefeldt, T., Shapera, W., Turner, T. and Uhler, J. (1997) Maternal, parental, and marital functioning in families of preadolescents with spina bifida. *Journal of Pediatric Psychology*, **22**(2), 167–81.

Hookham, V. (1985) Family constellations in relation to asthma. *Journal of Asthma*, **22**(2), 99–144.

Horner, S.D. (1997) Uncertainty in mothers' care for their ill children. *Journal of Advanced Nursing*, **26**(4), 658–63.

Horsch, U., Weber, C., Bertram, B. and Detrois, P. (1997) Stress experienced by parents of children with cochlear implants compared with parents of deaf children and hearing children. *American Journal of Otology*, **18** (Suppl. 6), S161–3.

Horwitz, S.M., Leaf, P.J. and Leventhal, J.M. (1998) Identification of psychosocial problems in pediatric primary care: do family attitudes make a difference? *Archives of Pediatrics and Adolescent Medicine*, **152**(4), 367–71.

Ievers, C.E., Drotar, D., Dahms, W.T., Doershuk, C.F. and Stern, R.C. (1994) Maternal child-rearing behavior in three groups: cystic fibrosis, insulin-dependent diabetes mellitus, and healthy children. *Journal of Pediatric Psychology*, **19**(6), 681–7.

Jellinek, M.S., Murphy, J.M., Little, M., Pagano, M.E., Comer, D.M. and Kelleher, K.J. (1999) Use of the Pediatric Symptom Checklist to screen for psychosocial problems in pediatric primary care: a national feasibility study. *Archives of Pediatrics and Adolescent Medicine*, **153**(3), 254–60.

Johnson, S.B. (1994) Health behavior and health status: concepts, methods, and applications. *Journal of Pediatric Psychology*, **19**(2), 129–41.

Johnson, S.B. and Tercyak, K.P. (1995) Psychological impact of islet cell antibody screening for IDDM on children, adults, and their family members. *Diabetes Care*, **18**(10), 1370–2.

Johnston, C.E. and Marder, L.R. (1994) Parenting the child with a chronic condition: an emotional experience. *Pediatric Nursing*, **20**(6), 611–14.

Kazak, A.E. (1989) Families of chronically ill children: a systems and social-ecological model of adaptation and challenge. *Journal of Consulting and Clinical Psychology*, **57**(1), 25–30.

Kazak, A.E. and Meadows, A.T. (1989) Families of young adolescents who have survived cancer: social-emotional adjustment, adaptability, and social support. *Journal of Pediatric Psychology*, **14**(2), 175–91.

Konstantareas, M.M. and Lampropoulou V. (1995) Stress in Greek mothers with deaf children: effects of child characteristics, family resources, and cognitive set. *American Annals of the Deaf*, **140**(3), 264–70.

Kovacs, M., Iyengar, S., Goldston, D., Obrosky, D.S., Stewart, J. and Marsh, J. (1990) Psychological functioning among mothers of children with insulin-dependent diabetes mellitus: a longitudinal study. *Journal of Consulting and Clinical Psychology*, **58**(2), 189–95.

Lampropoulou, V. and Konstantareas, M.M. (1998) Child involvement and stress in Greek mothers of deaf children. *American Annals of the Deaf*, **143**(4), 296–304.

Larson, R. and Richards, M.H. (1991) Daily companionship in late childhood and early adolescence: changing developmental contexts. *Child Development*, **62**(2), 284–300.

Martinson, I.M., Liu-Chiang, C. and Yi-Hua, L. (1997) Distress symptoms and support systems of Chinese parents of children with cancer. *Cancer Nursing*, **20**(2), 94–9.

Marvin, R.S. and Pianta, R.C. (1996) Parents' reaction to their child's diagnoses: relations with security of attachment. *Journal of Child Clinical Psychology*, **25**, 436–45.

Meadow-Orlans, K.P. (1995) Sources of stress for mothers and fathers of deaf and hard of hearing infants. *American Annals of the Deaf*, **140**(4), 352–7.

Melamed, B.G. and Ridley-Johnson, R. (1988) Psychological preparation of families for hospitalization. *Journal of Developmental and Behavioral Pediatrics*, **9**(2), 96–102.

Miller, A.C., Gordon, R.M., Daniele, R.J. and Diller, L. (1992) Stress, appraisal, and coping in mothers of disabled and nondisabled children. *Journal of Pediatric Psychology*, **17**(5), 587–605.

Murray, C.J.L. and Lopez, A.D. (1996) *Global Health Statistics: A Compendium of Incidence, Prevalence and Mortality Estimates for Over 200 Conditions. Vol. 2, Global Burden of Disease and Injury Series.* Cambridge: Harvard University Press.

Overstreet, S., Goins, J., Chen, R., Holmes, C.S., Greer, T., Dunlap, W.P. and Frentz, J. (1995) Family environment and the interrelation of family structure, child behavior, and metabolic control for children with diabetes. *Journal of Pediatric Psychology*, **20**(4), 435–47.

Perrin, E.C. and Gerrity, P.S. (1984) Development of children with a chronic illness. *Pediatric Clinics of North America*, **31**(1), 19–31.

Quittner, A.L., DiGirolamo, A.M., Michel, M. and Eigen, H. (1992) Parental response to cystic fibrosis: a contextual analysis of the diagnosis phase. *Journal of Pediatric Psychology*, **17**(6), 683–704.

Quittner, A.L., Espelage, D.L., Opipari, L.C., Carter, B., Eid, N. and Eigen, H. (1998) Role strain in couples with and without a child with a chronic illness: associations with marital satisfaction, intimacy, and daily mood. *Health Psychology*, **17**(12), 112–24.

Ray, L.D. and Ritchie, J.A. (1993) Caring for chronically ill children at home: factors that influence parents' coping. *Journal of Pediatric Nursing*, **8**(4), 217–25.

Roberts, M.C. and McNeal, R.E. (1995) Historical and conceptual foundations of pediatric psychology. In Roberts, M.C. (ed.) *Handbook of Pediatric Psychology*, 2nd edition. New York: Guilford Press, pp. 3–18.

Rodrigue, J.R., Geffken, G.R., Clark, J.E., Hunt, F. and Fishel, P. (1994) Parenting satisfaction and efficacy among caregivers of children with diabetes. *Children's Health Care*, **23**(3), 181–91.

Rodrigue, J.R., Hoffmann, R.G., Rayfield, A., Lescano, C., Kubar, W., Streisand, R. and Banko, C.G. (1995) Evaluating pediatric psychology consultation services in a medical setting: an example. *Journal of Clinical Psychology in Medical Settings*, **2**(1), 89–107.

Rodrigue, J.R., Geffken, G.R. and Streisand, R.M. (2000) *Child Health Assessment: A Handbook of Measurement Techniques*. Boston: Allyn and Bacon.

Rothenberg, M.B. (1968) Child psychiatry–pediatric liaison: a history and commentary. *Journal of the American Academy of Child Psychiatry*, **7**(3), 492–509.

Schobinger, R., Florin, I., Reichbauer, M., Lindemann, H. and Zimmer, C. (1993) Childhood asthma: mothers' affective attitude, mother–child interaction and children's compliance with medical requirements. *Journal of Psychosomatic Research*, **37**(7), 697–707.

Sharp, L., Pantell, R.H., Murphy, L.O. and Lewis, C.C. (1992) Psychosocial problems during child health supervision visits: eliciting, then what? *Pediatrics*, **89**(4), 619–23.

Silverberg, S.B. and Steinberg, L. (1990) Psychological well-being of parents with early adolescent children. *Developmental Psychology*, **26**(4), 658–66.

Singer, G.H.S., Irvin, L.K. and Hawkins, N. (1988) Stress management training for parents of children with severe handicaps. *Mental Retardation*, **26**(5), 269–77.

Speechley, K.N. and Noh, S. (1992) Surviving childhood cancer, social support, and parents' psychological adjustment. *Journal of Pediatric Psychology*, **17**(1), 15–31.

Spock, B. (1946) *The Common Sense Book of Baby and Child Care*. New York: Duell, Sloan and Pearce.

Stephenson, C. (1999) Well-being of families with healthy and technology-assisted infants in the home: a comparative study. *Journal of Pediatric Nursing*, **14**(3), 164–76.

Stevens, M.S. (1994) Parent coping with infants requiring home cardiorespiratory monitoring. *Journal of Pediatric Nursing*, **9**(1), 2–12.

Streisand, R., Rodrigue, J.R., Houck, C., Graham-Pole, J. and Berlant, N. (2000) Brief report: Parents of children undergoing bone marrow transplantation: documenting stress and piloting a psychological intervention program. *Journal of Pediatric Psychology*, **25**(5), 331–7.

Streisand, R., Braniecki, S., Tercyak, K.P. and Kazak, A.E. (2001) Childhood illness-related parenting stress: the Pediatric Inventory for Parents. *Journal of Pediatric Psychology*, **26**(3), 155–62.

Streisand, R., Kazak, A. and Tercyak, K.P. (in press) Pediatric-specific parenting stress and family functioning in parents of children treated for cancer. *Children's Health Care*.

Teare, J.F. (1984) Behavioral adjustment of children attending a residential school for the blind. *Developmental and Behavioral Pediatrics*, **5**(5), 237–40.

Tew, B.J., Payne, H. and Laurence, K.M. (1974) Must a family with a handicapped child be a handicapped family? *Developmental Medicine and Child Neurology*, **16** (Suppl. 32), 95–8.

Thomasgard, M. and Metz, W.P. (1997) Parental overprotection and its relation to perceived child vulnerability. *American Journal of Orthopsychiatry*, **67**(2), 330–5.

Thompson, R.J. Jr (1985) Coping with the stress of chronic childhood illness. In O'Quinn, A.N. (ed.) *Management of Chronic Disorders of Childhood*. Boston: G.K. Hall, pp.11–41.

Thompson, R.J., Gil, K.M., Gustafson, K.E., George, L.K., Keith, B.R., Spock, A. and Kinney, T.R. (1994) Stability and change in the psychological adjustment of mothers of children and adolescents with cystic fibrosis and sickle cell disease. *Journal of Pediatric Psychology*, **19**(2), 171–88.

Thompson, S.J., Auslander, W.F. and White, N.H. (2001) Comparison of single-mother and two parent families on metabolic control of children with diabetes. *Diabetes Care*, **24**(2), 234–8.

Tirosh, E., Shnitzer, M.R., Davidovitch, M. and Cohen, A. (1998) Behavioural problems among visually impaired between 6 months and 5 years. *International Journal of Rehabilitation Research*, **21**(1), 63–9.

Viner, R., McGrath, M. and Trudinger, P. (1996) Family stress and metabolic control in diabetes. *Archives of Disease in Childhood*, **74**(5), 418–21.

Walker, L.S., Ortiz-Valdes, J.A. and Newbrough, J.R. (1989) The role of maternal employment and depression in psychological adjustment of chronically ill, mentally retarded, and well children. *Journal of Pediatric Psychology*, **14**(3), 357–70.

Wallander, J.L. and Varni, J.W. (1995) Appraisal, coping, and adjustment in adolescents with a physical disability. In Wallander, J.L. and Siegel, L.J. (eds) *Adolescent Health Problems: Behavioral Perspectives*. New York: Guilford Press, pp. 209–31.

Wallander, J.L., Varni, J.W., Babani, L., DeHaan, C.B., Wilcox, K.T. and Banish, T. (1989) The social environment and the adaptation of mothers of physically handicapped children. *Journal of Pediatric Psychology*, **14**(3), 371–87.

Wasserman, A.L., Thompson, E.I., Wilimas, J.A. and Fairclough, D.L. (1987) The psychological status of survivors of childhood/adolescent Hodgkin's disease. *American Journal of Diseases of Children*, **141**(6), 626–31.

Wolfer, J.A. and Visintainer, M.A. (1979) Prehospital psychological preparation for tonsillectomy patients: effects on children's and parents' adjustment. *Pediatrics*, **64**(5), 646–55.

Young, M.H. and Schnee, A.D. (1997) Effect of psychological preparation on reducing behavioral distress and morbidity in children undergoing endoscopy. Poster presented at the 6th Florida Child Health Conference.

Youngblut, J.M. and Shiao, S.Y. (1993) Child and family reactions during and after pediatric ICU hospitalization: a pilot study. *Heart and Lung*, **22**(1), 46–54.

13

Parenting Influences on Intellectual Development and Educational Achievement

Sally M. Wade

SUMMARY

Parents, educators, and casual observers widely agree that parenting influences play an important role in determining the intellectual, educational, and social outcomes of children and youths. The purpose of this chapter is to provide an overview of research on the impact of parenting on intellectual development and academic achievement. The following broad areas will be discussed: landmark historical events over the past 30 years, including US legislation to promote parental involvement in public education; influences of parenting on early cognitive development, academic achievement, and vocational choices; and research-based recommendations for parents and educators. While sections of the chapter focus on the US (such as government policies), many of the issues discussed are applicable to parents, children, and educational systems in other countries.

HISTORICAL BACKGROUND

The effects of parenting on cognitive development and educational achievement have long been sources of interest and debate. Parents have not always been viewed as partners in the educational process. Historically, parents were often scapegoated as the cause of a child's 'deficiency' (Shores, 1998). More recently, parents appear to have found widespread acceptance as political advocates and service providers for their children (Turnbull and Turnbull, 1986). Developments in theory and research, such as the advent of 'ecological systems theory', have promoted understanding of parents as part of a complex system of variables, including biological, family, school, and community factors, that affect child development (Bronfenbrenner, 1979).

For nearly four decades, US federal policy has acknowledged the importance of parents to the educational process for all children (Shores, 1998). During the 1960s, US policy first turned in favor of parental involvement in public education. For example, the Head Start program included remediation for parents, as well as programs that empowered parents as educational decision-makers. In 1965, the Elementary and Secondary Education Act (ESEA) was established as part of President Johnson's War on Poverty (Tirozzi and Uro, 1997). Chapter 1 of ESEA, now commonly called Title I, represents the single largest allocation of federal funds to public education, and is intended to benefit economically disadvantaged children and youths. In fiscal year 1997, Title I served over seven million children in two-thirds of US elementary schools (Tirozzi and Uro, 1997).

While parental involvement has always been a vital component of Title I, under recent revisions, schools must keep parents informed about Title I and related standards, provide opportunities for parent training, and allow parents to help design and implement Title I programs in order to remain eligible for Title I funding.

The 1970s brought US federal legislation that began to focus on parents as educational decision-makers. The Education for All Handicapped Children Act of 1975 (PL 94-142) sought to empower parents, so that they might contribute to plans for their children's education. This legislation assumed that school districts would not meet the needs of exceptional children without parental input and advocacy. Under this law, parent–teacher conferences were an integral part of developing Individualized Education Plans (IEPs) for students in special education programs (Turnbull and Winston, 1984).

During the 1980s, US federal legislation emphasized the importance of family involvement in early intervention for infants and toddlers with special needs. The Education of the Handicapped Amendments of 1986 (PL 99-457) mandated Individualized Family Service Plans (IFSPs) for infants through two-year-olds with special needs. In 1990, PL 99-457 was renamed the Individuals with Disabilities Education Act (IDEA).

Throughout the last decade, US federal legislation has emphasized the importance of family involvement in the education of all children. In the Improving America's Schools Act of 1993, Congress declared that 'schools and parents must be encouraged to reach out to one another' (Shartrand et al., 1994, p. 6). Under Goals 2000 (US Department of Education, 1994), the federal government and all 50 states prioritized increased parental involvement as an important component of educational reform.

THE IMPACT OF PARENTING ON EARLY COGNITIVE DEVELOPMENT

Researchers in education and psychology agree that the home environment is a significant factor in the intellectual development of children. Considerable evidence suggests an association between parenting practices and early intellectual development in childhood, although the exact mechanisms and impact of the extent and quality of this relationship are still not entirely clear. Researchers have strived to develop theories to explain the factors that influence intellectual development in children, and it has been understood that investigation of this topic can lead to the development of numerous interventions to promote environmental enrichment in the home (Gottfried, 1984).

THE HISTORICAL DEBATE REGARDING THE IMPACT OF ENVIRONMENT ON CHILDHOOD DEVELOPMENT

Historically, theorists have been divided regarding the effect of a child's environment on his or her intellectual development. While some theories argue that the impetus of development is within the child and is largely unaffected by his or her environment and social interactions, others posit that a child's development is largely affected by environmental factors and interactions and may even be constituted by them (Meadows, 1996). The theoretical background on parenting and cognitive development can be illustrated by the views of developmental theorists Piaget and Vygotsky.

In Piagetian theory of childhood cognitive development, children actively construct knowledge as they manipulate and explore their surroundings (Berk, 2000). Marginalizing the role of adults in cognitive development, Piaget asserts that development takes place in stages and is uniform across individuals regardless of social environment. Emphasizing the biological nature of cognition, Piaget's cognitive-developmental theory suggests that children adapt to the external world as the structures of their minds develop, just as the structures of the body are adapted to fit with the environment. This adaptation is innate and inevitable, and is augmented with a need to maintain a balance between children's internal structures and information they gather in their everyday environments (Meadows, 1996; Berk, 2000).

According to Piaget, each sequential stage of cognitive development is characterized by distinct ways of thinking. During the *sensorimotor stage*, which occurs from birth until 2 years, children think by acting on the world with their senses. Between the ages of 2 and 7 years, children experience the pre-operational stage as they develop *symbolic but illogical thinking*. Until the age of 11 years, children experience a phase known as the *concrete operational stage*, in which thinking is transformed into more organized reasoning. Finally, during the *formal operational stage*, thought becomes a complex, abstract reasoning system, characteristic of adolescence and adulthood (Berk, 2000).

While Piaget did note that a child's environment could affect the rate of progress through stages and the detail of content in which the structures are applied, he asserted that the overall sequence and structure of cognitive stages is the same for all individuals. Although Piaget's theory is insightful and has contributed substantially to the field of developmental psychology, it has also sparked controversy and debate by other researchers, theorists, and groups such as parents and teachers, who believe that the environment is a critical factor in the intellectual development of children (Meadows, 1996).

Vygotsky's theory of cognitive development addresses the importance of environment in the development of children. In Vygotsky's sociocultural theory of development, the values, beliefs, customs, and skills of a social group affect development. Specifically, social interaction, such as co-operative dialogues between children and more knowledgeable adults, is necessary for cognitive development (Berk, 2000). In this relationship, the more expert partner, such as the parent, takes the responsibility for facilitating the child's learning of cognitive skills, such as language development. For example, when a child is learning a new task, the teacher or parent is responsible for providing a structure that allows the child to perform the task in increasingly complex ways, and then slowly decreases support as the child becomes more competent in the task (Meadows, 1996). This process, described as 'scaffolding', has a major formative influence on cognitive development. Like Piaget, Vygotsky believed children are active, constructive learners, constantly exploring and making sense of their environments. However, Vygotsky asserted that cognitive development is also a socially mediated process, dependent on the support adults provide for children as they learn new tasks.

EVIDENCE SUPPORTING THE IMPACT OF PARENTING ON COGNITIVE DEVELOPMENT

Cognitive development in children is a very large and theoretically intricate topic. While it is desirable to recognize and perhaps understand these perspectives, it is also important to recognize their practical implications, as shown in research endeavours. Considerable research has been conducted to explore the impact of the home environment on children's cognitive development. Many studies have focused on parenting practices, empirically addressing this issue with regards to age, developmental stage, socio-economic status, gender, and ethnicity. The following section

provides a brief review of this literature and suggestions for positive parenting practices found to promote cognitive development. Four broad parenting practices are addressed:

- emotional and verbal responsiveness of parents;
- cognitive stimulation;
- parental use of control and facilitation of independence; and
- the use of discipline and punishment.

Emotional and Verbal Responsiveness of Parents

Evidence shows that one parenting practice repeatedly found to influence the cognitive development of children is the emotional and verbal responsiveness of the parent or primary care-giver. Emotional and verbal responsiveness is characterized by a range of activities and ploys in which the parent communicates with the child, either in response to the child's cues or spontaneously. Specifically, responsiveness is often measured by observing the parent's vocalizations to the child, the distinctiveness and clarity of the parent's speech, the amount of kisses or caresses the parent bestows on the child, or the parent's use of a teaching style when interacting with the child. Other characteristics include the parent's use of praise, allowing the child to engage in messy types of play, and the warmth and encouragement the parent displays when responding to the child (Bradley and Caldwell, 1984).

A number of studies have concluded that the emotional and verbal responsiveness of a parent significantly influences the cognitive development of a child. One study shows that a parent's responsiveness to the child is positively correlated with indices of children's mental development at ages 12 and 24 months, and IQ scores at the age of 36 months (Bradley et al., 1989). Similarly, parental 'expressivity' (readiness to respond emotionally) and maternal responsiveness to the child were positively correlated with children's IQ scores at the age of 7 years (Coon et al., 1990). These findings suggest that the amount of time a parent spends interacting with a child, and the manner of this interaction, can significantly impact the child's cognitive development.

Research also indicates that parental responsiveness to the child has a major impact on children's cognitive development across various cultures. For example, a study exploring the social interactions of Embu children and their parents in a rural Kenyan community, found that children who were talked to frequently, whose vocalizations were responded to, and who engaged in sustained social interactions succeeded better on a cognitive achievement scale at 24 and 30 months of age, compared to children who had been less involved in verbal and social interactions (Sigman et al., 1988).

While it has been found that responsiveness can significantly influence the overall cognitive development of children, research also suggests that parental responsiveness influences language development and performance. For example, in a study involving children and their families, scores of the quality of home environment taken at 6 and 24 months were correlated with children's psycholinguistic abilities. In particular, maternal responsiveness showed a strong relationship with several aspects of language, such as auditory reception, auditory association, visual association, verbal expression, and 'grammatical closure' (Elardo et al., 1977). From the results of this and similar studies, it can be concluded that *responsiveness* in the home environment can significantly influence language growth during the early years of life.

Cognitive Stimulation in the Home Environment

A second aspect of parenting found to have a significant impact on the cognitive development of children is the amount of cognitive *stimulation* a parent provides within the home environment. While there are various tools that measure the level of cognitive stimulation in the home environment, most items are quite similar and measure comparable characteristics. During infancy, cognitive stimulation encompasses the full range of activities that take place between parents and children, from touching, gazing and smiling, presenting toys and making cooing noises. As the child grows older and more aware of the environment, toys and reading materials, visual and auditory stimulation, encouraging and playing with the child, and later, reading and talking to the child about his or her day become important (Bradley et al., 1989; McGroder, 2000).

Many studies have provided support for the strong influence stimulation has on the cognitive development of children. For example, infants who had experienced more mutual caregiver–infant gazing at one month, more interchanges of smiling during gazing at three months, and more general attentiveness at eight months achieved higher sensorimotor scores on a developmental schedule compared to infants who encountered less stimulation (Beckwith, 1976). Similarly, preschool children stimulated by their single, low-income African-American mothers with preschool-age children, scored higher on measures of cognitive school readiness compared to children whose mothers were considered below average in offering cognitive stimulation in the home (McGroder, 2000). Additionally, a study involving three different ethnic groups in North America, found that three sources of cognitive stimulation (availability of toys and learning materials; parent's involvement with and encouragement of the child; and the variety of experiences to which the child was exposed) were associated with mental test scores beginning at the age of 2 years (Bradley et al., 1989). Research also indicates that *variety* in stimulation is a necessary component when promoting cognitive development in early childhood. For example, opportunities for variety in daily stimulation, such as the father rather than the mother providing care every day, or the child receiving visits from relatives, was significantly correlated with scores on a mental development index and intelligence test scores at 36 and 54 months (Meadows, 1996).

The impact of home environment and parenting practices on early literacy experiences have also been researched. For example, a study, investigated the effects of the family literacy environment on over 500 kindergarten children's academic skills (Christian et al., 1998). Parents completed a measure that separated family literacy into various components:

- reading habits of the mother,
- reading habits of the father,
- who reads to the child and how often,
- number of books the child owns,
- how often someone in the family borrows books from the library,
- amount of television watched, and
- number of subscriptions to newspapers.

The family literacy environment, as assessed by these measures, was associated with the children's IQ and with their scores on measures of reading, receptive vocabulary, and knowledge of general information. Regardless of the family's socioeconomic status or the mother's educational level, children from families scoring high on family literacy environment scored higher on the academic measures than children from families who scored low on family literacy environment.

Parental Use of Control and Facilitation of Independence

Many studies have explored how parents' use of control and their facilitation of independence in the home environment contribute to cognitive development early in life. While it is understood that children at young ages need guidance and direction in their daily activities, research has also indicated that children whose parents promote autonomy, specifically those who adopt an authoritative style of child rearing, produce children who score higher on measures of intelligence and cognitive abilities compared to other children. Authoritative parents typically make reasonable demands of their children by setting limits and insisting that the child obeys. At the same time, they tend to express warmth and affection when setting these limits, and do so in a rational, democratic fashion (Berk, 2000). The mechanisms and processes underlying this relationship are not yet clear, but an element appears to be the quantity and style of verbal reasoning of such parents. This helps develop children's reasoning and gives them a better idea of 'cause and effect' relationships in the world.

Several studies have explored this style of parenting and have concluded that children whose parents provide structure and control, yet encourage independence, tend to score higher on measures of intelligence and cognitive abilities compared to other children. For example, a study of families with 3- to 4-year-old children in Bermuda found that mother's positive discipline and her positive control were significantly related to the children's IQ scores (Scarr, 1985). Further, in a study involving children from Kenya, it was discovered that children who were carried a great deal between 15 and 30 months of age scored poorly on the mental and motor scales at 30 months of age (Sigman et al., 1988). The reason is not immediately clear but may lie in the restricted stimulation of the carried children. Clinicians are often conscious that highly 'pampered children' – those not exposed to normal exploratory experiences – seem duller than those who are.

A recent study found a relationship between mothers' use of 'maintaining' and 'directiveness' when parenting and their children's later independent cognitive functioning (Landry et al., 2000). *Maintaining* is defined as a choice-providing strategy related to the object or activity in which the children are engaged in immediately prior to the mother's request, or as a direct response to the child's attempt to attract the mother's attention to an object or activity. *Directiveness* is defined as any verbal request, with or without a non-verbal behavior, that provides structured information about what is expected, but offers less choice, to the child. The results demonstrated that mothers' early maintaining establishes an important foundation to support children's later independence in cognitive functioning. Furthermore, directiveness positively supports children's early cognitive skills, but by 3.5 years, high levels of this behavior appear to have a direct, negative effect on children's cognitive development.

Parental Use of Discipline

Any discussion of child-rearing practices would be incomplete if the issue of discipline and punishment was not addressed. This is a facet of parenting that can sometimes create stress for parents, yet research has demonstrated that particular styles of positive discipline and punishment can support cognitive development in early childhood (Berk, 2000).

A study of mothers' 'positive' discipline, for example, was significantly related to children's IQ scores (Scarr, 1985). In this study, positive discipline was characterized by the use of a firm tone when addressing the child, but also explaining to the child the reasons for the discipline. Similarly, a number of studies using the measures of the quality of home environment have shown that the use of positive discipline significantly influences cognitive development.

Specifically, elements concerning the parent's use of discipline, such as how often the primary care-giver shouts at the child; displays of physical punishment; scolding of the child; and expression of overt annoyance or hostility toward the child appear to depress cognitive development. Others have found a significant positive relationship between reduced restriction and punishment and IQ scores (Bradley and Caldwell, 1984). More specifically, it has been shown that although some discipline should be used in the home, these practices should be used carefully and moderately, as inappropriate use (in quality and quantity) can lead to delays and deficits in cognitive development. For example, a number of studies have shown that children who were physically punished and abused in early childhood had poorer grades than their peers, performed poorly on standardized tests, and were more likely to have to repeat a grade (Eckenrode et al., 1993). The mechanisms of this relationship between punitive and restrictive approaches to children and depressed cognitive development are not known. There is the possibility that parents who adopt this approach may be limited or different in other key respects. A more probable reason appears to be that such approaches to children generate anxiety of a kind and level that blocks or depresses cognitive learning and inquisitiveness.

VARIATIONS IN PARENTING PRACTICES ACCORDING TO SOCIAL CLASS AND ETHNICITY

Although parenting practices have been addressed broadly thus far, it is important to acknowledge that they are dependent on demographic and contextual factors. For example, social class and ethnic parenting practices differ among cultures, as do the patterns of relationships between home environment and cognitive development (Bradley et al., 1989). These variations in the home environment and cognitive development of children must be addressed when exploring parenting practices. In any interdependent ecology, children's immediate surroundings and their developmental scores are interrelated, due to handling by their parents, exposure to stimulating environments and other sources of cognitive development (Berk, 2000). Children in poorer environments have been shown, for example, rarely to experience 'highly enriched' homes, as measured by a number of different criteria (Bradley et al., 1989). Further, even when lower socio-economic status children came from homes with an average level of enrichment, their intelligence test scores still declined between ages 1 and 3 years. Only in the few instances when these children lived in highly enriched home environments did their mental test scores increase.

Further support for variation in parenting practices by social class and ethnicity is demonstrated in the findings of a study involving low-income, single mothers (McGroder, 2000). Participants' parenting practices were clustered into four categories according to various characteristics. The most prevalent group was 'aggravated but nurturant', characterized by high scores on an aggravation factor, above-average scores on a nurturance factor, and below-average scores on cognitive stimulation. The second most prevalent group was 'low nurturance', characterized by average scores on aggravation and cognitive stimulation, and low scores on nurturance. The third most prevalent group was 'patient and nurturing', demonstrating below-average scores on aggravation and cognitive stimulation, and above-average scores on nurturance. The least prevalent group was 'cognitively stimulating', characterized by below-average scores on aggravation, average scores on nurturance, and high scores on cognitive stimulation. Results indicate that the two most prevalent groups among low-income, single mothers were those that demonstrated high levels of aggravation and those with low levels of nurturance. This is troubling because the children of the 'patient and nurturant' or 'cognitively

stimulating' mothers had average scores that were significantly higher than children of both 'aggravated but nurturant' or 'low nurturance' mothers.

These studies suggest that, not surprisingly, social class may be associated with parenting style, which may consequently affect cognitive development. A common trend emerging from studies is that many low-income families do not provide cognitively stimulating, enriched home environments. While this may be due to a lack of both financial and emotional support, especially among single mothers, it indicates that interventions and services are necessary to meet the needs of this population. Many children who live in environments that do not promote cognitive development, eventually experience academic difficulties and tend to score low on academic achievement measures. This is recognized at both national and local levels and warrants help which is enabled through legislation, as mentioned at the beginning of this chapter.

Regarding differences among ethnic groups, numerous studies have sought to determine variations among minority ethnic parenting practices and their impact on children's cognitive development. There is a general view that the strength of the relationship between home environment and intelligence may vary for different ethnic groups (Luster and Dubow, 1992). For example, in one study, there was a variable relationship between indices of quality of the home for whites, blacks, and Mexican-Americans (Bradley et al., 1989). All the relationships were weak.

Other research indicates that child-rearing practices often differ among ethnic groups and that influence on cognitive development in some groups is greater than in others. For example, compared to Caucasian Americans, Chinese adults describe their own parenting practices as 'more demanding'. Chinese parents tend to be more controlling of their children, often involving themselves in scheduling their children's time, beginning in early childhood. Furthermore, in many Hispanic and Asian Pacific Island families, there is a firm insistence on respect for parental authority. Specifically, a strong respect for the father is upheld in these families, with an unusually high level of maternal warmth present. While wide variation exists among the child-rearing practices of African-American parents, black mothers often rely on an adult-centered approach in which they expect immediate obedience from their children (Berk, 2000). Although African-American parents typically provide their children with cognitive stimulation in the home, black mothers usually tend to wait until the third year of life to begin this practice, whereas white mothers tend to do this from the early stages of infancy onwards (Bradley et al.,

1989). Thus, there may be cultural differences regarding the time when a baby is no longer considered a baby and given appropriate stimulation and preparation for later in life.

In general, the detailed information about minority ethnic parenting practices and dimensions of cognitive stimulation is missing, making sensible generalizations difficult. Clearly not all ethnic groups, and families within them, have the same value orientations regarding children's development. To raise these standards, therefore, it is necessary to give the parents the relevant information and skills, in a culturally sensitive manner.

DEFINITIONS AND DIMENSIONS OF PARENT INVOLVEMENT IN EDUCATION

In recent years, politicians, scholars, and popular media have emphasized the importance of 'parental involvement' in children's educational success. For example, the eighth US Education goal in 'Goals 2000' (US Department of Education, 1994) states, 'every school will promote partnerships that will increase parental involvement and participation in promoting the social, emotional, and academic growth of children'. However, without a specific definition, the concept of parental involvement remains nebulous and difficult to study or promote in a meaningful way (Epstein, 1996). Researchers have employed various incomplete measures of parental involvement, such as reading at home, providing homework assistance, and attending school functions (Grolnick et al., 1997). In a multidimensional model proposed by Grolnick and Slowiaczek (1994), parental involvement is broadly defined as 'the allocation of resources by the parent to the child in a given domain' (p. 538). More specifically, in the context of schooling, they describe three types of involvement:

- behavioral
- cognitive-intellectual
- personal

The behavioral aspect of parental involvement encompasses actual participation in such school activities as parent conferences and in home-based activities, such as helping with assignments. Cognitive-intellectual involvement includes exposing the child to intellectual stimulation, such as books and current events. Personal involvement refers to maintaining knowledge of the child's academic situation and activities. Obviously, these types of involvement are overlapping, rather than mutually exclusive sets of behaviors.

A model proposed by Epstein (1996) delineates six dimensions of parental involvement activities that schools can engage in:

- parenting;
- communicating;
- volunteering;
- learning at home;
- decision-making;
- collaborating with the community – this is important because it provides a ready structure for development of school-based parenting support.

The *parenting* dimension refers to the provision of assistance with parenting knowledge and skills, as well as to the school in helping parents develop a home environment supportive of age-appropriate learning. *Communicating* consists of providing families with information about how the school works and their children's academic progress. *Volunteering* refers to school-based efforts to engage parents in higher levels of volunteer work and attendance at school functions. *Learning at home* includes how families encourage, listen, react, praise, guide, monitor, and discuss schoolwork with their children. *Decision-making* involves sharing school leadership responsibilities with parents, often through such vehicles as parent organizations and school improvement teams. *Collaboration with the community* entails drawing upon community resources, such as universities and businesses, to strengthen educational services.

THE IMPACT OF PARENTAL INVOLVEMENT ON CHILDREN'S ACADEMIC ACHIEVEMENT

The positive impact of parental involvement on student achievement at all grades and levels has been extensively documented across several decades (e.g. Henderson, 1987; Henderson and Berla, 1994). At the most basic level, social learning theory (Bandura, 1977) indicates that children who observe their parents engaging in activities supportive of the educational process will learn to value education themselves. Parental involvement appears to be correlated with the age of the child. Parental involvement in elementary schools (ages 5–12 years) tends to be more welcomed and to occur more frequently than in secondary schools (ages 14–18 years), and includes such things as parents volunteering in the classroom and reading to their child at home (Epstein, 1987). In middle and high schools (ages 13–18 years), parental involvement declines

(Lucas and Lusthaus, 1978). This may be due to the adolescent's push for autonomy. It is also more difficult for parents to have contact with their child's teacher in middle and high school (ages 13–18 years) if the child no longer has one teacher but many (Hollifield, 1994). The following sections present a developmental perspective on the benefits of parental involvement in the educational process, from ages 3 through 18 years.

Ages 3–12 years

Findings from the Chicago Longitudinal Study indicate that parental involvement with inner-city children in preschool and kindergarten (ages 3–6 years) increases reading achievement, reduces years in special education, and reduces the number of grade retentions at age 14 years (Keith et al., 1993). Other findings suggest that mothers' levels of communication with teachers during the first three years of elementary school (ages 5–9 years) are associated with positive achievement trajectories in mathematics for children throughout the elementary grades (Jimerson et al., 1999). In addition, when elementary schools (ages 5–12 years) in three school districts implemented a new reading program, the district with the highest attainment of reading achievement scores had involved the parents in decision-making regarding the program and had informed them of ways in which they could reinforce the program's goals at home (Gillum, 1977).

Ages 12–14 years

Parental attitudes and expectations regarding school also play an important role in determining middle school educational outcomes. For example, data from the Longitudinal Study of Children at Risk revealed that sixth-graders' (ages 11–12 years) academic achievement and social adjustment were correlated with parental expectations for educational achievement and parental satisfaction with current educational services (Reynolds et al., 1993). Moreover, research has shown that what parents do at home is important in the middle and high school years (ages 12–18 years). Such actions as enforcing the completion of homework and restricting television viewing as important parent practices for adolescent students (Keith et al., 1986).

Ages 14–18 years

Parental involvement remains an important influence on student achievement at the high school level. It has been shown that students who have dropped out of high school report that their parents rarely helped them with homework or attended school functions (Rumberger et al., 1990). The impact of family socio-economic status, maternal employment patterns, family structure, and parental involvement (defined in terms of frequency of contact with teachers, involvement in planning for activities subsequent to high school graduation, and monitoring of academic work) on high school students' educational attainment has been evaluated (Eagle, 1989). Parental education, family income, and parental involvement are all associated with higher student achievement. However, when socio-economic status is controlled for, parental involvement is the only variable with an appreciable positive impact on high school students' educational attainment. High school students (ages 14–18 years) whose parents read to them during early childhood and set aside a special location for their children to study also demonstrated higher educational attainment than their peers. Most relevant, parental involvement has the greatest positive impact when initiated early in a child's educational career, and when meaningful. For example, attending a parent–teacher conference is more beneficial than paying money to join the parent–teacher association.

THE IMPACT OF CULTURE AND SOCIO-ECONOMIC STATUS ON PARENTAL INVOLVEMENT IN EDUCATION

Relationships between 'social address' factors (Bronfenbrenner, 1986) such as poverty, minority status, parental educational attainment, and family structure and parental involvement in education have been widely documented (Hoover-Dempsey and Sandler, 1997). For example, parents with lower levels of formal education and those who are employed, participate less in school-related activities than parents with more education and those who are not employed (Dauber and Epstein, 1993). While there does not appear to be a significant relationship between parents' marital status and involvement in education, evidence supports the notion that single, working parents have little time to devote to their children's educational pursuits. More recent research has confirmed that single parents are significantly less involved in most types of school-related activities than married, non-working mothers (Grolnick et al., 1997).

Because disadvantaged parents often have fewer and less fruitful contact with the schools than their middle-class counterparts, many educators have stereotyped them as unable or unwilling to serve as an educational resource for their children (Moles, 1993; Epstein, 1984). However, research on the attitudes of disadvantaged and minority parents tells a different story (Moles, 1993). Economically disadvantaged African-American and Latino parents in the US, for example, report a strong interest in participating in their children's school-related activities (Chavkin and Williams, 1985). Caucasian parents of lower socio-economic status also report a strong interest in participating (Lareau, 1987). In addition, despite low levels of parental involvement in school-based activities, an overwhelming majority of inner-city African-American middle school students (ages 12–14 years) report that their parents monitor and assist with their homework (Menacker et al., 1988). These findings appear to contradict 'culture of poverty' theories that disadvantaged students achieve less because their families value education less (e.g. Deutsch, 1967). A more accurate explanation of socio-economic differences in student achievement and parental involvement appears to be that schools utilize unevenly and inequitably the social and cultural resources of society (Lareau, 1987, p. 74). This notion of 'cultural capital' (Bourdieu, 1990) suggests that disadvantaged and minority parents bring to the school sets of knowledge and experiences different from those of their white, middle-class counterparts, and that schools lack the resources to draw upon their skills effectively (Lareau, 1987). For example, if a student struggles academically because he or she speaks a nonstandard dialect of English, or no English at all, it is likely that his or her parents speak in the same way. These parents may find involvement with the school more difficult and intimidating than other parents. In turn, teachers may not be enthusiastic about the 'extra work' necessary for meaningful partnerships with parents outside the dominant culture. In addition, other studies conclude that disadvantaged parents may avoid contact with teachers and administrators because of their own previous negative experiences in school settings (Lareau, 1987; Raffaele and Knoff, 2000).

When considering the influence of family status variables on parental involvement, it is important to remember that 'process variables' have a greater impact than matters of social address (Clark, 1983). For example, economically disadvantaged African-American students who succeeded in school are more likely than their less successful peers to have parents who monitored time use, set clear and consistent limits, encouraged academic pursuits, and engaged their children in frequent, warm, and nurturing dialogues. While minority and disadvantaged parents in the US almost uniformly report high levels of interest and desire to participate in their children's educational activities, educators often perceive them as uninvolved or unhelpful (Lareau, 1987). This incompatibility is especially problematic when viewed in light of a largely white, female, middle-aged, middle-class population of teachers, and ever-increasing ethnic, socio-economic, and family-structural diversity within the schools.

Rather than attribute failures in home–school collaboration with disadvantaged parents to a 'culture of poverty,' educators might seek new ways to tap into these families' unique strengths. Research has demonstrated that teachers often employ the same practices for attempting to engage parents and define effective parental involvement in similar ways, regardless of the parents' culture, class, or educational attainment (Raffaele and Knoff, 1999). Different cultural and socio-economic groups' views of the educational process and appropriate roles for parents and teachers suggest that a more flexible approach to home–school collaboration can promote greater involvement of diverse parents (Raffaele and Knoff, 1999).

In an ethnographic study of parental involvement attitudes and activities at two elementary schools, one serving a middle-class community and the other a working-class population, it has been shown that cultural differences between the two socio-economic groups appeared to influence the level and quality of parental involvement (Lareau, 1987). Home–school relationships were characterized by interdependence in the middle-class community, and by independence in the working-class community. For example, parents of lower socio-economic status often describe the roles of home and school as separate, rather than collaborative. Parents in the middle-class community are more likely to agree with the notion of shared responsibility between home and school, while working-class parents often viewed education as a 'discrete process' (Lareau, 1987, p. 79) and the sole responsibility of the teacher. Parents in the two socio-economic groups also differ in how they conceptualize the role of teachers. Working-class parents view the teachers as 'educated professionals', and are reluctant to 'tell them how to teach.' The middle-class parents, on the other hand, generally viewed the relationship between parents and teachers as a partnership between equals. One middle-class mother said of the teachers, 'They are not working for me, but they also are not doing something I couldn't do' (Lareau, 1987, p. 80).

Socio-economic status and culture are related to the degree to which parents become involved in the educational process, because economically disadvantaged and culturally diverse parents tend to shy away from direct, collegial interactions with school personnel (Lareau, 1987). However, some research has found no relationship between status variables and how much parents report caring about or desiring involvement with their children's education (Chavkin and Williams, 1985; Menacker et al., 1987). The discrepancy between the extent to which disadvantaged parents are actually involved in the educational process and the extent to which they report wanting to be involved indicates that educators could increase and expand the nature of parental involvement by these families.

Power and status issues play a critical role in determining whether students from 'dominated' minority groups succeed in school (Cummins, 1986). Minority students are most likely to succeed academically when they maintain positive feelings toward the dominant majority culture, remain connected to their own cultural identities, and are not made to feel inferior to members of the dominant group. It is suggested that to empower language-minority students, schools should incorporate aspects of the children's culture and language, collaborate with families and community agencies, encourage students to use language for personally relevant purposes, and promote advocacy for students (as opposed to labeling them as 'problems'). This is demonstrated by an experiential language development program based on this framework, in which Spanish-speaking parents in a Californian school district were encouraged to provide home-based language learning experiences for their children (Cummins, 1986). Students who participated in the program scored significantly higher on a school readiness inventory than Spanish-speaking peers who completed a traditional English-language immersion program. In addition, their parents remained more involved in the educational process. By empowering language-minority parents to serve as teachers for their own children, the schools promoted both increased academic achievement *and* greater parental involvement.

There are a number of ways in which educators can involve disadvantaged parents (Raffaele and Knoff, 2000). For example, if the parent's first language is not English, schools should provide translations of documents and issue invitations to school functions. It may be helpful to assist with transportation to and from school functions, and to consider making telephone calls to invite parents to events such as open house and conference night. Schools could also offer meetings with teachers at a variety of times, so parents with inflexible work schedules could still attend. Since even parents with little or no formal education have 'graduated from the university of life' (Raffaele and Knoff, 2000), educators can promote family involvement by recognizing all parents as sources of valuable knowledge and expertise. Schools can build collaborative relationships with parents by facilitating connections between families and community resources, such as counseling, mentoring programs, and career services (Chavkin, 1993).

PARENTING INFLUENCES ON VOCATIONAL CHOICES

Over the years, research has revealed that parents and families have a strong influence on adolescent involvement in career exploration and occupational choice. Early research studies found that factors including class, maternal employment, and family structure play roles in young adults' career development (e.g. Blau and Duncan, 1967; Zajonc and Markus, 1975; Smith, 1981). More recent research explores the influences of familial relationships and specific parental activities (e.g. Grotevant and Cooper, 1988; Young et al., 1988).

A recent study attempted to better understand the intent of parents' attempts to influence their children's career paths (Young and Friesen, 1992). Parents were asked to describe specific activities in which they engaged with their child that they felt influenced their child's career development. The participants consisted of over 200 parents from a large Canadian city. The parents were interviewed regarding their child's current career development and specific incidents they engaged in that influenced this development. Results of the study indicate that parents play an important role in helping their children develop specific skills, independent thinking or action, character, personal responsibility, and values and beliefs. This study illustrates the actively involved parents' point of view and provides a starting point for school counselors and teachers seeking to involve parents in the career exploration process.

Not only can parents play an important role in their child's career development, but studies also show that teenagers value their parents' input and advice on important life choices such as vocational decision (e.g. Wilks, 1986; Bregman and Killen, 1999). In one study, for example, researchers looked at adolescents' reasoning regarding career decisions and the role of their parents in these decisions (Bregman and Killen, 1999). The purpose of the study was to clarify the importance of parents and friends in the decision-making of Australian adolescents and to identify to whom they turn for particular types of advice. Analysis of the students' referent list indicated that mothers were ranked overall by students as the most important person but that they were most likely to turn to a same-sex friend for advice. Analysis of the students' rankings of the referent list showed that mothers and fathers received higher ratings than friends. However, in the student's rankings of how often they turned to parents and friends about problems, both male and female students indicated that they talked more frequently with friends. This finding indicates that young adults may turn to friends and parents for different situations.

Further analysis showed that parental guidance was rated most important by all participants in the areas of educational and vocational decisions. Friends were rated as most important in areas involving short-term decision-making. Thus, although students may turn to friends for minor everyday decisions such as what clothing to wear, adolescents recognize parents' special standing in providing advice on major decisions.

Young adults' completion of college appear to be related to the behavior modeled by their parents (Bank et al., 1990). For example, parents who work in a profession that requires an advanced degree pass on these educational and career values to their child. Furthermore, adolescents who are most successful in career development report strong parental attachments and support (Kenny, 1990). In another study, college students' security of attachment to parents was correlated with greater self-exploration (Ketterson and Blustein, 1997). On the other hand, strong involvement or enmeshment of the adolescent in the family system is related to difficulty in mastering career development tasks (Penick and Jepsen, 1992). Parental over-involvement may hinder high school and college-aged students' (ages 14–22 years) career development (Lopez and Andrews, 1987). For example, one study found that some adolescents are reluctant to explore career options openly in the presence of their parents (Amundson and Penner, 1998). Thus, a fine line exists between healthy involvement and unhealthy over-involvement: parents should support their child's career exploration and development while at the same time promoting autonomy and avoiding dictating to their children. The older the child, the more important it seems to engage in open-ended 'negotiations' and discussions that allow the child to make an informed choice.

OVERVIEW

An increasing body of literature and research demonstrates the importance of parental practices and beliefs in influencing their children's academic achievement, intellectual development, affective behavior and attitudes. It is well documented that parental involvement and parenting styles can predict a variety of intellectual, academic, and social outcomes as well as more subtle consequences. There are, therefore, strong reasons for increasing parental involvement in children's education. An important aspect of this is creating processes and environments that show parents how best to contribute to their children's education and cognitive development.

IMPLICATIONS FOR PRACTICE

When parents consider particular child-rearing practices, implications of research findings would be helpful to keep in mind. Overall, parental responsiveness can significantly promote cognitive and language development in children by providing them with emotional and verbal stimulation and support. Implications of these studies include the need for parents to provide their children with cognitive stimulation early in infancy and throughout childhood. Simply interacting with children on a daily basis can be most influential in their cognitive development and, through better educational achievement, their success later in life. Furthermore, providing an environment rich in cognitively stimulating materials, such as books and other learning materials, can be instrumental in promoting intellectual development and literacy skills.

These results suggest that implementing opportunities that give choice throughout childhood is beneficial. Thus, parenting practices that offer a great deal of direction need to decrease in relation to children's increasing competencies.

Evidence suggests that providing discipline in the home is essential and that certain disciplinary practices are more beneficial than others. Specifically, the effects of physical punishment have typically been found to be negative, at times contributing to delays in cognitive development. However, disciplining in a positive manner can lead to stability in the home and facilitate cognitive development.

More research is needed to document the characteristics of the relationship between parenting practices and academic achievement and to assist educators and parents in identifying and implementing those practices that have the most positive influence on school performance. Both research and common sense tells us that what parents do at home to promote learning will have a positive influence on their child's academic performance.

Ways Parents can Promote Academic Success

There are activities, suggested by research, that parents might use to promote their child's academic success:

- Talk, talk, talk with your child.
- Read to your child often – begin at an early age and continue as he or she ages.
- Teach your child letters and the sounds of letters.
- Have your child read to you.
- Role model reading for your child – let them see you reading.
- Reading aloud is not just for younger children – read aloud to older children and have them read aloud to you.
- Find a comfortable place to read together whenever possible, and snuggle up while reading.
- If the book is long, take turns reading with your child.
- Try to read for at least 15 minutes every day with your child.
- Read a variety of types of literature and material with your child. Let the child select what is to be read, even if it seems 'silly' to you.
- If you have a reluctant reader, try finding books or articles that relate to television shows, movies or hobbies that interest the child.
- If you have a computer or access to the internet, use this to encourage reading.
- Monitor and assist with your child's homework.
- Set aside a special 'study place' for your child.
- Encourage your child to write and draw pictures about his or her experiences.
- Establish frequent contact with your child's teachers, beginning as soon as he or she enters school.
- Maintain and communicate high expectations for your child's academic achievement.
- Help your child make academic and vocational plans for the future.
- If you are dissatisfied with some aspect of your child's education, work with his or her teacher to solve the problem.
- Praise your child often, conveying a positive feeling in your voice.

- Equip your home with lots of printed materials and things a child can play with. These do not need to be fancy or expensive toys – simple household items make great toys.
- Teach your child left and right.
- Play rhyming games with your child.
- Ask open-ended questions, such as 'What do you think will happen?' 'What would change the answer?' 'What do you think is important?'
- Ask why, and encourage your child to ask why of himself: 'Why did you/I do that?' 'Why did you/I make that decision?' 'Why would someone act that way?'
- Verbally review the process you went through to make a decision: 'First, I did _____, then I thought about my choices _____, and I chose to do _____ because of _____'.
- Limit the amount and type of television your child watches.
- Watch a television show with your child and discuss shows with them.
- Count everything, such as household items, brothers and sisters, food, money.
- Compare numbers/quantities: which is larger? Who has more? Who is younger? How many more? How much less?
- Talk about time. What time is it now? How much time did it take? How long has it been? Today is _____, yesterday was _____, tomorrow will be _____?
- Assist your child in planning: 'By when will you complete this chore?' 'What do you have to do tonight?' 'What steps do you have to take to complete this task?' 'How do you plan to complete the assignment by the due date?'
- Convey messages of confidence and competence to your child.
- Provide structure and routines in your home, but promote your child's increasing independence.
- Provide your child with opportunities to meet with other adults and children.
- Help your child learn study skills.
- Help your child learn organizational skills – use of a calendar, agenda, to-do lists, place for materials.
- Establish a homework routine – decide with the child the best time and place.
- If your child is overwhelmed with a task, help him break it down into manageable parts. This applies to homework as well as chores.
- Help the child identify the steps to complete an assignment. For example, the steps for a written report might be to: do some research, take notes, write an outline, write the report, revise and edit, finish the final report.

- Help your child learn to take a break from work. Studying for long periods of time can be more productive if you build in breaks. Your child can break for a quick snack, a ten-minute game or a walk.
- Make sure your child understands his or her assignments and behavioral expectations at school. Ask your child to repeat them to you.
- Ask questions about school and learning. Avoid asking 'What did you learn at school today?' Young children, aged 5–10 years, respond better to specific questions such as, 'What did you do in reading today?' or 'What did you have for lunch?' Older children respond better when the parent first shares something from their day and then asks about school.
- Keep homework supplies such as pencil, paper, ruler, sharpener, glue, scissors, eraser, etc., in one place. Much time can be wasted locating needed supplies.
- Discover the way your child learns best, then use his or her strength to learn a difficult assignment. Some children learn better by reading, some by writing, some while moving about, and some by talking. For example, mathematical facts can be written, sung, traced, read, or recited with a physical activity.
- Ask to see your child's homework and review it with him or her.
- Give help if needed, but don't do the work for your child. Remember that the goal is learning, not a grade on a specific assignment.
- Again, do not do your child's homework. This is similar to playing a sport *for* your child rather than letting them participate in the sport with you cheering and supporting his or her efforts.
- If homework is challenging, break it down into small time segments.
- You do not need to know how to complete a homework assignment or even know the language of the assignment in order to assist your child in learning the skill. Have your child explain and teach the skill to you.
- Establish good communication with your child's teacher.
- Have high standards for your children. Encourage them to work hard in school, have friends who are a positive influence, and to take part in healthy activities.
- Participate in school programs.
- Attend parent–teacher conferences.
- Learn what is expected of children in your child's grade.
- Obtain specific information about how your child is progressing.

- Do not wait until there is a problem before contacting your child's school. Establish early in the school year that you would like to have ongoing communication about classroom instruction.
- Have a positive attitude towards school.
- Remember that parents are the constant in a child's life and have a phenomenal influence on their child's success in the future.
- Take the 'long view' when thinking of your children's progress and remember how far they have come.
- Keep in mind what you want your child to be able to do as an adult. Work toward that goal each day, but remember not to be rigid in your ambition. Children change and develop their own career and other goals.

REFERENCES

Amundson, N.E. and Penner, K. (1998) Parent involved career exploration. *Career Development Quarterly*, **47**(2), 135–44.

Bandura, A. (1977) *Social Learning Theory*. Englewood Cliffs, NJ: Prentice-Hall.

Bank, B.J., Slavings, R.L. and Biddle, B.J. (1990) Effects of peer, faculty, and parental influences on students' persistence. *Sociology of Education*, **63**, 208–55.

Beckwith, L. (1976) Caregiver–infant interaction and early cognitive development in preterm infants. *Child Development*, **47**(3), 579–87.

Berk, L.E. (2000) *Child Development*, 5th edition. Needham Heights: Allyn & Bacon.

Blau, P.M. and Duncan, O.D. (1967) *The American Occupational Structure*. New York: John Wiley.

Bourdieu, P.J. (1990) *In Other Words: Essays Towards a Reflexive Sociology*; translated by Matthew Adamson. Stanford, CA: Stanford University Press.

Bradley, R.H. and Caldwell, B.M. (1984) 174 children: a study of the relationship between home environment and cognitive development during the first 5 years. In Gottfried, A.W. (ed.) *Home Environment and Early Cognitive Development: Longitudinal Research*. Orlando, FL: Academic Press, pp. 5–56.

Bradley, R.H., Caldwell, B.M., Rock, S.T., Barnard, K.E., Gray, C., Hammond, M.A., Mitchell, S., Siegel, L., Ramey, C.T., Gottfried, A.L. and Johnson, D.L. (1989) Home environment and cognitive development in the first 3 years of life: a collaborative study involving six sites and three ethnic groups in North America. *Developmental Psychology*, **25**(2), 217–35.

Bregman, G. and Killen, M. (1999) Adolescents' and young adults' reasoning about career choice and the role of parental influence. *Journal of Research on Adolescence*, **9**(3), 253–75.

Bronfenbrenner, U. (1979) *The Ecology of Human Development: Experiments by Nature and Design*. Cambridge, MA: Harvard University Press.

Bronfenbrenner, U. (1986) Ecology of the family as a context for human development: Research perspectives. *Developmental Psychology*, **22**, 723–42.

Chavkin, N.F. (1993) School social workers helping multi-ethnic families, schools, and communities join forces. In Chavkin, N.F. (ed.) *Families and Schools in a Pluralistic Society.* Albany, NY: State University of New York Press.

Chavkin, N.F. and Williams, D.L., Jr (1985) Parent involvement in education project. Executive summary of the final report. Austin, TX: Southwest Educational Development Lab (ERIC Document Reproduction Services No. ED 266 874).

Christian, K., Morrison, F.J. and Bryant, F.B. (1998) Predicting kindergarten academic skills: interactions among child care, maternal education, and family literacy environments. *Early Childhood Research Quarterly*, **13**(3), 501–21.

Clark, R.M. (1983) *Family Life and School Achievement: Why Poor Black Children Succeed or Fail.* Chicago: University of Chicago Press.

Coon, H., Fulker, D.W., DeFries, J.C. and Plomin, R. (1990) Home environment and cognitive ability of 7-year-old children in the Colorado Adoption Project: genetic and environmental etiologies. *Developmental Psychology*, **26**(3), 459–68.

Cummins, J. (1986) Empowering minority students: a framework for intervention. *Harvard Educational Review*, **56**(1), 18–36.

Dauber, S.L. and Epstein, J.L. (1993) Parents' attitudes and practices of involvement in inner-city elementary and middle schools. In Chavkin, N. (ed.) *Families and School in a Pluralistic Society*. Albany, NY: State University Press, pp. 53–71.

Deutsch, M. (1967) The disadvantaged child and the learning process. In Deutsch, M. (ed.) *The Disadvantaged Child.* New York: Basic Books.

Eagle, E. (1989) Socioeconomic status, family structure, and parental involvement: the correlates of achievement. Paper presented at the Annual Meeting of the American Educational Research Association, San Francisco, 27–31 March 1989.

Eckenrode, J., Laird, M. and Doris, J. (1993) School performance and disciplining problems among abused and neglected children. *Developmental Psychology*, **29**, 53–62.

Elardo, R., Bradley, R., and Caldwell, B.A. (1977) A longitudinal study of the relation of infants' home environments to language development at age three. *Child Development*, **48**, 495–603.

Epstein, J.L. (1984) School policy and parent involvement: research results. *Educational Horizons*, **62**, 70–2.

Epstein, J.L. (1987) Toward a theory of family–school connections: teacher practices and parent involvement. In Hurrelmann, K., Kaufmann, F. and Losel, F. (eds) *Social Interventions: Potential Constraints.* New York: Walter de Gruyter, pp. 121–35.

Epstein, J.L. (1996) Perspectives and previews on research and policy for family, school, and community partnerships. In Booth, A. and Dunn, J.F. (eds) *Family-School Links: How Do They Affect Educational Outcomes?* Mahwah, NJ: Erlbaum.

Gillum, R.M. (1977) The effects of parent involvement on student achievement in three Michigan performance contracting programs. Paper presented at the American Education Research Association Annual Meeting, New York.

Gottfried, A.W. (1984) Issues concerning the relationship between home environment and early cognitive development. In Gottfried, A.W. (ed.) *Home Environment and Early Cognitive Development: Longitudinal Research.* Orlando, FL: Academic Press.

Grolnick, W.S. and Slowiaczek, M.L. (1994) Parents' involvement in children's schooling: a multidimensional conceptualization and motivational model. *Child Development*, **65**, 237–52.

Grolnick, W.S., Benjet, C., Kurowski, C.O. and Apostoleris, N.H. (1997) Predictors of parent involvement in children's schooling. *Journal of Educational Psychology*, **89**, 538–48.

Grotevant, H.D. and Cooper, C.R. (1988) The role of family experience in career exploration: a life-span perspective. In Baltes, P.B., Featherman, D.L. and Lerner, R.M. (eds) *Life-span Development and Behavior.* Hillsdale, NJ: Erlbaum.

Henderson, A.T. (1987) *The Evidence Continues to Grow: Parent Involvement Improves Student Achievement.* Columbia, MD: National Committee for Citizens in Education.

Henderson, A.T. and Berla, N. (1994) *A New Generation of Evidence: The Family is Critical to Student Achievement.* Washington, D.C: Center for Law and Education.

Hollifield, J.H. (1994) High schools gear up to create effective school and family partnerships. Baltimore, MD: Center on Families, Communities, Schools, and Children's Learning, Johns Hopkins University (ERIC Document Reproduction No. Ed 380 229).

Hoover-Dempsey, K.V. and Sandler, H.M. (1997) Why do parents become involved in their children's education? *Review of Educational Research*, **67**, 3–42.

Jimerson, S., Egeland, B. and Teo, A. (1999) A longitudinal study of achievement trajectories: Factors associated with change. *Journal of Educational Psychology*, **91**, 116–26.

Keith, T.A., Reimers, T.M., Fehrmenn, P., Pottebaum, S. and Aubrey, L. (1986) Parental involvement, homework, and TV time: direct and indirect effects on high school achievement. *Journal of Educational Psychology*, **78**(5), 373–80.

Keith, T.Z., Troutman, G.C., Trivette, P.S., Keith, P.B., Bickley, P.G. and Singh, K. (1993) Does parental involvement affect eighth-grade student achievement? Structural analysis of national data. *School Psychology Review*, **22**(3), 474–96.

Kenny, M.E. (1990) College seniors' perceptions of parental attachments: the value and stability of family ties. *Journal of College Student Development*, **31**, 39–46.

Ketterson, T.U. and Blustein, D.L. (1997) Attachment relationships and the career exploration process. *Career Development Quarterly*, **46**(2), 167–78.

Landry, S.H., Smith, K.E., Swank, P.R. and Miller-Loncar, C.L. (2000) Early maternal and child influences on children's later independent cognitive and social functioning. *Child Development*, **71**(2), 358–75.

Lareau, A. (1987) Social class differences in family–school relationships: the importance of cultural capital. *Sociology of Education*, **60**, 73–85.

Lopez, F.G. and Andrews, S. (1987) Career indecision: a family systems perspective. *Journal of Counseling and Development*, **65**, 304–7.

Lucas, B.G. and Lusthaus, C.S. (1978) The decisional participation of parents in elementary and secondary schools. *Journal of High School*, **61**(5), 211–20.

Luster, T. and Dubow, E. (1992) Home environment and maternal intelligence as predictors of verbal intelligence: a comparison of preschool and school-age children. *Merrill-Palmer Quarterly*, **38**(2), 151–75.

McGroder, S.M. (2000) Parenting among low-income, African-American single mothers with preschool-age children: patterns, predictors, and developmental correlates. *Child Development*, **71**(3), 752–71.

Meadows, S. (1996) *Parenting Behaviour and Children's Cognitive Development*. East Sussex: Psychology Press.

Menacker, J., Hurwitz, E. and Weldon, W. (1988) Parent-teacher cooperation in schools serving the urban poor. *The Clearing House*, **62**, 108–12.

Moles, O. (1993) Collaboration between schools and disadvantaged parents: obstacles and openings. In Chavkin, N. (ed.) *Families and Schools in a Pluralistic Society*. Albany, NY: State University Press, pp. 21–49.

Penick, N.I. and Jepsen, D.A. (1992) Family functioning and adolescent career development. *Career Development Quarterly*, **40**, 208–22.

Raffaele, L.M. and Knoff, H.M. (1999) Improving home–school collaboration with disadvantaged families: organizational principles, perspectives, and approaches. *School Psychology Review*, **28**, 448–66.

Reynolds, A.J., Mavrogenes, N.A., Hagemann, M. and Bezruczko, N. (1993) *Schools, Families, and Children: Sixth Year Results from the Longitudinal Study of Children at Risk*. Chicago Public Schools: Department of Research, Evaluation, and Planning.

Rumberger, R.W., Ghatak, R., Poulos, G., Ritter, P.L. and Dornbusch, S.M. (1990) Family influences on dropout behavior in one California high school. *Sociology of Education*, **63**, 283–99.

Scarr, S. (1985) Constructing psychology: making facts and fables from our times. *American Psychologist*, **40**, 499–512.

Shartrand, A.M., Krieder, H.M., Erickson, L.S. and Warfield, M.E. (1994) *Preparing Teachers to Involve Parents: A National Survey of Teacher Education Programs*. Cambridge. MA: Harvard Family Research Project.

Shores, E.F. (1998) *A Call To Action: Family Involvement as a Critical Component of Family Education Programs*. Tallahassee, Florida South Eastern Regional Vision for Education (SERVE).

Sigman, M., Neumann, C., Carter, E., Cattle, D.J., D'Souza, S. and Bwibo, N. (1988) Home interactions and the development of Embu toddlers in Kenya. *Child Development*, **59**, 1251–61.

Smith, E.J. (1981) The working mother: a critique of the research. *Journal of Vocational Behavior*, **19**, 191–211.

Tirozzi, G.N. and Uro, G. (1997) Education reform in the United States. *American Psychologist*, **52**, 241–9.

Turnbull, A.P. and Turnbull III, H.R. (1986) *Families, Professionals, and Exceptionality: A Special Partnership*. Columbus, OH: Merrill.

Turnbull, A.P. and Winston, P.J. (1984) Parent involvement policy and practice: current research and implications for families of young severely handicapped children. In Blancher, J. (ed.) *Severely Handicapped Children and Their Families: Research in Review*. New York: Academic Press, pp. 377–97.

US Department of Education (1994) *Strong Families, Strong Schools*. Washington, DC:

Wilks, J. (1986) The relative importance of parents and friends in adolescent decision making. *Journal of Youth and Adolescence*, **15**(4), 323–34.

Young, R.A. and Friesen, J.D. (1992) The intentions of parents in influencing the career development of their children. *Career Development Quarterly*, **40**, 198–207.

Young, R.A., Friesen, J.D. and Pearson, H.M. (1988) Activities and interpersonal relations as dimensions of behavior in the career development of children. *Youth and Society*, **20**, 29–45.

Zajonc, R.B. and Markus, G.B. (1975) Birth order and intellectual development. *Psychological Review*, **82**, 74–85.

14

Parenting Exceptional Children

Susan McGaw

SUMMARY

There are in all societies, large numbers of parents and children with intellectual disability. They are a source of concern, for complex reasons. The more developed the society, the greater this concern, related to policies and procedures for supporting them. Because of their wide-ranging vulnerability, these policies present as a good litmus test of society's concern with parenting.

This chapter addresses, in some detail, the major issues in parenting and intellectual disability, historical background and landmark events that have shaped policy and practice. Consideration will be given to how the children fare, variations across cultures, current understanding, parental practices, an evaluation of support schemes and implications for practice.

PARENTS WHO HAVE AN INTELLECTUAL DISABILITY (ID)

Historically, the right and competence of intellectually disabled (ID) parents to produce and raise children has been questioned. Pejorative opinions have continuously expressed doubts regarding the capacity of these parents to manage the complexities of parenting and cited the risk of harm that their children might be exposed to if society does not intervene in some way. Current thinking, as expounded by the Disability Discrimination Act (1995)[1] and Human Rights Act (1998)[2] in the UK (and corresponding ones in most Western countries), reflects a shift in social attitude over time and an acceptance now (though not universal) that oppression of human rights and the fostering of discriminatory practices is unacceptable, especially when it relates to someone with a disability (Freeney et al., 1999). Ensuring that parents with ID are aware of and

receive their entitlements, as well as those of their children, can be difficult. This chapter raises some of the major issues in this area of work. An historical account of the 'exceptional' experiences of parents with ID and their children over time is provided, including past and present legislation that has channelled the passage of events. Epidemiological findings in respect of the children, and subsequently their parents will be discussed. Finally, the author's views and commentary on this topic will be given, based on her research and clinical experience in this field.

MAJOR ISSUES

Definitions of Intellectual Disability and Parental Competency

Whilst some researchers suggest that the provision of safe and adequate childcare requires a minimal level of intellectual capacity, it is unclear what that level actually is. In general, studies have not produced a convincing correlation between IQ and parenting capacity, although it has been suggested that when intelligence falls below the mild range (IQ < 60), parenting competency is brought into serious question. There is also an issue regarding parents whose IQ falls above an IQ cutoff of 70 (that is, within the borderline range of intellectual disabilities), many of whom have a specific ID embedded within a general IQ score. Further to this, contentious issues are raised as to whether intellectual disability *per se* increases the probability of child abuse, as many parents in this population share predisposing factors with parents of normal intelligence who abuse their children (Dowdney and Skuse, 1993).

In order to bring some clarification to this matter, the term 'intellectual disability' is adopted throughout this chapter to refer to parents who have been identified as having an IQ below 80. This term is synonymous with current terms such as 'learning disability', 'learning difficulties', 'mental retardation' and 'cognitive limitations', which vary according to cultural and political preference. Irrespective of these differences, there are three core criteria for ID that have been universally adopted by clinicians and encapsulated in both World Health Organisation and American Psychiatric Association classifications of mental disorder (AAMR, 1992: WHO, 1992; DSM – IV, 1994):

(a) significant impairment of intellectual functioning;
(b) significant impairment of adaptive/social functioning;
(c) age of onset before adulthood.

For the purpose of subclassification ID should reflect both intellectual and adaptive/ social functioning, taking into account the quality of support required by a person, to enable him or her to live independently in the community.

Defining the Term 'Disabled'

Collectively, there are many parents who can be described as 'disabled' because they have special needs and live with a disability of some kind – physical disability, chronic and temporary ill health, physical illness, disfigurements, sensory impairments, personality disorders, psychiatric disabilities, substance abuse disorders – as well as those parents diagnosed as having an ID (McConnell et al., 2000; Wates, 2001).

Current trends indicate that parents with disabilities are being identified collectively as

part of surveys and national strategies both in the UK (DoH, 2001) and US (Barker and Maralani, 1997). There are benefits to focusing on and addressing the needs of parents with disabilities as a whole. First, disabled parents comprise a sizeable population of parents who, when considered collectively, have greater opportunities to express their needs and seek representation within their community, across services and at government levels. Second, disabled parents may experience some common obstacles in their parenting, such as impoverishment, inadequate housing, limited mobility, negative stereotyped opinions and child protection issues, all of which require a collective approach from service providers (Wates, 2001). Third, user and advocacy groups comprising parents with various disabilities can become strong spokespeople for each other, subsequently compensating for some of the disabilities of a fellow parent. It is common to find parents with ID experiencing difficulties with expressive language, level and complexity of thinking, new concept formation and memory deficits, which a parent with physical disabilities, for example, may not experience.

However, confusion can arise when only certain categories of disability are reported in some studies (Goodinge, 2000), and on other occasions, reporting is generic and all encompassing (Barker and Maralani, 1997). Research highlights the need for intensive, specialist support to assist parents with ID because their needs frequently differ from those of other parents – including parents with other types of disability. They do not necessarily share all of the same needs and strengths as other disabled parents across this wide-ranging spectrum. It is therefore useful to establish commonality, as well as distinctions between parents with ID and other parents with disabilities, in both their functioning and capabilities.

PREVALENCE OF ID PARENTS

The number of parents with ID is unknown. Surveys that have attempted to track and estimate this population size have encountered a number of difficulties, including poor identification of a transitory parent population, incomplete records, inconsistent terminology and differing classification systems – all of which compound and bedevil this task. At best, 'guestimates' range from 0.004 to 1.7 per cent of the parent population across countries.

In the United States there are estimated to be 6.9 million (11 per cent) parents with disabilities between the ages of 18 and 64 (US Census Bureau, 1993) whose children are under 18 years of age. In another national survey, 1175 parents with disabilities (between the ages of 20 and 81) were identified from demographic data (Barker et al., 1997). Guestimates have been made from these surveys (on the basis of 1 in 5 respondents being identified has having a ID, proportionate to the total US population) that there are 1.4 million parents (20 per cent of 7 million) in the US between 18 and 64 years old with children under age 18 years old (Holburn et al., 2000). Evidently, this figure would be greater if the guestimate included parents whose children were 18 years and over. Authors acknowledge that these figures are not reliable or accurate, due to differences in diagnoses and because of sampling weaknesses, which include mismatches in ages and sampling year. There is, therefore, no reliable estimate of the number of parents with mental retardation in the US at present. The same uncertainties regarding incidence and prevalence remain consistent across other countries and should be borne in mind when interpreting the following figures.

In the UK, between 1.2 and 4 million parents have a disability of some kind (Goodinge, 2000). Of these, it is estimated that upwards of 250,000 (0.004 per cent) of parents may have an intellectual disability (McGaw, 1998). This crude estimate has been drawn from the ratio of parents referred and known to the Special Parenting Service (approximately 1000) over a 10-year period from 1987 to 1998), against the known general population in Cornwall, England (500,000 = 1:500) and the general parenting population in the UK as a whole (12 million). Since this estimate includes parents with borderline ID (IQ < 85), comparability with US estimates is made more difficult.

In Australia, approximately 0.99–1.7 per cent of families are headed by parents with an intellectual disability (Australian Institute of Health & Welfare, 1997). A rough estimate based on the prevalence of disabled adults in the population suggests that approximately 2.6–5.4 per cent of families are headed by parents with a psychiatric disability and less than 1 per cent of families are headed by parents with an intellectual disability (McConnell et al., 2000).

New Zealand figures are lower, with approximately 0.25 per cent of families headed by parents with an intellectual disability (Mirfin-Veitch et al., 1999).

Rights of Parents with ID

The current legal debate regarding consent issues is less frequent for parents with ID regarding their right to produce children. Historically, however, involuntary terminations and sterilization were mandatory and imposed upon many people with ID.

Today, parents with low IQs have parental rights, otherwise viewed as a collection of powers and duties (defined by the English Children Act 1989[3] as 'parental responsibility') which follow on from being a parent and bringing up a child. Although these rights are not enforceable by law, parents are expected to apply discretion to their interpretation and discharge of this parental responsibility, bar two limitations. They must provide (a) minimum standards of care, including the protection of children's welfare; and (b) diminishing parental responsibility as the child acquires sufficient understanding to make his own decisions. We can anticipate that difficulties will be experienced for some parents with ID in their interpretation and application of their parental responsibility, especially when this relates to basic care and child development (Tymchuk, 1992a; Feldman, 1994). However, how this is assessed and viewed by outsiders can be uncertain.

Divisions and tensions are commonplace for professionals who become involved in supporting parents with ID, especially where agencies differ in perspective, stage of intervention and whom they have identified as 'their' client – parent or child. Upholding the rights of parents with ID to enable them to make decisions about child-rearing practices is embedded within the philosophy and practice of some agencies. Others only become involved if there are child protection issues, with this focus becoming the determinant for the level and type of service provision offered to parents (McGaw, 2000). This is a difficult issue all round, especially as the rights of parents and individual rights of their children are not easily definable, and open to different interpretations both at ground level and in legal proceedings.

Rights of Children Whose Parents Have ID

The Convention on the Rights of the Child (1989)[4] identifies the right of children 'as far as possible ... to be cared for by his or her parents' (Article 7). This principle is expanded in Article 9 which states that 'a child shall not be separated from his or her family against their will except when ... such separation is necessary for the best interests of the child'. At the same time, the research clearly indicates that a child whose parents have a ID will be at increased risk of removal from their parent's care (either temporarily or permanently), and this risk is progressive as the child matures (Ray et al., 1994). However, the general principles, including the right of disabled parents to develop a family and live as other families, and the right of children to live in families that provide for their needs, remain the same as for parents without ID.

Court Intervention

Statutory intervention for the purpose of removing children from parents with ID is commonly reported across countries, regardless of variations in culture, legal process or legislation (Gillberg and Geijer-Karlsson, 1983; Accardo and Whitman, 1989; Mirfin-Veitch et al., 1999). It is widely reported that parents continue to be subject to professional discrimination, through negative prejudice and bias – which directly or indirectly influence judgements made about their parenting practices (Taylor et al., 1991; McConnell and Llewellyn, 2000). Where such discriminatory practices are evident, controversy and tensions follow, especially when the right of parents to exercise their parental responsibility is under scrutiny during care proceedings (Field and Sanchez, 1999).

Services and Interventions

In the UK, under the Children Act 1989, local authorities are guided to work 'in partnership' with parents and provide services for children in need. The duties and powers given to local authorities are appropriately set out. Provisions for children living with families include advice, home help and family centres. However, these duties appear to be qualified, in that local authorities shall take 'reasonable steps' and provide services that they consider appropriate. In reality, whilst practitioners willingly comply with such guidance, they often experience dissonance between endorsement of the rights of individuals with learning difficulties to become parents and the welfare rights of their children to receive 'good-enough' parenting (Glaun and Brown, 1999).

Typically, tensions increase as child protection issues manifest and the inadequacy of teaching programmes and support services available for these parents becomes apparent. Over time, research findings have been consistent: ID parents are over-represented across child welfare services, although it is unclear just how large this population is and the underlying reasons. The ability and capacity of low IQ parents to provide basic childcare appears to be influenced by a number of factors (academic functioning, mental/physical health, quality of relationships, size of family, children's health) including environmental and social components.

Research on the general parenting population has established a demonstrable link between material deprivation (including poverty, poor housing and public transport, poor-quality support services) and the chance of a child coming into public care (Bebington and Miles, 1989; Little and Mount, 1999). This symbiotic relationship between family functioning and the availability of a support programme becomes accentuated and even more critical when it relates to parents who have ID (Glaun and Brown, 1999). As a result, the timing, delivery and quality of professional support on offer to families, prior to or during legal public care proceedings often becomes contentious and fiercely debated between parties. Typically, local authorities are criticized for offering 'insufficient' family support programmes, failing to meet parent's needs and offering the appropriate level of support too late into the parenting process.

Parenting by adults with ID is a relatively new area for research, although the struggle to establish this status appears to have been pursued over many years. Over the past 20 years there has been a proliferation of studies that have tried to establish what impact an ID classification has on a parent's performance and their child's development and well-being. Clearly, an ID classification cannot be cited as the sole necessary *and* sufficient indicator of parental incompetence. A number of factors are influential in determining a parent's ability to cope. The rest of the chapter will explore these issues.

HISTORICAL BACKGROUND

This chapter focuses on the parenting role of adults with intellectual disabilities and their children, many of who may be considered to be 'exceptional' in terms of their existence within society today. Research evidence and commentaries bear witness to the precarious route that many parents with ID have been forced to take over the centuries, to ensure that their right to produce children is recognized and accepted by society. Historically, general concerns about genetic transmission of low intelligence and subsequent taboos relating to procreation have resulted in many adults being deprived of the right to parent following such a classification, although there has been some variability across countries. The following synopsis is a brief attempt to capture the essence of this learned work. It provides a brief chronology and historical examination of the struggle of adults with ID to become parents mainly in the UK and USA

(Field and Sanchez, 1999; Holburn et al., 2000), for whom the greatest evidence is available. This pathway reflects government policies, legislation and public attitudes from the early 19th century to the present day.

19th Century Parenting

During the Victorian era, institutions of different sorts developed rapidly, becoming the main service provision for many people with ID in the UK. Commonly referred to as 'idiots' or 'lunatics', many people with disabilities found themselves accommodated in institutions or asylums. During this period, Sir Francis Galton (1822–1911) coined the term 'eugenics' (the literal meaning is 'good birth') which espoused the notion of improving general as well as specific abilities of children by better selection of parents; that is, excluding ID people from procreating parents (Bambrick and Roberts, 1990).

Concurrently in the USA, a person considered to have ID in the early 1880s may have found himself or herself a 'ward of the state' (and residing in almshouses, workhouses, jails or mental hospitals); or even 'auctioneered-out' by the state to strangers who were paid by the person's family to 'care' for him or her (Field et al., 1999). Some were fortunate, coming from wealthy families who could afford to pay for their care at home, commissioning private tutoring to ensure that they received one-to-one instruction.

20th Century Parenting

The Eugenics Education Society was formed in the UK in 1907 and later adopted by eugenic groups in USA, where it gained momentum, fuelling a popular belief that ID was hereditary. This notion was supported by the Radnor Commission's report (UK) in 1908 which concluded that 'heredity was an important factor in mental deficiency, that defectives were exceptionally prolific, and that many current social problems were due to the fact that so many of the feeble-minded were free in the community'. Governments alike became concerned that the intelligence of their nation was under threat by the propagation of 'inferior' people who could contaminate the nation's gene pool. Women with ID were viewed as immoral, sexually active and at significant risk of producing 'inferior' offspring. The eugenic movement in the UK supported incarceration in sexually segregated institutions – a draconian solution adopted by the government at that time. It was heavily applied to women who had ID, as well as those suffering from physical disabilities and epilepsy. Institutionalization continued to be the main form of treatment in the UK, although voluntary sterilization was an additional option that could be considered and pursued (DHSS, Department of Health Select Committee, 1934).

In the USA, compulsory sterilization was the preferred main deterrent to the propagation of people who were referred to as 'inferior' and 'imbeciles' (Buck v Bell 1927). Institutionalization was also on the increase, rising from 9000+ persons placed in institutions in 1900 to over 68,000 by 1930 (Field and Sanchez, 1999). Also, compulsory sterilization was adopted by legislation across 30 states between 1907 and 1931, in respect of selected persons with ID or with mental illness, residing in institutions. Under these laws, over 12,000 people had been sterilized by 1931 (Bambrick and Roberts, 1990). The practice of sterilization continued up until 1942, after which time, opposing views started to permeate the court system and opinions were expressed that 'the right to procreate was a basic constitutional right' (Skinner v Oklahoma 1942).

In the 1960s the concept of 'normalization' was instrumental in dismantling institutionalized living and opening up opportunities for people with disabilities to live within the community (Wolfensberger, 1975). This concept was subsequently surpassed by 'social role valorization' which advocated that people with disabilities should receive special education and work opportunities to open up their life experiences. Since the 1970s, a variety of court orders have resulted in the shutting down of state institutions or have set deadlines for their closure, and greater emphasis has been placed on creating and supporting a normal lifestyle for people with disabilities of any kind.

Currently, sterilization is infrequently an option considered in the USA, although it is available through different channels according to the state in which the ID person lives (Roy and Roy, 1988). The UK position is that there are strict guidelines for applications for girls under 18 years of age to be sterilized. These include seeking leave of a High Court judge, representation by the Official Solicitor or appropriate guardian and guidance from expert evidence (giving reasons for the application, the history and foreseeable future of the girl, the risks and consequences of pregnancy and of sterilization, and the practicability of alternative precautions) (Roy and Roy, 1988). In respect of women aged 18 years and over, if they are unable to give personal consent, medical practitioners can proceed with sterilization in accordance with good medical practice, in 'exceptional circumstances, where there was no provision in law for consent and no one who could give consent and where the patient was suffering from such mental abnormality as to be unable to give consent' (Dyer, 1987).

The core issues that have dominated thinking and swayed current service provision for families headed by a parent with ID have often reflected (a) the culture and climate in which these parents have raised their children; (b) the available empirical research on the topic of parental competency and parental capacity; (c) the known effects of parenting on the children; and (d) government thinking around policy and practice for this population of parents. In the past, the courts have been instrumental in seeking solutions to some of the more controversial issues involving ID parents, especially when the plight of individual parents and their children have been the cause for statutory and public concern.

Landmark Events

Parenthood continues to be open to public scrutiny, especially in the light of government initiatives that target mass funding and intensive support to the most vulnerable families in our communities. Historically, in the UK, a number of family cases have attracted the attention of the courts and government alike, setting precedents in case law and becoming instrumental in shaping future service provision for many parents with ID.

JEANNETTE CASE: STERILIZATION ISSUES

The sterilization authorized by the High Court of Jeannette, a 17-year-old girl with ID in the UK in 1987 aroused considerable controversy at that time. It was considered to be the last option and in the best interests of the girl. Nevertheless, it was described as being 'Nazi-like' in its implications and an 'appalling denial of human rights' (Bambrick and Roberts, 1990). Rulings such as these have been infrequent since. This particular case established political and social non-acceptance of such decisions for subsequent cases.

JASMINE BECKFORD INQUIRY:

ABUSE AND NEGLECT ISSUES

The case of Jasmine Beckford, and the circumstances leading up to her death, has had longer term consequences. The inquiry into her death resulted in a widespread public reaction (London Borough of Brent, 1985). Jasmine's mother (Beverly Lorrington) was diagnosed as having a 'significant degree of intellectual handicap' with low 'expressed emotion'. She was struggling with raising two children by herself until she became pregnant again. Despite a history of violence she moved in with the father of her new child, a few months into the pregnancy. Subsequently, Jasmine suffered a numbers of assaults resulting in a bone fracture and bruising, and was eventually killed by her stepfather. She died aged 4 years in 1984. The inquiry concluded that the awful events leading up to her death could have been avoided and criticized professionals for failing to operate a co-ordinated approach to child protection, and for a complete absence of any surveillance by the health visitor and social worker.

JENKINS CASE: CONSENT ISSUES

Langley and Holman (2001) cite the case of David Jenkins (a care worker) who was charged with having 'unlawful sexual intercourse' with a woman with ID (with a mental age of less than 3 years), which drew public attention to the issues of informed consent. Their sexual encounter resulted in her pregnancy, confirmed after DNA testing. The issue of consent became the centre of debate in court in 2000. Tensions resulted from different interpretations of medical and legal guidance on 'capacity and consent' in relation to this woman. The Judge disagreed with the legal view that a woman must be able to understand 'what is proposed, and its implications and must also be able to exercise choice' when consenting to a sexual relationship. Instead, he considered that consent had to be given its ordinary English meaning.

DISABILITY DISCRIMINATION ACT 1995

In the UK, with effect from December 1996 it has been unlawful for a service provider to refuse unjustifiably to provide a service to a disabled person on the same terms as available to other people. Since October 1999, service providers have had to take 'reasonable steps' to change policies, practices or procedures that make it impossible or unreasonably difficult for disabled people to use a service. Further provisions coming into force in 2004 state that service providers will have to take reasonable steps to remove, alter or provide means of avoiding physical features that make it impossible or unreasonably difficult for disabled people to use a service.

A JIGSAW OF SERVICES[5]

During 1998–1999 the English Social Services Inspectorate (Scotland is different) conducted an inspection of eight councils across the UK in their provision of services to disabled parents (Goodinge, 2000). The intention was to identify population size and issues relating to parenting practice, problems and prospects for change. This disabled parent population included those with learning, physical and sensory impairments, as well as parents with chronic sickness and deteriorating illnesses. The inspection carried out an examination of the experiences of 621 disabled parents, using a key informant approach (asking Social Services to identify families falling within this classification) and studying 90 parents in detail. This landmark document is significant in promoting public and government's understanding of the provision of services for parents with ID.

Variation was apparent in the reporting of social service staff regarding the prevalence and categories of parents identified. In one such area, a service identified only one parent with ID receiving a service from them, compared to a much larger number of parents who had physical disabilities. Conversely, in another area, as many as 42 per cent of parents with ID were being supported by social service staff compared to only 27 per cent with physical disabilities. Within the sample group, parents with ID comprised the second largest group in terms of their main disability. None of these categories were mutually exclusive and some of these parents had more than one type of disability. Overall, more parents had physical disabilities (61 per cent) than any other type of disability, with parents with ID comprising the next largest group (12 per cent). Parents with a progressive illness comprised 10 per cent of the group; chronic sickness 8 per cent; deaf/hard of hearing 5 per cent; and blind/visually impaired parents 4 per cent.

Of all the parents with disabilities, child protection issues requiring social services' involvement were most frequently reported for parents who have ID (over 60 per cent of families with parents with ID). Across all other categories of disability, child protection issues featured in less than 20 per cent of all cases. This finding is alarming, when set against other information that staff were not routinely carrying out 'holistic assessments' on disabled parents. Adult services ('community care') tended to concentrate on developing a 'needs-led assessment' (prioritizing parent's needs, rather than limiting services to what was available). However, no real assessment was being conducted on the parents if the children's service team family had primary involvement.

Also, the range of services was problematic with little uniformity in approach or amount of social service provision available to disabled parents in general. In one area, 44 per cent of parents with ID (constituting the largest group) receive parenting courses. It was unclear from the report, however, whether the council had adapted a standard parenting programme or developed a specialist approach to accommodate the specific needs of parents with ID. In comparison, parenting courses were not available in a number of other councils.

Another concern was that many staff were unskilled and lacked the technical training to enable them to lead parenting courses and conduct an assessment with an ID parent. Further, the report conveyed concern that well-intentioned but ill-placed interventions and decision-making may be resulting from poor staff training in this specialism. As has already been stated, more critical decisions were being made regarding the care and future of the children from ID parents than for any other group. Alarmingly, the author reported that staff seemed unaware of their lack of skills in this area of work, being generally 'pleased with the training offered to them ... whilst only having a limited understanding of how to practice within a social model of disability' (Goodinge, 2000, p. 40).

Altogether, these findings indicate that there are significant differences in the process of identifying, engaging and supporting disabled parents across social services. Actual or perceived prevalence rates by social services were open to interpretation and error across the eight councils, in the absence of a database. Critical information as to whether a parent had a disability (in childcare terms) or if there were children in the family (adult services) compounded the difficulty faced by staff in identifying a parent with a disability.

CONSEQUENCES FOR CURRENT THINKING AND THRUST OF ACTIVITY

In 2001 the Government's White Paper 'Valuing People: A New Strategy for Learning Disability for the 21st Century'[6] outlined the new vision to improve life chances for people with ID. Embedded in this vision are four key principles, namely the recognition of rights, independence, choice and inclusion, to which ID children and their families are entitled. These principles are safeguarded by legislation. The new plans make reference to parents with ID, recommending closer integration of services, especially under new 'Partnership Boards' and better training for staff. Social services will be the lead agency, ensuring quality of services according to a published 'Quality Protects' framework.

Parenting Support Across the UK

A 'National Mapping of Parenting Services in England and Wales – Consultation Document' extracted information on parenting practices, problems and options for change through a survey of 6000 parenting services (statutory, private and voluntary) across the UK in 2001 (Henricson et al., 2001). The intention was to collate extensive data from parenting service providers across the UK to enable the Government to gain a fuller understanding of service provision to parents.

In terms of general services and their identification of the needs of people with ID, this was expressed in terms of parents accessing generic as opposed to specialized services. Most areas sampled considered that they made specific efforts to bring parents with ID into their service. Only a minority of providers felt that parents with ID would have trouble accessing their services, although this appears to be a matter of opinion rather than fact.

Evidently, this type of consultation process is helpful in informing government policy and in seeking solutions to supporting some of the most vulnerable parents in the community. However, caution needs to be exercised when the views of service providers are taken in isolation from parents with ID. The research is clear regarding the mismatch between the two perspectives – what the parents believe they need or what they are deemed to need by the services (Edmonds, 2000).

HOW DO CHILDREN FARE?

The Main Focus

The long-term welfare of children whose parents have an ID is poorly researched, with difficulties in the organization, implementation and analysis of studies (McGaw, 2000). Typical obstacles include problems in the sampling process, both in identifying and tracking parents and their children over long periods of time (Parish and Newman, 1994; Booth and Booth, 1997). Research is limited to small, non-random sample sizes. Also, many of these families are lost to studies because of their transitory lifestyle and the child's removal into care (Whitman et al., 1987). Methodological weaknesses in research design and a general lack of funding for longitudinal studies, for what is perceived to be a small population of vulnerable families, compounds this problem. Extraneous factors such as poverty, culture and the poor environment in which these families are often placed are confounding variables that undermine the integrity of the findings (Keltner, 1994; Feldman and Walton-Allen, 1997). Consequently, studies have been criticized for being of poor design, and therefore reducing replicability of findings to children of parents with ID as a whole (Taylor et al., 1991; Feldman, 1998; Field and Sanchez, 1999).

Despite these obstacles, researchers continue to investigate the welfare and plight of the children born to parents with ID, especially in relation to (a) the genetic risk of low intelligence, (b) the adequacy of care provided to them by their parents, and (c) the long-term effects on the children in their adulthood. This section attempts to gauge whether the children of parents with ID are truly 'exceptional' in terms of their parenting experiences.

Variations and Dimensions

The numbers of children born to parents with ID are unknown in the UK. There are estimated to be at least 120,000 children born annually to parents with intellectual disabilities in the USA (Keltner and Tymchuk, 1992). The absence of data and prevalence relating to numbers of children is of concern, especially as research highlights risks associated with their parenting. In contrast, far less reporting describes the more positive experiences of parenting for these children. This section draws attention to some of this positive research, in the knowledge that most negative aspects of the parenting (the children's exposure to neglect, maltreatment, developmental disabilities, behavioural and psychiatric disorders) are often extensively reported.

IQ and Chronological Variants in Children

Studies continue to report that there is a general 'regression to the mean' on intelligence for the children of parents with ID. In other words, the majority of children tend to function at a higher level of intelligence than their parents. However, more IQs are identified in the range of learning difficulties than would be expected from a random sample, but not necessarily lower than a disadvantaged sample from the general population (Scally, 1973; Feldman et al., 1985). Emerging ID are being identified in children as young as 2 years of age for up to 50 per cent of the sample group (Feldman et al., 1985). For older children (6–18 years old), researchers have identified that about 60 per cent of children have a disability of some kind. Of these, the vast majority have a learning difficulty (most within the mild classification). Less than half of these children are eventually placed outside of their home, though there is always an issue of supply and demand for provisions, which determines the percentage of outside family placements (Van Hove and Wellens, 1995).

Average to bright children are also born to parents with ID. Approximately 13 per cent of children were identified as of above-average intelligence when one parent was diagnosed as having an ID, and about 1 per cent of children when both parents had ID (Reed and Reed, 1965). Overall, these above-normal intelligence children represent about 0.75 per cent of the total population, although little confirmatory data exist to confirm or negate this. In one study that was drawn from a school population of 2600 children in New England (O'Neill, 1985) 13 families were identified where at least one parent had an intellectual disability and their children ($N = 23$) were identified as 'normal to superior intelligence. The findings revealed that 25 per cent of the children were well adjusted. Another quarter took over the parent's role with subsequent adjustment problems. The remaining children fared less well, with evidence of 'rebellion, lesser problems of socialization and control and pseudo-retardation'.

Vulnerability to Poor Physical Growth and Care

Despite concerns about the parenting abilities of persons with ID, relatively little is known about the general development of their children. The primary needs (food, warmth, health) of children have been reported as not being met across a number of studies involving parents with ID, some children being diagnosed with 'failure to thrive' (Seagull and Scheurer, 1986; Feldman et al., 1997). Also, these children have been known to be at increased risk of ill health from late or inappropriate treatment of childhood illnesses, in the absence of parenting training in symptom recognition and responses (Tymchuk, 1992b). Parents have been receptive to training to ameliorate the risks across all these areas of parenting care.

Vulnerability to Developmental Delays

In terms of their intellectual development, children whose parents have an ID are particularly vulnerable to developmental delay, especially in expressive language and cognitive skills (Feldman et al., 1989, 1993). Speech defects are going to be even more prevalent for those children who have a global learning difficulty (Dodd and Leahy, 1989), with the likelihood of a speech disorder rising as the measured level of intelligence falls (Schiefelebusch, 1972). Also, when children in these families are exposed to abuse and/or neglect, research indicates that there is an increased chance of developmental delay (Allen and Oliver, 1982). Neglect is considered to be more problematic for language development than the combined effect of abuse and neglect. Despite these findings, for the majority of the children (whose IQ will be higher than their parents') language delays may be remedied, especially for children under 3 years if their parents receive the appropriate training to address the identified deficits (Feldman and Case, 1993; McGaw, 1994). Poverty is also recognized as being a risk factor in child development and academic achievement (Campbell and Ramey, 1994). Research continues to experience difficulties in separating out the relative insignificance of these confounding variables.

Vulnerability to Behavioural Problems

Behavioural problems are common amongst children of parents with ID (Gillberg and Geijer-Karlsson, 1983; Seagull and Scheurer, 1986), with increasing susceptibility as they grow older (Accardo and Whitman, 1990). Studies reveal that parents may need more help in disciplining their children than parents with any other type of primary impairment (Berkeley Planning Associates, 1997). Child behaviour disorders are particularly prevalent amongst boys whose mothers are diagnosed as having an ID (Feldman et al., 1997). In a study involving 2-year-olds with or at risk of developmental delay, who were identified as vulnerable to behaviour problems, having a parent with intellectual disabilities (6 per cent of mothers; 8 per cent of fathers) was not the main risk factor by itself (Feldman et al., 2000). Parental stress, arising from a combination of family characteristics (maternal depression, paternal illness, an escape-avoidance coping strategy, family disharmony and financial stress, etc.), is more significant in the poor management of the child and the resulting behaviour problems.

Vulnerability to Abuse and/or Neglect

Whilst parental inadequacy is not predictable from parental IQ alone, there is substantial evidence to suggest that there are increased risks associated with lower levels of intelligence (IQ below 60). A child is at increased risk of unintentional neglect when his or her parents experience additional problems, over and above their intellectual disabilities (Tymchuk, 1992a), including poor parental education and the absence of supportive services (Schilling et al., 1982; Seagull and Scheurer, 1986). Neglect is the most frequently reported type of child maltreatment in studies: 80 per cent of ID parents having lost their children in care proceedings (in USA and Canada) because of actual or potential child neglect (Feldman et al., 1992, 1993). Physical and psychological neglect are reported more frequently than sexual or physical abuse (Feldman, 1997).

The risk of abuse for a child who has a parent with ID is less frequently reported than for neglect, although both are often cited as the reason for a child's removal from their birth family (Tymchuk, 1992a; Dowdney and Skuse, 1993). Purposeful abuse by an ID mother is infrequently observed or reported, although when it occurs the prognosis for change is poor (Tymchuk and Andron, 1990). It has not been possible to isolate single factors that are predictive of abuse, such as parent's childhood abuse/neglect, child characteristics or environmental stresses. However, investigators involved in maltreatment cases report that children of ID parents appear to be at less risk of continued mistreatment if the parent has an ID, than those children whose parents are diagnosed with serious emotional disorders or substance abuse (Taylor et al., 1991).

In comparison, across the general parenting population, children's low IQ or physical disabilities may render them at increased risk of abuse and/or neglect because of the special needs arising from their condition (McCormack, 1991; Sinason, 1992). It is unclear from the research whether this risk increases or remains the same when a child has special needs and the parent also has an ID.

Vulnerability to Poor Mental Health

Some studies have indicated that children may be vulnerable to psychiatric disorders associated with their parents' ID (Kohler et al., 1986) and disturbed parent–child relations (Kohler and Didier, 1974). Other studies (Seagull and Scheurer, 1986) report that children of low-functioning parents often present as depressed with their schools, continuously registering concerns over their intellectual and social functioning.

Conversely, there is some evidence that very 'bright' children born to parents with ID who are intellectually more capable than their parents (IQ in excess of 115) may be vulnerable to psychiatric

disturbance over time (O'Neil, 1985). Such children frequently present challenges to their parents as they question their parents' authority, override their decision-making and take over responsibility for their siblings. In one Swedish study that conducted a retrospective analysis of 41 offspring from 15 mothers with ID (Gillberg and Geijer-Karlsson, 1983), it was reported that 58 per cent of the children had required psychiatric services.

It is worth noting that across the general population, highly intelligent children who are labeled 'gifted' are vulnerable to emotional problems, regardless of their parent's status, ID or otherwise. Head banging (in small children), and insomnia and antisocial behaviours are commonly reported amongst older brighter children (Freeman, 2001). It appears that 'the mantle of giftedness lain on young shoulders can have serious repercussions' – many children fearing that they might be 'found out' and exposed as being of only average intelligence (Freeman, 2001).

Variations Across Social Class, Culture and Other Relevant Variables

Removal of children into public care is reported as being as high as 50 per cent for many families receiving services (Whitman et al., 1987; Ray et al., 1994). Some of the predictive factors cited in these studies relate to social class, culture and other variables. For example, the home environment and family variables have been identified as predictive of level of a child's development when other variables were controlled (Feldman et al., 1985). Nevertheless, few studies have attempted to separate out social class and cultural variables without encountering a number of difficulties.

Current Understanding of the Topic

Depending on how the above research is viewed, it can paint a picture of doom and gloom for many children raised by parents with ID. Some of the research outcomes and the statistics can shock and fuel pejorative opinions as to whether agencies should be spending valuable resources in supporting these families. Other research findings create optimism, providing evidence of positive improvements and changes in parents' abilities following intensive education and support. Also, children of parents with ID have expressed many positives about their childhood experiences (Faureholm, 1995). They love their parents and understand some of their difficulties with parenting. Family life is often perceived by these children to be 'unexceptional' when compared to the other children living within the same environment and community as themselves. Overall, longitudinal research is required to provide further understanding to the situation.

PARENTAL PRACTICES

This section intensifies its examination of parents with intellectual disabilities, their practice, problems and capacity for change. Early research identified that the parenting of mothers with ID could be unpredictable and often affected by extraneous variables including marital harmony between couples, impoverishment, numbers of children in the family and the presence of problems such as alcoholism or emotional disturbance (Mickelson, 1947, 1949). This situation remains the same today, with many families reported as living in the poorest housing stock available in the public sector (home ownership being a rare occurrence). The majority of parents with ID receive state benefits (unemployment is high) and are often described as having complex needs and requiring the support of multiple statutory agencies (Whitman and Accardo, 1990; Feldman, 1994). However, the literature in this area is guarded against drawing conclusions about the quality of life for the children of these parents based solely on their parents' low IQ. This section will investigate the influence of low intelligence or deficits in adaptive behaviour on parental competency, as distinct from other socio-economic, cultural factors that are commonly reported as being causal to many of their parenting difficulties.

Factors Affecting Parenting Competency

The heterogeneity of this parent population in terms of their competencies, difficulties and ability to look after their children, is well documented (New York State Commission on Quality of Care, 1993). Empirical research on this topic has striven to identify critical determinants or factors that might explain variations in parenting practice of those with ID, as distinct from the general parenting population. Poverty, cultural issues and prejudicial treatment by the courts have been highlighted by researchers as confounding variables in studies that report on the competency of parents with ID.

There is a paucity of research on the issue of social class, apart from projects that have controlled for poverty. It is widely reported across studies that parents with ID need family support benefits because of low income (Garber, 1988; McGaw, 1994; Feldman, 1997). It is infrequently reported otherwise. Denmark is the exception, where the majority of parents benefit from good housing and economic subsidies. However, even here it appears that more than 25 per cent of children of parents with ID are placed away from home between the ages of 0 and 11 years (Faureholm, 1996).

Elsewhere, income (or the lack of it) has been the main measure distinguishing between social classes across parenting groups with or without ID. When studies control for poverty, they report that the homes of mothers with IQs less than 75 are less stimulating as learning environments for their children than a low-income comparison group of parents with IQs of 85 or over (Keltner, 1994). Other evidence suggests that being raised by a mother with ID can have detrimental effects on child development that cannot be attributed to poverty alone (Feldman and Walton-Allen, 1997).

In addition to poverty, social support has also been identified as critical to child outcomes in families from low socio-economic (SES) backgrounds across the general parenting population (Bee et al., 1986) and in families of parents without ID who are raising children with disabilities (Dunst et al., 1986). Similarly, the level of the mother's social isolation and the quality of family/neighbourhood support seem to be important factors and predictors of parenting competency of ID adults (Llewellyn et al., 1999).

Closely associated with poor support are the problems of poor-quality housing available to parents on low incomes, the communities in which they are placed and the transitory lifestyles that result from dissatisfaction with their circumstances. In Belgium, one study identified that very few ID parents owned their own house, when compared to 70 per cent of the total Flemish population of homeowners (Van Hove and Broekaert, 1995). About one-third of such parents were living in 'community houses' (small group homes); about one-fifth were renting a house from a welfare renting society or housing association; and one-third were renting a house from the private sector. Researchers have expressed concerns about the mobility of this parent population (one in three moving at least twice in five years), which results in poor social integration within the community and a lack of permanency in their lives and the lives of their children, with all the additional stress of new adaptations.

These findings confirm previous findings of a survey conducted in the USA, which identified

421 parents with ID within a community, many of whom were transitory and highly mobile, moving from one area to the next (Whitman et al., 1987). Poor identification of families in need and a lack of networking across services for these families was the main reason why many of them appeared to 'fall through the services net'. Twenty-five per cent of over 1000 children were removed from their parent's care. Shortcomings in service provision for these families contributed significantly to the high removal rate of the children.

Further research has identified that the presence of social support may be insufficient by itself as a predictor of coping and competence for parents with ID (Tucker and Johnson, 1989). Support that promotes childcare-taking competence and that which inhibits competence can be identified and is distinguishable. However, identifying and controlling for multiple environmental, societal and familial variables in studies involving populations of needy, vulnerable adults and their children is fraught with difficulties, especially when the statutory agencies are involved with families. Some retrospective studies have attempted to gain understanding of the critical variables involved in the removal of children from parents with ID, using court records to assist them in this analysis.

Instead of bringing clarity to this analysis, many studies show that courts display prejudicial treatment in forming judgments regarding parental competency, and there is evidence that they have perpetuated the administrative tendency to remove children from the care of their parents on the basis of their ID. In one Australian study, the characteristics of 12 families were examined retrospectively, where it was known that the mother was diagnosed as having an ID (Glaun and Brown, 1999). All families were subject to child protection applications (going through the Children's Court Clinic in Australia) over an 18-month period. The purpose was to demarcate and isolate variables that may have contributed to the breakdown in care. In most instances, neglect rather than abuse was being alleged. The findings revealed a high prevalence of co-morbidity across this group of mothers, including medical disorder, psychiatric histories and drug use. Also, it was reported that during the project many parents disclosed histories of deprivation, neglect or sexual abuse in their own childhood. Fathers were infrequently involved in the parenting because of their intermittent absences from the home, and poor competencies resulting from health or intellectual problems of their own. The group of children appeared to be at high risk of developmental delays and learning

difficulties. Glaun and Brown (1999) concluded that the 'cumulative weight of stressful emotional, physical and social factors in combination with limited intellectual resources, precipitated a crisis in childcare'. Delineating and controlling for each of these factors was difficult, as has been the general experience of other researchers.

In another study, a review was conducted on all care and protection cases ($n = 407$) that were finalized in a Children's Courts in New South Wales, Australia, over a 9-month period (McConnell et al., 2000). The authors reported that almost one-third of all cases involved parents with a disability. Their work shows that parents with disabilities (including those with a psychiatric diagnosis) are overly represented in care and protection proceedings due to prejudicial treatment by the judiciary. They cite three instances for supporting this claim:

- Child protection agencies and courts intervene and remove children even though no evidence of maltreatment is present and even when evidence of neglect is not substantiated.
- Environmental, social and cultural factors may be the cause of parental incompetence, rather than the parent's disability. Poverty, low self-esteem, social isolation, poor housing, harassment and lack of appropriate services are contributory factors or even the etiology of many of their difficulties.
- Children are removed, in the absence of remedial support services. This presumes that parents are innately inadequate and their parenting deficiencies are irremediable.

In the extensive analysis of the assessment and judicial process that these families endured, the study is critical of the 'diagnostic-prognostic rationality' used by the courts and their reliance on 'expert opinion' adequately to explain parenting deficiencies or a prediction of parenting potential. It appears probable that courts wrongly attribute the parenting deficiencies to the disability itself, rather than from social factors that could be remedied.

Similarly, one American study that examined the court records of 206 seriously abused or neglected children and their families, reported that over half of the group comprised parents diagnosed as having low intelligence or an emotional disorder, with a sub-sample of substance abusers (Taylor et al., 1991). However, there was no difference between this parent group regarding mistreatment, higher predicted risk for continued mistreatment, or greater likelihood of permanent removal of the child by the court. Low IQ parents revealed significantly less prior court involvement and greater acceptance of court-ordered services. Parents diagnosed with serious emotional disorders were significantly more likely than less disturbed parents to have their children permanently removed, despite findings of no significant differences in risk or compliance factors.

Parental Engagement

The moral and ethical importance of seeking the views of people with intellectual disabilities on matters that involve them is well recognized, with clear differences being reported between the perception of need by the recipient of services and advocates for those services (Walton-Allen and Feldman, 1991; Llewellyn et al., 1998). Evidence shows that workers often feel that mothers need more services than they actually get, while mothers report that they are 'over-serviced' in some areas (e.g. childcare training) and 'under-serviced' in others (e.g. vocational and assertiveness training).

Other research has looked at levels of support for different groups, according to the families' need in areas of childcare, community living, and domestic skills. Significant differences have been found between the perceptions of parents, workers and significant others on the help parents need (Llewellyn et al., 1998). From the parents' perspective, their greatest unmet needs were in the community participation area, specifically with help to explore work options, to know which community services are available and how to access these, and to meet people and make friends. From the service worker's perspective, they perceived more parent needs on almost all items than the needs identified by parents themselves. It is unclear who held the most accurate perception of the parents' needs across these two groups, since there are no external validating criteria.

Regardless of these findings, in general, studies continue to ignore research findings, omitting parental consultation on preferred choice of venue for work, preferred worker, setting and methods of teaching. Services that fail to include parent consultation do so at their peril. Poor uptake of services from families can be costly in terms of the wasted resources, time and motivation of all those involved. Often, poor uptake indicates support that is imposed upon parents, rather than chosen by them. The viewpoints, opinions and influence of family members, neighbours and friends on a family's functioning are additional components that also need to be considered as they can have a detrimental as well as a facilitative effect on families (Tucker and Johnson, 1989; Booth and Booth, 1993).

Critical Aspects of Parental Involvement

Several factors appear to deter parents from accessing the services that they need:

- Anecdotal and clinical evidence suggests that parent who have ID are frequently reluctant to attend education programmes, particularly if these are perceived to be interlinked with care and protection services (Espe-Sherwindt and Kerlin, 1990; New York State Commission on Quality of Care, 1993).
- A history of parental deprivation and abuse in childhood may also be relevant, and impact on the support available to parents from their immediate and extended families. The ambivalent nature of such support has been reported extensively (Tucker and Johnson, 1989; Whitman and Accardo, 1990). Parent profiles often reveal childhood trauma, including alternative family placements in about half of families and documented histories of abuse or neglect in over one-third (Ray et al., 1994).
- Parental involvement, especially for parents with limited social skills, can sometimes be made more difficult because of multiple agency involvement, resulting in 'constant boundary invasion' and conflicting messages (Ziegler, 1989).

An important component of promoting parental involvement rests with the professionals taking time to understand the needs of parents and their children – a need that is forever undergoing change. Parenting competence appears to evolve over time, with new parenting knowledge, skills and practice continuously requiring updating and assimilation, as children's needs change. Parenting assessments appear critical to capturing the range of ability, as well as the specific needs of parents with ID, and their children. However, very few standardized assessments exist for this purpose and there are differences between researchers and service providers as to the preferred approach.

FUNCTIONAL PERSPECTIVE

This places importance on understanding the parents' aptitude and capability to learn (in the optimal learning environment for them) and their application of acquired skills to everyday situations. Often, this will involve measured observations, to determine where in the 'knowledge–skills–practice contingency'

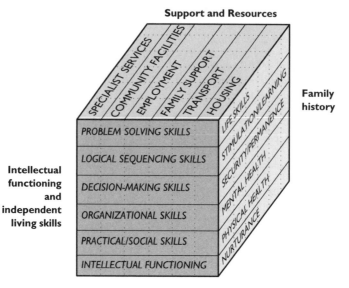

Figure 14.1 *Multi-dimensional parenting skills model*

difficulties may lie or gains have been made (McGaw, 1997, 1998, 2000). Advantages of the functional approach are that it highlights parents' abilities, rather than inabilities, and that it analyses the circumstances in which learning does, or does not, take place (Tymchuk, 1998). Individual, tailor-made programmes are the product of the functional perspective, enabling the specific needs of parents and their families to be catered for.

DIAGNOSTIC PERSPECTIVE

The diagnostic perspective is one frequently adopted by agencies and courts to aid understanding of a client's functioning and eligibility for services. Psychometric and non-psychometric assessments are used which provide standardized data from similar population pools (such as IQ, psychopathy, comprehension skills, working memory). The diagnostic approach can bring clarity to a situation regarding someone's level of functioning. Shortcomings of the diagnostic perspective are that it 'categorizes' and therefore labels vulnerable people. Furthermore, it cannot provide an adequate explanation of parenting deficiencies or a valid prediction of parenting potential (McConnell et al., 2000).

MULTI-DIMENSIONAL PARENTING SKILLS MODEL (MDPSM)

This all-encompassing model emphasizes multi-dimensional influences that directly or indirectly determine or influence the overall ability of parents. Based originally on the Parent Skills Model, which highlighted four specific areas requiring in-depth investigation (child and child development, life skills, family history, and support and

resources), the MDPSM incorporates cognitive functioning as well as environmental and cultural factors as central to any assessment (McGaw, 1993) (Figure 14.1). Using this model, 'mediating variables' can be identified which (a) buffer or exacerbate stress, and (b) are considered important to the coping and adaptation among families affected by ID (Keltner and Ramey, 1992).

Also, personal value judgements and beliefs about what constitutes 'normal' parenting practices and adequate parental competence is explored. The Parental Distribution Curve (Figure 14.2) model is used for this purpose in the training of the *Parent Assessment Manual* (McGaw et al., 1999). It addresses the issue of consensus parenting practices (the majority approach) and whether individual personal experiences (parent models, childhood and parenting experiences), professional specialisms (proactive versus reactive approaches; health, social or educational orientations) and cultural environments (religious, ethnic) result in deviations from the 'norm'. Neither majority nor minority parenting practices are necessarily right or wrong. A range of parenting practices can coexist, although this is not always perceived to be the case at an individual level.

Engaging and Improving Parenting Performance

Recent findings on parent training show that parents with intellectual disability can acquire knowledge and skills in both 'in vitro' and 'in

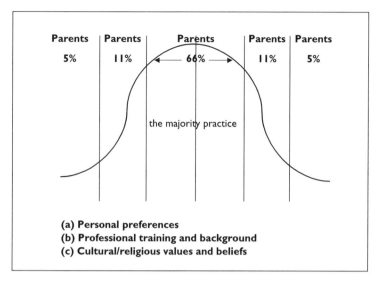

Figure 14.2 *Parental Distribution Curve*

vivo' situations (e.g. Feldman, 1992; Tymchuk and Andron, 1992). Feldman (1994), in a review of 'first-generation' parent training studies for parents with intellectual disability, shows that effective programmes comprise several components. First, interventions need to be matched to parental learning characteristics, for example by using illustrated materials (Feldman et al., 1999). Second, training must be highly concrete, incorporate simple guidelines, and promote generalization (Bakken et al., 1993; Griffiths et al., 1997). Third, staff must be well trained and have a gentle, patient and non-judgemental attitude (Espe-Sherwindt and Kerlin, 1990). Fourth, interventions need to be initially intensive, and then periodic over the long term (Feldman, 1994).

Home-based intervention programmes have been identified as the most effective approach, improving parents' learning in areas such as childcare, language development, health and safety (Whitman and Accardo, 1990; Tymchuk and Andron, 1992; Feldman et al., 1993; Feldman, 1994; McGaw, 2000). Optimal learning occurs when training is provided by highly trained professionals. Group instruction is a common provision for parents with intellectual disabilities as it appears effective and good value for money in terms of costs (Feldman et al., 1986). Self-instructional techniques, involving pictorial parenting manuals, to increase understanding of basic childcare and safety skills have been reported as effective across studies (Feldman and Case, 1999; Feldman et al., 1999).

Benefits of self-instructional approaches include high consumer satisfaction, a reduction in intensive training, and reduced service costs.

A review of ID parent training programmes has identified a group in which cognitive and other disabilities of the parent seem too great to overcome (Ray et al., 1994). This sub-group of parents are able to do particular tasks in isolation, but cannot cope with the accumulation of parenting demands and the organizational skills involved in matching these demands to the needs of the child. Transferring learning to a new or novel situation, multiple tasking and managing schedules were especially difficult for many parents. Outcome data on the generalization of parenting skills following training programmes for parents with intellectual disabilities is crucial, yet sparse (Feldman, 1994).

Shared Care

Unfortunately, the removal of a child from an ID parent is a common event, many of them having travelled this path before. Sadly, the emotional trail that follows the permanent removal of a child remains with a family, almost indefinitely. The agony of the single parent who is left 'childless', the anxiety of siblings who fear their own removal, and the guilt and apportioning of blame to parents for the loss of a child are common. Families require help to avoid the escalation of problems, the permanent removal of a child and, finally, family disintegration.

Looking to the extended family or an alternative 'parent' in the community is an issue that social services and the courts should consider, when parents are not coping well with their tasks. From the court reviews conducted so far, it appears that out-of-home placements could be averted in many instances if adequate resources were available to support parents with ID (McConnell et al., 2000). The courts often consider out-of-home placements, but will only do so if they feel that the alternative is ideal. When a suitable substitute parent cannot be found, the outcome of care proceedings can be uncertain. Shared care can be an option, but its success is dependent on choosing suitable foster-parents who can develop a positive relationship with the natural parents. Flexibility in arrangements appears critical to the success of family transition and reconstitution. Less draconian arrangements regarding post-adoption parent–child contact would allow both parent and child to come to terms with their separation. The majority of parents do not contest court proceedings aimed at establishing that their child is 'in need' as part of the 'care application' (McConnell et al., 2000).

Models such as family group conferencing (FGC) need exploration and possible adaptations to ID parents to find resolutions to problems within the family, especially when there are child protection issues. Family group conferences originated in New Zealand, where they have become part of primary legislation. Elsewhere FGCs are being adopted worldwide in an *ad hoc* fashion. A FGC is a decision-making process that has been developed to assist in family planning for a child's needs, with the assistance of a co-ordinator. In a FGC the child and his or her network form the primary planning group (often the child's immediate family). The need for a FGC is agreed by the family, the professionals and a co-ordinator, the latter two taking on the role of guiding the family in the decision-making process. The family is then left alone in private to agree (a) a plan, (b) a contingency plan and (c) how to review the plan for the child. This scheme seems ripe for adaptation for ID parents, whose (frequently) weak problem-solving skills may be strengthened using this type of family resolution. Experience to date suggests that FGCs can enable families to generate plans that provide a child with appropriate protection and the utilization of resources that professionals may not have been aware of. The model highlights the fact that neither professionals nor families alone can always keep children safe. FCGs may provide a real opportunity for partnership in protection. FCGs might also be useful for identifying acceptable processes and mechanisms of support for ID parents whose children are being taken into permanent care.

Does It Work?

In terms of whether children benefit from the training, guidance and support provided to their parents, the studies indicate that outcomes are variable. There are many successful reports of parent uptake of short-term interventions, with benefits to children, as indicated above. Long-term programmes are less positive, with high parent drop-out rates (averaging 40 per cent annually) (Ray et al., 1994). Up to approximately half the children of ID parents are also identified as being at risk of abuse/neglect, with approximately one-quarter of children being placed in alternative care (Whitman et al., 1989; Ray et al., 1994). Also, the chance of parents keeping their children appears to decrease as their children grow older (Sigurjonsdottir and Traustadottir, 2000). However, in general there are difficulties with the interpretation of these figures as they may be unrepresentative of this parent population as a whole. They do not account for the many parents with ID who are not known to the supporting agencies and who appear to fare well in their parenting – at least judged by not being known to the agencies. Also, most studies report that more could have been done to improve the training, support and engagement of parents. With an absence of longitudinal studies to furnish us with accurate data to supplement our present understanding, outcomes remain uncertain.

AUTHOR'S OVERVIEW

So far, this chapter has reported on the achievements and predicaments facing many parents with ID today. Their determination to achieve parenthood, despite the daily obstacles they face (impoverishment, abusive and neglectful childhood histories, poor housing, intermittent family support and social isolation) is admirable. Clearly, practical and sometimes specialist support is needed to help parents overcome many obstacles which threaten to undermine their parental competency. Lay or commonsense intervention is limited and insufficient for many families with parenting and can be particularly unsuitable for parents who have ID (Gray et al., 2001). Disparity between lay provision and specialist intervention for vulnerable families is an issue requiring careful attention from governments and service providers alike. In the current climate of new funding of parenting education and support, the argument that vulnerable parents may be 'stigmatized' by specialist provision needs to be viewed in the context of research findings which indicate that generic parenting training programmes are, more often than not, inadequate for these families.

Many parents are in the depths of despair by the time they reach our doors in the Special Parenting Service, Cornwall, UK. Often, they describe having been systematically 'processed' by the education system and 'serviced' by the statutory agencies, as well as having had many doubts cast on their ability to parent along the way. Regardless of whether these doubts are conveyed implicitly or explicitly, they undermine parents' confidence in themselves and promote insecurity about the family's future. The literature abounds with references to the poor self-esteem, self-concept and disempowerment of ID parents. Yet, despite the huge odds, I am constantly surprised by a parent's ability to change and to raise their parenting practice when a different approach is taken. Failure to make this change will probably result in their child being taken into care, so the stakes are high. My personal view is that professionals have a moral obligation to optimize parents' chances to improve their parenting skills, regardless of how poor the prognosis or apparent capacity to parent. There is only merit in trying, if this is not detrimental to the well-being of the child. So we need to be guided by our experience, and the research that shows short-term interventions (up to 2–3 years) can be successful for many of these families when they incorporate the following:

(a) User consultation to capture the parent's perceived need for intervention and support. Early identification of parents, including the timing and process by which parents access services, is critical to a programme's success (McGaw, 2000).
(b) Structured specialist assessments using a multi-dimensional model, which may or may not include diagnostic and functional elements.
(c) A holistic approach that is family-centred and all-encompassing. Such an approach will need to balance parents' choices, the primary needs of their children, the requirements of referring agencies and the expectations of the general public altogether. At ground level this will convert to support workers attending to the primary care needs of children at the same time as meeting the emotional, physical health and skill needs

of the parents, all within the context of the social environment in which families live (Ray et al., 1994). Continuity of service provision will be key, enabling parents to build on and retain easy access to the services with which they are already familiar. Equal importance will be placed on assisting parents to become involved with their local community, for the purpose of strengthening their social network and improving their access to neighbourhood support and resources.

Views Regarding Prospects

Many programmes appear to fall short of meeting the basic needs of families headed by ID parents, due to insufficient expertise in this topic and limited funding opportunities. Frequently, when service providers elect for creative options in family support they can find themselves restrained by national remits and professionals pressures to standardize their practice.

Of course, there is a need to establish and maintain quality services by setting benchmarks for professional practice. None the less, uniformity of practice should not result in stultification of creative and imaginative interventions, which might resolve the difficulties facing some parents. Innovation can be a catalyst for change if professionals choose this route. Exploration in areas such as parenting education in schools, supported living arrangements, shared-care and resiliency in children of ID parents are just a few topics that need to be developed in relation to ID parents.

Currently, schools provide personal, social and educational programmes (PSE) to teenagers through awareness raising on topics such as sex, protection against unwanted teenage pregnancies and sexually transmitted diseases. A golden opportunity exists to also include parenting within this curriculum, not only to benefit the general teenage population but also adolescents who might have special needs. Research indicates that the majority of teenagers have expectations of having and raising children when they become adults – this expectation is also held by adolescents with learning difficulties.

At the same time, many ID parents report on the inadequacies of their school education and how ill-prepared they felt for parenting. PSE programmes need to teach adolescents about the roles and responsibilities of parenthood and the skills required to do the job, including how to run a home, maintain a property, develop leisure activities (to share with their children), manage a job, access services (housing associations, crèche facilities, schools, DSS, parenting services), drive a car (so that they can transport their children around), and use financial services (mortgages, bank accounts, investments). Ultimately, these skills are best taught prior to having a family rather than in parallel, when the children's needs are imminent and there will be a sense of urgency driving any teaching programme.

Housing and supported living options for ID parents is another area requiring development for families who require a range of options to accommodate their changing needs and circumstances. Parents often want community support on an intermittent basis, as and when they need it. All too often they report being 'over-serviced' when they are in crises or 'under-serviced' when they appear to be coping. In general, parenting support is available throughout the UK through schemes such as Sure Start, Parent Line, Home Start and Pippin, but these are often inadequate in meeting the more complex and intensive needs of ID parents and their children. Within the learning disability specialism of both health and social services, support schemes such as Key Ring are good examples of flexible and continuous support that can be provided to adults with intellectual disabilities, at very little cost. This model provides 24-hour support to 10 ID people who live independently in scattered sites around a small community, with a support worker living centrally. Six of these schemes now exist in London and could be extended to parents with intellectual disabilities. However, they would not provide residential accommodation, a 'safe haven' or a teaching environment for families in crises or in transition.

Unfortunately, competing demands on limited resources have resulted in many local authorities closing residential units across the UK, which has narrowed placement opportunities available for ID parents who are not coping in their own home. In the USA, there are many charities who have developed specifically designed accommodation to meet the various and diverse needs of all parents with disabilities. However, in the absence of State funding and a national programme of support, the availability of such accommodation can be tenuous.

Lastly, longitudinal research is needed to identify risk and protective factors in children of ID parents. This will assist statutory agencies and support services in targeting service interventions and identifying children at increased risk of abuse/neglect or developmental delay. To date, the tracking of grown-up children of ID parents once they have been adopted has been problematic. Also, psychometrically robust tools need to be pioneered and standardized on an ID parent population, for general use across medical and healthcare professionals along with resilience- or asset-based prevention and youth development programmes for children of ID parents.

IMPLICATIONS FOR PRACTICE

Government, Societal and Cultural Considerations

Throughout this chapter, family and professional support has featured as a critical factor affecting the parenting competency of adults with learning disabilities. This section draws attention to the current fragmentation of service delivery which directly or indirectly impacts the quality and availability of service support provided to disabled families (Tymchuk, 1999; Goodinge, 2000). Surveys have revealed that disabled parents often become frustrated by disjointed service provision in the absence of a 'corporate approach' (Goodinge, 2000). In the absence of a central policy to integrate services, families with ID are placed at 'heightened health and safety risk status and lowered life satisfaction' (Tymchuk, 1999). Duplication of services, poor communication between agencies, inefficient spending of limited resources and poor specialist knowledge across front-line staff can result in the inappropriate matching of education and support programmes to a family's needs.

Generic Parenting Initiatives

Recommendations from the consultation document, *National Mapping of Family Services in England and Wales* (Henricson et al., 2001) include (a) integrating service arrangements for families at a government level whilst (b) allowing for local flexibility to develop services to meet local need and targeting requirements. Joint commissioning arrangements linked to the development of the 'Children and Families Plan' is viewed as the pathway, enabling this to happen at a local level. This should include universal as well as targeted services – such as for those needed by parents with ID. This useful document looks at creative ways of consolidating and funding services, whilst acknowledging various vulnerable parent populations, such as single and teenage parents, ethnic minority groups, fathers. One of the difficulties facing ID parents, and those of us who work alongside them, is that they appear to represent a minority population of parents, whose identification remains problematic.

At the same time, their numbers increase considerably if we include parents with borderline difficulties.

ID Specialism

The findings of the *Jigsaw of Services* report (Goodinge, 2000) has been particularly useful in guiding the UK Government with regard to the specific needs of parents with ID, which are now outlined in the *Valuing People: A New Strategy for Learning Disability* (Department of Health, 2001). This document sets out the Government's future intentions:

1   Place responsibility on the Director of Social Services to improve working arrangements (under a social care 'Quality Protects' Framework (DOH, 2000a) between children's and adults' teams. The *Jigsaw of Services* Report (Goodinge, 2000) highlighted that amongst the disabled parents as a whole, the children of parents with ID are the most vulnerable group. Service managers and front-line staff need to draw attention to the double-bind of not wishing to draw attention to the more negative aspects of the parenting, whilst needing to raise the profile of families' needs.

2   To make 'Partnership Boards' responsible for ensuring that services are available to support parents with ID at a local level. These Boards will be expected to promote and co-ordinate services for people with ID across specialist and general services, including housing, education, employment and leisure pursuits. Parents should benefit from such improved agency integration. Most importantly, parents will have an opportunity to become involved with these local partnerships boards and to represent themselves and other parents, if they so wish.

3   Staff training on the assessment of parents with ID, with a new adaptation of the *Assessment Framework (2000)* (DOH, 2000b), is being developed. This is a particularly important initiative since assessment of parenting skills is often undertaken by staff who do not have the necessary skills, whether from social services or health. The staff often still feel under-confident for working with parents with ID, even following training.

4   Collaboration between various parent support programmes and national policy organizations (such as the National Family and Parenting Institute in the UK) is necessary to ensure that the needs of parents with ID are recognized within the Government's wider initiatives to improve parenting and family support.

Sector Organization

The aim of government or macro-level initiatives will be to create opportunities for positive organizational changes at the operational level. One of the vehicles for change will be driven, in the UK, by the Disability Rights Commission Act (DRCA) which, apart from other important objectives, includes advising the public sector and businesses on best practice, which is based on user experiences and consultations. Another consideration is the research findings that reflect the experience of many service providers in the past.

Generic or Specialist Services

It is unclear whether generic or specialist services should be delivering support to parents with ID. Generally, surveys indicate that the majority of service provision is generic within the UK, with a scatter of professionals working across the statutory agencies within the ID sector, community healthcare trusts and social service teams (children or adult) (McGaw, 2000). At the same time, voluntary sector provision (St Michael's Fellowship, London; PALS, Birmingham; Respond, London) is diverse and on the increase, ranging from counselling and psychotherapy to a walk-in service providing practical support to families headed by a parent with ID. Guidance from the *Valuing People* document suggests that statutory specialist services will need to adopt a holistic approach in service delivery, and share their expertise with mainstream service providers through consultation and training. Voluntary sector provision may develop further, with funding becoming available to them through the ID Development Fund, or through partnership boards locally.

Supporting People

The need to support families in the UK is highlighted in the Supporting People framework, which was implemented in April 2003. This new policy aims to bring together resources under a new grant to provide greater flexibility to local authorities, to produce improved integration of planning and commissioning of support services, and to make an impact on the lives of parents with ID. This will open up many opportunities for the individual needs of families to be met at a service level. As has already been highlighted by the research, living arrangements appear to be a significant factor affecting parents' engagement with services, with distinctions made between different support networks (Llewellyn et al., 1999). An extensive review of services by the New York State Commission in 1993 drew the following conclusions:

1 Parents who have ID and who receive more formal support services and/or who have greater informal supports from families and friends are better able to meet basic parenting expectations.
2 Services that successfully help parents to engage in and commit to services, whilst strengthening the informal support of family and friends, can make a substantial positive difference in ensuring the well-being of both the children and the parents.
3 Access to early intervention preschool programmes for young children and supportive housing is particularly critical for parents who have ID. Service access agreements with local providers offering these services are essential to programmes that serve these families.
4 Parents with ID require life-long services to assist them in meeting the challenges of their children as they become older. Long-term funding needs to be adequate to offer training and in-home support services to families in the long term.
5 Programmes serving parents with learning disabilities need strong risk-management procedures to ensure that children are not neglected or abused and that they receive the proper nurturance, nutrition and medical care for normal physical, emotional and cognitive development.
6 Programmes serving parents with ID require professional supervisory staff skilled and experienced in working with parents with cognitive limitations who can assure proper training, supervision, and guidance for frontline staff helping the parents. Without this expertise, parenting and child preventive programmes are at risk of misunderstanding and/or overlooking the critical service needs of the parents and children.

Individual Level

There are many difficulties encountered when working with parents with ID. Progress can be made when we adopt a gentle approach, show respect to the families that we work with, and place importance on being flexible and creative about what we offer. The following pointers may help:

THE DOS OF WORKING WITH PARENTS WITH INTELLECTUAL DISABILITIES

- Take time to ask and listen to what parents want.
- Build on and emphasize parents' strengths rather than their weaknesses.
- Engage parents early, before child protection becomes an issue.
- Deliver services at the appropriate level of parents' understanding.
- Educate parents in child development at various stages of development.
- Help parents to provide structure, predictability and routine in their child's day.
- Teach parents to recognize and protect their child from abuse and neglect.
- Educate and support parents on how to react to the challenges of adolescence.
- Help parents to develop, facilitate and promote their informal support systems.
- Help parents to access mainstream services.
- Work with parents across multiple settings (home, centres, residential, foster-homes) to promote generalization and maintenance of parenting skills.
- Provide voluntary advocacy services that can offer practical and emotional support.

THE DON'TS OF WORKING WITH PARENTS WITH INTELLECTUAL DISABILITIES

- Do not guess at a parent's capacity to learn.
- Do not assume that parents can read, write, budget and cope without assistance.
- Do not make parents responsible for the failure of your teaching programme.
- Do not assume poor parent motivation. Disengagement with services may result from poor staff attitudes, environmental stresses or lack of emotional or practical support.
- Do not over-assess, over-service or overwhelm parents or their children.
- Do not underestimate, under-serve or undervalue parents or their children.
- Do not label, patronize or stigmatize.
- Do not assume quick fixes and miracle cures. Involvement can be long term.

NOTES

1 The Disability Discrimination Act (1995) UK legislates that it is unlawful for a service provider to refuse unjustifiably to provide a service to a disabled person on the same terms as available to other people.
2 The enactment of the Human Rights Act (1998) has meant that for the first time British courts must consider and decide human rights issues.

3 The Children Act 1989 (UK) requires local authorities to provide services to safeguard and promote the welfare of children as far as possible within their own families (DOH, 1990). This Act specifies that children should not necessarily be identified as in need because one or both parents is disabled. Conversely, it guides that the provision of services to a disabled parent may safeguard the welfare of the child sufficiently to enable the parent to continue looking after him or her at home.

4 The human rights of children and the standards to which all governments must aspire in realizing these rights for all children are espoused in one international human rights treaty, the Convention on the Rights of Children. As at 2002, this document has been ratified by 191 countries. Only two countries have not ratified: the United States which has signalled its intention to ratify by formally signing the Convention, and Somalia.

5 The Jigsaw of Services Report (Goodinge, 2000) was commissioned by the Department of Health (UK) to provide guidance during the government's development of a family policy.

6 The *Valuing People: A New Strategy for Learning Disability for the 21st Century* (2001) White Paper specified the UK Government's intentions to improve the life chances of people with learning disabilities through changes and better collaboration across public services and the voluntary sector.

REFERENCES

AAMR (1992) *Mental Retardation: Definitions, Classification and Systems of Support,* 9th edition. Washington, DC: American Association on Mental Retardation.

Accardo, P. and Whitman, B. (1989) Factors influencing child abuse/neglect in children of mentally retarded parents. *Paediatric Research,* 25(95) Abstract 556.

Accardo, P. and Whitman, B. (1990) Children of mentally retarded parents. *American Journal of Diseases of Children,* 144, 69–70.

Allen, R.E. and Oliver, J.M. (1982) The effects of child maltreatment on language development. *Child Abuse and Neglect,* 6, 299–305.

Australian Institute of Health & Welfare (1997) The definition and prevalence of intellectual disability in Australia. AIHW Catalogue Number DIS 2: Canberra.

Bakken, J., Miltenberger, R.G. and Schauss, S. (1993). Teaching parents with mental retardation: knowledge versus skills. *American Journal on Mental Retardation,* 97(4), 405–17.

Bambrick, M. and Roberts, G. (1990) Historical and current trends in sterilization of people with mental handicap. *British Journal of Clinical and Social Psychiatry,* 7, 145–8.

Barker, L.T. and Maralani, V. (1997) *Challenges and Strategies of Disabled Parents: Findings from a National Survey of Parents with Disabilities.* Berkeley, CA: Berkeley Planning Associates.

Bebington, A. and Miles, J. (1989) The background of children who enter local authority care. *The British Journal of Social Work,* 19, 5.

Bee, H.L., Hammond, M., Eyers, S., Barnard, K. and Snyder, C. (1986) The impact of parental life change on the early development of children. *Research in Nursing & Health,* 9, 65–74.

Booth, T. and Booth, W. (1993) Family Undoing. *British Journal of Learning Disabilities,* 21(4), 137–41.

Booth, T. and Booth, W. (1997) *Exceptional Childhoods, Unexceptional Children.* Family Policy Studies Centre.

Buch v. Buck. 274 U.S. 200 (1927) Quoted by Justice Oliver Wendell Holmes. Cited in Craft, M. and Craft, A. (1979) *Handicapped Married Couples.* London: Routledge & Kegan Paul.

Campbell, F.A. and Ramey, C.T. (1994) Effects of early intervention on intellectual and academic achievement: a follow-up study of children from low income families. *Child Development,* 65, 684–98.

Department of Health (1990) *An Introduction to the Children Act 1989.* London: HMSO.

Department of Health (2000a) Your Guide to Quality Protects. *A Chance to Life,* **November**.

Department of Health (2000b) *Framework for the Assessment of Children in Need and Their Families.* London: HMSO.

Department of Health (2001) *Valuing People: A New Strategy for Learning Disability for the 21st Century.* London: HMSO.

DHSS (1934) *Report of the Departmental Committee on Sterilisation.* London: HMSO.

Dodd, B. and Leahy, J. (1989) Phonological disorders and mental handicap. In Beveridge, M., Leuder, I. and Conti-Ramsden, C. (eds) *Language and Communication in Mentally Handicapped People.* London: Chapman Hall.

Dowdney, L. and Skuse, D. (1993) Parenting provided by adults with mental retardation. *Journal of Child Psychology and Psychiatry,* 34, 25–47.

DSM–IV (1994) *Diagnostic and Statistical Manual of Mental Disorders,* 4th edition. Washington, DC: American Psychiatric Association.

Dunst, C.J., Trivette, C.M. and Cross, A.H. (1986) Mediating influences of social support: personal, family, and child outcomes. *American Journal on Mental Deficiency,* 90, 403–17.

Dyer, C. (1987) Consent and the mentally handicapped. *British Medical Journal,* 295, 257–8.

Edmonds, J. (2000) On being a mother: a positive identity in the face of adversity. *Clinical Psychology Forum,* 137, 21–5.

Espe-Sherwindt, M. and Kerlin, S. (1990) Early intervention with parents with mental retardation: do we empower or impair? *Infants and Young Children,* 2(4), 21–8.

Faureholm, J. (1995) *Families of Parents with (ID).* National Danish School of Social Work, Denmark.

Faureholm, J. (1996) From lifetime client to fellow citizen. Paper presented at the Parenting with Intellectual Disability Conference, September 1996. Danish Ministry of Social Affairs, Denmark.

Feldman, M. (1992) Teaching child-care skills to mothers with developmental disabilities. *Journal of Applied Behavior Analysis,* 25, 205–15.

Feldman, M.A. (1994) Parenting education for parents with intellectual disabilities: a review of outcome studies. *Research in Developmental Disabilities*, **15**(4), 299–332.

Feldman, M.A. (1997) Parents with intellectual disabilities: implications and interventions. In Lutzker, J. (ed.) *Child Abuse: A Handbook of Theory, Research and Treatment*. New York: Plenum, pp. 401–19.

Feldman, M.A. (1998) Preventing child neglect: childcare training for parents with intellectual disabilities. *Informing Young Children*, **11**(2), 1–11.

Feldman, M.A. and Case, L. (1993) Effectiveness of home-based early intervention on the language development of children of mothers with mental retardation. *Research in Developmental Disabilities*, **14**, 387–408.

Feldman, M.A. and Case, L. (1999) Teaching child-care and safety skills to parents with intellectual disabilities through self-learning. *Journal of Intellectual & Developmental Disability*, **24**(1), 27–44.

Feldman, M.A. and Walton-Allen, N. (1997) Effects of maternal mental retardation and poverty on intellectual, academic, and behavioral status of school-age children. *American Journal on Mental Retardation*, **101**(4), 352–64.

Feldman, M.A., Case, L., Towns, F. and Betel, J. (1985) Parent education project I: the development and nurturance of children of mentally retarded parents. *American Journal of Mental Deficiency*, **90**, 253–8.

Feldman, M.A., Towns, F., Betel, J., Case, L., Rincover, A. and Rubino, C.A. (1986) Parent education project II: increasing stimulating interactions of developmentally handicapped mothers. *Journal of Applied Behavior Analysis*, **19**, 23–7.

Feldman, M.A., Case, L., Rincover, A., Towns, F. and Betel, J. (1989) Parent education project III: increasing affection and responsivity in developmentally handicapped mothers: component analysis, generalization, and effects on child language. *Journal of Applied Behavior Analysis*, **22**, 211–22.

Feldman, M.A., Case, L. and Sparks, B. (1992) Effectiveness of a child-care training program for parents at-risk for child neglect. *Canadian Journal of Behavioural Science*, **24**, 14–28.

Feldman, M.A., Sparks, B. and Case, L. (1993) Effectiveness of home-based early intervention on the language development of children of mothers with mental retardation. *Research Development Disability*, **14**, 387–408.

Feldman, M.A., Garrick, M. and Case, L. (1997) The effects of parent training on weight gain of non-organic-failure-to-thrive children of parents with intellectual disabilities. *Journal on Developmental Disabilities*, **5**(1), 47–61.

Feldman, M.A., Ducharme, J.M. and Case, L. (1999) Using self-instructional pictorial manuals to teach child-care skills to mothers with intellectual disabilities. *Behavior Modification*, **23**(3), 480–97.

Feldman, M.A., Hancock, B.A., Rielly, N., Minnes, P. and Cairns, C. (2000) Behavior problems in young child with or at risk for developmental delay. *Journal of Child & Family Studies*, **2**, 247–61.

Field, M.A. and Sanchez, V.A. (1999) *Equal Treatment for People with Mental Retardation*. Cambridge, MA: Harvard University Press.

Freeman, J. (2001) *Gifted Children Grown Up*. London: David Fulton.

Freeney, M., Cook, R., Hale, B. and Duckworth, S. (1999) Working in Partnership to Implement Section 21 of the Disability Discrimination Act 1995 Across the National Health Service. London: Department of Health.

Garber, H.L. (1988) *The Milwaukee Project. Preventing Mental Retardation in Children at Risk*. Washington, DC: American Association on Mental Retardation.

Gillberg, C. and Geijer-Karlsson, M. (1983) Children born to mentally retarded women: a 1–21 year follow-up study of 41 cases. *Psychological Medicine*, **13**, 891–4.

Glaun, D.E. and Brown, P.F. (1999) Motherhood, intellectual disability and child protection: characteristics of a court sample. *Journal of Intellectual & Developmental Disability*, **24**(1), 95–105.

Goodinge, S. (2000) A Jigsaw of Services, inspection of services to support disabled adults in their parenting role. London: Department of Health.

Gray, J., Spurway, P. and McClatchey, M. (2001) Lay therapy intervention with families at risk for parenting difficulties: The Kempe Community Caring Program. *Child Abuse & Neglect*, **25**, 641–55.

Griffiths, D., Feldman, M.A. and Tough, S. (1997) Programming generalization of social skills in adults with developmental disabilities: effects on generalization and social validity. *Behavior Therapy*, **28**, 253–69.

Henricson, C., Katz, I., Mesie, J., Sandison, M. and Tunstill, J. (2001) *National Mapping of Family Services in England and Wales – A Consultation Document*. National Family & Parenting Institute.

Holburn, S., Perkins, T. and Vietze, P. (2000) The Parent with Mental Retardation: A Review of the Research. *The International Review of Research in Mental Retardation*, **April**.

Keltner, B. (1994) Home environments of mothers with mental retardation. *Mental Retardation*, **32**, 123–7.

Keltner, B. and Ramey, S.L. (1992) The Family. *Current Opinion in Psychiatry*, **5**, 638–44.

Keltner, B. and Tymchuk, A. (1992) Reaching out to mothers with mental retardation. *American Journal of Maternal Child Nursing*, **17**, 136–40.

Kohler, C. and Didier, P. (1974) Reflections on the problems posed by children of mentally handicapped parents. *Revue de Neuropsychiatrie Infantile et d'Hygiene Mentale de l'Enfance*, **22**, 53–64.

Kohler, C., Brisson, S. and Charassin, R. (1986) An inquiry on the descendants of mentally deficient adults followed since childhood. *Annales Medico-Psychologiques*, **1**, 305.

Langley, H. and Holman, A. (2001) *Mother Knows Best*. London: Values Into Action.

Little, M. and Mount, K. (1999) *Prevention and Early Intervention with Children in Need*. Hampshire, UK: Ashgate.

Llewellyn, G., McConnell, D. and Bye, R. (1998) Perception of service needs by parents with intellectual disability, their significant others and their service works. *Research in Developmental Disabilities*, **19**(3), 245–60.

Llewellyn, G., McConnell, D., Cant, R. and Westbrook, M. (1999) Support network of mothers with an intellectual disability: an exploratory study. *Journal of Intellectual & Developmental Disability*, **24**(1), 7–26.

London Borough of Brent (1985) *A Child In Trust. The Report of the Panel of Inquiry into the Circumstances Surrounding the Death of Jasmine Beckford.*

McConnell, D. and Llewellyn, G. (2000) Disability and discrimination in statutory child protection proceedings. *Disability & Society*, **15**(6), 883–95.

McConnell, D., Llewellyn, G. and Ferronato, L. (2000) *Parents with a Disability and The NSW Children's Court.* Sydney, NSW: University of Sydney.

McCormack, B. (1991) Sexual abuse and learning difficulties (leader). *British Medical Journal*, **303**, 143–4.

McGaw, S. (1993) Identifying the needs of parents with (ID): a review. *Child Abuse Review*, **2**, 101–17.

McGaw, S. (1994) *Raising the Parental Competency of Parents with (ID).* PhD Dissertation, British Lending Library, Boston, Lincs.

McGaw, S. (1997) Practical support for parents with learning disabilities. In O'Hara, N.J. and Sperlinger, A. (eds) *Adults with Learning Disabilities.* John Wiley, pp. 123–38.

McGaw, S. (1998) Working with parents who happen to have intellectual disabilities. In Emerson, E., Hatton, C., Bromley, J. and Caine, A. (eds) *Clinical Psychology and People with Intellectual Disabilities.* Chichester: John Wiley, pp. 193–209.

McGaw, S. (2000) *What Works for Parents with Learning Disabilities.* Ilford, Essex: Barnardo's.

McGaw, S., Beckley, K., Connolly, N. and Ball, K. (1999) *Parenting Assessment Manual.* Cornwall & Isles of Scilly Health Authority, Trecare NHS Trust, Cornwall.

Mickelson, P. (1947) The feebleminded parent: a study of 90 family cases. *Journal of Mental Deficiency*, **51**, 644–53.

Mickelson, P. (1949) Can mentally deficient parents be helped to give their children better care? *American Journal of Mental Deficiency*, **3**, 516–34.

Mirfin-Veitch, B., Bray, A., Williams. S., Clarkson, J. and Belton, A. (1999) Supporting parents with intellectual disabilities. *New Zealand Journal of Disability Studies*, **6**, 60–74.

New York State Commission on Quality of Care (1993) *Serving Parents Who Are Mentally Retarded: A Review of Eight Parenting Programs in New York State.* New York State Developmental Disabilities Planning Council.

O'Neill, A.M. (1985) Normal and bright children of mentally retarded parents: The Huck Finn Syndrome. *Child Psychiatry and Human Development*, **15**, 155–268.

Parish, A. and Newman, T. (1994) Redditch Family Centre Study, Ilford: Barnado's.

Ray, N.K., Rubenstein, H. and Russo, N.J. (1994) Understanding the parents who are mentally retarded: guidelines for family preservation programs. *Child Welfare League of America*, **6**, 725–43.

Reed, E. and Reed, S. (1965) *Mental Retardation: A Family Study.* Philadelphia: W.B. Saunders.

Roy, M. and Roy, A. (1988) Sterilisation for girls and women with mental handicaps: some ethical and moral considerations. *Mental Handicap*, **16**, 97–100.

Scally, B.G. (1973) Marriage and mental handicap: some observations in Northern Ireland. In de la Cruz, F.F. and La Veck, G.D. (eds) *Human Sexuality and the Mentally Retarded.* New York: Brunner/Mazel, pp. 169–85.

Schiefelebusch, R.L. (1972) Language disabilities of cognitively involved children. In Irwin, J.V. and Marge, M. (eds) *Principles of Childhood Language Disabilities.* Appleton-Century-Crofts, New York: pp. 209–34.

Schilling, R., Schinke, P., Blythe, B. and Barth, R. (1982) Child maltreatment and mentally retarded parents: is there a relationship? *Mental Retardation*, **20**, 201–9.

Seagull, E.A. and Scheurer, S.L. (1986). Neglected and abused children of mentally retarded parents. *Child Abuse and Neglect*, **10**, 493–500.

Sigurjonsdottir, H.B. and Traustadottir, R. (2000) Motherhood, family and community life. In Traustadottir, R. and Johnson, K. (eds) *Women with Intellectual Disabilities* London: Jessica Kingsley, pp. 253–71.

Sinason, V. (1992) Therapy. Paper presented at the study day on Abuse of Young People with Learning Difficulties, January 1992, Salford Paediatrics Child Abuse Interest Group.

Taylor, C.G., Norman, D.K., Murphy, J.M., Jellinek, M., Quinn, D., Poitrast, F.G. and Goshko, M. (1991) Diagnosed intellectual and emotional impairment among parents who seriously mistreat their children: prevalence, type, and outcome in a court sample. *Child Abuse Neglect*, **15**, 389–401.

Tucker, M.B. and Johnson, O. (1989) Competence promoting vs. competence inhibiting social support for mentally retarded mothers. *Human Organisation*, **48**(2), 95–107.

Tymchuk, A. (1992a) Predicting adequacy of parenting by people with mental retardation. *Child Abuse & Neglect*, **16**, 165–8.

Tymchuk, A. (1992b) Do mothers with or without mental retardation know what to report when they think their child is ill? *CHC*, **21**, 1.

Tymchuk, A.J. (1998) The importance of matching educational interventions to parent needs in child maltreatment. In Lutzker, J.R. (ed.) *Handbook of Child Abuse Research and Treatment.* New York: Plenum Press, pp. 421–48.

Tymchuk, A.J. (1999) Moving towards integration of services for parents with intellectual disabilities. *Journal of Intellectual & Developmental Disability*, **24**(1), 3–6.

Tymchuk, A. and Andron, I. (1990) Mothers with mental retardation who do or do not abuse or neglect their children. *Child Abuse and Neglect*, **14**, 313–23.

Tymchuk, A. and Andron, L. (1992) Project parenting: child interactional training with mothers who are mentally handicapped. *Mental Handicap Research*, **5**(1).

US Census Bureau (1993) *Survey of Income and Program Participation.* United States.

Van Hove, G. and Broekaert, E. (1995) Independent living of persons with mental retardation in Flanders; a survey of research data. *European Journal on Mental Disability*, **2**(8), 38–46.

Van Hove, G. and Wellens, V. (1995) Ouders met een mentale handicap. Realiteit en begeleiding. *Orthopedagogische Reeks Gent/Special Education*, Ghent, **5**.

Walton-Allen, N. and Feldman, M.A. (1991) Perception of service needs by parents with mental retardation and their workers. *Comprehensive Mental Health Care*, **1**, 137–47.

Wates, M. (2001) Providing supportive services to disabled parents. Towcester: Disabled Parents Network.

Whitman, B. and Accardo, P. (1990) *When a Parent is Mentally Retarded*. Baltimore: Paul Brookes.

Whitman, B.Y., Graves, B. and Accardo, P. (1987) Mentally retarded parents in the community: identification method and needs assessment survey. *American Journal of Mental Deficiency*, **91**(6), 636–8.

Whitman, B., Graves, B. and Accardo, P. (1989) Training in parenting skills for adults with mental retardation. *Social Work*, September, 431–4.

WHO (1992) *ICD-10 Classification of Mental and Behavioural Disorders: Clinical Description and Diagnostic Guidelines*. Geneva: World Health Organisation.

Wolfensberger, W. (1975) *The Origin and Nature of Our Institutional Models*. Syracuse, New York: Human Policy Press.

Ziegler, M. (1989) A parent's perspective: implementing PL 99-457. In Gallagher, J.J., Trohanis, P.L. and Clifford, R.M. (eds) *Policy Implementation and PL 99-457*. Baltimore: Paul H. Brookes, pp. 85–96.

15

Parenting and Antisocial Behavior

Dana K. Smith, Peter G. Sprengelmeyer and
Kevin J. Moore

SUMMARY

In line with recent evidence that the family plays a central role in the development, maintenance, and treatment of antisocial behavior, this chapter will provide an overview of those investigations that have aided in understanding this developmental process. The role of individual child and parent factors, environmental factors, and contextual variables will be discussed in the context of the impact that each has, both individually and collectively, on parenting practices during three broad stages of child development: early childhood, middle childhood, and adolescence.

INTRODUCTION

Over the past 20 years, researchers have made substantial progress in understanding the development and treatment of antisocial behavior. They have identified a predictable developmental course (Patterson et al., 1992), showing that many factors influence the development of antisocial behavior. Although early studies in the development of problem behaviors focused on the isolated influence of unique individual and contextual factors (child, parent, environmental factors) on the development of antisocial behavior, more recent research has examined the contributions and complex interplay among these variables at individual, environmental, and social levels.

Longitudinal studies have been particularly instrumental in providing information on how individual characteristics, the environment, and social interactions all influence the development of antisocial behavior (Elliot et al., 1985; Wolfgang et al., 1987; Farrington, 1990; Patterson, 1992; Cairns and Cairns, 1994). Such studies have also helped to explain the cumulative influence of risk factors on the development of later problem behaviors (Sanson et al., 1991; Shaw et al., 1994; Reid and Eddy, 1997). The wealth of knowledge that these and other studies on the development of antisocial behavior have provided has not only contributed to a better understanding of the complex interplay of various individual and contextual factors that occur during the developmental process, but has also highlighted the central and key role that parenting plays in the development, maintenance, and treatment of antisocial behavior. More recent research has progressed to the point where specific parenting practices have been identified as key variables in the development and treatment of antisocial behavior and delinquency (Loeber and Dishion, 1983; Loeber and Stouthamer-Loeber, 1986; Eddy and Chamberlain, 2000).

EARLY CHILDHOOD

Individual Child Influences

Individual factors as early as infancy have been shown to play a role in the development of anti-social behavior. In particular, difficult temperament (Bates et al., 1985), early attachment problems (Erickson et al., 1985; Lyons-Ruth et al., 1993), and emotion regulation problems (intense inconsolability and irritability) (Thomas et al., 1968; Katz and Gottman, 1991), have been found to be predictive of later behavior problems and delinquency. In addition, parent-reported presence of early behavior problems has been shown to be related to later reports of problem behaviors (Campbell, 1990; Campbell et al., 1994), as well as teacher-reported (Campbell, 1994; Campbell et al., 1994) and observed problem behaviors (Cummings et al., 1989; Shaw et al., 1995), with some studies showing these relations as early as infancy (Richman et al., 1982; Rose et al., 1989; Keenan and Shaw, 1994).

Although these studies suggest a relationship between early individual child characteristics and the later development of problem behaviors, it should be noted that many studies have examined the direct effect of early child characteristics on the development of behavior problems by relying on parental reports of difficulties during infancy (difficult temperament, attachment problems), as well as during later development. Where parental reports of infant difficulties have been studied in conjunction with other methods (teacher reports, observations), results have been mixed (Thomas et al., 1968; Bates et al., 1985; Shaw et al., 2001).

The weak or inconsistent relationship between early temperamental difficulties and later problem behaviors found when additional methods of reporting are utilized may suggest that parents' reports of their child's behavior provide a biased perspective. It is possible that parents who have difficult infants may continue to see their child as 'difficult' as he or she develops (regardless of discrepant reports from others), which may create increased parental frustration, and, over time, may result in irritable parent–child interactions and decreasing frequency of proactive and supportive parenting practices.

Individual Parent Influences

Individual parent factors have also been found to be related to the development of child behavior problems. In particular, familial criminality and parental antisocial behavior have been found to be associated with the development of later child behavior problems (Robins et al., 1975), with some researchers demonstrating this relationship measured as early as age 2 years (Keenan and Shaw, 1994). Parental mental health, especially depressive symptomatology, has also been found to be related to the development of child behavior problems (Zahn-Waxler et al., 1988). In addition to genetic explanations, there are many other possible explanations for the relationship between parental mental health and the development of later child behavior problems. For example, researchers have suggested that depressive symptoms influence parental perceptions of child behavior (Zahn-Waxler et al., 1990) and parenting practices (O'Leary et al., 1999), both of which may, in turn, influence child behavior.

Contextual Influences

Research has shown that contextual factors occurring both within and outside of the home setting during early childhood may be related to the later development of child behavior problems. In particular, it has been suggested that the presence of multiple stressors (low socio-economic status, limited social support, and family adversity) may predict the development of child behavior problems (Rutter et al., 1975). In line with this suggestion, researchers have found that the likelihood of the development of behavior problems increases in accordance with the number of stressors a family experiences (Sanson et al., 1991; Shaw et al., 1994). Support for this hypothesis has been demonstrated in a recent study of 300 low-income, ethnically diverse families, where Shaw et al. (1998) found that family stress measured at 18 and 24 months predicted externalizing behavior problems at 24 and 42 months.

Although there is evidence that individual child, parent, and contextual factors in early childhood are each related to the development of later child behavior problems, these relationships are correlational and do not provide an explanation for the *cause* of antisocial behavior. In fact, there is evidence to suggest that many young children who show problems in one or more areas do not develop later antisocial behavior (Dishion and Patterson, 1997). It is more likely, therefore, that the development of antisocial and other problem behaviors is the result of a dynamic and interactive process between various combinations of variables occurring across individual, social, and environmental contexts. Several researchers have provided evidence of such a dynamic relationship (Martin, 1981; Patterson, 1982; Sroufe, 1983; Egeland and Farber, 1984; Greenberg and Speltz, 1988). In particular, researchers from a variety of perspectives have consistently identified parenting practices and parent–child relations as a central component in the development of antisocial behavior (Loeber and Dishion, 1983; Egeland and Farber, 1984; Lewis et al., 1984; Loeber and Stouthamer-Loeber, 1986; Eddy and Chamberlain, 2000).

Parent–Child Interactions

As research on antisocial behavior has taken a more developmental approach, family processes and contextual variables that interact to influence changes in behavior over time have come to the forefront. This process can be seen as reciprocal and transactional, where parent–child interactions influence parenting practices, which in turn, are simultaneously influenced by environmental and contextual factors – especially to the extent that parenting practices are disrupted. In this light, research that once focused on isolated individual parent and child characteristics has now broadened to include the interaction and reciprocity of these individual characteristics.

Expanding on early studies of temperament that focused solely on the role of the child, Bates (1980) found that difficult temperament influenced the course of later externalizing problem behaviors through the effect it had on care-giver attitudes and behaviors. These findings suggest that temperament in and of itself does not necessarily predict later behavior problems, but does so through an influence on parenting practices.

There is also evidence that how parents think about their children may shape the way in which they interact. For example, Baden and Howe (1992) found that mothers of problem-behavior children were more likely to view their child's misbehavior as 'intentional'. These mothers were also more likely than mothers of non-conduct-disordered children to attribute their child's negative behaviors to stable, global causes outside of their control and to view their own parenting as ineffective. These parents' feelings of blame and helplessness in regard to their child's misbehavior contribute to aversive and withdrawal responses by them, which sets the

stage for coercive parent–child interactions (Baden and Howe, 1992). Other researchers also provide support for an interactive parent–child process. In a study of 277 young children and their families, Nix et al. (1999) showed that mothers' hostile attributions of their children's behavior were predictive of later child behavior problems at school. Similar findings have been shown with regard to parental perception of the child's temperament (Fagot and Gauvain, 1997). A parent's belief that his or her child's behavior or temperament is stable may contribute to expectations for similar intentional or dispositional responses at later points in development. Together these studies suggest that parents' beliefs and interactions with their child may be central and guiding components in the relationship between early child characteristics and later externalizing behavior.

Evidence of this reciprocal shaping process has been demonstrated empirically. For example, Martin (1981) found that maternal non-responsiveness and infant demandingness, as well as the interaction of maternal non-responsiveness and infant demandingness, have been shown to be predictive of non-compliant behavior from the child at 22 months. Additionally, maternal non-responsiveness and infant demandingness were found to predict coercive behavior from the child at 42 months. However, other researchers have found non-significant effects of child behavior on parenting (O'Leary et al., 1999), which suggest that the exact magnitude of individual child and parent contributions to the development of behavior problems is still not well understood.

Parenting and Discipline Practices

As children mature from infancy to toddlerhood, discipline practices and limit-setting behaviors from the parent take on a more central role in parent–child interactions. As parents begin to respond to the increasing curiosity and mobility that toddlers naturally demonstrate, they are called upon to set more frequent limits. Although discipline and other socialization practices take on a more central role in toddlerhood, such practices are not developed in isolation from earlier parent–child interactions, but are built upon and influenced by parental attributions, child temperament, and parent–child interactions experienced during infancy.

Discipline practices examined during toddlerhood have been shown to be related to later child behavior problems. For example, McFayden-Ketchum et al. (1996) found that mother–child coercion and non-affection measured in preschool has been shown to be predictive of levels of aggression-disruption for boys and girls at school entry. Additionally, it has been found that children who experienced high levels of coercion (reactive, negative maternal control) at home were rated by teachers and peers as showing high levels of aggression-disruption at school. Those who experienced high levels of affection (positive maternal interest) at home showed decreased aggressive-disruption at school.

The protective role of positive parenting has been demonstrated in other studies as well. For instance, Pettit et al. (1997) found that supportive parenting (mother-to-child warmth, proactive teaching, reasoned discipline, and positive involvement) measured at the pre-kindergarten stage is predictive of adjustment (low behavior problems, social skills, and academic performance) seven years later. Another study found proactive parenting (supportive presence, clear instruction, and limit-setting) measured in preschool to be predictive of fewer behavioral problems at two- and four-year follow-ups (Denham et al., 2000).

The protective role that proactive and supportive parenting during early childhood serves in the development of behavior problems may extend further than immediate parent–child interactions. For example, some studies have shown that positive parenting practices can lessen or mediate the effects of some environmental and contextual factors. In a diverse sample of 376 children and their mothers, Dyer Harnish et al. (1995) found that the quality of mother–child interactions partially mediated the relation between maternal depressive symptomatology and child behavior problems, even when the effects of socio-economic status on both variables was taken into account. Pettit et al. (1997) found similar effects for family adversity, where supportive parenting practices during early childhood were found to lessen the effects of family adversity on later child behavior problems. Most recently, in their longitudinal study of 310 low-income infants, Shaw et al. (2001) found that the care-giving environment during infancy served as a protective factor in the development of externalizing disorders at school entry.

Parenting has also been found to moderate early individual child characteristics (difficult temperament, impulsivity, unmanageability) and the development of later externalizing behaviors (Bates et al., 1998; Rothbart and Bates, 1998). Although the relationship between individual,

contextual, and social factors in the development of behavior problems is clearly complex, it appears to be the consensus that parenting practices and the parent–child relationship during early childhood have a powerful role in guiding the developmental course of antisocial and prosocial behavior.

MIDDLE CHILDHOOD

Children who are at risk for persistent antisocial behavior by middle childhood (5–11 years old) have already experienced initial, but powerful, social-interactional learning in the family setting. As suggested in the developmental model presented by Reid and Eddy (1997), middle childhood is a time where parenting continues to play a central role in the development of antisocial behavior. During the middle childhood years, parents of antisocial children often demonstrate low involvement with their children, with their children's school (monitoring academic progress), and in monitoring their children's peer interactions. In addition, studies conducted by Patterson and colleagues suggest that these parents also tend to experience increasing difficulty in applying effective discipline and monitoring skills as their children continue to develop (Patterson, 1982; Patterson et al., 1989, 1992).

In the following section, the role that parenting plays in the development and maintenance of antisocial behavior during middle childhood will be discussed. Individual influences and contextual factors that have been shown to be related to the development of behavior problems through their impact on parenting and the family will be examined. In addition, we will present further evidence that the relationship between parenting and antisocial child behavior is part of a complex bi-directional process where parents and children who demonstrate antisocial behavior patterns appear to influence each other in a mutually reinforcing manner (Snyder et al., 1994; Snyder and Patterson, 1995; Stoolmiller, 2001).

Individual Child Influences

Similar to early childhood, individual child characteristics identified during middle childhood (child temperament, emotion regulation, early behavior problems, early maturation in girls) have also been found to be correlated with the later development of antisocial behavior (Olweus, 1980; Lerner et al., 1988). Recent research suggests that individual child characteristics observed during middle childhood are also greatly influenced by complex but observable interactions with parenting and other contextual factors rather than direct effects on antisocial behavior. For example, Hetherington (1991) found that families with early maturing daughters have higher conflict compared to families without early maturing daughters, with single-parent households of early maturing daughters demonstrating the highest conflict of all other family types. In this study, early maturation in girls was also found to be associated with weak mother–child bonds and greater involvement with older peers (a known risk factor for antisocial behavior). Hetherington (1991) also found that families of children with difficult temperaments had higher rates of negative startups, counter-attacks and continuance with their fathers compared to children with easy temperaments. Other researchers have shown similar interactional sequences with mothers and difficult children (Patterson, 1982; Webster-Stratton and Eyberg, 1982).

Individual child behavior demonstrated during middle childhood can influence the behavior of care-takers (Patterson, 1980, 1982, 1985; Scarr and McCartney, 1983; Brunk and Henggeler, 1984; Bell and Chapman, 1986; Lytton, 1990; Rutter et al., 1998). For example, a number of studies have shown that children demonstrating antisocial behavior patterns during middle childhood elicit more negative behavior from their own parents, as well as from other children's parents (Anderson et al., 1986). Parenting behaviors during middle childhood also influence child behavior. For example, in the same study (Anderson et al., 1986), parents of children with conduct problem behaviors have been found to be more negative with other children than mothers of children without conduct problem behaviors. These studies suggest that as children continue to develop, parent–child interactions continue to influence each other in a mutually reinforcing manner.

Parenting and Discipline Practices

Over the past few decades, a consensus has formed on a general developmental model where parenting is associated with the development and maintenance of antisocial behavior (Baumrind, 1967, 1971, 1991; McCord, 1979; Patterson, 1982; Loeber and Dishion, 1983; Laub and Sampson, 1988; Patterson et al., 1992). Several well-designed prospective longitudinal studies (Patterson et al., 1992; Huizinga et al., 1995) have shown that levels of parenting practices starting in early to middle childhood and continuing through pre-adolescence are associated with the reduced probability of delinquent behavior. These parenting practices include appropriate and consistent discipline, supervision, and the development of a positive relationship with the child.

In the programmatic studies of Patterson and his colleagues, parent management practices (discipline practices, monitoring across school, peer, and community settings) have been shown to influence the frequency, intensity, duration, and breadth (new forms) of antisocial behavior (Patterson, 1982; Patterson et al., 1992; Chilcoate et al., 1995). This finding highlights the importance of parental discipline and monitoring during middle childhood and has been replicated in several multi-agent, multi-method, correlational studies (Forgatch, 1991). In her study of three at-risk samples in different settings, Forgatch found that parental discipline and monitoring accounted for at least 30 per cent of the variance in antisocial behavior. Recently, this model has also been supported by several experimental studies where changes in parenting practices (supervision, discipline, positive parent– child relationship) have been shown to produce changes in children's antisocial behavior (Dishion et al., 1992; Forgatch and DeGarmo, 1999, 2000; Eddy and Chamberlain, 2000; Martinez and Forgatch, 2001). In summary, both sophisticated correlational studies and experimental tests (randomized trials) have provided strong evidence that parenting practices and family management skills such as monitoring, problem solving, and discipline are related to levels of antisocial and aggressive behavior in middle childhood.

Major reviews of the literature have consistently found that there is a strong correlation between 'harsh physical discipline' and aggressive-delinquent behavior (Welsh, 1976; Straus, 1991). However, other researchers (Belsky, 1984; Reid, 1986; Simions et al., 1994, 1995; Greenwald et al., 1997; Knutson and Schwartz, 1997; Stoolmiller et al., 1997), provide a somewhat compelling argument that it is not the harsh discipline itself that *causes* antisocial or aggressive behavior. Rather, it is suggested that physical and harsh discipline are part of a larger and more poweful construct of 'inept discipline', where micro-social (moment-by-moment) reinforcement contingencies have a significant relationship to the shaping, maintenance, and escalation of antisocial and aggressive behavior during early and middle childhood (Patterson, 1982; Patterson et al., 1992; Stoolmiller, in press).

The relationship of parental discipline practices (the contingent application of both positive and negative consequences) to children's antisocial behaviors within families has been demonstrated at the micro-social level in a series of studies by Patterson (1973, 1982, 1979a, 1979b), Snyder (1977), and Snyder and Patterson (1986, 1995). These studies strongly suggest that the rate and frequency of negative child behavior observed in families is related to the relative payoffs by parents for these behaviors. For example, in families with young and latency-age (6–10 years) children who demonstrate coercive or aggressive behaviors, children were found to match their relative rates of antisocial behavior (non-compliance) to the relative rates of payoff from others for performing these behaviors. Most often, the main payoff was a negative reinforcement response from the parent. That is, the parent removed an aversive stimulus such as a compliance demand or some other aversive intrusion. It is interesting to note that in the Snyder and Patterson (1995) study, differences were found between behaviors demonstrated by mothers from clinical pairs and mothers from non-clinical pairs. Mothers from non-clinical dyads provided payoffs for pro-social behaviors most often, and mothers from clinical dyads provided payoffs for negative verbal and other types of coercive behavior more often.

Researchers have made progress on the development of a theory for antisocial behavior through the study of contingencies that exist within family homes, using observational methods (Patterson, 1992). These methods have allowed them to account for childhood individual differences in the performance of antisocial behaviors and the relationships of individual differences to the family management practices described above. Although Maccoby (1993) found that a model based exclusively on negative reinforcement was unable to explain individual differences, Snyder and Patterson's (1995) results suggest that a model combining both negative and positive reinforcement patterns can more accurately predict individual childhood differences in the performance of antisocial behavior, than models based on either negative or positive reinforcement alone. That is, pro-social behavior of children in non-referred families worked as well as, or better than, coercion behavior to extinguish aversive behavior from a parent ('aversive intrusions'), whereas in families with children who demonstrate problem behaviors, only the child's coercive behavior worked to end the aversive exchange.

It appears that children who demonstrate antisocial behavior patterns get very little training or reinforcement during early and middle childhood for the performance of pro-social behaviors. So, as antisocial children mature, they are at risk of developing increasingly limited repertoires (cf. Staats, 1993) of pro-social behavior to cope with increasingly complex social environments and situations. Patterson (1982) has also shown that mothers of antisocial boys issue three to four times as many commands, threats, and scoldings as mothers of children who do not display high rates of antisocial behavior. There is some evidence to suggest that these relative rates of reinforcement within families are associated with the cross-setting generalization of antisocial behaviors. For example, Loeber and Dishion (1984) found that boys who are aggressive at home and at school have parents with significantly lower levels of competent parent management practices compared to boys who were aggressive in only one setting.

Parenting and Early-Onset Delinquency

Perhaps what is most important about the parenting model described above is that disrupted and coercive parenting practices have been associated with offspring's early arrest (before the age of 14 years), and early arrest, in turn, has been associated with chronic and violent offending (Patterson et al., 1992; Patterson and Yoerger, 1993; Patterson, 1995; Howell, 1997; Washington State Institute for Public Policy, 1997). For example, in the Oregon Youth Study, more than 76 per cent of the boys arrested before the age of 14 demonstrated chronic offending patterns by age 18 (Patterson, 1995). In addition, Blumstein et al. (1986) presented data from three longitudinal studies of juvenile offenders showing that once a youth had four or more arrests, the probability that the youths would become adult offenders was exceptionally high. Thus, it appears that children with early-onset delinquent behavior are most at risk for life-course persistent offending and antisocial behavior (Moffit, 1993).

Contextual and Familial Influences

Recent investigations (Laub and Sampson, 1988; Forgatch, 1989; Larzalere and Patteron, 1990; Capaldi and Patterson, 1991; Patterson et al., 1992; Bank et al., 1993; Sampson and Laub, 1994) suggest that the effect of contextual factors (poverty, divorce, high crime neighborhoods, stress, parental antisocial behavior and psychopathology) on child behavior is mediated through their disruptive effect on parenting practices and family functioning (parental depressed mood, poor parental discipline and monitoring, marital conflict). For example, parental stress may be correlated with child antisocial behavior primarily because such stress increases marital conflict or disrupts parenting. A recent review of the literature on the development of antisocial behavior by Rutter et al. (1998) suggests that when a significant combination of contextual family variables (teenage parent, antisocial parent, poverty, single-parent status, large family size) and poor parenting practices are present, they are associated with the development of a predictable pattern of developmental problems for children. Rutter et al. (1998) summarize this pattern as follows:

- First, the child's social development is impaired in the areas of relationships and social problem-solving.
- Second, the child has learned from his or her interactions with parents and other adults that aggressive behavior pays off.
- Third, the child has developed less social bonding, which then leads to low levels of social constraint for negative behaviors.
- Finally, inadequate supervision practices increase the probability that the child will become associated with a delinquent peer group and be placed in high-risk situations.

In a more specific example of this process, Hetherington (1991), using six-year follow-up data from the Virginia Longitudinal Study of Divorce and Remarriage, found that mothers in two-parent households were more vigilant in monitoring where their children were, who they were with, and what they were doing compared to mothers who were divorced. In addition, children with difficult temperaments appeared to be even more difficult to monitor and discipline for mothers who were divorced.

In this same study, boys from the divorced homes spent less time under adult supervision, both at home and in settings with other adults, and more time with peers or alone. Hetherington (1991) also found that mothers from two-parent families gave less controlling instructions, at lower rates, followed through more often, and were more successful in their attempts to control their sons compared to mothers who were divorced. In terms of parent–child interactions, mothers who were divorced were found to initiate negative interactions with their sons twice as often as mothers from two-parent families. In addition, if the boys were producing aversive behavior, mothers who were divorced were more likely than mothers from two-parent families to issue a counter-attack, and once these negative interaction patterns were initiated, they lasted significantly longer than they did for dyads of any other family type. Hetherington's study is a good example of how context, individual differences, and parenting can potentially coalesce during important developmental periods to increase the probability of antisocial behavior.

These data on middle childhood provide support for the potential development of 'coercive family interactions'; as children with antisocial behavior and their parents grow increasingly fatigued with each other, they ultimately may find it more reinforcing to be apart. Due to previous disciplinary defeats and frustration at repeated unsuccessful attempts to intervene with their child's negative behaviors, these parents may make fewer and fewer attempts to supervise their child's whereabouts, associations, and activities, resulting in increased risk for involvement in antisocial behaviors.

ADOLESCENCE

While research and treatment for antisocial behavior during early and middle childhood is focused primarily on child and family processes, as these youths become adolescents, the antisocial behaviors in which they engage spread out from the family into the school and community (Patterson et al., 1992; Reid and Eddy, 1997). These young people are also developing repertoires of increasingly dangerous behaviors as they grow physically, intellectually, and emotionally. The US Department of Health and Human Services' (2001) recent report on youth violence notes that illicit violent behavior peaks in the second decade of life, with 12 to 20 per cent of all adolescents engaging in some form of violent antisocial behavior. Part of the explanation for the high rates of adolescent antisocial behavior can be found in the fact that early childhood behavior problems remain relatively stable across time (Olweus, 1979; Cummings et al., 1989) and that additional youths begin antisocial behavior careers during adolescence (late-onset delinquency) without these prior warning signs.

By the time a youth has reached adolescence and young adulthood (12–18 years of age), interactional patterns that lead toward delinquent and antisocial behavior may be firmly entrenched. As these behaviors move out of the home and as the youth grows physically larger, there is increasing pressure for the youth's behaviors to be met with stronger consequences from parents, juvenile justice, and schools. Individual, family, and contextual influences begin to shift during this developmental period from initiating problematic behaviors to creating a social environment that can maintain antisocial behavior throughout the youth's early adult life.

Individual Youth Influences

Adolescence is a period that is typically characterized by a youth's increasing autonomy and involvement in social systems that span many settings (home, school, community, peer group). As adolescents become integrated in multiple social settings, they naturally become involved in interactions with increasing numbers of individuals across contexts, leaving parents to compete with strong socialization influences outside of the family setting. Although individual adolescent characteristics (temperament, behavior problems, intelligence, social competence) have been found to influence the development and maintenance of antisocial behavior, just as with early and middle childhood, it is likely that such individual influences do not act in isolation, but are influenced by the interactions and contexts in which they exist.

Researchers have long identified a relationship between low intelligence and delinquency (Hirschi and Hindelang, 1977; Quay, 1987), as well as a relationship between a verbal and performance intelligence discrepancy and delinquency (Quay, 1987; Walsh et al., 1987). However, researchers have also identified nonsignificant relationships between these and other individual characteristics and delinquency when other variables are taken into account (Dishion et al., 1984; Kendall and Fischler, 1984), suggesting that individual influences probably have their impact on the development and maintenance of antisocial behavior in combination with other social and environmental influences. Recent causal modeling studies (Henggeler, 1991, 1997; Rutter et al., 1998) have provided further clarification of the role that individual adolescent characteristics (low verbal skills, antisocial attitudes, mental health symptoms, hostile attributions) play in concert with environmental and contextual factors to impact the development and maintenance of antisocial behavior.

An example of the complex interplay between individual characteristics and contextual variables in the developmental process of antisocial behavior is the age of onset of delinquency. Capaldi and Patterson (1994) found a progression

in the sophistication of parenting skills in their comparison of non-offenders, early-onset offenders (youths who begin to show elevations in antisocial behavior prior to age 10 years), and late-onset offenders (youths who begin to show elevations in antisocial behaviors in late childhood and early adolescence) from the Oregon Youth Study, where parents of early-onset boys showed the lowest skill levels (supervision and monitoring). In addition, families of early-onset offenders ranked higher on contextual risk factors (low income, social disadvantage, parent unemployment, higher number of family transitions, and parent antisocial behavior) compared to later-onset offenders and non-offenders. Although early-onset offenders appear to be at greatest risk for chronic offending, late-onset youths also appear to be at risk for serious antisocial behavior. For example, in their longitudinal study of over 1500 boys (Pittsburgh Youth Study), Loeber et al. (1998) found that many boys (49 per cent of African-American boys and 72 per cent of Caucasian boys) who were later involved in serious delinquent behavior, had not committed a serious delinquent act by the age of 15. These findings suggest that child and adolescent behavior problems may interact with parenting and contextual variables in the onset and persistence of antisocial behavior. This highlights the importance of examining individual adolescent characteristics in combination with social and contextual factors (Henggeler, 1991, 1997) in order to fully understand the development and maintenance of antisocial behavior.

Parenting Influences

Supervision of the youth's whereabouts and peer associations appears to be a key parenting behavior associated with adolescent antisocial behavior. For example, in a study of the relationship between the amount of unsupervised time in the community, exposure to delinquent peers, and days spent detained in lock-up by boys from Oregon neighborhoods with higher than average rates of juvenile crime, Stoolmiller et al. (2000) found that associations with deviant peers and a greater amount of unsupervised time predicted the number of days spent in lock-up. In addition, the McCords (McCord et al., 1959; McCord, 1979), followed a sample of boys for 20 years and found that parents' poor supervision (along with harsh discipline) predicted their children's convictions for person crimes well into the children's forties. The connection between parental supervision, deviant peer associations, and antisocial behavior has also been demonstrated in intervention studies. For example, Eddy and Chamberlain (2000) found that the effect of treatment (comparisons of treatment foster care to group care) was mediated by the parents' family management skills (supervision, discipline, and a positive relationship with a mentoring adult) and deviant peer associations.

In addition to low levels of parental monitoring, researchers have identified other individual parent factors that appear to affect antisocial behavior in adolescents by affecting the parenting relationship. These factors are similar to those found in early and middle childhood and include the following:

- cognitive variables such as parent attributions of child behavior (Bugental and Shennum, 1984; Stern and Azar, 1998);
- behavioral variables such as parent criminality (Baker and Mednick, 1984; Farrington, 1989);
- emotional factors such as disengagement from or ambivalence about the relationship with the adolescent (Liddle, 1995); and
- parents' psychiatric status (Patterson et al., 1992).

Importantly, many of these parenting variables have been drawn from correlational studies wherein there may be a number of potential relationships between the variables measured. As mentioned early in this chapter, individual parent factors may be related to adolescent behavior as a consequence rather than as a cause. Researchers have found some support for this framing of events. For example, Lytton (1990) found that situational depression in parents decreases as child behavior improves.

Contextual Influences

Factors such as housing, poverty, and substance use in families have long been shown to be associated with adolescent antisocial and criminal behavior. However, as investigations have utilized better statistical modeling, it has become clear that the effects of these variables are not causal. Parenting behavior appears to drive the relationship between these contextual variables and negative adolescent behavior, and as discussed earlier, parenting practices such as supervision and discipline have been found to mediate up to 80 per cent of the variance in child behavior and environmental factors such as household overcrowding, father's drunkenness and criminality, and economic dependence (Laub and Sampson, 1988).

'Bonding' with family members is another construct that has been hypothesized to influence the development of antisocial behavior. However, there have been a number of studies that have shown a non-significant relationship between measures of family closeness and adolescent antisocial behavior (Elliott, 1994). Reviews of these studies suggest that types of bonding (bonding to pro-social versus antisocial family members) need to be distinguished before the relationship between bonding and the development of antisocial behavior can be fully understood (Foshee and Bauman, 1992).

As in early and middle childhood, exposure to high levels of marital and family conflict during adolescence appears to increase the risk of later antisocial behavior (McCord, 1979; Farrington, 1989; Elliott, 1994). Similar to research on the development of behavior problems in early childhood (Pettit et al., 1997), the influence of family adversity on the development of antisocial behavior in adolescence also appears to be mediated by parenting behavior (Reid and Eddy, 1997).

Contextual factors outside of the family home also appear to be related to antisocial behavior. For example, community factors such as poverty, low neighborhood attachment and community disorganization, the availability of drugs and firearms, exposure to violence and racial prejudice, laws and norms favorable to violence, and frequent media portrayals of violence have been suggested to contribute to antisocial behavior in adolescents (Brewer et al., 1995; Hawkins et al., 2000). These community factors may work together to create neighborhoods with elevated risk for individual adolescents to become involved in antisocial behavior. For example, poorer neighborhoods may have higher rates of street crime (Weis, 1986), and areas with higher crime rates may be more tolerant of crime in general and more preoccupied with other difficulties (Garbarino and Sherman, 1980). In addition, these factors may be linked to a lack of parental supervision for the adolescents who live in these areas (Hogan and Kitagawa, 1985). Taken together, these studies suggest that factors in the community may be related to antisocial behavior, both directly as well as through linkages with parenting behavior.

Interestingly, seemingly positive community factors may escalate antisocial behavior as an unintended side-effect. For example, in an urban center with a generally high poverty rate, Figueira-McDonough (1993) found that areas with lower ratios of males to females had higher rates of employment for males and lower rates of delinquency. However, areas with higher rates of employment for both males and females had higher rates of delinquency, possibly because there were lower rates of supervision due to adults being at work during the day. These findings highlight the complexity of predicting the relationship between employment, gender ratios, parenting, and adolescent behaviors.

School Involvement

As noted earlier in this chapter, youths involved in coercive processes tend to carry such interactional patterns from their homes into the school setting. These aggressive patterns serve to alienate the youths from teachers and pro-social peers. By the time these youths reach adolescence, they often routinely experience a relatively hostile school environment. Understandably, such youths receive less positive reinforcement and are less interested in the school environment (Catalano and Hawkins, 1996). At this critical point, many such youths drop out of school, and those who do not drop out are faced with frequent discipline problems, suspensions, and academic failure (Elliott et al., 1989). Although lack of interest in school has been shown to be related to delinquent behavior (Elliott and Voss, 1974), it should also be noted that a youth's relationship with school may also be bi-directional; school failure might contribute to delinquent behavior and/or delinquent behavior may contribute to school failure (McCord, 1993).

While the association between school difficulties and antisocial behavior has a long history, investigators have only recently begun to apply more sophisticated statistical approaches (causal modeling) to this domain. Findings from these analyses suggest that parenting, school difficulties, and relationships with negative peers are all associated. As demonstrated in a study by Dishion et al. (1991), academic failure, peer rejection, antisocial behavior, and poor parental monitoring have all been found to contribute significantly to the variance in early involvement with delinquent peers.

Peer Associations

As typical adolescents mature, they tend to spend more time away from the family. For the antisocial adolescent, this can mean additional time associating with deviant peers. By adolescence, peer status and position are relatively fixed, making it difficult for an antisocial adolescent to initiate pro-social peer relationships. What started

as non-compliance at home may now have become established associations with delinquent peers and substance use, which in turn appear to be related to increased probability of involvement in property and person-to-person crimes (Patterson et al., 2000). Hawkins et al. (2000) have demonstrated the increasingly important role that peers play in adolescent antisocial behavior. In a meta-analysis, they demonstrated that peer associations showed only a mild to moderate ability to predict antisocial behavior for children, aged 6 to 11 years old; for these children, prior offenses and family factors were far stronger predictors of antisocial behavior. For children between the ages of 12 and 14, however, the key predictor for antisocial behavior was negative peer associations.

Recently, researchers have begun to analyze the social processes that appear to shape antisocial behavior in these peer associations. For example, Dishion and Andrews (1995) showed that boys with a history of early arrests are more likely to reinforce each other's antisocial or rule-breaking talk with laughter than are non-arrested boys. Deviant peers have also been shown to be less likely to react positively to non-rule-breaking talk and more likely to have longer discussions about antisocial activities compared to non-arrested boys (Dishion et al., 1996). Dishion has labeled these types of interactions the 'deviancy training process' (Dishion and Patterson, 1997, p. 208), and found that these interactions predict adolescent initiation into delinquency as well as escalations in delinquent behavior.

Not only do negative peer associations result in the initiation and shaping of antisocial behaviors, but strong empirical evidence suggests that associations with negative peers also serve to maintain and escalate antisocial behavior. In a longitudinal study of over 1000 adolescents (The National Youth Survey), Elliott et al. (1985) found that delinquent peer associations strongly contributed to continued and escalated patterns of criminal behavior. When this variable (delinquent peer associations) was eliminated from the analyses, the growth in delinquency over time was virtually non-existent. These and other investigators (Dishion et al., 1999) highlight the potential negative effects of deviant peer associations on antisocial adolescent behavior, even when associations take place in controlled (treatment) settings.

Although research has shown that peers play an important role in the development and persistence of antisocial behavior during adolescence, peer relationships in and of themselves do not appear to cause antisocial behavior. Rather, peer relationships appear to influence deviant behavior in combination with adolescent characteristics and parenting practices. For example, it has been shown that delinquent behavior and deviant peer associations appeared to emerge and be exacerbated in the context of low parental involvement and monitoring (Stoolmiller, 1994). Further, parenting practices (monitoring) have both a direct and an indirect effect (mediated by delinquent peer associations) on delinquent behavior (Patterson and Dishion, 1985).

Gender

Existing literature suggests that there are different effects for parenting practices and sibling and peer relationships on female antisocial behavior (Kim et al., 1999). This evidence also shows that the developmental histories of antisocial boys and girls differ with respect to levels of abuse, neglect, and trauma (Kim et al., 1999; Lewin et al., 1999; Chamberlain and Moore, in press). These differences have led theorists to propose that there may be different predictors and mechanisms that explain gender variations in the development, maintenance, and performance of antisocial behavior.

Theories have long suggested that differences exist in the frequency and severity of male and female deviancy. Historically, it has been documented that female antisocial behavior is generally less severe than male antisocial behavior; however, data on gender differences in prevalence are mixed (reviewed in Zoccolillo, 1993). Although still relatively moderate, attention to female delinquency has increased over the past 20 years, resulting in challenges to previous theories regarding its development. In particular, patterns of delinquent behavior suggest that there are remarkable similarities in the range or types of crimes that males and females commit (Giordano et al., 1999; Liu and Kaplan, 1999). Although females are believed to commit fewer antisocial acts than their male counterparts (Giordano et al., 1999; Houtzager and Baerveldt, 1999), increases in female criminal behavior have been reported over the past several years (Austin, 1993). It is unclear whether reported increases in female antisocial behavior are a result of increased frequency and/or severity of female criminal involvement, or rather of an increased awareness regarding criminal acts committed by females. Research supports both perspectives (see Giordano, 1997).

Regardless of *why* increases in female antisocial behavior are being reported, the long-term detrimental effects of such behaviors are well documented (Robins, 1966; Sampson and Laub, 1993). In particular, female antisocial behavior has been linked to the development of later psychiatric problems (Lewis et al., 1991; Zoccolillo et al., 1992; Bardon et al., 1996), educational problems (Cairns et al., 1989; Lewis et al., 1991; Bardone et al., 1996), employment/occupational problems (Lewis et al., 1991; Zoccolillo and Rogers, 1991), substance abuse (Lewis et al., 1991; Bardone et al., 1996), early pregnancy (Robins, 1986; Cairns et al., 1989; Zoccolillo and Rogers, 1991; Kovacs et al., 1994; Underwood et al., 1995; Bardone et al., 1996, 1998; Woodward and Fergusson, 1999), selection of antisocial partners (Quinton and Rutter, 1988), early marriage (Robins, 1966; Rutter and Madge, 1976), and early death (Lewis et al., 1991; Zoccolillo and Rogers, 1991).

Despite a recent increase in attention to the study of female antisocial behavior, little attention has been given to the study of gender differences in the development of antisocial behavior, and intervention studies on female antisocial behavior are exceedingly rare. This gap in knowledge not only restricts the understanding of the development of female antisocial behavior, but also severely limits the implementation of theory-based treatment and prevention efforts. As a result, the development of female antisocial behavior is not well understood.

The few studies that have been conducted are limited by small sample sizes, lack of control groups, and lack of detailed treatment descriptions, which in turn limits the conclusions that can be drawn. In addition, studies on the treatment of antisocial behavior have generally been limited to pre- and post-test designs, where change processes during treatment have been virtually ignored. This lack of knowledge regarding the unique developmental trajectory of antisocial behavior in females results in a limited ability to answer urgent questions regarding treatment utility and prevention for this population. Empirical studies examining both treatment efficacy and gender differences in the development of intervention with conduct-problem males and females continues to be a necessity, if reductions in identified individual and societal implications of antisocial behavior are to be made.

PARENTING PRACTICES AND IMPLICATIONS FOR INTERVENTION

Recent research shows that it is highly likely that parenting practices mediate the effect of early conduct problems on later antisocial behavior (Olweus, 1980; Loeber and Dishion, 1983). This may be the primary reason why multifaceted interventions (e.g. Multisystemic Therapy: Henggeler et al., 1998; Multidimensional Treatment Foster Care: Chamberlain, 2003; Functional Family Therapy: Alexander et al., 2000; Perry Preschool Program: Berrueta-Clement et al., 1984; Helping the Noncompliant Child: Forehand and McMahon, 1981; The Incredible Years: Webster-Stratton et al., 2001), where antisocial behavior is targeted through interventions aimed at improving parenting practices (improving the parent–child relationship, increasing supervision, monitoring peer relations), have shown greater efficacy than interventions targeting individual youth factors in isolation. Specific parenting practices that are probably related to child antisocial behavior appear to vary during different developmental stages. These include the following:

- warmth and responsiveness in early childhood,
- limit-setting and active, positive involvement in middle childhood,
- monitoring and supervision, and
- a positive parent–youth relationship in adolescence.

However, the research reviewed in this chapter suggests that parents can strongly influence and alter the developmental course of antisocial behavior *at all time points*.

In looking at intervention paradigms, the most common approach to intervening with parental influences is to attempt to manipulate malleable factors that are hypothesized to decrease or prevent antisocial behavior. In this light, many practitioners attempt to improve the early care-giving environment (Olds et al., 1998), teach pro-social parenting (Webster-Stratton et al., 2001), and increase parental monitoring and involvement (Eddy and Chamberlain, 2000; Hawkins et al., 2000), based on recent reviews that have found that these parenting practices serve as a protective factors against the development and maintenance of antisocial behavior.

Understanding bi-directional relationships continues to be important for practitioners as well as for causal modeling investigators. While working with parents appears to be a necessary part of any effective treatment for antisocial behavior, deliberate care must be taken to engage parents in treatment endeavors in a supportive and caring manner and to avoid exacerbating any blame that many parents of antisocial youths may feel (Ambert, 1997).

It is helpful for practitioners to understand that many of the parent–child interactional processes involved in the development and maintenance of antisocial behavior often occur outside of parents' direct awareness. Moment-by-moment interactions are often so intricate that they are difficult for active participants, such as parents, to dissect. As primary care-takers, parents not only provide unique information on their child's behavior patterns, but are often the most powerful avenue for prevention and improvement.

CONCLUSION

The office of the US Surgeon General has recently released a report (2001) in which youth violence is considered from a public health perspective. Such a perspective appears logical not only because of the impact of youth violence on the health and safety of community members, but also because of the factors that appear to contribute to the genesis of antisocial and violent behavior. Many physical disease models see no single factor as causing illness, but rather see illness appearing when a critical number of conditions occur at the necessary intensity. The same can be said of antisocial behavior: there does not appear to be a single causative factor. Instead, the risk factors (individual, family, peer, and community factors) appear to join together to create an aggregate risk for each individual (Saner and Ellickson, 1996; Ellickson and McGuigan, 2000).

Although there is support for the association between individual and contextual variables (child temperament, attachment, child behavior problems, parental responsiveness, psychopathology, family stress, poverty) and the development of antisocial behavior, these relationships have been correlational in nature and do not provide causal evidence for the development of antisocial behavior. However, initial correlational research has been important in identifying significant relationships among variables at the individual, social, and environmental levels, which have in turn guided more complex research examining the interplay between variables at each of these levels. Although there now appears to be a consensus that parenting and parent–child interactions play a central role in the development and maintenance of antisocial behavior, the exact contributions that individual parent and child characteristics, contextual variables, and parenting practices have in the developmental process remain under investigation.

What the previous three decades of research on parenting and antisocial behavior does show, however, is that children influence, and are influenced by, the contingencies in their environments. In addition, parents appear to be particularly instrumental in helping their children develop levels of compliance commensurate with expectations of adults across settings (family, school, community). A parent's skill in providing positive, contingent parenting matched to his or her child's biological predisposition, is likely to reduce greatly the child becoming developmentally or socially deficient or acquiring antisocial habits (Patterson and Fisher, 2002). In addition, it appears that there is significant bi-directionality in the development of antisocial behavior, where children and parents shape each other's behavior in a manner that increases the likelihood of positive or negative outcomes throughout childhood and adolescence.

Fortunately, research to date points to potentially malleable variables, such as parenting practices, that may be developed as a focus of future prevention and change efforts. With the increasing popularity of more complex statistical methods (such as structural equation modeling and latent growth curve analysis) in the study of parenting, we have the ability to examine more closely the relationships and directionality of individual and contextual variables. It is our hope that as research methodologies continue to grow in complexity and clarity, so too will our understanding of the role that parenting plays in the development and treatment of antisocial behavior.

REFERENCES

Alexander, J., Pugh, C., Parsons, B. and Sexton, T. (2000) *Functional Family Therapy*. Boulder, CO: Center for the Study and Prevention of Violence.

Ambert, A.M. (1997) *Parents, Children, and Adolescents: Interactive Relationships and Development in Context*. New York: Haworth Press.

Anderson, K.E., Lytton, H. and Romney, D.W. (1986) Mothers' interactions with normal and conduct-disordered boys: Who affects whom? *Developmental Psychology*, **22**, 604–9.

Aos, S., Phipps, P., Barnoski, R. and Leib, R. (1999) *The Comparative Costs and Benefits of Programs to Reduce Crime: A Review of National Research Findings with Implications for Washington State*. Olympia WA: Washington State Institute for Public Policy.

Austin, R. (1993) Recent trends in official male and female crime rates: the convergence controversy. *Journal of Criminal Justice*, **21**, 447–66.

Baden, A.D. and Howe, G.W. (1992) Mothers' attributions and expectancies regarding their conduct-disordered children. *Journal of Abnormal Child Psychology*, **20**, 467–85.

Baker, R.L.A. and Mednick, B.R. (1984) *Influences on Human Development: A Longitudinal Perspective*. Boston, MA: Kluwer-Nijhoff.

Bank, L., Forgatch, M.S., Patterson, G.R. and Fetrow, R.A. (1993) Parenting practices of single mothers: mediators of negative contextual factors. *Journal of Marriage and the Family*, **55**, 371–84.

Bardone, A.M., Moffitt, T., Caspi, A. and Dickson, N. (1996) Adult mental health and social outcomes of adolescent girls with depression and conduct disorder. *Development & Psychopathology*, **8**(4), 811–29.

Bardone, A.M., Moffitt, T.E., Caspi, A., Dickson, N., Stanton, W.R. and Silva, P.A. (1998) Adult physical health outcomes of adolescent girls with conduct disorder, depression, and anxiety. *Journal of the American Academy of Child Adolescent Psychiatry*, **37**(6), 594–601.

Bates, J.E. (1980) The concept of difficult temperament. *Merrill-Palmer Quarterly*, **26**, 299–319.

Bates, J.E., Maslin, C.A. and Frankel, K.A. (1985) Attachment security, mother–child interaction, and temperament as predictors of behavior-problem ratings at age three years. In Bretherton, I. and Waters, E. (eds) *Monographs of the Society for Research in Child Development*, **50**(1–2), 167–93.

Bates, J., Pettit, G., Dodge, K. and Ridge, B. (1998) Interaction of temperamental resistance to control and restrictive parenting in the development of externalizing behavior. *Developmental Psychology*, **34**, 982–95.

Baumrind, D. (1967) Child care practices anteceding three patterns of preschool behavior. *Genetic Psychology Monographs*, **75**, 43–88.

Baumrind, D. (1971) Current patterns of parental authority. *Developmental Psychology Monographs*, **4**(1), Part 2, 1–103.

Baumrind, D. (1991) Effective parenting during the early adolescent transition. In Cowan, P.A. and Hetherington, M. (eds) *Family Transitions*. Hillsdale, NJ: Lawrence Erlbaum, pp. 111–59.

Bell, R.Q. and Chapman, M. (1986) Child effects in studies using experimental or brief longitudinal approaches to socialization. *Developmental Psychology*, **22**, 594–603.

Belsky, J. (1984) The Pennsylvania infant and family development project: I. Stability and change in mother–infant and father–infant interaction in a family setting at one, three, and nine months. *Child Development*, **55**, 692–705.

Berrueta-Clement, J.R., Schweinhart, L.J. Barnett, W.S., Epstein, A.S., Weikart, D.P. (1984) *Changed Lives: The Effects of the Perry Preschool Program on Youths Through Age 19*. Ypsilanti, MI: The High/Scope Press.

Blumstein, A., Cohen, J., Roth, J.A. and Visher, C.A. (1986) *Criminal Careers and 'Career Criminals'*. Washington, DC: National Academy Press.

Bowlby, J. (1969) *Attachment and Loss: Vol I. Attachment*. New York: Basic Books.

Brewer, D.D., Hawkins, J.D., Catalano, R.F. and Neckerman, H.J. (1995) Preventing serious, violent, and chronic juvenile offending: a review of evaluations of selected strategies in childhood, adolescence, and the community. In Howell, J.C., Krisberg, B., Hawkins, J.D. and Wilson, J.J. (eds) *Sourcebook on Serious,*

Violent, and Chronic Juvenile Offenders. Thousand Oaks, CA: Sage Publications, pp. 61–141.

Brunk, M.A. and Henggeler, S.W. (1984) Child influences on adult controls: an experimental investigation. *Developmental Psychology*, **20**(6), 1074–81.

Bugental, D.B. and Shennum, W.A. (1984) 'Difficult' children as elicitors and targets of adult communication patterns: an attributional-behavioral transactional analysis. *Monographs of the Society for Research in Child Development*, **49**, 1–81.

Cairns, R.B. and Cairns, B.D. (1994) *Lifelines and Risks: Pathways of Youth in Our Time*. Cambridge: Cambridge University Press.

Cairns, R.B., Cairns, B.D. and Neckerman, H.J. (1989) Early school dropout: configurations and determinants. *Child Development*, **60**, 1437–52.

Campbell, S.B. (1990) *Behavior Problems in Preschool Children: Clinical and Developmental Issues*. New York: Guilford Press.

Campbell, S.B. (1994) Hard-to-manage preschool boys: externalizing behavior, social competence, and family context at two-year follow-up. *Journal of Abnormal Child Psychology*, **22**, 147–66.

Campbell, S.B., Pierce, E., March, C., Ewing, L. and Szumowski, E. (1994) Hard-to-manage preschool boys: symptomatic behavior across contexts and time. *Child Development*, **65**, 836–51.

Capaldi, D.M. and Patterson, G.R. (1991) Relation of parental transitions to boys' adjustment problems: I. A linear hypothesis. II. Mothers at risk for transitions and unskilled parenting. *Developmental Psychology*, **27**, 489–504.

Capaldi, D.M. and Patterson, G.R. (1994) Interrelated influences of contextual factors on antisocial behavior in childhood and adolescence for males. In Fowles, D., Sutker, P. and Goodman, S.H. (eds) *Experimental Personality and Psychopathology Research*. New York: Springer, pp. 165–98.

Catalano, R.F. and Hawkins, J.D. (1996) The social development model: a theory of antisocial behavior. In Hawkins, J.D. (ed.) *Delinquency and Crime: Current Theories*. New York: Cambridge University Press, pp. 149–97.

Chamberlain, P. (2003) *Treating Chronic Juvenile Offenders: Advances Made Through the Oregon Multidimensional Treatment Foster Care Model*. Washington, DC: American Psychological Association.

Chamberlain, P. and Moore, K.J. (2002) Chaos and trauma in the lives of adolescent females with antisocial behavior and delinquency. In Greffner, R. (Series ed.) and Greenwald, R. (Vol. ed.) *Trauma and Juvenile Delinquency: Theory, Research, and Intervention*. Binghamton, NY: Haworth Press, pp. 79–108.

Cummings, E.M., Iannotti, R.J. and Zahn-Waxler, C. (1989) Aggression between peers in early childhood: individual continuity and developmental change. *Child Development*, **72**, 887–95.

Denham, S.A., Workman, E., Cole, P.M., Weissbrod, C., Kendziora, K.T. and Zahn-Waxler, C. (2000) Prediction of externalizing behavior problems from early to middle childhood: the role of parental socialization and emotion expression. *Development and Psychopathology*, **12**, 23–45.

Dishion, T.J. and Andrews, D.W. (1995) Preventing escalation in problems behaviors with high-risk young adolescents: immediate and 1-year outcomes. *Journal of Consulting and Clinical Psychology*, **63**, 538–48.

Dishion, T.J. and Patterson, G.R. (1997) The timing and severity of antisocial behavior: three hypotheses within an ecological framework. In Stoff, D.M., Breiling, J. and Maser, J.D. (eds) *Handbook of Antisocial Behavior*. New York: John Wiley, pp. 205–17.

Dishion, T.J., Loeber, R., Stouthamer-Loeber, M. and Patterson, G.R. (1984) Skill deficits and male adolescent delinquency. *Journal of Abnormal Child Psychology*, **12**, 37–54.

Dishion, T.J., Patterson, G.R., Stoolmiller, M. and Skinner, M. (1991) Family, school, and behavioral antecedents to early adolescent involvement with antisocial peers. *Developmental Psychology*, **27**, 172–80.

Dishion, T.J., Patterson, G.R. and Griesler, P.C. (1994) Peer adaptation in the development of antisocial behavior: a confluence model. In Huesmann, L.R. (ed.) *Aggressive Behavior: Current Perspectives*. New York: Plenum Press, pp. 61–95.

Dishion, T.J., Spracklen, K.M., Andrews, D.W. and Patterson, G.R. (1996) Deviancy training in male adolescent friendships. *Behavior Therapy*, **27**, 373–90.

Dishion, T.J., McCord, J. and Poulin, F. (1999) When interventions harm: peer groups and problem behavior. *American Psychologist*, **54**, 755–64.

Dishion, T.J., Patterson, G.R. and Kavanagh, K. (1992) An experimental test of the coercion model: linking theory, measurement, and intervention. In McCord, J. and Tremblay, R. (eds) *The Interaction of Theory and Practice: Experimental Studies of Intervention*. New York: Guilford, pp. 253–82.

Dyer Harnish, J., Dodge, K.A. and Valente, E. (1995) Mother–child interaction quality as a partial mediator of the roles of maternal depressive symptomatology and socioeconomic status in the development of child behavior problems. *Child Development*, **66**, 739–53.

Eddy, J.M. and Chamberlain, P. (2000) Family management and deviant peer association as mediators of the impact of treatment condition on youth antisocial behavior. *Journal of Consulting and Clinical Psychology*, **5**, 857–63.

Egeland, B. and Farber, E.A. (1984) Infant–mother attachment: factors related to its development and change over time. *Child Development*, **55**, 753–71.

Ellickson, P.L. and McGuigan, K.A. (2000) Early predictors of adolescent violence. *American Journal of Public Health*, **90**(4), 566–72.

Elliott, D.S. (1994) Serious violent offenders: onset, developmental course, and termination – The American Society of Criminology 1993 presidential address. *Criminology*, **32**, 1–21.

Elliott, D.S. and Voss, H.L. (1974) *Delinquency and Dropout*. Lexington, MA: Heath.

Elliott, D.S., Huizinga, D. and Ageton, S.S. (1985) *Explaining Delinquency and Drug Use*. Beverly Hills, CA: Sage.

Elliott, D.S., Huizinga, D. and Menard, S. (1989) *Multiple Problem Youth: Delinquency, Substance Use and Mental Health Problems*. New York: Springer-Verlag.

Erickson, M.F., Sroufe, L.A. and Egeland, B. (1985) The relationship between quality of attachment and behavior problems in preschool in a high-risk sample. In Bretherton, I. and Waters, E. (eds) Growing points of attachment theory and research. *Monographs of the Society for Research in Child Development*, **50**(1–2), 147–67.

Fagot, B.I. and Gauvain, M. (1997) Mother–child problem solving: continuity through the early childhood years. *Developmental Psychology*, **33**, 480–8.

Farrington, D.P. (1989) Early predictors of adolescent aggression and adult violence. *Violence and Victims*, **4**, 79–100.

Farrington, D.P. (1990) Implications of criminal career research for the prevention of offending. *Journal of Adolescence*, **13**, 93–113.

Figueira-McDonough, J. (1993) Residence, dropping-out, and delinquency rates. *Deviant Behavior*, **14**, 109–32.

Forehand, R. and McMahon, R.J. (1981) *Helping the Noncompliant Child: A Clinician's Guide to Parent Training*. New York: The Guilford Press.

Forgatch, M.S. (1989) Patterns and outcomes in family problem solving: the disrupting effect of negative emotion. *Journal of Marriage and the Family*, 115–24.

Forgatch, M.S. (1991) The clinical science vortex: a developing theory of antisocial behavior. In Pepler, D.J. and Rubin, K.H. (eds) *The Development and Treatment of Childhood Aggression*. Hillsdale, NJ: Erlbaum, pp. 291–315.

Forgatch, M.S. and DeGarmo, D.S. (1999) Parenting through change: an effective parenting training program for single mothers. *Journal of Consulting and Clinical Psychology*, **67**, 711–24.

Forgatch, M.S. and DeGarmo, D.S. (2000) Extending and testing the social interaction learning model with divorce samples. In Reid, J.B., Patterson, G.R. and Snyder, J. (eds.) *Antisocial Behavior in Children: Developmental Theories and Models for Intervention*. Washington DC: American Psychological Association.

Foshee, V. and Bauman, K.E. (1992) Parental and peer characteristics as modifiers of the bond-behavior relationship: an elaboration of control theory. *Journal of Health and Social Behavior*, **33**(1), 66–76.

Garbarino, J. and Sherman, D. (1980) High-risk neighborhoods and high-risk families: the human ecology of child maltreatment. *Child Development*, **51**(1), 188–98.

Giordano, P.C. (1997) Gender and antisocial behavior. In Stoff, D.M., Breiling, J. and Maser, J.D. (eds) *Handbook of Antisocial Behavior*. New York: John Wiley.

Giordano, P.C., Millhollin, T.J., Cernkovich, S.A., Pugh, M.D. and Rudolph, J.L. (1999) Delinquency, identity, and women's involvement in relationship violence. *Criminology*, **37**(1), 17–40.

Greenberg, M.T. and Speltz, M.L. (1988) Attachment and the ontogeny of conduct problems. In Belsky, J. and Nezworski, T. (eds) *Clinical Implications of Attachment*. Hillsdale, NJ: Erlbaum, pp. 177–218.

Greenwald, R.L., Bank, L., Reid, J.R. and Knutson, J.F. (1997) A discipline-mediated model of excessively punitive parenting. *Aggressive Behavior*, **23**, 259–80.

Hawkins, J.D., Herrenkohl, T.I., Farrington, D.P., Brewer, D., Catalano, R.F., Harachi, T.W. and Cothern, L. (2000) *Predictors of Youth Violence*. Office of Juvenile Justice and Delinquency Programs.

Henggeler, S.W., Borduin, C.M., Melton, G.B., Mann, B.J., Smith, L., Hall, J.A., Cone, L. and Fucci, B.R. (1991) Effects of multisystemic therapy on drug use and abuse in serious juvenile offenders: a progress report from two outcome studies. *Family Dynamics of Addiction Quarterly*, **1**(3), 40–51.

Henggeler, S.W., Melton, G.B., Brondino, M.J., Scherer, D.G. and Hanley, J.H. (1997) Multisystemic therapy with violent and chronic juvenile offenders and their families: the role of treatment fidelity in successful dissemination. *Journal of Consulting and Clinical Psychology*, **65**(5), 821–33.

Hetherington, E.M. (1991) The role of individual differences and family relationships in children's coping with divorce and remarriage. In Cowen, P.A. and Hetherington, M. (eds) *Family Transitions*. Hillsdale, NJ: Lawrence Erlbaum, pp. 165–94.

Hirschi, T. and Hindelang, M.J. (1977) Intelligence and delinquency: a revisionist review. *American Sociological Review*, **42**, 571–87.

Hogan, D. and Kitagawa, E. (1985) The impact of social status, family structure, and neighborhood on the fertility of black adolescents. *The American Journal of Sociology*, **90**, 825–55.

Houtzager, B. and Baerveldt, C. (1999) Just like normal: a social network study of the relation between crime and the intimacy of adolescent friendships. *Social Behavior and Personality*, **27**(2), 177–92.

Howell, J.C. (1997) *Juvenile Justice and Youth Violence*. London: Sage.

Huizinga, D., Loeber, R. and Thornberry, T. (1995) *Recent Findings from the Program on the Causes and Correlates of Delinquency*. Report to the Office of Juvenile Justice and Delinquency Prevention.

Katz, L.F. and Gottman, J.M. (1991) Marital discord and child outcomes: a social psychophysiological approach. In Garber, J. and Dodge, K.A. (eds) *The Development of Emotion Regulation and Dysregulation: Cambridge Studies in Social and Emotional Development*. New York: Cambridge University Press, pp. 129–55.

Keenan, K. and Shaw, D.S. (1994) The development of aggression in toddlers: a study of low income families. *Journal of Abnormal Child Psychology*, **22**, 53–77.

Kendall, P.C. and Fischler, G.L. (1984) Behavioral adjustment correlates of problem-solving: validational analyses of interpersonal cognitive problem-solving measures. *Child Development*, **55**, 879–92.

Kim, J.E., Hetherington, E.M. and Reiss, D. (1999) Associations among family relationships, antisocial peers, and adolescents' externalizing behaviors: gender and family type differences. *Child Development*, **70**, 1209–30.

Knutson, J.F. and Schartz, H.A. (1997) Evidence pertaining to physical abuse and neglect of children as parent child relational diagnoses. In Widiger, T.A., Frances, A.F., Pincus, H.A., Ross, R., First, M. and Davis, W. (eds) *DSM IV Sourcebook,* Vol. 3. Washington, D.C.: American Psychiatric Association Press, pp. 713–804.

Kovacs, M., Krol, R.M. and Voti, L. (1994) Early onset psychopathology and the risk for teenage pregnancy among clinically referred girls. *Journal of the American Academy of Child Adolescent Psychiatry*, **33**, 106–13.

Larzelere, R.E. and Patterson, G.R. (1990) Parental management: mediator of the effect of socioeconomic status on early delinquency. *Criminology*, **28**, 301–23.

Laub, J.H. and Sampson, R.J. (1988) Unraveling families and delinquency: a reanalysis of the Gluecks' data. *Criminality*, **26**(3), 355–79.

Lerner, J.V., Hertzog, C., Hooker, K.A., Hassibi, M. and Thomas, A. (1988) A longitudinal study of negative emotional states and adjustment from early childhood through adolescence. *Child Development*, **59**, 356–66.

Lewin, L.M., Davis, B. and Hops, H. (1999) Childhood social predictors of adolescent antisocial behavior: gender differences in predictive accuracy and efficacy. *Journal of Abnormal Child Psychology*, **27**(4), 277–92.

Lewis, M., Feiring, C., McGuffog, C. and Jaskir, J. (1984) Predicting psychopathology in six-year-olds from early social relations. *Child Development*, **55**(1), 123–36.

Lewis, E.O., Yeager, C.A., Cobham-Portorreal, C.S., Klein, N., Showalter, C. and Anthony, A. (1991) A follow-up of female delinquents: maternal contributions to the perpetuation of deviance. *Journal of the American Academy of Child Adolescent Psychiatry*, **30**(2), 197–201.

Liddle, H. (1995) Conceptual and clinical dimensions of a multidimensional, multi-systems engagement strategy in family-based adolescent treatment. *Psychotherapy*, **32**, 39–54.

Liu, X. and Kaplan, H.B. (1999) Explaining the gender difference in adolescent delinquent behavior: a longitudinal test of mediating mechanisms. *Criminology*, **37**(1), 195–215.

Loeber, R. and Dishion, T.J. (1983) Early predictors of male delinquency: a review. *Psychological Bulletin*, **94**, 68–99.

Loeber, R. and Dishion, T. (1984) Boys who fight at home and school: family conditions influencing cross-setting consistency. *Journal of Consultating and Clinical Psychology*, **52**, 759–68.

Loeber, R. and Stouthamer-Loeber, M. (1986) Family factors as correlates and predictors of juvenile conduct problems and delinquency. In Tonry, M. and Morris, N. (eds) *Crime and Justice: A Review of Research*, Vol. 7. Chicago: University of Chicago Press, pp. 29–149.

Loeber, R., Farrington, D.P., Stouthamer-Loeber, M., Moffit, T. and Caspi, A. (1998) The development of male offending: key findings from the first decade of the Pittsburgh Youth Study. *Studies in Crime and Crime Prevention*, **7**, 141–72.

Lyons-Ruth, K., Alpern, L. and Repacholi, B. (1993) Disorganized infant attachment classification and maternal psychosocial problems as predictors of hostile-aggressive behavior in the preschool classroom. *Child Development*, **64**, 572–85.

Lytton, H. (1990) Child and parent effects in boys' conduct disorder: a reinterpretation. *Developmental Psychology*, **26**, 683–97.

Maccoby, E.E. (1993) The role of parents in the socialization of children: an historical overview. *Developmental Psychology*, **28**(6), 1006–17.

Martin, J. (1981) A longitudinal study of the consequences of early mother–infant interaction: a microanalytic approach. *Monographs of the Society for Research in Child Development*, **46** (3, Serial No. 190).

Martinez, C.R., Jr and Forgatch, M.S. (2001) Preventing problems with boys' noncompliance: effects of a parent training intervention for divorcing mothers. *Journal of Consulting and Clinical Psychology*, **69**, 416–28.

McCord, J. (1979) Some child-rearing antecedents of criminal behavior in adult men. *Journal of Personality and Social Psychology*, **37**, 1477–86.

McCord, J. (1993) Descriptions and predictions: three problems for the future of criminological research. *Journal of Research in Crime & Delinquency*, **30**(4), 412–25.

McCord, W., McCord, J. and Zola, I.K. (1959) *Origins of Crime: A New Evaluation of the Cambridge–Somerville Youth Study*. New York: Cambridge University Press.

McFayden-Ketchum, S.A., Bates, J.E., Dodge, K.A. and Pettit, G.S. (1996) Patterns of change in early childhood aggressive-disruptive behavior: gender differences in predictions from early coercive and affectionate mother–child interactions. *Child Development*, **67**, 2417–33.

Nix, R.L., Pinderhughes, E.E., Dodge, K.A., Bates, J.E., Pettit, G.S. and McFadyen-Ketchum, S.A. (1999) The relation between mothers' hostile attribution tendencies and children's externalizing behavior problems: the mediating role of mothers' harsh discipline practices. *Child Development*, **70**, 896–909.

Office of the Surgeon General (2001) *Youth Violence: A Report for the Surgeon General*. Washington, DC: US Government Printing Office.

Olds, D., Hill, P., Mihalic, S. and O'Brien, R. (1998) *Blueprints for Violence Prevention, Book Seven: Prenatal and Infancy Home Visitation by Nurses*. Boulder, CO: Center for the Study and Prevention of Violence.

O'Leary, S.G., Smith Slep, A.M. and Reid, M.J. (1999) A longitudinal study of mothers' overreactive discipline and toddlers' externalizing behavior. *Journal of Abnormal Child Psychology*, **27**, 331–41.

Olweus, D. (1979) Stability of aggressive reaction patterns in males: a review. *Psychological Bulletin*, **86**, 852–75.

Olweus, D. (1980) Familial and temperament determinants of aggressive behavior in adolescent boys: a causal analysis. *Developmental Psychology*, **16**, 644–60.

Patterson, G.R. (1973) Changes in status of family members as controlling stimuli: a basis for describing treatment process. In Hamerlynck, L.A., Handy, L.C. and Mash, E.J. (eds) *Behavior Change: Methodology, Concepts, and Practice*. Champaign, IL: Research Press, pp. 169–91.

Patterson, G.R. (1979a) A performance theory for coercive family interactions. In Cairns, R. (ed.) *Social Interaction: Methods, Analysis, and Illustration*. Hillsdale, NJ: Lawrence Erlbaum Associates, pp. 119–62.

Patterson, G.R. (1979b) Treatment for children with conduct problems: a review of outcome studies. In Feshbach, S. and Fraczek, A. (eds) *Aggression and Behavior Change: Biological and Social Processes*. New York: Praeger, pp. 83–132.

Patterson, G. R. (1980) Mothers: the unacknowledged victims. *Monographs of the Society for Research in Child Development*, **45**, Serial No. 186.

Patterson, G.R. (1982) *A Social Learning Approach to Family Intervention: III. Coercive Family Process*. Eugene, OR: Castalia.

Patterson, G.R. (1985) A microsocial analysis of anger and irritable behavior. In Chesney, M. and Roseman, R. (eds) *Anger and Hositility in Behavioral and Cardiovascular Disorders*. Washington, D.C.: Hemisphere, pp. 83–99.

Patterson, G.R. (1992) Developmental changes in antisocial behavior. In Peters, R.DeV., McMahon, R.J. and Quinsey, V.L. (eds) *Aggression and Violence Throughout the Life Span*. Newbury Park, CA: Sage, pp. 52–82.

Patterson, G.R. and Dishion, T.J. (1985) Contributions of families and peers to delinquency. *Criminology*, **23**, 63–79.

Patterson, G.R. and Fisher, P.A. (2002) Recent developments in our understanding of parenting: bidirectional effects, causal models, and the search for parsimony. In Bornstein, M. (ed.) *Handbook of Parenting: Practical and Applied Parenting*, 2nd ed., Vol. 5. Mahwah, NJ: Erlbaum, pp. 59–88.

Patterson, G.R. and Yoerger, K. (1993) Developmental models for delinquent behavior. In Hodgins, S. (ed.) *Crime and Mental Disorders*. Newbury Park, CA: Sage, pp. 140–72.

Patterson, G.R., DeBaryshe, B.D. and Ramsey, E. (1989) A developmental perspective on antisocial behavior. *American Psychologist*, **44**, 329–35.

Patterson, G.R., Crosby, L. and Vuchinich, S. (1992) Predicting risk for early police arrest. *Journal of Quantitative Criminology*, **8**, 335–55.

Patterson, G.R., Reid, J.B. and Dishion, T.J. (1992) *Antisocial Boys*. Eugene, OR: Castalia.

Patterson, G.R., Dishion, T.J. and Yoerger, K. (2000) Adolescent growth in new forms of problem behavior: macro- and micro-peer dynamics. *Prevention Science*, **1**, 3–13.

Pettit, G.S., Bates, J.E., and Dodge, K.A. (1997) Supportive parenting, ecological context, and children's adjustment: a seven-year longitudinal study. *Child Development*, **68**, 908–23.

Quay, H.C. (1987) Intelligence. In Quay, H.C. (ed.) *Handbook of Juvenile Delinquency*. New York: John Wiley.

Quinton, D. and Rutter, M. (1988) *Parenting Breakdown: The Making and Breaking of Inter-generational Links*. Aldershot: Avebury.

Reid, J.B. (1986) Social–interactional patterns in families of abused and nonabused children. In Zahn-Waxler, C., Cummings, E.M. and Iannotti, R. (eds) *Altruism and Aggression: Biological and Social Origins*. New York: Cambridge, pp. 238–55.

Reid, J.B. and Eddy, J.M. (1997) The prevention of antisocial behavior: some considerations in the search for effective interventions. In Stoff, D.M., Breiling, J. and Maser, J.D. (eds) *Handbook of Antisocial Behavior*. New York: John Wiley, pp. 205–17.

Richman, M., Stevenson, J. and Graham, P.J. (1982) *Preschool to School: A Behavioral Study*. London: Academic Press.

Robins, L. (1966) *Deviant Children Grown Up*. Baltimore: Williams & Wilkins.

Robins, L. (1986) The consequences of conduct disorder in girls. In Olweus, D., Block, J. and Radke-Yarrow, M. (eds) *Development of Antisocial and Prosocial Behavior*. Orlando, FL: Academic Press, pp. 385–414.

Robins, L., West, P. and Herjanic, B. (1975) Arrests and delinquency in two generations: a study of Black urban families and their children. *Journal of Child Psychology and Psychiatry*, **16**, 125–40.

Rose, S.L., Rose, S.A. and Feldman, J.F. (1989) Stability of behavior problems in very young children. *Development and Psychopathology*, **1**, 5–19.

Rothbart, M. and Bates, J. (1998) Temperament. In Damon, W. and Eisenberg, N. (eds) *Handbook of Child Psychology: Social, Emotional, and Personality Development*, Vol. 3. New York: John Wiley, pp. 105–76.

Rutter, M. and Madge, N. (1976) *Cycles of Disadvantage*. London: Heinemann.

Rutter, M., Cox, A., Tupling, C., Berger, M. and Yule, W. (1975) Attainment and adjustment in two geographical areas: I. The prevalence of psychiatric disorder. *British Journal of Psychiatry*, **126**, 493–509.

Rutter, M., Giller, H. and Hagell, A. (1998) *Antisocial Behavior by Young People*. Cambridge, UK: Cambridge University Press.

Sampson, R.J. and Laub, J.H. (1993) *Crime in the Making: Pathways and Turning Points Through Life*. Cambridge, MA: Harvard University Press.

Sampson, R.J. and Laub, J.H. (1994) Urban poverty and the family context of delinquency: a new look at structure and process in a classic study. *Child Development*, **65**, 523–40.

Saner, H. and Ellickson, P.L. (1996) Concurrent risk factors for adolescent violence. *Journal of Adolescent Health*, **19**(2), 94–103.

Sanson, A., Oberklaid, F., Pedlow, R. and Prior, M. (1991) Risk indicators: assessment of infancy predictors of preschool behavioural adjustment. *Journal of Child Psychology and Psychiatry*, **32**, 609–26.

Scarr, S. and McCartney, K. (1983) How people make their own environments: a theory of genotype-environment effects. *Child Development*, **54**(2), 424–35.

Shaw, D.S., Vondra, J.I., Dowdell Hommerding, K., Keenan, K. and Dunn, M. (1994) Chronic family adversity and early child behavior problems: a longitudinal study of low income families. *Journal of Child Psychology and Psychiatry*, **35**, 1109–22.

Shaw, D.S., Keenan, K., Owens, E., Winslow, E.B., Hood, N. and Garcia, M. (1995) Developmental precursors of externalizing behavior among two samples of low-income families: Ages 1 to 5. Paper presented at the biennial meeting of the Society for Research in Child Development, Indianapolis, IN.

Shaw, D.S., Owens, E.B., Giovannelli, J. and Winslow, E.B. (2001) Infant and toddler pathways leading to early externalizing disorders. *Journal of the American Academy of Child and Adolescent Psychiatry*, **40**, 36–43.

Shaw, D.S., Winslow, E.B., Owens, E.B. and Hood, N. (1998) Young children's adjustment to chronic family adversity: a longitudinal study of low-income families. *Journal of the American Academy of Child & Adolescent Psychiatry*, **37**(5), 545–53.

Simons, R.L., Johnson, C. and Conger, R.D. (1994) Harsh corporal punishment versus quality of parental involvement as an explanation of adolescent maladjustment. *Journal of Marriage and the Family*, **56**, 591–607.

Simons, R.L., Wu, C.I., Johnson, C. and Conger, R.D. (1995) A test of various perspectives on the intergenerational transmission of domestic violence. *Criminology*, **33**, 141–72.

Snyder, J.J. (1977) A reinforcement analysis of interaction in problem and non-problem families. *Journal of Abnormal Psychology*, **86**, 528–35.

Snyder, J. and Patterson, G.R. (1986) The effects of consequences on patterns of social interaction: a quasi-experimental approach to reinforcement in natural interaction. *Child Development*, **57**, 1257–68.

Snyder, J.J. and Patterson, G.R. (1995) Individual differences in social aggression: a test of a reinforcement model of socialization in the natural environment. *Behavior Therapy*, **26**, 371–91.

Snyder, J., Edwards, P., McGraw, K., Kilgore, K. and Holton, A. (1994) Escalation and reinforcement in mother–child conflict: social processes associated with the development of physical aggression. *Development and Psychopathology*, **6**, 305–21.

Sroufe, L.A. (1983) Infant–caregiver attachment and patterns of adaptation in preschool: the roots of maladaptation and competence. In Perlmutter, M. (ed.) *Minnesota Symposium on Child Psychology*, Vol. 16. Minneapolis, MN: University of Minnesota Press, pp. 41–81.

Statts, A.W. (1993) Personality theory, abnormal psychology, and psychological measurement. *Behavior Modification*, **17**(1), 8–42.

Stern, S.B. and Azar, S.T. (1998) Integrating cognitive strategies into behavioral treatment for abusive parents and families with aggressive adolescents. *Clinical Child Psychology and Psychiatry*, **3**, 387–404.

Stoolmiller, M. (2001) Synergistic interaction of child manageability problems and parent-discipline tactics in predicting future growth in externalizing behavior for boys. *Developmental Psychology*, **37**, 814–25.

Stoolmiller, M., Patterson, G.R. and Snyder, J. (1997) Parental discipline and child antisocial behavior: a contingency-based theory and some methodological refinements. *Psychological Inquiry*, **8**(3), 223–9.

Stoolmiller, M., Eddy, J.M. and Reid, J.B. (2000) Detecting and describing preventive intervention effects in a universal school-based randomized trial targeting delinquent and violent behavior. *Journal of Consulting and Clinical Psychology*, **68**, 296–306.

Straus, M.A. (1991) Discipline and deviance: physical punishment of children and violence and other crime in adulthood. *Social Problems*, **38**(2), 133–54.

Thomas, A., Chess, S. and Birch, H.H. (1968) *Temperament and Behavior Disorders in Children*. New York: New York University Press.

Underwood, M.K., Kupersmidt, J.B. and Coie, J.D. (1995) Peer sociometric status and aggression as predictors of adolescent childbearing. *Journal of Research on Adolescence*, **6**(2) (for 1996), 201–23.

US Department of Health and Human Services (2001) *Youth Violence: A Report of the Surgeon General*. Rockville, MD, U.S. Department of Health and Human Services; Centers for Disease Control and Prevention; National Center for Injury Prevention and Control; Substance Abuse and Mental Health Services Administration; Center for Mental Health Services; and National Institutes of Health, National Institute of Mental Health.

Walsh, A., Petee, T.A. and Beyer, J.A. (1987) Intellectual imbalance and delinquency: comparing high verbal and high performance IQ delinquents. *Criminal Justice and Behavior*, **14**, 370–9.

Webster-Stratton, C. and Eyberg, S.M. (1982) Child temperament: relationship with child behavior problems and parent-child interactions. *Journal of Clinical Child Psychology*, **11**(2), 123–9.

Webster-Stratton, C., Mihalic, S., Fagan, A., Arnold, D., Taylor, T. and Tingley, C. (2001) *Blueprints for Violence Prevention, Book Eleven: The Incredible Years: Parent, Teacher and Child Training Series*. Boulder, CO: Center for the Study and Prevention of Violence.

Weis, J.G. (1986) Issues in the measurement of criminal careers. In Blumstein, A., Cohen, J., Roth, J.A. and Visher, C.A. (eds) *Criminal Careers and 'Career' Criminals*, Vol. II. Washington, DC: National Academy Press, pp. 1–51.

Welsh, R.S. (1976) Severe parental punishment and delinquency: a developmental theory. *Journal of Clinical Child Psychology*, **5**, 17–21.

Wolfgang, M.E., Thornberry, T.P. and Figlio, R.M. (1987) *From Boy to Man, from Delinquency to Crime*. Chicago, IL: University of Chicago Press.

Woodward, L.J. and Fergusson, D.M. (1999) Early conduct problems and later risk of teenage pregnancy in girls. *Development and Psychopathology*, **11**, 127–41.

Zahn-Waxler, C., Mayfield, A., Radke-Yarrow, M., McKnew, D., Cytryn, L. and Davenport, Y. (1988) A follow-up investigation of offspring of bipolar parents. *American Journal of Psychiatry*, **145**, 506–9.

Zahn-Waxler, C., Iannotti, R.J., Cummings, E.M. and Denham, S. (1990) Antecedents of problem behaviors in children of depressed mothers. *Development and Psychopathology*, **2**, 271–92.

Zoccolillo, M. (1993) Gender and the development of conduct disorder. *Development and Psychopathology*, **5**, 65–78.

Zoccolillo, M. and Rogers, K. (1991) Characteristics and outcome of hospitalized adolescent girls with conduct disorder. *Journal of the American Academy of Child Adolescent Psychiatry*, **30**(6), 973–81.

Zoccolillo, M., Pickles, A., Quinton, D. and Rutter, M. (1992) The outcome of childhood conduct disorder: implications for defining adult personality disorder and conduct disorder. *Psychological Medicine*, **22**, 1–16.

16

Parenting Antisocial Children and Adolescents

Beth A. Kotchick, Anne Shaffer,
Shannon Dorsey and Rex Forehand

SUMMARY

Countless studies have shown that one of the most consistent areas of a child's life found to contribute to both the development *and* the treatment of antisocial behavior is the family. Positive parenting practices, such as a supportive parent–child relationship, authoritative discipline methods, and close supervision, are major protective factors against the development of antisocial behavior.

In this chapter, we give a historical overview of how parents became involved in the treatment of child antisocial behaviors, followed by a review of the 'core issues' central to parenting interventions, including a discussion of developmental and contextual variables. The chapter presents an example of a well-established parent training program, and concludes with sections that address challenges frequently faced by clinicians in accessing and implementing these parenting programs, as well as our assessment of issues related to the future of parent training research.

HISTORICAL OVERVIEW OF PARENTING INTERVENTIONS

Antisocial behavior among young people was an area of professional concern as early as the turn of the 20th century. While our views of the causes, courses, and outcomes of antisocial behavior have been continually modified throughout the intervening years, the basic catalog of behaviors construed as 'antisocial' or 'delinquent' remains relatively unchanged. Treatment for the antisocial child, however, is an area that has seen tremendous changes in both its theoretical underpinnings and recommended applications. This section provides a brief historical review of the treatment of antisocial behavior problems in children, from the 1900s to the present day.

Two major scientific movements shaped the study of child problem behaviors in the early 1900s. As noted by Siegel and Scovill (2000), this period was characterized by the dominance of biological theories. In terms of delinquency, the 'degeneracy theory' held that antisocial behavior was genetically determined and, therefore, unalterable. So the relatively rare attempts that were made to treat delinquent youth were conducted by those holding more liberal views, believing that the child's environment may contribute to his or her behavior. Around the same time, Hall (1904) completed his seminal work on adolescence, the publication of which brought increased public attention to the new theories regarding the developmental tasks of youth. In the United States, early juvenile justice systems were established by the 1920s, which coincided with early efforts in the field of social work (such as Jane Addams and the Hull House in Chicago) toward the treatment and prevention of antisocial behaviors.

By the 1920s, theoretical principles were emerging that have continued to guide the treatment of antisocial youth today. Behavior modification techniques, still a mainstay in the treatment of child problem behaviors, were first developed in the 1920s. More importantly, researchers began to recognize the integral role that a child's environment plays in the development and maintenance of antisocial behavior. In a detailed review of thousands of case studies published in 1926, family environment (and parenting practices in particular) was identified as perhaps the most important predictor of delinquency (Healy and Bronner, 1926).

Given the current climate for treating antisocial youth, the conclusions of researchers in 1926 seem surprisingly modern. However, these conclusions were not immediately implemented, in part because the psychological treatment of children was not widely practiced. Treatment of children through the 1950s typically occurred via less empirically based psychodynamic approaches, employing a traditional one-on-one encounter between the therapist and child, and addressing more global, intrapsychic issues rather than specific behavior problems (e.g. Sternbach, 1947; Berman, 1959). While some practitioners continue to provide one-on-one psychotherapy with children, there were a number of reasons why, in the early 1960s, a 'paradigm shift' in child treatment occurred.

Traditional psychodynamic approaches were not very successful in addressing the immediate issues of a child's behavior problem. Any changes that did occur in the 'artificial' therapeutic situation did not generalize to settings outside the clinic (such as home or school). Perhaps most importantly, parents' non-involvement in the child's treatment meant that little change occurred in the home environment. In contrast, principles of behavior modification were beginning to find success in managing child behavior in multiple settings, such as classrooms, hospitals, and other institutions (Kazdin, 1978).

Due to this confluence of factors, the idea of therapists training parents in techniques to modify their children's behavior was met with much enthusiasm. This partnership between the parent and therapist was also possible because it was

Figure 16.1   *Triadic model of parent training*

concurrent with a broader trend toward the 'deprofessionalization' of psychotherapy (as shown by the increasing popularity of 'self-help' books), which has served to increase the efficiency and accessibility of treatment among a larger pool of consumers.

Although basic behavior modification techniques were effective for managing less severe problem behaviors, therapists and researchers quickly realized that they were not sufficient for dealing with more extreme, antisocial child behavior. According to Kazdin (1985), in these situations, 'it became evident that deviant behavior required more than simple alterations of a few consequences … Sequences of interaction between parents and children in the home emerged as important'. This led to the establishment of parent training, as it is widely known.

Parent training employs the therapist as a consultant who works directly with the parent (mediator) to alleviate the problem behavior of the child (target) (see Figure 16.1). In the clinic, the basic parent training presentation consists primarily of instruction by the therapist in parenting techniques, with structured modeling, role plays and practice sessions, as well as homework assignments for the parent to practice with the child. This format was based on the assumption that deficits in parenting skills are at least partly responsible for the development and/or maintenance of child problem behaviors. Thus parent training provides parents with a repertoire of skills with which to manage, and eventually improve, the child's behavior as well as broader parent–child interactional patterns (Forehand, 1993).

As noted elsewhere (e.g. McMahon and Forehand, 2003), the development of parent training as an empirically validated practice has occurred in three distinct stages: establishment, generalization, and enhancement. The first stage (from 1960 to 1975) involved the establishment of the parent training format, as discussed above, and tests of its efficacy as a treatment for child problem behaviors. Early studies, which included a large number of descriptive articles with single-case designs, found good support for the short-term efficacy of parent training in reducing negative child behaviors (e.g. noncompliance, aggression, destructiveness) and improving parenting practices. The second stage included research conducted in broader terms between 1975 and 1985; the long-term effects and generalization of parent training were the new areas for consideration.

Generalization of treatment effects has been shown to occur in at least four areas: setting (transfer of behavior changes from the clinic to home or school); temporal (maintenance for behavior change over time); sibling (application of new parenting skills with non-targeted children); and behavioral (concomitant improvements in non-targeted behaviors) (Forehand and Atkeson, 1977). The empirical demonstration of the generalization of treatment effects has served to enhance the perceived social validity of parent training (whether the treatment effects are considered to be 'clinically' or 'socially' important to the client) as well as the clients' satisfaction with the treatment (Kazdin, 1977).

While parent training is not universally effective in treating child problem behaviors, the research conducted between 1975 and 1985 greatly increased our understanding of the general mechanisms and outcomes of this treatment approach. Following this period, the third stage of parent training research began to examine ways to expand and enhance the parent training curriculum. This line of research has considered a wider range of factors that can impact the implementation and outcomes of parent training. For example, the role of developmental variables has been emphasized in designing and implementing behaviorally oriented interventions (Eyberg et al., 1998). Researchers have also considered the contextual factors that can affect parent training, thus broadening the perspectives for treating child antisocial behavior. The parent training paradigm may be enhanced to include multiple areas of family functioning as targets for intervention (parental and/or marital adjustment, socio-economic factors), in addition to the traditional teaching of parenting skills (Griest and Wells, 1983). More recently, interventions have been designed to involve and co-ordinate multiple levels of the child's environment, including the home, school, clinic, and community (e.g. Henggeler et al., 1998). Accompanying these changes in emphasis, recent reviews have found increased generalization of the positive outcomes of parent training.

CORE ISSUES IN TREATING ANTISOCIAL CHILDREN AND ADOLESCENTS

Central to the development and implementation of parent training programs for child antisocial behavior has been the study of how such behavior develops and is maintained. In order effectively to address child behavior problems, it is necessary to understand these issues, as they have direct application to all parenting interventions discussed in this chapter. Thus, in this section, we will briefly summarize from Forehand and Long (1996, 2002) how child characteristics and parenting can interact to create family processes that place a child on a trajectory to antisocial behavior.

The roots of antisocial behavior are sometimes found in a child's temperament. The work of Thomas and Chess (1977) identified some children as having 'difficult' temperaments early in life. From their infancy, these children are usually restless, intense, distractible, and moody, tend to sleep irregularly, and to have problems adjusting to changes. Longitudinal research has shown that, without intervention, a difficult temperament can be a predecessor to later antisocial behavior.

Fortunately, effective parenting can improve many of these negative behaviors. However, parenting a temperamentally difficult child is not an easy process and many parents unfortunately fall into unwise parenting practices, known as 'traps.' As parent training researchers have delineated, there are two reinforcement 'traps' that often disrupt parenting behavior. Both serve to exacerbate the child's problematic behavior, particularly noncompliance, which has been viewed as a keystone behavior in the development of antisocial behavior of children.

The negative reinforcement trap, as described by Patterson (1982), occurs when a parent issues a direction to a noncompliant child ('Johnny, please pick up your toys'). The child is likely to respond by whining, protesting, or refusing to comply with the command. A parent may 'give in' or 'give up' by withdrawing the direction, to stop the child's protesting or to complete the designated task in a more timely manner. However, doing so unintentionally reinforces the very behavior that the parent is attempting to avoid. The child learns that loud protestation and defiance nullify undesirable parental directions (negative reinforcement). Thus, not only does noncompliance increase, but so do other behaviors that are precursors of antisocial behavior.

Frustrated, the parent may then try to 'get tougher' by yelling or even becoming physically aggressive with the child when he or she is noncompliant. In this case, the child stops protesting or complies out of fear, thereby negatively reinforcing the parent's 'tough' behavior. Over time, both parent and child escalate their negative behavior via the negative reinforcement processes.

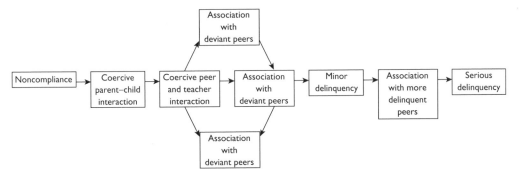

Figure 16.2 *The trajectory for the development of problem behaviors*

This results in a coercive and destructive cycle within the parent–child relationship. The goal of a parent training program is to stop this coercive cycle by teaching the parent better adaptive responses to noncompliant behavior. The effectiveness of such a program, in part, lies in how well these new parenting behaviors are learned and implemented.

Another factor contributing to the development of problem behaviors of children is the 'positive reinforcement trap', described by Wahler (1976). In such cases, oppositional behavior is reinforced because a parent responds with attention most frequently when the child misbehaves (spending time with the child talking about why he or she is not complying). Although parental attention is a necessary feature of good parenting, using it in response to undesirable behavior creates rather than solves problems. Even if given intermittently, parental attention to such behavior becomes a powerful reward for difficult children. As a result, the second goal of a parent training program is to help parents prevent the positive reinforcement trap by paying attention to positive, rather than negative, behaviors of their child. For example, attention is given to compliance instead of noncompliance and for co-operative play instead of fighting. Thus, effective parent training depends, in part, on how well parents can use positive reinforcement strategies to increase the frequency of appropriate child behaviors. As desirable behavior increases, negative behavior is likely to decrease.

The effectiveness of parent training is also determined by its timing, as far as the child's development is concerned. Early intervention with difficult behavior, particularly noncompliance, is important because such behavior can set a child on a path to increasingly antisocial behavior (Figure 16.2). Certainly not all difficult children

continue on this trajectory to its end. However, the longer that a child's misbehavior is addressed maladaptively, the more difficult it will become to modify both parenting and child behavior. In addition, research has shown that older children and adolescents who exhibit persistent antisocial behavior (as opposed to antisocial behavior that first begins in adolescence) tend to have behavior problems that are more severe and difficult to treat. When parenting programs intervene early and address the precursors to antisocial behavior, such as child noncompliance, increasingly serious problems can be prevented.

However, even with intensive intervention starting at an early age, it is important to point out that some children will continue to be difficult to treat. Attempts have been made to identify some characteristics of children who may be less amenable to any type of psychosocial intervention. Such children may be characterized as having a 'callous-unemotional' interpersonal style as, among other characteristics, they are low on empathy and guilt, and tend to manipulate others in a callous manner. Children with such tendencies have high rates of antisocial behavior, regardless of parenting quality. These children may not respond well to changed parental behavior as a result of training, though this hypothesis has not been tested (Wooton et al., 1997). In any case, clinicians are aware that some families will require substantially more effort than others when implementing a parenting program.

Implementation of Parenting Programs

ASSESSMENT

A significant first step in implementing a parenting program for child antisocial behavior is conducting a thorough assessment of relevant child, parent, family, and community variables that may need to be addressed in the intervention. Systematic assessment is vital for the identification of intervention targets as well as the measurement of change resulting from intervention (ascertained by pre- and post-intervention assessments).

As the focus of this chapter is on intervention, we provide only a brief overview of the most critical aspects of assessment. Readers should refer to the manual, *Helping the Noncompliant Child*, by McMahon and Forehand (2003) for more comprehensive discussions of assessment methods and available instruments.

The assessment of child or adolescent antisocial behavior must include the following elements:

- First, a detailed description of problematic behavior and the circumstances of its occurrence must be obtained. Specifically, information should be obtained regarding the nature of problem behavior, its frequency and severity, its history and development, and the contexts in which it tends to occur.
- Second, because the focus of parent training programs is on the modification of parent behaviors that may contribute to the development or maintenance of child antisocial behavior, assessment of parenting attitudes, styles, and skills should be very thorough. In particular, an assessment of the antecedents and consequences of child antisocial behavior, with an emphasis on parental responses, should be conducted.
- Third, the content of the assessment should also include measures of potential internalizing difficulties (depressive symptoms, anxiety symptoms), as these often co-occur with antisocial behavior.
- Fourth, specific areas of competence (sports, music), pro-social interactional skills (ability to form friendships, ability to relate to peers, teachers and coaches), and academic performance should be assessed, as the goal in treatment is not simply to eliminate antisocial behavior but also to increase the pro-social functioning of these children.
- Lastly, other risk factors often associated with child antisocial behavior, such as parental depressive symptoms, parental excessive alcohol/drug use, marital conflict, divorce, and community factors (neighborhood crime, gangs) should be assessed.

Assessment should also include the use of multiple reporters, meaning that parents, the child (when she or he is old enough to provide valid information), and, in some cases, others (grandparent, teacher) should serve as sources of data.

Each person provides a unique perspective, and each perspective is important to consider in designing an intervention. Furthermore, data should be collected through multiple methods of assessment: (a) interviews; (b) questionnaires; and (c) behavioral observation by the therapist or another person in the clinic and/or home. One method is not necessarily better than another, as each has strengths and weaknesses. By employing multiple methods, the strengths of each are utilized while the weaknesses are minimized.

In a later section, we describe one empirically validated parenting program (Helping the Noncompliant Child) for child antisocial behavior. Two assessment methods associated with this program are described here to illustrate the importance and utility of a thorough, multimodal assessment of both parenting and child behavior. First, typical daily situations, which frequently are problematic for noncompliant children, are assessed during the interview (e.g. going to bed at night, taking a bath, disrupting the parent during a telephone conversation). If a parent experiences a problem in any area, the parent is asked to describe in detail how he or she handles the situation, how the child responds, and how often the problem occurs. Such a detailed analysis of noncompliant behavior and parental responses often illuminates specific targets for intervention.

Second, the parent and child are observed in two situations, labeled 'Child's Game' and 'Parent's Game.' The Child's Game consists of basically free play, with the child determining the rules and activities of the interaction; the parent is told to let the child take the lead and play with the child in whatever activity he or she chooses (within reason). In the Parent's Game, the parent is told to engage the child in an activity and to make the rules and provide direction. These brief interactions give the clinician an idea of how the parent and child interact under conditions of both low and high structure. It is also helpful to note how often in the Child's Game a parent asks questions or gives directions to the child, despite being asked not to do so, and to compare this parental behavior with how frequently the parent praises the child's positive behaviors.

The former behaviors are typical of many parents with noncompliant children, because they have developed a pattern of bombarding the child with directions in hopes of obtaining occasional compliance. This is the opposite of what is taught in parent training programs: parents are asked to attend to and praise a child's appropriate behavior, while issuing fewer directions. In the Parent's Game, how a parent issues directions

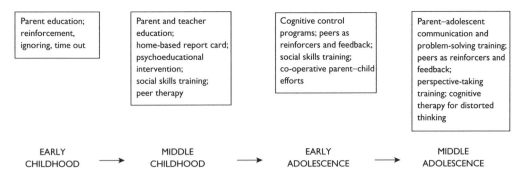

Figure 16.3   *Summary of interventions at each developmental age*

to the child (word choice, tone of voice, facial expression, body language), whether or not the child complies, and what the parent does in response to that compliance or noncompliance should be observed. Many parents of noncompliant children rely on ineffective methods of issuing directions (using questions or issuing multiple directives at one time) which reduce the likelihood that a child can or will comply. Thus, observations made during the Child and Parent Games can be very helpful aspects of assessment and treatment planning.

INTERVENTION

Parent training programs all share several common or core elements:

- focusing more on parents than the child;
- moving from a preoccupation with anti-social behavior to an emphasis on pro-social behavior;
- teaching parents to identify, define, and record child behavior;
- instructing parents in social learning principles (reinforcement of pro-social behavior, withdrawal of attention for misbehavior through the use of ignoring or time-out);
- teaching new parenting skills via didactic instruction, modeling, role playing, practicing with the child in the clinic and home;
- discussing ways to maximize generalization of skills from the clinic to the home; and
- when necessary, addressing parental (such as depressive symptoms), family (marital conflict), and community (neighborhood violence) risks, which may interfere with acquisition or maintenance of new parenting skills and adaptive child behavior.

Though the core elements are present in all parent training interventions, programs may differ in

their emphasis on each component. For example, the parent training program developed by Patterson (1975a, 1975b) has stressed the importance of parents learning the language of social learning principles, as well as learning to define and count behavior. In both the first and second editions of the book delineating their program, McMahon and Forehand (2003) stress the importance of teaching procedures (didactic instruction, modeling, role-playing, practice with child in clinic and at home, programming generalization to the home). In contrast, Webster-Stratton (1996) emphasizes the demonstration of parenting skills through videotaped modeling of skills rather than therapist teaching. In addition, Sanders et al. (2000) have used print and televised media as an avenue for intervention. It is important to point out that the variations across programs are probably of less significance than their common elements. A clinician choosing among programs should look at the available empirical support for a program more than these relatively minor variations across programs.

One characteristic that does influence the type of intervention utilized is the age of the child. Some changes in an intervention program that occur as the child grows older are summarized in Figure 16.3. As a child increases in age, her or his cognitive abilities and source of reinforcement (parents, peers) change, which leads to changes in intervention strategies. Several investigators have found that parent training is more effective with younger children, and their families are less likely to drop out of treatment. With older children, and particularly adolescents, parent training interventions may not only be less effective but are more difficult to implement. As a result, alternative family-based treatments for adolescent antisocial behavior have been designed in recent years.

In particular, Chamberlain has begun utilizing an alternative intensive intervention, Treatment Foster Care (TFC), for difficult-to-treat delinquent adolescents (Moore and Chamberlain, 1994). In this approach, adolescents are placed with community families who are experienced with teenagers, have good parenting skills in the form of behavior management strategies, and are willing to work as part of a treatment team. In most cases, the goal is to have the adolescent return to live with his or her family, which receives substantial intervention during and after the adolescent is in treatment foster care. Of importance, even with innovative programs such as the one developed by Chamberlain, the basic model of parent training remains the centerpiece component.

Clinicians working with children with antisocial behavior should give serious consideration to parent training. As a recent meta-analysis of 26 controlled studies indicates, behavioral parent training is associated with improvements in child behavior and parent personal adjustment (Serketich and Dumas, 1996). Furthermore, this approach has the most empirical support of any intervention for child antisocial behavior (Feldman and Kazdin, 1995). If parent training is selected as the intervention of choice for the treatment of antisocial behavior, the clinician must then choose among the various parenting programs that are currently available. In the final section of this chapter, we provide detailed guidelines for practitioners on the selection of an age-appropriate, empirically validated parent training intervention.

A PARENT TRAINING PROGRAM

In order to provide an example of one such parent training program, we now present a brief overview of the Helping the Noncompliant Child program, developed by McMahon and Forehand (2003). This is a program for young children (ages 2–8 years); as we have noted, modifications would occur for older children and adolescents (see Figure 16.3). The program has considerable empirical support demonstrating its short- and long-term effectiveness, and Forehand and his colleagues have adapted the program to be delivered in both a group format and a self-guided book for parents. The following overview explains the guiding principles of the program, the major intervention components, and the teaching procedures employed by the therapist in working with parents.

Basics of the Helping the Noncompliant Child (HNC) Program

This program makes use of the two primary situations in which parents interact with their child: times when the parent and child are enjoying mutual positive interactions, and times when there are tasks to accomplish and the parent needs or chooses to exercise his or her authority (assign chores, give directions, require attention, punish misbehavior). For most parents who come to a clinic with a noncompliant child, the second scenario is their primary focus. Usually the parent is mainly interested in acquiring more control over the child rather than improving the quality of his or her interactions with the child. However, our program focuses on *both* of these aspects of parenting. Thus, the HNC program consists of two major phases:

- teaching skills that are designed to improve the parent–child relationship, as well as to increase the child's desirable behaviors, and
- teaching skills that assist parents in dealing with noncompliance and other problematic child behavior.

It is best to teach the positive interactional skills first, and the procedures to enhance control or disciplinary efficacy only after those skills are genuinely in place. When taught in the reverse order, parents frequently learn to discipline their noncompliant child more effectively, but drop out of therapy before learning positive interactional skills. Without improvements in the parent–child relationship, future behavior problems are likely to develop.

The first phase of the program has three components: *attending*, *rewarding*, and *ignoring*. In the attending component, parents are taught simply to pay attention to their child's activities. The parent is taught to describe what the child is doing while refraining from giving directions or asking questions. This is designed to 'slow the parent down' and have him or her focus on the child's positive behavior. Parents often learn *for the first time* that their noncompliant child does display positive behaviors, at least sometimes. Sharing playtime also communicates to a noncompliant child that the parent is actively interested in what he or she is doing, and that the parent is paying attention in circumstances other than when the child misbehaves.

The second component involves teaching the parent to praise or reward the child's positive behavior. The types of rewards that are taught consist of verbal ('I really like it when you pick up your toys!') and physical (hug, pat, kiss) rewards. Parents are taught to reward pro-social rather than negative behaviors. The emphasis reiterated to the parent should be to focus attention on the positive behaviors of the non-compliant child and express approval when appropriate.

The third component of the initial phase of the program involves teaching a parent to ignore minor unacceptable behavior, such as whining, crying, and demanding attention. The parent is taught an ignoring procedure that involves no eye or physical contact, and no verbal recognition when minor unacceptable behaviors occur. The purpose of ignoring is to help the child differentiate between appropriate behaviors (which the parents attend/praise) and inappropriate behaviors (which the parents ignore). Parents commonly find ignoring their children a difficult skill to learn, but one that is ultimately effective in reducing minor problem behaviors.

In the second phase of the program, the therapist teaches the parent two disciplinary skills: how to issue directions and how to use a time-out procedure. Many parents give unclear directions, and, when the child does not comply, they become unfairly frustrated and angry. Therefore, parents are taught to give directions in simple, single units (rather than as a series) and to state them in a straightforward and positive manner.

Once a parent can issue effective directions, he or she is then taught to use a time-out sequence for instances when the child does not comply with the directions. Parents are asked to select a safe (and boring) place in their home to use for time out. Ideally, children in time out should not be able to see the television, toys, other people, or anything else that might be reinforcing or engaging. Time out is used when a child does not comply to a clear and simple direction issued by a parent, and after the child has received one warning. Parents are taught to lead their child to time out without lecturing, scolding, or arguing. In fact, during time out, parents are asked not to make any physical or verbal contact with their child, including eye contact, except what is minimally necessary to implement the time-out procedure. Children are then instructed to sit in the time out chair until a pre-designated time period is over. Generally speaking, children should remain in time out for one minute for each year of their age (five-year-olds stay in time out for five minutes). When the time out is over, the original direction is re-issued. Time out is implemented again if the child fails to comply a second time (and every time until compliance is achieved). Just as important as learning the procedures for time out

in response to child noncompliance, the parent is taught to praise the child when he or she does comply with the direction.

Teaching Procedures

The components of the parenting management program for noncompliant children are taught in a structured manner over the course of 8–12 sessions. The procedures by which a clinician teaches the parenting skills appear to be particularly important because parents who have difficulties interacting with their child cannot simply be told to change those interactions. Instead, skills have to be taught systematically either within a one-on-one session, a structured group, or via a self-guided parenting program.

The following procedures should be used by a clinician to teach the skills:

1 the skill and the rationale for the skill are described to the parent;
2 the clinician models the skill for the parent;
3 the parent practices the skill with the clinician;
4 the child is brought into the therapy room and the parent practices the skill with the child, while receiving feedback from the clinician;
5 ways to use the skill in various practical situations at home are discussed.

Each skill delineated in the preceding section is taught in this manner. Thus, the parent acquires one skill before moving to the subsequent skill. Similar procedures for skill acquisition can be used in the self-guided book for parents which is based on the HNC program, entitled *Parenting the Strong Willed Child* (Forehand and Long, 2002).

An additional part of the teaching procedures consists of the clinician's modeling of how the parent should interact with the child. For example, the clinician can interrupt his or her conversation with the parent to praise the child when he or she is playing quietly. In addition, the clinician can praise the parent for displaying good parenting skills. Both examples are effective ways of demonstrating the targeted skills to the parent.

OVERVIEW: THE CHALLENGES OF PARENTING INTERVENTIONS

Although parent training programs, such as the one just described, have been widely supported as efficacious interventions for preventing and treating child and adolescent antisocial behavior, there remain many barriers to their effective implementation by clinical practitioners. This section will review some of the challenges commonly faced by practitioners who are working with antisocial children and their families, and offer suggestions for overcoming these obstacles in order to deliver parent training interventions to those families who may benefit from them the most.

Challenge: The Broader Social Context in Which a Family Functions Interferes with Treatment or Maintenance of Treatment Gains

While parenting interventions may appear as though they were developed to be delivered in a vacuum, clinical researchers and practitioners alike have long recognized that broader social and environmental factors influence parenting behavior and response to treatment. Perhaps the best example of this is the socio-economic status (SES) of a family. Many researchers and clinicians have noted that greater socio-economic stress is associated with treatment dropout and poorer outcomes at the conclusion of parent training. Practitioners must recognize that families of lower SES face numerous stressors that may interfere with their ability to complete a parenting intervention and which may ultimately compromise any therapy gains. These stressors include poverty, substandard housing, residence in crowded and high-crime neighborhoods, lower education, and single parenthood.

Another contextual variable related to socio-economic status that may contribute to ineffective parent training efforts is *social insularity*, the experience of social alienation reported by many poor families (Wahler et al., 1979). It has been shown that the social networks of lower income families are often characterized not only by a lack of resources but also by the negative nature of social contacts that are available. Interactions with extended family are frequently more conflictual, and contacts with community supports are more often initiated by official agencies in response to a problem than self-initiated for support. Thus, for many families of antisocial youth, social networks that could provide support for dealing with child conduct problems are actually viewed as being highly stressful and do not provide the supportive scaffolding that may enhance parent training efforts with these highly stressed families.

When working with lower SES families, practitioners should keep in mind the following suggestions:

- Parenting programs that can offer on-site childcare while parents are in session or assist with transportation needs have had greater success in keeping parents in treatment.
- Interventions need to be delivered within the communities in which families reside, and must be offered at convenient times and locations. For example, use of community centers, churches, or schools located close to a family's home as places to deliver parent training interventions may greatly improve attendance and opportunities for success.
- Due to the negative nature of most social service contacts that families of lower income status experience, parenting interventions may be most effective when delivered by individuals and agencies trusted by parents. When this is not possible, establishing rapport prior to conducting any formal assessment or treatment is a critical first step to successful intervention.
- Parent trainers may need directly to address the broader needs of a family by either referring them to social service agencies or including a social work component in their treatment program.
- Enhancement of parents' social supports, particularly those that provide parenting support, may become a critical target of intervention. For some families, treatment for child problem behavior may end up looking more like case management at first. Parents cannot fully engage in parent training until their other basic needs have been adequately addressed.
- Working with socially isolated or highly stressed families that present for assistance in managing their children's antisocial behavior may require much more than parent training in order to be successful.

Challenge: Most Parenting Interventions Have Been Developed with Caucasian Families and Some Principles or Techniques May Not Generalize Well to Families of Other Ethnic Backgrounds

Parent training, and the conceptual models upon which it is based, were developed primarily with intact, middle-class families of European American descent. Little consideration has been formally given to how cultural factors, including ethnicity and social class, contribute to the development of parenting and the interventions designed to improve it. Indeed, parent training, as it has been described in this chapter and evaluated in the empirical literature, is based on the assumption that particular parenting behaviors (positive reinforcement, non-physical punishment) are associated with optimal child and adolescent development. However, little research has been directed to testing these assumptions in diverse ethnic groups. Culture and ethnicity do play critical roles in shaping child-rearing attitudes and practices, and to conduct parenting interventions without being sensitive to the cultural context of parenting leaves clinicians vulnerable to alienating the very families who seek their help (Forehand and Kotchick, 1996).

Little is known about the effectiveness of parent training with particular ethnic groups, or what factors best predict success in parent training with ethnically diverse populations. Without such data to guide decisions about treatment for antisocial behavior, practitioners are left with having to evaluate the 'fit' between parent training principles and techniques and a particular family's ethnic or cultural approach to parenting. Certainly, parent training leaves itself open to some modification based on a family's needs, and practitioners are encouraged to make such modifications, if cultural beliefs about parenting clash with the theoretical and practical underpinnings of the parent training programs currently available. In this spirit, we offer the following suggestions based on available literature and our own experiences with implementing parenting interventions in the increasingly culturally diverse United States.

- First and foremost, practitioners must have an awareness of the cultural attitudes and practices related to parenting that a family espouses before implementing parent training. Practitioners can learn from their clients by asking questions about minority cultural parenting beliefs, expectations, and practices during assessment. Some sample questions are presented in Table 16.1.
- Similarly, clinicians working with populations other than those typically studied in the realm of parenting and parent training may need to consult the work of colleagues in other social sciences, who have conducted research on parenting in diverse cultures, including anthropology, sociology, and political science.
- Aspects of parent training may need to be modified to match parenting beliefs and expectations.

For example, in our work with African-American families, we encountered substantial resistance to the notion of reinforcing or rewarding children for compliance with parental demands. The

Table 16.1 *Assessment of parenting in diverse cultures*

1	How did your parents raise you?
2	How do you feel about going to a professional who helps you deal with your child's problems?
3	What child behaviors are most appreciated by you as a parent?
4	What child behaviors are most difficult for you as a parent?
5	What parenting practices work best in changing your child's behavior?
6	What parenting practices do not work so well in changing your child's behavior?
7	What do you think about techniques, such as reinforcement and time out, which are taught in behavioral parenting programs?
8	What is the best way to teach new parenting practices/skills to you?
9	What are the stresses that interfere with you doing your best as a parent?

African-American families with whom we interacted seemed to consider compliance to be an expected behavior, and rewarding such behavior was viewed as undermining a central family theme of respecting authority. We dealt with this issue by changing our language: instead of referring to reinforcement as 'rewarding', we referred to the practice of overtly showing appreciation for child compliance as 'showing your child that you love her' and as a step to building stronger parent–child relationships. We also de-emphasized material and, to some extent, verbal rewards and stressed the importance of non-verbal and social reinforcement (giving hugs, granting special privileges).

Challenge: Other Family Processes May Interfere with the Delivery of Parenting Interventions

In addition to contextual factors outside the family, such as social class or culture, the internal family context may also affect the ability of the practitioner to effectively implement parent training. Factors that may interfere with the delivery of parent training as it has been presented in this chapter may include intrapersonal functioning (parental psychopathology) and interpersonal functioning (marital conflict) within the family. In terms of parental psychopathology, the best-studied topic has been parental depression or depressive symptoms. Although fathers are receiving more attention in recent research, most of the available literature focuses on maternal depressive symptoms and its relation to parenting and parent training outcomes. Maternal depressive symptoms have been found to relate to a number of disrupted parenting practices, including inconsistent or overly harsh discipline, poor responsiveness to children, and avoidance of conflict (see Cummings and Davies, 1994; Goodman and Gotlib, 1999, for reviews). Parental depression has also been found to relate negatively to parent training outcomes. Most notably, parental depressive symptoms are associated with premature dropout from treatment.

Marital difficulties, particularly conflict between parents, have also been extensively studied in terms of its relationship to parenting and parent training effectiveness (see Dadds et al., 1987; Emery, 1999). It has been proposed that conflict between parents may operate through disrupted parenting to affect children's behavior negatively. Parents engaging in high levels of conflict may be less responsive to children's needs, less likely to attend to children's behavior or provide positive reinforcement, or less consistent in terms of discipline. Research concerning the impact of marital conflict on parent training appears to support a long-term, rather than short-term effect. Specifically, conflict between parents and low marital satisfaction does not seem to affect immediate outcomes and the conflict may actually show improvement over the course of parent training. However, higher levels of marital conflict at the start of parent training have been shown to interfere with maintenance of treatment gains over time.

Parental depressive symptoms and marital conflict are included here as examples of the types of family processes that may contribute to child antisocial behavior and to difficulties in implementing parent training successfully. Indeed, there are many other family factors to consider before beginning parent training, including other forms of parental psychopathology (such as anxiety disorders), parental substance abuse, parental stress and anger coping skills, and relationships among other family members. To treat antisocial behavior in children and adolescents effectively, clinicians must first conduct a careful assessment of the family climate. After doing so, the practitioner may decide that parent training is the treatment of choice or, alternatively, that it should be deferred until after other family problems are addressed. While there are no firm guidelines for matching families with specific interventions, the available literature and our own clinical experience offer the following guidelines to assist practitioners in the treatment planning process:

- If parental depressive symptoms or marital problems are not severe and/or appear to be related to child behavior or its management, parent training itself may be an effective treatment. Indeed, marital satisfaction scores have improved after parent training, as has parental depression.

- Parent training may be enhanced to address other family problems, such as parental depressive symptoms or marital distress. *Parent Enhancement Therapy* has been developed as an adjunct to Helping the Noncompliant Child. This program includes components to enhance communication between parents, problem-solving skills, and pleasant activities shared by spouses. These components are intended to target both marital conflict and parental depressive symptoms. Similarly, parent training programs may be modified to include components that address other family problems as well.

- If other family problems are severe enough to warrant more immediate or intensive attention, parent training could be conducted concurrently with treatment for the other problems of concern. It is recommended that such treatment be conducted with an independent therapist so that the clinician working on parent training may remain focused on the issues around child behavior and parenting practices.

- Finally, if depressive symptoms, marital conflict, or other family problems are very severe (e.g. a parent is suicidal; divorce is imminent), it may be better to delay parent training until those problems have received sufficient attention. Parent training is more likely to be effective if these issues have already been addressed in therapy.

Challenge: Parental Expectations of Child Behavior, and of the Therapy Process, May Interfere with Their Ability to Adhere to the Treatment Regimen

Engaging families in parent training requires that parents view the intervention as an appropriate and potentially useful one for dealing with their concerns. Often parents of antisocial children arrive at the therapist's door with biased, distorted, or unrealistic expectations or attributions about their child's problem behavior, its causes, their own parenting efficacy, or the therapy process. Sometimes, parents have unrealistic expectations about the developmental appropriateness (or inappropriateness) of their children's behavior, or they are so focused on the negative interactions with their child that they ignore or fail to recognize the child's good qualities. In addition, exasperated parents initially may not agree with the 'philosophy' of parent training: here they are, bringing their child to the clinician to be 'fixed', and they are told that they have to do all the work!

Several clinical researchers have written about the engagement process in parent training (see Prinz and Miller, 1996). For example, four domains have been found to be associated with engagement in parent training:

- parental expectations, attributions, and beliefs;
- situational demands and constraints (financial and social stressors, marital and personal adjustment);
- intervention characteristics (group versus individual parent training, type of intervention, scheduling of sessions, homework); and
- relationship with the therapist.

Webster-Stratton and her colleagues have utilized qualitative research methods to describe the process of parent training interventions from the perspective of the parents going through it (e.g. Webster-Stratton and Herbert, 1994). In her formulation, the initial stage parents went through involved their acknowledgement that their children were engaging in behaviors that they were not able to control. Later, parents had to embrace the long-term commitment required in parent training approaches in order for the treatment to be successful.

As such, assessing, validating, and, when necessary, correcting parent's perceptions of their children's behavior and their expectations of therapy become a critical part of the treatment process. There are several ways to accomplish this:

- First, ask parents to share their ideas on the nature of their child's behavior, as well as their expectations about what needs to be done to alter it. This assessment will provide important information about 'where parents are coming from,' and how much ground they need to cover before skills training may be initiated.
- Second, parents who hold inappropriate expectations regarding child behavior (temper tantrums are unacceptable after age 2; young children should be able to follow multiple directions given at one time) should be educated about appropriate developmental expectations.
- Third, for parents who have become overly focused on the negative aspects of their child's behavior, model recognition and

acknowledgement of the child's strengths, and assist parents in identifying their child's positive qualities.

- Fourth, offer an explanation of social learning principles behind parent training techniques. Parents who have some understanding of why they are being asked to do certain things and how parent training works may not be as frustrated by the demands placed on them or by setbacks in later sessions.

Challenge: Parents May Not Comply with the High Demands Placed on Them in Most Parenting Interventions

Success in parent training relies on parents' willingness to comply with homework assignments (completing behavioral observations at home, practicing skills in between sessions; reading materials that are often lengthy or complex) and regular attendance (often once per week) at sessions for up to several months. Some programs also require frequent telephone contacts with therapists between sessions. Relative to other therapies, behaviorally based parent training places high demands on parents. The cost paid by parents, though well worth it in the long run, may seem overwhelming at the outset.

Parents' failure to comply with parent training requirements has been the subject of study by Patterson, Chamberlain and colleagues (e.g. Patterson and Chamberlain, 1988, 1994). *Parental resistance*, as it has been termed, may occur both within-session (refusing to perform tasks in session, stated inability to perform) and out-of-session (failure to complete homework assignments). Contextual variables, such as social disadvantage and parental psychopathology are associated with initial resistance, and continue to play a role in parental investment in therapy over the long run. According to Patterson and Chamberlain's 'struggle hypothesis,' parental resistance is expected to increase in early sessions, but eventually decrease as parents begin to meet with success in implementing their new skills. However, initial resistance is dangerous; high levels of resistance in the first two sessions of parent training have been associated with subsequent dropout.

The quality of the relationship between parents and the therapist has been identified as a critical factor in parental compliance or resistance. Research with a family-based intervention for adolescents with conduct problems indicates that relationship characteristics such as affect-behavior integration, warmth, and humor accounted for much of the treatment outcome. Another study revealed that the directive behavior of parent trainers (teaching and confronting) actually increased parental resistance in session, whereas supportive and facilitative therapist behaviors had the opposite effect. Thus, it is clear that practitioners employing parent training must be able to successfully combine the directive, *teaching skills* intrinsic to the approach with *relationship building skills*, such as empathy, warmth, and humor.

Although establishing a collaborative, supportive therapeutic relationship will certainly go a long way in promoting parental investment in treatment, there still remain the practical costs of parent training, including the time demanded by treatment and the expense of attending sessions. Overcoming these barriers, particularly for families most likely to present for treatment (highly stressed, with fewer available resources), can be difficult. However, being creative and flexible often generates potential solutions, such as the following:

- Offer incentives or rewards for progress and compliance in therapy. For example, returning portions of a refundable deposit, engaging in phone calls with clients, and actually conducting treatment sessions can be made contingent on completion of assigned tasks. Alternatively, paying parents a small 'parenting salary' upon completion of assigned tasks may increase compliance and reduce dropout, particularly for lower-income families. Such a 'salary' could involve a small reduction in the weekly therapy fees charged.
- Being flexible in terms of where and when sessions are conducted may increase parental co-operation. As stated earlier, holding sessions at a trusted, local community center or offering services such as transportation or childcare may be particularly powerful incentives for parents at high risk for dropout due to the level of competing demands for their time.
- Employing with parents some of the same techniques they are expected to use with their children (e.g. attending, positive reinforcement) not only models these skills for parents, but also may serve to increase compliance with treatment demands.

Challenge: Because Antisocial Behavior is More Common Among Families Who Face a Variety of Other Stressors, Therapists May Feel Incapable of Effecting Real and Lasting Change

Parent training has never been characterized as a particularly taxing form of therapy for those who practice it. Indeed, since most of the real effort is made by parents, parent training may even be considered by some to be an 'easy' treatment to implement. However, for those who work with severely antisocial children, burnout is a real issue. Often the odds are stacked against treatment success; families are overburdened or overstressed, or the child's own behavior (severe antisocial/delinquent behavior) makes parenting interventions difficult to administer. In addition, true treatment success is often dependent upon the presence and strength of family and community supports, forces which are often beyond the control of the therapist.

To counter feelings of powerlessness and exhaustion, practitioners working with severely antisocial children are encouraged to follow the lead of Linehan and her colleagues, who identified therapist support systems as being critical to success in her 'dialectical behavior therapy' for adults with borderline personality disorder (Linehan and Kehrer, 1993). Additionally, parent trainers can work toward building a network within the community to implement multi-level interventions. For example, Pro-social Family Therapy (Blechman, 1998) specifies a close working relationship and treatment involvement among all adults who serve care-taking roles in the target child's life (at school, in the juvenile justice system).

FUTURE DIRECTIONS IN PARENT TRAINING

The following section will serve as a forum for discussing the future directions of parent training research and dissemination, based in part on the current status of parenting interventions for child antisocial behavior problems. To this end, the section is divided into a guide for practitioners, a guide for researchers, and a guide for policymakers. However, as will be discussed, one of the barriers encountered in promoting the value of parenting programs among practicing clinicians is that these three groups of professionals operate separately and rarely communicate with each other. While we do not wish to exacerbate these divisions, we have organized the section in this fashion for clarity of presentation.

A Guide for Clinicians

As stated earlier, parent training is the best *empirically evaluated intervention* for child and adolescent antisocial behavior. Unfortunately, treatment programs that have the best empirical support are often the ones that are most poorly disseminated among practitioners. Often, the 'publicity' directed toward such programs is limited to the attention they receive in peer-reviewed scientific journals or professional conferences. What many practitioners have easy access to, however, are various parenting programs that are advertised by mailings or brochures designed to catch the clinician's eye, but which have few or no data supporting their efficacy. Fortunately, there are now several resources to help clinicians select an age-appropriate, empirically validated program.

First, a review published in the *Journal of Clinical Child Psychology* in 1998 identified treatment programs that were 'well established' or 'probably efficacious' based on their empirical support (Brestan and Eyberg, 1998). Among the programs with the best empirical support for treating child behavior problems were those based on Patterson's program, Living with Children (designed for parents of pre-adolescents); Webster-Stratton's The Incredible Years (designed for parents of 3–10 year olds), Forehand and McMahon's Helping the Noncompliant Child (designed for parents of 2–8 year olds), Eyberg and colleagues' Parent–Child Interaction Therapy (designed for parents of 2–8 year olds), Tremblay and colleagues' Delinquency Prevention Program (designed for parents of preschoolers through adolescence), and Henggeler and colleagues' Multisystemic Therapy (designed for parents of adolescents).

Second, in 2000, the Office of Juvenile Justice and Delinquency Prevention and the Center for Substance Abuse Prevention published *Strengthening America's Families: Model Family Programs for Substance Abuse and Delinquency Prevention*, which showcases research-based prevention programs that are family-focused and have demonstrated effectiveness (Alvarado et al., 2000). Seven programs have been assigned the highest rating (Exemplary I) because of the use of an experimental design with a randomized sample, replication by an independent investigator, and multiple studies demonstrating clear evidence of program effectiveness. Seven programs are designated as Exemplary II in that they meet all criteria for Exemplary I programs except independent replication.

The Exemplary I and II programs are presented in Table 16.2. Designation of Exemplary I or II status is noted and programs are classified by age of child for which they were designed. There is also a Strengthening America's

Families website (http://www.strengthening-families.org) which may be used as a reference to select an empirically validated parenting program.

Certainly, clinical researchers who develop and validate treatment programs have traditionally failed adequately to promote their products, often leaving practitioners to rely on less validated, but better marketed, interventions. However, this breakdown in communication between science and practice may also be due to the lack of a viable avenue through which clinicians can communicate with the researchers about any difficulties encountered in the implementation of a laboratory-tested treatment program with real clients. Clearly, there is a need for a dialogue whereby researchers can be made aware of these difficulties firsthand. Then, as the individuals most familiar with the treatment, they can partner with clinicians in developing solutions similar to those presented in the challenges section of this chapter. However, it would also be beneficial for clinicians to be more involved in the research process so that these parent training programs can be better fitted to real-world practice. One potential path for this involvement is for clinicians using empirically supported parent training programs to submit case studies of treatment implementation in journals that specialize in issues related to clinical treatment, such as *Cognitive and Behavioral Practice* or *Clinical Case Studies*.

A Guide for Researchers

With parent training emerging as one of the best-studied child and family treatment, researchers now find themselves in an unprecedented position: they have the opportunity to move research objectives beyond establishing efficaciousness in clinical trials. This extension is somewhat uncommon in social and behavioral sciences. However, in other fields, establishing efficaciousness in clinical trials is only one of several steps involved in fully examining a treatment (see Duan and Rotheram-Borus, 1999). In the biomedical field, for example, testing for efficaciousness comes after first establishing that programs do no harm (Phase I) and, second, might have beneficial effects (Phase II). Then, efficaciousness is established in Phase III trials, after which dissemination trials (Phase IV) begin. Phase IV trials involve implementing treatment under less controlled conditions and exploring how effectively treatment can be integrated into actual treatment settings with a range of providers and with more heterogeneous populations. This step is crucial, as every intervention that has

Table 16.2 *Strengthening America's families: Exemplary I and II programs[a]*

Age of child for which Program is designed	Exemplary I	Exemplary II
0–5		Prenatal and Early Childhood Nurse Home Visiting Program (Obrien.ruth@tchden.org)
2–8	Helping the Noncompliant Child (McMahon@u.washington.edu)	
3–10	The Incredible Years (www.incredibleyears.com)	
4–7		Raising a Thinking Child (Mshure@drexel.edu)
6–10	Strengthening Families Program (Vmolgaar@iastate.edu)	
6–18	Functional Family Therapy (Jfafft@psych.utah.edu)	
8–14	Preparing for the Drug Free Years (Moreinfo@drp.org)	
6–18		Parenting Wisely (www.familyworksinc.com)
8–17		Brief Strategic Family Therapy (not available)
10–18	Multisystemic Therapy (Keller@mstservices.com)	
10–14		Strengthening Families Program for Parents and Youth 10–14 (www.exnet.iastate.edu)
11–18		Multidimensional Family Therapy (hliddle@med.miami.edu)
11–18		Adolescent Transition Programs (Katek@hevanet.com)
12–18	Treatment Foster Care (Pattic@tigger.oslc.org)	

[a]Email or web addresses for programs are presented in parentheses.

been supported in research has not always been supported in practice.

Parent training programs for treating child antisocial behavior are clearly 'ready' for Phase IV trials, and in some cases, Phase IV trials are being carried out. In moving beyond clinical trials, it appears that parent training researchers should now focus on three areas: (1) identifying alternative methods of packaging or delivering parent training programs to diverse families; (2) developing effective methods for training clinicians in established intervention programs; and (3) disseminating programs so that they will reach the necessary audiences.

PACKAGING AND DELIVERING INTERVENTIONS

A longstanding concern of both researchers and clinicians has been how to best 'package' programs so that they are accessible to families who do not traditionally present for treatment in clinics and mental health centers. In research studies, treatment is typically administered either by individuals with graduate degrees in clinical psychology or by individuals who are highly trained in treatment delivery. Research is needed to determine how treatment might be implemented in settings (schools, social service agencies, housing authorities) where parents are already involved and which are administered by individuals with whom the parents are already familiar. As an example of the type of research needed, Miller and her colleagues are currently evaluating ParentCorps, which is a parent training program administered by individuals from the communities in which the participating parents reside (Calzada et al., 2000). Training for facilitators is time-consuming and intensive, as they have varying levels of experience in working with families and acting in leadership roles. However, these facilitators will probably have the best chance of success in engaging parents and quickly establishing rapport. The outcomes from projects such as this one will begin to provide some answers to questions about community implementation of parenting programs.

In addition, it is likely that treatment in community settings will progress quite differently from the standard 12 weekly one-hour sessions that occur in clinics. In our experience, attempting to adhere to 12 one-hour sessions can be a challenge even when working with middle-class families in the structured environment of the clinic. Research is needed to determine how both the treatment pace and didactic skill delivery may need to differ from that of the clinic when implemented in community settings. It is often unreasonable to expect that low-income families can commit to three months of weekly sessions at the same time each week due to irregularity of times when they may be working and previously mentioned challenges such as difficulty obtaining childcare and transportation. With highly stressed families, it may be necessary to distill the information taught in a parenting program and focus only on a few 'effective ingredients'. While we recognize these challenges to treatment, as scientist-practitioners we also recognize the need for systematic research that will identify those crucial skills or pieces of knowledge that parents must know to adequately modify their children's behavior.

Other potential options for the delivery of interventions include utilization of the less-intensive treatment methods mentioned previously, including group interventions, books, and computer-based programs, and these options are in need of further empirical validation. While traditional therapist–client interventions are quite successful, the costs of one-on-one treatment are relatively high. Alternatives deserve consideration, as they offer several benefits that may make them worthwhile if one-on-one treatment is not realistic or otherwise possible. For example, while parents in a group setting may not receive as much individual therapist attention, they may benefit significantly from interacting with other parents experiencing similar difficulties with their children. Books, as noted earlier, can be used either independently or as a supplement to traditional interventions. Computer-based programs are a more recent innovation. However, at least one such program has met with empirical support and successful outcomes. Parenting Wisely (http://www.family-worksinc.com) is an interactive and self-administered CD-ROM program that requires no outside intervention in order to be implemented. Clearly, more research attention is needed to evaluate programs such as these, both as stand-alone interventions and as a way to augment more traditional parenting interventions.

TRAINING CLINICIANS

In order for programs to be implemented smoothly by practitioners, they need to be packaged in a way that allows for thorough assimilation of the skills by the therapist. However, determining the most thorough method of instruction must also be balanced by considerations regarding monetary costs and the time required to learn the programs. Treatment manuals, which most programs provide, are quite thorough and low-cost but may involve time-intensive self-study and do not provide opportunities to have questions answered or to obtain supervision and feedback on implementation. Workshops, which some programs offer, provide intensive training on the material covered in the treatment manuals and typically offer opportunities to role play skills and even obtain feedback on skill use, but are usually costly and may require travel. One option that complements the training manuals involves videos of therapists conducting each of the parent training sessions with a family. These videos are useful both for clinicians and for parents as both can see how treatment will probably progress.

An excellent example of an effective training method is currently being conducted in Norway. The government is funding a group of clinicians to receive training in a parenting program by individuals from Patterson's laboratory. The trainees have a series of seminars/training sessions with the specialists and then in between training sessions the trainees send videotapes of their implementation to the United States in order to receive supervision. In this model of training, practitioners receive group didactic instruction and then individual supervision on their use of the skills learned in didactic sessions. Clearly this method provides thoroughness of training, but is costly for the individual whose training is not funded by an external source. None the less, a very pertinent research question involves how to best package programs so that practitioners can quickly learn the program and be ready to implement it.

DISSEMINATING PROGRAMS

As in most fields, becoming highly skilled in treatment outcome research requires a high level of devotion and commitment to that one area. Unfortunately, the skill set for conducting research does not translate well into the field of marketing: those who do an excellent job of developing and testing treatments typically do a poor job of promoting them outside the traditional academic outlets. In fact, the skills required for effectively disseminating a treatment program can almost be considered opposite to the skill set typically held by researchers. In order to be effectively marketed, research findings about empirically supported programs need to be translated into succinct, easily readable, and engaging summaries that do not resemble results sections of research papers. Programs need recognizable logos, descriptive names, and attractive brochures and handouts. Furthermore, either the researcher, or someone knowledgeable about the program, needs to focus on attending conferences for practitioners and obtaining interviews on talk shows and in magazines that will reach the target audience of program consumers (such as practitioners and parents).

For empirically supported programs to be implemented by practitioners, they have to be readily available and accessible. Even when a particular program's efficaciousness is presented in a scientific journal, information is rarely included regarding how the program manual might be obtained. Including this information would be a relatively easy step for researchers. In addition, more efforts need to be made to use web resources, practitioner-focused conferences, mailings, and state and local psychology associations to disseminate programs.

As this discussion suggests, much is left to be done in the field of parent training research. If empirically validated programs are going to be implemented in real-world practice, researchers must find ways to accomplish the goals of improved dissemination and marketing of their products. One potential avenue involves researchers themselves developing skills in dissemination and marketing. However, this investment may be prohibitive, both in terms of financial cost and time. A second avenue involves partnering with a company or organization that specializes in marketing and dissemination. Outside the fields of academia and research, businesses are increasingly utilizing consultants who focus on completing specific projects, such as developing a packaged program that could be disseminated, or developing a route of dissemination. Borrowing again from medicine, a biomedical researcher who develops a new drug for the treatment of hypertension would not be responsible for ensuring that the drug was well-marketed and disseminated. A separate division, even a different company, takes on this task. In fact, it is unlikely that the company would even want the researcher to undertake this task, given how likely he or she would be to go about the task in an inefficient manner.

A Guide for Policy-makers

Beyond partnering with businesses, additional changes need to occur on a more global level. Government programs need to take a proactive stance towards adolescent, young adult, and adult antisocial behavior by funding early parenting interventions. For example, in the United States, the government funds numerous programs (juvenile detention centers, boot camp programs) that punish antisocial behavior or seek to deter its occurrence, but less money is devoted to preventing the behavior from occurring initially. Once adolescent externalizing behavior goes untreated and develops into delinquency and criminal behavior, it requires a much greater economic investment to contain and reduce it. Countries that fund parent training programs, like the program in Norway mentioned previously, invest more initially but will probably have less need for later spending to address antisocial behavior as children age.

A second public policy issue, in the US specifically, involves the health care insurance industry. When government funding for the prevention and treatment of child antisocial behavior does not exist, parents must rely on private health insurance to cover the costs of treatment. While most insurance providers cover such services now, managed health care agencies have recently begun moving toward eliminating payment for therapy addressing clinically relevant but undiagnosed child behavior problems, such as noncompliance. If this trend continues, many children in need of services will go untreated when families cannot afford to pay for treatment. Ironically, insurance programs will probably continue to fund treatment for those diagnosed with conduct disorder later in childhood or adolescence. However, at that point treatment will probably be less effective than it would have been earlier in the developmental trajectory of antisocial behavior and the costs to society may already be more expensive than would have been the initial investment in early intervention. Mental health professionals and local, regional, and national psychology associations need to become more involved in ensuring that legislators and policy-makers are aware of the implications of reduced payment for treatment of externalizing problems and the potential costs to the government in terms of court involvement, incarceration, and the loss of human capital.

In Western Europe, child behavioral difficulties are dealt with by a range of agencies, including largely free health services. However, given the pressure on agencies, children's noncompliant behavior is often not dealt with unless it is part of a wider problem (such as Attention-Deficit Hyperactivity Disorder, ADHD) and until it is already well established. So the same issues around the cost of not intervening early enough arise.

The US and some other governments are to be commended, however, in the level of research funding provided to advance parent training programs to the current state. At present, additional funds need to be directed towards the tasks of making these programs more widely available. Governments may also play a role in encouraging universities to provide funds for engaging independent companies to assist researchers in packaging, marketing, and disseminating their programs. Alternatively, incentives or rewards need to be provided for academic researchers who work with professionals in disciplines outside of social science for the purposes of dissemination.

CONCLUDING COMMENTS

Clearly, parent training has a long history which establishes it as one of the best studied, and most effective interventions for childhood and adolescent conduct problems. The basic model of parent training provides a format for intervening with mild to severe behavior problems, and has proven to be flexible and adaptable in a wide range of clinical settings and to a wide variety of child difficulties beyond acting-out behavior. While its core principles and methods have been supported as both efficacious and modifiable, several challenges remain to be conquered. As we have outlined in this chapter, clinicians, researchers, and policy-makers face important

tasks in furthering the development of parent training. Specifically, clinicians and researchers must find avenues through which they may collaborate more easily to remedy and refine aspects of implementation beyond laboratory walls. Researchers are charged with identifying viable and efficacious alternatives for delivery, including the exploration of the potential offered by the internet and other computer-based intervention modalities.

Further research is sorely needed to identify the best options for dissemination, marketing, and training of practitioners so that empirically validated parent training approaches are utilized by those families who need them.

Finally, clinical researchers, practitioners, and child and family advocates must unite in their efforts to effect changes in government policies that affect funding for and access to parent training programs across the world. Parent training may be in the enviable position of being a well-established and widely utilized program, but, in the ever-evolving social and political climate of modern society, there is always more work to be done.

ACKNOWLEDGMENTS

The authors would like to acknowledge the support of the William T. Grant Foundation and the University of Georgia's Institute for Behavioral Research.

REFERENCES

Alvarado, R., Kendall, K., Beesley, S. and Lee-Cavaness, C. (2000) *Strengthening America's Families: Model Family Programs for Substance Abuse and Delinquency Prevention*. Salt Lake City: University of Utah.

Berman, S. (1959) Antisocial character disorder: its etiology and relationship to delinquency. *American Journal of Orthopsychiatry*, **29**, 612–21.

Blechman, E.A. (1998) Parent training in moral context: prosocial family therapy. In Briesmeister, J.M. and Schaefer, C.E. (eds) *Handbook of Parent Training: Parents as Co-therapists for Children's Behavior Problems*. New York: John Wiley, pp. 508–48.

Brestan, E.V. and Eyberg, S.M. (1998) Effective psychosocial treatments of conduct-disordered children and adolescents: 29 years, 82 studies, and 5,272 kids. *Journal of Clinical Child Psychology*, **27**, 180–9.

Calzada, E., Caldwell, M. and Miller, L. (2000) Creating and maintaining a community-research partnership. Paper presented at the Society for Community Research and Action Biennial Conference, Atlanta, GA.

Cummings, E.M. and Davies, P.T. (1994) Maternal depression and child development. *Journal of Child Psychology and Psychiatry*, **35**, 73–112.

Dadds, M.R., Schwartz, S. and Sanders, M.R. (1987) Marital discord and treatment outcome in behavioral treatment of child conduct disorders. *Journal of Consulting and Clinical Psychology*, **55**, 396–403.

Duan, N. and Rotheram-Borus, M.J. (1999) Development and dissemination of successful behavioral prevention intervention: safety, innovation, essential ingredients, robustness, and marketability. Paper presented at Prevention Research Center at the University of Washington School of Social Work. (http://depts.washington.edu/swprc/translation/Rotheram.html)

Emery, R.E. (1999) *Marriage, Divorce, and Children's Adjustment*, 2nd edition. Thousand Oaks, CA: Sage.

Eyberg, S.M., Schuhmann, E.M. and Rey, J. (1998) Child and adolescent psychotherapy research: developmental issues. *Journal of Abnormal Child Psychology*, **26**, 71–82.

Feldman, J.M. and Kazdin, A.E. (1995) Parent management training for oppositional and conduct problem children. *The Clinical Psychologist*, **48**(4), 3–4.

Forehand, R. (1993) Twenty years of research: does it have practical implications for clinicians working with parents and children? *Clinical Psychologist*, **29**, 104–7.

Forehand, R. and Atkeson, B.M. (1977) Generality of treatment effects with parents as therapists: a review of assessment and implementation procedures. *Behavior Therapy*, **8**, 575–93.

Forehand, R. and Kotchick, B.A. (1996) Cultural diversity: a wake-up call for parent training. *Behavior Therapy*, **27**, 187–206.

Forehand, R. and Long, N. (1996) Programs to assist parents of strong-willed children. *Directions in Child and Adolescent Psychotherapy*, **3**, 3–19.

Forehand, R. and Long, N. (2002) *Parenting the Strong-Willed Child*, 2nd edition. Chicago: Contemporary Books.

Goodman, S.H. and Gotlib, I.H. (1999) Risk for psychopathology in the children of depressed mothers: a developmental model for understanding mechanisms of transmission. *Psychological Review*, **106**, 458–90.

Griest, D.L. and Wells, K.C. (1983) Behavioral family therapy with conduct disorders in children. *Behavior Therapy*, **14**, 37–53.

Hall, G.S. (1904) *Adolescence: Its Psychology and Its Relations to Physiology, Anthropology, Sociology, Sex, Crime, Religion, and Education*, Vols I–II. New York: Appleton.

Healy, W.J. and Bronner, A.F. (1926) *Delinquents and Criminals: Their Making and Unmaking*. New York: MacMillan.

Henggeler, S.W. Schoenwald, S.K., Bordrun, C.M., Rowland, M.D. and Cunningham, P.H. (1998) *Multisystemic Treatment of Antisocial Behavior in Children and Adolescents*. New York: Guilford.

Kazdin, A.E. (1977) Assessing the clinical or applied importance of behavior change through social validation. *Behavior Modification*, **1**, 427–52.

Kazdin, A.E. (1978) *History of Behavior Modification: Experimental Foundations of Contemporary Research*. Baltimore: University Park Press.

Kazdin, A.E. (1985) *Treatment of Antisocial Behavior in Children and Adolescents*. Homewood, IL: Dorsey Press.

Linehan, M.M. and Kehrer, C.A. (1993) Borderline personality disorder. In Barlow, D. (ed.) *Clinical Handbook of Psychological Disorders*. New York: Guilford, pp. 396–444.

McMahon, R.J. and Forehand, R. (2003) *Helping the Noncompliant Child: A Clinician's Guide to Effective Parent Training*, 2nd edition. New York: Guilford.

Moore, K.J. and Chamberlain, P. (1994) Treatment Foster Care: toward development of community-based models for adolescents with severe emotional and behavioral disorders. *Journal of Emotional and Behavioral Disorders*, **2**, 22–30.

Patterson, G.R. (1975a) *Families: Applications of Social Learning to Family Life*, revised edition. Champaign, IL: Research Press.

Patterson, G.R. (1975b) *Professional Guide for 'Families' and 'Living with Children'*. Champaign, IL: Research Press.

Patterson, G.R. (1982) *Coercive Family Process*. Eugene, OR: Castalia.

Patterson, G.R. and Chamberlain, P. (1988) Treatment process: a problem at three levels. In Wynne, L.C. (ed.) *The State of the Art in Family Therapy Research: Controversies and Recommendations*. New York: Family Process Press, pp. 189–223.

Patterson, G.R. and Chamberlain, P. (1994) A functional analysis of resistance during the parent training therapy. *Clinical Psychology: Science and Practice*, **1**, 53–70.

Prinz, R.J. and Miller, G.E. (1996) Parental engagement in interventions for children at risk for Conduct Disorder. In Peters, R. and McMahon, R.J. (eds) *Preventing Childhood Disorders, Substance Abuse, and Delinquency*. Thousand Oaks, CA: Sage, pp. 161–83.

Sanders, M.R., Markie-Dadds, C., Tully, L.A. and Bor, W. (2000) The Triple-P Positive Parenting Program: a comparison of enhanced, standard, and self-directed behavioral family intervention for parents of children with early-onset conduct problems. *Journal of Consulting and Clinical Psychology*, **68**, 624–40.

Serketich, W.J. and Dumas, J.E. (1996) The effectiveness of behavioral parent training to modify antisocial behavior in children: a meta-analysis. *Behavior Therapy*, **27**, 171–86.

Siegel, A.W. and Scovill, L.C. (2000) Problem behavior: the double symptom of adolescence. *Development and Psychopathology*, **12**, 763–93.

Sternbach, O. (1947) Arrested ego development and its treatment in conduct disorders and neuroses of childhood. *Nervous Child*, **6**, 306–17.

Thomas, A. and Chess, S. (1977) *Temperament and Development*. New York: Brunner/Mazel.

Wahler, R.G. (1976) Deviant child behavior within the family: developmental speculations and behavior change strategies. In Leitenberg, H. (ed.) *Handbook of Behavior Modification and Behavior Therapy*. Englewood Cliffs, NJ: Prentice-Hall.

Wahler, R., Leske, G. and Rogers, E.S. (1979) The insular family: a deviance support system for oppositional children. In Hamerlynch, L.A. (ed.) *Behavioral Systems for the Developmentally Disabled: Vol. 1. School and Family Environments*. New York: Brunner/Mazel.

Webster-Stratton, C. (1996) Early intervention with videotape modeling: programs for families of children with Oppositional Defiant Disorder or Conduct Disorder. In Hibbs, E.S. and Jensen, P.S. (eds) *Psychosocial Treatments for Child and Adolescent Disorders: Empirically Based Strategies for Clinical Practice*. Washington, DC: American Psychological Association, pp. 435–74.

Webster-Stratton, C. and Herbert, M. (1994) Strategies for helping parents of children with conduct disorders. In Hersen, M. and Eisler, R.M. (eds) *Progress in Behavior Modification*. Belmont, CA: Brooks/Cole Publishing Co., pp. 121–42.

Wootton, J.M., Frick, P.J., Shelton, K.K. and Silverthorn, P. (1997) Ineffective parenting and childhood conduct problems: the moderating role of callous-unemotional traits. *Journal of Consulting and Clinical Psychology*, **65**, 301–08.

17

Parenting and Mental Health

Colleen S. Conley, Melissa S. Caldwell,
Megan Flynn, Alison J. Dupre and Karen D. Rudolph

SUMMARY

This chapter will summarize theory and research on the impact of parental mental health, broadly construed, and associated circumstances on parenting. A brief overview of historical trends and theories in the domain of parenting research will be provided, followed by a review of relevant research on personal and contextual influences on parenting. This background will then be used as a basis for discussion concerning how intervention programs and social policy can be directed toward mental health promotion in the context of parenting.

A critical goal of many family-oriented mental health professionals is to maximize the quality of relationships between parents and children. Understanding how to modify these relationships requires answers to several questions. How does parental psychological well-being hinder or enhance parenting? Which environmental influences promote optimal parent–child interactions and relationships, and which interfere with warm, supportive, and effective parenting? What types of prevention and intervention programs can be developed to enhance healthy parenting, and how can social policy initiatives support such programs?

HISTORICAL PERSPECTIVES ON PARENTING

Decades of scientific inquiry about parenting have yielded a wealth of information about the impact of different parenting practices on child health and development (for reviews, see Bornstein, 1995). Surprisingly, theory and research only more recently have begun to consider the antecedents, or determinants, of parenting – that is, *why* and *under what circumstances* parents adopt particular caregiving styles. Three major trends characterize the evolution of knowledge about why parents engage in certain types of parenting.

First, models of parenting have evolved from exclusively person-centered to ecologically based views that consider how certain circumstances or contexts contribute to parenting. These parenting contexts may range from macro-level influences (such as living in poverty), to micro-level processes (such as dealing with daily stresses and strains), and may include socio-cultural factors (such as ethnicity or social class) (Belsky, 1984; McLoyd, 1990). Understanding how such contexts influence and are influenced by the characteristics of parents has become an increasingly important goal in elucidating the determinants of parenting.

Second, models of parenting have matured from unidimensional to multidimensional paradigms, which take into account the complex interactions among the elements (for reviews, see Belsky, 1984; McLoyd, 1990; Kendziora and O'Leary, 1993). For example, early research on parenting and parental mental health reflected a heavy emphasis on the implications of maternal depression for parenting and child adjustment. Gradually, models of parenting have expanded to consider the joint contribution of many different aspects of parental mental health and well-being. In the present chapter, a broad conceptualization of mental health will be applied to allow for a comprehensive understanding of the interacting influences on parenting, and to provide a backdrop for considering the areas at which parenting interventions may be targeted.

Third, models of parenting have progressed from a focus on parents as the sole agents of socialization to a focus on the joint contributions of parents and children (Belsky, 1984; Scarr, 1992; Eder and Mangelsdorf, 1997). These transactional models consider the interactions or 'goodness of fit' between children and their caregivers in predicting the nature of parent–child relationships and child adjustment (Mangelsdorf et al., 1990).

Inconsistency on the part of a parent, for example, may be more detrimental to a child who benefits from regularity and predictability than to a child with an easygoing and flexible temperament. Moreover, transactional models propose that children actively *elicit* particular types of parenting, resulting in reciprocal processes of socialization (Belsky, 1984; Scarr, 1992; Darling and Steinberg, 1993). For instance, a child with a difficult temperament may evoke more controlling behavior and harsher discipline from a parent. Because the present focus lies on the characteristics of parents and their contexts that guide parenting, this third trend in research on parenting will not be further broached.

THEORIES AND DIMENSIONS OF PARENTING

Parenting involves a wide spectrum of goals, behaviors, and interactions. Parents convey a set of values, standards, and beliefs to children about themselves and others, train children how to express and regulate their emotions, transmit certain styles of communication, model particular behaviors, and teach a variety of skills, competencies, and ways of interacting in the world. Consequently, theories of parenting focus on a range of dimensions through which parents explicitly and implicitly influence their children,

including such features as the emotional climate of the parent–child relationship, the provision of instrumental support and guidance, and the use of discipline practices designed to teach appropriate behaviors. These dimensions typically incorporate a combination of parent socialization goals and values (such as the goal of raising a compassionate child), particular parenting practices (as in teaching a child to be empathic when a friend is distressed), and a generalized parenting style (for example, engaging in warm and supportive parent–child interactions) (see Darling and Steinberg, 1993).

Some theories of parenting focus primarily on the emotional context of parent–child relationships. For example, attachment theory holds that parents who provide emotionally supportive caregiving, characterized by warmth, sensitivity, nurturance, and contingent responsiveness, cultivate secure attachment with their children, which in turn promotes positive developmental outcomes (Bowlby, 1969; Ainswort et al., 1972). Other theories of parenting (Baumrind, 1971; Maccoby and Martin, 1983; Darling and Steinberg, 1993; Skinner et al., 1998) expand on this perspective by viewing parenting in terms of:

- an affective dimension, characterized by warmth, involvement, nurturance, and acceptance versus rejection and criticism; and
- an instrumental dimension, characterized by autonomy granting versus control and discipline.

Control has been further differentiated into two forms (Barber, 1996; Pomerantz and Ruble, 1998):

- behavioral control, which involves efforts to regulate children's behavior through guidance and limit setting; and
- psychological control, which involves efforts to regulate children's psychological development through constraint of verbal or emotional expression.

Understanding the impact of parental mental health and associated contexts on parenting thus requires a consideration of how these different dimensions and processes of parenting may be influenced.

OVERVIEW

This chapter explores theory and research regarding personal characteristics, mental health status, environments and resources, all of which shape the various dimensions of parenting.

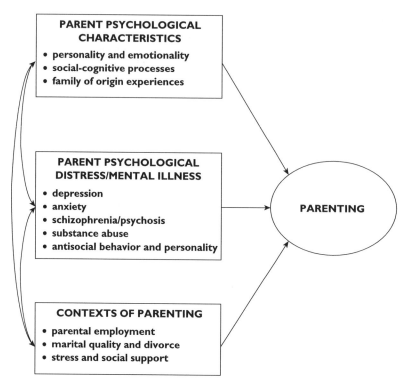

Figure 17.1 *An ecological model of parenting and mental health, which draws from work by Belsky (1984), McLoyd (1990), and Steinberg (Darling and Steinberg, 1993)*

Figure 17.1 presents a schematic model of parenting that incorporates basic elements from several well-elaborated models (Belsky, 1984; McLoyd, 1990; Conger et al., 1992; Darling and Steinberg, 1993). This model, along with relevant empirical research, will be used as a framework for considering how intervention and social policy can be used to promote healthy parenting and child development.

PERSONAL AND CONTEXTUAL INFLUENCES ON PARENTING

Parent Psychological Characteristics

The psychological characteristics of parents are likely to play a prominent role in parent socialization goals and behaviors and in the quality of parent–child relationships. Three characteristics that have received attention in research on parenting include: (a) personality and emotionality, (b) social-cognitive processes, and (c) family of origin experiences.

PERSONALITY AND EMOTIONALITY

Personality, by definition, is a relatively stable and pervasive pattern of traits that influence behavior. Thus, it is likely that parents' personalities affect their parenting. Research on personality and parenting has linked three major components of personality – agreeableness or positive affectivity, extraversion or sociability, and emotional stability – with positive parenting. Specifically, parents who are high in positive affectivity or agreeableness have more positive interactions with their children, are more warm, expressive, sensitive, involved, responsive, and supportive toward them, are more competent during interactions with their children, and have a more positive mood during parent–child interactions (Belsky et al., 1995; Goldstein et al., 1996; Szewczyk et al., 2001). In contrast, parents who are low in agreeableness tend to show more negative affect toward their children, to be more controlling and less nurturing, and to foster less secure attachment with their children (Kochanska et al., 1987). Similarly, parents who are extraverted tend to show more sensitivity, positive affect, and cognitive stimulation with their children than do parents who are introverted (Belsky et al., 1995).

Emotional stability and emotionality may influence several aspects of parenting. Less emotionally stable parents tend to overreact to negative events or circumstances, such as their children's misbehaviors (Belsky et al., 1995). Even emotionally stable parents get moody at times, however, and these transient moods may influence parenting. Mood states may affect the way parents view interactions with their children, as well as how they respond to their children's behaviors (Belsky et al., 1995). For example, sad or angry moods may lead parents to attend less to their parenting role, make inappropriately negative attributions for their children's behavior, or overreact to minor misbehaviors. Interestingly, one parent's emotionality may be associated with the other parent's child-rearing behavior. In particular, recent research has revealed that positive affect in fathers is the best predictor of mothers' positive engagement with their children (Szewczyk et al., 2001).

Although these findings touch on only a few broad aspects of personality, the link between personality and parenting is likely to hold for more specific aspects of personality as well. For example, parents with an internal locus of control and a high sense of interpersonal trust demonstrate more warm, accepting, respectful, and helpful interactions with their children (Mondell and Tyler, 1981). Furthermore, because personality is so pervasive and is a strong predictor of behavior, many other personality attributes are likely to generalize to parenting. For example, more responsible adults are likely to be more responsible parents; more insecure adults are likely to be less confident in their parenting; more caring adults are likely to be more caring as parents. In addition, parents' personality and moods affect their parenting not only indirectly, by influencing parenting behaviors, but also directly, by providing models of emotional expression and interactional styles for their children. Research demonstrates that parents' and children's levels of emotionality are highly correlated (Bronstein et al., 1993), suggesting that children may internalize their parents' emotional displays. Moreover, research indicates that the ways parents express, regulate, and talk about emotions shape their children's expression and regulation of emotions (Eisenberg et al., 1996, 1998; Parke and McDowell, 1998). Similarly, children may learn ways of interacting with others by modeling parent behaviors. Thus, parents' personality and emotions may be transmitted across generations through specific parenting behaviors and through the quality of parent–child interactions.

SOCIAL-COGNITIVE PROCESSES

Several models have been proposed to explain the specific social-cognitive processes underlying parenting behavior (see Bugental, 1993; Crittenden, 1993; Milner, 1993; Strassberg, 1997). Consistently, this research indicates that social information-processing systems, which guide parents' attention, perception, interpretation, and responses in the context of parent–child interactions, are critical determinants of parenting (for a review, see Werkerle and Wolfe, 1996). Disturbances in social information processing related to parenting may occur at several stages. For example, parents may misperceive children's needs or behaviors, make interpretive errors, and fail to respond, or enact inappropriate responses, leading to a range of maladaptive parenting behaviors. Three particular aspects of social cognition and information processing that have been shown to influence parenting practices and behaviors include attributions, perceived self-efficacy, and coping styles.

Attributions involve judgments about the intent of behaviors or the causes of particular events. Typically, the tendency to attribute negative behavior or events to internal, stable, and global causes and to attribute positive behavior or events to external, unstable, and specific causes has been found to correlate with poorer mental health (Tiggemann et al., 1992). In the context of child rearing, parental attributions for children's emotional states and behaviors are associated with parental emotional arousal and discipline practices. In particular, negative attributions and appraisals of ambiguous child misbehavior or noncompliance have been linked to greater physiological arousal and feelings of anger in response to the behavior (Dix and Lochman, 1990; Slep and O'Leary, 1998), as well as to harsh and coercive disciplinary practices (Dix et al., 1989; Scott and Dembo, 1993; Smith and O'Leary, 1995; Strassberg, 1997; Slep and O'Leary, 1998; Nix et al., 1999).

At an extreme level, misattributions may leave parents at risk for abusive parenting. For example, research has shown that abusive parents possess threat-oriented relationship schemas. These schemas lead parents to be overly sensitive to children's challenges to their authority and to attribute high levels of power to their children, which then results in aversive parenting practices (Bugental, 1993). In contrast, parents who more accurately perceive their children's thoughts, feelings, and behaviors, especially during disagreements, are more likely to base their disciplinary tactics on the child's emotional state, which leads to greater contentment with conflict resolution (Hastings and Grusec, 1997). Attributions may therefore influence several dimensions of child-rearing practices.

Perceived self-efficacy involves personal evaluations of one's ability to perform competently or effectively in a particular environment (Bandura, 1995). A high level of perceived self-efficacy fosters self-confidence, thereby promoting persistent problem solving, optimistic predictions, high expectancies for performance outcomes, and active responses to stress (Bandura, 1995). High self-efficacy has been linked to parenting competence (Teti and Gelfand, 1991; Jackson and Huang, 2000). In fact, it has been suggested that self-efficacy may act as a buffer against difficult child temperaments and may represent a final common pathway in predicting parenting sensitivity (Teti et al., 1996). When self-efficacy is diminished, minor parenting hassles or child non-compliance might overwhelm one's parenting capabilities, causing caregiving to be interpreted as an unmanageable and distressing task and creating diminished parental involvement, warmth, and sensitivity. In addition to affecting parenting behavior directly, self-efficacy beliefs may influence other social information-processing mechanisms that guide parenting. For instance, parents with low self-efficacy may overestimate children's power or misattribute misbehavior to parental incompetence, which may interfere further with parenting processes.

Coping styles also may contribute to parenting beliefs and behavior. Whereas proactive coping, which involves approaching and dealing directly with adversity, has been linked to positive mental health, avoidance coping, which involves cognitive and behavioral efforts aimed at escaping from adversity, has been linked to mental health difficulties (Endler et al., 1993; Kohn et al., 1994). Coping efforts are likely to influence parent–child interactions and parenting behaviors (Kurtz and Derevensky, 1994). For instance, problem-focused coping is associated with increased perceived control in the parenting role, more parental warmth, and more authoritative parenting (Holloway and Machida, 1991). An active approach to child-rearing challenges may therefore enhance adaptive parenting. Alternative coping responses that involve distancing, escaping, and avoiding are associated with parental distress, which in turn interferes with effective discipline practices (Holloway and Machida, 1991; Tein et al., 2000).

FAMILY OF ORIGIN EXPERIENCES

A comprehensive picture of the personal determinants of parenting requires a consideration of how parents' own history and experiences in the context of parent–child and other close relationships influence their parenting. How does the experience of an insecure attachment relationship, a history of abuse, or exposure to parent–child or marital conflict during one's own childhood affect subsequent parenting beliefs and behavior?

Child-rearing patterns tend to remain consistent across generations. This intergenerational transmission of parenting may in part reflect common genetic forces that shape interpersonal behavior. However, early experiences within interpersonal relationships may play a crucial role in forming the basis for beliefs, emotional experience and regulation, and ways of interacting in future relationships. That is, internal representations or schemas of intimate relationships that originate within early family relationships may be reactivated in parents' relationships with their own children (Lyons-Ruth, 1992). Consistent with this view, the security of attachment between parents and their children has been demonstrated to remain somewhat consistent across generations (Fonagy et al., 1991; Lyons-Ruth et al., 1996). These representations of relationships may form a database of stored information that guides ongoing information processing and emotion regulation in the parenting context, thereby driving the types of social-cognitive and emotional influences on parenting described earlier. Indeed, parents' experience within their family of origin has been found to be one of the strongest contributors to parenting (Cox et al., 1985; Belsky et al., 1986; Elder et al., 1986; Lyons-Ruth, 1992).

Parents' Psychological Distress and Mental Illness

A considerable amount of research has examined the implications of psychological disorders in parents for parenting and child development. A variety of parenting processes may be compromised by severe and chronic parental mental illness, as well as by more mild and transient forms of psychological distress.

DEPRESSION

Maternal depression is one of the most widely studied influences on parenting (for reviews, see Beardslee et al., 1983; Gelfand and Teti, 1990; Gotlib and Hammen, 1992; Hammen and Rudolph, 1996; Cicchetti et al., 1998; Radke-Yarrow, 1998; Cummings and Davies, 1999; Goodman and Gotlib, 1999). Depressive symptoms may range from mild feelings of sadness and low self-worth to severe emotional, cognitive, behavioral, and physiological impairment, including a decreased interest or pleasure in activities, significant appetite or weight fluctuations, sleep problems, restlessness or sluggishness, a loss of energy, difficulty concentrating, and recurrent feelings of worthlessness or guilt. Depressed individuals commonly express flat affect, a lack of interest in social interactions, feelings of hopelessness, and a heightened self-focus.

Not surprisingly, depression is associated with problematic parenting behavior and maladaptive parent–child interactions. One might imagine multiple pathways through which depression interferes with parenting competence. For example, feelings of sadness or flat affect may be reflected in impaired emotional expression and regulation within parent–child interactions; hopelessness and low self-worth may diminish parenting self-efficacy and thus cause frustration with, or disengagement from, the parenting role; a heightened self-focus may hinder contingent responsiveness, reciprocal interactions, effective communication, and joint problem solving; irritability may result in decreased warmth and sensitivity and increased criticism; and fatigue may lead to inconsistent responses, lack of guidance or limit setting, and withdrawal. Indeed, depression in mothers has been linked to negative affect and irritability, criticism, insensitivity, and poor conflict resolution during parent–child interactions. Depression also has been found to be associated with maternal disengagement, as reflected in decreased verbalization and responsiveness to children's speech and diminished involvement and provision of structure (Radke-Yarrow et al., 1985; Hops et al., 1987; Kochanska et al., 1987; Gordon et al., 1989; Field et al., 1990; Goodman and Brumley, 1990; Teti et al., 1996; for reviews, see Hammen, 1991; Gotlib and Hammen, 1992).

Depressed parents also may convey negative messages to children about themselves and the world, either through modeling or through the type of feedback they provide to children. For example, negative attributions, low self-worth, and hopelessness – characteristics of depressed individuals – may be adopted by the offspring of depressed parents (Garber and Flynn, 2001). Moreover, parental feedback and explanations of child-focused events are associated with children's attributions, suggesting that children learn to interpret events based on parents' beliefs (Garber and Flynn, 2001).

ANXIETY

Experiences of anxiety may range in severity from the worries of everyday life to extreme levels of nervousness, physiological arousal, and inhibited behavior or avoidance that are characteristic of clinical disorders. Furthermore, anxiety may assume multiple forms. For example, anxiety may involve general worries about many areas of one's life, often accompanied by physical symptoms such as muscle tension, restlessness, and sleeplessness. Alternatively, anxiety may be circumscribed to particular situations, such as performance and social situations, or to particular objects. At extreme levels, anxiety may be severely debilitating, as in the case of agoraphobia, which is characterized by an intense fear and avoidance of situations in which immediate escape may be difficult, or obsessive-compulsive disorder, which is characterized by recurrent intrusive thoughts and rituals. In such cases, anxiety may interfere with day-to-day functioning across multiple roles, including the parenting role.

Once again, a range of parenting processes may be disrupted by the presence of anxiety in parents. For instance, generalized anxiety may lead to overly protective and cautious parenting styles (Capps et al., 1996); preoccupation with one's own worries or physical symptoms may interfere with engagement in consistent and warm interactions with children (Fellow-Smith, 2000); even circumscribed anxiety, such as a fear of social situations, may impair parents' ability to actively engage in the parenting role by restricting activities such as attendance at school or social events (Fellow-Smith, 2000). The type of disruptions in parenting that occur will likely depend on the form and severity of parental anxiety.

Although empirical evidence is scarce concerning the influence of parental anxiety on particular parenting processes, research supports the presence of parenting and parent–child relationship difficulties in anxious parents. In terms of direct effects on parenting, anxious parents respond less warmly and positively to their children, allow their children less independence, and express more critical child-directed comments (Whaley et al., 1999). Anxious parents have been shown to minimize communication with their children and to discourage children's expression of thoughts and ideas, thus inhibiting the development of emotional ties and causing feelings of disappointment and dejection in children (Rao and Ram, 1984). Research also has demonstrated less secure attachment in the children of anxious parents (Manassis et al., 1995). Even moderate levels of anxiety may affect parenting. For example, one study demonstrated that parents who worried about their children's academic performance were more likely to engage in intrusive-support practices that undermined children's autonomy (Pomerantz and Eaton, 2001).

Anxious parents also may model maladaptive cognitive styles and problematic behaviors that reflect their fears and insecurities. Anxious mothers report diminished confidence in their child-rearing competence and coping in response to child-related stresses (Barnett and Parker, 1986). These decreased perceptions of efficacy may then be adopted by children. Indeed, anxious parents appear to transmit their lower levels of perceived control and lack of global optimism to their children; such modeling may help to explain the intergenerational transmission of anxiety within families (Capps et al., 1996). These preliminary studies indicate the presence of a range of parenting difficulties in individuals with anxiety.

SCHIZOPHRENIA/PSYCHOSIS

Schizophrenia and related psychotic disorders typically begin during the child-bearing and early child-rearing years and are characterized by a severe and chronic course of debilitating thoughts and behaviors. Thus, these disorders may have serious consequences for parenting. Some symptoms involve decreases in typical behaviors, such as flat affect, decreased speech, and decreased motion. Such symptoms may affect parents' ability to communicate with their children, display affection, foster intimacy, and provide children with age-appropriate stimulation. Other symptoms involve the appearance of atypical behaviors and experiences, such as hallucinations and unusual beliefs. These symptoms may limit parents' capacity to appropriately socialize their children. For example, delusional parents may model maladaptive belief systems to their children, who may then adopt these beliefs into their own thinking (Seeman, 1996). Indeed, studies consistently have indicated that individuals with schizophrenia or other psychotic disorders exhibit significantly more parenting difficulties compared to parents without a mental illness. For example, mothers with schizophrenia have been found to be more withdrawn and emotionally uninvolved during interactions with their children (Cohler et al., 1977; Goodman and Brumley, 1990).

Schizophrenia and psychosis in parents also may exert indirect effects on parenting. For example, as we will discuss later, supportive marital relationships and a strong parenting alliance play an important role in promoting adaptive parenting. One parent's support in the marital relationship may be particularly important as a buffer against the other parent's mental illness. Yet, severe mental illness may pose serious challenges to establishing and maintaining positive marital relationships, thus decreasing the likelihood of a stable family environment.

SUBSTANCE ABUSE

Research has consistently demonstrated the negative effects of substance use and addiction on parenting. Alcohol consumption and addiction have been found to be associated with a wide range of cognitive deficits and maladaptive behaviors, such as impairment in perceptual-motor skills, difficulties with appropriate emotional expression, and deficits in problem solving (Sparadeo et al., 1983; Eliason and Skinstad, 1995), which have substantial implications for interpersonal functioning and child rearing. For example, alcohol intoxication influences parents' judgments of child misbehaviors and adversely affects parental efficacy in managing children (Lang et al., 1999). Alcoholism has been associated with inconsistent discipline, poor monitoring of child behavior, and decreased nurturance and emotional availability. Of further detriment to parent–child relations, alcoholic parents tend to value and use corporal punishment, exhibit less empathy for their children's needs, and hold inappropriate expectations of their children. Alcoholic parents also tend to engage in frequent parent–child role reversals (Gallant et al., 1998). Similarly, drug-dependent mothers display less responsive, more negative, and more rejecting parenting behaviors than do non-substance abusing parents (Hans et al., 1999).

Parental substance abuse also exerts indirect effects on parenting and parent–child relationships. For instance, engaging in substance use models ineffective coping strategies and other problem behaviors to children (Windle, 1996) and undermines parents' ability to maintain a household or adequate employment. Substance use also interferes with the capacity to maintain positive marital relations and a healthy home environment (Windle, 1996). Moreover, substance-dependent parents are likely to invest much of their time and resources into obtaining and consuming substances, thus neglecting their parenting role. In sum, substance use itself, combined with a compromised family environment and a failure to allocate adequate time and money to the act of parenting, are likely to have serious consequences for parenting and child well-being.

ANTISOCIAL BEHAVIOR AND PERSONALITY

The essential feature of antisocial behavior and personality is disregard for and violation of the rights of others, including deception and manipulation, perpetration of criminal acts, and failure to conform to social norms. Antisocial individuals tend to be impulsive, irresponsible, and aggressive, and have difficulty empathizing with the feelings and experiences of others. Antisocial personality may therefore impede individuals from forming meaningful interpersonal relationships (Milan, 1990).

Because optimal parenting requires parents to exhibit empathy and to anticipate the needs of their children, antisocial behavior and personality are likely to have detrimental effects on parenting. For instance, studies have revealed that mothers with antisocial personality traits typically display unresponsive parenting (Cassidy et al., 1996) and ineffective monitoring of children's activities (Patterson and Capaldi, 1991). Moreover, individuals with antisocial personality traits exhibit excessively punitive disciplinary tactics with children, which increase the likelihood of child abuse and injury (Wolfe, 1987).

Antisocial characteristics also may influence the societal context in which parents and children interact. Because parents with antisocial personality traits may engage in a wide range of destructive and potentially criminal behaviors, they may be incarcerated and thus separated from their children. Furthermore, antisocial parents may model criminal and aggressive behaviors, leading to poor socialization and consequent antisocial behaviors on the part of the child.

Contexts of Parenting

A comprehensive model of parenting and mental health requires an ecological perspective that situates parenting within the broader context of people's lives. This perspective considers how contextual factors directly and indirectly influence the process of parenting. Other chapters in this volume consider wider contexts of parenting, such as social and economic adversity and culturally divergent settings. Here we consider the influence of proximal contexts within and outside of the family, including chronic strains and daily stresses created by parental employment and marital conflict or divorce, as well as the impact of general stresses and social support networks on parenting. This contextual perspective considers how the multiple roles that parents need to negotiate in their daily lives may pose challenges to their parenting.

PARENTAL EMPLOYMENT

Parents' jobs, although they contribute to the financial resources of the family, also may add stress to family dynamics. Many parents deal with stressful, emotional, demanding, or high-pressure jobs, or face conflict in their work environments. These and other stresses associated with parental employment often carry over into family life, possibly contributing to family conflict and undermining adaptive parenting. Parents with high levels of work-related stress are likely to evidence their stress in strained parenting interactions. For example, they may express more negative affect with their children (Repetti, 1994), use harsh, coercive, or disruptive disciplinary tactics, such as yelling, hitting, and severe punishment (Almeida et al., 1999), or withdraw from parenting physically (such as by speaking less or paying less attention to children) and emotionally (such as by expressing less affection, or appearing less caring and loving) (Repetti and Wood, 1997).

In addition to the 'spillover' effect (Repetti and Wood, 1997, p. 92) of work stress into parenting, research implicates participation in multiple roles as a contributor to mental health difficulties, such as depression and anxiety, in both men and women (Repetti et al., 1989; Greenberger and O'Neil, 1993; Windle and Dumenci, 1997). That is, the more roles parents have to balance, the fewer physical and emotional resources they have available to devote to parenting. Despite some support for the negative effect of multiple roles, there is also evidence that, in some instances, multiple roles may buffer parents from stress and psychological distress (e.g. Sprock and Yoder, 1997). In fact, employment that is valued and that offers social support actually may increase mental health and life satisfaction (Pleck, 1985; Repetti et al., 1989), which may exert a positive influence on parenting.

What, then, determines whether employment will have positive or negative consequences for parenting and mental health? The impact of employment may depend on multiple factors, such as parents' level of participation in their roles (such as time at work versus time necessary/ available for parenting), commitment to and satisfaction with these roles, and support in these roles (such as shared parenting responsibilities) (Greenberger and O'Neil, 1993). The consequences of employment may also depend on the intensity of parenting demands, which are higher for younger, multiple, and special-needs children. Thus, although stress at work can carry over into stress at home, it does not always do so. Responses will depend on a combination of individual circumstances, including the nature and supportiveness of home and work environments, and various psychological factors, including parents' values, attitudes, and coping styles.

MARITAL QUALITY AND DIVORCE

Marital satisfaction and closeness are related both to positive mental health and to effective parenting (Cox et al., 1989; Deal et al., 1989). A close, engaging, and satisfying marriage may encourage a parent's investment or involvement in parenting, as well as improve the quality of parenting by increasing child-directed warmth, responsiveness, support, sensitivity, and positive attitudes, and by decreasing hostility (Cox et al., 1989; Floyd et al., 1998; Szewczyk et al., 2001). This pattern, in turn, should facilitate more secure parent–child attachment and more positive child outcomes (Frosch et al., 2000; Frosch and Mangelsdorf, 2001). Furthermore, parents who unite in a parenting alliance — by co-parenting with equal involvement and commitment, providing mutual support and agreement over parenting strategies and expectations, and respecting each other's parental roles — also tend to individually parent in consistent, confident, competent, and effective ways (Deal et al., 1989; Mahoney et al., 1997; Floyd et al., 1998).

Conversely, parents in conflictual, distressed, or dissatisfying marriages are likely to exhibit a variety of maladaptive parenting practices, including a lax disciplinary style, decreased acceptance of children's assertiveness, and more unreasonable commands. They also tend to display more negative affect toward their children, have stressful or tense interactions with their children, and even reject or withdraw from their parenting role (Bond and McMahon, 1984; Fauber et al., 1990; Kerig et al., 1993; Almeida et al., 1999). Marital conflict also undermines parental warmth, support, and emotional availability, thus leading to less secure parent–child attachment (Frosch et al., 2000). In terms of the parenting alliance, marital discord disrupts parents' ability to establish respectful, supportive, consistent patterns of co-parenting, which in turn detracts from warm and involved parenting (Floyd et al., 1998). Finally, some research indicates that parenting itself may have adverse consequences for marital satisfaction (Almeida et al., 1999), suggesting a bi-directional, or even cyclical, relation between parenting stress and marital stress. Thus, the harmony of marital relations seems to be integral to parenting.

In addition to direct effects of marital quality on parenting, the former may influence the latter through its impact on parental mental health. Although marriage is associated with lower rates of psychological distress overall (Gotlib and Hammen, 1992), marriage with conflict or low levels of satisfaction and cohesion is linked to compromised mental health, including a higher incidence of depression, anxiety, and substance abuse problems (Windle and Dumenci, 1997; Whisman, 1999). This relation also appears to be bi-directional: higher marital dissatisfaction and conflict predict onset of mental health problems, and mental health problems predict marital dissatisfaction and conflict (Gotlib and Hammen, 1992).

In some cases, serious marital discord may end in divorce. Stress associated with divorce often leaves parents less physically and emotionally available for their children (for reviews, see Hines, 1997; Hetherington et al., 1998). The stress of divorce is associated with both physical and psychological health risks in parents, such as medical problems, depression, anxiety, anger, loneliness, impulsivity, and substance use. These problems, in turn, are likely to undermine parental perceptions of competence and to increase apprehension about parenting efficacy, leading to compromised parenting, as discussed earlier (Hines, 1997; Hetherington et al., 1998) (see also chapter 8).

In addition to its effects on parental mental health, divorce disrupts family dynamics and resources, which inevitably compromises the divorced couple's parenting. For example, parents who separate no longer have an alliance to discipline and parent their children together, which increases the opportunity for inconsistent parenting (Hines, 1997). Divorced parents also tend to remain in conflict with one another, which may make them more irritable, less supportive, and less involved in their parenting roles (Hetherington et al., 1998). Specifically, divorced mothers show parenting difficulties in control and assignment of household tasks, whereas divorced fathers tend to have problems with communication, self-disclosure, and monitoring their children's activities (Hetherington et al., 1998).

Despite the range and depth of parenting problems associated with divorce, the effects of divorce are not all negative. First, unsatisfied and argumentative parents who stay together, rather than divorce, foster a hostile, unsupportive parenting environment that may have worse parenting consequences than a divorce (Hines, 1997). Second, although rocky at first, parenting practices and family relationships tend to stabilize within two years of divorce (Hetherington et al., 1998). Third, although divorce often is associated with problems both in parental mental health and in parenting, this is not always the case. For example, divorced parents who co-parent their children in their dual residences tend to have more positive outcomes (Hetherington et al., 1998). In addition, although many parenting practices change during the divorce transition, some parents manage to maintain close, supportive, and authoritative parenting, which makes the transition easier for parents and children (Hines, 1997; Hetherington et al., 1998). Thus, although research indicates that, in general, divorce has negative consequences for parenting and mental health, individual circumstances such as the intensity of marital conflict, family structure and dynamics, and resiliency of both parents and children will determine the effects of divorce.

STRESS AND SOCIAL SUPPORT

Beyond the challenges of employment and marital relationships, parents face a variety of stresses in their everyday lives, including the stress of parenting itself. Although parenting, for many, is a rewarding and fulfilling life experience, it also may be stressful, and this stress can have a negative impact on personal well-being and parenting. Some research finds that parents may be less happy and satisfied with their lives, worry more, and experience higher levels of psychological distress than non-parenting adults (McLanahan and Adams, 1987; Bird, 1997). Parenting tends to be particularly stressful and to be associated with more severe psychological distress in the context of children with special needs (Teti et al., 1996), young children (Oyserman et al., 2000), and children who are perceived as more demanding or less reinforcing (Kwok and Wong, 2000). The strains of parenting can, therefore, heighten psychological distress and undermine functional parent–child relationships and family interaction (Patterson, 1983; Crnic and Greenberg, 1990). More general stress in other areas of parents' lives also appears to lead to maladaptive parenting styles such as negativism, criticism, and irritability (Burge and Hammen, 1991; Conger et al., 1992).

Social support systems may buffer the impact of stressful contexts on both parental mental health and parenting. Social support in the context of parenting may involve a range of processes, including the provision of emotional support (love, empathy, encouragement, understanding, and advice); instrumental support (concrete assistance with tasks, such as parenting, childcare, and household tasks); informational support (such as advice or information concerning parenting or childcare); and economic support (giving concrete material help) (Cochran and Niego, 1995; Henly, 1997).

Social support can help parents cope with difficult life circumstances, such as employment demands and marital conflict or divorce (Sprock and Yoder, 1997), which in turn may alleviate parenting difficulties and parental distress. In addition to these indirect effects, much research

indicates a direct positive effect of social support on the psychological well-being of parents (see Belsky, 1984) and on parenting skills (Taylor and Roberts, 1995; Henly, 1997). Certain aspects of support – particularly emotional and instrumental support – are most strongly associated with maternal well-being and positive parenting skills. Specifically, a parent's level of social support predicts a stronger sense of competence in the caregiving role, more parental responsiveness and nurturance, and decreased restrictiveness, punitiveness, and hostility (for reviews, see Belsky, 1984; McLoyd, 1990). Of course, the types and levels of support that are most beneficial will vary from parent to parent, and from situation to situation.

However, some forms of social 'support' may create conflict or stress. For example, intergenerational or extended-family networks may offer parenting support and advice, but when family members disagree about child-rearing beliefs and practices, these networks may become more distressing and undermining than helpful (Cochran and Niego, 1995; Sonuga-Barke et al., 1998). In fact, a key element in determining the benefit provided by social networks is the goodness of fit between parents and their networks, in terms of ideological views, expectations, and practices, as well as in the level and quality of support desired and provided (see Belsky, 1984).

Commentary: Personal and Contextual Influences on Parenting Processes

A burgeoning body of research points to multiple influences on parenting, including processes associated with psychological characteristics of parents, parental psychological distress and mental illness, and contextual factors. Yet, many challenges and questions need to be addressed to construct a comprehensive picture of parenting and mental health. Here we highlight a few neglected or only recently emerging areas of study: (1) the impact on parenting of varying degrees of parental psychological distress and mental illness; (2) the particular impact of fathers' mental health on parenting processes and practices, and; (3) the mediational role of parenting contexts in the path from psychological well-being to parenting.

Much research on parenting and mental health focuses on severe cases of mental illness that incapacitate parents, rather than on more common mental health challenges that parents face from time to time. Mild symptoms of psychological distress, such as transitory depression and anxiety, are often left untreated and accepted as 'hassles' that only minimally interfere with parenting. However, even mild distress may have significant implications for parenting. Without recognition of the impact of this distress on parenting, both parents and children may inaccurately interpret difficulties in family interactions and relationships.

Although research on normative parenting processes has begun to examine the specific role of fathering (Pleck, 1995), research on fatherhood and mental health is relatively limited. Recent changes in paternal roles (such as becoming more involved in parenting) have put strains on fathers that seem to increase their psychological distress (Dickstein et al., 1991; Pleck and Pleck, 1997). Paternal psychological distress, in turn, is likely to alter family relationships and to strain family resources. For example, a few studies have begun to illuminate the specific consequences of mental illness in fathers. These investigations have revealed that difficulties such as depression and substance abuse in fathers are linked to problematic parent–child interactions and less secure attachment in children (for a review, see Phares and Compas, 1993). To date, studies of fathering have focused on mental health difficulties more common among men, such as substance abuse and antisocial behavior, and on employment stress, and thus additional research is needed on the impact of other psychological and contextual difficulties on fathering.

Despite parental mental illness and parenting contexts being frequently studied topics, researchers are only now beginning to link them together explicitly. It is important to note that psychological distress and mental illness may affect parenting not only through the direct expression of symptoms, but also through the contexts or circumstances of a person's life (such as employment, finances, and romantic relationships). Severe depression, debilitating anxiety, psychosis, substance abuse, and antisocial behavior all may be associated with impairments in living that have significant ramifications for an individual's parenting capacity. For example, antisocial personality frequently is associated with criminal behaviors considered punishable and subject to incarceration. Such behaviors and the consequent separations from one's family may have serious consequences for parenting. Likewise, anxiety and depression may interfere with marital quality and satisfaction. Thus, mental health difficulties not only have a direct effect on parenting processes, but also have an indirect effect through their impact on the family environment. Paradoxically, treatment of severe mental illness, in some cases, may pose serious challenges to an individual's parenting abilities.

For example, severe mental illness may necessitate psychiatric hospitalization, resulting in the parents' separation from their children. Also, medication commonly prescribed to alleviate symptoms of mental illness may seriously impair parents' capacity through deleterious side-effects (Anthony and McGinnis, 1978). Medication and other treatment also can be quite costly, in terms of both time and money, and further diminish family resources. Thus, it is important to consider the effects of intervention in the further exacerbation of parenting difficulties.

IMPLICATIONS FOR PRACTICE: INTERVENTION AND SOCIAL POLICY

Knowing that parental mental health and parenting are intricately related, an essential issue becomes how to address problems in these areas. To do this, we may benefit once again from an ecological perspective. Within such a framework, multiple levels of parents' personal resources and environments must be addressed to contribute to their mental health and parenting needs. At the individual level, prevention and intervention programs targeted at parents and their children can be tailored to address particular parenting and mental health issues. At an intermediate level, social support networks, friends, and extended family members can offer an additional layer of support. At a more broad-based level, local resources, such as schools and community centers, may provide group-focused programs for parenting and mental health issues. And finally, at a large-scale level, social policy may help to address parenting and mental health issues in ways that directly or indirectly benefit parents and families. Each of these levels of influence, alone or in combination, can be a focus for addressing the issues in parenting and mental health that we discussed earlier. Possible goals and practices that can be incorporated into these intervention approaches are described below.

Individual Approaches

As already seen, parents with mental health concerns face many challenges in their parenting roles. Depending on the severity and context of these challenges, one or a combination of several parent-centered intervention methods may be appropriate. These include teaching basic parenting skills, engaging parents in positive interactions with their children, and providing counseling to reduce parents' psychological distress.

Parents who are coping with psychological or environmental stresses may seek assistance with their parenting skills. Programs can help parents to address specific aspects of their child-rearing interactions, such as emotional engagement, responsiveness, discipline, and dealing with issues of control and autonomy (Puckering et al., 1994; Luthar and Suchman, 2000). Beyond building child-rearing knowledge and skills, some programs focus on the parent–child pair, and thus seek directly to enhance parent–child interactions and relationship capacities, such as attachment quality, positive interactions, and dealing with negative emotions (Oyserman et al., 1994; Clark et al., 1998). These programs may offer structured time and opportunities for parents to have positive, enjoyable interactions with their children, with the supportive guidance of care providers. Nurses or other assistants often help parents to engage with their children (such as by establishing eye contact or fostering communication) and to respond to children's cues and needs. Beyond fostering positive contact between parents and children, these *in vivo* interactions provide an optimal setting for building parenting skills, by allowing mental-health workers to assess parenting strengths and weaknesses, provide supervision, training, and guidance in the immediate parenting context, and model appropriate parenting skills for parents to implement (Oyserman et al., 1994).

Although many parenting programs work directly on enhancing parenting skills and interactions, other programs focus on improving parents' mental health, and thus indirectly on fostering better child-rearing skills. Programs may address particular mental health issues (such as through psychotherapy for depression or anxiety, or treatment for substance abuse), as well as their impact on parenting, using a variety of therapeutic approaches. Several of these approaches draw on current understanding of parenting processes, such as those reviewed earlier in the chapter. For example, in line with evidence supporting the influence of information-processing deficits on parenting, cognitive-behavioral approaches to parenting interventions are specifically designed to address maladaptive social-cognitive processes, such as low self-efficacy, negative attributions, and coping difficulties (Clark et al., 1998). In a recently developed program for abusive parents, an attribution-retraining approach is used to target parents' maladaptive attributions about their children, rather than specific parenting behaviors. This intervention

has demonstrated parenting improvements beyond support-based home visitation programs (Bugental, 2001). Success of this type of program highlights the importance of integrating research on the determinants of parenting into intervention efforts.

Other programs address the interpersonal context of parenting and mental health. Interpersonal approaches are designed to restructure parents' negative self-schemas, negative expectations, and negative emotional expression, particularly within the parenting relationship (Klerman, et al., 1995; Clark et al., 1998). Drawing again from research on the determinants of parenting, interpersonal approaches also may involve exploring the parents' family of origin and its impact on current parent–child and family relationships. For example, programs may attempt to modify maladaptive internal models of relationships in parents who lacked effective role models, such as those who grew up with abusive or neglectful parents (Nicholson and Blanch, 1994).

More intensive types of intervention may be required for parents with severe mental illness. These parents may undergo chronic or episodic hospitalization, and thus may lose consistent contact with their children. In some cases, legal authorities may deem mentally ill parents too incompetent, neglectful, or mentally unstable to look after their children, and may remove them from their custody. These approaches take a deficit approach to parenting and mental health that focuses on parents' incompetence. In contrast, some programs take a skill-development approach that bolsters parenting skills and confidence. For example, residential treatment centers or home-visit programs allow parents to continue parenting under the supervision of mental health providers, who not only can address their mental health needs, but also can assess and help develop their parenting skills and confidence (Oyserman et al., 1994). In addition to skill-building, the educational component of these programs may provide information on child development, health care, and educational needs. For parents who are severely incapacitated by mental illness, these programs may further assist with or teach them about maintaining a household, obtaining and preparing food, and providing for children's health and hygiene. Furthermore, programs may offer contingency planning or respite care services during hospitalization or acute symptom phases for parents who experience periods of severe mental illness.

Although quite varied in approach and content, parent-centered interventions, in general, recognize the social-cognitive and interpersonal contributors to mental health and parenting difficulties, and address those needs educationally and therapeutically with parents and their children. There is some evidence that parenting programs improve parents' self-esteem, decrease levels of stress, anxiety, and depression (Puckering et al., 1994; Day and Davis, 1999), and improve parenting skills and interactions (Puckering et al., 1994; Luthar and Suchman, 2000). Yet, the long-term benefits of these programs for both parental mental health and parenting processes have not yet been established (Golding, 2000).

Group or Network Approaches

Programs that take a broader ecological approach may extend resources to include social support networks. Whether by tapping into existing resources, such as spouses, other family members, and neighbors, or helping to build new social support networks, such as through parent support groups, this approach helps parents to reduce their sense of isolation and to cope with the challenges of parenting.

Although many individual intervention programs focus solely on the parent with mental health issues, family-oriented interventions may include both spouses and even other family members. These programs are helpful in addressing the broader contexts of parenting, such as possible marital issues or family stresses contributing to mental health and parenting problems, and may provide marital or family therapy if relevant. Spouses or other family members also may seek education on relevant mental health issues (for example, learning about depression, or understanding the impact of anxiety on parenting) and may learn ways to cope with mental illness in the family. These approaches encourage supportive spouse and family interactions as a therapeutic tool. As such, these programs may help foster communication, connectedness, support, and joint problem-solving between parenting pairs or other family members (Beardslee et al., 1992, 1997; Goldstein and Miklowitz, 1995; Clark et al., 1998), thereby addressing some of the parenting processes that are compromised by a conflictual or unsupportive family environment. Family intervention approaches appear to be quite successful for parents with depression (Beardslee et al., 1992, 1997; Clark et al., 1998) and schizophrenia (Goldstein and Miklowitz, 1995).

Group interventions are likely to have a didactic component similar to individual interventions (such as learning about parenting interactions, skills, and resources), but they also provide opportunities for parents to exchange experiences, coping strategies, and parenting ideas with others, and to build mutual support networks with parents facing similar difficulties. Although research on the efficacy of such group intervention approaches is limited, one group therapy program documented improvements in a few of the targeted parenting behaviors (including affective interactions and parenting satisfaction), but not others (including limit setting and autonomy) (Luthar and Suchman, 2000).

Community Approaches

Some researchers advocate more broadly focused parenting interventions that involve community resources, or are delivered within community settings. Community-based service programs come in many forms, with varying agendas, methods, and outcomes. What they have in common is a focus on parenting *in context*, within the community. Ecologically based or community programs may aim to increase social support networks, involve parents in community resources, and even address the needs of particular socio-cultural groups (Golding, 2000) or parents with particular circumstances, such as teen parents, single parents, or divorced parents (Goodman, 1984). By working with parents in their communities, these programs may foster peer support, reduce feelings of isolation, and empower parents to make contacts with and engage in local community resources.

Although rare, some programs establish connections and foster communication between parents and schools or daycare services, and even help to arrange for these services. Community intervention programs could be very helpful in assisting parents in building relationships with service providers (for example, pediatricians, teachers, school counselors) and social networks (such as neighbors, other parents). Unfortunately, though, this level of support is rarely included in parenting intervention programs. In a review of community mental health services for parents with mental illness, Oyserman et al. (1994) state that 'environmental supports outside the home were not considered, and treatment did not include development of natural support systems to provide informational, emotional, or instrumental assistance after the crisis' (p. 138).

In addition to helping individual parents within community contexts, community-based programs may address parenting issues on a large scale, by delivering services to many parents and even taking a preventive approach. Whereas many individual- and family-based programs assist parents with evidenced difficulties in parenting and mental health, community interventions or group-based programs can be more proactive, taking an early intervention approach that identifies at-risk populations (such as parents with a history of abuse, unstable marriages, or low self-efficacy), and intervenes before difficulties arise, or a primary prevention approach that provides community-wide services to all parents to curb the incidence of parenting deficits on the whole. The methods of these programs vary, but may include direct education by specialists, home visits, parent or family counseling, parenting skills training, and support groups.

Although little research has tested the efficacy of community approaches to parenting and mental health, some claim that they are just as effective as individually focused programs (Golding, 2000). Certainly, both individual- and community-based programs have advantages, and one may be more beneficial than the other for particular circumstances and goals. A combination of individual and community approaches, though, may be most effective in addressing issues of parenting and mental health. Indeed, some service providers and health policy-makers have advocated such a multi-level model that integrates individual approaches (addressing parents' psychological and parenting needs), family and group approaches (attempting to improve interactions between parents and children; building on family and social support networks), and community approaches (helping parents to utilize local mental health services and school and daycare resources) (Luthar and Suchman, 2000). Furthermore, a tiered service model may draw on resources from many levels, including direct service providers, such as health visitors and general practitioners, professional consultants, such as mental-health specialists who can offer support, training, and consultation to service providers, and, in some cases, physical services, such as social welfare, health care services, and daycare personnel (Day and Davies, 1999). This type of collaborative approach would allow parents to gain support in their immediate surroundings, while benefiting from the expertise and services of more specialized programs.

Commentary: Recommendations for Service Providers and Social Policy

Both basic research on parenting and analysis of current interventions point to a few key themes and recommendations regarding service delivery for parenting difficulties. First, parenting interventions should have a clear theoretical foundation, specific goals, specific treatment objectives and techniques focused on particular parenting behaviors, and clarity in applying those concepts to the treatment approaches (Clark et al., 1998). Second, a whole-parent model of intervention should address not only specific parenting difficulties and mental illness but also the potentially stressful contexts of parenting, and should build strengths, motivation, skills, and knowledge in a way that fits with those contexts or circumstances. Such programs should take into account the familial, social, and environmental contexts of parenting (such as employment, financial status, marital problems, and social support), and should respond to individual parents' and families' needs and circumstances (Warfield et al., 2000). Third, several researchers recommend moving away from a deficit or disorder model of parenting and mental health (that is, viewing parents as incompetent and needing to be reformed by 'expert' service providers), and instead taking a strength-building or empowerment approach, by working with parents and their individual circumstances, tapping into their strengths, and helping them function in their environments (Puckering et al., 1994; Mowbray et al., 2000). For example, one program's philosophy is built on respect for individual parents and their experiences and knowledge of their children, and thus advocates mutual support and partnership between parents and service providers in addressing parenting difficulties (Puckering et al., 1994). Thus, instead of using their expertise solely to guide how parents should parent, service providers can use their expertise to help parents develop their strengths, tap into and maximize benefits from existing resources, and advocate for themselves in their communities.

Although current efforts to address parenting and mental health issues are promising, much remains to be developed in this area. Most importantly, many existing programs focus on addressing difficulties once they have arisen, but neglect to build resiliency in parents and families to help them prevent future problems. Existing parenting programs typically take a reactive *intervention* approach, which targets parents who already show mental health or parenting difficulties and intervenes with these problems, rather than a *prevention* approach, with the aim of preventing problems by promoting mental health and adaptive parenting for all parents. Even among parents who show difficulty, early intervention approaches can be implemented before maladaptive parenting processes become set and difficult to change (Lyons-Ruth et al., 2000).

Thus far, we have discussed individual, group, and community levels of intervention. However, perhaps the best venue for taking a prevention approach to parenting and mental health is through changes to social policy, or the goals and guidelines for how a society operates in a given area. In the case of parenting, social policy governs how parents are expected to parent children, how and when society should intervene, what programs are available for such intervention, and who has access to those programs. Social policy also extends beyond policy-making into programming and funding. Employing social policy initiatives as a means of addressing parenting difficulties has the potential for substantial benefits. Social policy efforts may enable prevention and intervention programs to reach larger populations, thereby not only benefiting those at risk but also improving parenting for those not currently experiencing difficulties.

Social policy also may be used to make programs more accessible to parents. As discussed earlier, many parents with mental health difficulties face special challenges. For instance, parents who struggle with mental illness are more likely to have stressful life circumstances, financial difficulties, or inadequate social support (Mowbray et al., 2000). Social policy initiatives can help parents to overcome these obstacles by encouraging funding, transportation, and childcare for participation in parenting programs or by offering home visit/outreach programs for engaging isolated or incapacitated parents (Lyons-Ruth et al., 2000).

Parents with mental health difficulties also may find themselves facing lengthy or repeated separations from their families resulting from crisis admissions to the hospital or criminal incarceration. Under those circumstances where separation is unavoidable, policy changes may help to maintain parent–child relationships by providing contact opportunities and within-institution services for parents and their children. Similarly, because abusive, neglectful, or severely mentally ill parents risk temporarily or permanently losing custody rights, they may avoid seeking help for fear of losing their children or facing legal incrimination. Social policy may address such barriers to service by providing child visit programs for parents in these situations, or by offering incentives to parents who independently seek help with their children.

Social policy also can be directed toward reducing the stigma surrounding mental illness and parenting difficulties by promoting parenting programs and increasing social awareness of mental health issues and the implications for parenting, thus making parents more likely to seek available services. Furthermore, instead of targeting programs for 'incompetent' parents or those having difficulties, social policy-makers can bring parenting services and interventions to a community-based level, directed toward *all* parents, thus alleviating the stigma associated with seeking help. For example, parenting or family living classes that provide preventive education as well as intervention services may be provided to the community as part of an accepted routine of childcare (as in birthing classes, maternity wards, well-baby clinics, pediatrician offices). As such, these programs not only can help parents with current difficulties, but also can build resiliency in parents who may otherwise show difficulties later on.

Finally, addressing parenting at the level of social policy has several advantages for increasing our understanding of parental mental health and parenting. To develop and provide effective prevention and intervention services for parents, it is crucial that program developers possess adequate information about the factors that result in parenting deficits, as well as those factors that promote adaptive parenting. Such information can only be obtained through high-quality research on parenting processes and intervention efficacy. Social policy-makers can develop policies and programs that encourage research on the determinants of adaptive and maladaptive parenting, which in turn can inform more effective programming and policies.

CONCLUSION

Research on parenting and mental health has demonstrated that certain characteristics of parents and their contexts can present a challenge to adaptive parenting. Viewing this research in light of transactional, ecologically based, and multidimensional models of parenting illuminates new perspectives on the potential pathways linking parent psychological characteristics, psychological distress and mental illness, and parenting contexts with the process of parenting.

Figure 17.1 illustrates two key elements of these pathways, as highlighted in this chapter. First, bi-directional relations exist among the many determinants of parenting. For example, maladaptive social-cognitive processes may contribute to parental mental illness, which in turn may affect parents' emotionality. Further, stressful contexts may exacerbate mental illness, which in turn creates more stress. Second, Figure 17.1 shows how parent psychological characteristics and contexts can influence parenting both directly and indirectly. For example, family stress and social support not only affect parenting directly by virtue of creating stressful or supportive home environments, but also indirectly through their effects on parents' level of psychological distress, which in turn influences parent–child interactions and relationships. As another example, growing up in a positive home environment may enhance parenting through both direct and indirect pathways. Parents' own childhood experiences may directly influence their current child-rearing styles, or adaptive early experiences may promote current mental health, which then fosters strong parenting skills.

Although this complex web of linkages at first may seem to complicate attempts at prevention and intervention, it actually may help to uncover pathways to adaptive parenting. By recognizing the varied influences on parenting and mental health, parenting programs can intervene not only at the level of parenting processes or mental health difficulties, but also at the level of antecedent variables. For example, therapeutic approaches may address early childhood experiences or life stresses that contribute to mental illness; family or group interventions may build social support and reduce family stress, which in turn may alleviate psychological distress and thus improve parenting; and cognitively based treatments may modify maladaptive social-cognitive mechanisms, so as to intercept the damaging attributions or efficacy beliefs that mediate the effect of parental mental illness on parenting. Based on this increasing awareness of the complicated interplay among various parenting processes and contexts, families, service-providers, and policy-makers can look forward to effective collaboration to promote positive mental health as well as adaptive parent–child relationships.

ACKNOWLEDGMENTS

The authors would like to thank Julie Eisengart and Alison Groot for their assistance in preparation of this chapter, and Joe Pleck for his helpful feedback. Writing of this chapter was supported by a William T. Grant Foundation Faculty Scholars Award and National Institute of Mental Health Grant MH59711–01 awarded to Karen D. Rudolph.

REFERENCES

Ainsworth, M.D., Bell, S.M. and Stayton, D.J. (1972) Individual differences in the development of some attachment behaviors. *Merrill-Palmer Quarterly*, **18**, 123–43.

Almeida, D.M., Wethington, E. and Chandler, A.L. (1999) Daily transmission of tensions between marital dyads and parent–child dyads. *Journal of Marriage and the Family*, **61**, 49–61.

Anthony, E.J. and McGinnis, M. (1978) Counseling very disturbed parents. In Arnold, L.E. (ed.) *Helping Parents Help Their Children*. New York: Brunner/Mazel, pp. 328–41.

Bandura, A. (1995) Exercise of personal and collective efficacy in changing societies. In Bandura, A. (ed.) *Self-efficacy in Changing Societies*. New York: Cambridge University Press, pp. 1–45.

Barber, B.K. (1996) Parental psychological control: revisiting a neglected construct. *Child Development*, **67**, 3296–319.

Barnett, B. and Parker, G. (1986) Possible determinants, correlates and consequences of high levels of anxiety in primiparous mothers. *Psychological Medicine*, **16**, 177–85.

Baumrind, D. (1971) Current patterns of parental authority. *Developmental Psychology Monograph*, **4**, 1–103.

Beardslee, W.R., Bemporad, J., Keller, M.B. and Klerman, G.L. (1983) Children of parents with major affective disorder: a review. *American Journal of Psychiatry*, **140**, 825–32.

Beardslee, W.R., Hoke, L., Wheelock, I., Rothberg, P.C., van de Velde, P. and Swatling, S. (1992) Initial findings on preventive intervention for families with parental affective disorders. *American Journal of Psychiatry*, **149**, 1335–40.

Beardslee, W.R., Versage, E.M., Wright, E.J., Salt, P., Rothberg, P.C., Drezner, K. and Gladstone, T.R.G. (1997) Examination of preventive interventions for families with depression: evidence of change. *Development and Psychopathology*, **9**, 109–30.

Belsky, J. (1984) The determinants of parenting: a process model. *Child Development*, **55**, 83–96.

Belsky, J., Hertzog, C. and Rovine, M. (1986) Causal analyses of multiple determinants of parenting: empirical and methodological advances. In Lamb, M., Brown, A. and Rogoff, B. (eds) *Advances in Developmental Psychology*, Vol. 4. Hillsdale, NJ: Lawrence Erlbaum, pp. 153–202.

Belsky, J., Crnic, K. and Woodworth, S. (1995) Personality and parenting: exploring the mediating role of transient mood and daily hassles. *Journal of Personality*, **63**, 905–29.

Bird, C.E. (1997) Gender differences in the social and economic burdens of parenting and psychological distress. *Journal of Marriage and the Family*, **59**, 809–23.

Bond, C.R. and McMahon, R.J. (1984) Relationships between marital distress and child behavior problems, maternal personal adjustment, maternal personality, and maternal parenting behavior. *Journal of Abnormal Psychology*, **93**, 348–51.

Bornstein, M.H. (ed.) (1995) *Handbook of Parenting*. Mahwah, NJ: Lawrence Erlbaum.

Bowlby, J. (1969) Disruption of affectional bonds and its effects on behavior. *Canada's Mental Health Supplement*, **59**, 12.

Bronstein, P., Fitzgerald, M., Briones, M., Pieniadz, J. and D'Ari, A. (1993) Family emotional expressiveness as a predictor of early adolescent social and psychological adjustment. *Journal of Early Adolescence*, **13**, 448–71.

Bugental, D.B. (1993) Communication in abusive relationships: cognitive constructions of interpersonal power. *American Behavioral Scientist*, **36**, 288–308.

Bugental, D.B. (2001) Parental attributions as predictors of caregiving outcomes. Paper presented at the biennial meeting of the Society for Research in Child Development, Minneapolis, MN.

Burge, D. and Hammen, C. (1991) Maternal communication: predictors of outcome at follow-up in a sample of children at high and low risk for depression. *Journal of Abnormal Psychology*, **100**, 174–80.

Capps, L., Sigman, M., Sena, R., Henker, B. and Whalen, C. (1996) Fear, anxiety and perceived control in children of agoraphobic parents. *Journal of Child Psychology and Psychiatry*, **37**, 445–52.

Cassidy, B., Zoccolillo, M. and Hughes, S. (1996) Psychopathology in adolescent mothers and its effects on mother–infant interactions: a pilot study. *Canadian Journal of Psychiatry*, **41**, 379–84.

Cicchetti, D., Rogosch, F.A. and Toth, S.L. (1998) Maternal depressive disorder and contextual risk: contributions to the development of attachment insecurity and behavior problems in toddlerhood. *Development and Psychopathology*, **10**, 283–300.

Clark, R., Paulson, A. and Seidl, M.E. (1998) Relationship-focused group intervention for at-risk families with infants and young children. In Stoiber, K.C. and Kratochwill, T.R. (eds) *Handbook of Group Intervention for Children and Families*. Boston: Allyn and Bacon, pp. 401–23.

Cochran, M. and Niego, S. (1995) Parenting and social networks. In Bornstein, M.H. (ed.) *Handbook of Parenting: Vol. 3. Status and Social Conditions of Parenting*. Mahwah, NJ: Lawrence Erlbaum, pp. 393–418.

Cohler, B.J., Grunebaum, H.U., Weiss, J.L., Gamer, E. and Gallant, D.H. (1977) Disturbance of attention among schizophrenic, depressed and well mothers and their young children. *Journal of Child Psychology and Psychiatry*, **18**, 115–35.

Conger, R.D., Conger, K.J., Elder, G.H., Jr, Lorenz, F.O., Simons, R.L. and Whitbeck, L.B. (1992) A family process model of economic hardship and adjustment of early adolescent boys. *Child Development*, **63**, 526–41.

Cox, M., Owen, M., Lewis, J., Riedel, C., Scalf-McIver, L. and Suster, A. (1985) Intergenerational influences on the parent–infant relationship in the transition to parenthood. *Journal of Family Issues*, **6**, 543–64.

Cox, M.J., Owen, M.T., Lewis, J.M. and Henderson, V.K. (1989) Marriage, adult adjustment, and early parenting. *Child Development*, **60**, 1015–24.

Crittenden, P.M. (1993) An information-processing perspective on the behavior of neglectful parents. *Criminal Justice and Behavior*, **20**, 27–48.

Crnic, K.A. and Greenberg, M.T. (1990) Minor parenting stresses with young children. *Child Development*, **61**, 1628–37.

Cummings, E.M. and Davies, P.T. (1999) Depressed parents and family functioning: interpersonal effects and children's functioning and development. In Joiner, T. and Coyne, J.C. (eds) *The Interactional Nature of Depression: Advances in Interpersonal Approaches*. Washington, DC: American Psychological Association, pp. 299–327.

Darling, N. and Steinberg, L. (1993) Parenting style as context: an integrative model. *Psychological Bulletin*, **113**, 487–96.

Day, C. and Davis, H. (1999) Community child mental-health services: a framework for the development of parenting initiatives. *Clinical Child Psychology and Psychiatry*, **4**, 475–82.

Deal, J.E., Halverson, C.F. and Wampler, K.S. (1989) Parental agreement on child-rearing orientations: relations to parental, marital, family, and child characteristics. *Child Development*, **60**, 1025–34.

Dickstein, L.J., Stein, T.S., Pleck, J.H. and Myers, M.F. (1991) Men's changing social roles in the 1990s: emerging issues in the psychiatric treatment of men. *Hospital and Community Psychiatry*, **42**, 701–5.

Dix, T. and Lochman, J.E. (1990) Social cognition and negative reactions to children: a comparison of mothers of aggressive and nonaggressive boys. *Journal of Social and Clinical Psychology*, **9**, 418–38.

Dix, T., Ruble, D.N. and Zambarano, R.J. (1989) Mothers' implicit theories of discipline: child effects, parent effects, and the attribution process. *Child Development*, **60**, 1373–91.

Eder, R.A. and Mangelsdorf, S.C. (1997) The emotional basis of early personality development: implications for the emergent self-concept. In Hogan, R., Johnson, J. and Briggs, S. (eds) *Handbook of Personality Psychology*. San Diego, CA: Academic Press, pp. 209–40.

Eisenberg, N., Fabes, R.A. and Murphy, B.C. (1996) Parents' reactions to children's negative emotions: relations to children's social competence and comforting behavior. *Child Development*, **67**, 2227–47.

Eisenberg, N., Cumberland, A. and Spinrad, T.L. (1998) Parental socialization of emotion. *Psychological Inquiry*, **9**, 241–73.

Elder, G.H., Caspi, A. and Downey, G. (1986) Problem behavior and family relationships: life course and intergenerational themes. In Sorensen, A., Weinert, F. and Sherrod, L. (eds) *Human Development: Interdisciplinary Perspectives*. Hillsdale, NJ: Lawrence Erlbaum, pp. 293–340.

Eliason, M.J. and Skinstad, A.H. (1995) Drug/alcohol addictions and mothering. *Alcoholism Treatment Quarterly*, **12**, 83–96.

Endler, N.S., Parker, J.D.A. and Butcher, J.N. (1993) A factor analytic study of coping styles and the MMPI-2 content scales. *Journal of Clinical Psychology*, **49**, 523–7.

Fauber, R., Forehand, R., Thomas, A.M. and Wierson, M. (1990) A mediational model of the impact of marital conflict on adolescent adjustment in intact and divorced families: the role of disrupted parenting. *Child Development*, **61**, 1112–23.

Fellow-Smith, L. (2000) Impact of parental anxiety disorder on children. In Reder, P., McClure, M. and Jolley, A.

(eds) *Family Matters: Interfaces between Child and Adult Mental Health*. London: Routledge, pp. 96–106.

Field, T., Healy, B.T., Goldstein, S. and Guthertz, M. (1990) Behavior-state matching and synchrony in mother-infant interactions of non-depressed versus depressed dyads. *Developmental Psychology*, **26**, 7–14.

Floyd, F.J., Gilliom, L.A. and Costigan, C.L. (1998) Marriage and the parenting alliance: Longitudinal prediction of change in parenting perceptions and behaviors. *Child Development*, **69**, 1461–79.

Fonagy, P., Steele, H. and Steele, M. (1991) Maternal representations of attachment during pregnancy predict the organization of infant–mother attachment at one year of age. *Child Development*, **62**, 891–905.

Frosch, C.A. and Mangelsdorf, S.C. (2001) Marital behavior, parenting behavior, and multiple reports of preschoolers' behavior problems: mediation or moderation. *Developmental Psychology*, **37**, 502–19.

Frosch, C.A., Mangelsdorf, S.C. and McHale, J.L. (2000) Marital behavior and the security of preschooler–parent attachment relationships. *Journal of Family Psychology*, **14**, 144–61.

Gallant, W.A., Gorey, K.M., Gallant, M.D., Perry, J.L. and Ryan, P.K. (1998) The association of personality characteristics with parenting problems among alcoholic couples. *American Journal of Drug Alcohol Abuse*, **24**, 119–29.

Garber, J. and Flynn, C. (2001) Vulnerability to depression in childhood and adolescence. In Ingram, R.E. and Price, J.M. (eds) *Vulnerability to Psychopathology: Risk Across the Lifespan*. New York: Guilford, pp. 175–225.

Gelfand, D.M. and Teti, D.M. (1990) The effects of maternal depression on children. *Clinical Psychology Review*, **10**, 329–53.

Golding, K. (2000) Parent management training as an intervention to promote adequate parenting. *Clinical Child Psychology and Psychiatry*, **5**, 357–71.

Goldstein, L.H., Diener, M.L. and Mangelsdorf, S.C. (1996) Maternal characteristics and social support across the transition to motherhood: associations with maternal behavior. *Journal of Family Psychology*, **10**, 60–71.

Goldstein, M.J. and Miklowitz, D.J. (1995) The effectiveness of psychoeducational family therapy in the treatment of schizophrenic disorders. *Journal of Marital and Family Therapy*, **21**, 361–76.

Goodman, C. (1984) The PACE family treatment and education program: a public health approach to parental competence and promotion of mental health. *New Directions for Mental Health Services*, **24**, 53–77.

Goodman, S.H. and Brumley, H.E. (1990) Schizophrenic and depressed mothers: relational deficits in parenting. *Developmental Psychology*, **26**, 31–9.

Goodman, S.H. and Gotlib, I.H. (1999) Risk for psychopathology in the children of depressed mothers: a developmental model for understanding mechanisms of transmission. *Psychological Review*, **106**, 458–90.

Gordon, D., Burge, D., Hammen, C., Adrian, C., Jaenicke, C. and Hiroto, D. (1989) Observations of interactions of depressed women with their children. *American Journal of Psychiatry*, **146**, 50–5.

Gotlib, I.H. and Hammen, C.L. (1992) *Psychological Aspects of Depression: Toward a Cognitive-Interpersonal Integration*. Chichester, UK: Wiley.

Greenberger, E. and O'Neil, R. (1993) Spouse, parent, worker: role commitments and role-related experiences in the construction of adult's well-being. *Developmental Psychology*, **29**, 181–97.

Hammen, C. (1991) *Depression Runs in Families: The Social Context of Risk and Resilience in Children of Depressed Mothers*. New York: Springer-Verlag.

Hammen, C. and Rudolph, K.D. (1996) Childhood depression. In Mash, E. and Barkley, R.A. (eds) *Child Psychopathology*. New York: Guilford, pp. 153–95.

Hans, S.L., Bernstein, V.J. and Henson, L.G. (1999) The role of psychopathology in the parenting of drug-dependent women. *Development and Psychopathology*, **11**, 957–77.

Hastings, P. and Grusec, J.E. (1997) Conflict outcome as a function of parental accuracy in perceiving child cognitions and affect. *Social Development*, **6**, 76–90.

Henly, J. R. (1997) The complexity of support: the impact of family structure and provisional support on African American and White adolescent mothers' well-being. *American Journal of Community Psychology*, **25**, 629–55.

Hetherington, E.M., Bridges, M. and Insabella, G.M. (1998) What matters? What does not? Five perspectives on the association between marital transitions and children's adjustment. *American Psychologist*, **53**, 167–84.

Hines, A.M. (1997) Divorce-related transitions, adolescent development, and the role of the parent–child relationship: a review of the literature. *Journal of Marriage and the Family*, **59**, 375–88.

Holloway, S.D. and Machida, S. (1991) Child-rearing effectiveness of divorced mothers: relationship to coping strategies and social support. *Journal of Divorce and Remarriage*, **14**, 179–201.

Hops, H., Biglan, A., Sherman, L., Arthur, J., Friedman, L. and Osteen, V. (1987) Home observations of family interactions of depressed women. *Journal of Consulting and Clinical Psychology*, **55**, 341–6.

Jackson, A.P. and Huang, C.C. (2000) Parenting stress and behavior among single mothers of preschoolers: the mediating role of self-efficacy. *Journal of Social Service Research*, **26**, 29–42.

Kendziora, K.T. and O'Leary, S.G. (1993) Dysfunctional parenting as a focus for prevention and treatment of child behavior problems. *Advances in Clinical Child Psychology*, **15**, 175–206.

Kerig, P.K., Cowan, P.A. and Cowan, C.P. (1993) Marital quality and gender differences in parent–child interaction. *Developmental Psychology*, **29**, 931–9.

Klerman, G.L., Weissman, M.M., Rounsaville, B. and Chevron, E.S. (1995) Interpersonal psychotherapy for depression. *Journal of Psychotherapy Practice and Research*, **4**, 342–51.

Kochanska, G., Kuczynski, L., Radke-Yarrow, M. and Welsh, J.D. (1987) Resolutions of control episodes between well and affectively ill mothers and their young children. *Journal of Abnormal Child Psychology*, **15**, 441–56.

Kohn, P.M., Hay, B.D. and Legere, J.J. (1994) Hassles, coping styles, and negative well-being. *Personality and Individual Differences*, **17**, 169–79.

Kurtz, L. and Derevensky, J.L. (1994) Adolescent motherhood: an application of the stress and coping model to child-rearing attitudes and practices. *Canadian Journal of Community Mental Health*, **13**, 5–24.

Kwok, S. and Wong, D. (2000) Mental health of parents with young children in Hong Kong: the roles of parenting stress and parenting self-efficacy. *Child and Family Social Work*, **5**, 57–65.

Lang, A.R., Pelham, W.E., Atkeson, B.M. and Murphy, D.A. (1999) Effects of alcohol intoxication on parenting behavior in interactions with child confederates exhibiting normal or deviant behaviors. *Journal of Abnormal Child Psychology*, **27**, 177–89.

Luthar, S.S. and Suchman, N.E. (2000) Relational psychotherapy mothers' group: a developmentally informed intervention for at-risk mothers. *Development and Psychopathology*, **12**, 235–53.

Lyons-Ruth, K. (1992) Maternal depressive symptoms, disorganized infant–mother attachment relationships and hostile-aggressive behavior in the preschool classroom: a prospective longitudinal view from infancy to age five. In Cicchetti, D. and Toth, S. (eds) *Developmental Perspectives on Depression*. Rochester, NY: University of Rochester Press, pp. 131–69.

Lyons-Ruth, K., Zeanah, C.H. and Benoit, D. (1996) Disorder and risk for disorder during infancy and toddlerhood. In Mash, E. and Barkley, R.A. (eds) *Child Psychopathology*. New York: Guilford, pp. 457–91.

Lyons-Ruth, K., Wolfe, R. and Lyubchik, A. (2000) Depression and the parenting of young children: making the case for early preventive mental health services. *Harvard Review of Psychiatry*, **8**, 148–53.

Maccoby, E.E. and Martin, J. (1983) Socialization in the context of the family: parent–child interaction. In Mussen, P.H. (series ed.) and Hetherington, E.M. (vol. ed.) *Handbook of Child Psychology: Socialization, Personality, and Social Development*, 4th edition. New York: Wiley, pp. 1–101.

Mahoney, A., Jouriles, E.N. and Scavone, J. (1997) Marital adjustment, marital discord over childrearing, and child behavior problems: moderating effects of child age. *Journal of Clinical Child Psychology*, **26**, 415–23.

Manassis, K., Bradley, S., Goldberg, S., Hood, J. and Swinson, R. (1995) Behavioural inhibition, attachment and anxiety in children of mothers with anxiety disorders. *Canadian Journal of Psychiatry*, **40**, 87–92.

Mangelsdorf, S., Gunnar, M., Kestenbaum, R., Lang, S. and Andreas, D. (1990) Infant proneness-to-distress temperament, maternal personality, and mother–infant attachment: associations and goodness of fit. *Child Development*, **61**, 820–31.

McLanahan, S. and Adams, J. (1987) Parenthood and psychological well-being. *Annual Review of Sociology*, **13**, 237–57.

McLoyd, V.C. (1990) The impact of economic hardship on Black families and children: psychological distress,

parenting, and socioemotional development. *Child Development*, **61**, 311–46.

Milan, M.A. (1990) Antisocial personality in adulthood. In Hersen, M. and Last, C.G. (eds) *Handbook of Child and Adult Psychopathology: A Longitudinal Perspective*. New York: Pergamon, pp. 307–21.

Milner, J.S. (1993) Social information processing and physical child abuse. *Clinical Psychology Review*, **13**, 275–94.

Mondell, S. and Tyler, F.B. (1981) Parental competence and styles of problem solving/play behavior with children. *Developmental Psychology*, **17**, 73–8.

Mowbray, C., Schwartz, S., Bybee, D., Spang, J., Rueda-Riedle, A. and Oyserman, D. (2000) Mothers with a mental illness: stressors and resources for parenting and living. *Families in Society*, **81**, 118–29.

Nicholson, J. and Blanch, A. (1994) Rehabilitation for parenting roles for people with serious mental illness. *Psychosocial Rehabilitation Journal*, **18**, 109–19.

Nix, R.L., Pinderhughes, E.E., Dodge, K.A., Bates, J.E., Pettit, G.S. and McFadyen-Ketchum, S.A. (1999) The relation between mothers' hostile attribution tendencies and children's externalizing behavior problems: the mediating role of mothers' harsh discipline practices. *Child Development*, **70**, 896–909.

Oyserman, D., Mowbray, C.T. and Zemencuk, J.K. (1994) Resources and supports for mothers with severe mental illness. *Health and Social Work*, **19**, 132–42.

Oyserman, D., Mowbray, C.T., Meares, P.A. and Firminger, K.B. (2000) Parenting among mothers with a serious mental illness. *American Journal of Orthopsychiatry*, **70**, 296–315.

Parke, R.D. and McDowell, D.J. (1998) Toward an expanded model of emotion socialization: new people, new pathways. *Psychological Inquiry*, **9**, 303–7.

Patterson, G.R. (1983) Stress: a change agent for family process. In Garmezy, N. and Rutter, M. (eds) *Stress, Coping, and Development in Children*. New York: McGraw-Hill, pp. 235–64.

Patterson, G.R. and Capaldi, D.M. (1991) Antisocial parents: unskilled and vulnerable. In Cowan, P.A. and Hetherington, E.M. (eds) *Family Transitions. Advances in Family Research Series*. Hillsdale, NJ: Lawrence Erlbaum, pp. 195–218.

Phares, V. and Compas, B.E. (1993) Fathers and developmental psychopathology. *Current Directions in Psychological Science*, **2**, 162–5.

Pleck, E.H. and Pleck, J.H. (1997) Fatherhood ideals in the Unites States: historical dimensions. In Lamb, M.E. (ed.) *The Role of the Father in Child Development*, 3rd edition. New York: Wiley, pp. 33–48.

Pleck, J.H. (1985) *Working Wives/Working Husbands*. Beverly Hills, CA: Sage.

Pleck, J.H. (1995) The gender role strain paradigm: an update. In Levant, R.F. and Pollack, W.S. (eds) *A New Psychology of Men*. New York: Basic Books, pp. 11–32.

Pomerantz, E.M. and Eaton M.M. (2001) Maternal intrusive support in the academic context: transactional socialization processes. *Developmental Psychology*, **37**, 174–86.

Pomerantz, E.M. and Ruble, D.N. (1998) The multidimensional nature of control: implications for the development of sex differences in self-evaluation. In Heckhausen, J. and Dweck, C.S. (eds) *Motivation and Self-Regulation Across the Life-Span*. New York: Cambridge University Press, pp. 159–84.

Puckering, C., Rogers, J., Mills, M., Cox, A.D. and Mattsson-Graff, M. (1994) Process and evaluation of a group intervention for mothers with parenting difficulties. *Child Abuse Review*, 3, 299–310.

Radke-Yarrow, M. (1998) *Children of Depressed Mothers: From Early Childhood to Maturity*. New York: Cambridge University Press.

Radke-Yarrow, M., Cummings, E.M., Kuczynski, L. and Chapman, M. (1985) Patterns of attachment in two- and three-year-olds in normal families and families with parental depression. *Child Development*, 56, 884–93.

Rao, V.N. and Ram, P.K. (1984) Impact of disturbed parents on the children. *Child Psychiatry Quarterly*, 17, 133–8.

Repetti, R.L. (1994) Short-term and long-term processes linking job stressors to father–child interaction. *Social Development*, 3, 1–15.

Repetti, R.L. and Wood, J. (1997) Effects of daily stress at work on mothers' interactions with preschoolers. *Journal of Family Psychology*, 11, 90–108.

Repetti, R.L., Matthews, K.A. and Waldron, I. (1989) Employment and women's health: effects of paid employment on women's mental and physical health. *American Psychologist*, 44, 1394–401.

Scarr, S. (1992) Developmental theories for the 1990s: development and individual differences. *Child Development*, 63, 1–19.

Scott, J.W. and Dembo, M.H. (1993) Maternal attributions regarding children's noncompliant behavior. *Child Study Journal*, 23, 187–207.

Seeman, M.V. (1996) The mother with schizophrenia. In Goepfert, M. and Webster, J. (eds) *Parental Psychiatric Disorder: Distressed Parents and Their Families*. Cambridge, England: Cambridge University Press, pp. 190–200.

Skinner, E.A., Zimmer-Gembeck, M.J. and Connell, J.P. (1998) Individual differences and the development of perceived control. *Monographs of the Society for Research in Child Development*, 63 (2–3, Serial No. 254).

Slep, A.M.S. and O'Leary, S.G. (1998) The effects of maternal attributions on parenting: an experimental analysis. *Journal of Family Psychology*, 12, 234–43.

Smith, A.M. and O'Leary, S.G. (1995) Attributions and arousal as predictors of maternal discipline. *Cognitive Therapy and Research*, 19, 459–71.

Sonuga-Barke, E.J.S., Mistry, M. and Qureshi, S. (1998) The mental health of Muslim mothers in extended families living in Britain: the impact of intergenerational disagreement on anxiety and depression. *British Journal of Clinical Psychology*, 37, 399–408.

Sparadeo, F.R., Zwick, W.R. and Butters, N. (1983) Cognitive functioning of alcoholic females: an exploratory study. *Drug and Alcohol Dependence*, 12, 143–50.

Sprock, J. and Yoder, C.Y. (1997) Women and depression: an update on the report of the APA task force. *Sex Roles*, 36, 269–303.

Strassberg, Z. (1997) Levels of analysis in cognitive bases of maternal disciplinary dysfunction. *Journal of Abnormal Child Psychology*, 25, 209–15.

Szewczyk, M., Neff, C., Dranger, E.A., Mangelsdorf, S.C. and Schoppe, S.J. (2001) Personality, social-contextual, and child temperament correlates of mother's parenting quality. Poster presented at the biennial meeting of the Society for Research in Child Development, Minneapolis, MN.

Taylor, R.D. and Roberts, D. (1995) Kinship support and maternal and adolescent well-being in economically disadvantaged African-American families. *Child Development*, 66, 1585–97.

Tein, J., Sandler, I.N. and Zautra, A.J. (2000) Stressful life events, psychological distress, coping, and parenting of divorced mothers: a longitudinal study. *Journal of Family Psychology*, 14, 27–41.

Teti, D.M. and Gelfand, D.M. (1991) Behavioral competence among mothers of infants in the first year: the mediational role of maternal self-efficacy. *Child Development*, 62, 918–29.

Teti, D.M., O'Connell, M.A. and Reiner, C.D. (1996) Parenting sensitivity, parental depression and child health: the mediational role of parental self-efficacy. *Early Development and Parenting*, 5, 237–50.

Tiggemann, M., Winefield, H.R., Goldney, R.D. and Winefield, A.H. (1992) Attributional style and parental rearing as predictors of psychological distress. *Personality and Individual Differences*, 13, 835–41.

Warfield, M.E., Hauser-Cram, P., Krauss, M.W., Shonkoff, J.P. and Upshur, C.C. (2000) The effect of early intervention services on maternal well-being. *Early Education and Development*, 11, 499–517.

Werkerle, C. and Wolfe, D.A. (1996) Child maltreatment. In Mash, E.J. and Barkley, R.A. (eds) *Child Psychopathology*. New York: Guilford, pp. 492–537.

Whaley, S.E., Pinto, A. and Sigman, M. (1999) Characterizing interactions between anxious mothers and their children. *Journal of Consulting and Clinical Psychology*, 67, 826–36.

Whisman, M.A. (1999) Marital dissatisfaction and psychiatric disorders: results from the national comorbidity survey. *Journal of Abnormal Psychology*, 108, 701–6.

Windle, M. (1996) Effect of parental drinking on adolescents. *Alcohol Health and Research World*, 20, 181–4.

Windle, M. and Dumenci, L. (1997) Parental and occupational stress as predictors of depressive symptoms among dual-income couples: a multilevel modeling approach. *Journal of Marriage and the Family*, 59, 625–34.

Wolfe, D.A. (1987) *Child Abuse: Implications for Child Development and Psychopathology*. Newbury Park, CA: Sage.

18

Parenting Children with Mental Health Problems

Fiona K. Miller and Jennifer M. Jenkins

SUMMARY

The parenting of children who are experiencing problems in development is a major challenge. In this chapter we focus on the specific difficulties of parenting children with emotional and behavioral disturbance. They are children who, for instance, suffer from unusual levels of anxiety when approaching new situations. They may frequently worry, be afraid of sleeping alone, or in more extreme cases, avoid challenging situations such as school. The anxiety they experience makes it difficult for them to cope with everyday tasks. Other children may feel unhappy and tearful much of the time, such that it is not easy for them to function in their everyday lives.

How can parents help children who are struggling with these kinds of difficulties? We consider recent research findings on the etiology of children's mental health disorders to help us understand the key role that parents and other people who are close to children play in exacerbating or ameliorating these problems. We also consider the research evidence on the types of treatments that are effective for children with emotional and behavioral difficulties. We then build on such treatment evidence to suggest ways that parents can help their children who are suffering from such disturbance.

INTRODUCTION

Mental health difficulties in children fall into two broad categories of internalizing and externalizing disturbance. Internalizing disorders involve disturbances of affect; they include emotional disorders (feelings of sadness, depression, guilt, and dysphoria), anxiety (feelings of fearfulness, worry, or nervousness), and separation anxiety (clinging, dependent, and distressed behavior upon separation from parents). In contrast, externalizing disorders typically involve negative behaviors that are problematic for the child and disturbing to others. They include conduct disorders (threatening or physically attacking people, and cruelty), physical aggression (getting into many fights, hitting, kicking, biting), and hyperactivity (fidgety and impulsive behavior). Parenting children with externalizing problems is the focus of chapter 19 and will not therefore be covered in this chapter.

Our discussion of effective treatments and the role of parents will focus mainly on parenting children with internalizing disturbances, such as anxiety and depression. Anxiety and depression are the most common types of internalizing disorders. They often co-occur and their symptoms may intensify as children become adolescents (Strauss et al., 1988; Zahn-Waxler et al., 2000). The mental health problems that children can show during the preschool period are is more diffuse than in later years, and there is considerable overlap in internalizing and externalizing difficulties (Richman et al., 1982).

HISTORICAL BACKGROUND

Clinical theories and research findings have been influential in shaping the views of developmentalists on the role of parenting in children's emotional and behavioral problems. Cross-fertilization has occurred between the clinical and research domains over time such that research on parenting has affected clinical practice. In turn, researchers have been intrigued by the richness of clinical theories and have subsequently used them to inform the hypotheses to be tested in their research studies (Vuchinich et al., 1988; Patterson et al., 1993). This interplay between clinical work and research has been essential for developing the understanding that most parenting researchers and clinicians now share. The consensus view that now informs both clinicians and researchers is characterized by two main elements, which maintain that children's mental health difficulties are influenced by multiple factors and that these are reciprocal and bi-directional influences (Collins et al., 2000).

First, mental health problems in children are multi-determined. Children contribute constitutional and genetic vulnerabilities (Rutter et al., 1999), as well as sequenced experiences that make them more vulnerable to the development of mental health disorders (Rutter, 1996). Factors outside children, such as different aspects of their context, also influence their development. Although the family context has been a focus of interest for both clinicians and researchers for six decades, schools (Mortimore, 1998), neighborhoods (Sampson et al., 1997), and peer groups (Hogue and Steinberg, 1996), have recently been identified as central factors influencing the development of emotional and behavioral problems in children.

Second, although much research work involves the presentation of linear relationships and unidirectional influences, most clinicians and researchers operate from a bi-directional model that emphasizes reciprocal parent–child influences on the development of child disturbance. Until recently the statistics and research methods that allow for the investigation of more dynamic models have not been available or within the competence of non-statisticians. Developments, both theoretical (Kenny, 1994) and statistical (growth curve modeling, structural equation modeling) (Snijders and Kenny, 1999; Boyle and Willms, 2001), have meant that it is now possible to test models that have bi-directional processes at their core (Conger and Conger, 1994).

Before describing such a model we consider some of the clinical perspectives informing treatment of children between the 1930s and 1960s. Reflected in these early perspectives is a continuum, where at one end, parents have *no* role in children's disturbance, and at the other end, parents and the more general care-giving context have a *significant* role in children's disturbance. Today most people would operate in the middle of this continuum, where both child and parent effects are seen as important factors in children's mental health. Tensions continue to exist, however, around the extent of child and parent contributions to child well-being.

The earliest psychotherapeutic treatments for child disturbance occurred within a psychoanalytic framework. Initially, parents were not seen to play an important role in either why children became disturbed or how to help them once such disturbance developed. Freud (1916/17) hypothesized that children's anxiety resulted from the existence of their unconscious infantile aggressive or libidinous wishes about their parents. Melanie Klein's early formulation of childhood disturbance involved the mechanism of splitting. Splitting occurred when the infant had an intense need that was not immediately met. The intensity of the child's own affect led to splitting, and the external world (that is, the parents) was thought to have very little role in this.

This view of the parental role, however, changed with Winnicott (1960), one of the founders of object relations theory. He was influential in directing attention from the intrapsychic experience of the baby to the quality of the care-giving environment. He argued that mothers (they were seen as much more central to the emotional well-being of the developing child than fathers, siblings or extended family) could influence the affective or intrapsychic experience of their babies by the ways in which they interacted with them. Through 'good enough mothering' mothers could moderate their babies' experience of challenging environments. Although there would be challenges from the external world when infants would be frustrated and unhappy, mothers could provide a source of comfort that would affect how these experiences were stored in memory to affect subsequent experience. This is effectively a moderation model, an issue that we return to in a later section.

Attachment theory, which is essentially a modern extension of object relations theory, differs from that theory in articulating a more central role for primary care-givers in the etiology of children's disturbance (Ainsworth et al., 1978). Attachment researchers have argued that parenting in the first year of life influences children's attachment security, which is related in turn to the development of emotional and behavioral problems. The aspect of parenting thought to be most important for attachment security is maternal sensitivity (van Ijzendoorn, 1995). For attachment researchers it is not that maternal sensitivity moderates the relationship between stressors and child well-being, but that without sensitive parenting the child's well-being will be compromised.

What is the legacy of psychoanalytic thinking that affects how we understand the role of parents in children's mental health today? There are several elements to emphasize. Infants and young children are thought to compile emotional experience into mental models that affect their responses to later events (Baldwin, 1992; Stern, 1994). These mental models reflect parent–child interactional history, but they also reflect the intrapsychic and meaning-making processes (such as attributional processes) that are idiosyncratic to that particular child. These ideas have generated empirical studies of the ways in which early attachment status influences the development of mental health difficulties such as anxiety and depression (Zahn-Waxler et al., 2000), the quality of later intimate relationships (Owens et al., 1995), and one's capacity to parent (Fonagy et al., 1991).

The psychoanalytic framework has had a profound impact on practice. Much of the work in children's mental health centers today has the child's mental models as a focus of treatment (psychoanalytic and cognitive) as well as the mother–child relationship. The less beneficial aspect of this impact is that bi-directional influences are often minimized such that child effects in the development of the attachment relationship are minimized (Goldsmith and Alansky, 1997). Another drawback is that this has led to a treatment and research focus on the mother–child dyad, with other aspects of the family and broader social systems being neglected.

Another clinical model that was influential both historically and presently in how practitioners think about the role of parents in children's mental health is the behavioral model. This model is based on principles of learning theory. Parents are seen to have an important role in the etiology and treatment of problem behavior (Patterson, 1971). If a child engages in problematic behavior it is thought that behavior is more or less likely to be repeated, based on how people in the environment have responded to it. From the vantage point of operant conditioning, the parental role in behavior disturbance is that parents inadvertently encourage problematic behaviors or emotions by rewarding them. Thus the anxious behavior of a three-year-old child,

displayed when the parents leave to go out for the evening, is reinforced when the parents abandon their plans and stay home. In such a case the parents are involved in therapy in order to modify their own behavior to change environmental contingencies that are reinforcing specific behavior patterns.

It is also possible that the elements of a child's context relevant to the problem may not involve the parents. The rewards for the problematic behavior may come from the child, peers, teachers, and others. In this case the parental role involves observation of children's behavior to identify environmental contingencies. The behavioral framework has been very useful in our understanding of the role of parents in children's mental health problems by emphasizing the need to view behavior as intrinsically linked to the context in which it occurs. The careful analysis of the function of behavior means that contingencies to behavior are carefully analyzed and parents are not automatically assumed to be implicated in children's emotional and behavioral problems. Other contextual influences may prove to be more important.

Contemporary Understanding of the Relationship between Parenting and Children's Mental Health

Currently, many practitioners and family researchers have integrated concepts from psychoanalytic thinking and behavioral models to conceptualize development within a systemic framework. Mental health problems in children are seen as part of a dynamic process, involving many different components of a complex system. Most practitioners believe that aspects of children that are intrinsic to them influence how their family treats them, but at the same time they would maintain that behavior of parents and siblings directed towards the child, has a further influence on future behaviors and emotional states of the child. Most practitioners would also agree that family members are influenced by forces outside the family. Schools and neighborhoods contribute to how children develop, but they also influence how supported parents feel, and how easy it is for them to parent.

Although most practitioners will agree on such a systemic view of the etiology of disturbance in children, many focus on one element of this system when trying to help the child and family. This is because changing one element of the system has been shown to result in improved outcomes for other aspects of the system (Kazdin and Wassell, 2000). Thus effective therapeutic outcomes for children have been demonstrated for cognitive behavioral interventions that focus on children's cognitions (Silverman et al., 1999), for pharmacological treatments that focus on change in children's biochemistry (Bernstein et al., 2000), and for parent training that focuses on change in parental behavior towards children (Webster-Stratton and Hammond, 1997). It would be a mistake, however, to argue back from effective treatment to understanding causal mechanisms in etiology. In the section on the Practice of Parenting, we review three principles that have emerged from the research literature on parenting and child mental health that speak to the role of parents in children's mental health.

CORE ISSUES

As stated earlier, the main focus of this chapter is on parenting children with internalizing disturbances, such as anxiety or depression. The types, incidence rates, and variants will be reviewed first for anxiety disorders and second for depression or dysthymia.

Anxiety Disorders

Anxiety disorders are one of the most common types of disorders experienced by children and adolescents; they are often associated with problems in other areas of functioning (i.e. school), and other psychiatric difficulties such as dysthymia and depression (Albana et al., 1996; Kendall et al., 2000; Vasey and Dadds, 2001). The Diagnostic and Statistical Manual of Mental Disorders, Fourth Edition (DSM-IV), which is the classification system used to make diagnoses in North America, identifies three main subtypes of anxiety disorders, including separation anxiety disorder (SAD), social phobia (SP), and generalized anxiety disorder (GAD) (American Psychiatric Association, 1994).

Separation anxiety disorder is the only one of these three subtypes that can be diagnosed in children and not in adults. SAD is characterized by feelings of extreme anxiety, fear, panic, and concerns about danger or death, and these feelings occur when a child is separated or about to be separated from his/her attachment figure. Such feelings may prevent separation from the attachment figure or limit a child's activity (Kendall et al., 2000). Social phobia is characterized by a child's avoidance or withdrawal from new situations or unfamiliar people (Kendall et al., 2000), and generalized anxiety disorder is

characterized by pervasive worries about performance, relationships, and health (Kendall et al., 2000). Other types of anxiety disorders found in the DSM-IV include obsessive compulsive disorder, panic disorder, and specific phobias (American Psychiatric Association, 1994).

The incidence rates of anxiety disorders and their subtypes vary according to a number of factors, including sample (community versus clinic), type of disorder, respondent (child versus parent), age, and gender. Weiss and Last (2001) recently summarized a body of evidence to estimate these incidence rates. In community samples, rates of childhood anxiety disorders range from approximately 10 to 20 per cent (Kashani and Orvaschel, 1988; McGee et al., 1990; Weiss and Last, 2001). The rates are much higher in clinical samples and range from approximately 27 to 45 per cent (Last et al., 1992; Weiss and Last, 2001). The prevalence rate for SAD ranges from 2 to 12 per cent; for SP the prevalence rate is approximately 1 per cent; and for GAD, the prevalence rate ranges from 2 to 5 per cent among adolescents. Children report more anxious symptoms than their parents do. These incidence rates are reduced, however, when functional impairment is required for a diagnosis (Zahn-Waxler et al., 2000).

Specific types of anxiety disorders also appear to vary according to children's age and gender. SAD is more common in early and middle childhood, while panic disorders, and GAD are more common in older children and adolescents. Animal phobias are more common in early childhood while social phobias are more common in adolescence (Marks and Gelder, 1966; Zahn-Waxler et al., 2000). In terms of gender differences, rates of anxiety disorder in non-referred samples are higher for girls than for boys (Costello, 1989; Kashani and Orvaschel, 1990; Weiss and Last, 2001). Gender differences should be interpreted with caution, however, given that cultural variations may lead to increased awareness and referral rates of anxiety disorders in girls rather than boys (Kendall et al., 2000). The form of anxiety experienced by children may also change with age, although the level of anxiety remains consistent (Weiss and Last, 2001). For example, preschool difficulties such as shyness and behavioral inhibition predict later childhood anxiety disorders (Dadds and Roth, 2001), while child and adolescent anxiety disorders predict impairment in adulthood and adult anxiety disorders (Ollendick and King, 1994; Vasey and Dadds, 2001). In a longitudinal study of clinically referred children, only 18 per cent of children met the criteria for their original diagnosis 3–4 years later (Last et al., 1996).

However, 30 per cent of these children had developed other psychiatric problems, including 16 per cent who displayed different types of anxiety disorders (Last et al., 1996).

Depressive Disorders

Major depressive disorder (MDD) and its milder version dysthymic disorder (DD) are the most common types of depressive disorders in children and adolescents (Zahn-Waxler et al., 2000). MDD and DD occur less often than anxiety disorders and more often than manic-depressive disorder (MD) (Zahn-Waxler et al., 2000). Major depressive disorder involves a period of time that is characterized by depressed mood, feelings of sadness, irritability, anhedonia, fatigue, suicidal ideation, and difficulty concentrating (American Psychiatric Association, 1994). Dysthymic disorder is less severe than MDD and is characterized by a chronically depressed mood, irritability, low energy, and poor concentration (American Psychiatric Association, 1994). Dysthymia occurs more frequently than depression, lasts longer than depression (3 years versus 8–9 months), is more resistant to treatment than depression, and likely has a more negative impact on later psychosocial adjustment than depression (Kovacs et al., 1984; McCauley et al., 1993; Harrington et al., 1996; Stark et al., 2000). Depressive episodes are recurrent, suggesting that depressed children will likely experience further depressive episodes (Stark et al., 2000).

Akin to anxiety disorders, the incidence of depressive disorders also varies according to age and gender (Stark et al., 2000). Depression occurs rarely in preschool, and in approximately 2 per cent of school-age children and pre-adolescents. There is a marked increase in depressive symptoms associated with age through to the end of adolescence where depression reaches adult levels of 15–20 per cent (Rutter et al., 1970; McGee et al., 1990; Lewinsohn et al., 1994; Stark et al., 2000). For dysthymic disorder, the rate in childhood ranges from 0.6 to 2.5 per cent, and the rate in adolescence ranges from 3 to 8 per cent. Research on the prevalence rates for depression and dysthymia is somewhat limited because the disorders are sometimes assessed separately and sometimes assessed in combination (Stark et al., 2000). The rate of depression is significantly higher in clinic samples (42 per cent) and in children who have additional medical or academic difficulties (Peterson et al., 1993; Stark et al., 2000).

The specific symptoms or precursors of depression experienced by children also vary with age. Prepubertal children tend to experience more separation anxiety, phobias, somatic complaints and psychomotor agitation, while adolescents experience more hypersomnia, hopelessness, and anhedonia (Ryan et al., 1987; Zahn-Waxler et al., 2000). In terms of gender differences, the prevalence rates for boys and girls are similar until early adolescence, at which point females experience depression more often than males and for longer periods of time (Stark et al., 2000).

The prevalence and expression of internalizing disorders also appear to vary according to culture, although the scarcity of research in this area makes it difficult to draw conclusions (Zahn-Waxler et al., 2000). Cultural norms that guide the expression of emotion and patterns of coping with stress likely influence the type of mental health difficulties that develop and the prevalence rate of such difficulties in different cultures (Zahn-Waxler et al., 2000). One finding that does appear to generalize across cultures is that girls are more likely than boys to have internalizing disorders (Crijnen et al., 1997).

In summary, research to date indicates that a substantial proportion of children and adolescents suffer from internalizing disorders. Anxiety and depression frequently co-occur and the co-morbidity rate has been estimated to fall between 20 and 50 per cent (Brady and Kendall, 1992; Angold et al., 1999; Zahn-Waxler et al., 2000). Internalizing disorders are also co-morbid with externalizing disorders. This co-morbidity amongst anxiety, depression, and externalizing disorders and the cyclical nature of depression highlight the challenge that parents face when parenting children with mental health difficulties.

PRACTICE OF PARENTING

We now consider the role of parents in the genesis, continuation, and amelioration of mental health difficulties and internalizing disorders. With regard to the role of parents in the genesis and continuation of child internalizing disorders, three potential sources of influence are discussed: independent parent and child effects; joint or bi-directional parent and child effects; and moderation effects, which involve potential risk factors that operate in conjunction with other factors to contribute to the development of mental health difficulties. Finally, we briefly review research examining the effectiveness of involving parents in treatment aimed at reducing child internalizing disorders.

Child and Parent Effects in
Children's Mental Health Problems

It has long been recognized that children with mental health problems have more problematic relationships with their parents. Many different aspects of problematic parenting have been found to be associated with increased mental health problems in children. For instance, when parents are more critical towards their children and less supportive (Pettit and Bates, 1989; Hibbs et al., 1992; Ge et al., 1996; Pettit et al., 1997), when they expose the children to violence (Sternberg et al., 1993), and when they show less sensitivity and emotional involvement (Garber et al., 1995), their children show more difficulties with anxiety and depression, and other mental health problems. Evidence to date suggests that family stress and problematic parenting are unlikely to predict uniquely to specific disorders (Williams et al., 1990). Instead, they are more likely to provide a general stress for the child, which in interaction with individual characteristics of children, such as temperament, age, gender and other factors, results in an internalizing or externalizing disorder. We first review evidence demonstrating that the quality of the parent–child relationship is influenced both by parents and by children, and then we go on to consider genetic effects in children's mental health problems.

One of the important shifts that has taken place in people's thinking about parenting and mental health problems in children is the extent of the child's contribution to the quality of the relationship that grows up between parent and child. Although the idea that children influence their parents has been present in the clinical and research literature for a long time (Bell and Harper, 1977), the ways that such effects are differentiated from parent effects or from other contextual effects has become more sophisticated and convincing. Consider an example. Typically, when behavioral geneticists do twin studies they examine the similarities between twins, who differ on their degree of genetic relatedness, on outcomes such as personality, psychiatric disturbance, levels of achievement and so on. An innovative twist to these studies involves the examination of the parent–child relationship as the outcome. A study by Rowe and Plomin (1981) compared the parenting received by monozygotic twins (who share 100 per cent of their genes) with that received by dizygotic twins (who share 50 per cent of their genes). Monozygotic twins have been found to be more similar in their behavior and temperaments than dizygotic twins. If parents were not influenced

in their parenting by characteristics of their babies then we would expect monozygotic and dizygotic twins to be parented similarly. In fact, monozygotic twins were parented much more similarly than dizygotic twins. This suggests that characteristics of babies elicit different responses from parents.

The 'child effect' that has received the most attention is an aspect of temperament that has been called behavioral inhibition or shyness. Behaviorally inhibited children show high levels of fear to novelty. They attempt to avoid whatever it is that is threatening to them. Children who are temperamentally shy as toddlers or young children are more at risk of developing anxiety and depression later in their lives (Rubin, 1993) and of showing patterns of social avoidance as adults (Caspi et al., 1988; Gest, 1997). Behavioral inhibition has been found to show at least some degree of heritability. Emde et al. (1992) examined 200 pairs of 14-month-old twins, half monozygotic and half dizygotic. Different aspects of emotionality and temperament were assessed by parental report and independent observation. The evidence for genetic influence was stronger for shyness (also called behavioral inhibition) than for any other temperamental construct as genetic influence was evident both for observational measures and parental report measures, a pattern not seen for other measures.

Behaviorally inhibited children have been found to elicit particular patterns of behavior from their parents and thus to play their part in shaping the relationship. Behaviorally inhibited children elicit more comforting as well as more intrusiveness from mothers in the form of encouragement to approach novel stimuli (Nachmias et al., 1996). It may be that parental behaviors such as intrusiveness, particularly in highly fearful children, may operate against the development of successful coping strategies in the face of novelty, on the part of the child.

As well as genetic effects being evident for behavioral inhibition as an aspect of temperament that may predispose to anxiety disorders, genetic influences are also evident for anxiety and depressive disorders in children. Heritability estimates for depression and anxiety vary markedly depending on the study design and study informants (Rutter et al., 1999). A study by Thapar and McGuffin (1995) examined twin pairs between 8 and 16 years of age and had parents and children report on children's anxiety. A significant genetic component was found, based on parental ratings, but no significant genetic component was found that was based on adolescent ratings. The largest twin study, including

1412 twins, reported a significant genetic influence on anxiety symptoms based on child, mother and father report (Topolski et al., 1997), but estimates varied as a function of informant, type of anxiety disorder, and child age. The heritability estimate for childhood depression has also been found to vary by child age and other factors. Thapar and McGuffin (1995) reported that significant heritability for depression has been found in adolescence but not in childhood. Although genetic estimates vary considerably as a function of the factors outlined above, the likelihood is that they are important in understanding children's individual vulnerabilities to mental health problems.

As well as characteristics of children influencing the quality of the relationship that grows up between parents and their children, characteristics of parents also contribute to the formation of these relationships and in turn relate to mental health problems in children. Parents' histories of being parented have been found to be related to their abilities to care for their children. For instance, work by Quinton and Rutter (1988) has found that women who had been raised in institutions and looked after by multiple care-givers were less effective with their own children than women who had been raised with their own mothers. Attachment researchers have shown that there are striking similarities in the relational style that mothers have with their own mothers and that mothers have with their babies (Benoit and Parker, 1994). Personality characteristics have also been found to affect parenting. For instance, Clark et al. (2000) found that maternal neuroticism and extraversion, assessed when children were 8–10 months old, were both positively related to power assertive parenting when infants were between 13 and 15 months of age. Even more interesting from the standpoint of child and parent effects is the observation that parenting at 13–15 months was predicted by a combination of child and parent personality effects. Maternal personality was differentially related to later parenting, depending on the temperament of the baby being parented.

Bi-directional Influences

Many of the studies linking mental health problems in children with the quality of parenting that they receive are carried out cross-sectionally rather than longitudinally. When children's behavior and parental behavior is assessed at the same point in time it is not possible to untangle whether problematic parenting has caused anxious or depressed child behavior, whether difficult children have elicited problematic responses from their parents, or whether these two variables are linked only because of their relationship to a third variable. Two kinds of research designs have enabled researchers to get a clearer picture of how these associations come about. One design involves the collection of longitudinal data, with child behavior and parenting behaviors assessed at two or more time points. It is then possible to examine whether a change in child behavior is predicted by earlier parenting or whether a change in parenting behavior is predicted by earlier child behavior. When such mutual influence models have been tested there is evidence that effects between parents and children go in both directions (Conger and Conger, 1994).

The second design involves sequential analysis of observations (Gottman, 1980; Patterson, 1982). In this type of study, sequences of interaction are coded, allowing one to see how person A's behavior elicits B's response, which in turn elicits A's subsequent behavior. Although such sequences can still be influenced by genetic effects, the main mechanism involved in such patterns is assumed to be based on social learning theory. These problematic sequences have been found to revolve around emotion expressions and responses. In experimental tasks, anger expressions are more likely to elicit anger and aggression than sadness and fear. Sadness and fear expressions are most likely to elicit comforting behaviors and concern (Biglan et al., 1985, 1989; Jenkins and Ball, 2000). It may be that internalizing emotions such as depression and anxiety function to suppress aggression and elicit increased care. Examinations of the interactions of depressed mothers, their children and their husbands have found that mothers' depressed moods resulted in the suppression of fathers' and children's aggression (Hops et al., 1987). These moods functioned to win respite from the anger of other family members. When the fathers and children did express anger to the mothers, this temporarily suppressed her distressed mood. Dadds et al. (1996) studied the family interaction sequences of anxious children, who were compared to aggressive and non-clinic children during a problem-solving task that asked families to solve anxiety-provoking interpersonal situations. During this task, parents of anxious children were more likely than the other parents to respond by offering encouragement to children's avoidant solutions and by offering fewer prosocial solutions. Such responses led anxious children to adopt avoidant solutions as their final solutions.

As well as contextual effects in families playing a role in the maintenance of children's symptoms, social groups may also play a similar role. There is evidence to suggest that more anxious children choose more anxious friends, and that having more anxious friends increases children's own anxieties over time (Hogue and Steinberg, 1996). It may be therefore, as suggested by behavioral models, that the functional consequences of behavior are important to consider when thinking about how depressed and anxious emotions are maintained or exacerbated within the social group in which children operate.

Moderation Effects

There is a third important role that parents may play in children's mental health. It arises from the fact that factors that put children at risk may operate contingently. The same factor can have quite different effects when it occurs in two different circumstances, such that the effects of one factor modify the effects of another factor. This is important for understanding the relationship between parenting and children's mental health for several reasons.

Parenting styles have been found to be differently associated with outcomes in children depending on the temperament of the children. Consider, for instance, the internalization of values in children. Kochanska (1997) examined children's temperament and maternal socialization when children were 2–3 years old and children's consciences when they were 4 years old, and showed that for children who were fearful as toddlers, conscience was best promoted by gentle maternal discipline. For children fearless as toddlers, secure attachment and maternal responsiveness promoted conscience development. The observation that temperamental differences in children necessitate different parental treatment for optimal child development has also been borne out with respect to externalizing outcomes in children. Bates et al. (1998), for example, found that children with different degrees of resistance to control needed different parenting for optimal outcomes. Children who were very resistant in infancy showed less externalizing behavior at 7 years old if their mothers were low on restrictive parenting than if they were high on restriction. Children who were low resistant in infancy showed less externalizing behavior if mothers were more restrictive during their infancy.

Not all children exposed to environmental risks develop mental health problems. There are characteristics of children, or characteristics of their environment, that help them to withstand the stress. This area of research is known as the study of protective factors and is based on the premise that risk factors operate contingently – negatively affecting some children but not those who are 'protected.' Factors that have been found to be protective for children include children's social relationships, their IQs, and as we have seen above, their temperaments (Jenkins and Smith, 1990; Werner, 1993; Masten et al., 1999; Luthar et al., 2000). The reason that such findings are important in thinking about the role of parents in children's mental health is that elements of children's lives combine together in complex ways. Although we have been able to identify certain common risk factors in children's lives related to family and peer relationships, biological and genetic factors within individuals, schools and communities, as well as positive elements in their lives that may help them to withstand adversity, too many questions remain about the ways in which such elements combine for us to be able to be accurate in our predictions of who will develop mental health problems.

With specific regard to the development of internalizing problems, Rapee (1997) reviewed the literature on the potential role of child-rearing practices in anxiety and depression. It is difficult to draw conclusions from this area of work because there are too few studies that have originated from varied theoretical perspectives and have used multiple methods. More research is required to distinguish between the roles that general parent psychopathology and specific parenting behaviors play in the development of anxiety and depression. Initial evidence suggested that rejecting parenting behavior was associated with child depression while controlling parenting behavior was related to child anxiety (Rapee, 1997). More research is also required to examine the bi-directional effects of child temperament, parent personality, and parenting behaviors in the development of internalizing disorders.

Role of Parenting in the Amelioration of Internalizing Symptoms

Although there is some research examining parent and child effects as sources of influence in the development of children's mental health problems, there is comparatively little research examining the role of parental involvement in treatment outcomes, particularly for internalizing disorders (Kendall et al., 2000). Thus far, treatment research in child and adolescent psychotherapy has focused on the effectiveness of specific treatment techniques and not the potential contributions of other factors, such as child, parent, and family involvement (Kazdin, 1997).

Most practitioners adhere to a systemic view of the etiology of child disturbance, yet despite this view, treatment typically focuses on one element of the system, such as a parent or child. This is due, in part, to the finding that treatment that focuses on one element of the system can improve other parts of the system (Kazdin and Wassell, 2000). It may also be due to the logistical and financial implications of attempting to treat multiple parts of a system. Given the lack of research in this area, there are very few evidence-based recommendations that can be made at this time to suggest how to involve parents in the effective treatment of children's internalizing difficulties. Parenting behavior, however, likely plays a significant role in the treatment and amelioration of children's mental health difficulties and inferences can be drawn from research examining the role of parenting in the etiology of child disturbance and from anecdotal observations of the role of parents in effective treatment programs (Kendall et al., 2000; Manassis, 2001).

Given that 40–60 per cent of children and adolescents drop out of treatment before its completion and that those who drop out have more severe difficulties than those who remain, it is important to solicit and encourage parents' ongoing involvement in their children's treatment programs (Wierzbicki and Pekarik, 1993; Armbruster and Kazdin, 1994; Kazdin, 1997). Retention in treatment programs may be achieved by reducing parental stress. This may occur if parents have an opportunity to discuss their own concerns (Prinz and Miller, 1994), if they receive financial support for covering the cost of attending treatment, if childcare services are provided for their children who are not in treatment, and if the therapist forges a strong alliance with all family members, including the parent (Kazdin, 1997). Success early in treatment is a predictor of early discontinuation (Kazdin, 1997), suggesting that it is important to emphasize the role that ongoing treatment is likely to play in children and adolescents' ability to sustain the gains that they make early in the treatment process.

Consistent with a systemic view of the etiology and treatment of children's mental health difficulties, it is important to investigate the potential sources of the disorder. Problems within the family context, maternal stress or depression, insecure attachments, and behavioral inhibition or shyness are all factors that may put children at risk for the development of either anxious or depressive disorders (Duggal et al., 2001; Manassis, 2001; Vasey and Dadds, 2001). Knowledge about the potential sources of child and adolescent anxiety or depression has treatment implications in that it can guide decisions about the nature and course of treatment. Most clinicians thoroughly investigate children's developmental histories when completing a mental health assessment. During this process, it would be useful to consider the specific role that etiological factors have played in the development of children's internalizing difficulties. For example, when working with a child who has an anxiety disorder, one might look for signs of early attachment difficulties, behavioral inhibition, or shyness (Manassis, 2001).

Evidence suggests that differential parenting styles, insecure attachment patterns, and temperamental vulnerabilities (for example, shyness or behavioral inhibition) interact to contribute to the development of sub-clinical and clinical anxiety disorders. Longitudinal research by Warren et al. (1997) has found that adolescents who had shown anxious-resistant attachment patterns at one year of age were twice as likely to have an anxiety disorder in adolescence than non-anxiously attached infants. Moreover, anxious-resistant attachment patterns in infancy were stronger predictors of adolescent anxiety disorder than were measures of maternal anxiety or child temperament (Warren et al., 1997). Insecure infant attachment relationships may be one mechanism through which childhood anxiety disorders are developed and maintained (Manassis, 2001).

It may be useful for clinicians working with children and their families to explore clients' attachment histories. Clinicians may also ask parents about their children's temperament, how they have coped or responded to their child's temperament, and how the parents themselves cope with anxiety. Parents whose children are securely attached to them, for instance, will likely be able to participate in their child's treatment by being empathic toward their child and helping them to face desensitization procedures designed to help their children overcome anxiety (Manassis, 2001). If a secure attachment relationship does not exist between a client and his/her parents, then this information is useful in that the clinician could act as a secure attachment figure for a child or adolescent who is attempting to cope with anxiety. Further, if an anxious child or adolescent has a disorganized attachment that has resulted from unresolved loss or trauma, then it would be appropriate to deal with that loss or trauma in the treatment of the anxiety disorder (Manassis, 2001). Similarly, if an anxious child or adolescent has an ambivalent attachment style, then it would be important to explore how consistently parents respond to and cope with their child's need for and bids for attention. If parents respond inconsistently to their children's cues when their children are feeling threatened or distressed, then it may be useful for therapists to work with parents and deal with factors that play a role in inconsistent parenting behavior, such as stress, depression, or lack of awareness.

Research on the etiology of depression also has implications for the treatment of children and adolescents with dysthymia or depression. A recent study by Duggal et al. (2001) examined the antecedents of child and adolescent depression in a prospective longitudinal study of children at risk, who were from families with lower socio-economic backgrounds. Analyses of the factors predicting the onset of child versus adolescent depression showed that depression in each age group was predicted by different variables. Depressed children were more likely to have come from adverse family environments, where their mothers were depressed and experiencing high levels of stress. These children received less supportive care in early childhood and were more likely to have experienced abuse (Duggal et al., 2001). In contrast, adolescents who first became depressed in adolescence were more likely to have experienced early care that was characterized more specifically by a lack of emotional support (Duggal et al., 2001).

Moreover, gender differences emerged in adolescence, such that depressed adolescent girls were more likely to have had a depressed mother while depressed adolescent boys were more likely to have experienced less emotional support in preschool years (Duggal et al., 2001). This gender difference was consistent with earlier findings suggesting that adolescent girls may identify with and become over-involved with their depressed mothers. They may also be more likely than adolescent males to worry about, feel responsible for, and support their depressed parents (Klimes-Dougan and Bolger, 1998; Duggal et al., 2001). Again, the different etiological pathways leading to depressive symptomatology in childhood and adolescence suggest that clinicians continue to explore potential historical and current sources of the disorder and offer treatment to both parents and children. Treatment aimed at reducing the levels of maternal depression, stress, and adversity experienced by young children may reduce the likelihood that such children will develop depressive disorders. Treatment for depressed adolescent girls might include mothers and focus on issues around adolescent identity formation and individuation.

Despite the lack of empirical evidence evaluating the role of parents in the treatment of anxiety disorders, work by Kendall et al. (2000) highlights the importance of parent participation in their child-focused cognitive behavior therapy (CBT) program. In general, they suggest that clinicians involve parents as much as possible in their children's assessment and treatment. With the understanding of the role that parenting behavior can play in the development of anxiety disorders, clinicians need to strike a balance between parental under- or over-involvement in the treatment process. Clinicians should obtain information on familial problems, parents' concerns, and their perceptions of their children's difficulties. Compared with other children, anxious and depressed children report that their families are less supportive, more conflictual, and more controlling when making decisions (Stark et al., 1990). Parents of anxious children often experience guilt and anxiety about the presence of their child's disorder and past events that may have led to it (Kendall et al., 2000; Manassis, 2001). As such, therapists might work with parents alone, as well as together with their children, to deal with the role that the parents may be playing in the maintenance of their children's anxiety disorders.

In striking a balance between parent over- and under-involvement, therapists could discourage parental over-protectiveness and help parents and families to be more supportive and cope better with conflict (Kendall et al., 2000). They could also help parents deal with the feelings of guilt or anxiety about the presence of a child's anxiety disorder and encourage them to refocus their attention on coping with the present situation. As such, clinicians might actively encourage parent involvement in children's therapy by soliciting their participation and by identifying the importance of the role that parents can play in keeping appointments and helping a child to organize and follow through on homework activities. Clinicians might also encourage parents to pursue their own treatment; help parents to identify and change any parent–child interaction patterns that may be contributing to a child's anxiety; help parents to set realistic expectations for their children's behavior and achievement; and help parents to teach their children to cope with anxiety by helping their child with treatment homework, such as relaxation exercises. Given that anxious children often have high standards and low self-confidence, it is particularly important for therapists to teach parents to reward children's partial success. Throughout the therapeutic process, parents need to learn how to grant their children more autonomy and increase their confidence in coping with distressing situations (Kendall et al., 2000).

Soliciting parental involvement in a child-focused CBT program is one way of helping parents to more effectively parent children with anxiety disorders. A study by Barrett et al. (1996) compared the efficacy of a child-only CBT treatment program for anxiety disorders with and without a family anxiety management (FAM) module. Parents involved in the FAM treatment program learned to identify and modify their anxious reactions and they were taught how to communicate, problem solve, and contingently manage their child's behavior. When rates of anxiety disorders in children from both groups were compared one year after treatment completion, the results showed that children from the combined child and family treatment program were 25 per cent less likely to have an anxiety disorder diagnosis than children whose families did not receive treatment (Barrett et al., 1996).

Akin to research on the role of parenting in the treatment of anxiety disorders, there is also very little research examining the role of parenting in the treatment of depression or dysthymia in children and adolescents (Stark et al., 2000). There is some evidence to suggest that parent training does not add significantly to the reduction of child depressive symptoms, beyond that achieved by child focused cognitive behavior therapy (Lewinsohn et al., 1990). However, most clinicians and researchers would argue that it is important to involve parents in their children's treatment for depression, for multiple reasons. Parents can help children generalize the coping skills that they learn in therapy to other contexts, such as home or school. Moreover, given the cyclical nature of depression, parents can learn to recognize signs indicating the onset of a depressive episode. They might be able to obtain therapeutic support for their child at the start of an episode, which may, in turn, reduce the length of the episode (Stark et al., 2000).

Therapists should consider the role that parents and the family context could play in the maintenance or amelioration of child depression. For instance, therapists could work with families to reduce the level of stress experienced by a child and work with a child to improve his/her ability to deal with stress. If family conflict is a source of stress, then an important goal is to reduce that stress. Given the role that negative thoughts or a maladaptive schema play in the maintenance of child depression, it would be useful for a therapist to examine, and attempt to alter, familial verbal and non-verbal communication patterns that are contributing to a child's negative world view (Stark et al., 2000).

In addition to psychosocial treatments for depression and anxiety, parents may wish to pursue pharmacological treatments. Pharmacological treatments should be used as part of a comprehensive treatment plan, involving psychosocial interventions for depressed and anxious children and youth (Kutcher et al., 1995; Stark et al., 2000). When blood levels are monitored, tricyclic medications are moderately effective in treating depression in children, but not adolescents (Stark et al., 2000). Selective serotonin reuptake inhibitors (SSRIs) are effective in treating depressed adolescents, although there is little research examining their effectiveness with children. Busiprone may be effective in treating GAD (Kutcher et al., 1995). Future research is needed to examine the effectiveness of pharmacological treatments and psychosocial treatments that involve parents and children so that clinicians can intervene effectively when working with anxious and depressed children and youth (Kutcher et al., 1995; Stark et al., 2000).

AUTHORS' OVERVIEW

Findings from developmental and clinical research examining the role of parenting in the promotion and amelioration of children's mental health problems, and internalizing problems in particular, present a complex and incomplete picture. Clearly, children's mental health difficulties result from the complex and reciprocal interactions of multiple elements in a developmental system involving parents, children, and their environment. Although tensions will continue to exist around the nature and extent of parent, child, and environmental contributions to children's mental health difficulties, there is sufficient evidence to conclude at this point that they are all important influences. When working with individual children and their families, it is important for clinicians to consider how the particular pattern of parent, child, and environmental factors are operating to promote, maintain, or ameliorate specific child mental health difficulties. The following implications for practice are based on current developmental and clinical research findings and on suggestions from clinical researchers working with children and youth.

IMPLICATIONS FOR PRACTICE

- Consider a systemic view of the etiology and presenting symptomatology by specifically examining the current and historical roles that parent, child, and environmental effects may play in the child's anxiety or depression. Also consider the specific way in which parent characteristics, behavior, and environ-mental factors moderate or interact with child characteristics to promote anxiety or depression.

- Consider the potential role that parents may play in their children's treatment programs.
- Consider the need for parents to be involved in their own treatment program, especially if they are demonstrating rejecting or control-ling parenting behavior, or if they are feeling guilty about the existence of their child's symptoms.
- Reduce the financial and logistical barriers to treatment that prevent parents from partici-pating in their children's treatment or prevent them from helping their child to receive treat-ment. Search for other ways to support par-ents in their attempts to obtain treatment for their child.
- Early in the therapeutic process, emphasize to parents the importance of treatment com-pletion, including the role that it will play in increasing therapeutic benefits. Solicit parents' help in teaching children to generalize skills acquired in therapy to other settings, such as school.
- Consider both psychosocial (e.g. CBT) and pharmacological interventions when treating anxious and depressed children and youth.

REFERENCES

Ainsworth, M.D.S., Belhar, M.C., Walters, E. and Wall, S. (1978) *Patterns of Attachment: A Psychological Study of the Strange Situation*. Hillsdale, NJ: Erlbaum.

Albana, A.M., Chorpita, B.F. and Barlow, D.H. (1996) Childhood anxiety disorders. In Mash, E.J. and Barkley, R.A. (eds) *Child Psychopathology*. New York: Guilford Press, pp. 196–241.

American Psychiatric Association (1994) *Diagnostic and Statistical Manual of Mental Disorders*, 4th edition. Washington, DC: American Psychiatric Association.

Angold, A., Costello, E.J. and Erkanli, A. (1999) Comor-bidity. *Journal of Child Psychology and Psychiatry*, **40**, 57–87.

Armbruster, P. and Kazdin, A.E. (1994) Attrition in child psychotherapy. In Ollendick, T.H. and Prinz, R.J. (eds) *Advances in Clinical Child Psychology*, Vol. 16. New York: Plenum, pp. 81–108.

Baldwin, M. (1992) Relational schemas and the processing of social information. *Psychological Bulletin*, **112**, 461–84.

Barrett, P.M., Dadds, R.M. and Rapee, R.M. (1996) Family treatment of childhood anxiety: a controlled trial. *Journal of Consulting and Clinical Psychology*, **64**, 333–42.

Bates, J.E., Dodge, K.A., Pettit, G.S. and Ridge, B. (1998) Interaction of temperamental resistance to control and

restrictive parenting in the development of externalizing behavior. *Developmental Psychology*, **34**, 982–95.

Bell, R.Q. and Harper, L.V. (1977) *Child Effects on Adults*. Lincoln: University of Nebraska Press.

Benoit, D. and Parker, K. (1994) Stability and transmis-sion of attachment across three generations. *Child Development*, **65**, 1444–56.

Bernstein, G., Borchardt, C.M., Perwien, A.R., Crosby, R.D., Kushner, M.G., Thuras, P.D. and Last, C.G. (2000) Imipramine plus cognitive-behavioral therapy in the treat-ment of school refusal. *Journal of the American Academy of Child and Adolescent Psychiatry*, **39**, 276–83.

Biglan, A., Hops, H., Sherman, L., Friedman, L.S., Arthus, J. and Osteen, V. (1985) Problem solving inter-actions of depressed women and their husbands. *Behavior Therapy*, **16**, 431–51.

Biglan, A., Rothlind, J., Hops, H. and Sherman, L. (1989) Impact of distressed and aggressive behavior. *Journal of Abnormal Psychology*, **98**, 218–28.

Boyle, M. and Willms, J.D. (2001) Multilevel modeling of hierarchical data in developmental studies. *Journal of Child Psychology and Psychiatry*, **42**, 141–62.

Brady, E. and Kendall, P.C. (1992) Co-morbidity of anxiety and depression in children and adolescents. *Psychological Bulletin*, **111**, 244–55.

Caspi, A., Elder, G.H. and Bem, D.J. (1988). Moving away from the world: life-course patterns of shy children. *Developmental Psychology*, **24**(6), 824–31.

Clark, L.A., Kochanska, G. and Ready, R. (2000) Mothers' personality and its interaction with child tem-perament as predictors of parenting behavior. *Journal of Personality and Social Psychology*, **79**, 274–85.

Collins, W.A., Maccoby, E.E., Steinberg, L., Hetherington, E.M. and Bornstein, M.H. (2000) Contemporary research on parenting: the case for nature and nurture. *American Psychologist*, **55**(2), 218–32.

Conger, K. and Conger, R. (1994) Differential parenting and change in sibling differences in delinquency. *Journal of Family Psychology*, **8**, 287–302.

Costello, E.J. (1989) Child psychiatric disorders and their correlates: a primary care pediatric sample. *Journal of American Academy of Child and Adolescent Psychiatry*, **28**(6), 851–5.

Crijnen, A.A.M., Achenbach, T.M. and Verlhulst, F.C. (1997) Comparisons of problems reported by parents of children in 12 cultures: total problems, externalizing, and internalizing. *American Academy of Child and Adolescent Psychiatry*, **36**, 1269–77.

Dadds, M.R. and Roth, J.H. (2001) Family processes in the development of anxiety problems. In Vasey, M.W. and Dadds, M.R. (eds) *The Developmental Psycho-pathology of Anxiety*. New York, NY: Oxford Univer-sity Press. pp. 3–26.

Dadds, M.R., Barrett, P.M., Rapee, R.M. and Ryan, S. (1996) Family process and child anxiety and aggres-sion: an observational analysis. *Journal of Abnormal Child Psychology*, **24**, 715–34.

Duggal, S., Carlson, E.A., Sroufe, L.A. and Egeland, B. (2001) Depressive symptomatology in childhood and adolescence. *Development and Psychopathology*, **13**, 143–64.

Emde, R.N., Plomin, R., Robinson, J., Corley, R., DeFries, J., Fulker, D.W., Reznick, J.S., Campos, J., Kagan, J. and Zahn-Waxler, C. (1992) Temperament, emotion and cognition at fourteen months: the MacArthur Longitudinal Twin Study. *Child Development*, **63**, 1437–55.

Fonagy, P., Steele, H. and Steele, M. (1991) Maternal representations of attachment during pregnancy predict the organization of infant–mother attachment at one year of age. *Child Development*, **62**, 891–905.

Frued, S. (1916/1917) General Theory of the Neuroses. Reprinted in *Introductory Lectures on Psychoanalysis*. 1973. London: Pelican Books.

Garber, J., Braafladt, N. and Weiss, B. (1995) Affect regulation in depressed and non-depressed children and young adolescents. *Development and Psychopathology*, **7**, 93.

Ge, X., Conger, R.D., Simons, R.L. and Best, K.M. (1996) Parenting behaviors and the occurrence and co-occurrence of adolescent depressive symptoms and conduct problems. *Developmental Psychology*, **32**, 717–31.

Gest, S.D. (1997) Behavioral inhibition: stability and associations with adaptation from childhood to early adulthood. *Journal of Personality and Social Psychology*, **72**, 467–75.

Goldsmith, H.H. and Alansky, J.A. (1987) Maternal and infant temperamental predictors of attachment: a meta-analytic review. *Journal of Consulting and Clinical Psychology*, **55**, 805–16.

Gottman, J. (1980). Analyzing for sequential connection and assessing inter-observer reliability for the sequential analysis of observational data. *Behavioral Assessment*, **2**, 361–8.

Harrington, R., Rutter, M. and Fombonne, E. (1996) Developmental pathways in depression: multiple meanings, antecedents, and endpoints. *Development and Psychopathology*, **8**, 601–16.

Hibbs, E.D., Zahn, T.P., Hamburger, S.D., Kruesi, M.J.P. and Rapoport, J.L. (1992) Parental expressed emotion and psychophysical reactivity in disturbed and normal children. *British Journal of Psychiatry*, **160**, 504–10.

Hogue, A. and Steinberg, L. (1996) Homophily of internalized distress in adolescent peer groups. *Developmental Psychology*, **31**, 897–906.

Hops, H., Biglan, A., Sherman, L., Arthur, J., Friedman, L. and Osteen, V. (1987) Home observations of family interactions of depressed women. *Journal of Consulting and Clinical Psychology*, **55**, 341–6.

Jenkins, J.M. and Ball, S. (2000) Distinguishing between negative emotions: children's understanding of the social regulatory aspects of emotion. *Cognition and Emotion*, **14**, 261–82.

Jenkins, J.M. and Smith, M.A. (1990) Factors protecting children living in disharmonious homes: maternal reports. *Journal of the American Academy of Child and Adolescent Psychiatry*, **29**, 60–9.

Kashani, J.H. and Orvaschel, H. (1988) Anxiety disorders in mid-adolescence: a community sample. *American Journal of Psychiatry*, **145**, 960–4.

Kazdin, A.E. (1997) Practitioner review: psychosocial treatments for conduct disorder in children. *Journal of Child Psychology and Psychiatry*, **38**(2), 161–78.

Kazdin, A.E. and Wassell, G. (2000) Therapeutic changes in children parents and families resulting from treatment of children with conduct problems. *Journal of the American Academy of Child and Adolescent Psychiatry*, **39**, 414–20.

Kendall, P.S., Chu, B.C., Pimentel, S.S. and Choudhury, M. (2000) Treating anxiety disorders in youth. In Kendall, P.S. (ed.) *Child and Adolescent Therapy: Cognitive-Behavioral Procedures*, 2nd edition. New York, NY: Guilford, pp. 235–87.

Kenny, D.A. (1994) Using the social relations model to understand relationships. In Erber, R. and Gilmour, R. (eds) *Theoretical Frameworks for Personal Relationships*. Hillsdale: Lawrence Erlbaum, pp. 111–27.

Klimes-Dougan, B. and Bolger, A.K. (1998) Coping with maternal depressed affect and depression: adolescent children of depressed and well mothers. *Journal of Youth and Adolescence*, **27**, 1–15.

Kochanska, G. (1997) Multiple pathways to conscience for children with different temperaments: from toddlerhood to age 5. *Developmental Psychology*, **33**, 228–40.

Kovacs, M., Feinberg, T.L., Crouse-Novak, M., Paulauskas, S.L. and Finkelstein, R. (1984) Depressive disorders in childhood: II. A longitudinal study of the risk for subsequent major depression. *Archives of General Psychiatry*, **41**, 643–9.

Kutcher, S., Reiter, S. and Gardner, D. (1995) Pharmacotherapy: approaches and applications. In March, J.S. (ed.) *Anxiety Disorders in Children and Adolescents*. New York, NY: Guilford Press, pp. 341–85.

Last, C.G., Perrin, S., Hersen, M. and Kazdin, A.E. (1992) DSM-III-R anxiety disorders in children: sociodemographic and clinical characteristics. *Journal of the American Academy of Child and Adolescent Psychiatry*, **31**(6), 1070–6.

Last, C.G., Perrin, S., Hersen, M. and Kazdin, A.E. (1996) A prospective study of childhood anxiety disorders. *Journal of the American Academy of Child and Adolescent Psychiatry*, **35**(11), 1502–10.

Lewinsohn, P.M., Clarke, G., Hops, H. and Andrews, J. (1990) Cognitive-behavioral treatment for depressed adolescents. *Behavior Therapy*, **21**, 385–401.

Lewinsohn, P.M., Clarke, G.N., Seeley, J.R. and Rohde, P. (1994) Major depression in community adolescents: age at onset, episode duration, and time to recurrence. *Journal of the American Academy of Child and Adolescent Psychiatry*, **33**, 809–18.

Luthar, S.S., Cicchetti, D. and Becker, B. (2000) The construct of resilience: a critical evaluation and guidelines for future work. *Child Development*, **71**, 543–62.

Manassis, K. (2001) Child–parent relations: Attachment and anxiety disorders. In Silverman, W.K. and Treffers, P.D.A. (eds) *Anxiety Disorders in Children and Adolescents: Research, Assessment and Intervention*. New York, NY: Cambridge University Press, pp. 255–72.

Marks, I.M. and Gelder, M.G. (1966) Different ages of onset in varieties of phobia. *American Journal of Psychiatry*, **123**(3), 218–21.

Masten, A., Hubbard, J., Gest, S., Tellegen, A, Garmezy, N. and Ramirez, M. (1999) Competence in the context of adversity: pathways to resilience and maladaptation from childhood to late adolescence. *Developmental Psychopathology*, **11**, 143–69.

McCauley, E., Myers, K., Mitchell., J., Calderon, R., Schloredt, K. and Treder, R. (1993) Depression in young people: initial presentation and clinical course. *Journal of the American Academy of Child and Adolescent Psychiatry*, **32**, 714–22.

McGee, R., Feehan, M., Williams, S., Partridge, F., Silva, P.A. and Kelly, J. (1990) DSM-III disorders in a large sample of adolescents. *Journal of the American Academy of Child and Adolescent Psychiatry*, **29**, 611–19.

Mortimore, P. (1998) *The Road to Improvement*. Lisse, The Netherlands: Swets and Zeitlinger.

Nachmias, M., Gunnar, M., Mangelsdorf, S., Parritz, R.H. and Buss, K. (1996) Behavioral inhibition and stress reactivity: the moderating role of attachment security. *Child Development*, **67**, 508–22.

Ollendick, T.H. and King, N.J. (1994) Diagnosis, assessment, and treatment of internalizing problems in children: the role of longitudinal data. *Journal of Consulting and Clinical Psychology*, **62**, 918–27.

Owens, G., Crowell, J., Pan, H. and Treboux, D. (1995) The prototype hypothesis and the origins of attachment working models: adult relationships with parents and romantic partners. *Monographs of the Society for Research in Child Development*, **60**, 133–45.

Patterson, G.R. (1971) *Families: Application of Social Learning Theory to Family Life*. Champaign, IL: Research Press.

Patterson, G.R. (1982) *Coercive Family Process*. Eugene, OR: Castalia.

Patterson, G.R., Dishion, T. and Reid, J. (1993) *Antisocial Boys*. Eugene, OR: Castalia.

Peterson, A.C., Compas, B.E., Brooks-Gunn, J., Stemmler, M., Ey, S. and Grant, K.E. (1993) Depression in adolescence. *American Psychologist*, **48**, 155–68.

Pettit, G.S. and Bates, J.E. (1989) Family interaction patterns and children's behavior problems from infancy to 4 years. *Developmental Psychology*, **25**, 413–20.

Pettit, G.S., Bates, J.E. and Dodge, K.A. (1997) Supportive parenting, ecological context, and children's adjustment: a seven-year longitudinal study. *Child Development*, **68**(5), 908–23.

Prinz, R.J. and Miller, G.E. (1994) Family-based treatments for childhood antisocial behavior: experimental influences on dropout and engagement. *Journal of Consulting and Clinical Psychology*, **62**, 645–50.

Quinton, D. and Rutter, M. (1988) *Parenting Breakdown: The Making and Breaking of Inter-generational Links*. Aldershot: Avebury.

Rapee, R.M. (1997) Potential role of childrearing practices in the development of anxiety and depression. *Clinical Psychology Review*, **17**, 47–67.

Richman, N., Stevenson, J. and Graham, P.J. (1982) *Preschool to School*. London: Academic Press.

Rowe, D.C. and Plomin, R. (1981) Environmental and genetic influences on dimensions of perceived parenting: a twin study. *Developmental Psychology*, **17**, 517–31.

Rubin, K.H. (1993) The Waterloo longitudinal project: correlates and consequences of social withdrawal from childhood to adolescence. In Rubin, K.H. and Asendorpf, J. (eds) *Social Withdrawal, Inhibition and Shyness in Childhood*. Hillsdale, NJ: Erlbaum, pp. 291–314.

Rutter, M. (1996) Transitions and turning points in developmental psychopathology: as applied to the age span between childhood and mid-adulthood. *International Journal of Behavioral Development*, **19**, 603–26.

Rutter, M., Tizard, J. and Whitmore, K. (1970) *Education, Health and Behavior*, Harlow, UK: Longman.

Rutter, M., Silberg, J., O'Connor, T. and Simonoff, E. (1999) Genetics and child psychiatry: II. Empirical research findings. *Journal of Child Psychology and Psychiatry and Allied Disciplines*, **40**, 19–56.

Ryan, N.D., Puig-Antich, J., Ambrosini, P., Rabinovich, H., Robinson, D., Nelson, B., Iyengar, S. and Twomey, J. (1987) The clinical picture of major depression in children and adolescents. *Archives of General Psychiatry*, **44**, 854–86.

Sampson, R.J., Raudenbush, S., Earls, F. and Holton, J. (1997) Neighborhoods and violent crime: a multilevel study of collective efficacy. *Science*, 15 August 1997.

Silverman, W., Kurtines, W.M., Ginsburg, G.S., Weems, C.F., Lumpkin, P.W. and Carmichael, D.H. (1999) Treating anxiety disorders in children with group cognitive-behavioral therapy: a randomized clinical trial. *Journal of Consulting and Clinical Psychology*, **67**, 995–1003.

Snijders, T. and Kenny, D.A. (1999) The social relations model for family data: a multilevel approach. *Personal Relationships*, **6**, 471–86.

Stark, K.D., Humphrey, L.L., Crook, K. and Lewis, K. (1990) Perceived family environments of depressed and anxious children: child's and maternal figure's perspectives. *Journal of Abnormal Child Psychology*, **18**, 527–47.

Stark, K.D., Sander, J.B., Yancy, M.G., Bronik, M.D. and Hoke, J.A. (2000) Treatment of depression in childhood and adolescence: cognitive-behavioral procedures for the individual and family. In Kendall, P.S. (ed.) *Child and Adolescent Therapy: Cognitive-Behavioral Procedures*, 2nd edition. New York, NY: Guilford, pp. 173–233.

Stern, D. (1994) One way to build a clinically relevant baby. *Infant Mental Health Journal*, **15**, 9–25.

Sternberg, K.J., Lamb, M.E., Greenbaum, C., Cicchetti, D., Dawud, S., Cortes, R.M., Krispin, O. and Lorey, F. (1993) Effects of domestic violence on children's behavior problems and depression. *Developmental Psychology*, **29**, 44–52.

Strauss, C., Lease, C., Last, C. and Francis, G. (1988) Overanxious disorder: an examination of developmental differences. *Journal of Abnormal Child Psychology*, **16**, 433–43.

Thapar, A. and McGuffin, P. (1995) Are anxiety symptoms in childhood heritable? *Journal of Child Psychology and Psychiatry and Allied Disciplines*, **36** (3), 439–47.

Topolski, T.D., Hewitt, J.K., Eaves, L.J., Silberg, J., Meyer, J.M., Rutter, M., Pickles, A. and Simonoff, E. (1997) Genetic and environmental influences on child reports of manifest anxiety and symptoms of separation anxiety and overanxious disorders: a community-based twin study. *Behavior Genetics*, **27**, 15–28.

Van Ijzendoorn, M.H. (1995) Adult attachment representations, parental responsiveness and infant attachment: a meta-analysis of the predictive validity of the adult attachment interview. *Psychological Bulletin*, **117**, 387–403.

Vasey, M.W. and Dadds, M.R. (2001) An introduction to the developmental psychopathology of anxiety. In Vasey, M.W. and Dadds, M.R. (eds) *The Developmental Psychopathology of Anxiety*. New York, NY: Oxford, pp. 3–26.

Vuchinich, S., Emery, R. and Cassidy, J. (1988) Family members as third parties in dyadic and family conflict: strategies, alliances and outcomes. *Child Development*, **59**, 1293–302.

Warren, S.L., Huston, L., Egeland, B. and Sroufe, L.A. (1997) Child and adolescent anxiety disorders and early attachment. *Journal of the American Academy of Child and Adolescent Psychiatry*, **36**, 637–44.

Webster-Stratton, C. and Hammond, M. (1997) Treating children with early-onset conduct problems: a comparison of child and parent training interventions. *Journal of Consulting and Clinical Psychology*, **65**, 93–109.

Weiss, D.D. and Last, C.G. (2001) Developmental variations in the prevalence and manifestation of anxiety disorders. In Vasey, M.W. and Dadds, M.R. (eds) *The Developmental Psychopathology of Anxiety*. New York, NY: Oxford University Press, pp. 27–42.

Werner, E. (1993) Risk, resilience and recovery: perspectives from the Kauai Longitudinal Study. *Development and Psychopathology*, **5**, 503–15.

Wierzbicki, M. and Pekarik, G. (1993) A meta-analysis of psychotherapy dropout. *Professional Psychology: Research and Practice*, **24**, 190–5.

Williams, S., Anderson, J., McGee, R. and Silva, P.A. (1990) Risk factors for behavioral and emotional disorder in preadolescent children. *Journal of the American Academy of Child and Adolescent Psychiatry*, **29**, 413–19.

Winnicott, D. (1960) Ego distortion in terms of true and false self. Published in *The Maturational Processes and the Facilitating Environment: Studies in the Theory of Emotional Development*. 1979. London: The Hogarth Press.

Zahn-Waxler, C., Klimes-Dougan, B. and Slattery, M.J. (2000) Internalizing problems of childhood and adolescence: prospects, pitfalls, and progress in understanding the development of anxiety and depression. *Development and Psychopathology*, **12**, 443–66.

Part III

PARENT SUPPORT

19

Assessing and Delivering Parent Support

Harriet Heath

SUMMARY

Parents who receive support as well as parents who perceive themselves as supported tend to be physically and mentally healthier than those who do not. This chapter focuses on issues related to support, beginning with a review of how the concept has developed. Support is defined as a quality of an interaction between either two people or a person and some entity (such as government policy) in which usually the recipient perceives the interaction as supportive. The functions of support are described, recognizing that 'supportive' interactions have the potential to be detrimental as well as beneficial. A broad range of potential sources of support is identified, including a person's immediate relationships; networks among social relationships; government and corporate policies; and cultural attitudes and beliefs. The chapter concludes by reviewing the issues involved in assessing parents' support, for the purposes of program-planning and of measuring a program's effectiveness.

INTRODUCTION

Support is meeting the social, emotional and intellectual needs of people (Bradley, 1995). The most important thing about having support is that it is good for us. Research has shown the benefits of having support on physical health and even mortality, on mental health and happiness (Argyle, 1992), and even in specific situations such as preventing depression following childbirth (Cutrona, 1984). Numerous investigations have sought to identify the characteristics of support and how it is provided. They have looked at the function of support and its perception by the receiver (Wills and Shinar, 2000). They have researched social networks (Brissette et al., 2000) and social relationships (Reis and Collins, 2000). They have also come to recognize that all of these, social support, social networks and social relationships, have the potential for harm (Cohen et al., 2000). Drawing from this vast amount of research, this chapter focuses on the concepts and issues most relevant to parent support and to providing programs for parents:

- the functions of support;
- the potential sources of parental support;
- identification of a parent's or a group of parents' support system as guides to developing programs for parents;
- assessment of the effectiveness of a program or intervention.

Understanding the role of support in the lives of parents is important for several reasons. First, such understanding in turn engenders an understanding of the parent and his or her strengths, and helps parents identify what they want to know and to achieve. In other words, understanding parents' supports helps them and practitioners to plan programs. Second, assessing the supports that parents have and how those supports change as a result of intervention is a means of demonstrating the strengths of programs. This knowledge is useful for future program planning and for fund-raising. Lastly, understanding support is useful simply for the information and insights gathered, and for the further study of parenting. Although these areas are not distinct, differentiating between them makes for clearer descriptions of what support parents have.

This chapter begins with a brief history of support and how it has been provided before turning to defining the concept, identifying the sources of support, and assessing its presence and effectiveness.

HISTORICAL PERSPECTIVE

Early History

Society has a long history of concern over how its children are being reared. Plato in his *Republic*, and Rousseau in *Emile*, both describe the duties of parents (Schlossman, 1979). In the American colonies in the late 17th century, under the supervision of government and the church, 'tithing men' conducted home visits to supervise parents' moral education of their young (Schlossman, 1983). The late 19th century 'Settlement House' movement included parent education as a part of their programs which were intended to address the needs of the poor, particularly poor immigrants (Erickson and Kurz-Riemer, 1999).

Less well documented was the passage of information and support from parent to child and from friend to friend (Buchmueller, 1968; Kagan and Seitz, 1988; Long, 1997). These informal sources provided parents with direct assistance both during the birth process and while actually caring for a child (Benedek, 1956; Carter, 1996).

Parents themselves also sought information. As early as 1815 there were groups of parents meeting to discuss child-rearing. Some, especially those in north-eastern America, were particularly concerned with the religious and moral improvement of their children and how to 'break their children's will' (Brim, 1965, p. 323). In 1888, a group of women started meeting in New York to discuss how they could become better parents. This group would evolve into the Child Study Association of America, funded largely by the Laura Spelman Rockefeller Memorial and later by the Spelman Fund (Auerbach, 1968). Magazines such as *Ladies Home Journal* and *Woman's Home Companion* carried articles on child-rearing. By the end of the 19th century, such information was reaching large numbers of parents (Brim, 1965).

The early 20th century was a period of great activity in the field of parenting. Universities in Iowa, California, and Minnesota, as well as Cornell and Columbia Teacher's College, created centers for the study of child development and welfare with the responsibility 'of transmitting sound research directly to parents' (Brim, 1965, p. 330; Ross, 1996; Smuts, 1996). Under the aegis of the Department of Agriculture, the federal government of the United States established 2000 county Home Demonstration Agents who demonstrated approved methods of home-making, home management, and childcare. Schools, stimulated by the National Congress of Parents and Teachers, began sponsoring parent education programs. The National Council of Parent Education, also funded by the Laura Spelman Rockefeller Memorial, became the forum integrating all activities related to parenting education. These were summarized in a 350-page volume published in 1932 (Brim, 1965). With the advent of World War II and the discontinuation of the Laura Spelman Rockefeller Memorial funding, however, social concerns moved away from parenting education.

1950 to Present – Informational Support Available

The current renewed interest in parenting education stems from many sources:

- Beginning in the 1950s, changes occurred in the structure of the American family. Parents frequently had no relatives living nearby. Large numbers of immigrants continued to arrive, bringing different customs and expectations. As family units became less stable, it became more common for single parents to raise children alone. Both parents were more likely to be working outside of the home. Many parents were raising their children in poverty (Carter, 1996).
- The burgeoning body of research relating to human development raised parents' interest in understanding its implications for child-rearing and in wanting to do well by their children. Benjamin Spock's book of child-rearing advice, based on psychoanalytic theory, current research, and a pediatrician's experience, became a bestseller. 'Research generally confirms significant levels of interest in more parenting information, across socioeconomic categories' (Simpson, 1997, p. 23).
- Parents' realization that they face different issues than those their own parents faced has also furthered interest in parenting education. When communities seem less safe, and when it becomes difficult to protect children from exposure to risks such as AIDS, violence, and war, parents want to discuss how to cope with these changes (Carter, 1996; Chenoweth, 2000).
- Society's interest in bettering the lives of children has also contributed to the parent education movement (Nedler and McAfee, 1979). Head Start, the Parent Child Development Centers, and Home Start all include a parent education component (Schlossman, 1979). Programs were developed to address specific problems such as teen pregnancy and developmental disabilities (Carter, 1996; Fine and Lee, 2001).

Today, parents are deluged with information from multiple sources about what they should and should not do with their children. Infants' routine medical check-ups include information about feeding, sleeping, and general baby care (Brazelton, 1992). School counselors are expected to provide parents with information (Einzig, 1996; Lew, 1999). The number of parenting books, magazines, and newsletters has increased steadily in recent years (Simpson, 1997). Electronic media offer new sources of information such as videos, talk shows, interviews, and internet sites (Simpson, 1997).

The number and diversity of parent education programs exemplifies this trend. Hetty Einzig (1996) lists ten national universal programs in the United Kingdom ranging from home-centered programs to group programs to helplines. Nick Carter (1996) estimates that there are more than 50,000 parenting programs in the United States alone. These programs range from small 'mom and pop' gatherings to large multimillion-dollar operations funded by state and federal governments. There are non-profit parenting programs with hundreds of replicated sites, as well as a growing number of for-profit businesses (Carter, 1996). Some programs are oriented to the needs of specific groups, such as parents of children with disabilities or autism or at risk of being abused (Fine and Lee, 2001). Some have a theoretical basis for their work. Systematic Training for Effective Parenting (STEP) is based on Adlerian psychology, while STEEP is based on the psychoanalytic theory of Mahler (Egeland and Erickson, 1993). Many are quite eclectic in their approach though Carter (1995) concluded that even so, 75 per cent of their contents were similar.

Some programs, continuing the early tradition of self-help groups, evolved because parents sought specific kinds of parenting experiences for which they needed specialized information. The childbirth education movement of the 1950s and 1960s, which used information about natural childbirth, prepared couples for childbirth and initiated practices that are now common in American hospitals (decreased use of anesthesia, fathers in delivery rooms, rooms that are home-like rather than institutional, etc.) (Pizzo, 1990). The LeLeche League started when a few women in Chicago gathered, from their own experiences, information about successful breastfeeding. They subsequently made that information available both to other women through nursing mothers' groups, and to the medical profession (Heath, 1976; Merrill, 1987). The fathers' movement has incorporated elements of 'basic support, parent education, information and referral, and networking' for dads (Kagan and Seitz, 1988, p. 320). These kinds of programs grew when parents themselves (sometimes working with professionals, sometimes not) collected the information needed for a specific experience or situation.

This stream of information and advice, though well-intentioned, produced some negative consequences:

- Often the information and advice from different sources was conflictual. Experts did not agree (Auerbach, 1968; Simpson, 1997), which sometimes caused parents to dismiss all information (Zero to Three, 1997).

- Parents sometimes followed advice, only to find that it 'didn't work' and they stopped listening (Darling, 1990; Carter, 1996).
- The tendency of professionals to tell parents what to do established a pattern of 'talking down' to parents (Brim, 1965), or parents were supposed to listen to the 'all-knowing professional' who 'knew best' (Hecimovic et al., 1999, p. 263). As the civil rights and women's movements placed more emphasis on equality in relationships, this approach became increasingly unacceptable (Carter, 1996).
- A trend emerged of blaming parents for all a child's problems (Johnson et al., 2000). 'Children's emotional and social difficulties were often blamed on parents, particularly mothers, who eagerly sought advice and education from teachers and child development experts' (Bowman, 1997, p. 163). Instead of feeling empowered and respected, parents were often left guilt-ridden and made uncertain by this approach (Bowman, 1997).
- The 'professionalization' of parenting sometimes made parents feel inadequate but also caused them to become advocates (Darling, 1990; Long and Leonard, 1992).

1950 to Present – Other Supportive Functions

Efforts to provide information to parents were accompanied by an increasing recognition that for healthy development, people needed other kinds of support. Erik Erikson hypothesized in 1950 that people needed a fund of 'traditional reassurance' (emotional support) to resolve the crisis of the generative (parenting) stage (Erikson, 1968, p. 139). According to Veiel and Baumann (1992), the term 'support' did not occur in the scientific literature until the early 1970s. In the early research, 'social support' 'was primarily used in a concrete sense to denote a personal relationship or transaction' (Veiel and Baumann, 1992, p. 2). Early studies analyzed the positive impact of social support on the ability to deal with stressful situations such as the transition to parenthood (Cutrona, 1984; Gottlieb and Pancer, 1988).

Since then, terms and their meanings have proliferated. Alan Vaux summarized the process when he wrote 'social support refers to a complex and dynamic process involving transactions between individuals and their social networks within a social ecology' (Vaux, 1992, p. 194). He recommended using 'more precise terms, support resources, behavior and appraisals' (p. 214). In this chapter, *social support* refers to 'any

process through which social relationships can influence health positively' (Cohen et al., 2000). *Support functions* are 'a broad range of interpersonal behaviors by members of a person's social network [that] may help him or her successfully cope with adverse life events and circumstances' (Cutrona and Russell, 1990, p. 319; see also Wills and Shinar, 2000). Support is an 'inferred characteristic or function of social relationships or transactions.' It carries the notion of a supportive quality, 'which can be abstracted from particular relationships and transactions and can be used to characterize them' (Veiel and Baumann, 1992, p. 2). Changing the purpose from prevention to development, Garbarino and Kostelny (1995) wrote that when they spoke of 'opportunities for development' they meant 'interpersonal and institutional relationships (with kith and kin, with professionals, with neighbors, with community authorities, etc.) in which parents find material, emotional, and social encouragement compatible with their needs and capacities as they exist at a specific point in their parenting career' (1995, pp. 419–20).

In their efforts to define support more exactly, researchers began defining its functions. By the late 1970s, researchers such as Cobb, Kahn, Antonucci, and Caplan had identified at least three functions of support – emotional, informational, and appraisal – that seemed to mitigate stressful situations (House, 1981, p. 16). Based in part on Weiss's (1976) model of the assets that can be gained from relationships, Cutrona (1984, p. 379) expanded the list to six functions of social support: attachment, social integration, opportunity for nurturance, reassurance of worth, reliable alliance, and guidance. Benjamin Gottlieb and Mark Pancer developed a similar list experientially by categorizing the responses of 40 single Canadian mothers receiving social assistance to questions about their problems and the people who helped them cope. Their classifications fitted 'reasonably well with prior definitions and conceptions of support' (House, 1981, pp. 18 and 22). The two approaches to identifying the functions of support with their similar outcomes added strength to the assumption that the concept of supportive functions was relevant to everyday life.

In 1988 a major change came to the lists of supportive functions when Gottlieb and Pancer presented social network as a means of delivering support rather than one of the functions. Descriptions of the network vary. Gerald Caplan, for example, included 'professions and formal community institutions as well as natural systems (such as the family; non-professional and informal social units, particularly mutual aid organizations; and person-to-person care giving efforts both spontaneous and organized)' (House, 1981, p. 17). In contrast, Cochran and Niego (1995, p. 396) limits personal social networks to those anchored to a specific individual, including only 'those persons outside the household who engage in activities and exchanges of an affective and/or material nature with members of the immediate family.' For our purposes, all of these people and groups of people will be considered as potential sources of support.

Carl Dunst integrated Gottlieb and Pancer's network system into a more complex view, incorporating the following (Dunst and Trivette, 1990, p. 331):

- a consideration of the availability of support and the type or function provided, with a measure of the quality and quantity available;
- a constitutional factor that included the indicated need and its congruence with the support proposed; and
- a measure of the satisfaction reported regarding the helpfulness of the support.

This structure can be used both to plan intervention programs and to meet the needs (particularly the instrumental needs) of individual parents.

As early as the 1880s, the idea of support was present in the parent education movement, though the word was not. Early self-help groups saw the group leader's role as that of an 'enabler, who used his knowledge to help them function as individuals, evolving their own answers in feelings responses and behavior' (Auerbach, 1968, p. 30). Leaders, in other words, were to help parents feel competent and to provide emotional support. Research documented the need for social contact. One study (Minturn et al., 1964) compared the social contexts of parents in six cultures and found that only the Gusii mothers of Nyansongo in Kenya were more isolated than American mothers. Descriptions of programs focused on the social contexts of groups (Braun et al., 1984) and on the inclusion of parent support as well as education (Walker and Riley, 2001).

The family support movement grew in response to several criticisms of the parent education and social improvement efforts of the 1960s and 1970s (Solomon, 1987; Gerris et al., 1998). Beginning in the 1970s, the movement adopted the principles of working with families as partners, gaining acceptance as a community asset, acting as a resource for all families, and building trusting relationships with families who participated in their programs (FSA, 2000). The movement evolved in part 'from concerns over the ability of existing social-welfare programs to promote the healthy development of children and families by preventing problems

rather than waiting until a crisis emerged' (FSA, 2000, p. 2; Ferguson, 2001; Kluger, 2001). It also developed in part as a response to the family changes and research findings cited above. Family support centers are increasingly involved in helping parents to learn job skills, in adult education and support, and in reducing child abuse and neglect (FSA, 2000). By tailoring their missions to local concerns, such centers can provide instrumental and tangential, as well as emotional and informational, support.

As we have seen, parents wanting to rear their children well, being encouraged to do so, and providing parents with relevant information and support has a long history. Concerns about the impact of support on the parents receiving it have emerged relatively recently. Recognition that parents need *personal* support has come to the fore even more recently. Despite these evolutions, the ultimate goal of all programs and methods has always been the same: to facilitate the rearing of healthy children, however the concept of 'healthy children' is defined at a given time.

Moving from this review of the development of the concept of support, this chapter now gives a more precise definition of the functions of support, describes a model that illustrates how support is delivered to parents, and finally, discusses examples of how both function and delivery are assessed.

DEFINING AND ANALYZING SUPPORT

With the increasing recognition that support is necessary for healthy development, researchers have sought to define more precisely the quality of the interaction that is supportive (Veiel and Baumann, 1992; Wills and Shinar, 2000) by identifying its separate functions. In the process they have also identified some issues important to understanding support in people's lives.

Functions of Support

Although different researchers have developed their own categories and labels for the various functions of support, there is sufficient similarity between them to make the following list. The list includes all functions found in the literature though the first three are those most commonly discussed (Dunst and Trivette, 1990; Wills and Shinar, 2000). Each entry contains the definitions of different researchers. To further explain the function, entries may also include relevant theory, empirical findings, and/or pragmatic implications.

EMOTIONAL SUPPORT

- Consists 'of expressions of attachment to and esteem for the individual that are typically communicated in confiding interactions that foster the ventilation of feelings and insecurities in particular' (Gottlieb and Pancer, 1988, p. 241).
- 'Information which leads you to believe that you are cared for and loved as a person' (Cooke et al., 1988, p. 213).
- 'Comfort and security during times of stress, leading the person to feel that he or she is cared for by others' (Cutrona and Russell, 1990, p. 322).

James House observed that when individuals think of people being 'supportive' toward them, they think mainly of emotional support (House, 1981; see also Turner, 1992) and find this the most effective kind of support (Cohen, 1992). This category subsumes the largest number of specific acts of support mentioned in discussions of support (House, 1981, p. 24) Emotional support is related to people's needs for *attachment*, the deep, loving, ongoing relationship with another person that is assumed to underlie healthy personality development (Erikson, 1968; Bowlby, 1969). Some current political thought questions whether the recent emphasis on meeting individual needs has not moved too far from recognizing the importance of the reaching out to others, which is necessary if attachment and the feelings of community are to develop (Kraemer and Roberts, 1996).

INFORMATIONAL SUPPORT

- 'Cognitive guidance consists of advice, counsel and normative information about the individual's handling of his or her situation or about his or her plans for handling situations' (Gottlieb and Pancer, 1988, p. 241).
- 'Providing a person with information that the person can use in coping with personal and environmental problems' (House, 1981, p. 25).

Erik Erikson (1950) spoke of the needs of healthy people to have available 'proven methods,' that is they need information and guidance about how to do what needs to be done. Anthropological studies show that all societies studies have systems for educating their children into the ways of the group (LeVine, 1975). Although the systems vary from culture to culture, the fact that they exist does not. The importance of having factual information and relevant skills is very apparent to parents when they are facing a newborn for the first time (Minde et al., 1982; Gottlieb and Pancer, 1988); or ways of changing children's disruptive behavior (Brown,

1998); or a child with severe brain damage (Rosenthal and Geckler, 1997). The drive for accurate information is demonstrated by the efforts of groups that, finding such information unavailable, develop and disseminate their own (Merrill, 1987). Parents ask for information (Bitsika and Sharpley, 1999; Chenoweth, 2000) and report satisfaction with having received it (Bitsika and Sharpley, 2000) as well as being dissatisfied when it does not meet their needs (Darling, 1990).

When measuring informational support, researchers have identified three separate components:

- its usefulness in (Dunst and Trivette, 1990) or relevance to (Heath, 1976) a given situation;
- its accuracy (Heath, 1976) or helpfulness (Dunst and Trivette, 1990); and
- the expectations it can create (Heath, 1976).

The present author, for example, demonstrated the importance of accuracy and relevance of information in a study of lactation, at a time when information was readily accessible that was detrimental to establishing breast-feeding (Heath, 1976). In contrast to women following accurate information, women following inaccurate information were no longer breast-feeding when their babies were four months old even though they had planned prenatally to do so.

Although advising parents has a long history, and although parents request such advice, including information as a component of support has been tenuous. There are several reasons for this. For one, conflicting views on what makes for healthy development make it difficult to measure the effects of having information (Hauser-Cram, 1990; Tolan et al., 1998). Parenting is viewed as a personal matter. Telling people what to do is viewed as intrusive and not helpful (Einzig, 1996). Another reason is that the current trend toward parent groups being supportive and peer-led, rather than instructive, has de-emphasized the importance of information as a function of support, as has the cultural assumption that if they are mentally healthy, parents (i.e. mothers) will know how to parent (Deutsch, 1945; Carter, 1996).

INSTRUMENTAL/TANGIBLE SUPPORT

- 'Providing aid in kind, money, labor, time, or any direct help' (House, 1981, pp. 24–5).
- 'Tangible aid consists of services and material resources that are extended by network members free of charge' (Gottlieb and Pancer, 1988, p. 241).
- 'Concrete instrumental assistance, in which a person in a stressful situation is given the necessary resources (e.g. financial assistance,

physical help with tasks) to cope with the stressful event' (Cutrona and Russell, 1990, p. 322).

Current systems of support differ in how they organize this function. Some list two: *material assistance*, such as money, food, clothing, and shelter; and *instrumental help*, such as childcare, respite care, and labor (Dunst and Trivette, 1990). Others include both as instrumental (Cooke et al., 1988; Cutrona and Russell, 1990).

Instrumental support with its pragmatic input ranks high in supporting parents through stressful periods such as the transition to parenthood (Gottlieb and Pancer, 1988) and when children have disabilities (Dunst and Trivette, 1990).

ALTRUISM

- Opportunity for nurturance where a person is 'responsible for the well-being of another' (Cutrona, 1984, p. 379).
- Information that leads people to believe that they are worthwhile because of what they have done with and for others (Cooke et al., 1988, p. 213).

Although being cared for is accepted as vital for human development, the need to provide such care is seldom mentioned in psychological theory. It is not, for example, included in Maslow's hierarchy of needs (Maslow, 1962). An exception is Erikson's (1968) theory of healthy development, in which he writes of nurturing the next generation. (See Noddings, 1984, for a further development of these themes.) This function is a vital part of the group process, particularly with groups of parents (Braun et al., 1984). It is part of the phenomenon of how parents help each other. For many, the giving and sharing are a benefit to both the giver and the receiver.

APPRAISAL

- A person's 'skills and abilities are acknowledged' (Cutrona, 1984, p. 378). 'Esteem support' (Cutrona and Russell, 1990, p. 322; see also Minde et al., 1982; Cowan and Cowan, 1988).
- 'Provides feedback about how a person is doing and has ideas for resolving difficulties' (Cooke et al., 1988, p. 213).
- 'The information involved is relevant to self-evaluation — what social psychologists have termed social comparison' (House, 1981, p. 25).

Appaisal, another infrequently mentioned function of support, is related to the need to feel good about oneself, and to feeling competent through feedback (Maslow, 1962; Erikson, 1968). Recognition

of these needs fueled the empowerment movement in social service work. Givers who realize the importance of positive appraisal aim to structure interchanges to leave recipients feeling in charge (Dunst and Trivette, 1990).

COHERENCE

- The 'global orientation that expresses the extent to which one has a pervasive, enduring though dynamic feeling of confidence that one's internal and external environments are predictable and that there is a high probability that things will work out as well as can reasonably be expected' (Antonovsky, as quoted by Gottlieb and Pancer, 1988, p. 242).
- Gives person an 'ability to withstand or come to terms with environmental turbulence and adversity' and a reassurance of worth. Conditions couples' appraisals of the significance of the transition for the stability, continuity, and meaning of each partner's life and the couple's relationship (Gottlieb and Pancer, 1988, p. 241).
- Programs that seek to adapt to cultural values such as integrating traditional patterns into the program (Gonzales-Mena, 1997; Red Horse, 1997).

Coherence is another of the functions seldom mentioned in the literature. However, recognizing the importance of providing people with a sense of coherence is one factor driving the current emphasis in parent education to be 'culturally sensitive' (Bavolek, 1997).

COMPANIONSHIP AS SUPPORT

- Shared leisure and other social activities that are initiated primarily for the intrinsic goal of enjoyment (Wills and Shinar, 2000).
- Companionship may not be a component of support in the sense that support implies buffering effects that would be expected when the social contact involves problem-focused help. It is included here because companionship may contribute to well-being through recreation, humor, and affection and thus should help elevate a person's current level of contentment (Rook, 1990, pp. 222–3).

Companionship may be the least mentioned of the functions of support. Even Erikson's (1968) personality theory does not mention companionship as one of the expectations of marriage.

Issues Related to the Definition of Support

Researchers have not succeeded in developing scales that independently measure these different functions (Cutrona and Russell, 1990; Dunst and Trivette, 1990; Wills and Shinar, 2000). This difficulty has raised questions of whether there is perhaps only one overarching support function, and whether several of the above functions, as opposed to only one, are involved in most supportive behaviors. The idea that an act of support often serves several functions simultaneously is intuitively sound. For example, in a discussion group where information is forthcoming, a person may also gain an emotional sense of being accepted and nurtured. Indeed, this is a goal that many parent groups set for themselves early in their development (Auerbach, 1968; Garbarino and Kostelny, 1995). Similarly, information may be perceived as being cohesive, i.e. fitting into one's own beliefs, and thus measurements will factor out as being both informational and cohesive.

Even though the functions are statistically and experientially interrelated, they are conceptually distinct (Cutrona and Russell, 1990; Dunst and Trivette, 1990; Wills and Shinar, 2000). Research participants have no difficulty distinguishing between information and instrumental help when asked (Heath, 1976). Measuring them separately continues to be relevant when attempting to understand the support available to a person or group and when planning programs (Wills and Shinar, 2000).

The value of a function varies with the situation (Dunst and Trivette, 1990; Sarason et al., 1992). Cutrona was one of the early researchers to question whether certain functions were more supportive than others in certain situations. She found reliable alliance and guidance (tangible and informational support) a significant negative predictor of postpartum depression (Cutrona, 1984, p. 387).

It might be tempting to conclude from how the functions of support have been described here that non-supportive behaviors either do not exist or are unimportant. They do and they are important. Research documents that activities planned to provide support are not always beneficial (Cohen et al., 2000) and that networks can 'be inimical to health' (Brisette et al., 2000, p. 64; Reis and Collins, 2000). Both Harris (1992) and Rook (1992) conclude that negative effects of seemingly supportive relationships do exist, and that it is important for both effective program development and definitive research to recognize which inputs from the environment are perceived as supportive and by whom.

Listening to comments frequently made to parents demonstrates the unsupportive quality possible in interactions. 'If you knew how to parent, the baby would stop crying.' 'If you spent more time with that teenager she wouldn't be so obnoxious.' 'Parents are too involved.' 'Parents are not involved

enough.' These are all common statements from well-meaning people. (See Reis and Collins, 2000, for descriptions of tools for measuring.)

Putting each of the functions of support defined earlier onto a continuum results in the following scheme:

- *Emotional support*
  from emotionally supportive to emotionally non-supportive (which could include demeaning, emotionally undermining)
- *Informational*
  from accurate to inaccurate
  from relevant to irrelevant
  sets acceptable expectations to sets stressful expectations
- *Instrumental*
  from helpful to unhelpful
  from useful to useless
- *Altruistic*
  from giving to non-giving
- *Appraisal*
  from positive to negative
- *Coherence*
  from coherent to disjointed
- *Companionship*
  from companionable to non-companionable

Research participants are able to rate the degree of support received or not received in various interactions and activities. In the author's early research (Heath, 1976), parents rated how supportive they experienced many events to have been, using a scale from one to five. Parents whose baby cried continually reported feeling inadequate in their roles, while those whose babies settled into life with happy smiles reported feeling good about their parenting. Parents questioned information they received, identifying what was obviously incorrect as well as what was right and that which could have been either. Parents perceived differences in their degree of support and were able to report them.

Researchers recognizing that actions meant to be supportive are not always received as such have further analyzed those individual characteristics that make people less able to accept support (Harris, 1992) and social attitudes that make it permissible to do so (Kraemer and Roberts, 1996).

Having identified the functions of support and their positive to negative potential, we now turn to describing the input of the other person in the transaction, or how support is delivered.

DELIVERING PARENT SUPPORT

If support is a quality characterizing an interaction, we must now describe where and with whom that interaction might occur, that is, the way that support is delivered.

Potential Sources of Support

Urie Bronfenbrenner's (1979) ecology of human development places such interaction within a multi-level ecological system. This framework can be diagrammed as a nested arrangement of concentric structures, the micro-, meso-, exo- and macrosystems, each contained within the next and each influencing the interaction at the core or in the microsystem. The quality of interaction in the microsystem may or may not support the parent. Before examining the factors that influence the nature of these interactions, we must identify the other in that interaction. In that process we will continue to be inclusive.

Bronfenbrenner's (1979) theory accommodates the social support system or network customarily defined in the research on support, that is, a person's immediate circle of contacts. It also provides a means of including larger events, situations or cultural attitudes that have tended to be ignored in the support research but that are increasingly recognized for their impact on parents and parenting (Gottlieb, 1992; Garbarino and Kostelny, 1995). Examples of these are 'back-to-work' legislation, 'flexi-time' policies, and cultural attitudes toward parenting (Erickson and Kurz-Riemer, 1999). Recognizing the influence of the exo- and macrosystems makes more realistic the descriptions of parents' support systems and expands both the potential sources of support available to parents and the means of intervention available to program planners.

Microsystem

Represented by the center circle in Bronfenbrenner's diagram, the microsystem consists of 'a pattern of activities, roles and interpersonal relations experienced by the developing person in a given setting with particular physical and material characteristics' (Bronfenbrenner, 1979, p. 22). Here occur the molar activities, the 'ongoing behavior possessing a momentum of its own and perceived as having meaning or intent by the participants in the setting' (p. 45). The quality of that behavior can be supportive or otherwise.

For our purposes of identifying potential sources of parental support, it is necessary to list more specifically who takes these roles and participates in the interpersonal relationships Bronfenbrenner mentions. Conceptually, the partner in the interaction may be one of numerous people, including:

- the parenting partner (Gottlieb and Pancer, 1988)
- the parent's own parents (Hunter, 1997)
- children (Bronfenbrenner, 1979)
- kin (Hunter et al., 1998)
- friends (Gottlieb and Pancer, 1988)
- fellow workers (Kerr and McIntosh, 2000)
- other parents (Kerr and McIntosh, 2000)
- parent support group (Scott, 1999)
- home visitor (Pesoff, 1998)

Professionals are seldom included, but have been found very relevant in predicting outcomes (Heath, 1976). The person is identified by asking the question, 'Who makes a difference in your life?' (Cochran and Niego, 1995).

Various support studies have excluded many of the potential partners in the interaction. These exclusions are generally made based on the research issues in question. For example, one researcher found the implications of spousal support different from those of support by others, so parenting partners were excluded from consideration (Cochran and Niego, 1995). Family members living in the household were viewed as having a different kind of relationship (Cochran and Niego, 1995), as did people paid for their services (Gottlieb and Pancer, 1988). Other research has been inclusive, listing innumerable people and groups of people, the parenting partner, parents, children, kin, friends, fellow workers, and professionals as being potential partners in supportive interaction (Dunst and Trivette, 1990; FSA, 2000). For our purposes, all of these people and groups of people will be considered as potential sources of support.

The assumption is that social relationships in and of themselves are usually viewed as healthly (Reis and Collins, 2000). Much research shows that people who are socially integrated live longer and survive various medical problems better than do people less socially integrated (Brissette et al., 2000; Cohen et al., 2000).

Social integration is defined as 'the extent to which an individual participates in a broad range of social relationships' (Brissette et al., 2000, p. 54). There are a number of elements in measuring the concept, assessing:

- 'the number of different types of social relationships an individual participates in;'
- 'the frequency with which the individual engages in various activities;'
- 'the extent to which individuals believe they are embedded in a stable social structure and identify with their fellow community members and social positions;' and
- 'combined information regarding social ties, community involvement, and frequency of

contact with friends and relatives into a single summary index' (Brissette et al., 2000).

In Bronfenbrenner's system all these interactions occur at the microsystem level.

Increasing attention is being paid to the impact of the media on parents, even though the media are non-personal in nature (Simpson, 1997; Fine and Lee, 2001). Using Bronfenbrenner's (1979) definition that the ongoing behavior is perceived as having meaning, a person reading from a book or watching television is seeing meaning in the interchange. — The media functions as a passive partner in an interchange and must be considered as a potential deliverer of support. Rae Simpson's summary of the influence of the media includes both printed material, such as books, magazines, newspapers, newsletters, pamphlets, posters, brochures, and parenting newsletters, and the electronic media, including radio, television, video, and computer technologies and websites. Gregory Brock and his colleagues (1993) report a study that found that parents most preferred reading as the method for learning about child-rearing, documenting the widespread use of popular print materials such as magazines by parents for obtaining child-rearing advice. Researchers have found that print materials such as newsletters are used in a variety of ways: one provided parents with information to encourage discussions about child-rearing within their social networks (Walker and Riley, 2001); another gave parents suggestions of what they could do to curb their children's violence (Murray et al., 1999). Thus, to include all potential sources of support we will consider all of the relevant people listed above as well as the media to be parts of the microsystem.

Another part of the microsystem is the setting or location of the activities. Settings include homes, schools, hospitals, doctor's offices, daycare centers, playgrounds, churches, colleges and universities, work places, community centers, libraries, family support centers, shopping malls, and supermarkets.

The Mesosystem

The mesosystem, the next concentric circle in the diagram, comprises the interrelations among two or more settings in which the developing person actively participates. For the child, the mesosystem would include the relations among home, school, and the neighborhood peer group. For an adult, it would include relations among the family, work, and social life (Bronfenbrenner, 1979, p. 25).

Benjamin Gottlieb and Mark Pancer (1988) have expanded Bronfenbrenner's rather quick description of the mesosystem to include specific measurable properties of the social network. Their analysis includes two main factors (Gottlieb and Pancer, 1988, p. 238):

- structural properties: size of network, its composition (the close friends and closest family relations), and its density (degree of internal connectedness);
- characteristics of the ties within the social network: the intensity (frequency of contact), the multiplexity (members of the network share more than one role or interest), the durability (length of time the relationships have existed), and opportunities for reciprocity (members of the network providing support for each other).

This structure proposed by Gottlieb is frequently referred to in the literature as the 'social network' and 'the integration of social networks', and has been widely used in research to measure support.

Gottlieb and Pancer (1988) have successfully used their system to predict the amount of stress parents will experience as they move into parenthood. The larger the social network and the more integrated the parents, the less stress. Carl Dunst integrated Gottlieb and Pancer's system into a more complex one, incorporating the following:

- a consideration of the availability of support and the type or function provided, with a measure of the quality and quantity available;
- a constitutional factor that included the indicated need and its congruence with the support proposed; and
- a measure of the satisfaction reported as to its helpfulness and usefulness (Dunst and Trivette, 1990, p. 331).

Being able to measure and to use in research the above organization of the mesosystem, demonstrates the validity of the theoretical structure and its usefulness in understanding people's support systems.

The Exosystem

The exosystem, the third concentric circle in Bronfenbrenner's (1979) framework, refers to areas of human endeavor in which the developing person is not actively involved but in which events occur and decisions are made that affect or are affected by the developing person (Bronfenbrenner, 1979). Examples are policy decisions made by governments, employers, social agencies, school boards, mental health centers, family support centers and such. A more specific example would be decisions made by the administration of one's place of employment about working conditions which will affect parents who have had no input in their determination (Galinsky, 1999). For example, the board of directors of the company where a parent works might instigate a policy of flexible work-time, or the local hospital might institute a policy allowing parents to stay with their children during emergency procedures (Garbarino, 1990; Garbarino and Kostelny, 1995). There are many more examples of policy-making that affect parents and families, including the following:

- the Family and Medical Leave Act, signed into US law in 1993, which provides up to 12 weeks of unpaid leave each year for the care of a newborn or adopted child, a seriously ill child, spouse or parent, or because of the worker's own illness (Phillips, 1997, p. 17; Zigler and Hall, 2000);
- social security laws that provide no benefits for work done in the home, even those related to rearing children, who will be the future workers who will keep the social security system solvent in the future (Burggraf, 1997; Crittenden, 2001);
- policy decisions, such as de-institutionalizing patients from mental hospitals (Ursprung, 1990);
- The current emphasis on welfare-to-work (Behrman, 1997, 2002) and the widespread 'failure to support the work of caring for children and other family members' (Kurz, 1997, p. 94);
- the reconstructing of the role of fathers (Gerson, 1997).

A complete list of possible sources of support at the exosystem level is beyond the scope of this chapter. However, even this small number of somewhat randomly selected items demonstrates the impact activity can have at this level on parenting. Using simple relevant questions about parents' reactions to the policy or event make the impact on parents measurable (Halpern, 1992).

The Macrosystem

Finally, the outer circle in Bronfenbrenner's system, the macrosystem, refers to 'consistencies, in the form and content of lower-order systems (micro-, meso-, and exo-) that exist, or could exist, at the level of the subculture or the culture as a whole, along with any belief systems or ideology underlying such consistencies' (Bronfenbrenner, 1979, p. 26). 'Macrosystems,' writes Garbarino, 'serve as the master blueprints

for the ecology of human development. These blueprints reflect a people's shared assumptions about how things should be done, as well as the institutions that represent those assumptions' (Garbarino, 1990, p. 83). Examples are numerous: patterns of violence or affluence as described by Gabarino and Kostelny (1995) and Phillips (1997); cultural definitions of parental roles (Belksy, 1984; Belksy and Kelly, 1994); beliefs and practices associated with the socio-economic status of the parent (Beckman, 1984; Halpern et al., 1992); attitudes toward parenting as implied by economic decisions (Burggraf, 1997; Crittendon, 2001); the current idealization of the American family of the 1950s, and the assumption that the 'socially desirable' family structure including two parents (mother and father) is always the preferable one (Kurz, 1997). Folk beliefs may also fall into this category. In the Rural Alabama Pregnancy and Infant Health Project, for example, the home visitors found that some of their clients believed it was dangerous for a mother to wash her hair in the four weeks after childbirth (Nagy et al., 1992). Finally, Einzig (1996) has noted the impact of Victorian parenting styles on modern parenting, particularly in the United Kingdom.

In summary, people interact with numerous potential sources of support. These sources include all the people in their environment, many kinds of media, relevant social/governmental/employer policies, and the themes about parents and parenting that run through the social structure of a society (Cochran and Niegro, 1995; Brissette et al., 2000). With recognition of the potential sources of support must also be the recognition of the sources of potential toxicity. (See Garbarino and Kostelny (1995) for an excellent development of this theme.)

The Relationship Between the Sources and Functions of Support

As discussed in the sections on the micro- and mesosystems, further study of the sources of support is frequently done to identify relationships among the sources or social networks by considering properties of structure and density, both of which have been found to contribute to health. This additional analysis, however, does not assess the qualitative aspects of the interaction (Brissette et al., 2000). (See Einzig (1996) and Garbarino and Kostelny (1995) for a further development of this theme.)

For clarity, in this chapter, support and its functions have been kept as separate entities from social networks or sources of support, though not all research and writing does so. Some research projects have developed intricate measures that combine the two. The process of developing these measures is long and complex. The results may be very useful for a specific program, but frequently must be adapted if applied elsewhere (Brissette et al., 2000).

There are several advantages to keeping the two concepts separate. One is that the support coming from a resource can be recorded, such as the social worker who complimented the parent on how she talked to her two-year-old. Every interaction at the microsystem level can be analyzed as to who was involved, the function of support implied in the interaction, and its intensity. Another advantage is that keeping the two separate allows for specific questions to be asked about how functions may be tied to settings. For example, many parents are reluctant to enter their children's schools because of their own negative emotional experiences in school (Berger, 1981). A rationale for home-visiting is that the home is where some parents are most comfortable (FSA, 2000). A third reason is that one can investigate the influence of a person's sources of support on a supportive interaction. Gottlieb and Pancer (1988), for example, predict that the information will be more easily accepted if the network does so (size of network and its intensity). Birkel and Reppucci (1983) report that parents with tight kin relationships attend fewer parent group discussion sessions than do those with less tight kin networks. Solomon's (1987) research takes the impact a step further, describing how the social network directly influenced infant socialization, a finding with which Cochran and Niego's (1995) work concurs. Lastly, keeping the two concepts differentiated allows for a precise description of parents' support that is particularly useful when developing programs (Thoits, 1992; Wills and Shinar, 2000).

We shall consider evidence that uses both the distinctly defined support and resources and the composite to illustrate to the reader the usefulness of both approaches. This way readers will better understand the literature, and will be able to adopt the most useful approach to whatever work they undertake.

Having identified potential sources of support, we now turn to the issue of determining how we can assess their impact.

ASSESSING SUPPORT

Identifying the role of support in the lives of parents requires assessing its presence. It means answering such questions as whether this parent or group of parents is receiving support, and if so, what function is it providing and who or what are the sources?

There are several reasons for wanting to identify the support parents have. First, doing so allows parents to understand themselves and their situations more clearly, and for practitioners to understand also. Such understanding is imperative for program planning, and generates information that is necessary for fund-raising (Halpern, 1992; FSA, 2000).

A second reason for assessing parents' support is to measure the effectiveness of a program or an intervention. Here the question being researched is: has the program or intervention been helpful to the parent? This information is important for ongoing program planning, and for raising funds to continue the work (FSA, 2000).

A third reason is to attain a better understanding of the role of support in the lives of people. Parenting is challenging and frequently stressful. Increased understanding of how support can lessen stress and improve the health of both parents and children will benefit both groups in the future.

Whatever the reason for assessing parents' support, assessment requires one to identify the content to be covered, the measurements to use, and the research design. The following discussion is an overview of some current methods in use.

Identify the Source of the Assessment

One fact has to be clarified first. For an accurate assessment of a parent's or a group's available support, information must include information about the source of assessment and the condition under which it is given. A piece of advice, a gift, a program or a policy – any interaction can be assessed differently by the person receiving it, the person giving it, or an outside observer (Wills and Shinar, 2000). A court-mandated parenting program will be viewed by the judge, presumably, as supportive to parents who have been abusing their children. The parents may view the same program negatively because it requires them to spend more time away from their children after working all day. Telling a woman who wants to breast-feed that she can easily do so for three months is supportive but the same words are not supportive if the woman thinks breast-feeding is repulsive. Differences are also found between parents' perceptions of the support they expect to receive and the support they actually receive (Wills and Shinar, 2000).

An outside observer may add a criterion, an empirically based standard, on which to base the assessment (Cohen et al., 2000). The accuracy of a culture's attitude toward bottle-feeding, for instance, may be determined by comparing the respective health of groups of infants who differ only in manner of feeding. Or, the accuracy of a culture's emphasis on infant stimulation may be assessed by comparing the school-readiness of children who participated in an infant stimulation program with that of those who did not. This approach, as the examples illustrate, is frequently used when assessing the supportive quality of policy decisions and/or cultural patterns and beliefs.

Dissimilarities in the assessment of support can occur at the 'exo-level' even when the assessment is empirically based (Cohen et al., 2000). Zigler and Styfco's (1996) research on Head Start reports evidence of cognitive and academic advances made by Head Start children. African-American colleagues, however, have shared with the author that their communities feel the Head Start program contributes to the breakdown of families. From their perspective, young children are taken away from their mothers, or other kin, for schooling. As a consequence, since their children were in school, parents were encouraged to work full-time. The children then had to be placed in daycare, and time away from their mothers increased. It was this long-term separation of very young children from their mothers and kin that these professional colleagues saw as eroding the strong emotional ties that had been part of their traditional family life. In assessing parent support systems, consideration must be given to whose perceptions are being recorded.

An assessment of the support of a parent or a group, must include information about the person making the assessment.

Reasons for Assessing Support

As outlined earlier, there are three basic reasons for assessing parents' support. One is to identify the strengths, interests, and situations of the parents involved for program development. The second is to evaluate the effectiveness of a program in meeting parents' needs. And the third is to understand more fully the role of support in the lives of parents.

Different reasons tend to aim for different outcomes of the assessments. The first requires a general, overall (even exhaustive) view of the parents in their environment. The second, and typically the third, look for definitive evidence of consequences or output as a result of following a program or intervention. The latter assessment

tends to be more specialized than the former. Programs have already identified their goals, which are usually drawn from a general overall assessment and are therefore fewer. To demonstrate the impact of a program accurately, the assessment design is usually a more traditional one using control groups and pre- and post-testing.

The following discussion describes some ways used to assess parents' support systems, and present ways to evaluate intervention programs. References mentioned throughout the text will suggest additional resources. Note, however, that both types of assessment use similar instruments for gathering data. These will be described first before going into the other details.

Instruments for Assessing Parents' Support

Instruments used to assess parents' support include checklists, questionnaires, interviews, diaries, observations, and any combination of the above (Erickson and Kurz-Riemer, 1999). The sophistication of the instruments ranges from the simple (checklists) to the highly developed (questionnaires with measures of reliability and validity reported). The process may involve a combination of instruments, including a semi-structured interview that probes for further discussion of information reported elsewhere. Many researchers strongly suggest that data collection include an interview, during which the interviewer can individualize the parents' description of their support systems and needs (Dunst and Trivette, 1990; Cochran and Niego, 1995).

One of the simplest instruments may be a checklist which can be an effective way to find out about the support people have. Simple statements can tell whether or not a parent has experienced certain events, and how often. For instance, parents can respond to statements such as 'My baby eats at the same time every day,' or 'My mother frequently takes the baby,' on a five-point scale ranging from always to never (Heath, 1976).

Somewhat more complex direct questions can focus on the sources of support available to the parent, such as 'Please give me the names of all of the people who are important to you in one way or another' (Cochran and Niego, 1995, p. 399). This kind of question builds information about the parent's network. Questions can also focus on the kind of support available, as follows: 'Do you have close relationships that provide you with a sense of emotional security and well-being,' 'Can you count on anyone to provide you with emotional support (talking over problems and helping you make a difficult decision)?' 'Can you count on anyone to help you with daily tasks like grocery shopping, house cleaning, cooking, telephoning, giving you a ride?' (Wills and Shinar, 2000, p. 90). Responses to the above can be indicated on a seven-point scale ranging from 'completely true' to 'not at all true', reflecting the extent to which the statement describes their current social support (Cutrona, 1984). Such questions can even determine the kind of support that social policies or cultural beliefs provide for parents: 'The current emphasis on providing infants and young children quality daycare makes me feel confident in my ability to rear my children.' Here, a rating of '5' indicates that the emphasis makes the parent feel competent.

Interviews are a powerful method of gathering precise information. Parents can describe a time when someone told them that they were doing a good job of raising their child, and give details about the event such as who that person was, the tie that the parents have with that person, and how the parents felt about the interaction. Interviews can also follow a questionnaire. If a parent indicates on a questionnaire that the current emphasis on daycare does not make her feel confident, a follow-up interview question can allow her to describe more of her feelings, and explain what about the statement gave her concern.

Carl Dunst and Carol Trivette (1990), investigators with a long history of researching parental support, advise potential interviewers regarding how best to gather information. They suggest that interviewers do the following:

- Tell the family or person being interviewed the reasons why the data are being collected. For example, 'Could you please take the time to fill out this scale about what you might need so that I can be of assistance to you and your family?'
- Be very clear about how the results will be used. For example, 'After you complete the scale, I'd like us to go over your responses to get a better idea about your concerns and needs'.
- Use responses as a way of helping the family clarify and define what they perceive to be a concern or need. For example, 'You indicated that childcare is a need. Can you tell me more about what types of childcare you feel would be most beneficial?'
- Restate needs as they are expressed, in order to clarify that the family agrees with the interviewer's perceptions. For example, 'If I understand you correctly, you are saying that because you will be going back to work, you must find daycare that is available during hours that fit with your work schedule.'

The researchers conclude that, 'Attention to these four considerations help specify needs and the types of resources required to meet needs' (Dunst and Trivette, 1990, p. 337).

One of the more complex methods of gathering very specific information is that of Dunst and Trivette (1990). By repeatedly testing their assumptions and scales, they have developed a well-documented system called the Systematic Assessment of Social Support Inventory (SASSI), which uses both interview and self-report methods for obtaining five classes of social support information:

1 indication of need for particular types of support;
2 identification of an individual's or a family's personal social network;
3 description of types of support generally offered by personal social network;
4 description of the nature of social ties with personal social network members;
5 a measure of satisfaction with aid and assistance obtained from personal social network.

The SASSI is outstanding in its ability to help the respondents, by gentle questioning, to identify their specific needs and their sources of support for meeting those needs.

The above has covered a description of various tools used to identify and measure support and sources of support. For information beyond the scope of this chapter, Wills and Shinar (2000) provide an in-depth discussion of the issues involved in measuring perceived and received social support, an annotated list of tools, and a guide for developing a plan for assessing support for a specific program or research project (see also Brissette et al., 2000).

Assessing Support for Purposes of Program Planning

Two features help make for assessing a community effectively. One is to include the future participants in the assessment process, to ensure their wants and needs are addressed (Dunst and Trivette, 1990; Long, 1997). The other is to realize that the more detailed and inclusive the assessment is of a parent, group of parents, or community, the better the chances of planning an effective program or intervention (Erickson and Kurz-Riemer, 1999). A detailed, inclusive assessment of the support, interests, and life space of a parent, group of parents, or community would include information about the functional support received from the following:

- personal/social network members, such as spouse or partner, relatives, friends, neighbors, childcare providers, or clergy members;
- associational groups, such as church groups, interest clubs, self-help groups, block clubs, school groups, or sports leagues;
- community programs and professionals, such as public or private schools, senior citizens' programs;
- specialized professional services, such as public health clinics, early intervention programs, family preservation programs, substance abuse programs, or respite care (Erickson and Kurz-Riemer, 1999, p. 122).

Well-worded questions would obtain information about the functional support that each of these groups might provide. Questions such as: who from among these groups can you count on to provide childcare? Who from these groups says you are doing a good job raising your children? From whom can you get reliable information about raising children?

Knowledge about parents' information, interests, and needs related to child-rearing is part of any in-depth assessment for program planning (Debord et al., 1999). Figure 19.1 presents such a list. It includes information about parents' preferences as to how they like to receive or share knowledge as well as the information and skills they have. This list is based on an analysis of what society expects parents to do and a description of how parents go about doing what is expected of them (Heath, unpublished). It can be used as a checklist for parents to record the information and skills they have, or they can be given choices to mark what they have, and would like to discuss and their preferred kinds of programs. Professionals also can use the list to record the strengths and needs of the parents as they perceive them to be.

More and more planners are doing broad community assessments (FSA, 2000) gaining information about the exo- and macrosystems. Such an assessment should include the following potential community resources (adapted from Dunst et al., 1994, p. 146):

- econmic (money for necessities and emergencies);
- physical and environmental (adequate housing, safe neighborhood);
- food and clothing (at least two meals a day, enough clothes for each season);
- Health care (availability of general and emergency medical and dental care);
- vocational (opportunity to work, satisfaction with work);
- transportation and communication (means of getting to places and of contacting relatives and friends);
- adult education (available and accessible educational opportunities);
- child education (opportunities to play with other children, appropriate toys, good schools);
- childcare (help in routine dailycare, childcare while employed);
- recreational (opportunities for relaxing and fun activities);
- cultural (opportunities to share value-related experience).

This thorough assessment of the strengths and interests of a parent and a community is required to obtain the necessary information for effective detailed planning to establish a program that will be effective. It has two major difficulties: one, the list of such issues is too long for any one person to complete; and two, the assessment process can become so long and so laden with information that it is unmanageable.

Family Support America (2000) has outlined an approach to avoiding the pitfalls of too much information and overly lengthy questionnaires. FSA suggests incorporating the people of the community where a program may evolve into the assessment process. Resembling a form of strategic planning, this approach incorporates members of the community to identify jointly with program staff the strengths and needs of the people in the community. It recommends establishing a planning committee that draws from all segments of the community, including parents whom the program might serve, community and neighborhood leaders, representatives of social agencies and community organizations, and anyone in the community who has significant contact with children and families. The committee should also include potential funders.

The committee does the assessment of the community following the guide *Know Your Community: A Step-by-Step Guide to Community Needs and Resource Assessment* (Samuels, et al., 1995). Data are collected by using statistics about the community from secondary sources and by gathering information about the perspectives of residents. The latter may be gathered using checklists, interviews, and, most frequently, focus groups. The information gathered focuses on the assets and strengths of the community, as well as on its needs. Even with this comprehensive design there may not be enough attention given to the policy issues and cultural patterns that affect parents and their functioning in a specific community. (See Webster-Stratton (1998) for a description of

Information

___ Attachment, building and maintaining relationships
___ Developmental stages
___ Families of origin
___ Feelings and how to deal with them
___ Parent's goals
___ Beliefs systems
___ Learning styles
___ Needs people have in order to survive and to live happily
___ Using needs to motivate children

___ The parental role
___ Relevance of past experience
___ Safety issues
___ Self-esteem
___ Sibling and peer relationships
___ Temperament patterns
___ Values and ways of integrating them into family life.
___ Other

Skills
___ Advocate for children
___ Anticipate
___ Balance demands of work and family
___ Brainstorm
___ Calm self–take a perspective
___ Communicate effectively
___ Design an appropriate environment
___ Discipline
___ Empathize
___ Enjoy
___ Implement life skills
___ Manage stress
___ Negotiate
___ Observe objectively
___ Plan effectively

Play with:
___ young children
___ adolescents
___ Problem solve
___ Reflect, assess about situations
Relate to, respond to, interact with:
___ young children
___ adolescents
Resolve conflict with:
___ young children
___ adolescents
Teach and guide:
___ young children
___ adolescents
___ Think through an issue
___ Use community resources
___ Other

Preferred method of presenting content

___ Lectures, having information given me
___ Opportunities to integrate the knowledge into my situations
___ Sharing my situations
___ Hearing others' experiences
___ Being given solutions
___ Figuring out solutions
___ Videos
___ Reading material

Preferred kind of leadership

___ comes from group
___ trained in specific curriculum
___ highly trained in content
___ has effective group skills

Figure 19.1 *List of parents' information, skills, interests and preferences (Heath, 1998a)*

how another program followed the family support principles in developing a program.)

The strength of this approach is that as it gathers the information needed for effective planning, it involves many community members whose input is invaluable in identifying the strengths and needs of the community.

For program planning that is more circum-spect, this kind of in-depth analysis may not be needed. In some research or planning it often is not necessary to have detailed information regarding the extent and intensity of every social relationship. Dunst and Trivette (1990, p. 330) concluded that 'rather, the goal is to gain insight about the ways in which resources and support flow between the family and personal network members'. Consequently, Dunst and Trivette (1990, p. 330) developed a system for obtaining specific information about the following:

- relationship support, by assessing it 'in terms of the existence and quantity of social relationships;'
- structure support, assessed 'in terms of the structural features that exist among and between sets of social relationships;'
- constitutional support, assessed 'in terms of the need for certain types of aid and assistance and the congruence between what is needed and offered;'
- functional support, assessed 'in terms of the particular types of aid; and
- assistance that are offered by personal social network members and the manner in which support is offered;'
- satisfaction with support, 'as assessed in terms of the subjective evaluation of the degree to which one feels "supported".'

This system of assessing support has proven effective in helping parents obtain the support, especially instrumental support, that they need. By limiting detail, Dunst and Trivette (1990) found that they were able to analyze the properties of the social network more efficiently for a specific purpose. This approach illustrates another way of assessing the needs of a parent or group of parents for program development that is less extensive than the general assessment. However, to gain this specificity took an extensive research project of testing groups, planning interventions, and measuring their effectiveness that is not appropriate if the idea is to understand a community's needs.

We have presented as examples two methods of obtaining information about parents' support or the need thereof for the purposes of program planning. We now turn to the process of assessing the effectiveness of a program or intervention.

Assessing the Effectiveness of a Program or Intervention

In assessing the effectiveness of a program or intervention, researchers continue frequently to implement a modified classical design of pre- and post-testing with intervention and control groups. Randomly assigning subjects to experimental or control groups is usually not possible (Hauser-Cram, 1990). Edward Brown (1998), for example, investigated whether training parents could have an effect on their children's disruptive school behavior. The supportive content of the intervention was information, focusing on parenting skills presented in a warm, friendly, emotionally supportive environment. A group of volunteer parents, whose children qualified as

disruptive, were divided into an experimental and a control group. The experimental group of parents attended four training sessions focusing on parenting skills. The children of the two groups had received the same number of referrals for defiant behaviors in the nine weeks before their parents received training. Nine weeks following the training the two groups of students differed significantly, with the experimental group receiving significantly fewer referrals (Brown, 1998). Other research using this modified classical design has looked at a parent education intervention to protect children following divorce (Shifflett, 1998), and to change attitudes toward children of incarcerated parents (Spring, 1999).

Using a traditional research design has some serious drawbacks. For one, traditional research design is expensive, time-consuming, and requires a large number of subjects to obtain significant results. A sound design demands that a control group be used for comparison, yet since control groups do not receive treatment, problematic ethical issues arise concerning the denial of services (Hauser-Cram, 1990). 'Objective' behavioral measures involve observations that are difficult to obtain and to score reliably. Such detailed research can interfere with other programs or work in the setting. Lastly, current writing on research design recognizes the diversity of variables involved in preventive work, such as the personality characteristics of the people involved. These cannot be accommodated in the traditional design (Hauser-Cram, 1990).

Consequently, current views on research design suggest that one evaluation should not attempt to incorporate all possible variations. Rather evaluators should 'aim for the development of a series of carefully designed studies with well-chosen outcomes on a tightly determined set of subgroups' (Hauser-Cram, 1990, p. 599; see also Tolan, et al., 1998, for further discussion of issues related to program development and assessment). From data derived from such studies, patterns of relationships can be identified. Carl Dunst and his associates used such an approach to develop a conceptual framework for defining the major components of social support and their separate dimensions, and for depicting the direct and indirect influences of social support on parent, family, parent–child, and child functioning (Dunst and Trivette, 1990). Neil Guterman's (1997) meta-analysis of 18 controlled early intervention studies is an example of this trend. The families in these studies were at risk of abusing or neglecting their children. Several trends emerged from the meta-analysis, including the essential role of parenting education support, and directions for future program design and study, particularly with respect to addressing parental powerlessness. Another such analysis reviewed parenting education interventions for parents with intellectual disabilities identified in 20 published studies. This analysis also found interesting trends, such as the importance of training parents in basic childcare and of using behavioral approaches (Feldman, 1994). (See Hauser-Cram, 1988, for a review of meta-analysis.)

An example of the effectiveness of this approach is the Fair Start Initiative. Launched in seven diverse communities in the early 1980s, it differs from the studies mentioned above in that the programs reported were conducted simultaneously, with a common funder, and with some contact among the various sites. All had a similar objective: 'to improve chances for the survival and healthy development of infants and young children in disadvantaged low-income families' (quoted in Larner et al., 1992, p. 6). The reports of each of the initiatives included a description of the program design and implementation, a review of the costs of implementation, and a summary of the findings. As a consequence, the report not only presents an overview but can offer more insight into some findings because they were repeated in several locations or under similar circumstances. For example, projects held in medical settings were more effective in having the parents take their children to well-baby clinics and in having them immunized than did projects situated away from clinics. In three of the projects, the staff had a great deal of contact with the families after the babies' birth, during which they emphasized parent education. Babies in these projects tended to be more alert and to function better on a screening measurement (Larner, 1992).

These studies are examples of the current trend toward *meta-analysis*, an analysis that combines the results of other studies, to identify trends that could not be identified in a single study. The move to meta-analysis has come with the increased understanding of the complexity of measuring support and the new sophisticated statistical procedures that can be easily calculated on modern computers, making meta-analyses simpler to perform.

Assessment of parents' support achieves two purposes. It creates a description of the support a parent or group of parents have. This information is an integral part of any program development and is useful when seeking funding. It also evaluates the effectiveness of an intervention or validates a research assumption. This information is important for both validating programs and ensuring continued funding, and for adding to our general understanding of the role of support in the health of parents and their children. The two purposes require different kinds of information and arrive at different kinds of conclusions. Both are needed for the understanding of and providing for parents' needs for support.

CONCLUSION

When reviewing research on support, it is easy to get involved in attempting to identify different kinds of support, to become entranced by significant relationships between interventions and results, to be enthused about the potential for children's development, and to lose sight of the role of parents in the process of providing support to improve children's opportunities. Parents are the intervening factor between the provision of support and the outcome.

Parents, to use the support offered them, must be thinking and reflective people. They are the ones deciding what components in the environment are helpful to their child-rearing efforts and what are not. As the work of Bandura (2000) is demonstrating, the 'self system is not merely a conduit for external influences.' He continues, 'human agency operates generatively and proactively rather than just reactively' (Bandura, 2000, p. 29). Parents are not only an important buffer between their children and their environment (Belsky, 1984), they create, especially for the young child, a major part of the environment in which the child grows. Many perform this task conscientiously through a process that includes complex cognitive skills (Heath, unpublished). Support is not accepted or rejected on a random basis but, for many, through a conscious decision-making process (Holden and Hawk, 2003).

The current trend of including parents in program planning and intervention recognizes the parents' cognitive ability to know what may be useful to a specific group of parents and what may not. As described above, the work of Carl Dunst and Carol Trivitte (1990) as well as Family Support America (2000) uses this perspective of parents by giving them an active role in any program planning. Both Star Parenting (Crary, 1994) and Parenting Creatively (Heath, 1983, 1998b) have done the same in parent education. Their programs provide a framework for parents to figure out how they themselves want to handle specific situations. More than simple problem-solving, these approaches draw systematically on the developmental literature to serve as guides for parents. Encouraging parents to decide how they want to raise their children gives parents a feeling of competence (appraisal) and acceptance (emotional support), while still providing them with the information and skills they seek.

This chapter is a summary of the literature on parent support, the meanings of the term, the ways support is provided and the means of measuring its effectiveness. The review has revealed the importance of the role of parents as thinking reflective people in the support process.

REFERENCES

Argyle, M. (1992) Benefits produced by supportive social relationships. In Veiel, H. and Baumann, U. (eds) *The Meaning and Measurement of Social Support.* New York: Hemisphere, pp. 13–32.

Auerbach, A. (in Cooperation with Child Study Association of America) (1968) *Parents Learn through Discussion: Principles and Practices of Parent Group Education.* New York: John Wiley.

Bandura, A. (2000) Self-efficacy: the foundation of agency. In Perrig, W. and Grob, A. (eds) *Control of Human Behavior, Mental Processes, and Consciousness: Essays in Honor of the 60th Birthday of August Flammer.* Mahaw, NJ: Lawrence Erlbaum, pp. 17–34.

Bavolek, S. (ed.) (1997). *Multicultural Parenting Educational Guide: Understanding Cultural Parenting Values, Traditions and Practices.* Park City: UT: Family Development Resources.

Beckman, P. (1984) A transactional view of stress in families of handicapped children. In Lewis, M. (ed.) *Beyond the Dyad: Genesis of Behavior,* Vol. 4. New York: Plenum Press, pp. 281–98.

Behrman, R. (ed.) (1997) Welfare to work. *The Future of Children,* **7**(1). The David and Lucile Packard Foundation, 308 Second St, Suite 102, Los Altos, CA 94022.

Behrman, R. (ed.) (2002) Children and welfare reform. *The Future of Children,* **12**(1). The David and Lucile Packard Foundation, 308 Second St, Suite 102, Los Altos, CA 94022.

Belsky, J. (1984) The determinants of parenting: a process model. *Child Development,* **55**, 83–96.

Belsky, J. and Kelly, J. (1994) *The Transition to Parenthood: How a First Child Changes a Marriage.* New York: Delacorte Press.

Benedek, T. (1956) 'Psychobiological aspects of mothering. *American Journal of Orthopsychiatry,* **25**, 272–8.

Berger, E. (1981) *Parents as Partners in Education: The School and Home Working Together.* St Louis, MO: The C.V. Mosby Co.

Birkel, R. and Reppucci, N. (1983) Social networks, information-seeking, and the utilization of services. *American Journal of Community Psychology,* **11**(2), 185–205.

Bitsika, V. and Sharpley, C. (1999) An explanatory examination of the effects of support groups on the well-being of parents of children with autism: general counseling. *Journal of Applied Health Behavior,* **1**(2), 16–22.

Bitsika, V. and Sharpley, C. (2000) Development and testing of the effects of support groups on the well-being of parents of children with autisim II: specific stress management techniques. *Journal of Applied Health Behavior,* **2**(1), 8–15.

Bowlby, J. (1969) *Attachment: Volume I of Attachment and Loss.* New York: Basic Books.

Bowman, B. (1997) Preschool as family support. In Dunst, C. and Wolery, M. (eds) *Advances in Early Education and Day Care: Family Policy and Practice in Early Child Care.* Greenwich, CO: Jai Press, pp. 157–70.

Braun, L., Coplan, J. and Sonnenschein, P. (1984) *Helping Parents in Groups: A Leader's Handbook.* Boston, MA: Resource Communications.

Brazelton, T.B. (1992) *Touchpoints: Your Child's Emotional and Behavioral Development.* Reading, MA: Addison-Wesley.

Brim, O. (1965) *Education for Child Rearing.* New York: Free Press.

Brissette, I., Cohen, S. and Seeman, T. (2000) Measuring social integration and social networks. In Cohen, S., Underwood, L. and Gottlieb, B. (eds) *Social Support Measurement and Intervention: A Guide for Health and Social Scientists.* New York: Oxford University Press, pp. 53–85.

Brock, G., Oertwein, M. and Coufal, J. (1993) Parent education: theory, research, and practice. In Arcus, M., Schvaneveldt, J. and Moss, J. (eds) *Handbook of Family Life Education: Foundation of Family Life Education,* Vol. 2. Newbury Park, CA: Sage Publications, pp. 87–114.

Bronfenbrenner, U. (1979) *The Ecology of Human Development: Experiments by Nature and Design.* Cambridge, MA: Harvard University Press.

Brown, E. (1998) The effects of a parent education training program on the classroom behavior of openly defiant middle school students. *Dissertation Abstracts International Section A: Humanities and Social Sciences,* **59**(1–a), 0090.

Buchmueller, A.D. (1968) Introduction. In Auerbach A. (ed.) in Cooperation with Child Study Association of America, *Parents Learn through Discussion: Principles and Practices of Parent Group Education.* New York: John Wiley, pp. xi–xii.

Burggraf, S. (1997) *The Feminine Economy and Economic Man: Reviving the Role of Family in the Postindustrial Age.* Reading, MA: Addison-Wesley.

Carter, N. (1996) *See How We Grow: A Report on the Status of Parenting Education in the US.* Philadelphia, PA: The Pew Charitable Trusts.

Chenoweth, L. (2000) Grandparent education. In Hayslip, B. (ed.) *Grandparents Raising Grandchildren: Theoretical, Empirical, and Clinical Perspectives.* New York: Springer, pp. 307–26.

Cochran, M. and Niego, S. (1995) Parenting and social networks. In Bornstein, M. (ed.) *Handbook of*

Parenting. Vol. 3 Status and Social Conditions of Parenting. New York: Lawrence Erlbaum, pp. 393–418.

Cohen, S. (1992) Stress, social support and disorder. In Veiel, H. and Baumann, U. (eds) *The Meaning and Measurement of Social Support.* New York: Hemisphere, pp. 109–24.

Cohen, S., Gottlieb, B. and Underwood, L. (2000) Social relationships and health. In Cohen, S., Underwood, L. and Gottlieb B. (eds) *Social Support Measurement and Intervention: A Guide for Health and Social Scientists.* New York: Oxford University Press, pp. 3–25.

Cooke, B., Rossmann, M., McCubbin, H. and Patterson, J. (1988) Examining the definition and assessment of social support: a resource for individuals and families, *Family Relations,* **37**, 211–16.

Cowan, A.P. and Cowan, C. (1988) Changes in marriage during the transition to parenthood: must we blame the baby? In Michaels, G. and Goldberg, W. (eds) *The Transition to Parenthood: Current Theory and Research.* Cambridge, England: Press Syndicate of the University of Cambridge, pp. 114–54.

Crary, E. (1994) *Love and Limits: Guidance Tools for Creative Parenting.* Seattle, WA: Parenting Press.

Crittenden, A. (2001) *The Price of Motherhood: Why the Most Important Job in the World is Still the Least Valued.* New York: Henry Holt.

Cutrona, C. (1984) Social support and stress in the transition to parenthood, *Journal of Abnormal Psychology,* **93**(4), 378–90.

Cutrona, C. and Russell, D. (1990) Type of social support and specific stress: toward a theory of optimal matching. In Sarason, B., Sarason, I. and Pierce, G. (eds) *Social Support: An Interactional View.* New York: John Wiley, pp. 319–66.

Darling, R. (1990) Parental entrepreneurship: a consumerist response to professional dominance. In Nagler, M. (ed.) *Perspectives on Disability: Text and Readings on Disability.* Palo Alto, CA: Health Markets Research, pp. 287–301.

Debord, K., Heath, H., McDermott, D. and Wolfe, R. (1999) *Family Support and Parenting Education.* Chicago, IL: Family Support America.

Deutsch, H. (1945) *The Psychology of Women,* Vol. II. New York: Greene and Stratton.

Dunst, C. and Trivette, C. (1990) Assessment of social support in early intervention programs. In Meisels, S. and Shonkoff, J. (eds) *Handbook of Early Childhood Intervention.* Cambridge, MA: Cambridge University Press, pp. 326–49.

Dunst, C., Trivette, C.M. and Deal, A.G. (eds) (1994) *Supporting and Strengthening Families: Vol. 1. Methods, Strategies, and Practices.* Cambridge, MA: Brookline Books.

Egeland, B. and Erickson, M. (1993) Implications of attachment theory for prevention and intervention. In Parens, H. and Kramer, S. (eds) *Prevention in Mental Health.* Northvale, NJ: Jason Aronson, pp. 23–50.

Einzig, H. (1996) Parenting education and support. In Bayne, R., Horton, I. and Bimrose, J. (eds) *New Directions in Counselling.* New York: Routledge, pp. 220–34.

Erickson, M. and Kurz-Riemer, K. (1999) *Infants, Toddlers, and Families: A Framework for Support and Intervention.* New York: Guilford Press.

Erikson, E. (1950) *Childhood and Society.* New York: W.W. Norton.

Erikson, E. (1968) *Identity Youth and Crisis.* New York: W.W. Norton.

Feldman, M. (1994) Parenting education for parents with intellectual disabilities: a review of outcome studies. *Research in Developmental Disabilities,* **15**(4), 299–302.

Ferguson, H. (2001) Promoting child protection, welfare and healing: the case for developing best practice. *Child and Family Social Work,* **6**(1), 1–12.

Fine, M. and Lee, S.W. (eds) (2001) *Handbook of Diversity in Parent Education: The Changing Faces of Parenting and Parent Education.* San Diego, CA: Academic Press.

FSA (2000) *Family Support Centers: A Program Manager's Toolkit: Program Planning and Evaluation,* Vol. 1. Chicago IL: Family Support America.

Galinsky, E. (1999). *Ask the Children: What America's Children Really Think About Working Parent.* New York: William Morrow.

Garbarino, J. (1990) The human ecology of early risk. In Meisels, S. and Shonkoff, J. (eds) *Handbook of Early Childhood Intervention.* Cambridge, MA: Cambridge University Press, pp. 78–96.

Garbarino, J. and Kostelny, K. (1995) Parenting and public policy. In Bornstein, M. (ed.) *Handbook of Parenting. Vol. 3 Status and Social Conditions of Parenting.* New York: Lawrence Erlbaum, pp. 417–36.

Gerris, J., Van As, N., Wels, P. and Janssens, J. (1998) From parent education to family empowerment programs. In L'Abate, L. (ed.) *Family Psychopathology: The Relational Roots of Dysfunctional Behavior.* New York: Guilford Press, pp. 401–26.

Gerson, K. (1997) The social construction of fatherhood. In Arendell, T. (ed.) *Contemporary Parenting: Challenges and Issues.* London: Sage Publications, pp. 119–53.

Gonzales-Mena, J. (1997) *Multicultural Issues in Child Care,* 2nd edition. Mountain View, CA: Mayfield Publishing.

Gottlieb, B. (1992) Quandaries in translating support concepts to intervention. In Veiel, H. and Baumann, U. (eds) *The Meaning and Measurement of Social Support.* New York: Hemisphere Publishing, pp. 293–312.

Gottlieb, B. and Pancer, S.M. (1988) Social networks and the transition to parenthood. In Michaels, G.Y. and Goldberg, W.A. (eds) *The Transition to Parenthood: Current Theory and Research.* Cambridge, England: Press Syndicate of the University of Cambridge, pp. 235–69.

Guterman, N. (1997) Early prevention of physical child abuse and neglect: existing evidence and future directions. *Child Maltreatment: Journal of the American Professional Society on the Abuse of Children,* **2**(1), 12–34.

Halpern, R. (1992) Issues of program design and implementation. In Larner, M., Halpern, R. and Harkavy, O. (eds) *Fair Start for Children: Lessons Learned from Seven Demonstration Projects.* New Haven, CO: Yale University Press, pp. 179–97.

Halpern, R., Larner, M. and Harkavy, O. (1992) The child survival/fair start initiative in context. In Larner, M., Halpern, R. and Harkavy, O. (eds) *Fair Start for Children: Lessons Learned from Seven Demonstration Projects.* New Haven, CO: Yale University Press, pp. 246–56.

Harris, T. (1992) Some reflections on the process of social support and nature of unsupportive behaviors. In Veiel, V. and Baumann, U. (eds) *The Meaning and Measurement of Social Support.* New York: Hemisphere Publishing, pp. 171–90.

Hauser-Cram, P. (1988) The possibilities and limitations of meta-analysis in understanding family program impact. In Weiss, H. and Jacobs, F. (eds) *Evaluating Family Programs.* Hawthorne, NY: Aldine de Gruyter, pp. 445–60.

Hauser-Cram, P. (1990) Designing meaningful evaluations of early intervention services. In Meisels, S. and Shonkoff, J. (eds) *Handbook of Early Childhood Intervention.* Cambridge, MA: Cambridge University Press, pp. 583–602.

Heath, H. (1976) Determinants of parenting behavior: the effect of support and information on the breast feeding experience. Unpublished dissertation, University of Michigan.

Heath, H. (1983) *Parents Planning: A Manual.* Haverford, PA: Conrow Publishing.

Heath, H. (1998a) *Choosing Parenting Curricula Based on the Interests, Needs, and Preferences of the Parents Who will Use It.* Internet resource URL: http://parenthood.library.wisc.edu

Heath, H. (1998b) *Planning: A Key to Mastering the Challenge of Parenting.* Haverford, PA: Conrow Publishing.

Heath, H. (Submitted for publication) *Deciphering the Parenting Experience: A Theory.*

Hecimovic, A., Powell, T. and Christensen, L. (1999) Supporting families in meeting their needs. In Zager, D. (ed.) *Autism: Identification, Education and Treatment.* Mahway, NJ: Lawrence Erlbaum, pp. 261–300.

House, J. (1981) *Work Stress and Social Support.* Reading, MA: Addison-Wesley.

Hunter, A. (1997) Counting on grandmothers: black mothers' and fathers' reliance on grandmothers for parenting support. *Journal of Family Issues,* 18(3), 251–69.

Hunter, A., Pearson, J., Ialong, N. and Kellam, S. (1998) Parenting alone to multiple caregivers: child care and parenting arrangements in black and white Urban Families. *Family Relations: Interdisciplinary Journal of Applied Family Studies,* 47(4), 343–53.

Johnson, H., Cournoyer, D., Fisher, G., McQuillan, B., Moriarty, S., Richerts, A., Stanek, E., Stockford, C. and Yhirigian, B. (2000) Children's emotional and behavioral disorders: attributing of parental responsibility by professionals. *American Journal of Orthopsychiatry,* 70(3), 327–39.

Kagan, S. and Seitz, V. (1988) Family support programs for new parents. In Michaels, G. and Goldberg, W. (eds) *The Transition to Parenthood: Current Theory and Research.* New York: Cambridge University Press, pp. 311–41.

Kerr, S. and McIntosh, J.B. (2000) Coping when a child has a disability: exploring the impact of parent-to-parent support. *Child: Care, Health and Development,* 26(4), 309–21.

Kluger, M. (2001) What works in family support services. In Kluger, M., Alexander, G. and Curtis, P. (eds) *What Works in Child Welfare.* Washington, DC: Child Welfare League of America, pp. 3–9.

Kraemer, S. and Roberts, J. (eds) (1996) *The Politics of Attachment: Towards a Secure Society.* London: England: Free Association Books.

Kurz, D. (1997) Doing parenting: mothers, care work, and policy. In Arendell, T. (ed.) *Contemporary Parenting: Challenges and Issues.* London: Sage Publications, pp. 92–118.

Larner, M. (1992) Realistic expectations; review of evaluation findings. In Larner, M., Halpern, R. and Harkavy, O. (eds), *Fair Start for Children: Lessons Learned from Seven Demonstration Projects.* New Haven, CO: Yale University Press, pp. 218–45.

Larner, M., Halpern, R. and Harkavy, O. (1992) The fair start story: an overview. In Larner, M., Halpern, R. and Harkavy, O. (eds) *Fair Start for Children: Lessons Learned from Seven Demonstration Projects.* New Haven, CO: Yale University Press, pp. 3–10.

LeVine, R. (1975) Parental goals: a cross-cultural view. In Leichter, H. (ed.) *The Family as Educator.* New York: Teachers College Press, pp. 52–65.

Lew, A. (1999) Parenting education: selected programs and current and future needs. In Watts, R. (ed.) *Interventions and Strategies in Counseling and Psychotherapy.* Philadelphia, PA: Accelerated Development.

Long, N. (1997) Parent education/training in the USA: current status and future trends. *Clinical Child Psychology and Psychiatry,* 24, 501–15.

Long, N. and Leonard, L. (1992) Parents perspective of the desirability of pediatricians being able to provide information on various child/parenting issues. *Clinical Research,* 40, 815A.

Maslow, A. (1962) *Toward a Psychology of Being.* New York: D. Van Nostrand.

Merrill, E. (1987) Learning how to mother. *Anthropology & Education Quarterly,* 18, 222–40.

Minde, K., Shosenberg, N. and Marton, P. (1982) The effects of self-help groups in a premature nursery on maternal autonomy and caretaking style 1 year later. In Bond, L. and Joffe, J. (eds) *Facilitating Infant and Early Childhood Development.* Hanover, NH: University Press of New England, pp. 240–58.

Minturn, L. and Landbert, W. (1964) *Mother of Six Cultures.* New York: John Wiley.

Murray, N.G., Kelder, S.H., Parcel, G.S., Frankowski, R. and Orpinas, P. (1999) A randomized trial of a parent education intervention to prevent violence among middle school children. *Health Education Research*, **14**(3), 421–6.

Nagy, M.C., Leeper, J. Hullett-Robertson, S. and Northrup, R. (1992) The Rural Alabama Pregnancy and Infant Health Project: a rural clinic reaches out. In Larner, M., Halpern, R. and Harkavy, O. (eds) *Fair Start for Children: Lessons Learned from Seven Demonstration Projects*. New Haven, CO: Yale University Press, pp. 218–45.

Nedlar, S. and McAfee, O. (1979) *Working with Parents: Guidelines for Early Childhood and Elementary Teachers*. Belmont, CA: Wadsworth Publishing.

Noddings, N. (1984) *Caring: A Feminine Approach to Ethics and Moral Education*. Berkeley, CA: University of California Press.

Pesoff, J. (1998) Poverty and early childhood developmental delay: perspectives from hispanic mothers. *Dissertation Abstract International, Section A: Humanities and Social Sciences*, **59**(4–A).

Phillips, N. (1997) Growing up in the urban environment: opportunities and obstacles for children In Phillips, N. and Straussner, S. (eds) *Children in the Urban Environment: Linking Social Policy and Clinical Practice*. Springfield, IL: Charles Thomas, pp. 5–24.

Pizzo, P. (1990) Parent advocacy: a resource for early intervention. In Meisels, S. and Shonkoff, J. (eds) *Handbook of Early Childhood Intervention*. New York: Cambridge University Press, pp. 668–78.

Red Horse, J. (1997) Traditional American indian family systems. *Families, Systems and Health*, **15**(3), 243–50.

Reis, H. and Collins, N. (2000) Measuring relationship properties and interactions. In Cohen, S., Underwood, L. and Gottlieb, B. (eds) *Social Support Measurement and Intervention: A Guide for Health and Social Scientists*. New York: Oxford University Press, pp. 136–92.

Rook, K. (1992) Detrimental aspects of social relationships: taking stock of an emerging literature. In Veiel, H. and Baumann, U. (eds) *The Meaning and Measurement of Social Support*. New York: Hemisphere Publishing, pp. 157–69.

Rosenthal, M. and Geckler, C. (1997) Family intervention in neuropsychology. In Horton, A., Wedding, D. and Webster, J. (eds) *The Neuro-Psychology Handbook, Vol. 2: Treatment Issues and Special Populations*, 2nd edition. New York: Springer, pp. 47–72.

Samuels, B., Ahsan, N. and Garcia, J. (1995) *Know Your Community: A Step-by-Step Guide to Community Needs and Resources Assessment*. Chicago, IL: Family Support America.

Sarason, I., Sarason, B. and Pierce, G. (1992) Three context of social support. In Veiel, H. and Baumann, U. (eds) *The Meaning and Measurement of Social Support*. New York: Hemisphere Publishing, pp. 143–54.

Schlossman, S. (1979) The parent education game: the politics of child psychology in the 1970s. In Leichter, H. (ed.), *Families and Communities as Educators*. Columbia University, NY: Teachers' College Press, pp. 224–44.

Schlossman, S. (1983) The formative era in American parent education: overview and interpretation. In Haskins, R. and Adams, D. (eds) *Parent Education and Public Policy*. Norwood, NJ: Ablex Publishing, pp. 7–39.

Scott, K. (1999) Parenting boys identified as having learning disabilities: a meaning-making perspective. *Dissertation Abstracts International, Section B: The Sciences and Engineering*, **60**(6–B), 3021.

Shifflett, K. (1998) A program for educating parents about the effects of divorce and conflict on children. *Dissertation Abstracts International, Section B: The Sciences and Engineering*, **58**(12–B), 6849.

Simpson, R. (1997) *The Role of the Mass Media in Parenting Education*. Boston: Center for Health Communication, Harvard School of Public Health.

Smuts, A. (1996) Science discovers the child: a history of the early scientific study of children. *Dissertation Abstracts International, Section A: Humanities and Social Sciences*, **56**(12–A), 4919.

Solomon, B. (1987) Empowerment: social work in oppressed communities. *Journal of Social Work Practice*, **2**(4), 79–91.

Spring, J. (1999) The effect of parent education on knowledge of parenting skills and attitude change of incarcerated mothers. *Dissertation Abstracts International, Section B: The Sciences and Engineering*, **60**(6–B), 3022.

Thoits, P. (1992) Social support functions and network structures: a supplemental view. In Veiel, H. and Baumann, U. (eds) *The Meaning and Measurement of Social Support*. New York: Hemisphere Publishing, pp. 57–62.

Tolan, P., Quintana, E. and Gorman-Smith, D. (1998) Prevention approaches for families. In L'Abate, L. (ed.), *Family Psychopathology: The Relational Roots of Dysfunctional Behavior*. New York: The Guilford Press, pp. 379–400.

Turner, R.J. (1992) Measuring social support: issues of concept and method. In Veiel, H. and Baumann, U. (eds) *The Meaning and Measurement of Social Support*. New York: Hemisphere Publishing, pp. 217–33.

Ursprung, A. (1990) Family crisis related to the deinstitutionalization of a mentally retarded child. In Nagler, M. (ed.) *Perspectives on Disability: Text and Readings on Disability*. Palo Alto, CA: Health Markets Research, pp. 302–8.

Vaux, A. (1992) Assessment of social support. In Veiel, H. and Baumann, U. (eds) *The Meaning and Measurement of Social Support*. New York: Hemisphere Publishing, pp. 193–216.

Veiel, H. and Baumann, U. (1992) The many meanings of social support. In Veiel, H. and Baumann, U. (eds) *The Meaning and Measurement of Social Support*. New York: Hemisphere Publishing, pp. 1–9.

Walker, S. and Riley, D. (2001) Involvement of the personal social network as a factor in parent education effectiveness. *Family Relations: Interdisciplinary Journal of Applied Family Studies*, **50**(2), 186–93.

Webster-Stratton, C. (1998) Parent training with low-income families: promoting parental engagement through a collaborative approach. In Lutzker, (ed.) *Handbook of Child Abuse Research and Treatment.* New York: Plenum Press, pp. 183–210.

Weiss, R. (1976) Transition states and other stressful situations: their nature and programs for their management. In Caplan, G. (ed.) *Support Systems and Mutual Help: Multidisciplinary Explorations.* New York: Grune and Stratton, pp. 213–32.

Wills, T. and Shinar, O. (2000) Measuring perceived and received social support. In Cohen, S., Underwood, L. and Gottlieb, B. (eds) *Social Support Measurement and Intervention: A Guide for Health and Social Scientists.* New York: Oxford University Press, pp. 86–135.

Zero to Three (1997) Parents Speak: Findings from Focus Group Research on Early Childhood Development.

Report by Belden & Russonello Research and Communications. Washington, DC: Zero to Three, 17 April.

Zigler, E. and Hall, N. (2000) *Child Development and Social Policy: Theory and Applications.* Boston, MA: McGraw Hill.

Zigler, E. and Styfco, S. (1996) Head start and early childhood intervention: the changing course of social science and social policy. In Zigler, E., Kagan, S. and Hall, N. (eds) *Children Families and Government: Preparing for the Twenty-first Century.* Cambridge, MA: Cambridge University Press, pp. 32–155.

20

Community-based Support for Parents

Judy Hutchings and Carolyn Webster-Stratton

SUMMARY

Rearing children is one of the hardest jobs facing adults in our society and one for which there is least preparation. Moreover, several aspects of the job of parenting have become more difficult in recent years. Much has been learned about the risk and protective factors associated with different developmental outcomes for children and the important role parents can play in promoting children's social, emotional and academic capacity and competence. Our current understanding is that many parents are not well prepared to do their best for their children.

In this chapter we consider factors that can make parenting more challenging and describe the growing number of interventions, in statutory and voluntary services, that have been developed to support parents and children within their own communities. We describe how working preventively and collaboratively with families within their own communities and building their links with schools can achieve good outcomes for children. Some of the information on practice has been drawn from work in Britain, where the first author is based. There is also a description of the work of the second author who is based in Seattle, USA. The principles, however, readily apply to and are informed by other settings.

The challenge facing parents today is growing. The increase in childhood conduct disorders, now involving up to 20 per cent of all children in Britain and the USA (Rutter et al., 1975), is one example of the problems faced by many parents. Early childhood conduct problems are occurring in increasing numbers and, if unresolved, lead to delinquency and subsequent adult mental health problems and/or violent criminal behaviour. These difficulties are costly to society (Kazdin, 1993; Scott et al., 2001a) and resistant to intervention if they are left untreated for too long. In financial terms these children cost ten times more than other children in regard to their demands on education, social welfare, community and mental health services and the judicial and penal systems (Robbins, 1981).

This growing problem is being tackled by public services in health, education and social welfare and by voluntary agencies, many of whom depend to a significant extent on state funding for many of their activities. The demand for effective programmes to curb and prevent children's disruptive, unruly and antisocial behaviour has never been greater. All developed countries are struggling to deal with the rise in antisocial behaviour, particularly involving substance use and often involving crime. As an example, juvenile arrests for serious violent crimes in the US have increased by 50 per cent in a ten-year period (Cook and Laub, 1998).

Conduct disorders are the most common reason for referral to children's mental health services (Offord et al., 1987) and the most frequent problem domain in clinical practice (Kazdin, 1990). Even when a service is available, only 10 per cent of these children get access to a specialist service (Hutchings, 1996) and even fewer find their way to one where practice is well developed and evidence based (Scott et al., 2001b). Referred children are not necessarily those most in need of help. Many of the most needy families simply do not seek referral for mental health services or accept help because they perceive these services as stigmatizing and inaccessible.

The search for effective ways to prevent the costly problem of childhood conduct disorders has become a priority in most Western countries. Given the numbers involved, governments recognize that early community-based interventions are the most cost-efficient and effective way to approach this problem. 'Head Start' programmes in the US, and the newer 'Sure Start' programmes in the UK are attempting to do this. Interventions that begin in the early school years are a strategic and long-term attempt to prevent or reduce anti-social and rule-breaking behaviours before they lead to well-established negative reputations, academic failure and escalating problems in adolescence, of which persistent and violent crime are the extremes. Few services, however, succeed in addressing specific issues associated with recruiting parents who, by virtue of their multiple problems, have traditionally been hard to engage.

In the UK, the Sure Start programme, launched in 1999, provides community support for all families with children under the age of 4 years in designated high social-exclusion areas. The Head Start programme in the US, which was established in the 1960s, is shifting its focus from providing early enrichment for 'at risk' 4-year-old children, four hours, four days a week, to providing more comprehensive family support starting in infancy and extending to full day programmes. Unlike Sure Start, however, it is predominantly a means-tested, particularized (not universal) service in designated areas. Both Sure Start and Head Start are important services through which wide-ranging resources are directed to support families whose children are identified as being at risk. Both are currently being developed and researched.

Over the last century there have been huge social changes. Family size has fallen and 50 per cent of new mothers report not having had contact with a small baby before having their own. Many new parents have limited experience of young children, which restricts their knowledge of what to expect of their child and can result in unrealistic expectations. Many new parents no longer live near their families of origin, thus restricting their access to helpful advice and support. When this is coupled with increasing breakdown in couple relationships, single parenthood, unemployment, poverty and social isolation, child-rearing becomes disrupted and parenting more challenging.

We are now aware, more than at any other time in the past, that poverty is an increasingly common experience for large numbers of families, of whom many are single mothers. This is, in part, a result of growth of inequality in income, and loss of jobs in traditional industries resulting in declining unskilled and semi-skilled work. Families with children are over-represented among the poorest households in Western countries. Despite fiscal and other policies, an increasing number depend on means-tested benefits, and on loans and credit, for the money they need to survive. Low-income households are at greatest risk of falling into debt and those with larger families, and lone mothers in particular, are vulnerable both to debt and to the problems of borrowing money to pay off debts. The gap between the living standards of rich and poor households is growing steadily wider in the UK, even under a Labour Government, and the poorest households are not only losing out relatively but perhaps also becoming poorer in absolute terms.

There are increasing concentrations of poor families in specific geographical areas and escape from poverty is becoming increasingly rare. Poverty and unemployment diminish resources to resolve problems in child mental health and welfare through their effects on parents. Neighbourhoods with concentrations of marked vulnerability have child abuse and infant mortality rates many times higher than those found in better off local communities. At a time when the pressures and demands of parenting have become more complex, struggling with other socio-economic difficulties makes parenting yet more difficult.

Other aspects of society's development have contributed to added stresses for parents. For example television, which can be a valuable educational tool for children, also presents problems for parents. Since television shows how the other half live, children can demand things that are advertised on television and some of their peers have, which parents cannot afford. Children may demand to see programmes, because their friends watch them, but the suitability of which parents cannot judge, often until it is too late. Hundreds of studies have now documented the negative effects of aggressive television programmes (Huesmann et al., 2003) and computer programs on children's aggressive behaviours with peers and adults. Today, many children have unsupervised access to television in their own bedrooms. Sometimes television has replaced the need for babysitters and most certainly has reduced family communication, playing time and reading opportunities, as well as increasing exposure to violent programmes.

In fact the average British child spends more time watching television than engaging in activities in the classroom or with their parents.

Not only has television (and computer usage) reduced children's time interacting with peers and parents but convenience foods enable children to eat when, and where, they want. Family mealtimes have disappeared in many homes. Many poorer families no longer have a table at which to eat and the many occasions for family communication and interaction that having a meal entailed have disappeared. Parents frequently find themselves in uncharted territory.

THE HISTORY OF SUPPORT TO FAMILIES IN BRITAIN

In 19th century Britain, concern about child welfare focused primarily on the child. There had been 'Poor Laws' since Elizabethan times, but the Poor Law Amendment Act of 1834 forced unemployed, though able-bodied, people to enter workhouses in order to receive their keep, so that 'idleness' would not be reinforced. Conditions in workhouses were harsh, and husbands, wives and children were separated. Yet, despite the awful conditions, by 1848 there were over 300,000 inmates in workhouses. Those children who entered workhouses were treated in ways that respected neither their rights nor their individuality. At the same time, hundreds of children survived on the streets by begging, stealing or prostitution.

During the second half of the 19th century, recognition of the need for more humane care for children led to the foundation of voluntary children's societies. The philosophy of these philanthropic societies was that children had to be 'rescued' from parents who were failing to meet their needs (LSPCC, cited in Hendrick, 1994). Over a 40-year period Barnardo's (the major children's charity) alone sent almost 20,000 children overseas to Canada, Australia and New Zealand, and other childcare societies did the same. These children mostly entered domestic service or labouring work and this practice continued well into the 20th century.

Although guided by different philosophies, both state and voluntary sectors at that time were operating on the basis that children had to be removed and protected from inadequate parents. Their different solutions ignored the rights of families and failed to consider the possibility that, with support, many parents could care for their children. The idea of removing and protecting children from parents had a long history, going back at least to Plato who, around 300 BC,

recommended that children be raised by the state to avoid inconsistency on the part of (incompetent) parents (Hammer and Turner, 1985).

The 19th century saw some important advances in family health and health care but these were mainly due to public health measures, such as improved sanitation and the prevention of disease related to lack of clean water. The origins of health visiting go back to 1852 and the 'sanitary visitors' employed by the 'Manchester and Salford Sanitary Reform Association' (Owen, 1982). Their role, over many decades up to the Second World War, was mainly concerned with promoting physical health (Clark, 1981). This was a far cry from their current central and increasingly recognized role in supporting families to understand and cope with their young children within their own communities.

After the Second World War, in 1948, with the birth of the welfare state, the Poor Law was finally abolished. Local Authority Children's Departments were established and the rising cost of residential care, and high rates of foster care placement breakdown, led to the provision of the resources necessary to support families and prevent children from being taken out of their homes into care. Bowlby's (1953) views on the importance of mother–child early attachment relationships contributed to this change in thinking and by the mid-1950s the Government was seeking to prevent the admission of children into care through the introduction of comprehensive social welfare legislation. The 1969 Children and Young Person Act required interventions to support families. The responsibility for the prevention and treatment of delinquency fell to the newly formed Social Services Departments (SSDs). In the post-war years, when state-funded services were becoming conscious of the need to support the child within its family, the voluntary bodies were also moving in the same direction and it was from them that much of the innovative work came. Despite good intentions, little preventive work was undertaken by statutory agencies as, mainly due to rising poverty in the 1970s, demand for community services outstripped resources and statutory agencies were forced to put their main effort into child protection from physical and sexual abuse. The death of Maria Colwell in 1973, who had been removed from foster care to be reunited with her birth mother, and the public outcry and damning subsequent enquiry all contributed to this shift.

During the 1980s poverty continued to rise, a record number of people were dependent on supplementary benefit and family breakdown was increasing. Some specialist services to support families with children with behavioural difficulties through parenting interventions, were showing good outcomes. However, the numbers of children with difficulties were such that it was impossible for specialist services to respond comprehensively or effectively. The problems presented at a rate that could not be met by specialist services, and families living in the poorest parts of the country, mainly in depressed inner cities, with housing and relationship problems and mental ill health, had the worst outcomes. These families were also those for whom preventive services were least available and, when available, least used. Professionals and voluntary bodies alike saw that children in circumstances of 'social exclusion' were at greatest risk of developing physical, behavioural and emotional difficulties. It was clear that effective ways of providing community-based support for families who do not benefit from traditional statutory services was the main challenge facing service providers.

SUPPORT TO PARENTS OF YOUNG CHILDREN

The Sure Start initiative has provided a structure that allows a more comprehensive provision of support to families. This includes work to enhance parental health and mental health, support in dealing with issues such as housing, job training and job finding, the provision of childcare, and resources for parents and families to develop their competence and confidence in their role as parents early in their child's life. In their work in Seattle, the Webster-Stratton Incredible Years programmes, discussed later in more detail, provide meals, childcare and transport for families involved in community-based Head Start parenting programmes, as well as shopping vouchers.

In one local Sure Start area (the Isle of Anglesey), where the first author works, the Sure Start service includes the following:

- a community child-minding scheme
- a 'Home Start' volunteer family support scheme
- preschool support services for families of children identified as having developmental difficulties
- a 'Book Start' project bringing local library services to the community and including a free book as an incentive to join
- an exercise and parenting initiative offering free supervised relaxation and exercise sessions (yoga, swimming and aqua aerobics) for parents with crèche facilities provided
- the funding of playgroups and mother and toddler groups to increase social contact for both mothers and children

- a dedicated Sure Start health visitor within the designated area offering 'sleep' clinics, individual consultations for parents, accident prevention courses and a series of guest speakers on topics relevant to parents
- community classes in computing and information technology
- a community 'Fun Bus' and activity days for children and families where families could also get advice on housing, further education or other problems
- parent survival courses, using the Webster-Stratton Incredible Years Basic Parenting programme

The first author has recently undertaken an evaluation of the Anglesey Sure Start project, mainly through participant satisfaction questionnaires. All aspects of the service have proved very popular with users, and data from the parent survival courses (the Webster-Stratton basic parenting programme) are showing good outcomes for parental mental health and child behaviour.

There are a number of excellent and methodologically sound studies demonstrating the value of support during pregnancy and the first year of life. The Community Mothers programme developed in Dublin (Johnson and Molloy, 1995) supported first-time mothers in disadvantaged and deprived areas. Experienced mothers from the same communities were recruited to support first-time mothers whose children were born during six months in 1989. Programme co-ordinators were responsible for recruiting and supporting the community mothers. These mothers were recruited as having a caring and sensitive nature, reasonable literacy, and an interest in the community. They trained for approximately six hours in their own homes. First-time mothers were randomly allocated to intervention or control groups. Community mothers visited target mothers monthly for the first year of the child's life. The control group received standard support from the public health nurse. Mothers in the intervention group reported a better diet, and more positive and fewer negative feelings. The results are evidence for a model of empowerment as it comes from a programme delivered by mothers from the same communities who shared experiences.

The Social Support and Pregnancy Outcomes study (Oakley et al., 1990) demonstrated the effectiveness of a social support intervention provided by midwives in high-risk pregnancies. Women with a history of low birth-weights were randomly allocated to receive social support in pregnancy in addition to standard antenatal care, while others received only the latter. Social support was given by four research midwives and included 24-hour contact telephone numbers and home visits to provide a listening service. The babies of intervention group mothers had a higher mean birth-weight and there were fewer very low birth-weight babies in the group. Children in the intervention group were more likely to have received all of their primary inoculations, and were more likely to be read to, to play more cognitive games and to hear more nursery rhymes. The differences between the two groups were maintained, and at seven years, there were fewer behaviour problems among the children and less anxiety among the mothers in the intervention group.

In the Edinburgh Study of Post-natal Depression (Holden et al., 1989), women were screened for depression six weeks after giving birth, and by psychiatric interview, 13 weeks after giving birth. Women identified as depressed were randomly allocated to either eight, weekly, contact sessions by health visitors, who had received a short training in counselling for post-natal depression, or a no-treatment group. Standardized psychiatric interviews were used to identify depression before and after intervention. The majority of the women in the treatment group fully recovered compared with a minority of the controls.

Whilst few studies have looked at parenting support in diverse cultures, the Link worker project (Dance, 1987, cited in Oakley, 1992) targeted Pakistani women with one low birth-weight baby during a subsequent pregnancy. This was a randomized controlled trial study in which intervention mothers were visited three to five times during pregnancy. Intervention mothers had fewer medical problems, higher birth-weight babies, shorter labours, less analgesia and fewer babies with feeding problems.

In a review of programmes for children aged 0–8 years to prevent substance abuse, delinquency and violence in adolescence, Webster-Stratton and Taylor (2001) identify a study by Olds et al. (1986, 1998) as one for which there is the best evidence base. The study evaluated a home-visiting intervention by nurses to mothers in their prenatal months and during the first two years of their child's life afterwards. This study was important both because it was a randomized controlled trial study and because of its 15-year follow-up. Olds et al.'s intensive and comprehensive programme was designed to improve maternal prenatal health, pregnancy outcomes, childcare, children's health and development, and the women's own personal development and participation in the work force. Results indicated that nurse-visited women and children fared better than those assigned to control groups in each of the outcome domains. Home visits during pregnancy resulted in mothers having heavier babies, stopping smoking, and having

fewer pre-term deliveries. The 15-year follow-up showed that intervention mothers had, in contrast to those in the comparison and control groups, fewer verified reports of child abuse or neglect, fewer subsequent births, received less welfare, had fewer maternal problems due to alcohol and drug abuse, and fewer arrests. Children of these mothers had fewer arrests, fewer instances of running away, and lower alcohol consumption.

This programme has been replicated by Kitzman (1997) and others in Memphis with 1139 African-American mothers (primarily poor and unmarried). Results showed that nurse-visited children suffered fewer injuries in the first two years of life. Similar results from nurse visiting interventions were obtained by Larson (1980) in a home-visiting programme in Montreal and by Barnard et al. (1988) in Seattle.

PARENTING SKILLS AND CHILD BEHAVIOUR PROBLEMS

Many children have problem behaviours because their parents lack key parenting skills (Patterson, 1982), use them inconsistently (Patterson and Forgatch, 1989), or fail to use them at the appropriate times (Gardner et al., 1999). Evidence shows that while most children aged 20 months exhibit antisocial behaviours such as tantrums, mainly arising from their lack of communication skills at that age, these are generally replaced with more socially appropriate behaviours within a very short time. However, some children fail to move on and learn to use more socially appropriate behaviour.

Research has repeatedly demonstrated that parenting practices contribute to early antisocial behaviour and later delinquency (Reid, 1993; Campbell, 1995). Inconsistent parental discipline, poor commands, and harsh and inconsistent punishment play a significant role in the development and maintenance of child behaviour problems (Kochanska and Aksan, 1995). When this also includes little positive parental warmth and little involvement with, and poor monitoring of, the child both within and outside the home, the outcome is likely to be problematic for the child.

Patterson (1982), whose early work first described the relationship between parenting and child behaviour, describes a 'coercive family process' that is established when parents are unpredictable in their use of both positive reinforcement for pro-social behaviours and punishment for deviant behaviours.

A wide variety of programmes have been developed to support parents of young children by giving them effective behaviour management skills through structured training sessions, reading material and attendance at groups. Many of these programmes are designed for 'normal parents' rather than as a crisis intervention. Community-based parenting support is provided in the home, in the community or in school, on a one-to-one or group basis by statutory or voluntary agencies. In Britain, for example, over 600 family centres provide a wide range of support to parents and children.

Voluntary organizations have been important in the promotion of the group approach to parenting education. In the UK, most influential are Parent Network, Exploring Parenthood and Family Caring Trust. Community education programmes have also been developed, for example by the Open University.

In a review of Parenting Programmes in Britain, Celia Smith (1996) identified 38 programmes. Many were relatively small scale and local in delivery, reaching few, sometimes fewer than 100, parents per annum. A few studies were reaching 200–300 parents per year. Parent Network reaches around 2000 parents per year and the Family Caring Trust estimates that at least 20,000 parents per year are reached by its range of programmes. However, provision is patchy and dependent on the interest of particular individuals or organizations. Smith concluded that, in 1996, approximately 4 per cent of parents in Britain were in receipt of a programme. Whilst Sure Start funding will have increased these numbers, still only a small proportion of parents have access to this form of support.

Most parenting programmes have the core principles of helping parents to increase positive child behaviour and at the same time to set clear, consistent and non-violent limits for children. Parent effectiveness training (PET) (Gordon, 1975) was started in 1962 in California and has been influential on both sides of the Atlantic. This is a group-based programme and, in addition to the core behaviour management principles, the programme includes 'active listening' and 'conflict resolution', which is seen as a problem-solving skill. Unfortunately much of the research into PET is unpublished or has methodological difficulties, making it hard to establish the effectiveness of this programme. Systematic Training for Effective Parenting (STEP) (Dinkmeyer, 1979) is based on psychodynamic principles and attempts to create a democratic family atmosphere focused on encouragement, mutual respect, discipline that is consistent with behaviour, time limits and choices. This, like PET, emphasizes reflective listening and the use of natural and logical consequences. This programme has also been developed into a teacher programme but unfortunately,

as with PET, systematic research has been sparse.

Other programmes include: How to Talk So Kids Will Listen (Faber and Mazlish, 1980), a self-administered course for use by groups of 6–12 parents; Responsive Parenting which has individual or group programmes; and Canter and Canter's (1985) Assertive Discipline, to help parents and teachers to engage children in more appropriate behaviour.

One of the most impressive programmes is the Triple P – Positive Parenting Programme – developed by Sanders in Australia (Sanders, 1999). This is one of the better evidence-based programmes and is a multilayered intervention which includes both universal and targeted approaches (see chapter 21). The Mellow Parenting programme developed in Britain has good reported outcomes and is described in chapter 3.

There are strengths and limitations to each of these programmes, the significant overriding limitation being the relatively limited amount of reliable evidence of effectiveness and durability for many of them. The Webster-Stratton Incredible Years programmes, discussed later in this chapter are probably the best evidence-based interventions in this field.

SUPPORT FOR PARENTS OF ADOLESCENTS

Support for parents of teenagers has received much less attention than for parents of younger children, yet this is an issue of considerable importance to most societies. In Britain, the Government has tried to make parents accountable for their youngsters' misdemeanours and crimes through the Parenting Orders, part of the Crime and Disorder Act 1998. It has also established a Connections programme, with similarities to Sure Start, to reach teenagers.

Many of the services that currently exist for adolescents are therapeutic in nature and occur after the child is in trouble. There is very little evidence of effective strategies for this work. Patterson et al. (1993) at the Oregon Social Learning Centre have undertaken some of the best-evaluated parenting programmes with parents of children of a variety of ages. However, their success rates for children under the age of 10 years are much higher (75 per cent success) as compared with only 25 per cent with adolescents. Those interventions for adolescents with a good evidence base are achieved by removing the youngsters from their families (Chamberlain, 1990).

It is not surprising that interventions for conduct disorders (CD) are of limited effect when offered in adolescence, when delinquent and aggressive behaviours have persisted for many years, and when secondary risk factors such as academic failure, school drop-out, and affiliation to deviant peer groups have developed (Ruma et al., 1996; Werry, 1997). In fact, interventions targeting adolescents with CD can result in worsening of symptoms through exposure to delinquent peers (Dishion et al., 1999). There have been a number of demonstration projects for treatment of conduct disordered adolescents through specialized residential treatment and foster placements. However, these are costly, because they require skilled and intensive human input and are no real solution to such a widespread problem that have their origins in early childhood.

The increased treatment resistance in older CD children and young people (Webster-Stratton, 1991; Reid, 1993) results in part from delinquent behaviours becoming embedded in a broader array of rewarding systems, including those at the family, school, peer group, neighbourhood, and community levels (Lynam et al., 2000). Thus, the payoff or contingencies in all of these systems must be altered for interventions to become effective for adolescents – an endeavour that requires the co-ordination and expertise of myriad service providers and explains why the outcomes from such endeavours are so poor (Henggeler et al., 1998).

A number of programmes have versions for the parents of adolescents, including PET and STEP. A verson of the Triple P programme for parents of teenagers is being evaluated by Sanders in Australia. The Family Caring Trust has a programme designed for the parents of teenagers; it is a flexible self-help programme run by a range of community organizations including schools and churches. Parent Network courses are for (parents of) children of all ages. They provide an opportunity for parents to talk to each other about the problems they are experiencing. Parents who have received 150 hours of training over six months lead the groups, as experienced fellow parents.

Parent Time (Cohen and Irwin, 1983) is a programme for parents of adolescents who are not experiencing serious difficulties. Results suggest that it gives parents an enhanced capacity to listen, to set limits and to confide in other parents. Parents Who Care (Hawkins and Catalano, 1996) is a book and video presentation with instructions and exercises for parents and families, with guidance on how to involve adolescents in family decision-making. Family Systems Programmes are offered as both group and individual family-based units to empower families 'from within' to direct, monitor and change. Growing up Fast (Gavacci, 1995) was designed to help the whole family to recognize their strengths and set appropriate goals for themselves to bring the young person through adolescence to maturity. The programme recognizes that the young person is an active agent in the process.

A study providing adolescent-focused newsletters (Bogenschneider and Stone, 1997) demonstrated that, following receipt of a series of three newsletters, parents had a higher level of monitoring compared with the control group and were more responsive to their children, engaging in more intimate discussion with them about adolescent risk behaviours. A number of voluntary agencies have telephone helplines for adolescents themselves. 'Parent line', for example, is a government-funded, national helpline for parents seeking advice with their children, of all ages. Relate has developed a Relate Teen Service for adolescents experiencing difficulties as a result of parental separation.

Unfortunately few of these services have demonstrated effective outcomes in scientifically rigorous ways. Most have the benefit of face validity and some, such as Parentline, are extensively used. However, there is no evidence that these services reach those parents who, by virtue of the range and severity of their problems, are in the most urgent need of help.

BEHAVIOURAL APPROACHES TO SUPPORT CHILDREN WITH BEHAVIOURAL DIFFICULTIES

Among all the programmes for children with behavioural difficulties, the 'social-cognitive' and behavioural parenting approaches have been most extensively researched over the last 30 years and their therapeutic effectiveness is well established.

Behavioural parent training approaches have many elements in common. Treatment is based on 'social learning theory' and utilizes the concepts of modelling, positive reinforcement, time out and contingency contracting (Kazdin, 1993). The aim is to increase positive behaviours through a variety of rewards, whilst reducing unwanted behaviours through response cost or other strategies, resulting in their disappearance and 'extinction'. A most influential parent training programme was developed by Patterson and colleagues (Patterson et al., 1975; Patterson, 1982). This is based on extensively researched models of parent–child interactions and designed to alter the pattern of exchanges between parent and child so that pro-social and co-operative, rather than coercive and disruptive, behaviour is directly reinforced and supported within the family.

Some programmes include work to enhance the parent–child relationship, with a focus on play and other relationship-enhancing activities which has been shown to be an essential component (Taylor and Biglan, 1998).

A parenting programme that combines a focus on relationship-building with cognitive, affective and behavioural components was developed by the second author initially for treating young children with diagnosed oppositional disorder or conduct disorder. This programmme is described in more detail below, but extensive evaluation indicates that the short- and long-term success of treatment has demonstrated significant improvements in child behaviours and improved child adjustment for at least two-thirds of treated children. It has also proved acceptable to the service users. An important by-product of this particular programme appears to be a significant improvement in parental mental health, particularly depression, and improved anger-management skills following parent training. This and other evidence has led to recognition at UK government level that parenting programmes enhance both child and maternal mental health.

Parenting programmes have been delivered in a variety of formats including television programmes, DIY programmes with videotapes, individual consultations and in groups. Local circumstances, such as rurality and the nature of the target group, dictate what is feasible. Many studies show direct evidence that changes in parent behaviour, the target of the intervention, are associated with changes in child behaviour.

Despite the success of behavioural and social learning theory based approaches with the parents of CD children, some studies report parent dropout of up to 40 per cent and some children do not continue to show clinically significant responses over time. Long-term follow-up studies show that 30–40 per cent of parents who have received parent training continue to have children with behaviour problems in the clinical range (Patterson, 1982; Webster-Stratton, 1985). Furthermore, those with the most difficult social circumstances are less likely to engage in these programmes, and if they do, are more likely to drop out (Dumas and Wahler, 1983). Despite these limitations, parenting programmes are by far the most effective forms of intervention at the present time.

A number of the factors influence treatment outcome. Early intervention and longer duration of treatment are both associated with positive outcomes. Success declines with increasing child age; the older the child at the start of treatment, the poorer the outcome. Where a family is experiencing extreme socio-economic disadvantage or if the mother is depressed, in conflict with her huuband/partner, is a single parent or is socially isolated with respect to her family and her community, some parent training programmes have proved to be ineffective in resolving difficulties with the child. Many programmes find that recruitment rates for parent training from low-income families with children with conduct problems are low. Even when recruited, these multi-stressed parents are the most likely to drop out of treatment and later to relapse, to fail to make clinically significant improvements following treatment, or to maintain treatment effects over time (Wahler et al., 1993). Parent training programmes have to address these issues and evidence from studies by the second author shows how this can be done (e.g. Webster-Stratton et al., 2001a).

The effectiveness of parent training is dependent on the acceptability of the service provided to parents since it affects their willingness to follow advice and to adhere to agreed child management strategies and techniques. Therapist behaviours that are perceived as 'directive' appear to increase the likelihood of parental resistance and lack of co-operation. Non-directive trainers, on the other hand, engaging in such behaviours as 'facilitating' and 'supporting', appear reliably to decrease client non-compliance.

The second author (Webster-Stratton, 1998a) points out that families who fail to engage with services may have been seen to workers to be

> unmotivated, resistant, unreliable, disengaged, chaotic, in denial, disorganized, uncaring, dysfunctional, and unlikely candidates for this kind of treatment – in short, unreachable.

She goes on to remind us that

> However these families might equally describe many of the programmes as 'unreachable', too far away from home, too expensive, insensitive, unrealistic, inflexible in terms of timing and content, hard to understand and/or blaming or critical of parents' lifestyle (Webster-Stratton, 1998a).

The 'calculus' used by these parents is no different from those of the more compliant. It is likely that the costs to these clients of receiving treatment outweigh any possible benefits, even though they want to do what is best for their children. It seems possible, she contends, that this population has been 'unreachable' not because of their own characteristics but mainly because of the characteristics of the interventions that they have been offered.

Child Interventions

Because of the difficulties in engaging the parents of many high-risk children, a number of child programmes have been developed and researched in recent years. Some programmes focus specifically on social skills deficits such as friendship and/or play skills, whereas others have relied more on cognitive–behavioural methods to teach child problem-solving, self-control and positive 'self-talk'. Few of these programmes have involved parents, many have not targeted conduct problem children, few have used observational measures of change, and more difficult children seem to benefit less from these programmes.

School-based Interventions

Efforts to involve parents in school programmes are not new and attempts to create a link between home and schools have been in operation in the UK through parent–teacher associations for many years. However, they have been mainly successful with middle-class parents and parents of children who are already 'doing well in school'. Linking the Interests of Families and Teachers (LIFT), an Oregon Social Learning Centre project, showed the benefits of offering a parent training programme in the school and of strategies to make teachers more accessible to parents (Reid, 1993). Despite some programmes that are successful in linking parents and teachers, they are, for the most part, independent agents of children's socialization.

Engaging parents is the first priority. Parents spend the greatest amount of time with their children and have generally the greatest influence. The research literature suggests that parenting programmes offered as a preventive measure, before children are diagnosed as having conduct disorder, are more cost-effective, more pervasive in impact, and less stigmatizing. Community-based interventions must have the support of, and from, parents at their heart. Universal programmes, provided in the community, are more likely to engender a collaborative approach to the practice of positive parenting and to build strong and supportive parent communities and partnerships with schools.

THE 'INCREDIBLE YEARS' PROGRAMMES

While not all risk factors for childhood emotional and behavioural difficulties are easily amenable to intervention, some such as poor parenting skills, social isolation, lack of support networks for parents, and lack of school involvement are. If these risk factors can be modified, parents can build up protective strategies that may help buffer some of the adverse effects of poverty and other adversity and their accompanying stressors. Growing recognition of the failure of treatment programmes with

older children, coupled with the recognition of the growing numbers of children with problems, has led to the provision of community-based parenting programmes focused on parents of younger children.

Based on her work with referred children, the second author developed a model that suggested the benefit of intervening at the parent, child and school level, and a series of programmes named 'The Incredible Years'. These programmes are described in some detail because of the strong, replicated evidence base.

The Incredible Years programmes include parents, children and teachers (see Figure 20.1) and have been developed and researched over the last 20 years, in a number of randomized controlled group studies as well as in replications by independent researchers. Her programmes have been identified, using strict criteria, as a 'Blueprint Programme' (Webster-Stratton et al., 2001b) for the prevention of violence and, using similar criteria, by the US Office of Juvenile Justice and Delinquency Prevention (OJJDP, 2000). Additionally, in a recent report from the American Psychological Association, the Incredible Years series was identified as one of only two effective treatments for conduct disorder. There are three interlocking programmes for parents, children and teachers, all of which have been used both as therapeutic interventions and in high-risk Head Start communities. All three programmes, parent, child and teacher, use manuals, and protocol adherence is stressed. Leaders are trained in a collaborative problem-solving style in which the specific goals, issues and life circumstances of each group member are used in group discussions. The curriculum of each programme is, therefore, placed in context in relation to particular families, classrooms, and characteristics of the group. This is a culturally sensitive approach that has proven effective for children.

Since developing these programmes as treatment programmes for referred children, community-based preventive parent, child and teacher interventions in high-risk communities have been evaluated, demonstrating that these are strongly evidence-based community programmes. Whilst the parenting component is regarded as important in improving parent–child relationships, programmes to help parents improve their relationship with their child's education providers and help schools to promote children's social competence are also emphasized.

The Parenting Programme

Addressing the issue of how to engage high-risk families and enable them to 'take ownership' of

THE INCREDIBLE YEARS PARENT, CHILD, AND TEACHER PROGRAMS		
Population & Intended use	Minimum "Core" Program	Recommended Supplemental Programs For Special Populations
For use as Prevention Programs for Selective Population (i.e., high-risk populations without overt behavior or conduct problems) Settings: Pre-school, Daycare, Head Start schools Public Health Centers	BASIC (12 to 14, two-hour weekly sessions)	• ADVANCE Parent Programs for Highly stressed families • SCHOOL Parent Program for Children (Kindergarten to Grade 3) • CHILD Program if child's problems are pervasive at home and at school • TEACHER Classroom Management Program if teachers have high numbers of students with behavior problems or if teachers lack these skills
For use as Treatment Programs for Indicated Populations (i.e., children exhibiting behavior problems or diagnosed conduct disorders) Settings: Mental Health Centers Pediatric Clinics, HMOs	BASIC and ADVANCE (22 to 24, two-hour weekly sessions)	• SCHOOL Program for parents if child has academic problems • CHILD Program if child's problems are pervasive at home and at school • TEACHER Program if child's problems are pervasive at home and at school

Figure 20.1   *The Incredible Years Programmes and their use with selective populations (From Webster-Stratton et al., 2001b).*

the central programme ideas is of critical importance. Many early parent training programmes relied largely on verbal methods such as didactic lectures, brochures, and group discussions. These methods have been shown to be generally ineffective in producing behavioural changes in parents (Chilman, 1973). In addition, such methods are not optimal for parents whose level of literacy, educational or general intellectual ability is limited. 'Performance training' methods such as live modelling, role rehearsal, and individual video feedback have, on the other hand, proved effective in producing behavioural changes in parents and children (O'Dell, 1985; Hutchings et al., 2004). However, implementation is time-consuming and costly, making such programmes impractical for large-scale use. Furthermore, they cannot directly address other risk factors, such as social isolation, or improving home school links.

The 'Incredible Years' training programmes are all based on videotape modelling and have proved to be both practicable and cost-effective. Parents watch video clips of parents and children and practice interacting with their children in ways that promote pro-social behaviours and/or decrease inappropriate behaviours. This flexible modelling approach results in better generalization of the training content and, therefore, better long-term maintenance, which is a better method of learning for less verbally sophisticated parents.

The method also has the advantage not only of low individual training cost when used in groups, but of potential for mass dissemination.

The model is used for working with families, children and teachers actively and collaboratively. In a collaborative relationship, the facilitator does not set him/herself up as an 'expert', dispensing advice to parents about how they should parent more effectively. The collaborative model (Webster-Stratton and Herbert, 1994) implies a reciprocal relationship based on utilizing equally the facilitator's and the parent's knowledge, strengths and perspectives. It is non-judgemental and non-hierarchical. The provision of transport, daycare, meals and flexible course times are built in to take account of families' circumstances and enable them to participate.

The partnership between parents and group facilitators gives back dignity, respect and self control to parents who, because of their particular situation, may have low self-confidence and intense feelings of guilt and self-blame (Baydar et al., 2003). A collaborative approach is more likely to increase parents' confidence and perceived self-efficacy than 'top-down' and 'expert' therapeutic approaches. Parents with high self-efficacy will tend to persist at tasks until they succeed. Also, people who have determined their own priorities and goals are more likely to persist in the face of difficulties. This model is likely to increase parents' engagement in the intervention, and evidence suggests that the collaborative process has the advantage of reducing drop-out rates and increasing motivation and commitment.

For low-income single mothers, who are often socially isolated with little support and few friends, parent groups can become an 'empowering' environment, decreasing their insularity and giving them new sources of support. The programme helps groups to become support systems by assigning everyone a 'buddy' in the second session. Buddies are asked to call each other during the week to share how the homework assignment is going. This assignment is carried out every few weeks with a different buddy. Parents are initially hesitant about making these calls but, as they experience the support they receive from these telephone conversations, they continue to make calls to one another. By utilizing powerful group processes, the programme is cost-effective and addresses an important risk factor for children with conduct problems, namely, the family's isolation and stigmatization. The parent groups provide support which can become a model for parent support networks.

The 'Basic' parenting programme is designed for parents of children aged 2–8 years and aims to promote modelling effects for parents by creating positive feelings about the videotape models. The videotapes show parents and children of differing ages, cultures, socio-economic backgrounds and temperaments, so that parents perceive at least some of the models as similar to themselves and their children, and therefore accept the tapes as relevant. Videotapes show parent models in natural situations with their children 'doing it wrong' and 'doing it right', to illustrate how one can learn from one's mistakes. This approach emphasizes a coping and interactive model of learning (Webster-Stratton and Herbert, 1994). Parents view a videotape vignette of a parent 'doing it wrong' and then discuss and role play how the parent might have handled the interaction more effectively. This enhances parents' confidence in their own ideas and their ability to analyse different situations with their children and select an appropriate parenting strategy. In this respect, the training differs from most other parent training programmes in which the therapist is 'the expert' and provides the analysis and recommending a particular strategy. The collaborative context is designed to ensure that the intervention is sensitive to individual cultural differences and personal values. The programme is 'tailored' to each family's individual needs and goals (identified in the first session) as well as to each child's personality and behaviour problems. This is theoretically a complex task, but in practice an adequate working approximation can be developed.

The first two segments of the 'Basic' programme focus on teaching parents to play with their children, building interactive and reinforcement skills. The third and fourth segments teach parents a specific set of non-violent discipline techniques including commands, time out and ignoring (Forehand and McMahon, 1981), as well as logical and natural consequences, and the importance of monitoring their child. The fourth segment also shows parents how to teach their children problem-solving skills (Shure, 1994).

There are two other parenting programmes. The 'Advance' programme emphasizes adult interpersonal skills, such as effective communication skills, anger management, problem-solving between adults, and ways to give and get support. The 'Supporting Your Child's Education' programme emphasizes parenting approaches that promote children's academic skills, including fostering reading skills, setting up predictable homework routines, and building collaborative relationships with teachers.

The process of disseminating this work has been carefully planned. Basic parent group leader training is a three-day workshop to familiarize potential group leaders with the programme content and to introduce them, through experience, to the collaborative approach. There is also a certification process for leaders through which they gain feedback to enable them to ensure that they are delivering the evidence-based programme. This is important, because it maximizes the quality of the performance of the group facilitator. Certified leaders, implementing the full programme, achieve results similar to those in the published literature. The certification requirements are clearly specified. Few, if any, other programmes are supported as well to give new leaders confidence that they are delivering an evidence-based programme.

The parenting programmes have been shown to be effective in significantly improving parental attitudes and parent–child interactions, along with reducing parents' reliance on violent and critical disciplinary approaches and reducing child conduct problems (Webster-Stratton et al., 2001a). These results have been replicated by independent investigators in mental health clinics with families of children with conduct problems (Spaccareli et al., 1992; Taylor et al., 1998; Scott, 2001b). The Scott study was conducted in real life in an applied setting, where the therapists were typical personnel of the centre.

Two prevention programmes have been researched in high-risk Head Start communities designed to address the problems of early starter 'at risk' children through a parent training. These have demonstrated that parent training is a highly useful intervention for promoting increased positive parent–child interactions (Webster-Stratton, 1998b; Office of Juvenile Justice and Delinquency Prevention, 2000).

The programme is effective in recruiting families from circumstances in which other studies have shown little success. In a recent analysis of the Head Start studies over 75 per cent of mothers attended more than 75 per cent of the sessions offered. Additionally, those parents with mental health difficulties (depression, anger, substance abuse and a history of having been abused as children) had good programme attendance and were actively engaged in the homework. They also showed significant improvements in their parenting interactions relative to controls and did as well as mothers without mental health problems (Webster-Stratton, 1998b).

Data from two Head Start samples were combined in order to compare the effectiveness of intervention according to ethnic group, with analyses differentiating between Caucasian, African-American, Asian-American and Hispanic participants (Reid et al., 2001). Results indicated that significant changes occurred regardless of the ethnicity of the family, and all ethnic groups had high 'consumer' satisfaction for the programme. However, some differences emerged when scores on the consumer satisfaction survey were rank-ordered, with Caucasian mothers consistently rating the programme somewhat more critically than the other three groups. In terms of attendance, Asian mothers had the highest rates and Caucasian parents attended significantly fewer sessions than Hispanic and African-American parents. The significance and generalizability of these findings is not immediately apparent.

The findings from these Head Start studies have been replicated by independent investigators as prevention programmes with different populations, including with Hispanic (Miller and Rojas-Flores, 1999) and low-income African-American families (Gross et al., 1999) in different cities. Studies using the basic programme have shown that parent training is highly promising as an effective therapeutic method for producing significant behaviour change in children within high-risk, socio-economically disadvantaged populations. These findings provide support for the view that parenting practices play a key role in children's social and emotional development. However, the long-term data suggests that, to improve the potency of this intervention, it is imperative to address child skill deficits and collaboration with teachers to promote more sustained effects across the home and school setting.

The Teacher Programme

On entering school, disruptive children quickly become socially excluded and may elicit the same negative patterns of response from teachers that they experienced at home. For high-risk children to benefit from intervention programmes, healthy bonds or 'supportive networks' are necessary between teachers and parents, and children and teachers. Family–school networks are of benefit to children due to parents' increased expectations, interest in, and support for their child's social and academic performance and create a consistent socialization process across home and school settings.

Effective classroom management reduces disruptive behaviour and enhances social and academic competence (Walker et al., 1995; Brophy, 1996). Well-trained teachers help aggressive, disruptive and uncooperative children to develop the appropriate social behaviour that is a prerequisite for success in school.

The IY teacher programme was developed to teach effective classroom management skills (Webster-Stratton, 1999). It is a six-day group-based training. It targets teachers' use of effective classroom management strategies for dealing with misbehaviour, promoting positive relationships with difficult students, strengthening social skills and strengthening teachers' positive communication with parents. The programme emphasizes the importance of positive home telephone calls, regular meetings with parents, home visits, and successful parent conferences. It uses the same collaborative process skills that were developed for the parenting programme, with vignettes, role play and homework assignments.

The parent and the teacher training curriculum have been evaluated with Head Start teachers and mothers. Following the programme, experimental mothers had significantly lower negative parenting and significantly higher positive parenting scores than control mothers. Parent–teacher 'bonding' was significantly higher for experimental mothers. Experimental children showed significantly fewer conduct problems at school than control children. Children of mothers who attended six or more intervention sessions showed significantly fewer conduct problems at home than control children. Children who were the 'highest risk' at baseline (high rates of non-compliant and aggressive behaviour) showed clinically more significant reductions in these behaviours than high-risk control children. After training, experimental teachers showed significantly better classroom management skills than control teachers. One year later the experimental effects were maintained for parents who attended more than six of the group sessions. The clinically significant reductions in behaviour problems for the highest risk experimental children were also maintained.

The Child Programme

Despite these improved outcomes achieved by combining the parent and teacher programmes, it was deemed necessary to improve further on the success rate by developing, in addition, a curriculum for the children in their early years in the classroom. This was done by adapting the 'Dinosaur School' programme (Webster-Stratton and Reiad, 2003), originally developed as a small group programme for referred children, into a programme for early school years, delivered to the whole classroom.

The Dinosaur School curriculum (Webster-Stratton and Reid, in press) is guided by child risk factor research and aims to enhance children's appropriate classroom behaviour (such as a quiet hand up, listening to teacher). It also promotes social skills, positive peer interactions (for example, waiting, taking turns, asking to enter a group and complimenting), empathy skills and emotional language to help children develop appropriate conflict management skills and reduce conduct problems. The programme is designed to dovetail with the parent and teacher training programmes. The curriculum can be used by a therapist as a 'pull out' small group programme for treating children with conduct problems. These small group sessions are offered once a week for two hours for 18–20 sessions (usually when parents are in parent groups). In addition, the curriculum can be used as a classroom-wide prevention programme offered by teachers of children aged 3–8 years. It is offered to all children in 15–30 minutes 'circle time' discussions followed by small group practice activities, two to three times a week over the school year.

The Dinosaur School programme uses child sized puppets, Wally and Molly, who share their difficulties and successes with the children. Dina Dinosaur is the principal of Dinosaur School and comes out to review progress. The programme promotes child problem-solving through children becoming problem-solving detectives. As with the parent and teacher programmes, it uses vignettes to promote identity with other children, role play to give practice of new skills, and homework assignments.

A recent evaluation by the second author has compared different combinations of training including parent, teacher and child programmes with a waiting list control group for referred children (Webster-Stratton and Hammond, 1997). Outcomes from this study indicate that classroom observation of teachers who received the teacher training showed trained teachers to have better classroom atmospheres and to be less harsh and critical and more nurturing. In short, when the teacher training component was added to either the parent or child programmes the effects on children's behaviour were significantly enhanced. The combined training for parent, teacher and child showed more effects across settings on multiple variables (parent and teacher report and observations at home and in school).

This study is currently being repeated as an early intervention initiative in Head Start. There are already many issues to be resolved regarding the use of this programme across larger geographical areas, persuading professionals to adopt it in preference to either home-grown or other off-the-shelf programmes and the insertion of such a programme for a large enough group of children in schools which are typically the least resourced and most stressed. There are also issues of cultural compatibility. For these reasons, it may be worthwhile describing the application of this programme in a different country and quite a different (though not extremely so) culture.

WORK IN WALES

The first author has worked with children and families in Wales for over 25 years. She has researched outcomes of a standard and structured, intensive practice-based behavioural programme for children with severe behavioural problems (Hutchings et al., 2002). The intensive programme utilized video feedback to parents of their own interactions with children and repeated practice of new management skills (parents doing things rather than being given advice). Four-year follow-up (Hutchings et al., 2004) has shown that only the gains made by the intensive treatment group have been maintained. These findings demonstrate that video feedback and coaching help parents but are costly and require highly skilled personnel, thus making the intervention available to very few children and families. This led to the development of a practice-based training programme for health visitors (nurses with statutory duties for health care of young children), which has been researched and demonstrated evidence of positive outcomes for health visitors, parents and children (Lane and Hutchings, 2002). This is now an accredited Masters level module within the University of Wales.

For the last five years the first author's main focus has been on developing the use of the Webster-Stratton Incredible Years programmes in Wales. The programmes have been delivered both for referred children and as preventive interventions. More than one hundred professional staff across Wales have undertaken the three-day basic parent group leader training course and are running the parenting programme in a range of services. A recent survey found them to be very satisfied with the training and highly motivated to run the programme. Running the IY parenting programmes is challenging, as modelling respect for, and acceptance of, group members by leaders is highly skilled. In addition, providing facilities to make groups accessible requires resources that are rarely provided within services.

The three-day parent group leader training is a thorough introduction to the programme but, even with this training, it takes considerable skill to run the programmes as designed. The programme content is clearly defined and the materials explicitly presented. However, experience suggests that a thorough grounding in social learning theory is an important prerequisite to successful group leadership, as are collaborative leader skills.

A high level of skill and organization is needed to deliver the programmes. The first two parent groups run by the first author had a drop-out rate of almost 50 per cent. It would be easy to dismiss this as not untypical of parents of children referred with such problems. However, all of these parents are experiencing difficulties with a child and need help and support. Many of the programme components are difficult for busy clinicians to achieve but improvements in attendance and homework compliance are achieved by following programme requirements, such as weekly telephone calls to all group members, and rigorously following up absentee parents on the same day. Also, where possible, make-up sessions are provided for parents who miss sessions.

As leaders have become more skilled, we maintain higher levels of attendance, with the majority attending over 75 per cent of sessions, as well as almost 100 per cent homework compliance. Homework compliance is a good predictor of successful delivery of the programme and homework results were initially poor. The strategies for encouraging compliance with homework activities need to be used systematically, including parent completion of the weekly self-monitoring checklist, which helps them to set homework goals and to evaluate their own performance.

Initially too little time was allowed for discussion of homework for the coming week. Since greater emphasis has been given to the importance of homework, compliance has significantly improved and, while barriers are discussed with parents who fail to complete homework, attention

focuses primarily on those parents who have completed homework.

The settings in which services are delivered in North Wales are very different from those in Seattle. The rural bilingual (Welsh and English) communities pose difficulties in terms of gathering together groups of people, even within services such as Sure Start, who are delivering community-based support to scattered populations.

The small group therapeutic Dinosaur School and the Classroom Dina programmes have been run in a number of NHS and Education Service settings across Wales.

A recent development has been the establishment of the classroom-based Dinosaur School programme in Gwynedd, North West Wales in reception classes with rising 5-year-old children. At the same time, their parents are offered the basic parenting programme to encourage them to support their children at the difficult transition point at which they enter school. This has involved collaboration across agencies and commitments at management level to facilitate the maintenance of these activities. The teachers delivering this programme undertook a shortened version of the teacher training programme, learning the basic classroom management skills on which the school programme is based. The success of this programme in its first year (2001/02) led to its expansion into a further six schools in 2002/03 and a further four schools in 2003/04. The plan is to deliver the Classroom Dina programme throughout the first three years of children's schooling. In 2002/03 the six-day teacher classroom management programme was introduced in North West Wales and run for two groups of 12 teachers. This was highly valued by the teachers and is being run again in 2003/04.

The IY programmes in Wales have been promoted through the university based 'Child Behaviour Project', through which basic training in the delivery of all the programmes and some advanced consultation has been organized. The project provides a focus for staff to learn together to deliver these evidence-based programmes. An IY Support Group has been established and meets every three months to help less experienced leaders to deal with common problems and pair up with more experienced leaders to run their first group. As the project has now devoted itself entirely to promoting the IY programmes, it has just (September 2003) become The Centre for Promoting the Incredible Years Programmes in Wales.

The co-ordination of training and the provision of research resources has enabled some evaluation of outcomes. Positive outcomes have been reported from parent, child, and teacher programmes, in terms of parent and teacher satisfaction and reported improvements in child behaviour. This enables positive feedback to be given to agency managers about the programmes, which helps to ensure the future availability of resources for the programme.

CONCLUSION

Early childhood conduct problems are occurring in large numbers and, if unresolved, lead to delinquency and subsequent costly adult mental health problems and/or criminal behaviour. The search for effective ways to prevent this violence has become a national priority. There is a need to get services to high-risk families in their own communities during children's early years. The way in which services are delivered influences whether families accept, ignore or reject what is available. Parents and children need to be active participants in health care. Services have to pay attention to parents' life styles, and needs and services must be modified to meet these needs so that parents can be contacted and engaged.

The history of work to support families within their own communities is short and it has occurred in the context of rapidly changing society and one in which the challenges of parenting have grown significantly. At the start of the 21st century British government policy is making the 'community' the focus of health care through the establishment of Local Health Groups. These will have responsibility for commissioning statutory services at a local level, with representatives of other agencies. Sure Start services, supporting families 'at risk' and other innovative work from voluntary groups, parent support groups and media resources all have a contribution to supporting parents at a community level. Successful implementation of support to parents in their own communities requires workable methods, and available trained and appropriately supervised staff. The Sure Start programme will only reach some of the families of children at risk and we need a strategy that will meet the needs of all children and families. Health visitors, in Britain, are well placed to work with other agencies to engage all families in a collaborative way during the preschool years but they need both training and for this work to be given sufficient priority in their schedule.

There are serious gaps in research. Few investigators have used randomized controlled studies. This is particularly important when programmes are prescribed by the Courts, as they can be in Britain under the provisions of the Children Act 1989 and the Crime and Disorder Act 1998.

Under these acts, Parenting Orders can require parents of young people in trouble to attend parenting classes.

While many programmes are available for children at risk of developing conduct disorder, few address the problem with parents, children and teachers together and have evidence-based validation from well-designed trials. We need to engage parents in high-risk communities whilst their children are still young and to build partnerships between parents and schools using evidence-based interventions.

The work of the second author has been a major influence on services delivering parenting programmes in the UK, and is currently being implemented and researched in both treatment and preventive settings (Scott et al., 2001). The community programmes incorporate interventions with parents, teachers and children (Webster-Stratton et al., 2001b). The Incredible Years parenting programme has demonstrated how to engage many high-risk families and enable most to assimilate the ideas. In the 'early intervention' setting when they are offered to communities and combined with the child and teacher programmes, they are perceived as non-stigmatizing and offer one of the best available models for supporting parents and enhancing children's social and emotional competence. Parents of high-risk children can be engaged when services recognize their needs and provide for them, for example providing childcare, transportation and meals.

Such community-based programmes can reduce factors that place children at risk for conduct disorders. However, to be most effective they need to encompass various levels of society – the children and their peers, the school, the family and wider society. Both sense and evidence suggest that the earlier that difficulties are tackled, the better they will be ameliorated Programmes are likely to be most effective if delivered early in the child's life and include the parent, the child and the school. The evidence from the Incredible Years early intervention programmes in Head Start centres is demonstrating just this and beginning to be replicated in Britain where a significant number of Sure Start services are incorporating them into their range of services to support families.

Effective parenting programmes require skilled group leaders with knowledge of social learning theory and practical parenting skills as well as effective collaborative communication skills. The task is to engage parents as problem solvers through a collaborative approach that recognizes the strengths and knowledge of the participants as a valuable contribution to the shared problem-solving task of rearing children in a complex modern world (Webster-Stratton and Hammond, 1994).

Parenting is one of the factors associated with problematic child outcomes and programmes need to address this, as well as other parental physical and emotional health issues and the other by-products of social exclusion. Governments on both sides of the Atlantic are recognizing the urgent need to implement evidence-based support to families within their own communities.

REFERENCES

Barnard, K.E., Magyaru, D., Summer, G., Booth, C.L. Mitchell, S.K. and Spieker, S. (1988) Prevention of parenting alterations for women with low social support. *Psychiatry*, **51**, 248–53.

Baydar, N., Reid, J.B. and Webster-Stratton, C. (2003) Who benefits from school-based preventive parent training programs? The role of mother mental health factors and program engagement. *Child Development*, **74**, 433–53.

Bogenschneider, K. and Stone, M. (1997) Delivering parent education to low and high risk parents of adolescents via age-paced newsletters. *Family Relations*, **46**, 123–34.

Bowlby, J. (1953) *Child Care and the Growth of Love*. Harmondsworth: Penguin.

Brophy, J.E. (1996) *Teaching Problem Students*. New York, NY: Guilford Press.

Campbell, S.B. (1995) Behaviour problems in pre-school children: a review of recent research. *Journal of Child Psychology and Psychiatry*, **36**, 113–49.

Canter, L. and Canter, M. (1985) *Assertive Discipline for Parents*. New York: Harper and Row.

Chamberlain, P. (1990) Comparative evaluation of specialized foster care for seriously delinquent youths: a first step. *Community Alternatives: International Journal of Family Care*, **2**, 21–36.

Chilman, A. (1973) Programs for disadvantaged parents. In Caldwell, B.U. and Riccuiti, W.N. (eds) *Review of Child Development and Research*, Vol. 3. Chicago: University of Chicago Press.

Clark, J. (1981) *What Do Health Visitors Do? A Review of the Research 1960–1980*. London: Royal College of Nursing.

Cohen, M. and Irwin, C.E. (1983) Parent-time: psychoeducational groups for parents of adolescents. *Health and Social Work*, **8**, 196–202.

Cook, P.J. and Laub, J.H. (1998) The unprecedented epidemic in youth violence. In Tonry, M. and Moore, M.H. (eds) *Crime and Justice: A Review of Research, Vol. 24*. Chicago: University of Chicago Press, pp. 27–64.

Dinkmeyer, D.C. (1979) A comprehensive and systematic approach to parent education. *Journal of Family Therapy*, **7**(2), 46–50.

Dishion, T.J., McCord, J. and Poulin, F. (1999) When interventions harm: peer groups and problem behavior. *American Psychologist*, **54**, 755–64.

Dumas, J.E. and Wahler, R.G. (1983) Predictors of treatment outcome in behavioural parent training. *Journal of Consulting and Clinical Psychology*, **52**, 117–34.

Faber, A. and Mazlish, E. (1980) *How to Talk So Kids Will Listen so Kids Will Talk*. New York: Avon.

Forehand, R.L. and McMahon, R.J. (1981*) Helping the Non-compliant Child: A Clinicians Guide to Parent Training*. New York, NY: Guilford Press.

Gardner, F.E.M., Sonuga-Barke, E.J.S. and Sayal, K. (1999) Parents anticipating misbehaviour: an observational study of strategies parents use to prevent conflict with behaviour problem children. *Journal of Child Psychology and Psychiatry*, **40**(8), 1185–96.

Gavacci, S.M. (1995) The growing up FAST: families and adolescents surviving and thriving program. *Journal of Adolescence*, **18**, 31–47.

Gordon, T. (1975) *Parent Effectiveness Training*. New York: New American Library.

Gross, D., Fogg, L., Webster-Stratton, C. and Grady, J. (1999) Parent training with low-income multi-ethnic parents of toddlers. Paper presented at the Society for Research in Child Development, Albuquerque, NM.

Hammer, T.J. and Turner, P.H. (1985) *Parenting in Contemporary Society*, 2nd edition. NJ: Prentice Hall.

Hawkins, J.D. and Catalano, R.F. (1996) *Parents Who Care: A Guide for Families With Teens*. Washington: Developmental Research and Programs.

Hendrick, H. (1994) *Child Welfare, England 1872–1989*. London: Routledge.

Henggeler, S.W., Schoenwald, S.K., Borduin, C.M., Rowland, M.D. and Cunningham, P.B. (1998) *Multisystemic Treatment of Antisocial Behavior in Children and Adolescents*. New York: Guilford Press.

Holden J.M., Sagovskiy, J.R. and Cox, J.L. (1989) Counseling in a general practice setting: a controlled study of health visitor intervention in the treatment of postnatal depression. *British Medical Journal*, **298**(6668), 223–6.

Huesmann, L.R., Moise-Titus, J., Podolski, C. and Eron, L.D. (2003) Longitudinal relations between children's exposure to TV violence and their aggressive and violent behavior in young adulthood: 1977–1992. *Developmental Psychology*, **39**, 201–21.

Hutchings, J. (1996) The personal and parental characteristics of pre-school children referred to a child and family mental health service and their relation to treatment outcome. Unpublished D.Clin.Psy. Thesis, University of Wales, Bangor.

Hutchings, J., Appleton, P., Smith, M., Lane, E. and Nash, S. (2002) Evaluation of two treatments for children with severe behaviour problems: child behaviour and maternal mental health outcomes. *Behavioural and Cognitive Psychotherapy*, **30**, 279–95.

Hutchings, J., Lane, E. and Kelly, J. (2004) Comparison of two treatments for children with severely disruptive behaviours: a four-year follow-up. *Journal of Behavioural and Cognitive Psychotherapy* (in press).

Johnson, Z. and Molloy, B. (1995) The community mothers programme – empowerment of mothers by mothers. *Children and Society*, **9**(2), 73–83.

Kazdin, A.E. (1990) Premature termination from treatment of children referred for antisocial behaviour.

Journal of Child Psychology and Psychiatry, **31**, 415–25.

Kazdin, A.E. (1993) Treatment of conduct disorder: progress and directions in psychotherapy research. *Development and Psychopathology*, **5**, 277–310.

Kitzman, H. (1997) Effect on prenatal and infancy home visitation by nurses on pregnancy outcomes, childhood injuries and repeated childbearing: a randomised controlled trial. *Journal of the American Medical Association*, **278**, 644–52.

Kochanska, G. and Aksan, N. (1995) Mother–child mutually positive affect, the quality of child compliance to requests and prohibitions, and maternal control as correlates of early internalization. *Child Development*, **66**, 236–54.

Lane, E. and Hutchings, J. (2002) Evaluation of a course in behavioural analysis for health visitors: the benefits for health visitors and the families with whom they worked. *British Journal of Nursing*, **11**(10), 702–14.

Larson, C.P. (1980) Efficacy of pre-natal and post-partum home visits on child health and development. *Pediatrics*, **66**, 191–7.

Lynam, D.R., Caspi, A., Moffitt, T.E., Wikström, P.H., Loeber, R. and Novak, S. (2000) The interaction between impulsivity and neighborhood context on offending: the effects of impulsivity are stronger in poorer neighborhoods. *Journal of Abnormal Psychology*, **109**, 563–74.

Miller, L.S. and Rojas-Flores, L. (1999) *Preventing Conduct Problems in Urban, Latino Preschoolers through Parent Training: A Pilot Study*. New York, NY: New York University Child Study Center.

Oakley A. (1992) *Social Support and Motherhood*. Oxford: Blackwell.

Oakley, A., Rajan, L. and Grant, A. (1990) Social support and pregnancy outcome. *British Journal of Obstetrics and Gynaecology*, **79**, 155–61.

O'Dell, S.L. (1985) Progress in parent training. In Hersen, M., Eisler, R.M. and Miller, P.M. (eds) *Progress in Behavior Modification*. New York: Academic Press, **19**, 57–107.

Office of Juvenile Justice and Delinquency Prevention (2000) *The Incredible Years Training Series*. Washington, D.C: Office of Juvenile Justice and Delinquency Prevention.

Offord, D.R., Boyle, M.C. and Szatmari, P. (1987) Ontario child health study: II, six month prevalence of disorder and rates of service utilization. *Archives of General Psychiatry*, **44**, 832–6.

Olds, D.L. (1986), Preventing child abuse and neglect: a randomized trial of nurse home visitation. *Pediatrics*, **78**, 65–78.

Olds, D.L. (1998) Long-term effects of nurse home visitation on children's criminal and antisocial behavior: 15-year follow-up of a randomized trial. *Journal of the American Medical Association*, **280**, 1238–44.

Owen, G.M. (1982) Health visiting. In Allen, P. and Jolley, M. (eds) *Nursing, Midwifery and Health Visiting Since 1900*. London: Faber and Faber.

Patterson, G.R. (1982) *Coercive Family Process*. Eugene, OR: Castalia.

Patterson, G.R. and Forgatch, M.S. (1989) *Parent and Adolescents Living Together, Part 2: Family Problem Solving*. Eugene, OR: Castalia Publishing.

Patterson, G.R., Reid, J.B., Jones, R.R. and Conger, R.E. (1975) *A Social Learning Approach to Family Intervention: Families with Aggressive Children*, Vol. 1. Eugene, OR: Castalia.

Patterson, G.R., Dishion, T.J. and Chamberlain, P. (1993) Outcomes and methodological issues relating to the treatment of antisocial children. In Giles, T.R. (ed.) *Effective Psychotherapy: A Handbook of Comparative Research*. New York: Plenum Press, pp. 43–88.

Reid, J.B. (1993) Prevention of conduct disorder before and after school entry: relating interventions to developmental findings, *Development and Psychopathology*, **5**, 243–62.

Reid, M.J., Webster-Stratton, C. and Beauchaine, T.P. (2001) Parent training in Head Start: a comparison of program response among African American, Asian American, Caucasian and Hispanic Mothers. *Prevention Science*, **2**(4), 209–27.

Robbins, L.N. (1981) Epidemiological approaches to natural history research: antisocial disorders in children. *Journal of the American Academy of Child Psychiatry*, **126**, 493–509.

Ruma, P.R., Burke, R.V. and Thompson, R.W. (1996) Group parent training: is it effective for children of all ages? *Behavior Therapy*, **27**, 159–69.

Rutter, M., Cox, A., Tupling, C., Berger, M. and Yule, W. (1975) Attainment and adjustment in two geographical areas, 1: The prevalence of child psychiatric disorder. *British Journal of Psychiatry*, **126**, 493–509.

Sanders, M.R. (1999), Triple P-Positive Parenting Program: towards an empirically validated multi-level parenting and family support strategy for the prevention of behaviour and emotional problems in children. *Journal of Clinical Child and Family Psychology Review*, **2**(2), 71–89.

Scott, S. (2001) Parent training programmes. In Rutter, M. and Taylor, E. (eds) *Child & Adolescent Psychiatry*, 4th edition. Oxford: Blackwell Science.

Scott, S., Knapp, M., Henderson, J. and Maughan, B. (2001a) Financial costs of social exclusion: follow-up study of children into adulthood. *British Medical Journal*, **323**(7306), 191–3.

Scott, S., Spender, Q., Doolan, M., Jacobs, B. and Aspland, H.C. (2001b). Multicentre controlled trial of parenting groups for childhood antisocial behavior in clinical practice. *British Medical Journal*, **323**, 194–203.

Shure, M. (1994) *I Can Problem Solve (ICPS): An Interpersonal Cognitive Problem-Solving Program for Children*. Champagn, IL: Research Press.

Smith, C. (1996) *Developing Parenting Programmes*. London: National Children's Bureau.

Spaccareli, S., Cotler, S. and Penman, D. (1992) Problem-solving skills training as a supplement to behavioural parent training. *Cognitive Therapy and Research*, **16**, 1–18.

Taylor, T.K. and Biglan, A. (1998). Behavioural family interventions for improving child-rearing: a review for clinicians and policy makers. *Clinical Child and Family Psychology Review*, **1**, 41–60.

Taylor, T.K., Schmidt, F., Pepler, D. and Hodgins, H. (1998) A comparison of eclectic treatment with Webster-Stratton's parent and children series in a mental health center: a randomized controlled trial. *Behaviour Therapy*, **29**, 221–40.

Wahler, R.G., Cartor, P.G., Fleischman, J. and Lambert, W. (1993) The Impact of synthesis teaching and parent training with mothers of conduct-disordered children. *Journal of Abnormal Child Psychology*, **21**, 425–40.

Walker, H.M., Colvin, G. and Ramsey, E. (1995) *Antisocial Behavior in School: Strategies and Best Practices*. Pacific Grove, CA: Brooks/Cole.

Webster-Stratton, C. (1985) Comparisons of behaviour transactions between conduct disordered children and their mothers in the clinic and at home. *Journal of Abnormal Child Psychology*, **13**(2), 169–84.

Webster-Stratton, C. (1991) Annotation: strategies for helping families with conduct disordered children. *Journal of Child Psychology and Psychiatry*, **32**(7), 1047–62.

Webster-Stratton, C. (1998a) Parent training with low-income families: promoting parental engagement through a collaborative approach. In Lutzker, J.R. (ed.) *Handbook of Child Abuse Research and Treatment*. New York, NY: Plenum Press, pp. 183–210.

Webster-Stratton, C. (1998b) Preventing conduct problems in Head Start children: strengthening parent competencies, *Journal of Consulting and Clinical Psychology*, **66**, 715–30.

Webster-Stratton, C. (1999) *How to Promote Children's Social and Emotional Competence*. London: Sage Publications.

Webster-Stratton, C. and Hammond, M. (1997) Treating children with early-onset conduct problems: a comparison of child and parent training interventions. *Journal of Consulting and Clinical Psychology*, **65**(1), 93–109.

Webster-Stratton, C. and Herbert, M. (1994) *Troubled Families – Problem Children, Working with Parents: A Collaborative Process*. Chichester: John Wiley.

Webster-Stratton, C. and Reid, M.J. (2003) Treating conduct problems and strengthening social emotional competence in young children (ages 4–8 years): The Dina Dinosaur treatment program. *Journal of Emotional and Behavioral Disorders*, **11**, 130–43.

Webster-Stratton, C. and Reid, M.J. (in press) Strengthening social and emotional competence in young children—the foundation for early school readiness and success: Incredible Years Classroom Social Skills and Problem Solving Curriculum. *Journal of Infants and Young Children*.

Webster-Stratton, C. and Taylor, T. (2001) Nipping early risk factors in the bud: preventing substance abuse, delinquency, and violence in adolescence through interventions targeted at young children (ages 0–8 years). *Prevention Science*, **2**(3), 165–92.

Webster-Stratton, C., Reid, M.J. and Hammond, M. (2001a) Preventing conduct problems, promoting social competence: a parent and teacher training partnership in Head Start. *Journal of Clinical Child Psychology*, **30**, 283–302.

Webster-Stratton, C., Mihelic, C., Fagan, A., Arnold, D., Taylor, T. and Tingley, C. (2001b) *Blueprints For Violence Prevention, Book 11: The Incredible Years: Parent, Teacher and Child Training Series*. Golden, CO: Venture Publishing.

Werry, J.S. (1997), Severe conduct disorder – some key issues. *Canadian Journal of Psychiatry*, **42**, 577–83.

21

Towards a Multi-level Model of Parenting Intervention

Matthew R. Sanders and Alan Ralph

SUMMARY

This chapter outlines the conceptual and empirical basis for the development of a multi-level approach to parent training and family intervention, as an integral component of programmes designed to prevent and treat behavioural and emotional problems in children and adolescents. Specifically, we argue for the value of developing a multi-level, preventively oriented, population health approach to parent education. We have deliberately restricted our exploration of the parenting literature and have constrained our attention to the models of parenting that have the strongest evidence base, namely behaviourally oriented family interventions that are based on social learning models. We begin by discussing the historical context within which these family interventions developed, review the evidence supporting their efficacy and effectiveness, and discuss possible implications for policy-makers, service providers and consumers. Finally, we identify some challenges for future research.

THE CASE FOR PARENT EDUCATION

Increasing attention is being given to the importance of better preparation for parents to undertake their role in raising children. This is partly in response to public alarm about the high prevalence of behavioural and emotional problems in children and the increased recognition of the role of parenting and family factors in influencing whether children develop serious problems in adolescence and beyond. Parents generally receive little preparation beyond the experience of having been parented themselves, with most learning 'on the job' through trial and error (Risley et al., 1976; Sanders et al., 1999). The changing social ecology of parenthood is also complicating the task of raising children. The already demanding role of parenthood is further complicated when parents do not have access to extended family support networks (such as grandparents, trusted family friends) for advice on child-rearing, or when they experience the stress of separation, divorce or re-partnering (Lawton and Sanders, 1994; Sanders et al., 1997). The experience of parental divorce affects parents' abilities to socialize their children and results in more children being raised in single-parent households, with consequently greater risk for adverse developmental outcomes (Amato and Booth, 1996; Martinez and Forgatch, 2001).

The rationale for parent training stems from evidence linking dysfunctional parenting practices with an increased risk of children developing behavioural and emotional problems. Research into the prevention and treatment of psychological disorders in children and adolescents has increasingly highlighted the critical importance of working with parents in a family context. The family provides the first and most important, social, emotional, interpersonal, economic and cultural context for human development. As a result, family relationships have a pervasive influence on the well-being of children. Disturbed family relationships are a generic risk factor, and positive family relationships a protective factor, related to a wide variety of mental health problems that occur from infancy to old age (Sanders, 1995). Many significant mental health, social and economic problems are linked to disturbances in family functioning and the breakdown of family relationships (Patterson, 1982; Chamberlain and Patterson, 1995; Sanders and Duncan, 1995).

Epidemiological studies indicate that family risk factors such as poor parenting, family conflict, and marriage breakdown strongly influence children's development (e.g. Dryfoos, 1990; Robins, 1991; Cummings and Davies, 1994). Specifically, these adverse influences which increase the risk of children developing major behavioural and emotional problems, include the following:

- the lack of a warm positive relationship with parents;
- insecure attachment;
- harsh, inflexible, rigid, or inconsistent discipline practices;
- inadequate supervision of and involvement with children;
- marital conflict and breakdown; and
- parental psychopathology, particularly maternal depression and parental criminality (e.g. Coie, 1996; Loeber and Farrington, 1998).

HISTORICAL BACKGROUND

While many different theoretical approaches to parent training and family intervention have emerged, the approach that has received the most empirical support is 'behavioural family intervention' (BFI: see Sanders, 1998; Horne, 2000). This social learning approach has drawn heavily on traditional concepts from learning theory, particularly applied behaviour analysis, and has, from its inception, emphasized the reciprocal and bi-directional nature of parent–child interactions. The key tenet of the social learning approach is that children learn to relate to others through primarily social interactions within the family (Horne, 2000). Behaviours are initially acquired by watching others, by using an already learned behaviour in a new situation, or simply by experimentation. Over time, behaviours are gradually strengthened or weakened as a consequence of the way that parents, siblings and others respond to that behaviour.

Over the years, however, BFI has also drawn extensively on other theoretical perspectives in psychology. There is now a wealth of information about the various factors that impact on children's development. In particular, research on parenting has identified children's competencies in naturally occurring everyday contexts, and traces the origins of social and intellectual competence to early parent–child relationships. Social psychology has also produced considerable advances in our knowledge of the development of social skills and how children manage social situations. These advances have helped to produce behavioural family interventions that target skills and behaviours that contribute to the appropriate development of children and adolescents.

Particular emphasis is placed on using child-initiated interactions as a context for the use of incidental teaching by parents. Cognitive psychology has also expanded in ways that now provide greater knowledge about cognitive processing in children that greatly informs the way interventions can maximize children's learning and skills acquisition. Social information processing models also highlight the important role of parental cognitions such as attributions, expectancies and beliefs as factors that contribute to parental self-efficacy, decision-making, and behavioural intentions.

More recently, ecological and contextual perspectives have been developed that view parent–child relationships in a broader social setting such as in the neighbourhood, media, work and schools (Biglan, 1992). Attempts are made to 'normalize' parenting experiences, and particularly the process of participating in parent education, by breaking down parents' sense of social isolation, increasing social and emotional support from others in the community, and validating and acknowledging publicly the importance and difficulties of parenting. Active community involvement in and support for the programme are also sought by the engagement of key community stakeholders.

Thus behavioural family interventions now have a far broader conceptual and structural focus than ever before. However, it is worth briefly examining more closely the stages through which BFI passed to reach the current situation.

Early applications of parent training are most commonly associated with Gerald Patterson and his colleagues at the Oregon Social Learning Center in the United States (e.g. Patterson et al., 1975; Patterson, 1982; Patterson et al., 1992). With its historical roots firmly embedded within the field of behaviour modification and applied behaviour analysis, this skills-oriented approach contrasted strongly with prevailing psychodynamic views on child therapy.

The development of training procedures to manage conduct problem behaviours in the home took place in the 1960s and early 1970s. Numerous single case studies illustrated the short-term effects of parent-implemented behavioural techniques such as praise, clear instructions, and time-out in reducing verbal and physical aggression (e.g. Wahler et al., 1965).

The second stage in the late 1970s and early 1980s involved examining more carefully the generalization and maintenance effects of parent training interventions. Four levels of generalization were differentiated (e.g. Forehand and Atkeson, 1977) that were relevant to the effects of parent training as it became clear that the main challenge was to transfer the treatment gains beyond the clinic and into the natural environment. The four levels of generalization were as follows:

- Setting generalization was said to occur when the treatment effects were demonstrated at home, in the school, or in other places remote from where training occurred.
- Time generalization (sometimes referred to as 'maintenance') occurred when the effects were observed to continue into the future, once training had been terminated.
- Behaviour generalization occurred when corollary improvements were observed in behaviours that were not targeted during treatment (e.g. improvements in sharing after a child had been taught to refrain from hitting).
- Sibling generalization occurred when behaviour improvements were noted in siblings who had not been the subject of an intervention.

As well as considering and programming for the generalization of children's behaviour, the generalization effects of parent training also needed to be addressed to assess the extent to which changes in parenting behaviours generalized across settings, time, behaviours and parents (Sanders and James, 1983). Several studies showed that parent training often results in strong generalization effects and that many of these changes are maintained over time (e.g. Koegel et al., 1978; Sanders and Glynn, 1981; Sanders and Dadds, 1982).

The third stage, which began in the mid-1980s, involved the development of 'adjunctive interventions' such as marital communication skills training, stress management, self-management and coping skills to enhance the effects of parenting skills training (e.g. Dadds et al., 1987). This research extended the focus of intervention beyond the parent–child dyad and resulted in a more comprehensive form of behavioural family intervention that addressed a range of other family risk variables.

A fourth stage in the evolution of BFI dated from around the mid-1990s and featured the adoption of a 'population health' perspective to supporting parents and families (Biglan, 1992; Sanders and Dadds, 1993; Spoth et al., 2001). Although the need for widespread dissemination and application of parenting programmes in the community had been identified very early, few actual demonstrations of how this could be achieved had been reported. Our own work at the University of Queensland has adopted a population perspective since the mid-1990s where comprehensive multi-level parenting interventions targeting entire populations have been developed (Sanders, 1999, 2001; Zubrick et al., in press). This current phase potentially involves significantly increasing the exposure of parents to evidence-based parenting interventions. This is accomplished by increasing the numbers of community-based practitioners being trained to deliver parenting education and support programmes across a range of existing health and educational services, including community and child health centres, general practices, kindergartens, preschools, primary and high schools.

Our recent review has highlighted the relative efficacy that behavioural family interventions show when compared to other treatment approaches such as client-centred therapy, systemic family therapy, and psychodynamic therapy for families. Parents receiving BFIs reported higher satisfaction, greater rates of improvement for their children's behaviour, and were more willing to recommend the programme to others.

TYPES OF PARENTING INTERVENTIONS

As parent training evolved over the past 30 years, it became apparent that behavioural family interventions could be delivered through a variety of therapeutic modalities in addition to individually administered programmes. Several randomized controlled trials have demonstrated that improved parenting can be effectively learned by parents participating in groups. Other studies have demonstrated that parenting groups can provide parents with a highly cost-effective option that is often preferred to an individual family-based service. This has been shown to be particularly attractive to immigrant families, families with English as their second language, and parents of children with severe behaviour problems, especially where materials are presented using videotaped examples. Self-directed or self-administered parent training through the use of well-designed materials including videotapes and workbooks has also proven moderately effective and highly cost-efficient. This approach appears to become even more effective with the addition of telephone assistance from a trained therapist. Effects have also been reported where parents merely viewed videotapes depicting common parenting problems and solutions (Webster-Stratton, 1984; Connell et al., 1997; Sanders et al., 2000b).

These programme modifications have the potential to substantially extend the reach of parenting programmes. However, low participation rates of parents in evidence-based parenting interventions have proven to be a major problem. A large-scale survey of 1218 Australian parents showed that only 10 per cent of parents had accessed any form of parent education (Sanders et al., 1999). Furthermore, in another comprehensive child health survey, only 2 per cent of parents of children with identifiable behavioural and emotional problems received mental health interventions of any sort (Zubrick et al., 1995).

Another emerging theme has been the development of parenting interventions of varying intensity. Universal preventive approaches to parenting programmes are generally designed to reduce family-related risk factors, such as discord, and enhance family protective factors, such as attachment. The use of the media to bring these issues to the attention of parents and care-givers in the community, plus those who come into contact with them, is considered crucial. While some families may require intensive interventions, others require quite minimal assistance. The development of minimally sufficient interventions for the latter type of family has led to the development of brief, primary care-based 'parent consultation' models involving two to four sessions of intervention. Originally conceived of as an early intervention strategy for mild cases, and typically delivered by specially trained general or allied health practitioners, it has become apparent that brief models of intervention can also benefit parents of children with more severe behaviour problems. They can also be implemented where more intensive interventions, though desirable, may not be immediately available.

Many families with child behaviour problems are functioning well enough that they can satisfactorily embrace and implement strategies and skills taught them during parent training programmes. However, for others, there is increasing evidence that other family risk factors such as marital conflict, parental depression and stress are implicated in parents' difficulties with their children, and may well prevent them from making full use of such strategies and skills. Related interventions targeting these additional risk factors were, therefore, developed and evaluated. For example, research has shown that the provision of brief marital communication skills training enhanced outcomes for maritally discordant parents of oppositional preschool children, but conversely did not improve outcomes for non-maritally discordant parents (Dadds et al., 1987). It has also been demonstrated that clinically depressed mothers benefited from additional modules providing cognitive coping skills training (Sanders and McFarland, 2000). Furthermore, the addition of anger management and 'attributional retraining' (where parents are taught alternative cause and effect reasoning) has been shown to improve outcomes for parents at risk of child maltreatment (Sanders et al., in press). These studies have extended the range and intensity of interventions for parents of conduct problem children.

Another difficulty has been the ability to predict in advance what level or intensity of treatment will be appropriate for different families. Although parent training was originally conducted either in the home or in a clinic environment, parents often have multiple competing demands, and parent trainers need to be more flexible in terms of where and when these interventions are delivered. For example, parenting interventions have been delivered in a variety of contexts including parents' homes, primary health care settings, childcare centres, schools, and as a work-site intervention.

Furthermore, the adoption of a contextual approach argues for the importance of seeking other opportunities for parenting interventions including the use of the media, primary health care settings, schools, places of work, and religious organizations. Although the evaluation of the media for parenting interventions and use of primary care settings is very recent, early results from several current trials are promising (e.g. Sanders et al., 2000b; Sanders and Turner, 2002).

EVIDENCE SUPPORTING PARENTING INTERVENTIONS

There have been several recent comprehensive reviews that have documented the efficacy of behavioural family intervention (BFI) as an effective means of assisting parents to raise children (Lochman, 1990; Sanders, 1996, 1998; Taylor and Biglan, 1998; McMahon, 1999). This literature will not be revisited here in detail. Its historical development has been briefly reviewed earlier. However, in summary, BFI can be described as a flexible, action-oriented, educationally focused intervention that aims to provide family members with the skills and knowledge required to resolve family problems that are causing distress to one or more family members. It allows practitioners to tailor solutions to family problems according to the complexity of the presenting problems and the conditions that maintain them.

There is clear evidence that BFI can educate parents about ways to manage children with disruptive behaviour disorders, particularly those with oppositional defiant disorders (ODD: Forehand and Long, 1988; Webster-Stratton, 1994; McMahon and Wells, 1998). The empirical basis of BFI is strengthened by evidence that the approach can be successfully applied to many other clinical problems and disorders, including attention deficit hyperactivity disorder (ADHD: Barkley et al., 1992), persistent feeding difficulties (Turner et al., 1994), pain syndromes (Sanders et al., 1994), anxiety disorders (Barrett et al., 1996), autism and developmental disabilities (Schreibman et al., 1991), achievement problems, and habit disorders, as well as everyday problems of normal children (see Sanders, 1996; Taylor and Biglan, 1998, for reviews of this literature). Parenting and family-oriented interventions have also been increasingly used to help educate parents of adolescents about ways to address the risk of drug abuse, conduct problems and delinquency, attention deficit disorder, eating disorders, depression, and chronic illness (Dishion and Andrews, 1995; Irvine et al., 1999).

Meta-analyses of treatment outcome studies of family focused interventions often report large effect sizes (Serketich and Dumas, 1996), with good maintenance of treatment gains (Forehand and Long, 1988). Treatment effects have been shown to generalize to school settings (McNeil et al., 1991) and to various community settings outside the home (Sanders and Glynn, 1981). Furthermore, parents participating in these programmes are generally satisfied 'consumers' (Webster-Stratton, 1989).

It is also becoming increasingly evident that the benefits of BFI are not restricted to children, with several studies now reporting effects in other areas of family functioning, including reduced maternal depression and stress, increases in parental satisfaction and efficacy,

and reduced marital conflict over parenting issues (e.g. Webster-Stratton, 1998; Nicholson and Sanders, 1999; Sanders and McFarland, 2000; Sanders et al., 2000a, 2000b).

BFIs have met a number of important scientific and clinical criteria which strengthen confidence in the intervention approach. These include the following:

- *Replicated findings*: primary treatment effects, which have shown that decreases in negative disciplinary behaviour by parents and increased use of a variety of positive attending and other relationship-enhancing skills lead to improved child behaviour. These findings have been replicated many times in different studies involving different investigators, in different countries, and with a diverse variety of client populations (Sanders, 1999; Scott et al., 2001).

- *Demonstrations of clinically meaningful outcomes for families*: clinically significant outcomes have been demonstrated by applying rigorous criteria for clinical improvement such as the Reliable Change Index for child outcomes (RCI: Jacobson and Truax, 1991). These have shown that as many as 75 per cent of children display evidence of clinically reliable change. Furthermore, there is little evidence that parenting interventions produce negative side-effects, symptom substitution, or other adverse family outcomes.

- *The effectiveness of different delivery modalities*: there is increasing evidence showing that a variety of delivery modalities can produce similar positive outcomes for children, including individual, group, telephone-assisted, and self-directed variants of parenting programmes (e.g. O'Dell, 1974; Connell et al., 1997; Sanders et al., 2003).

- *High levels of consumer acceptability*: high levels of consumer satisfaction have been repeatedly demonstrated in different controlled evaluations of BFI and for specific advocated parenting techniques (see Webster-Stratton, 1989; McMahon, 1999).

- *Effectiveness with a range of family types*: in the area where the strongest support for BFI is evident, namely for disruptive behaviour problems in pre-adolescent children, interventions have been successfully used with two-biological-parent families, step-parents, and single parents.

Until relatively recently there were few well-controlled studies examining family intervention with adolescents. This situation has changed and it is reasonable to conclude that family intervention is potentially effective with a variety of adolescent problems, including substance abuse (Alexander et al., 1994; Liddle and Dakof, 1995), antisocial behaviour (Henggler et al., 1993), and eating disorders (Le Grange et al., 1992).

In sum, these findings confirm that BFI is a powerful clinical resource for effecting change in family relationships that in turn are related to a wide range of behavioural and emotional problems in children.

THE PRACTICE OF PARENTING

BFI is conceptually and clinically justified as a basis for educating parents, as a strategy to address both the prevention and treatment of behavioural and emotional problems in children and adolescents. This justification stems from evidence that parenting factors, such as dysfunctional discipline and family conflict, are major risk factors for the development of psychopathology in children. The relationship between parenting variables and child development has been well established, with four types of research powerfully demonstrating the effects of parenting practices on children (Collins et al., 2000). These include the following:

- behaviour-genetic research studies which included direct observation measures of parenting behaviour;
- studies of children with different genetic predispositions, who differ in their response to different rearing environments;
- studies which show that child behaviour changes follow experimental manipulation of parent behaviour after controlling for children's initial characteristics; and
- research showing that effects of broader ecological contexts on children (such as social disadvantage) are mediated through changes in parenting behaviour. These studies have employed cross-sectional, longitudinal and experimental designs and have used sophisticated statistical techniques to analyse interaction effects.

Parenting practices are also related to a variety of contextual factors, including socio-demographic and interpersonal adjustment variables of parents. For example, lower socio-economic status is associated with greater use of corporal punishment and coercive discipline strategies (e.g. Zubrick et al., 1995; Sanders et al., 1999). Many of the negative effects of poverty on children's development are mediated through the effects of poverty on parental behaviour, with studies showing that economic stress and disadvantage increase parental punitiveness, which in turn adversely affects children (e.g. Conger et al., 1994).

Family support and attachment are also significant predictors of positive adjustment in childhood and adolescence. Indirect evidence suggests that family support is a protective factor for adolescent substance abuse and conduct problems (Cohen and Wills, 1985; Cauce et al., 1990; Wills et al., 1992). Where children display non-compliant and antisocial behaviour, parents are often poorly equipped to provide consistent affection and discipline to their children. There is also good evidence that the onset and maintenance of adolescent substance abuse and conduct disorders are associated with a number of family practices such as disrupted, coercive or nonexistent parenting; inappropriate discipline; and inadequate parental monitoring (Loeber and Stouthamer-Loeber, 1987; Block et al., 1988; Farrington et al., 1990; Hawkins et al., 1992; Steinberg et al., 1994).

Parenting variables related to adolescent highrisk sexual behaviour include limited parental availability to the children, low levels of parent monitoring and support, and coercive and negative family exchanges (Biglan et al., 1990). Poor parental supervision in middle childhood has also been shown to be a significant factor in children's movement into a deviant peer network in early adolescence (Dishion et al., 1991), and higher levels of monitoring have been associated with lower levels of adolescent deviance (Lamborn et al., 1996). 'Parental monitoring' is a strong predictor of male adolescent delinquency (Loeber and Dishion, 1983; Loeber and Stouthamer-Loeber, 1987) and differences in parents' monitoring practices correlated directly with levels of antisocial behaviour in boys and indirectly via increased contact with delinquent peers (Patterson and Dishion, 1985). There is also evidence that inadequate parental monitoring has been implicated in fire-setting and early substance use.

Recent studies have provided perhaps the clearest picture yet of the parenting constructs that could be targeted when developing early interventions to prevent severe adolescent problems. Conflict with parents has been shown to be strongly associated with contact with deviant peers, substance use, and engaging in antisocial behaviour. On the other hand, high levels of positive family relations, parental supervision, rule setting, and positive reinforcement appear to be associated with less contact with deviant peers, less engagement in antisocial behaviour, and less substance use (Metzler et al., 1998).

OVERVIEW: CONCLUSIONS REGARDING THE STATE OF THE ART

Over recent years, BFI has become a much more sophisticated endeavour that now provides practitioners with a rich array of clinical tools and strategies to assist parents to promote their children's development. With the advent of different delivery modalities and multi-level models which provide support for parents at differing levels of intensity, a more diverse range of practitioners has become involved in the delivery of parenting interventions. The following conclusions seem warranted on the basis of the evidence.

- BFI is one of the most thoroughly researched treatment approaches for childhood conduct problems. Research evaluating the use of behavioural family interventions for child conduct problems has supported the efficacy of this approach both in the short term, and over follow-up periods of up to 17 years after the termination of treatment (Forehand and Long, 1988; Long et al., 1994). There is increasing evidence to support the efficacy of behavioural family intervention as a treatment for anxiety, recurrent pain syndromes, social skills deficits, language problems and for children with developmental disabilities.
- Despite the evidence supporting the effectiveness of BFI, there is little room for complacency. There are several significant limitations with current approaches that must be addressed by researchers and practitioners if these interventions are to have a significant impact on family relationships at a population level. A major concern for the family intervention field in general is that empirically supported interventions are under-utilized by professionals. Nor are they readily accessible to families who might benefit from them (Taylor and Biglan, 1998). Most children with behavioural problems receive no assistance from mental health professionals (Zubrick et al., 1995). Furthermore, there are low participation rates in parent education and support schemes, particularly in families who are considered most at risk for the development of serious problems (Sanders et al., 1999). Non-evaluated parent education and family support programmes continue to dominate the field, where programmes are offered to the public with no known effects. In the absence of any meaningful form of accountability or quality control to ensure evidence-based family interventions are promoted,

families are exposed to a diverse range of untested and in some instances even potentially harmful interventions.
- Empirically supported family intervention programmes generally have limited reach. It is also of continuing concern that indigenous and ethnic minority groups have low representation in clinical outcome trials. These groups are among the most disadvantaged sectors of the community and are more likely to drop out from treatment (Kazdin, 1997). Access problems are compounded by the relative inflexibility of delivery formats required by most interventions, particularly the requirement for face-to-face session attendance during regular working hours. For families with both parents working or families living in rural, remote or otherwise isolated areas, meeting this attendance requirement can be an insurmountable problem.
- Another criticism of family intervention as a risk reduction approach is that it may simply be insufficient as an intervention on its own, particularly for complex problems such as severe conduct disorder, ADHD and drug abuse, where there are multiple interacting risk factors. Based on epidemiological evidence, some researchers have argued that longer, more intensive, multi-risk factor interventions covering home, school, peer groups and the child themselves are required to prevent conduct disorders (McMahon and Slough, 1996; Kazdin, 1997). However, it has still to be convincingly demonstrated, through long-term outcome studies, that such an approach will be more effective than targeting a more limited subset of risk and protective factors such as parenting skills, maternal depression or marital discord.
- One of the major problems for families with limited resources is that receiving multiple interventions can add to the burden of care already experienced by them (such as additional appointments, more professionals to deal with and extra costs), particularly if the child has special needs such as those arising from a chronic disability.

IMPLICATIONS FOR PRACTICE

The practice of parent training has evolved substantially over the past decade to the extent that practitioners now have access to a range of high-quality empirically supported interventions to assist parents and their children. There has been increasing recognition that the family plays a critical role in determining developmental outcomes for children and adolescents. We believe that there is strong enough evidence available for governments to support the wide-scale implementation of evidence-based parenting programmes. However, to move beyond the stage of political rhetoric regarding the importance of the family to making any significant impact on the quality of parenting children receive, major changes are required in how parenting and family support services are provided for the community.

Perhaps the most important challenge facing the field of parent education is to reorient our focus from treatment outcome studies to the development and evaluation of a *population perspective on family problems*, including the effective dissemination of what is known to work in promoting effective parenting and positive family relationships. A comprehensive population-based strategy is required. This strategy needs to be designed to enhance parental competence, prevent dysfunctional parenting practices, promote better teamwork between partners, and thereby reduce an important set of family risk factors associated with behavioural and emotional problems in children.

Early parent training programmes focused on assisting parents to manage problem behaviours, but more recently the trend has been to provide early intervention programmes, and more latterly, prevention programmes. These are typically conceptualized as falling into one of three categories: universal, selective or indicated (Mrazek and Haggerty, 1994):

- *a universal* prevention strategy targets an entire population (e.g. national, local community, neighbourhood or school);
- *selective* prevention programmes refer to strategies that target specific subgroups of the general population that are believed to be at greater risk than others for developing a problem (such as low-income families, young single mothers); and
- *indicated* preventive interventions target high-risk individuals who are identified as having detectable problems, but who do not yet meet diagnostic criteria for a behavioural disorder (e.g. disruptive and aggressive children).

The Triple P – Positive Parenting Programme – is a multi-level, parenting and family support strategy developed by the first author and colleagues. One of the programme's aims is to prevent severe behavioural, emotional and developmental problems in children by enhancing the knowledge, skills and confidence of parents. It incorporates universal, selective and indicated interventions, organized across five levels, on a tiered continuum of increasing strength (see Table 21.1) for parents of children from birth to age 12 years. Recently the programme has been extended to provide the same levels of information and support for parents of teenagers aged 12–16 years.

- *Level 1*, a universal parent information strategy, provides all interested parents with access to useful information about parenting, through a co-ordinated promotional campaign using print and electronic media, as well as user-friendly parenting 'tip sheets', and videotapes which demonstrate specific parenting strategies. This level of intervention aims to increase community awareness of parenting resources, receptivity of parents to participating in programmes, and to create a sense of optimism by depicting solutions to common behavioural and developmental concerns.
- *Level 2* is a brief, one- or two-session, primary health care, selective intervention providing anticipatory developmental guidance to parents of children with mild behaviour difficulties.
- *Level 3*, a four-session, more intensive selective intervention, targets children with mild to moderate behaviour difficulties and includes active skills training for parents.
- *Level 4* is an indicated intensive eight- to ten-session, individual or group training programme, for parents of children with more severe behavioural difficulties.
- *Level 5* is an enhanced behavioural family intervention programme, for families where parenting difficulties are complicated by other sources of family distress (such as marital conflict, parental depression, high levels of stress, or teenage relationship problems). This multi-level model is depicted in Figure 21.1.

The different levels of the model are all supported by resources that include 14 professionally produced videotapes depicting common problems and solutions for a range of children's ages and issues; a series of over 50 'tip sheets' providing advice and information to parents on common problems faced from infancy to adolescence; parent workbooks for use in face-to-face, group or self-directed intervention modes; wallcharts summarizing key parenting principles; and practitioner kits and manuals to facilitate the delivery of the various levels of the programme. To increase parents' access to the

Table 21.1   *The Triple P model of parenting and family support*

Level of intervention	Target population	Intervention methods	Programme materials	Possible target behaviours
1 Universal Triple P	All parents interested in information about promoting their child's development	Anticipatory well childcare involving the provision of brief information on how to solve developmental and minor behaviour problems. May involve self-directed resources, brief consultation, group presentations and mass media strategies	*Positive Parenting* booklet; *Positive Parenting* tip sheet series; *Families* video series; *Every Parent Triple P Programme Guide*	Common everyday behaviour difficulties
2 Selected Triple P	Parents with a specific concern about their child's behaviour or development	Provision of specific advice for a discrete child problem behaviour. May be self-directed or involve telephone or face-to-face clinician contact or group sessions	Level 1 materials; *Primary Care Triple P Practitioner's Manual*; developmental wall chart; consultation flip chart	Bedtime routine difficulties; temper tantrums; meal-time behaviour problems; toilet training
3 Primary Care Triple P	Parents with specific concerns about their child's behaviour or development that require active skills training	Brief therapy programme (1–4 clinic sessions) combining advice, rehearsal and self-evaluation to teach parents to manage a discrete child problem behaviour	Level 1 and 2 materials	As for Level 2; persistent eating problems; pain management
4 Standard Triple P	Parents of children with more severe behaviour problems; parents wanting intensive training in positive parenting skills	Intensive programme focusing on parent–child interaction and the application of parenting skills to a broad range of target behaviours. Includes generalization enhancement strategies. May be self-directed or involve telephone or face-to-face clinician contact or group sessions	Level 1 to 3 materials; *Every Parent's Self-Help Workbook*; *Standard Triple P Practitioner's Manual and Every Parent's Family Workbook*; *Group Triple P Facilitator's Manual and Every Parent's Group Workbook*	General behaviour management concerns; aggressive behaviour; oppositional defiant disorder; conduct disorder learning difficulties
5 Enhanced Triple P	Parents of children with concurrent child behaviour problems and family dysfunction	Intensive programme with modules including home visits to enhance parenting skills, mood management strategies and stress coping skills, and partner support skills	Levels 1 to 4 materials; *Enhanced Triple P Practitioner's Manual and Every Parent's Supplementary Workbook*	Persistent conduct problems; concurrent child behaviour problems and parent problems (such as relationship conflict, depression); child maltreatment

different intervention levels, a coherent system of training and accreditation is provided to a diversity of practitioners including general practitioners, community and child health nurses, social workers, occupational therapists, physiotherapists, teachers, school counsellors, psychologists, psychiatrists and paediatricians.

The programmes for parents of teenagers, known as Teen Triple P, mirror those for parents of younger children, but with a stronger emphasis on the importance of parents acknowledging and encouraging the growing autonomy and independence of teenagers relative to younger children. Recognition is also given to the likelihood

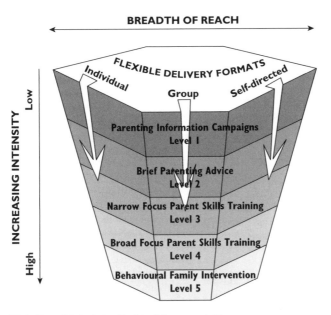

Figure 21.1   *Triple P model depicting flexible delivery modalities*

of teenagers engaging in risky behaviour that may put their current or future health, education and general well-being in jeopardy, and providing parents with ways of assisting their teenagers to negotiate and manage these challenges effectively.

In summary, this tiered multi-level strategy recognizes that there are differing levels of dysfunction and behavioural disturbance in children and adolescents, and parents have differing needs and desires regarding the type, intensity, and mode of assistance they may require. The multi-level strategy is designed to maximize efficiency, contain costs, avoid waste and over-servicing, and ensure the programme has wide reach in the community. The programme targets five different developmental periods from infancy to adolescence, and within each developmental period the reach of the intervention can vary from being very broad (targeting an entire population) to quite narrow (targeting only high-risk children). Also the multidisciplinary nature of the programme involves the better utilization of the existing professional workforce in the task of promoting competent parenting. It stands in marked contrast to the traditional approach which is typically based around more narrowly focused programmes that make few allowances for differing parental needs, different developmental challenges, or are not directly linked to the reduction of known risk factors. Furthermore, it directly challenges the *ad hoc* way that parenting services are often fragmented

with many competing approaches across different service delivery domains.

TOWARDS A MODEL OF EFFECTIVE PARENT CONSULTATION

Reports of clinical trials documenting the effects of family intervention programmes often mask the complexity of the therapeutic process issues involved in successful family intervention. In addition to relevant theoretical and conceptual knowledge on psychopathology, family relationships, life-long human development, principles and techniques of behaviour, and attitude and cognitive change, practitioners must be interpersonally skilled. They require well-developed communication skills, with advanced level training in the theory and principles of family intervention. On this basis, several principles that optimize the effectiveness of parenting interventions are proposed.

Parenting Interventions Should Empower Families

Interventions should aim to enhance individual competency and the families' ability as a whole to solve problems for themselves. In most (but not all) instances, families will have a lessening need for support over time. The Triple P programme is based on a strong self-regulatory framework. Goals include children developing emotional self-regulations, and parents becoming resourceful independent problem-solvers. Family interventions that promote dependency are ill-informed and potentially destructive. Equally, parenting programmes need to steer clear of being too prescriptive about the values and beliefs individual parents want to instil in their children, while advising parents about effective strategies they can choose from to achieve those goals.

Parenting Interventions Should Build on Existing Strengths

Successful interventions build on the existing competencies of family members, however meagre they may be. It is assumed that individuals are capable of becoming active problem-solvers, even though their previous attempts to resolve problems may not have been successful. This may be due to lack of necessary knowledge, skills or motivation. It is not the case that parenting education programmes are only useful for educated, middle-class families. Major validation studies with Triple P have been conducted with high-risk, low-income families where appropriate parenting behaviours were shaped and strengthened.

The Therapeutic Relationship is an Important Part of Effective Family Intervention

Regardless of theoretical orientation, most family intervention experts agree that the therapeutic relationship between the clinician and relevant family members is critical to successful long-term outcome (Sanders and Lawton, 1993; Patterson and Chamberlain, 1994). Clinical skills such as rapport building, effective interviewing and communication skills, session structuring, and the development of empathic, caring relationships with family members are important to all forms of family intervention. Such skills are particularly important in face-to-face programmes, but are also important in models of support that involve brief or minimal contact, including telephone advice or correspondence programmes. Consequently, mental health professionals undertaking family intervention work need advanced level training and supervision in both the science and the clinical practice of family intervention.

The Goals of Intervention Should Address Known Risk Variables

Family interventions vary according to the focus or goals of the intervention. Interventions that have proven most successful address variables that are known to increase the risk of individual psychopathology and those that are known to protect against such psychopathology. Some interventions focus heavily on behavioural change (e.g. Forehand and McMahon, 1981), whereas others concentrate on cognitive, affective and attitude change as well (e.g. Sanders and Dadds, 1993; Webster-Stratton, 1994).

The focus of the intervention depends greatly on the theoretical underpinnings and assumptions of the approach. However, a common goal in most effective forms of family intervention is to improve family communication, problem-solving, conflict resolution, and parent management skills. This does not mean that parents are simply taught how to control their children more effectively. A critical focus of Triple P is the strong emphasis on using positive parenting strategies that promote appropriate child development, including increased communication, impulse-control, emotional regulation, problem-solving, and skills development on the part of the child, particularly as they become older and more autonomous.

Intervention Services Should be Designed to Facilitate Access

It is essential that interventions be delivered in ways that increase, rather than restrict, access to services. Professional practices can sometimes restrict access to services. For example, inflexible clinic hours during 9 am to 5 pm may be a barrier to working parents' participation in family intervention programmes. Family intervention consultations may take place in many different settings, such as in clinics or hospitals, family homes, kindergartens, preschools, schools and worksites.

The type of setting selected should vary depending on the goals of the intervention and the needs of the target group. It is also important that programme materials should not require high levels of literacy skills. For example, Triple P programme materials are designed for a grade 6–7 reading level that could be read by an average 11 year old, and are supplemented by videos and behavioural rehearsal. Practitioners must become more flexible to allow better tailoring of services to meet individual family needs.

Family Intervention Programmes Should be Timed Developmentally to Optimize Impact

The developmental timing of the intervention refers to the age and developmental level of the target group. Family intervention methods have been used across the life-span including pre-birth, infancy, toddlerhood, middle childhood, adolescence, early adulthood, middle adulthood, and late adulthood. Developmentally targeted family interventions for particular problems may have a greater impact than if delivered at another time in the life-cycle. For example, premarital counselling may be more effective in reducing subsequent relationship breakdown than a marriage enrichment programme delivered after marital distress has already developed. There is still much to be learnt regarding such developmental 'timing'.

Parenting and Family Interventions can Complement and Enhance Other Interventions

Family intervention can be an effective intervention in its own right for a variety of clinical problems. Programmes that focus on parenting variables are not necessarily limited when more complex cases are encountered. Triple P has produced successful outcomes with clinically depressed, maritally discordant, and highly distressed parents, and with stepfamilies. However, for other more complex problems, such as schizophrenia and bipolar disorder, family intervention can be successfully combined with other interventions such as drug therapy, individual therapy, social and community survival skills training, classroom management, and academic instruction.

Family intervention can complement other interventions for individuals by increasing compliance with medication, and by ensuring the co-operation and support of family members. Family intervention should therefore be an integral component of comprehensive mental health services for all disorders.

Parenting Interventions Should be Gender Sensitive

Family interventions have the potential to promote more equitable gender relationships within the family. Intervention programmes may directly or indirectly promote inequitable relationships between marital partners, by inadvertently promoting traditional gender stereotypes and power relationships that increase dependency and restrict the choices of women. In addition, the modelling of such stereotypic behaviour by parents will have a strong influence on children's adoption of those stereotypes, thus furthering inequality. Consequently, family intervention programmes should strongly promote gender equality.

Theories Underlying Family Interventions Should be Scientifically Validated

Family interventions should be based on coherent and explicit theoretical principles that allow key assumptions to be tested. This extends beyond demonstrating that an intervention works, although that may be an important first step. It involves showing that the mechanisms purported to underlie improvement (specific family interaction processes) actually change and are responsible for the observed improvement, rather than other non-specific factors. As governments become increasingly concerned with funding programmes to reduce the social costs of delinquency, drug abuse, domestic violence, child abuse, depression and suicide, it becomes increasingly important to adopt a 'culture of evaluation' to demonstrate outcomes that justify spending of public funds.

Family Interventions Should be Culturally Appropriate

Family intervention programmes should be tailored in such a way as to respect and not undermine the cultural values, aspirations, traditions and needs of different ethnic groups. This does not necessarily involve developing different interventions, but being sensitive to issues of engagement and presentation. The Triple P programme has been translated into several community languages with considerable success.

The selective use of culturally relevant and appropriate examples depicting the use of empirically supported procedures as part of a generic parenting programme such as Triple P appears to overcome concerns that such programmes are not culturally appropriate for ethnic minority groups. However, there is still much to learn about how to achieve this objective although there is increasing evidence from other countries that sensitively tailored family interventions can be effective with minority cultures (Myers et al., 1992).

IMPLICATIONS FOR POLICY

Not only do governments need to support evidence-based parenting initiatives, they need to do so on such a scale as to achieve a population level reduction in the prevalence of dysfunctional parenting. However, as governments could easily be criticized for appearing to meddle in the lives of families, they cannot accomplish the task on their own. Community-level support and participation from industry, professional, non-government and consumer organizations would also be desirable. Meaningful partnerships between various sectors in the community are based upon shared recognition that supporting children and families is for the benefit of the entire community. Examples include local businesses funding the delivery of parenting programmes in the workplace as part of 'Employee Assistance Schemes'.

Another important consideration for governments is to decide whether programmes without a definable evidence base should be funded. Although it may seem provocative to suggest that governments should de-fund some existing programmes, limited resources and the need for proper public accountability demand that professionals delivering programmes to the public use the best available evidence to develop 'best' practice guidelines.

Implications for Schools and Health Services

Many parents turn to their family doctors and to schools for advice regarding parenting and behaviour management issues. Transition to school programmes that make group parenting programmes available to parents have the potential, if well promoted, to substantially extend the reach of parenting interventions at a developmentally sensitive transition point.

Similarly, the development of training programmes for primary health care practitioners provides an important opportunity for the provision of brief parent consultation models in a destigmatized, anticipatory, 'well-childcare' context. This can be particularly important in providing a response to families where abuse is occurring. It has often been thought that parents need to be highly motivated to seek parenting advice and assistance. However, Triple P has now been widely used as an abuse-prevention strategy with encouraging preliminary findings. When coupled with primary care, good parenting support programmes can offer a non-stigmatizing

and non-coercive response to this significant problem area.

Implications for Parents and Children

With the proliferation of parenting programmes offered in the community, parents need to be better informed regarding the goals, methods, outcomes and costs involved in participating in various types of parenting programmes. In addition, the acceptability of different parenting strategies with problems of children of various ages (such as use of incidental teaching, time-out, having rules, planned ignoring) should become an increasing focus of research inquiry. Unless variables affecting parental judgements of acceptability are identified, potentially effective strategies may be overlooked and weak or ineffective procedures used in their place.

CONCLUSIONS

There are now a number of well-established, empirically supported parenting and family intervention programmes that have met basic scientific and clinical criteria to be considered as effective interventions for a range of child behaviour problems. Parent educators are being increasingly confronted by information showing that many clinical assumptions about the necessary and sufficient conditions required to produce change in families are not true. For example, the view that face-to-face, talk-oriented approaches are needed is now being challenged by well-controlled research findings.

The next generation of parenting programmes will increasingly look to use modern communication technologies, particularly the worldwide web, to improve access and reduce costs to consumers. While such initiatives are already occurring, it remains critical that such innovations are subjected to careful evaluative scrutiny. An important challenge for future research is to identify the profiles of parents who are responders and non-responders to different intensities and modalities of parenting intervention.

REFERENCES

Alexander, J.F., Holtzworth-Munroe, A. and Jameson, P.B. (1994) The process and outcome of marital and family therapy: research review and evaluation. In Bergin, A.E. and Garfield, S.L. (eds) *Handbook of Psychotherapy and Behavior Change*, 4th edition. New York: John Wiley, pp. 595–630.

Amato, P.R. and Booth, A. (1996) A prospective study of divorce and parent–child relationships. *Journal of Marriage and The Family*, **58**, 356–65.

Barkley, R.A., Guevremont, D.C., Anastopoulos, A.D. and Fletcher, K.E. (1992) A comparison of three family therapy programs for treating family conflicts in adolescents with attention-deficit hyperactivity disorder. *Journal of Consulting and Clinical Psychology*, **60**(3), 450–62.

Barrett, P.M., Dadds, M.R. and Rapee, R.M. (1996) Family treatment of childhood anxiety: a controlled trial. *Journal of Consulting and Clinical Psychology*, **65**, 627–35.

Biglan, A. (1992) Family practices and the larger social context. *New Zealand Journal of Psychology*, **21**(1), 37–43.

Biglan, A., Metzler, C.W., Wirt, R., Ary, D., Noell, J., Ochs, L., French, C. and Hood, D. (1990) Social and behavioural factors associated with high-risk sexual behavior among adolescents. *Journal of Behavioral Medicine*, **13**, 245–61.

Block, J., Block, J.H. and Keyes, S. (1988) Longitudinally foretelling drug usage in adolescence: early childhood personality and environmental precursors. *Child Development*, **59**, 336–55.

Cauce, A., Reid, M., Kandesmann, S. and Gonzales, N. (1990) Social support in young children: measurement, structure, and behavioral impact. In Sarason, B.R., Sarason, I.R. and Pierce, G.R. (eds) *Social Support: An Interactional View*. Wiley Series on Personality Processes. New York: John Wiley, pp. 64–94.

Chamberlain, P. and Patterson, G.R. (1995) Discipline and child compliance in parenting. In Bornstein, M.H. (eds) *Handbook of Parenting, Vol. 4: Applied and Practical Parenting*. Mahwah, NJ: Lawrence Erlbaum, pp. 205–25.

Cohen, S. and Wills, T.A. (1985) Stress, social support, and the buffering hypothesis. *Psychological Bulletin*, **98**, 310–57.

Coie, J.D. (1996) Prevention of violence and antisocial behavior. In Peters, R.D. and McMahon, R.J. (eds) *Preventing Childhood Disorders, Substance Abuse, and Delinquency*. Thousand Oaks, CA: Sage Publications, pp. 1–18.

Collins, W.A., Maccoby, E.E., Steinberg, L., Hetherington, M.E. and Bornstein, M.H. (2000) Contemporary research on parenting: the case for nature and nurture. *American Psychologist*, **55**(2), 218–32.

Conger, R.D., Ge, X., Elder, G.H. and Lorenz, F.O. (1994) Economic stress, coercive family process and developmental problems of adolescents. *Child Development*, **65**, 541–61.

Connell, S., Sanders, M.R. and Markie Dadds, C. (1997) Self-directed behavioral family intervention for parents of oppositional children in rural and remote areas. *Behavior Modification*, **21**(4), 379–408.

Cummings, E.M. and Davies, P. (1994) *Children and Marital Conflict: The Impact of Family Dispute and Resolution*. New York: Guilford Press.

Dadds, M.R., Schwartz, S. and Sanders, M.R. (1987) Marital discord and treatment outcome in the treatment of childhood conduct disorders. *Journal of Consulting & Clinical Psychology*, **55**, 396–403.

Dishion, T.J. and Andrews, D.W. (1995) Preventing escalation in problem behaviour with high-risk adolescents: Immediate and 1-year outcomes. *Journal of Consulting and Clinical Psychology*, **63**, 538–48.

Dishion, T.J., Patterson, G.R., Stoolmiller, M. and Skinner, M.L. (1991) Family, school, and behavioral antecedents to early adolescent involvement with antisocial peers. *Developmental Psychology*, **27**, 172–80.

Dryfoos, J.G. (1990) *Adolescents at Risk: Prevalence and Prevention*. New York: Oxford University Press.

Farrington, D.P., Loeber, R., Elliott, D.S., Hawkins, J.D., Kandel, D.B., Klein, M.W., McCord, J., Rowe, D.C. and Tremblay, R.E. (1990) Advancing knowledge about the onset of delinquency and crime. In Lahey, B.B. and Kazdin, A.E. (eds) *Clinical Child Psychology*, Vol. 13. New York: Plenum, pp. 283–342.

Forehand, R.L. and Atkeson, B.A. (1977) Generality of treatment effect with parents as therapists: a review of assessment and implementation procedures. *Behavior Therapy*, **8**, 575–93.

Forehand, R.L. and Long, N. (1988) Outpatient treatment of the acting out child: procedures, long term follow-up data, and clinical problems. *Advances in Behavior Research and Therapy*, **10**, 129–77.

Forehand, R.L. and McMahon, R.J. (1981) Suggestions for evaluating self-administered materials in parent training. *Child Behavior Therapy*, **3**, 65–8.

Hawkins, J.D., Catalano, R.F. and Miller, J.Y. (1992) Risk and protective factors for alcohol and other drug problems in adolescence and early adulthood: implications for substance abuse prevention. *Psychological Bulletin*, **112**, 64–105.

Henggler, S.W., Bourdin, C.M. and Mann, B.J. (1993) Advances in family therapy: empirical foundations. *Advances in Clinical Child Psychology*, **15**, 207–41.

Horne, A.M. (2000) *Family Counseling and Therapy*, 3rd edition. Itasca, IL: F.E. Peacock Publishers.

Irvine, A.B., Biglan, A., Smolkowski, K., Metzler, C.W. and Ary, D.V. (1999) The effectiveness of a parenting skills training program for parents of middle school students in small communities. *Journal of Consulting and Clinical Psychology*, **67**, 811–25.

Jacobson, N.S. and Truax, P. (1991) Clinical significance: a statistical approach to defining meaningful change in psychotherapy research. *Journal of Consulting and Clinical Psychology*, **59**, 12–19.

Kazdin, A.E. (1997) A model for developing effective treatments: progression and interplay of theory, research and practice. *Journal of Clinical Child Psychology*, **26**, 114–29.

Koegel, R.L., Glahn, T.J. and Nieminen, G.S. (1978) Generalization of parent-training results. *Journal of Applied Behavior Analysis*, **11**, 95–109.

Lamborn, S.D., Dornbusch, S.M. and Steinberg, L. (1996) Ethnicity and community context as moderators of the relations between family decision-making and adolescent adjustment. *Child Development*, **67**, 283–301.

Lawton, J.M. and Sanders, M.R. (1994) Designing effective behavioral family interventions for stepfamilies. *Clinical Psychology Review*, **14**(5), 463–96.

LeGrange, D., Eisler, I., Dare, C. and Russell, G.F. (1992) Evaluation of family treatments in adolescent anorexia nervosa: a pilot study. *International Journal of Eating Disorders*, **12**, 347–57.

Liddle, H.A. and Dakof, G.A. (1995) Therapy for drug abuse: promising but not definitive. Special issue: The effectiveness of marital and family therapy. *Journal of Marital and Family Therapy*, **21**(4), 511–43.

Lochman, J.E. (1990) Modification of childhood aggression. In Hersen, M., Eisler, R.M. and Miller, P.M. (eds) *Progress in Behavior Modification*, Vol. 25. New York: Academic Press, pp. 47–85.

Loeber, R. and Dishion, T.J. (1983) Early predictors of male delinquency: a review. *Psychological Bulletin*, **94**, 68–99.

Loeber, R. and Farrington, D.P. (1998) Never too early, never too late: risk factors and successful interventions for serious and violent juvenile offenders. *Studies on Crime and Crime Prevention*, **7**(1), 7–30.

Loeber, R. and Stouthamer-Loeber, M. (1987) Family interaction as antecedent to the direction of male aggressiveness. *Journal of Abnormal Social Psychology*, **66**, 239–42.

Long, P., Forehand, R., Wierson, M. and Morgan, A. (1994) Does parent training with young non-compliant children have long-term effects. *Behavior Research and Therapy*, **32**, 101–7.

Martinez, C.R. and Forgatch, M.S. (2001) Preventing problems with boys' non-compliance: effects of a parent training intervention for divorcing mothers. *Journal of Consulting and Clinical Psychology*, **69**, 416–28.

McMahon, R.J. (1999) Parent training. In Russ, S.W. and Ollendick, T. (eds) *Handbook of Psychotherapies with Children and Families*. New York: Plenum Press.

McMahon, R.J. and Slough, N.M. (1996) Family-based intervention in the Fast-Track Program. In Peters, R.D. and McMahon, R.J. (eds) *Preventing Childhood Disorders, Substance Abuse and Delinquency*. Banff International Behavioural Science Series, Vol. 3. Thousand Oaks, CA: Sage Publications, pp. 90–110.

McMahon, R.J. and Wells, K.C. (1998) Conduct problems. In Mash, E.J. and Barkley, R.A. (eds) *Treatment of Childhood Disorders*, 2nd edition. New York: The Guilford Press, pp. 111–207.

McNeil, C.B., Eyberg, S., Eisenstadt, T.H., Newcomb, K. and Funderbunk, B. (1991) Parent–child interaction therapy with behaviour problem children: generalization of treatment effects to the school setting. *Journal of Clinical Child Psychology*, **20**(2), 140–51.

Metzler, C.W., Biglan, A., Ary, D.V. and Li, F. (1998) The stability and validity of early adolescents' reports of parenting constructs. *Journal of Family Psychology*, **12**, 600–19.

Mrazek, P. and Haggerty, R.J. (1994) *Reducing the Risks for Mental Disorders*. Washington: National Academy Press.

Myers, H.F., Alvy, K.T., Arrington, A. and Richardson, M.A. (1992) The impact of a parent-training program on inner-city African American families. *Journal of Community Psychology*, **20**, 132–47.

Nicholson, J.M. and Sanders, M.R. (1999) Behavioural family intervention with children living in step families. *Journal of Marriage and Divorce*, **30**, 1–20.

O'Dell, B.N. (1974) Accelerated entry into the opportunity structure: a sociologically-based treatment for delinquent youth. *Sociology and Social Research*, **58**, 312–17.

Patterson, G.R. (1982) *Coercive Family Process*. Eugene, OR: Castalia Press.

Patterson, G.R. and Chamberlain, P. (1994) A functional analysis of resistance during parent training therapy. *Clinical Psychology Science and Practice*, **1**, 53–70.

Patterson, G.R. and Dishion, T.J. (1985) Contributions of families and peers to delinquency. *Criminology*, **23**, 63–79.

Patterson, G.R., Reid, J.B., Jones, R.R. and Conger, R.E. (1975) *A Social Learning Approach to Family Intervention, Vol. 1. Families with Aggressive Children*. Eugene, OR: Castalia Publishing.

Patterson, G.R., Reid, J.B. and Dishion, T.J. (1992) *A Social Interactional Approach, Vol. 4. Antisocial Boys*. Eugene, OR: Castalia Publishing.

Risley, T.R., Clark, H.B. and Cataldo, M.F. (1976) Behavioral technology for the normal middle class family. In Mash, E.J. Hamerlynck, L.A. and Handy, L.C. (eds) *Behavior Modification and Families*. New York: Brunner/Mazel, pp. 34–60.

Robins, L.N. (1991) Conduct disorder. *Journal of Child Psychology and Psychiatry and Allied Disciplines*, **32**(1), 193–212.

Sanders, M.R. (ed.) (1995) *Healthy Families, Healthy Nation: Strategies for Promoting Family Mental Health in Australia*. Queensland: Australian Academic Press.

Sanders, M.R. (1996) New directions in behavioral family intervention with children. In Ollendick, T.H. and Prinz, R.J. (eds) *Advances in Clinical Child Psychology*, Vol. 18. New York: Plenum Press, pp. 283–330.

Sanders, M.R. (1998) The empirical status of psychological interventions with families of children and adolescents. In L'Abate, L. (eds) *Family Psychopathology: The Relational Roots of Dysfunctional Behavior*. New York: The Guilford Press, pp. 427–65.

Sanders, M.R. (1999) Triple P Positive Parenting Program: Towards an empirically validated multi-level parenting and family support strategy for the prevention of behavior and emotional problems in children. *Clinical Child and Family Psychology Review*, **2**, 71–90.

Sanders, M.R. (2001) Helping families change: from clinical interventions to population-based strategies. In Booth, A. and Crouter, A.C. (eds) *Couples in Conflict*. Mahwah, NJ: Lawrence Erlbaum, pp. 185–219.

Sanders, M.R. and Dadds, M.R. (1982) The effects of planned activities and child management training: an analysis of setting generality. *Behaviour Therapy*, **13**, 1–11.

Sanders, M.R. and Dadds, M.R. (1993) *Behavioral Family Intervention.* Boston: Allyn and Bacon.

Sanders, M.R. and Duncan, S.B. (1995) Empowering families: policy, training, and research issues in promoting family mental health in Australia. *Behaviour Change,* **12,** 109–21.

Sanders, M.R. and Glynn, E.L. (1981) Training parents in behavioural self-management: an analysis of generalization and maintenance effects. *Journal of Applied Behaviour Analysis,* **14,** 223–37.

Sanders, M.R. and James, J.E. (1983) The modification of parent behavior: a review of generalization and maintenance. *Behavior Modification,* **7,** 3–27.

Sanders, M.R. and Lawton, J.M. (1993) Discussing assessment findings with families: a guided participation model of information transfer. *Child and Family Behavior Therapy,* **15,** 5–35.

Sanders, M.R. and McFarland, M.L. (2000) The treatment of depressed mothers with disruptive children: a controlled evaluation of cognitive behavioural family intervention. *Behavior Therapy,* **31,** 89–112.

Sanders, M.R. and Turner, K.M.T. (2002) The role of media and primary care in the dissemination of evidence-based parenting and family support interventions. *Behavior Therapist,* **25,** 156–66.

Sanders, M.R., Shepherd, R.W., Cleghorn, G. and Woolford, H. (1994) The treatment of recurrent abdominal pain in children: a controlled comparison of cognitive-behavioural family intervention and standard pediatric care. *Journal of Consulting and Clinical Psychology,* **62,** 306–14.

Sanders, M.R., Nicholson, J.M. and Floyd, F.J. (1997) Couples' relationships and children: In Halford, W.K. and Markman, H.J. (eds) *Clinical Handbook of Marriage and Couples Interventions.* Chichester: John Wiley, pp. 225–53.

Sanders, M.R., Tully, L.A., Baade, P., Lynch, M.E., Heywood, A., Pollard, G. and Youlden, D. (1999) *Living with Children: A Survey of Parenting Practices in Queensland.* Brisbane: School of Psychology, University of Queensland and Epidemiology Services, Queensland Health.

Sanders, M.R., Markie-Dadds, C., Tully, L. and Bor, B. (2000a) The Triple P – Positive Parenting Program: a comparison of enhanced, standard and self-directed behavioral family intervention for parents of children with early onset conduct problems. *Journal of Consulting and Clinical Psychology,* **68,** 624–40.

Sanders, M.R., Montgomery, D.T. and Brechman-Toussaint, M.L. (2000b) The mass media and child behaviour problems: the effect of a television series on child and parent outcomes. *Journal of Child Psychology and Psychiatry and Allied Disciplines,* **41**(7), 939–48.

Sanders, M.R., Markie-Dadds, C. and Turner, K.M.T. (2003) *Theoretical, Scientific and Clinical Foundations of the Triple P – Positive Parenting Program: A Population Approach to the Promotion of Parenting Competence.* Parenting Research and Practice Monograph No. 1, Brisbane: Parenting and Family Support Centre, University of Queensland.

Sanders, M.R., Pidgeon, A.M., Gravestock, F., Connors, M.D., Brown, S. and Young, R.W. (in press) Does attributional retraining and anger management enhance the effects of the Triple P – Positive Parenting Program with parents at risk for child maltreatment.

Schreibman, L., Kaneko, W.M. and Koegel, R.L. (1991) Positive affect of parents of autistic children: a comparison across two teaching techniques. *Behavior Therapy,* **22**(4), 479–90.

Scott, S., Spender, Q., Doolan, M., Jacobs, B. and Aspland, H. (2001) Multicentre controlled trial of parenting groups for childhood antisocial behaviour in clinical practice. *British Medical Journal,* **323,** 1–6.

Serketich, W.J. and Dumas, J.E. (1996) The effectiveness of behavioral parent training to modify antisocial behavior in children: a meta-analysis. *Behavior Therapy,* **27,** 171–86.

Spoth, R.L., Redmond, C. and Shin, C. (2001) Randomized trial of brief family interventions for general populations: adolescent substance use outcomes 4 years following baseline. *Journal of Consulting and Clinical Psychology,* **69,** 627–42.

Steinberg, L., Fletcher, A. and Darling, N. (1994) Parental monitoring and peer influences on adolescent substance abuse. *Pediatrics,* **93,** 1–5.

Taylor, T.K. and Biglan, A. (1998) Behavioral family interventions for improving child-rearing: a review of the literature for clinicians and policy makers. *Clinical Child and Family Psychology,* **1,** 41–60.

Turner, K.M.T., Sanders, M.R. and Wall, C.R. (1994) Behavioural parent training versus dietary education in the treatment of children with persistent feeding difficulties. *Behaviour Change,* **11**(4), 242–58.

Wahler, R.G., Winkerl, G.H., Peterson, R.F. and Morrison, D.C. (1965) Mothers as behavior therapists for their own children. *Behavior Research and Therapy,* **3,** 113–24.

Webster-Stratton, C. (1984) Randomized trial of two parent training programs for families with conduct-disordered children. *Journal of Consulting and Clinical Psychology,* **52,** 666–78.

Webster-Stratton, C. (1988) Mothers' and fathers' perceptions of child deviance: roles of parent and child behaviors and parent adjustment. *Journal of Consulting and Clinical Psychology,* **56,** 909–15.

Webster-Stratton, C. (1989) Systematic comparison of consumer satisfaction of three cost-effective parent training programs for conduct problem children. *Behavior Therapy,* **20,** 103–15.

Webster-Stratton, C. (1994) Advancing videotape parent training: a comparison study. *Journal of Consulting and Clinical Psychology,* **62**(3), 583–93.

Webster-Stratton, C. (1998) Preventing conduct problems in Head Start children: strengthening parenting competencies. *Journal of Consulting and Clinical Psychology,* **66,** 715–30.

Williams, C.D. (1959) The elimination of tantrum behavior by extinction procedures. *Journal of Abnormal and Social Psychology,* **59,** 269.

Wills, T.A., Vaccaro, D. and McNamara, G. (1992) The role of life events, family support, and competence in adolescent substance use: a test of vulnerability and protective factors. *American Journal of Community Psychology*, **20**, 349–74.

Zubrick, S.R., Silburn, S.R., Garton, A., Burton, P., Dalby, R., Carlton, J., Shephard, C., and Lawrence, D. (1995) *Western Australia Child Health Survey:* *Developing Health and Well Being in the Nineties.* Perth, WA: Australian Bureau of Statistics and the Institute for Child Health Research.

Zubrick, S.R., Northey, K., Silburn, S.R., Lawrence, D., Williams, A.A., Blair, E., Robertson, D. and Sanders, M.R. (in press) Prevention of child behaviour problems via universal implementation of a group behavioural family intervention. *Prevention Science*.

22

e-Parenting

Nicholas Long

SUMMARY

This chapter will introduce you to the concept of 'e-parenting' and the profound impact that emerging technologies will have on parents, children, and those of us who work with families. It is hoped that by the time you finish reading this chapter you will have a greater understanding of e-parenting and agree that this is a topic of growing importance and one that warrants the attention of professionals in the field of parenting.

INTRODUCTION

In recent years terms such as 'e-mail' and 'e-business' have become part of our common language. The emergence of such terms clearly reflects our society's growing use of electronic technology. While the electronic age has already begun, we are just in the early stages of this technological revolution. Futurist Alvin Toffler (2000) believes that technology today is a Stone Age version of what we are likely to have within the next 20 years. In the same way that engines revolutionized the 20th century, it is predicted that computer technology will transform the 21st century. This transformation will impact many areas of our lives, including our roles as parents. Parents in growing numbers will be utilizing electronic technology to assist them in rearing their children. As such, 'e-parenting' refers to the use of electronic technology to assist in the parenting role.

The use of electronic technology is growing at a rapidly accelerating rate. We do not have to look very far back in time to witness examples of what was once thought to be a new or emerging technology that is now considered part of our normal way of life. It was not too long ago that we did not have copiers, pagers, calculators, fax machines, video cameras/players, voice mail, and cell phones – let alone personal computers, e-mail, and the Internet. While the 'business world' has been the primary focus of most of these advances over the past two decades, future advances will be increasingly aimed at our 'personal and family world.'

We have already witnessed a rapid adoption of computer and Internet technology by the general public over the past several years. According to a 2001 report from the US Census Bureau, the majority of households (51 per cent) in the United States had one or more computers in 2000 (US Census Bureau, 2001). This represented a *25 per cent increase in under two years*. The number of households with Internet access was increasing at an even faster rate. There was *over a 50 per cent increase in household Internet access during this same time period*, with more than 2 in 5 households with access. The census bureau also reported that in the US approximately

94 million people use the Internet at home. Unofficial estimates indicated that by 2002 this number was well over 100 million.

It is also important to note that having a child in the home increases the likelihood that there is a computer in that home (US Census Bureau, 2001). Approximately two-thirds of US homes where there are children between the ages of 3 and 17 years had computers in 2000. However, there are disparities across ethnic groups. Seventy-seven per cent of white non-Hispanic children, 72 per cent of Asian and Pacific Islander children, 43 per cent of black children, and 37 per cent of Hispanic children had computers in the home. Similar discrepancies exist for Internet use at home. At least parts of these discrepancies are related to family income and educational-level of the parents, both of which are related to computer ownership and Internet access at home. However, it is encouraging to note that recent research from the Pew Foundation's Internet and American Life Project (www.pewinternet.org) has found that the digital divide is narrowing and the Internet population in the US is increasingly reflecting American demographics.

The growth of the Internet has been phenomenal. As of September 2002, it was estimated that there were 605.6 million Internet users worldwide (NUA, 2003). The number of websites on the Internet grew from 50 sites in 1992 to over 8.7 million unique sites by 2002 (OCLC, 2003). The Internet is increasingly being viewed as a primary avenue to get information. While accurate information concerning how frequently parents go on-line for parenting information is not available, numbers are available for other areas such as health care. An estimate, based on a 2002 survey (Fox and Rainie, 2002), suggests that 73 million people in the US had gone on-line in search for health-care information. On a typical day more people in the US go on-line for medical advice (approximately 6 million per day) than visit a health-care provider.

Although accurate usage numbers related to accessing parenting information are not available, there is no shortage of parenting information on the web. For instance, a search engine (Google) was used to search for information on parenting in 2003. The search word 'parenting' yielded 4,830,000 web pages. Even if only 1 per cent of these web pages were of value to parents this still translates to over 48,000 web pages! There is little doubt that parents are turning to the Internet in increasing numbers for information related to their roles as parents.

It is predicted that technology will cause a power shift in our culture, in part due to improved information accessibility. As the saying goes 'knowledge is power,' and technology will increasingly assist the individual in acquiring both knowledge and skills that have traditionally been relegated to professionals. As part of this power shift, parents will have an increasing capability, with the assistance of technology, to rapidly access information about parenting, to analyze this information, to communicate with others outside their traditional social network about parenting issues, to acquire skills through interactive and individualized learning activities in the area of parenting, and to have on-line support networks. Many other, yet unknown, technological breakthroughs will occur over the coming decades that will impact parenting in unforeseen ways. There is little doubt that technology will be interfacing with parenting.

HISTORICAL BACKGROUND

Electronic technology has been impacting the area of parenting for many decades. Radio, television, and other electronic entertainment media have had an impact in multiple ways. During the early stages of their introduction both radio and television were considered to increase family interaction. Family members would often gather around the radio, or later in front of the television, to listen to or watch a program. It was often considered a social event that, given the limited number of radios and television sets initially, sometimes included several families. In many homes family members would gather together and discuss the program after it was over, and the medium was seen as actually stimulating family interactions. As multiple channels became available, with non-stop programming, as well as families having multiple radios and televisions in the home, the use of these media became an activity that promoted isolation rather than socialization. The 'connection' with media has resulted in a more 'disconnected' family structure, because members pursue interests in isolation.

Over the years parents have been exposed to various models of parenting through television shows that involve families. In the US, these models have evolved from Ozzy and Harriett Nelson in the 1950s to Ozzy Osbourne in 2002. Needless to say, the parenting examples portrayed in television shows have changed significantly over the years. While the impact of such shows on the actual parenting practices of the general public is not known, they have at least opened the public's eyes to a wide range of parenting styles.

Perhaps the greatest impact that electronic technology has had in the area of parenting is in the area of parenting education. Radio and television have provided parents with much information about parenting (Simpson, 1997). Shows that discuss parenting and child-rearing issues, although not as common as would be ideal, reach millions of parents. Videotapes have been developed on numerous parenting topics. Although such videotapes are often used as part of a broader intervention (as Hutchings and Webster-Stratton discuss in this handbook), self-administered, video-taped parent training programs can also be effective in helping parents of young children with behavior problems (Webster Stratton, 1990, 1994). In another area of parenting, researchers have examined a self-administered videotape program called the Family Depression Program which targets parents who are depressed (Butler et al., 2000). The focus is to de-stigmatize depression, improve family communication, and encourage resilience in children. Initial field trials of the program have been encouraging. However, it is computer technology that offers the greatest promise to help parents. Initial studies examining some technology-driven interventions for parents have been very promising. What is perhaps most encouraging is that various studies show that technology-driven interventions can be effective with individuals from various socio-economic groups and not just computer-literate middle-class parents.

Phillip Dunham and colleagues at Dalhousie University in Canada have been exploring the use of a computer-mediated social support network to help young single parents (Dunham et al., 1998). This computer network included a public messaging area, e-mail, and text-based teleconferences for up to eight participants at a time. Participants in this study were between the ages of 15 and 20 years of age, single, and had at least one child under the age of one year. None of the mothers were employed full-time outside the home, and all but three received some form of social assistance. The participants were what many would consider a high-risk group and not likely to benefit from, or even utilize, such a technological approach. However, during the six-month study, the 42 women accessed the network over 16,670 times. A descriptive analysis of the messages exchanged on the network found that 98 per cent of the messages provided positive social support. The majority of this support was emotional followed by informational and tangible support. The researchers reported that a qualitative review of the on-line discussions indicated that close personal relationships and a sense of community

developed as a function of this computer network. Findings also show mothers who participated regularly in this activity were more likely to report a decrease in stress.

Interactive videodisk technology has been used in private industry training for many years. This type of instruction has been found to be superior to reading, lectures, general computer instruction, and the passive viewing of video-tapes (Niemiec and Walberg, 1987; Fletcher, 1990). The use of this technology outside private industry (e.g. Martin and Wienke, 1998) has been slower to develop because of cost and equipment needs. Fortunately, costs have been falling rapidly and CD-ROM technology has replaced the need for more expensive videodisk technology. We are already seeing the initial use of CD-ROM technology to teach parents how to manage their children's behavior effectively. Don Gordon and colleagues at Ohio University in the USA have developed a program called 'Parenting Wisely' that utilizes this technology to teach parents such skills as active listening, contracting, monitoring children's behavior, problem-solving, positive reinforcement, and contingency management (Kacir and Gordon, 1999; Lagges and Gordon, 1999; Gordon, 2000). This interactive, multimedia program is contained on a CD-ROM. The parent is exposed to case studies via video clips. Each case opens with video clip of a common family problem, such as a child not doing homework or not following a parental direction. Each problem is followed by three possible responses. Parents choose the response that is most similar to the way they would probably handle the situation. They then see a video portrayal of their solution followed by a critique of both the positive and negative consequences of that particular solution. If the chosen solution was not particularly effective the parent then receives information on responses that may be preferable. The program also includes a tutorial on how to work through the cases. For parents with low literacy skills, an option allows for the computer to read text aloud. Parents typically spend 2–3 hours working through the cases.

Studies conducted by the researchers (Kacir and Gordon, 1999; Lagges and Gordon, 1999; Gordon, 2000) demonstrate this approach to be effective up to six months following completion of the program. They found parents increased their knowledge of parenting principles and skills, increased the use of parenting skills taught in the program, and also reported reductions in problem behaviors of their children. The program has been used effectively with low-income families, teenage parents, and court-ordered families. The effectiveness of this CD-ROM program is remarkable given its brief duration. It is believed that its effectiveness is due to several factors, including the high-quality videotape modeling of relevant issues, a high level of user interaction, and the self-paced, private, and non-judgmental computer format. Gordon and his colleagues have recently been developing similar programs for foster parents, and parents of younger children, and making cultural adaptations such as their United Kingdom version which uses UK families in the videos. They also plan to offer these programs over the Internet within the next few years.

Studies such as the above have led some entrepreneurs to think about ways of using technology on a wide-scale basis. One group of individuals representing the fields of mental health, business, and technology have recently started an enterprise called Epotec. Epotec (www.Epotec.com) is an Internet-based service that is attempting to combine 'proven psychotherapeutic techniques with cutting edge technology.' They are contracting with managed health-care organizations and employee assistance plans to provide employees access to their services. Their services include on-line information on mental health issues and prevention, on-line support/chat groups, and interactive multi-session programs. They are developing several hundred of these interactive programs on such topics as anxiety, depression, pain management, interpersonal relationships, workplace problems, personal finance, and several parenting topics. Most of these interactive programs consist of 8–10 sessions with a 'coach' (such as a mental health professional) being available on-line or by telephone to assist the individual as they work through a program. Epotec has already secured multi-million dollar contracts and it is anticipated that we will be seeing many other similar programs develop in the coming years.

We are now beginning to see a convergence of different technologies (e.g. computers and television will become more closely linked) that will impact parenting education. As an example of the initial stages of this convergence the Canadian Institute of Child Health, a government-sponsored program, operates the 'e-Parenting Network' (www.eparentingnetwork.ca). This innovative multimedia network involves interactive web TV modules that contain evidence-based parenting information on various topics including child safety, nutritional issues, and positive parenting. Parents are able to watch the video modules, download information, e-mail questions to guest experts, and follow links to other resources.

CORE ISSUES

Accessibility

Many emerging technologies are initially viewed as having only limited potential because large segments of society do not have access to technologies in their early stages of development. This concern is not unique to computers and the Internet. Historically, such concerns have been expressed about the limited impact such innovations as the telephone and television would have, given their limited applications and access during the early years after their development.

Although a rapidly growing number of parents have computer and Internet access, many do not. There are great variations across countries, with parents in the United States, Canada, Western Europe, and Australia generally having the greatest access. A recent study in the US found that 70 per cent of parents with children under 18 were Internet users compared to 53 per cent of non-parents (defined as those without a minor child living at home) (Allen and Rainie, 2002). Access varies by many socio-demographic variables including parental income and education. Fortunately, this digital divide is constantly narrowing as costs decline and access becomes easier.

A factor that will further facilitate the greater use of computers and the Internet is the movement in many countries to increase the computer literacy of children. In some cases, this movement has been funded by politicians and others who believe that computer literacy will be as important as reading and writing for a child's future employability. As early as 1999, almost every teacher (99 per cent) at government-funded schools in the United States had access to computers in the school (84 per cent had computers available in their classrooms) (National Center for Education Statistics, 2000a, 2000b). In 1999, Internet access was available to students in 95 per cent of these schools. As these children become adults, it is more likely that they will use computers and the Internet in their personal lives than their parents. It is anticipated that in the future the use of computer technology and the Internet (or later variations) in the home will be as common as the use of telephones and televisions are today.

Another issue related to accessibility is the content of many websites. The literacy requirements of the material found on many websites is at a level many parents cannot understand. One study found that the materials on the majority of English-language consumer health-care websites were written at the university level (Berland et al., 2001). As the Internet becomes more accessible, website developers need to take into consideration the diversity of users. Future advances in technology will make it easier to communicate with computers through voice commands and options, allowing two-way verbal communication to become more common.

Potential Benefits

The impact of general parenting information obtained over the Internet has not been well studied. However, based on information from the Pew Foundation's project on the Internet and American Life (www.pewinternet.org), there is hope that information obtained over the Internet can have a positive impact. Their research has found that people view the Internet as a major source of health-care information (Fox and Rainie, 2002). Seventy per cent of Internet users surveyed stated that information they accessed through the Internet influenced their medical care decisions, and 48 per cent reported that on-line information improved the way they cared for themselves. These positive results combined with several research studies that have examined the use of written information such as booklets and handouts to change parenting practices support the potential benefit of providing accurate parenting information over the Internet. A key is having accurate, empirically sound, easily available information that serves effectively to educate parents.

It is realized, of course, that written information on parenting is often not enough to change parenting practices. As a result, there has been a tremendous growth in the development of parent support and education programs (Long, 1997). Many parents want to participate in face-to-face individual or group parenting programs; however, there are many barriers that prevent participation in such center-based traditional parenting programs. These barriers include issues such as transportation, childcare, scheduling around work and/or other activities, and lack of local availability of such services in rural areas. As a result, many parents do not get involved in parent programs until their issues become so significant that they are dealing with treatment interventions rather than prevention. Technology offers the potential of being able to meet the needs of large numbers of parents around the globe in terms of the prevention of child problems, the treatment of mild to moderate problems, and the enhancement of the parent–child relationship. Internet-based programs previously discussed, such as the interactive parenting program developed by Gordon and the network support project of Dunham, show great potential.

Technology also offers the potential to train large numbers of practitioners in evidence-based family strengthening and parenting programs. Often empirically validated parenting programs are poorly disseminated. Technological advances will make it easier for program developers and researchers who are often at academic institutions to neatly package and disseminate materials and train others over the Internet. This clearly streamlines the development aspect of programs. The emphasis will shift to the dissemination of empirically sound information, not just on commercial marketing.

Concerns about Technology Dependence

For over a hundred years scholars have debated the impact that new technologies will have on society and families. Computers and the Internet are merely the latest topics of such debates. A primary concern with these latest technologies is that they have made it increasingly easier to socialize, shop, work, learn, and be entertained all from the privacy of our homes, thus further isolating us from 'real-world,' face-to-face contact. Supporting this viewpoint is Norman Nie, a Stanford University researcher, who asserts that individuals who use the Internet frequently tend to socialize less with family and friends (Nie, 2001). On the other hand, research from the Pew Foundation's Internet and American Life Project and others suggests that the Internet may actually reduce isolation and enlarge and enrich most users' social worlds. Keith Hampton, a specialist in cyber-sociology currently at the Massachusetts Institute of Technology, argues that the social impact of on-line technologies may in fact result in more social ties, diverse ties, and more support (Hampton and Wellman, 2000). For example, computer networks allow individuals to develop supportive interactive relationships with others that are often not prejudiced by such things as physical appearance and race or limited by geography. The study described earlier by Dunham is an early example of the potential for on-line social support.

Researchers examining the impact of computers and the Internet on communities often struggle with the issue of how to define 'community.' Are communities defined by physical proximity or as social networks? In today's world we often interact most with individuals who are not our physical neighbors. Communication and transportation systems have allowed us to live within social networks that are not based on physical proximity. The computer and Internet allow these networks to expand into 'virtual' or 'cyber communities.' A concern about such Internet-based communities is that they lead to a decline in traditional face-to-face relationships and contact to the detriment of society.

There is no doubt that the debate on the social impact of newer technologies on families and communities will continue for years. However, the advantages and disadvantages of 'virtual communities' will become clearer over time. Research projects such as the Netville project in Canada may help in this regard (Hampton and Wellman, 2000; Hasse et al., 2002). The Netville project has focused on a suburban neighborhood that was built from the ground up to utilize some of the most advanced communication technologies available, including a broadband high-speed local network. Residents have access to high-speed Internet services, videophones, on-line health services, on-line jukebox, local discussion forums, and on-line entertainment and educational applications. This 'wired' community is being studied by Hampton and others to better understand the impact of electronic technology on communities.

Concerns about Privacy

Internet users are rightly concerned about privacy. Initial concerns about the privacy of information shared on-line focused on areas such as the security of credit card information. It was not until such security and privacy issues were assured that e-shopping and e-commerce took off. Current privacy issues include concerns about the confidentiality of information regarding which specific sites an individual visits. Currently, such information can often be collected and shared with others. In fact, one of the most interesting findings from the Pew Foundation project on the Internet and American Life indicated that 89 per cent of individuals who used the Internet to access health-care information were concerned that these websites might pass on personal information about what they did on-line (Fox and Rainie, 2000). Eighty-five per cent were worried that insurance companies might deny them health-care coverage or raise their health insurance premiums based on the health sites they visited. Obviously, such concerns about privacy will need to be addressed before many parents will feel free to use the Internet on a wide-scale basis not only to obtain potentially sensitive information, but also to participate in interactive programs and openly communicate on-line.

Reliability and Validity of Information

There are significant concerns about the reliability and validity of parenting information on the Internet. The concern about the reliability and validity of parenting information is not unique to the Internet, but the ease of disseminating information over the web, relative to other methods such as the print media, makes it a spawning ground for inaccurate and incomplete information. A study conducted in Italy examined the reliability of health-care information given to parents regarding a child's fever, on 41 websites (Impicciatore et al., 1997). The results showed that only a few of these websites gave complete and accurate information when compared to professional guidelines. Subsequent studies support the belief that people using the Internet have a difficult time finding complete and accurate health-related information (Berland et al., 2001).

Fortunately, there *is* evidence that Internet users are becoming more discriminating about information they find on-line. In regard to health-care information, the Pew project found that many people question the validity of some of the information found on the Internet (Fox and Rainie, 2002). They found that 73 per cent of individuals who search for health information on the Internet have, at some point, rejected some of the information they discovered because of its questionable validity. They found that many of these people decided not to use information they found on a website because the site 'appeared' to be too commercial and more concerned with selling products than providing accurate information. Additionally, others have turned away from information on a particular website because they could not determine the source of the information. Finally, 37 per cent turned away from a website because they could not determine when the information was last updated. This skepticism on the part of these Internet users is good and likely to lead to better information.

The accuracy with which parents can judge the validity of parenting information found on the Internet is unknown. Given the difficulty we as professionals can often have in determining the validity of parenting advice, it is unlikely that most parents would be able to make consistently accurate judgements. One way to assist parents is for a well-regarded entity to develop a 'seal of approval' that could be given to websites providing empirically sound advice. This concept will be discussed more thoroughly later in the chapter.

Ethical Concerns

We will need continually to evaluate the effectiveness of technology-driven services. While these services may be cost-effective and intriguing, they may not always be in the best interests of many parents and children. Commercial interests in technology-driven services (e.g. commercial sponsorship of websites) and financial incentives also raise ethical concerns. Subtle, and sometimes not so subtle, pressures for commercial and financial gain may influence the content of services. As of yet there are no specific well-established 'ethical guidelines' for the development of technology-driven services for parents. While professionals in the area of parenting are often guided by ethical principles of their discipline, we must remember that many of the websites for parents are being developed by entrepreneurs who are not bound by such a code of ethics.

AUTHOR'S OVERVIEW

Given the recent advances in electronic technologies, it is impossible accurately to predict what will transpire over the coming decades. What is known is that the movement to advance these technologies is being driven by powerful public, political, educational, commercial, and financial forces. There will be advances that we cannot even imagine today. However, perhaps the most important issue we face is not how technology will change but how we manage the change itself. The next section of the chapter will discuss the implications for practice of the current changes we are witnessing in electronic technologies.

As several other chapters in this handbook point out, parenting and society are interrelated and it is not possible to think of parenting in isolation from society. As electronic technologies become increasingly part of our society it will become more difficult to think about parenting, and especially parenting services, in isolation of electronic technology.

IMPLICATIONS FOR PRACTICE

Need to be Open to the Use of Technology-Driven Services

Practitioners and policy-makers will need to be open to the fact that technology-driven services

do have a legitimate place in the field of parenting education and support. Many practitioners have strongly held beliefs that personal instruction/relationship and/or group discussion/process is absolutely necessary for a parenting intervention to be successful. However, the studies cited earlier in this chapter and others (e.g. Long et al., 1993) suggest otherwise. This is not to say that technology-driven services are appropriate and effective for all parents, but that they can be effective for many parents. In a more general sense we need to acknowledge that different parents have different preferred learning methods. For example, some parents are reluctant to attend parent education or support groups due to being uncomfortable in groups. They may fear being judged if they ask questions. Even if they do attend parenting groups, they may not interact and benefit as much from the group experience. Such parents may benefit most from services that are technology-based, such as an interactive CD-ROM program or on-line network. Many other parents want and need the interpersonal contact that parenting groups and individual services offer.

Integration into Traditional Services

There is a tendency to view technology-based services for parents as a replacement for traditional services. However, it is really more appropriate to view technology as supplementing and enhancing traditional services rather than replacing them. Electronic technologies offer a different medium for providing information to, communicating with, and teaching parents. Some parents will be naturally drawn to technology-driven services while others will prefer and benefit more from traditional services. In most cases services will involve a combination approach that includes both face-to-face services and technology. Just as the videotape worked its way into many parenting programs rather than replacing parent educators and parent support practitioners, so will the new technologies.

Need to Help Parents Utilize Electronic-Technology Effectively

Most parents go on-line without a definite plan on how to research a parenting topic or evaluate the information they obtain. Practitioners can provide information to parents regarding what websites they recommend for different types of parenting information and how to conduct effective web searches for specific topics (suggesting keywords to use). As stated previously, there is no generally accepted 'authority' that provides their 'seal of approval' indicating that a particular website provides relevant, accurate, valid information. Therefore, practitioners can help parents by suggesting guidelines that they can use to evaluate websites and on-line information. These guidelines should include questions such as the following to guide them in their evaluation process:

- Is the author of the material clearly identified? What is his/her training and experience?
- Is contact information provided that would allow you to ask questions about the site?
- Does the website have the type of sponsor that suggests it provides objective information?
- If it is a commercial site, does it appear to be more interested in selling things than providing valuable information?
- If it is a commercial site, does it have an advisory board, experts or consultants that endorse the content of the site?
- Is the information provided primarily factual or primarily opinions?
- Is the information provided dated in some way to allow you to determine if the information has been recently updated?

Practitioners should also help parents utilize technology in moderation. Parents need clearly to understand that their time and attention will always be the most important issue in being an effective parent. A parent's interpersonal relationship with their child should not be compromised by a dependence on technology.

Guidelines for Developers

Some practitioners will become involved in developing or helping to develop websites as well as other technology-based services for parents. In developing such information it is important to remember that in order for parents to use technology-based programs, they must be easy to use, be visually appealing, and address their specific needs and preferences. We also know that data-driven interactive learning experiences that allow learners to 'interact' and receive experiential feedback tend to be more successful than passive learning experiences in facilitating learning.

While there are no generally accepted guidelines for the development of parenting websites at the present time, guidelines do exist for the development of health-care websites. These guidelines should be scrutinized by those developing websites for parents. The American Medical Association has guidelines for health-related websites (Winker et al., 2000). These guidelines contain principles that address such issues as content, privacy, advertising and sponsorship. Health On the Net (HON) Foundation is a not-for-profit International Swiss Organization that has developed a code of conduct that specifies eight principles for medical and health websites (www.hon.ch/HONcode/Conduct.html). These principles address areas such as authority, attribution, transparency of authorship, and transparency of sponsorship. Websites that follow this code of conduct are permitted to display the foundation's symbol on their website. It is hoped that similar guidelines will be developed by a widely accepted organization for parenting websites in the near future.

Challenged by Parents

As parents become more informed about parenting issues via the Internet they will be more likely to challenge the advice or information offered by practitioners. The accuracy of information parents obtain will likely become a bigger issue in the near future as more 'fringe' advice is marketed by commercial sites whose primary goal is to make a profit. This problem is most likely to occur around specific problems for which parents are desperate for solutions (such as ADHD, developmental problems, and bedwetting). Practitioners will increasingly need to be able to address the accuracy of information obtained by parents. In many cases the information parents obtain will be accurate and much better educated consumers will require more informed practitioners.

The Importance of Research

Just as practitioners should emphasize evidence-based practices in the traditional services they provide parents, they should also do the same with technology-based services. As the use of such services grows, there will be a growing research base indicating which services are most effective and which services work best for which types of parents. Practitioners will need to keep up with this research and become educated consumers themselves in terms of what technology-based programs and services they recommend to parents.

Expansion of Learning Opportunities for Practitioners

The use of technology will greatly facilitate the training of professionals, including those who work in the area of parenting. Many universities are now focusing a great deal of effort in the area of 'distance learning.' This approach to learning is being advanced due to the potential for tremendous cost savings and increased accessibility. Most of these 'distance learning' programs utilize either the Internet or a compressed-video system that operates over telephone lines. Although Internet-based programs are quite flexible and can reach a tremendous number of individuals without regard to location or meeting space limitations, they often fall short at present on the ability of participants to interact with the instructor or other participants except through written messages. Compressed-video technology, on the other hand, allows participants to see and hear each other. However, compressed-video technology has not been perfected and video images currently appear as if they are in slow motion. Compressed-video programs also have the disadvantage of requiring fixed sites and expensive equipment.

In the future we will witness the development of technology that has the advantages of both current systems. Undoubtedly, we will be able easily to hold video-conferences over the Internet. While this is currently possible, it is only in the initial stages of development. Eventually, such systems will not require computers. We will probably be able to buy very inexpensive cameras to mount on top of our televisions and interact with one another through cable television lines. This will open up not only the opportunity to 'attend' classes, professional workshops, or conferences while sitting in front of our television but also an opportunity to provide direct services to the children and families we serve. We will be able to make 'house calls' from the comfort of our office or home. Such a practice will likely, from a policy perspective, be an outgrowth of the current practice of 'tele-medicine' where physicians, usually specialists, can see and talk to patients at a distant site over a compressed-video system. The specialists are currently able to listen through a stethoscope or view X-rays via sounds and images transmitted over the system. Tele-medicine systems are now being used by some mental health professionals to interview clients or patients in rural areas. While this approach will not totally replace personal contact, it does offer promise in certain situations (such as providing services to parents in remote areas, or as an adjunct to traditional services).

The Internet also provides an incredible opportunity for dissemination of information to professionals. Present technology allows for easy sharing of information via Listservs and websites. Library research can now be done from your personal computer. Full-text articles from a growing number of journals can now be accessed over the Internet. In addition to information available on websites, there are a growing number of chat rooms that allow practitioners to discuss various issues with other practitioners. Future technologies will make it increasingly easier to communicate and share information with other practitioners around the globe.

BACK TO THE FUTURE

It is hard to even fathom the technological advances that will take place in this new millennium based on what we have witnessed in recent years. The current frenzy with the Internet will probably be dwarfed by new, yet unknown, technologies. Those involved in the field of parenting services will need to be ready to seize new, currently unknown, opportunities as a result of technological breakthroughs. We need to become future-smart or at least future-aware. If we, as professionals with expertise in the area of parenting, do not take advantage of future technologies, others with solely commercial and financial motivation will.

Many futurists believe that there will be a growing convergence of technologies in the near future. For example, computers, cell phones, digital televisions, and the Internet will merge into something new. James Canton, a highly regarded technology futurist, believes that this convergence of leading-edge technologies will be the single most powerful driver of change in the next century (Canton, 1999).

Computers will become voice-activated and video-communication enabled. Artificial intelligence will make computers 'smarter' than humans over the next couple of decades (Canton, 1999; Martin, 2000). Computers will become powerful extensions of human beings that will augment intelligence, learning, and communication. They will be designed more like living organisms that evolve, learn, and adapt. Canton believes that in the future the human–machine interface will be one that is based on trust, integrity, and intimacy; in other words, human qualities. He draws the analogy to pilots of today's technology-loaded jet fighter planes where the line between human control and computer control of the aircraft is seamless and at times unclear.

However, it is important for us to realize that technology can be intoxicating. It is mysterious, attractive, and addictive, but it is not a panacea for all ills and needs. There is a negative side. In the opinion of some, technology distracts us from the emotional connections to others, including our children. Futurist John Naisbitt and his colleagues in their book *High Tech High Touch* (Naisbitt et al., 1999) discuss the need for us to make the most of the benefits of technology while minimizing its detrimental effects. It is this challenge that will be most important to the future of e-parenting.

REFERENCES

Allen, K. and Raine, L. (2002) *Parents On-line.* Report from the Pew Internet & American Life Project. Washington, DC.

Berland, G.K., Elliott, M.N., Morales, L.S. et al. (2001) Health information on the Internet: accessibility, quality, and readability in English and Spanish. *Journal of the American Medical Association*, **285**(20), 2612–21.

Butler, S.F., Budman, S.H. and Beardslee, W. (2000) Risk reduction in children from families with parental depression: a videotaped psychoeducation program. *National Academies of Practice Forum*, **2**(4), 267–76.

Canton, J. (1999) *Technofutures: How Leading-Edge Technology Will Transform Business in the 21st Century.* Carlsbad, CA: Hay House.

Dunham, P.J., Hurshman, A., Litwin, E., Gusella, J., Ellsworth, C. and Dodd, P. (1998) Computer-mediated social support: single young mothers as a model system. *American Journal of Community Psychology*, **26**(2), 281–306.

Fletcher, G.D. (1990) Effectiveness and cost of interactive videodisc instruction in defense training and education. Report No. P-2372, Institute for Defense Analysis.

Fox, S. and Rainie, L. (2000) *The On-line Health Care Revolution: How the Web Helps Americans Take Better Care of Themselves.* Report from the Pew Internet & American Life Project. Washington, DC.

Fox, S. and Rainie, L. (2002) *Vital Decisions: How Internet Users Decide What Information to Trust When They or Their Loved Ones are Sick.* Report from the Pew Internet & American Life Project. Washington, DC.

Gordon, D.A. (2000) Parent training via CD-ROM: using technology to disseminate effective prevention practices. *Journal of Primary Prevention*, **21**(2), 227–51.

Hampton, K.N. and Wellman, B. (2000) Examining community in the digital neighborhood: early results from Canada's wired suburb. In Ishida, T. and Isbister, K. (eds) *Digital Cities: Technologies, Experiences, and Future Perspectives.* Lecture Notes in Computer Science 1765. Heidelberg: Springer-Verlag.

Hasse, A.Q., Wellman, B., Witte, J. and Hampton, B. (2002) Capitalizing on the Internet: social contact, civic engagement, and sense of community. In Wellman, B. and Haythornthwaite, C. (eds) *The Internet and Everyday Life.* Oxford, UK: Blackwell, pp. 291–324.

Impicciatore, P., Pandolfini, C., Casella, N. and Bonati, M. (1997) Reliability of health information for the public on the world wide web: systematic survey of advice on managing fever in children at home. *British Medical Journal*, **314**, 1875–81.

Kacir, C. and Gordon, D.A. (1999) Parenting Adolescents Wisely: the effectiveness of an interactive videodisk parent training program in Appalachia. *Child and Family Behavior Therapy*, **21**(4), 1–22.

Lagges, A. and Gordon, D.A. (1999) Use of an interactive laserdisc parent training program with teenage parents. *Child and Family Behavior Therapy*, **21**(1), 19–37.

Long, N. (1997) Parent education/training in the USA: current status and future trends. *Clinical Child Psychology and Psychiatry*, **2**(4), 501–15.

Long, N., Rickert, V. and Ashcraft, E. (1993) Bibliotherapy as an adjunct to stimulant medication in the treatment of Attention Deficit Hyperactivity Disorder. *Journal of Pediatric Health Care*, **7**, 82–8.

Martin, J. (2000) *After the Internet: Alien Intelligence.* Washington, DC: Capitol Press.

Martin, S.M. and Wienke, W.D. (1998) Using cutting edge technology to prepare teachers to work with children and youth who have emotional/behavioral disorders. *Education and Treatment of Children*, **21**(3), 385–95.

Naisbitt, J., Naisbitt, N. and Philips, D. (1999) *High Tech High Touch: Technology and Our Search for Meaning.* New York: Broadway Books.

National Center for Education Statistics (2000a) *Teacher's Tools for the 21st Century: A Report on Teachers' Use of Technology.* Washington, DC: US Department of Education, Office of Educational Research and Improvement.

National Center for Education Statistics (2000b) *Stats in Brief: Internet Access in U.S. Public Schools and Classrooms: 1994–1999.* Washington, DC: US Department of Education, Office of Educational Research and Improvement.

Nie, N.H. (2001) Sociability, interpersonal relations, and the Internet: reconciling conflicting findings. *American Behavioral Scientist*, **45**(3), 420–35.

Niemiec, R. and Walberg, H.J. (1987) Comparative effects of computer-assisted instruction: a synthesis of reviews. *Journal of Educational Computing Research*, **3**(1), 19–37.

NUA (2002) How many on-line? Retrieved 31 January 2003 from http://www.nua.ie/surveys/how_many_online/

OCLC (2002) Number of websites. Retrieved 31 January 2003 from http://wcp.oclc.org/stats/size.html

Simpson, A.R. (1997) *The Role of the Mass Media in Parenting Education.* Boston: Center for Health Education, Harvard School of Public Health.

Toffler, A. (2000) Commentary. In Sikes, A.C. and Pearlman, E. (eds) *Fast Forward: America's Leading*

Experts Reveal How the Internet is Changing Your Life. New York: William Morrow/Harper Collins.

US Census Bureau (2001) *Home Computers and Internet Use in the United States: August 2000.* Current Population Reports, September 2001. Washington: US Department of Commerce.

Webster-Stratton, C. (1990) Enhancing the effectiveness of self-administered videotape parent training for families with conduct-problem children. *Journal of Abnormal Child Psychology,* **18,** 479–92.

Webster-Stratton, C. (1994) Advancing videotape parent-training: a comparison study. *Journal of Consulting and Clinical Psychology,* **62,** 583–93.

Winker, M.A., Flanagin, A., ChiLum, B. et al. (2000) Guidelines for medical and health information sites on the Internet. *Journal of the American Medical Association,* **283**(12), 1600–6.

Epilogue

Towards a Parenting Society

Nicholas Long and Masud Hoghughi

This book has brought together evidence to show that every aspect of a child's functioning – physical and mental health, intellectual and educational achievement and social behaviour – are all fundamentally affected by parenting practices. Chapters have also set out a fairly comprehensive overview of the prerequisites of 'good enough' parenting, both in general and specific areas and what happens when they are not met.

And yet, at the beginning of the 21st century we are witnessing high levels of family problems such as poverty, homelessness, infant mortality, malnutrition, drug and alcohol abuse, family and youth violence, child and adolescent mental health problems, and youth suicide in many countries around the world. Such ills are not confined to developing countries but are starkest in the most 'powerful' or 'rich' nations, by virtue of the differences between the 'haves' and 'have nots'. These difficulties show that, judged by their results, many significant efforts put into parenting assistance still goes awry.

As previous chapters have shown, parenting does not occur in isolation but rather within a larger framework of interdependent elements. It is influenced by numerous factors encompassing individual characteristics of children and parents, families, and the societies in which they live. When working with families, we typically focus attention on individuals, often losing sight of the wider ecological perspective. However, it is important to remember that parents and children often reflect the problems of the wider society and that families do not develop independently of the prevailing culture. In this final chapter we will briefly discuss family trends, social issues, and our recommendations for moving toward a society that is more supportive of effective parenting. Our predictions of family trends, and our subsequent recommendations, have been gleaned over the years from our own experiences and observations and the writings of many others (e.g. Louv, 1992; Garbarino, 1995; Walsh, 1995; Rickel and Becker, 1997; Hewlett and West, 1998; Matathia and Salzman, 1999; Freely, 2000; Golombok, 2000; Bumpass, 2001; Garbarino and Bedard, 2001; Kaslow, 2001; Westman, 2001).

TRENDS

In the 21st century we will probably witness a continuing shift from multigenerational family units to individual family units, particularly in the West. This will result in greater isolation and perhaps alienation from the extended family, decreasing both the practical and emotional support available to parents. Due to issues such as the lack of time, parents are becoming less likely to join organizations and become active in their communities. The trend is for parents to live increasingly isolated and unconnected lives.

In recent decades we have also seen the amount of time parents spend interacting with their children gradually decline. Parents have less and less time to devote to active parenting. Stressed-out parents have to survive in an increasingly competitive society. They are spending more of their time working to provide the basic necessities of food, shelter and leisure for their children and less time providing for their emotional needs. As a result, many are becoming disengaged from their children, though the primeval, physically protective tendencies remain.

The structure and composition of families is changing. There is consequently growing dilution and confusion in defining what constitutes a family and who is a parent. The 'traditional' family consisting of a mother and a father who naturally conceived their children and who are 'satisfactorily' married, though still the norm, is becoming less common. Thus, new terms have emerged to describe different types of families. Terms such as 'nuclear', 'extended', 'single-parent', and 'blended' have become integrated into our language.

As previous chapters have indicated, growing trends in the diversity of family structure and composition include trends such as the increasing numbers of grandparents serving as their grandchildren's primary parents and an increasing number of gay and lesbian couples raising children. Changes in patterns of conception also make defining 'family' more difficult. As a growing number of couples turn to artificial reproductive technologies to help them have children, a child may end up with a biological father (sperm donor), a biological mother (egg donor), a surrogate mother, and a social mother and father who rear the child. The picture becomes even more complicated if the parents who are rearing the child divorce and re-marry and step-parents are introduced. The net result is that during the 21st century it will become progressively more difficult to define 'family' and 'parent'. As a society we will increasingly struggle both emotionally and legally to make sense of this confusion, though the basic needs of children for secure attachment, nurture and guidance will remain.

In the most developed industrial societies, it seems that the interplay between increasing individualism and pressures of the market economy have fuelled many of the family changes we are witnessing. Often individuals are judged by their job, their productivity and how much they are paid rather than their commitment to their children and community. Material values and media-driven trends increasingly shape personal relationships, which strain under the wider availability of choices even in partners, and the pressure towards getting the most out of one finite life. As a consequence, we become more self-centred, placing our own needs above those of others, including our children, though paradoxically our concern for the poor and dispossessed of other countries is at an all-time high. Within such a cultural framework, parenting is at best passively valued and often has to be actively defended by parents and others. The market economy and corporate voracity which place the focus on survival through profit, use people as production units, creating time and financial pressures which are at the core of many adults' struggle to be better parents.

Most business leaders have moved away from the informal 'social contract' that employers had with employees in past generations. These often meant that as long as the employee performed well in the job then the employer would look after him in terms of job security and benefits. In many ways, such a relationship utilized family values such as commitment, caring and trust. Times have changed. In the US, there are now companies that hire individuals at 49 per cent time so they do not have to give them benefits such as health insurance that would be required at 50 per cent. In the United States, Western Europe, Canada, Australia and New Zealand, although workers are better protected than in many other regions of the world, we still see large corporations laying off groups of workers at the same time as they provide huge bonuses to executives. Given their prominence and impact, we should not be surprised that cynicism and self-centredness percolate down to families and other social institutions.

Government polices also often add to business practices and cultural influences in working against parents. Proportionate to their income, the rich are taxed less than the poor. Although in most countries the state acknowledges and to some extent compensates parents for children's expenses, the economic burden on parents seems to be growing. This points to a critical contemporary dilemma: as a society we expect parents to invest huge amounts of time, energy and expense in child-rearing, but it is society at large that reaps the much greater material benefits. In developed societies, children are now rarely a source of economic benefit to parents. Therefore an argument could be made for proposing that the necessary survival and educational costs for children should be borne by the state, out of equitable taxation, so that at least this major pressure on parents is removed.

At the heart of much of the divided political debate on government support for parents and children is the basic issue of how families are viewed. Are families basically private domains for whose care the role of government should be minimal? Or, are families the core unit of society and thus the prime focus for any attempts at improving it? Most developed nations appear to be moving in directions that contain elements of both positions, while remaining wary of committing themselves. The closest approximations to the latter position can be seen in Nordic countries, where family welfare is at the core of the political agenda and kept above party politics.

One of the most significant trends in recent decades has been the tremendous increase of single-parent families. This is one consequence of growing divorce rates and the trend for women to have children outside marriage or a stable relationship. As discussed elsewhere in this handbook, children who are reared by one parent tend to have more problems than those reared in two-parent families. It appears that the greatest risk comes not from the absence of a second parent *per se* but from the difficulties that are associated with it, such as decreased income, lack of partner support in child-rearing issues and parental practices.

The increasing formal and legal equality between men and women has perhaps been the most significant positive social change of the last century. However, it has had a downside in terms of parenting. In the past, within traditional families in many Western cultures, mothers often stayed at home to care for their children while fathers worked outside the home financially to support the family. As, under economic and social pressures, more women have pursued jobs outside the home, at least two major difficulties in regard to child-rearing have become prominent.

Firstly, for the most part, women continue to carry the major burden of their traditional responsibilities for child-rearing and housekeeping, in addition to working outside the home. Thus, we witness the changing role of women but relatively unchanging role of men. While there has been some recent shifting toward a more equitable sharing of parenting responsibilities between mothers and fathers in dual-income families, there is the need for much more. The second difficulty arises from the loss of vast amounts of unpaid labour previously devoted to the care and nurture of our children. With both parents in the workforce, we are struggling as a society to find effective substitute care for children and how to pay for it. In most Western countries, there is variable assistance with provision and cost of childcare, but rarely enough. The issue of whether childcare should be paid for by the government or employers remains very much alive.

In recent years, there has been a growing debate on the relative importance of the influence of parenting versus the influence of genes on children. While it is important to recognize that genes have a significant influence on many child characteristics including personality features, future debates in this area will probably focus more on the interaction between genetic and environmental factors rather than whether a particular child characteristic is the result of 'nature' or 'nurture'. A related area of research that will see growth is the genetic influences on specific parenting behaviors. Do genes influence the type of parent one becomes, such as authoritarian or permissive? Such research will be greatly facilitated by the Human Genome Project, which recently achieved a major breakthrough in developing a map of the human genome. Research will now move swiftly from examining gene sequencing to gene function. The ability to identify everyone's genetic fingerprint will also eventually become possible, making it possible to identify those persons, both parents and children, who are most at risk genetically for adverse reactions to environmental influences. How we respond to such knowledge will be complex and as yet unpredictable. Will we look to providing additional support to those at most risk or will we look to genetic engineering for help?

Other Trends

- The amount of time parents spend interacting with their children has been declining in most countries over recent decades and may well continue.
- Families will continue to face mounting economic pressures in trying to parent their children effectively.
- Society will become more multiracial.
- Economic pressures will result in a growing number of infants to be cared for outside the home at younger ages, in order to allow parents to return to work.
- Most of the population movement in the past decades has involved people moving from rural areas to large cities for jobs. Electronic technologies are allowing more individuals to work from their homes or facilities outside large cities. This trend will have, as yet, unpredictable consequences for parenting.
- Children are becoming sexually active at earlier ages and parents need to play an increasing role in sex education. This will be so, particularly because of social and political resistance in some countries to introducing sex education at younger age levels in the schools.
- The entertainment media will have an increasing influence on the lives of children as new technologies and methods of accessing them are developed. Parents' messages about violence, sex, drugs and other issues will need to be correspondingly more powerful in order to compete with movies, television, music, video games, the Internet, targeted print media and other yet-unknown technologies.

- There is also a trend in how parents are portrayed in the media. Television and the movies used to celebrate families and show strong models of parenting. We are now increasingly exposed to parenting models that are dysfunctional.
- There is a trend for children in their early twenties to continue living, or return to live, with their parents. Whether this is good for either party is as yet an unanswered question.
- Due to parent work schedules and economic pressures, more children at younger ages are being left alone, especially after school hours, to care for themselves. Studies of young teenagers show that the more hours that they are left alone after school, the greater the risk of alcohol and drug use. These unsupervised after-school hours are also a prime time for sexual activity.
- The legislative liberalization of soft drug use, already evident in parts of Europe, will spread.
- Advances in genetic engineering will provide the technology for parents to create 'designer babies', notwithstanding current prohibition. Society will have to sort out the ethical and legal implications.
- Due to various stressors, parents are not supervising their children and adolescents as closely as in the past. This is a problem as it decreases the level of control necessary to curb youth problems such as drug and alcohol use, delinquency and unsafe sex.
- Neighbourhood ties among families have been eroding as families have become increasingly mobile and isolated.
- In recent decades there has been a trend in many countries indicating that children's emotional and behavioral problems are becoming more frequent and severe.
- The significant impact of problems with alcohol and drug abuse will continue and perhaps grow.
- Surveys in Europe and the US indicate that parents' greatest concerns for their children are related to safety (crime/violence), exposure to drugs, need for quality schools, declining morals and negatively changing values in society. There is no indication that any of these concerns will become less serious.

Although there are some positive trends, such as healthier and educationally more competent children, most of the trends described above are negative. Fortunately, both parents and children are quite resilient. Most of the time they are able to cope effectively with the many issues and stressors that they confront in their daily lives.

However, we are also learning that there are limits to resiliency and coping. Individuals are typically able to cope with a limited number of stressors but as the number of stressors they are exposed to increases, their ability to cope effectively decreases. As a growing number of parents confront multiple stressors, especially in the absence of adequate support, their effectiveness as parents is compromised.

MOVING TOWARD A PARENTING SOCIETY

We use the term 'parenting society' to denote a number of component approaches and also to imply that such a society is a good and desirable one. A parenting society not only promotes the care, control and development of all citizens at a macro-strategic level and organization of relevant structures, but also helps individual parents and families to look after their children optimally.

The need for a parenting society is based on two fundamental premises:

- No society can survive without order. Although order can be imposed, it will only endure if citizens are imbued with a sense of its necessity and are supportive of legally enforced structures created to maintain it. Parenting is the most powerful, life-long means of inculcating respect for social order in children.
- A society with order but lacking in appropriate values to animate it is arid and not fit for humanity. Most social legislation is based on a macro projection of the chief values such as co-operative care, loyalty and commitment, which animate most families. Parenting is the strongest possible single influence, shaping the values children adopt and enact.

It therefore seems to us that a society that does not actively promote parenting is likely to undermine the very foundations of its own progressive enrichment and even survival. If such survival and enhancement are the overarching goals, what should we do to optimize the prospects of a parenting society? There are three broad areas of enablement:

- reducing the number and impact of those factors that undermine 'good enough' parenting;
- supporting the status quo in those areas that are adequate and appropriate and do not warrant changing;

- promoting those areas that, although already positive, would benefit from further opportunities for enhancement.

These three sets of interrelated activities can be brought together and addressed in a number of overarching objectives.

Given the wide range of factors that influence parenting, it is obvious that if we are to move society toward being more supportive of it, strategies must be multifaceted and address a wide range of issues. We must above all regard 'family' as broadly as possible to include any setting that provides opportunities for care, control and development of the child. This will embrace all those adults who engage in the 'primary parenting' of the child, whether they are biological parents, grandparents, or other persons. The 'extended' family should include all those outside of the immediate family who are actively involved in caring for the child, including teachers. It is important to recognize the important and interactive role that teachers and others play in a child's development.

We need to redefine the traditional parenting roles of men and women. There needs to be more flexibility with child-rearing responsibilities within families. In families where both parents are employed outside the home, this will mean that responsibilities will be shared more equitably. However, specific roles will vary from family to family and we as a society should strive to accommodate more flexible parenting responsibilities. We can think of policies, such as those in Sweden, where paternity leave has to be taken alternately with maternity leave, to ensure that fathers have equal opportunity for parenting in the early years and are seen by society at large to have a facilitated responsibility in this area.

To be successful we must aim toward a convergence of political, business, service, and research ideas regarding parenting. Convergent messages from various segments of society including the government, businesses, entrepreneurs, scientists, journalists, religious leaders, and parents themselves regarding the crucial importance of this process will be a prerequisite for developing comprehensive and effective strategies. They and we, after all, share the one common 'connective tissue' that we are all either parents or children of parents and no common interest is greater than ensuring the welfare of families.

As we have suggested, one of the greatest issues facing parents in Western countries is their diminishing time spent interacting with their children. We know that effective parenting not only entails financial and emotional commitment but also requires an immense amount of time and focal energy. Given current and probable social pressures, time is an ever more scarce commodity. However, the greatest positive impact and richness of parenting is typically found in the 'quality time' parents and their children spend together, where attachment deepens. We need to encourage parents to slow down so that they may find and share the wonders of life with their children.

How do we create more time for parenting? Several countries provide long-term paid maternity and paternity leave for new parents. Other strategies include laws that would allow a certain amount of flexible leave for parenting responsibilities, such as attending parent–teacher meetings at schools. Tax incentives could be offered to employers who offer flexi-time and compressed work weeks. Policies could be enacted that would allow employees to take compensatory time off instead of overtime pay for extra hours worked, as already happens in some enlightened enterprises. Other possibilities include policies that allow employees to take extra weeks of unpaid vacation during the year when their children are at home. Incentives, tax or otherwise, should be offered to family-friendly businesses that provide on-site childcare, which also allow parents more time with their children.

Governments are the most influential force in parenting. The timid ones just respond to pressure. The enlightened ones lead and shape social attitudes. Their influence is exerted in a multitude of obvious and subtle ways. Recognizing the dangers of a 'nanny state' is not incompatible with active intervention.

Fiscal policies can either strengthen or impede the parenting process. Parents need economic security of a kind and level that will not undermine their functioning. Many families face significant economic stressors that negatively influence their ability to parent effectively. Individuals who work need to be assured a 'living wage' that will allow them, and their children, to live above the poverty line. Those families in economic distress need assistance with housing. No family in a civilized country should be allowed to become and remain homeless, given the long-term corrosive effects of this status on both parents and children.

The pressures of globalized market economies result in business plans that focus on the *financial* 'bottom line'. In a parenting society, the time and effort that parents spend in child-rearing would be viewed as having a large economic value in producing productive tax-paying citizens for the future. Although the value of effective parenting should be recognized, it is critical that children are not viewed purely as capital and considered only in economic terms. Their emotional health and behavioural propriety according to core positive values is what will ensure their productive citizenship.

Before enacting any public programme, its impact on parenting and children should be examined. Questions need to focus on whether the proposed measures will increase positive interaction between adults and children. As we have seen, a wide range of benevolent adults (such as grandparents) act as parenting figures. With the increasing break up of families, the importance of maintaining continuity of contact with such figures should be recognized and promoted.

Community planning and development needs to take into consideration the impact on families. There is a growing recognition that many community development practices of the past decades have had a detrimental social impact. There is a growing and welcome return to town-planning traditions that promote sidewalks, front porches, shopping within walking distance and common grounds for children and families to interact. In a parenting society, developers and urban planners would design communities that encourage social interaction and connectedness for families, rather than isolate them.

It is understandable that governments place so much importance on economic health ('It's the economy, stupid'), because without it much else is imperilled. But we seem to have reached a point where a society's success seems to be measured more by financial indices than by the well-being of children and families. In the end, it may be possible to have both economic prosperity and family well-being. We may learn that greater co-operation between work and home can transform company culture and lead to healthier and better motivated employees. That in turn will benefit companies economically, through lower employee turnover and related costs, as well as more productive (because of increased stability and commitment) employees. Economic security may enhance family stability and its absence lead to greater family stress and child vulnerability. However, in Western societies, governments recognize the complexity of adult intimate relationships and keep clear of trying to legislate for them.

In the face of 'globalization' and 'market economy', most Western governments seem to be fighting a rearguard and largely passive fight against influences that most agree are harmful to children's interests. Increases in the consumption of tobacco, alcohol, soft and some classified drugs and violent, antisocial films, video games and the like are examples of these. In the absence of countervailing forces, many children succumb to these influences, particularly those who seem to be particularly vulnerable.

The most powerful countervailing force, as research has repeatedly demonstrated, is the quality of parenting. Most parents desperately express the need to know how best to counter such influences on their children, but do not know whom to ask. Government and social agencies' advice is often vapid and unhelpful, in being both generalized and weak.

A parenting society, bringing together government, parents and social agencies, would unite in controlling the spread of commercially motivated damaging activity, by recognizing that any of the doctrinal and economic advantages of a 'free market' are vastly outweighed by its impact on vulnerable children. Such a society would also utilize the considerable amount of good knowledge and experience available to teach parents how better to insulate their children against adverse experiences. Many of the chapters in this book encapsulate such advice.

Given the critical and formative influence of schools, as arenas for both teacher/parenting figures and increasingly powerful peers, a parenting society would enhance and project the role of schools accordingly. There is evidence of growing recognition of this, but not yet as the result of a focal policy in many countries. In a parenting society the government would sufficiently fund and support schools due to the recognition of the central importance of schools not only in terms of academic education but also in terms of broader child development.

A parenting society would also provide comprehensive health care to all family members, irrespective of income, as is already done in many countries such as those in Western Europe. Parents who face serious or chronic illnesses for any member of their family should not be forced into financial ruin as, unfortunately, often happens in countries that do not have a government-supported universal health-care system.

Given the complexity of parenting and the diversity of parenting roles, it is not surprising that numerous academic subjects touch on the study of and/or application of knowledge to parenting. Disciplines with interests in parenting include child development, family studies, psychology, education, social work, sociology, pediatrics, nursing, anthropology, religion, communication and many others. It is important to recognize that the study of parenting has not traditionally been considered an independent discipline, but rather an area of interest embedded within other disciplines. Although a distinct discipline of 'parenting studies' may be emerging, its absence is a major contributing factor to the fragmentation of the field and its poor impact. It would immeasurably help the move toward a parenting society if scholars from different disciplines collaborate, so as to gain a broader, multi-dimensional and better focused understanding of parenting.

Practitioners in the area of 'parenting services' are also often isolated from others working with parents. Parenting support services are quite diverse and include intensive home-visiting programmes, parenting classes and support groups, clinical parenting therapy programmes, brief interventions in health care or social service settings. These practitioners have often been trained in different disciplines and at varying levels. Considerable fragmentation of approaches remains. Service providers who see themselves as part of a parenting society, like a good family, are more likely to co-operate and provide more co-ordinated and better focused services.

The isolation between practitioners and scholars/ researchers in the area of parenting is perhaps the most important. The roles of the scholar/ researcher and the practitioner, while at times overlapping and complementary, often have conflicting goals that reduce the impact of their work. From the scholar/researcher perspective, a major goal is to understand more clearly, through basic research, the process of parenting or the effectiveness of parenting services. This often involves carefully controlled studies that address specific questions. Much of this research is complex and theoretically driven, its findings difficult to understand and not clearly relevant to service providers in the field. The motivation for such research is often the desire for valid findings that can be used as small building blocks towards a better knowledge base for parenting and parenting services. It would seem to us critical that grant-awarding bodies should insist that research into parenting should have practitioners involved as advisers and that studies clearly set out the potential practice/use implications of their findings.

Other Characteristics of a Parenting Society

- Recognition that children learn what they live.
- Acknowledgement of the astonishing variety of effective family forms and parenting practices around the globe.
- Grassroots movements and political action groups that advocate for parents.

- A comprehensive, well-funded and co-ordinated approach to providing parent-support services.
- A focus on the use of evidence-based parenting-support programmes.
- Access to home-visiting programmes provided by appropriate professionals for all new parents.
- Parenting education and support programmes that are readily accessible to all parents. These programmes should be fully integrated into communities, family resource centres, and placed where parents spend their time (such as workplaces, schools, churches, shopping areas). These centres should provide information and offer support and development programmes for parents.
- Recognition that a single model for parenting education and support will not be appropriate or effective. Parenting programmes must be adapted to a community's needs and strengths, and should target the specific needs of individual families. A wide variety of programmes will be needed to address the varied needs of parents.
- Provision of parenting programmes that are culturally appropriate.
- Increased and appropriate access of parents to supportive social networks.
- Better social detection systems that trigger help appropriate to need.
- A mentoring system for new parents who do not have extended family members or friends readily available.
- Professionals that really listen to concerns and suggestions of parents rather than behave as if they already know what the problems and best solutions are.
- Widespread recognition of the importance of facilitating access to parks, libraries, museums, and open spaces.
- Family-friendly employers.
- Accessible and affordable high-quality child-care programmes.
- Strong schools that encourage parental involvement.
- Arriving at a core political consensus regarding the central importance of parenting support, that puts it outside party politics.
- Recognizing the limits of influence of parenting; it is not sensible to blame parents for all their children's problems.
- Recognition that children also impact parenting and that the parent–child relationship is bi-directional.
- Development of an index of parenting support, to measure a country's success in supporting parents. While numerous financial indices exist to measure a country's financial

prosperity, few indices exist to measure social capital and prosperity, and none that focus specifically on parenting. Such an index could be used to advocate for change.

We are aware that many of the above recommendations may appear to be gratuitous advice to governments which daily struggle to curb the most corrosive forces in society and ensure that families are not exposed to them. However, we believe that the many government actions, as for example those against drugs and crime, are often ill-focused and ineffectual precisely because they do not place the creation of a strong and well-functioning family, and a parenting society that would support it, at centre stage.

The parent–child bond is the heart of humanity. It is the most powerful of all human attachments and what keeps it going. When a society does not support this bond, its very existence is put in jeopardy. We must support parents in nurturing their children's physical, emotional, social, cognitive and spiritual growth. If we do not, their failure will be magnified in becoming ours.

An African proverb, popularized in recent years by Hillary Clinton, says, 'It takes a village to raise a child.' But, this village appears to be crumbling, leaving parents increasingly alone to nurture their children – to ensure that they are safe, healthy, economically secure, and imbued with positive values. It is difficult to inculcate such socially necessary virtues as tolerance, helpfulness, fairness, caring, courage, respect, loyalty, honesty, responsibility, self-reliance, trustworthiness and self-discipline when wider political and corporate forces cynically flout them.

It is evident from this handbook that effective parenting cannot occur in isolation. We, as citizens and professionals, must aspire to better times and move forward, however slowly, making better use of available and improving evidence. We *can* make a difference. As Margaret Mead said, 'Never doubt that a small group of thoughtful, committed citizens can change the world; indeed, it is the only thing that ever has.' It should not be beyond our wit to elevate parenting to a central position in society, for our present sakes and the sake of all our future. There is, after all, little that is more important than raising the next generation and doing it better.

REFERENCES

Bumpass, L. (2001) The changing contexts of parenting in the United States. In Westman, J. (ed.) *Parenthood in America: Undervalued, Underpaid, Under Siege*. Madison, WI: The University of Wisconsin Press, pp. 211–19.

Freely, M. (2000) *The Parent Trap: Children, Families, and the New Morality*. London: Virago Press.

Garbarino, J. (1995) *Raising Children in a Socially Toxic Environment*. San Francisco: Josey-Bass.

Garbarino, J. and Bedard, C. (2001) *Parents Under Siege*. New York: Simon & Schuster.

Golombok, S. (2000) *Parenting: What Really Counts?* London: Routledge.

Hewlett, S.A. and West, C. (1998) *The War Against Parents*. Boston: Houghton Mifflin.

Kaslow, F.W. (2001) Families and family psychology at the Millennium. *American Psychologist*, **56**(1), 37–46.

Louv, R. (1992) *Childhood's Future*. New York: Anchor Books.

Matathia, I. and Salzman, M. (1999) *Next: Trends for the Near Future*. New York: Overlook Press.

Rickel, A.U. and Becker, E. (1997) *Keeping Children from Harm's Way: How National Policy Affects Psychological Development*. Washington, DC: American Psychological Association.

Walsh, D. (1995) *Selling Out America's Children*. Minneapolis, MN: Fairview Press.

Westman, J.C. (ed.) (2001) *Parenthood in America: Undervalued, Underpaid, Under Siege*. Madison, WI: The University of Wisconsin Press.

Index

Notes, As the subject of this book is parenting, entries have been kept to a minimum under this term. Readers are advised to seek more specific entries.